On the Origin of Languages

On the Origin of Languages

---- ✳ ----

Studies in Linguistic Taxonomy

Merritt Ruhlen

Stanford University Press

Stanford University Press
Stanford, California

© 1994 by the Board of Trustees of the
Leland Stanford Junior University

Printed in the United States of America

Original printing 1994
Last figure below indicates year of this printing:
04   03   02   01   00   99   98   97   96   95

CIP data appear at the end of the book

Stanford University Press publications are distributed exclusively by Stanford University Press
within the United States, Canada, Mexico, and
Central America; they are distributed exclusively
by Cambridge University Press throughout the
rest of the world.

For my parents,

Florence Ennis Ruhlen

Frank Merritt Ruhlen

Preface

For most of the twentieth century, and for a variety of reasons, some of which are discussed in this book, the field of taxonomy, or classification, has provoked little interest in the linguistic community. Yet the past decade has witnessed a renaissance in linguistic taxonomy that has brought this once moribund field from obscurity to center stage—not only in scientific circles, but in the mass media as well. In just the past three years the field has seen lengthy articles in *U.S. News and World Report* (November 5, 1990), *The Atlantic* (April 1991), and *Scientific American* (April 1991), as well as television shows in England (April 1992) and Germany (June 1992). Within the academic community few topics are today more controversial—or more heatedly argued—than the current debates over Joseph Greenberg's Amerind proposal, the Nostratic hypothesis recently reinvigorated by Russian scholars, or, indeed, virtually *any* proposal of genetic affinity that goes beyond the obvious.

The sources of this renaissance are multiple. In the broader context it represents simply the latest episode in a century-long debate over the limits of the comparative method in linguistics. Certainly the publication of Greenberg's *Language in the Americas* in 1987 was a major factor in this revival of interest in taxonomy, as was to a lesser extent the publication of my book on classification that same year. But even before these two books appeared, other events had signaled a reawakening of interest in classification. In March 1986, at Rice University, Sydney Lamb and Douglas Mitchell had organized a Symposium on the Genetic Classification of Languages to celebrate the two-hundredth anniversary of Sir William Jones's famous pronouncement on

Indo-European—the crux of which, "sprung from some common source," became the title of the published proceedings. The conference brought together
for the first time Greenberg, his associates, and the Russian Nostraticists,
and this single event led to continued cooperation between the two groups,
both informally and at several subsequent conferences. In the years since
this conference—and perhaps largely as a consequence of it—the work of the
Russian Nostraticists has come to be much better known in this country.

Later that same year—and independently of the Rice conference—Harold
Fleming began distributing a newsletter, *Mother Tongue*, devoted to the study
of language in prehistory, that has served ever since as a forum for debate on
topics considered too controversial for establishment journals like *Language*.
Fleming too had been stimulated by his discovery of the Russian Nostratic
work, during a conference in Moscow, a discovery that had rekindled his long-
held interest in classification. The impetus given to linguistic taxonomy by
the Rice conference, the founding of *Mother Tongue*, and Greenberg's classification of the American Indian languages soon attracted several other scholars
interested in developing more comprehensive classifications of the world's languages. These linguists, who had been working essentially in isolation, were
quickly integrated into the emerging network of scholars; among them, John
Bengtson, Václav Blažek, and Allan Bomhard have been the most prolific
contributors.

In 1988 this renewed interest in linguistic taxonomy gained an added boost
from an unexpected quarter, when biologists—especially L. L. Cavalli-Sforza
and his colleagues—found that a classification of the human population based
on genetics bore a striking resemblance to the linguistic classification advocated by Greenberg and the Nostraticists. At a time when Greenberg's
adversaries were unremittingly assailing his tripartite classification of New
World languages, Cavalli-Sforza discovered exactly the same classification,
on the basis of human genetics. This independent confirmation of Greenberg's findings—drawing upon wholly different data and a wholly different
methodology—posed a problem for his critics that they have yet to address.
In reality, the revolution in taxonomy had begun some four decades earlier
with Greenberg's classification of African languages, but in retrospect it is
now clear that the revolutionary aspect of that classification was not fully
appreciated at the time.

The high degree of correlation between the linguistic and genetic evidence
for the spread of humans in prehistory led archaeologists, in particular Colin
Renfrew, to propose that perhaps the time had come for a concerted interdisci-
plinary approach to the problems of human prehistory, in which the findings
of comparative linguistics, human genetics, and archaeology would be inte-

grated into a single overall hypothesis concerning the origin and spread of modern humans from Africa to the rest of the world, over the last 100,000 years. Renfrew called this endeavor the "Emerging Synthesis," and this book is intended as a linguistic contribution to this collective enterprise. Over the past five years scholars from these three disciplines have participated in joint conferences in Turin, Italy (1988), Ann Arbor, Michigan (1988), Orono, Maine (1989), Santa Fe, New Mexico (1989), Sapporo, Japan (1989), Boulder, Colorado (1990), Cold Spring Harbor, New York (1990), Florence, Italy (1991), and Tokyo, Japan (1992). For those interested in the Emerging Synthesis, these conferences provided a forum for the exchange of ideas and a running debate over differences of opinion, and some of the papers in the present volume represent my participation in the conferences.

I cannot in fact sufficiently emphasize the importance of these conferences for my own work. They have afforded me opportunities to discuss questions of mutual interest with some of the world's most distinguished linguists, biologists, and archaeologists. In particular, I would like to acknowledge the friendly counsel of the following linguists, none of whom necessarily agrees with any of the views expressed in this book: Lionel Bender, John Bengtson, Václav Blažek, Claude Boisson, Allan Bomhard, Bernard Comrie, Aron Dolgopolsky, Sheila Embleton, Harold Fleming, Joseph Greenberg, John Hawkins, Mary Ritchie Key, Sydney Lamb, Vitaly Shevoroshkin, Sergei Starostin, and William S.-Y. Wang. I have also profited from discussions with many biologists, among whom Kenichi Aoki, L. L. Cavalli-Sforza, Jared Diamond, André Langaney, Alberto Piazza, Vincent Sarich, Robert Sokal, Christy Turner, and Steven Zegura deserve special thanks. And I must thank, as well, the archaeologists Takeru Akazawa and Colin Renfrew, and the physicist Murray Gell-Mann, for their support and advice. As in the past, Stanford University Press has been supportive in a difficult and controversial volume, and I would particularly like to thank my editors Muriel Bell and William Carver. Finally, I would like to express my appreciation to Donald Knuth for creating the TEX typesetting language, which made the difficult material in this book typographically possible.

M. R.
Palo Alto, California
10 May 1993

Contents

On the Origin of Languages

If we possessed a perfect pedigree of mankind, a genealogical arrangement of the races of man would afford the best classification of the various languages now spoken throughout the world; and if all extinct languages, and all intermediate and slowly changing dialects, were to be included, such an arrangement would be the only possible one.

—Charles Darwin, *On the Origin of Species,* 1859

Introduction

Linguists are justifiably proud that the evolutionary explanation for similarities among languages was clearly enunciated in the late eighteenth century, by Sir William Jones, more than 70 years before Darwin offered such an explanation for biological similarities. Furthermore, the nineteenth century saw major advances in linguistic taxonomy, including a meticulous in-depth investigation of the Indo-European family that remains to this day the standard by which historical studies are measured. But this auspicious beginning notwithstanding, the twentieth century has witnessed a decline in interest in such matters, which most linguists consider to have been essentially resolved—to the extent that any resolution is possible—in the last century. Indeed, linguistic taxonomy in the twentieth century has actually regressed in many respects, and an elaborate mythology about how classification is carried out—and what is actually known—has been allowed to capture the field. What is being done to move beyond that mythology is the unifying theme of the present collection of essays.

Until recently most linguists viewed the tenets of linguistic taxonomy roughly as follows. Though the Indo-European family had been established beyond doubt, it had never been shown to be related to any other family—and cannot be, because the rate of linguistic change is so rapid that all trace of genetic affinity is eroded after around 6,000 years. Many other families have also been identified (e.g. Uralic, Dravidian, Australian, Algonquian, Siouan, Arawakan), but none of them can be convincingly connected either with each other or with other families. Linguistic taxonomy, according to this view, has simply gone as far as it can, and this temporal limit, 6,000 years, just happens to coin-

cide with the presumed time depth of the Indo-European family discovered
by Jones over two centuries ago. Not only did Jones discover the method of
comparative linguistics, we are told, he discovered the limits of that method
as well. It is as if Galileo's telescope was not only the *first* telescope, but also
the most powerful telescope that could ever be built. Incredible as it may
seem, this is the commonly accepted view of linguistic taxonomy today.

The reality, however, is quite different, and were a taxonomist from Mars
to visit the Earth and consult our literature she would be at a loss to explain
why the Australian family is universally accepted as valid, while the Amerind
family is almost universally rejected, when there is in fact far more evidence
supporting Amerind than there is in support of Australian. The claim that
Indo-European has not been shown to be related to any other family would be
equally incomprehensible, and the claim that all linguistic evidence evaporates
after 6,000 years would be immediately seen to be contradicted by the Indo-
European evidence itself. What the Martian taxonomist would make of all this
is hard to imagine. What *we* should make of it, however, is clear: concerning
linguistic classification, most linguists know what they have been taught; and
few have ever examined the evidence firsthand.

It is my goal, in this book, to demonstrate that the field of linguistic taxonomy, far from having been exhausted in the nineteenth century, and notwithstanding decades of neglect, is ripe for the production of more penetrating
analyses. The field, in fact, has only begun to move beyond the obviously
valid families identified in the preliminary stages of research so long ago; and,
although much is firmly established, much also remains to be worked out. In
short, linguistic taxonomy was arrested before it had a chance to flower. This
book seeks to reopen these vital questions, and to show that their exploration
will lead ultimately to a better understanding of the structure of the human
population, on the basis of linguistic evidence. That endeavor is not only a
goal for comparative linguistics, but also a debt that linguists have long owed
to the other human sciences. To continue pretending that there is no evidence
for linguistic prehistory prior to 4,000 B.C. will no longer do.

Each of the essays in this volume was written to answer a certain question,
to respond to a particular criticism, or to assemble or develop material useful to those seeking to construct more comprehensive classifications of human
languages. The first chapter, a revised version of a paper from the Santa Fe
Institute workshop on the evolution of language, offers a general introduction to the methods and results of genetic linguistics, as I now see them. It
is intended to be accessible to a broad audience, and it provides a general
background for the other, more specialized essays.

Chapter 2 is a paper presented at the Cold Spring Harbor Centennial
Symposium in September 1990. The organizers of this symposium, Richard

Dawkins and Jared Diamond, brought together scholars from six different fields in which evolution plays a prominent role (molecular biology, functional morphology, animal behavior, sexual selection, human society, and historical linguistics) and asked each group to explain to the others how its field distinguishes descent from a common ancestor from borrowing, convergence, and accidental resemblance. My paper attempted to address this question for language, and for linguistics the question essentially becomes, "What is the basis for the genetic classification of languages?"

The Khoisan family of languages, indigenous to southern Africa, is renowned for its click consonants, almost universally lacking in other language families. When Greenberg presented evidence for the Khoisan family in his pioneering classification of African languages in 1963, he provided etymologies connecting Hadza and Sandawe, two divergent languages of eastern Africa, with the more homogeneous Khoisan languages of southern Africa, which are themselves divided into three subgroups, Northern, Central, and Southern Khoisan. Thus Greenberg did not bother to provide etymologies connecting these three subgroups, believing their relationship was obvious. Yet the validity of even this southern African Khoisan family has been questioned by the South African linguist E. O. J. Westphal. In Chapter 3 I compare the three Khoisan subgroups, using material gathered by Dorothea Bleek, and try to identify probable cognate forms among the three branches. The several hundred suggested etymologies have two purposes: first, they show that the three subgroups are genetically related, beyond any doubt; and, second, they provide material from Khoisan that may be compared with similar data from other families in the ongoing endeavor to determine the place of the Khoisan family within the world's languages.

The Yeniseian family, a half-dozen attested languages, now reduced to a single extant language, Ket, has long been considered a mysterious isolate, and information on the family has been sparse in languages other than Russian. In the early 1980's the Russian scholar Sergei Starostin reconstructed the Proto-Yeniseian language on the basis of available materials; at the same time he suggested connections with the Sino-Tibetan and (North) Caucasian families, forming a higher-level family that he named Sino-Caucasian, now usually called Dene-Caucasian (see Chapter 1). Chapter 4 presents a translation of Starostin's Proto-Yeniseian reconstructions, the supporting evidence in the Yeniseian languages, and Starostin's extra-Yeniseian comparisons. I have added a few comparisons with Na-Dene, Nahali, Burushaski, and Basque, but otherwise the work is entirely Starostin's.

A little over a decade ago several linguists called into question the validity of Edward Sapir's Na-Dene family, which is scattered across western North America, chiefly in the northwest. They argued that the Haida language did not belong to this family, contrary to Sapir's claim. In his book on the classification of New World languages, Greenberg devoted a chapter to the "Na-Dene problem," arguing that Sapir's original evidence was fully sufficient to show the affinity of Haida with Na-Dene. Greenberg had, in fact, compiled a Na-Dene notebook, a mine of data that he might have used to demonstrate further the affinity of Haida with Na-Dene, had he felt it necessary. In Chapter 5 I have used his Na-Dene notebook to identify probable cognates among the constituents of Na-Dene: Haida, Tlingit, Eyak, and the Athabaskan family. The resulting etymologies leave little doubt that Haida belongs with the other Na-Dene languages, as claimed by Sapir. They also provide material from this poorly documented family that may be compared with that of other families, material that is in fact employed in the preceding chapter.

The publicaton of Greenberg's classification of native American languages in 1987 unleashed a torrent of invective from specialists in American Indian languages, not unlike the reception accorded Darwin's *Origin of Species* in 1859. Even before the book appeared, one scholar called for Greenberg's classification to be "shouted down," and after publication, another scholar called it "subversive." Chapter 6 attempts to place this ongoing controversy in its proper historical context, tracing its origins to similar debates waged at the turn of this century. The essay also analyzes the criticisms of Greenberg's opponents, showing that they are often methodologically unsound, and at times even intellectually dishonest. The dynamics of their assault, seen against Greenberg's prior record of achievement, are grist for historians and pathologists of science.

In his classification of Native American languages, Greenberg listed each etymology under a semantic gloss, without a corresponding phonetic gloss. As a consequence of this decision there was no overall semantic index carrying the associated phonetic glosses for the 2,000-odd etymologies contained in the book. Chapter 7 provides such an index, and also indicates cases where etymologies from Amerind subbranches should be combined in a higher-level Amerind etymology (see Chapter 8).

In all of the scathing reviews of Greenberg's book *Language in the Americas,* its chief defect was hardly mentioned, namely, that the book contained *more* evidence for Amerind than he had claimed. Not infrequently, etymologies that Greenberg posited for one or more Amerind subfamilies are semantically and phonologically similar to etymologies in other branches, and all should thus have been combined as additional Amerind etymologies. Chapter 8 lists these additional etymologies.

In *Language in the Americas* Greenberg posited a root TANA 'child,' whose distribution was apparently restricted to North America; he also pointed out an -*i*- (masc.)/-*u*- (fem.) alternation in South American Amerind languages.

Chapter 9 extends Greenberg's original analysis by showing that both the lexical item in question and its phonological alternation are found throughout the Americas. Furthermore, the item and the alternation are intimately connected, in the sense that extant languages suggest that Proto-Amerind originally had three distinct forms of the lexical item: *TINA 'son, brother,' *TUNA 'daughter, sister,' and *TANA 'child, sibling.' The widespread distribution of this morphologically complex pattern throughout the Americas, and its absence elsewhere in the world, demonstrates the obvious validity of Amerind no less than does the celebrated n- 'I'/m- 'thou' pronominal pattern.

One element in the mythology of twentieth-century comparative linguistics has been the notion that there are no recognizable genetic connections between the language families of the Americas and those of the Old World. The logic of this view is impeccable: if all trace of genetic affinity disappears after 6,000 years, then there cannot be recognizable connections between the Americas and Asia, since the New World is known to have been inhabited for at least 12,000 years. The empirical evidence, however, belies the logic. Of the three families that Greenberg posited for the Americas, each is more closely related to certain Old World language families than it is to the other two, thus yielding evidence for three distinct migrations from Asia to the Americas. The third, most recent migration brought to the New World the Eskimo-Aleut, whose closest relatives are the various language families spread across northern Eurasia that Greenberg groups together under the name Eurasiatic, and that Russian scholars call Nostratic. The second, prior migration had brought the Na-Dene family, whose Asian connections are with the other members of the Dene-Caucasian family (see Chapters 1 and 4). Chapter 10 presents linguistic evidence for the first migration, that which had brought the speakers of Proto-Amerind to the New World. This essay argues that Amerind is most closely related to the Eurasiatic family; but whereas Eskimo-Aleut is simply the easternmost constituent of Eurasiatic itself, Amerind is related at greater remove to the higher-level taxon Eurasiatic.

Chapter 11 traces the distribution of a single lexical item from North Africa, across Eurasia, and throughout the Americas. The length of the item in question—the item is triconsonantal—and its presence in so many different families with similar, but slightly different meanings, argue strongly for a common origin for all the forms. In addition, this essay shows how the wider comparative picture may at times clarify certain problems within specific families, problems that cannot be resolved on a family-internal basis.

It has long been recognized that first- and second-person singular pronouns are among the most stable semantic meanings in human language. Indeed, such pronominal similarities are often among the first characteristics noticed in the more ancient linguistic families, such as Eurasiatic, Dene-Caucasian, and Amerind. During the debate over Amerind between Greenberg and his critics, the meaning—and even the existence—of the widespread Amerind pattern n- 'I' vs. m- 'thou' was much discussed, and Greenberg's critics offered a bewildering variety of possible explanations in their determination to avoid accepting Greenberg's simple explanation of common origin. It was even claimed by some, though without any supporting evidence, that such nasal sounds might persist naturally in many parts of the world, and thus that their prevalence in the Americas should not be thought unusual. To test this hypothesis I collected these two pronouns for all of the world's established linguistic families, according to the best information at my disposal. These data are given in Chapter 12; they show quite clearly, I believe, that there is no support for the conjecture of worldwide nasality. The Amerind pronominal pattern is a characteristic specific to the Amerind family, one found nowhere else in the world. As such it remains one of the bedrock foundations of Amerind, as has been recognized throughout this century by Trombetti, Sapir, Swadesh, Greenberg, and others.

The question of the possible monogenesis of human language has, during this century at least, been virtually taboo. Of course, if one accepts the thesis that the Indo-European family has no recognizable genetic connections with any other family, as most linguists do, then such questions do not even arise. But if one does accept the idea that Indo-European is clearly related to a whole host of other families, as demonstrated beyond any reasonable doubt by the Russian Nostraticists, then one faces the hard question of just how far one might go. The final two chapters discuss these questions from somewhat different perspectives. Chapter 13 seeks to understand the almost fanatical opposition that these questions have engendered, such that to the present day even the discussion of broad genetic connections remains a taboo topic in the pages of *Language*. The origins of this unreasoning hostility are traced to similar debates at the beginning of this century.

Chapter 14, written in collaboration with John Bengtson, approaches the question from a strictly empirical perspective. We have sought to compare all of the world's language families simultaneously in order to see whether they do, or do not, share common elements that would imply a common origin for all extant languages. We found, as did such predecessors as Alfredo Trombetti and Morris Swadesh, that there are in fact many such elements, and in this essay we present etymologies for 27 of what seem to us the most widespread of these. In addition to presenting evidence for the monogenesis of (extant) human languages, this chapter also seeks to reconcile the Greenberg approach of multilateral comparison with what is usually described as "traditional historical linguistics." We argue that Greenberg's approach—which in reality is simply linguistic taxonomy—is a necessary first stage in the comparative method, one that must be undertaken before the second stage, traditional historical linguistics, can begin its task of the reconstruction of proto-languages and the discovery of sound correspondences like Grimm's Law. The confusion of these two stages, and the mistaken belief that reconstruction and sound correspondences play a crucial role in linguistic taxonomy, are pervasive in the writings of Greenberg's critics.

Historians of science will, I believe, one day focus on the peculiar development of comparative linguistics in the twentieth century. During this century historical linguists have persistently belittled both the methodology and the empirical data of their own field, protesting that they have nothing to contribute to an understanding of the origin and evolution of our species before roughly the historical epoch. According to this traditional view, the world contains literally hundreds of language families among which there are no visible genetic connections. This book addresses the underlying causes of this collective myopia and the evidence that demonstrates just how mistaken these received views are. The various chapters do not provide final answers to all of the questions of linguistic classification, but they do suggest that answers more comprehensive than those now commonly accepted are possible. If this book serves merely to reopen the debate on linguistic taxonomy, after a century of stagnation, it will have served its purpose.

1

An Overview of Genetic Classification

The past decade has witnessed a reawakening of interest in the genetic classification of languages and the implications of such a classification for the prehistory of the human species.* Here I shall review several lines of recent research that bear on these questions. In particular, I will argue that the notion that Indo-European is unrelated to any other family is little more than a linguistic myth, as is the parallel idea that the New World contains scores of independent families. Contrary to the almost universal belief that linguistic families such as Indo-European, Uralic, Dravidian, Sino-Tibetan, Austronesian, Australian, etc., share no recognizable cognates, there are in fact numerous etymological connections among the world's language families (see Chapter 14), and they should be investigated in depth to see what import they may have for the prehistory of modern humans.

THE DISCOVERY OF COMPARATIVE LINGUISTICS

The evolutionary explanation for linguistic diversity was discovered some time before Darwin's parallel discovery of evolution by natural selection in

---

* This essay originally appeared in *The Evolution of Human Languages,* ed. by John A. Hawkins and Murray Gell-Mann, 1992, Reading, Mass. It is reprinted here with minor modifications. I would like to thank Joseph Greenberg for allowing me to use data from his forthcoming book, *Indo-European and Its Closest Relatives: The Eurasiatic Language Family,* Stanford, Calif., Stanford University Press. I would also like to express my appreciation to Lionel Bender, John Bengtson, Allan Bomhard, Joseph Greenberg, and John Hawkins for critical comments on an earlier version of this paper.

TABLE 1 Indo-European Cognates

Word	Anatolian	Tocharian	Armenian	Albanian	Indo-Iranian
I	uk		es		ahám
me	ammuk		es		mā́m
thou		twe	du	ti	tuvám
who?	kuis	kuse	ov	kush	kás
what?	kuit	kuse	z-i	çë	kím
that		te	da		tát
not	natta				ná
one				një	ékas
two	twi-	wi	erku	dy	duvā́
three	tri-	trey	erekʻ	tre	tráyas
foot	pat(a)-	paiyye	otn		pā́d-
eye		ek	akn	sü	ákṣi-
tooth		keme		dhëmp	dán
nose					nās-
heart	kart-		sirt		
knee	kenu	keni	cunr	gju	jā́nu
flesh/meat		misa	mis	mish	mā́ṅsa-
water	watar	war		ujë	udakám
fire	paḫḫur	puwar	hur		
tree/wood	taru				dā́ru
month/moon		meñe	amis	muai	mā́s-
cow		keu	kov		gā́v-
dog	śuwana-[2]	kwen-	šun		śvā́n-
wolf				ulk	vŕ̥ka-
sheep			hoviw[8]		ávi-
mouse			mukn	mī	mū́ṣ-
father		pācer	hayr		pitár-
mother		mācer	mayr		mātár-
name	lāman	ñem	anun	émën	nāman-
old			hin		sánas
new	newas	ñuwe	nor		návas
is	estsi	ste	ē	është	ásti
eats	etstsi		utē		átti
carries		parän	berē	bie[4]	bhárati
die/death	merta		mah		mr̥tá-

Notes: Unless specified otherwise, Anatolian is represented by Hittite, Tocharian by Tocharian B, Indo-Iranian by Sanskrit, Italic by Latin, Celtic by Old Irish, Baltic by Lithuanian, Slavic by Old Church Slavonic, and Germanic by Gothic. [1]Latvian, [2]Hieroglyphic Luwian, [3]'oak,' [4]'brings,' [5]'alone,' [6]in compounds, [7]'evil,'

Greek	Italic	Celtic	Baltic	Slavic	Germanic
egō	ego		àš	azŭ	ik
eme	mē	mé[22]	manè	mę	mik
su	tū	tú	tù	ty	θu
tis	quis	cía	kàs	kŭto	hwas
ti	quid	cid	kàs	čĭto	hwa
to			taĩ	tŭ/ta	θa
	ne-	ní-	ne-	ne	ni
oi(w)os[5]	ūnus	oín	víenas	ino-[6]	ains
duo	duo	dó	dù	dŭva	twai
treis	trēs	trí	trȳs	trĭje	θrija
pod-	ped-		pėda[18]	pěšĭ[19]	fōtus
ópsomai[10]	oculus	enech	akìs	oko	augō
odón	dēns		dantìs	zǫbŭ	tunθus
	nāsus		nosis	nosŭ	nasa[9]
kardiā	cord-	cride	širdìs	srŭdĭce	hairtō
gonu	genū	glún			kniu
	membrum[14]	mīr[15]	mésa	męso	mimz
hudōr		uisce	vanduõ	voda	wato
pūr	pir[16]				fōn
doru		daur[3]		drěvo	triu[17]
mén	mēnsis	mī	mėnuo	měsęcĭ	mēna
bous	bōs	bó	gùovs[1]	govędo	kuo[9]
kuōn	canis	con-	šuo-		hunds
lúkos	lupus	olc[7]	vilkas	vlŭkŭ	wulfs
ó(w)is	ovis	ōi	avìs	ovĭca	ouwi[9]
mûs	mūs			myšĭ	mūs[9]
pater-	pater	athair			faðar
māter-	māter	máthair	mótina	mati	muotar[9]
onoma	nōmen	ainm	emmens[13]	imę	namo
hénos[12]	senex[21]	sen	sēnas		sineigs
ne(w)os	novus	nue	naũjas	novŭ	niujis
esti	est	is	ẽsti	jestŭ	ist
edei	ēst		éda	jasti	itan
pherei	fert	berid		berǫ[20]	bairan
ámbrotos[11]	mortuus	marb	mir̃ti	mĭrǫ	maúrθr

[8]'shepherd,' [9]Old High German, [10]'I will see,' [11]'immortal,' [12]'last year's,' [13]Old Prussian, [14]'limb, part of the body,' [15]'portion, morsel,' [16]Umbrian, [17]'stick of wood,' [18]'foot-track,' [19]'on foot,' [20]'bring together,' [21]'old man,' [22]'I.'

biology. It is customary to recognize as the starting point of comparative linguistics Sir William Jones's lecture in 1786, in which he asserted that Sanskrit, Greek, and Latin bear "a stronger affinity, both in the roots of verbs and in the forms of grammar, than could have been produced by accident; so strong that no philologer could examine Sanskrit, Greek, and Latin, without believing them to have sprung from some common source, which, perhaps, no longer exists. There is a similar reason, though not quite so forcible, for supposing that both the Gothic and the Celtic had the same origin with the Sanskrit" (quoted in Robins 1968: 134). In time, the linguistic family that Jones had perceived came to be known as Indo-European, and during the nineteenth century its investigation was one of the principal focuses of linguistic scholarship. A sample of Indo-European cognates is given in Table 1.

In reality, a number of linguistic families had been recognized even before Indo-European, and during the nineteenth century many other families were recognized in various parts of the world. Moreover, pioneering Indo-Europeanists such as Rasmus Rask, one of the founders of comparative Indo-European linguistics at the beginning of the nineteenth century, did not hesitate to apply the comparative method to other languages around the world, and it was in fact Rask who first recognized that Aleut and Eskimo form a family in the same manner as do the Indo-European groups enumerated by Jones. Nor did Rask hesitate to compare the families he identified *with each other,* and in this regard made a number of startling discoveries, one of which was the connection between the Eskimo-Aleut family and the Samoyed family (located in northwestern Asia), both of which exhibit a dual suffix in -k and a plural suffix in -t. We shall see below that this k/t contrast between duals and plurals is even more widespread than Rask had noticed, and is in fact one of the characteristics of a language family that Joseph Greenberg calls Eurasiatic (Greenberg, to appear), which will be discussed below.

Twentieth-century linguistics, with its emphasis on synchronic (ahistorical) explanations, has had a flavor wholly different from that of nineteenth-century scholarship, which prized the diachronic (historical) explanation above all else. Furthermore, during the twentieth century, genetic linguistics has, with several notable exceptions, stagnated and even retrogressed, for reasons that are discussed in Chapter 13. Twentieth-century Indo-Europeanists, again with a few notable exceptions, have been consistently hostile toward all attempts to connect Indo-European with *any* other linguistic family. In Asia a connection between the Uralic (Finno-Ugric, Samoyed) and Altaic (Turkic, Mongolian, Tungus) families, which was widely accepted in the nineteenth century, has fallen into disrepute, and even the genetic affinity of the three Altaic families is now questioned by some specialists. Similarly, scholars studying Native American languages have taken pride in the bewildering number of supposedly

Khoisan (S Africa)

Niger-Kordofanian (C&S Africa)

Nilo-Saharan (C Africa)

Afro-Asiatic (N Africa)

(North) Caucasian (SE Europe)

Kartvelian (S Europe)

Indo-European (S&W Eurasia)

Uralic-Yukaghir (N Eurasia)

Dravidian (S India)

Altaic (C Asia)

Yeniseian (C Asia)

Korean-Japanese-Ainu (E Asia)

Chukchi-Kamchatkan (NE Asia)

Eskimo-Aleut (N America)

Sino-Tibetan (E Asia)

Austroasiatic (SE Asia)

Miao-Yao (SE Asia)

Daic (= Kadai) (SE Asia)

Austronesian (Oceania)

Indo-Pacific (New Guinea)

Australian (Australia)

Na-Dene (N America)

Amerind (N&S America)

Figure 1. The World's Language Families (adapted from Ruhlen [1987])

independent language families in the Americas, which by some accounts would surpass 200.

The major counterweight to this general apathy toward genetic classification has been the work of Joseph Greenberg, who over a period of forty years (1950–90) classified the languages of Africa (Greenberg 1963), New Guinea (Greenberg 1971), and the Americas (Greenberg 1987) into small numbers of families: four for Africa, two for New Guinea, and three for the Americas. Before Greenberg's work these areas were believed to contain dozens—if not hundreds—of independent language families, among which there were no apparent connections. In the light of Greenberg's findings we may now classify all of the world's languages into fewer than two dozen families, as shown in Figure 1, excepting only a few isolated languages (Basque, Burushaski, Gilyak, Nahali) without any apparent relatives, and even those isolates are beginning to find their way into global classifications.

OPPOSITION TO LONG-RANGE COMPARISON

In one sense the term "long-range comparison" is infelicitous and misleading, for it implies that comparison of linguistic families is in some sense different from the "short-range comparison" of individual languages. Sometimes this fictional dichotomy is phrased in terms of "phylum linguistics" vs. "family linguistics," where by the latter is meant standard comparative linguistics as worked out by Indo-Europeanists, while the former is regarded as little more than "broad-based guesses about distant linguistic and other relationships whose ultimate nature is in fact very uncertain" (Hopper 1989: 818). In reality, the comparative method proceeds in the same way at *all* levels of classification and should be applied in the same manner to comparisons between Indo-European and other families as it was to the Indo-European languages themselves. From a theoretical point of view, *nothing changes* in the higher levels of classification, except perhaps the density of the evidence.

During the late nineteenth and early twentieth centuries a reaction set in against all forms of long-range comparison. Although similarities between Indo-European and other Eurasian families had been noted by many scholars in the nineteenth century, their work has been largely overlooked and forgotten during the present century. Instead, linguists adopted the convenient fiction that Indo-European has no recognizable relatives. According to this view the comparative method is useful for only 5,000–8,000 years, which just happens to be the assumed age of Indo-European! Beyond this time depth, phonetic and semantic erosion have obliterated, so we are told, whatever traces of relationships Proto-Indo-European might once have had with other linguistic families, and cognates between such families will simply not be recognizable. According to Terrence Kaufman, "a temporal ceiling of 7,000 to 8,000 years is inherent in the methods of comparative linguistic reconstruction. We can recover genetic relationships that are that old, but probably no earlier than that" (Kaufman 1990: 23). Catherine Callaghan is no less dogmatic when she claims that "languages apparently lack such nonuniversal markers of remote genetic relationship" (Callaghan 1990: 16).

In support of such a view, the critics of attempts to find Indo-European's relatives will point out that in less than 2,000 years Latin *aqua* 'water' has drifted into French *eau,* phonetically a single vowel [o], and in 5,000 years Proto-Indo-European **dwo* 'two' has been transformed into Armenian *erku* 'two.' Real cognates, according to this view, do not look alike and can be recognized only through a knowledge of the historical sound laws that have produced all the contemporary forms. And since we do not know what sound correspondences connect different families, we cannot possibly recognize what real cognates between families would look like. The chief fallacy with this argument is that, although French and Armenian did change in the ways indicated, other languages did not. Italian *acqua* 'water' is very close to the Latin form, and Greek and Latin *duo* are all but identical with the reconstructed form in Proto-Indo-European (PIE). Or consider PIE **nepōt* 'nephew,' which is reflected in modern Rumanian as *nepot,* virtually identical with the PIE form. Forms such as this, which are by no means exceptional, show just how far from the truth is the idea that after several thousand years all evidence of genetic relationship has changed beyond recognition. But even though the widely held notion that the comparative method is limited to the last 5,000–8,000 years can be shown to be little more than a cherished myth of twentieth-century linguistics, it still does not follow that Indo-European is *necessarily* related in any obvious way to other families. This question can only be answered empirically, by actually comparing Indo-European with the rest of the world's language families.

EURASIATIC/NOSTRATIC

The search for the missing relatives of the Indo-European family has had a long and checkered history, and I will deal here chiefly with certain twentieth-century developments. From the beginning, the search has been plagued by certain methodological errors. First, because most scholars sought to find a *single* relative of Indo-European, most proposals tended to be of a binary nature. Whereas Indo-Europeanists would never dream of comparing Albanian and Armenian, by themselves, to prove they are related, it is precisely such an approach that was adopted in many of the attempts to prove that Indo-European is related to some family or other. The multilateral approach, which had been used exclusively in the study of Indo-European ever since Jones's lecture, was in time discarded in the comparison of language families in favor of a binary approach, but the weaknesses of binary comparison are by now so well known that we need hardly dwell on them (Ruhlen 1987).

The binary approach leads also into a second kind of error, namely, the belief that low-level families are more obvious than (and must be established prior to) the more remote higher-level families. Many scholars who study Native American languages believe, for example, that Amerind itself is the most weakly supported of Greenberg's proposed families in the New World, when in fact it is really more robust than some lower-level branches of Amerind. Consider the case of Austronesian, which parallels Amerind in several interesting ways. Both families resulted from a *rapid* expansion over a *vast* territory that was previously *uninhabited* by man (partially so in the case of Austronesian). Archaeological evidence indicates that the Amerind radiation is about twice as old as the Austronesian radiation, or perhaps even older. Now despite considerable work on the Austronesian family, its internal subgrouping remained largely unknown until recently, but the validity of Austronesian itself was never in doubt. Precisely parallel is the case of Amerind, whose validity no more than Austronesian's should be seen as depending on the prior validity of its components—for example, Almosan-Keresiouan, Almosan, Mosan, or even Salish—as some scholars claim.

A third major error, within the context of binary proposals, was that Indo-European was usually compared with language families that were seen as "worthy" relatives of Indo-European. Because nineteenth-century Indo-Europeanists were decidedly ethnocentric—in many cases even racist—not

TABLE 2 Eurasiatic Cognates

Word	Indo-European	Uralic	Turkic	Mongolian	Tungus
I_1[32]	*mē-[1]	*-m	men[2]	mini[3]	mini[3]
I_2[32]	-x[33]	*-k			
thou	*tu~te	*ti~te		*ti	-ti
pronoun base	*e-g(h)o-m[58]	en-ge-m[79]			
who?	*kʷi~kʷo	ken[15]	*kim	ken	*xa-[17]
what?	*jo~je[24]	*jo-[24]	je-[19]	jaɣun	ja
this	kū-[33]		ku[31]	-ku[81]	
that	*to	*to	-ti	*te-[8]	*ta-
not	*ne	*ne			
dual	-k'[12]	*-k	iki[13]	ikire[77]	
plural		*-t	-t[14]	*-t	-te
two	*dwō-				d'ur[76]
eye		nugie[55]		ńundun	ńundun
bark		*kopa	*kāp[59]		
feather		*tulka	tülüg[88]		
star	*(s)tēr				
fish	*(s)kʷalo-s	*kala			*xol-sa
wolf	*wĺkʷo-s	loqa[27]		noqa[28]	luka[29]
older brother		aka[48]	*āka	aqa	akā
edge		*käćä[43]		keči[44]	
wet		*ńorV	nurě[31]	*nōr(u)-	*ńāru-[30]
dark	*pol-[51]	*piĺmV	boz[52]	bora[52]	balu[53]
speak	*kel[68]	*kele[69]	*kāla	kele(n)[69]	
think	*med-	met[82]		*mede-[83]	mede[84]
sleep		uni[64]		no[65]	
eat	tap[46]	tēp[47]			dzəb
arrive	*tek-[62]		teg-[14]		
take	*kap-	*kapa-	*kʰapa-	qaba-	*xapki-[39]
sharpen	*(s)pik-[37]		*pākä		*pākä
wash	arra-[33]		ari[34]	arun[35]	

Notes: Adapted from *Indo-European and Its Closest Relatives: The Eurasiatic Family,* by Joseph H. Greenberg, Stanford University Press, to appear. [1]'me,' [2]Uzbek, [3]'my,' [4]expresses an emphatic wish on the part of the speaker, [5]Old Japanese, [6]'we,' [7]'thy,' [8]'this,' [9]'there,' [10]occurs marginally in expressions such as *to mo kaku mo* 'this and that,' [11]plural, [12]Armenian plural in nouns, pronouns, and verbs, [13]'two,' [14]Old Turkish, [15]Archaic Finnish, [16]Kamchadal, [17]interrogative base, [18]indefinitizer, [19]interrogative enclitic, [20]coordinating conjunction, [21]privative suffix, [22]negative suffix, [23]'not to be,' [24]relative pronoun, [25]sentence interrogative, [26]Kerek, [27]'fox,' [28]'dog,' [29]'lynx,' [30]'swamp,' [31]Chuvash, [32]first-person *m* is generally ergative or active, while first-person *k*- is absolutive, passive, or stative, where

Korean	Japanese	Ainu	Gilyak	Chukchi-Kamchatkan	Eskimo-Aleut
-ma[4]	mi[5]		me-[6]	-m	-ma
				-k	-k
			ti	-t	-t[7]
				i-ɣə-m[58]	*-m-kə-t[78]
-ka[19]	ka[18]	-ka[18]	-ka[19]	k'e[16]	*kina
ja[25]	i[17]~ja[25]	ja[25]	ja-	jaq[26]	
ki[80]	ko-no	ku-ri	ku[80]		
tjə	to[10]	to[9]		tiʔ-[8]	*ta-[8]
ani[23]	-na[22]	-nak[21]			na-
		-ki	-gi	-k[11]	-k
		*-ti	-t	-ti	-t
tu		tu			
nun	nū-ŋ[56]	nu-	ńü-n[57]	nannin[16]	
këpcil[61]	kapa	sik-kap[60]	xip		
thʌlʌk[88]		trax		ičelčlx[16]	tˢuluk[66]
tal[74]	teru[75]	tolibi[73]		tirkətir[73]	
			q'ol	klxin[16]	iqaluk
		horokew	łiɣ-s		
	aka[50]	aki[49]	ikin		
*kɔtˢ	kisí[45]	kese			
	nure[5]		ŋur		
			polm[54]	pylm	
			qlai[70]	kel[71]	kiliɣā[72]
mit[85]				mitəlhən[86]	misiɣaa[87]
nuŭ	nun-uŋ[50]	enunui	nax[67]		*inaɣ
	tabe-ru				tamaxta
tah	tukú				tikippuq[63]
kaph-[40]	kapu[41]		kip	ɣɣvalʔyn[42]	kiputi[41]
	pikú[38]				*piɣ-
	ara-u	ruye[36]			

[33]Hittite, [34]'become clean,' [35]'clean,' [36]'rub gently,' [37]'point, nail,' [38]'grind,' [39]'seize by the neck,' [40]'repay,' [41]'buy,' [42]'booty,' [43]'end,' [44]Dagur, [45]'shore,' [46]Tokharian, [47]'food,' [48]Yukaghir, [49]'younger brother,' [50]Ryukyuan, [51]'gray, pale,' [52]'gray,' [53]'blind,' [54]'make blind,' [55]Yukaghir 'I have seen,' [56]Ryukyuan 'see,' [57]'see,' [58]'I,' [59]'cover,' [60]'eyelid,' [61]Middle Korean, [62]'reach,' [63]Greenlandic, [64]Finnish, [65]Dunshan, [66]'quill of a feather,' [67]'sleeping place,' [68]'call,' [69]'tongue, speech,' [70]'converse,' [71]'cry out, shout,' [72]Kuskokwim, [73]'sun,' [74]'moon,' [75]'shine,' [76]Evenki, [77]'twins,' [78]the bipersonal form of transitive verbs ("I . . . thee"), [79]Hungarian 'me,' [80]'that,' [81]emphatic suffix, [82]Yukaghir 'inform,' [83]'know,' [84]'knowledge,' [85]'believe,' [86]'expert,' [87]'he perceives it,' [88]'hair.'

just any relative would do for their august language family. What followed from their ethnocentrism was that Indo-European would inevitably be compared first with the Semitic family, which includes Arabic, Hebrew, and Aramaic, and thus had long been seen as Indo-European's most prestigious neighbor. This choice was unfortunate, for two reasons. First, Semitic is without any doubt more closely related to other language families of North Africa, in a family known as Afro-Asiatic, than it is to Indo-European. Thus comparing Indo-European, a *family,* with Semitic, a *branch* of another family, was methodologically unsound from the outset. At best it is Afro-Asiatic as a whole that should be compared with Indo-European. Second, Afro-Asiatic is not as closely related to Indo-European as are numerous other families spread across northern Eurasia. Indo-Europeanists would have found much more substantial linguistic connections had they directed their attention to the Eskimo in his kayak, or to the Chukchi reindeer herders of easternmost Siberia, but these were not the kind of relatives they were looking for.

The first to move beyond binary comparisons was the Dane Holger Pedersen, who, early in the twentieth century, proposed that Indo-European was related not just to one family, but to several, in a higher-level family he called Nostratic. Originally, Pedersen's Nostratic included Indo-European, Semitic, Finno-Ugric, Samoyed, Yukaghir, Altaic, and Eskimo-Aleut, but its membership was never precisely defined, leaving open the possibility that other Nostratic languages might later be discovered. (I will return to this problem below.)

During the 1960's two Russian scholars revived and elaborated Pedersen's Nostratic hypothesis. Vladislav Illich-Svitych and Aron Dolgopolsky, at first independently and later together, set out to show that Indo-European is related to Afro-Asiatic, Kartvelian, Uralic, Altaic, and Dravidian. Over 700 etymologies, involving both grammar and lexicon, have now been published in support of these relationships (Illich-Svitych 1965, 1971–84; Dolgopolsky 1964, 1984). A summary of Nostratic work to date is given in Kaiser and Shevoroshkin (1988).

Recently, a family along the lines of Nostratic—with important differences— has been proposed by Greenberg (to appear). (See Figure 2.) Greenberg calls this family Eurasiatic and includes within it Indo-European, Uralic, Altaic (Turkic, Mongolian, Tungus), Korean-Japanese-Ainu, Gilyak, Chukchi-Kamchatkan, and Eskimo-Aleut. Evidence for this family is provided by 64 grammatical etymologies and over 500 lexical etymologies, many of which, it should be noted, overlap with Nostratic etymologies. A small sample of Eurasiatic cognates, adapted from Greenberg's book, is given in Table 2.

Even this brief table leaves little doubt that Indo-European is intimately related to a whole host of families running across northern Eurasia and into

North America. For example, no description of Indo-European has ever failed to note that the family as a whole is characterized by first-person *m-* 'I' and second-person *t-* 'you' (sing.), but Table 2 shows that these particular pronouns are of Eurasiatic origin, and are thus not unique to Indo-European. Furthermore (see the table), Eurasiatic distinguished two first-person pronouns, the aforementioned *m-* and another in *k-*, the original distinction being that *m-* was basically ergative or active, whereas *k-* was absolutive, passive, or stative, as can be seen in those families that maintain the distinction. Eurasiatic also possessed two interrogative pronouns, *ki* and *ja,* the former being generally personal ("who?"), the latter usually impersonal ("what?"). The demonstrative system also included two pronouns, a near demonstrative *ku* 'this' and a far demonstrative *to* 'that.' Finally, we might note the widespread distribution within Eurasiatic of a dual suffix *-k* and a plural suffix *-t,* a connection noted by Rask almost two centuries ago. In addition to such grammatical evidence there are numerous lexical items that run through Eurasiatic, a few of which are given in Table 2. Grammatical and lexical similarities such as these (and many others) cannot be the result of either chance or borrowing, but can be reasonably explained only as the result of common origin and subsequent diversification.

But what are we to make of the *differences* between Nostratic and Eurasiatic? As seen in Figure 2, both groupings include Indo-European, Uralic, Altaic, and Korean, but Eurasiatic adds to these Japanese, Ainu, Gilyak, Chukchi-Kamchatkan, and Eskimo-Aleut, while Nostratic adds not these, but Afro-Asiatic, Kartvelian, and Dravidian. The differences in the two groupings reflect the different methodologies used in their construction. The goal of Nostraticists has been to demonstrate that Indo-European is related to other language families; indeed, demonstrating that it is not an isolate is the very definition of Nostratic. Furthermore, Nostraticists place great emphasis on comparing only families that have been reconstructed, preferring not to take into account those that have not. Greenberg, by contrast, has approached the problem of Indo-European relatives from a totally different vantage point. As in all of his taxonomic work, he has not tried to prove that X is related to Y, but rather has simply *classified* the world's languages (and language families). Relationships are a derivative property of a classification, not a primary goal. Thus in determining the constituency of Eurasiatic, Greenberg considered *all* potentially relevant families, reconstructed or not, and came to the conclusion that certain Eurasian families are more closely related to each other than they are to other language families, and thus collectively define Eurasiatic. Greenberg does not doubt that Afro-Asiatic, Kartvelian, and Dravidian are related to Eurasiatic, but considers these relationships more distant.

Figure 2. Comparison of the Nostratic and Eurasiatic Language Families

Thus Eurasiatic is intended to be first and foremost a valid linguistic taxon, or family. Nostratic, by contrast, at least in its classic six-family version, is definitely not a valid taxon, since it leaves out certain families (all of them families that Greenberg includes in Eurasiatic) that are clearly more closely related to Indo-European than is, for example, Afro-Asiatic. Sergei Starostin (1989: 43) expresses a similar view regarding Afro-Asiatic: "I prefer presently to exclude Afro-Asiatic material from the Nostratic comparisons. This does not mean, of course, that Afro-Asiatic parallels for Nostratic roots . . . are all accidental 'look-alikes.' They may purely reflect a relationship between Afro-Asiatic and Nostratic at some deeper level."

Still, because at one time or another Nostraticists have included within Nostratic all the families Greenberg includes in Eurasiatic, the inclusion of these families in Nostratic presents no real problems. What *is* disturbing is the continual addition of more and more families to Nostratic as scholars perceive that etymological connections run even deeper than classical Nostratic. Recently, Kaiser and Shevoroshkin (1988) have suggested adding Nilo-Saharan and Niger-Kordofanian to Nostratic. At this level there would be little, if any, difference beween Nostratic and Proto-World. And indeed Nostratic might well be interpreted in just this manner, as a metaphor for long-range comparison, which when followed to its logical conclusion leads to a single human family.

Nostraticists have certainly proved what they set out to show, namely, that Indo-European is in no sense an isolated family without demonstrable relatives. But by largely overlooking the crucial initial step in the comparative method—classification—they have reconstructed, with regular sound correspondences, a linguistic family that never existed. This is not to disparage the very valuable work that the Nostraticists have produced, but simply to cast it in a different light, suggesting that it needs to be examined in an even broader context before we can determine the true meaning of each Nostratic trait.

AMERIND

Probably the most important contribution to genetic linguistics in the 1980's, and certainly the most controversial, was the appearance of Greenberg's (1987) classification of the indigenous languages of the Americas. In this work Greenberg presented evidence that the New World languages are to be classified into just three families: Eskimo-Aleut, Na-Dene, and Amerind. Since Eskimo-Aleut and Na-Dene had long been accepted, what was controversial was Greenberg's proposal to classify all other Native American languages, which cover most of North America and all of South America, into a single Amerind family. In support of this family Greenberg proposed over 300 etymologies, and on the basis of the etymologies given by Greenberg for the 11 separate Amerind subgroups I have suggested an additional 150 Amerind etymologies (see Chapter 8). Given the prevailing opinion of American Indian specialists that the New World contains some two hundred independent families (Campbell and Mithun 1979, Kaufman 1990), Greenberg's amalgamation of all these families save two has met with incredulity, outrage, and dismay. Space does not permit an extended discussion of the controversy provoked by Greenberg's Amerind proposal, but a general history of Amerindian classification is given in Ruhlen (1987), and a discussion of the issues involved in the ongoing controversy over Amerind may be found in Chapter 6.

Rather than entering into the often obscure argumentation over Amerind, I will instead briefly review the most persuasive piece of evidence that Amerind is a valid linguistic taxon within the world's language families, despite the generally negative reception from the establishment experts. We have seen that Eurasiatic is characterized by the pronominal system *m*- 'I' and *t*- 'you' (sing.), but except for Eskimo-Aleut in the far north, this pronominal pattern is virtually absent in the New World. In its place we find a different pattern, *na* 'I' and *ma* 'you' (sing.), that is perhaps the most salient characteristic of the Amerind family, widely attested throughout North and South America. By reviewing how this particular pronominal pattern has been viewed by various scholars during this century, we may render in miniature the outlines of the Amerind controversy itself.

The first to call attention to the high frequency of this pattern in the New World (as far as I have been able to determine) was Alfredo Trombetti, who documented the pattern in numerous American Indian languages, throughout North and South America, in his 1905 book. Moreover, Trombetti did not

TABLE 3 Amerind Cognates

Word	Almosan-Keresiouan	Penutian	Hokan	Central Amerind	Chibchan-Paezan
I	*ne-[1]	na?	na	nã[2]	nan
thou	-m	ma	mai	am[4]	ma
who?	?aqi-[51]	gu	kī	*haka	kin
where?	mana[8]	mani			mani
that	-t-[13]	t-[12]	t-[11]		
not	*kaθ-	kwa?	kam	*ka	ka
two	ma?ɫ	palo-		pahn	palu
hand	maχwa[6]	makan	mane	*maka	man
tooth	tˢaäm[54]	tsam[55]	i?tˢaw	*tam	dau
eye	-tu?	tu	-ītu	*te	ičui[56]
mouth	i?ə/iha		ja?		
foot	*si	sija?	sa?je	siha	
leg	*-θōk-an-	ṭa?	tek	tˢaku	
knee	*-ketekʷ-i	ikat			ikuet
vagina	-nɛ?ɛ	ne?ēs	i'un?		
girl	tuña	tūne[48]		*tun[49]	tuntu[34]
aunt		pinūkin	pane-	*pan	puna[57]
snake		kan	xanʲ-[59]	kunze	
ant	tˢ'aχuna	tˢokun		sikuwi	
bird	tˢitˢipe/tˢ'ēk	č'ik'	šīk	tsikie	eš'ɛka-
fly (n.)	tˢ'âpi	čap	-komo-		
urine	ošewa[32]	wiuš	wisāk		wisi
water₁	pa?ah	bai[35]		p'ãide	pui
water₂	*akwā[43]	oka?	aqa	*gʷa[42]	aka
tree₁	tepō	tumaj[29]		tebe[31]	jutube
tree₂	ondata	ito		*tua[16]	
thorn		ōnoxk			
covering			šīk'o[20]		teka-ra[21]
good	čema		tˢama	*tˢam	tˢama
dark	atek	tek[40]		tukɨ[41]	tsix-
left (hand)	qatˢ/kes-	kets	kasark	kuč'ē	kuts-
swallow	m'lχʷ[38]	mülk'	malqi?[39]		murki
see	tˢ'iɨ[63]	tˢ'elei[23]		tsi[24]	tili
say	-wāɫ	wili			
go	wa[25]	waŋ[26]	wan		wan

Notes: [1]'my,' [2]'I, we,' [3]'we,' [4]'thou, you,' [5]'thy,' [6]'give a potlatch,' [7]'give,' [8]'who?,' [9]'he,' [10]'he, she, it, they,' [11]a stage III article, i.e. a mere marker of nominality,' [12]'his, her, its,' [13]a petrified article appearing between third-person possessive pronouns and nouns beginning with a vowel, [14]'leg,' [15]'see,' [16]'oak tree,' [17]'say,' [18]'younger sister,' [19]'woman,' [20]'blanket,' [21]'poncho,' [22]'woman's shirt,' [23]'look,' [24]'eye,' [25]'come,' [26]'walk,' [27]'tell,' [28]'speak,' [29]'stick, wood,' [30]'firewood,' [31]'wood,'

Andean	Macro-Tucanoan	Equatorial	Macro-Carib	Macro-Panoan	Macro-Ge
naja	en³	no	ana³	no	nu
-ma⁵	ma	ma	ama	em	ma
kunna				kine-	huna
					manẽ-⁵²
maj	-mãni	mañi			
ta¹⁰	toho	tu	da	ta	ti⁹
kaa	kai	kaoka		ka	ka
pula⁵³	p'ālin				
maki	-muka	*me?eŋ	emekun	moken	mako⁷
		iti	itie	*e-tˢe	i-tio
	etu	tu	etoj	e-tua	toi
ja	ia?a	iahoj	ííxa	*jo?i¹⁷	ia
		-šej	iši	ise¹⁴	
čaki⁴⁷	to?a⁴⁷	taxu⁴⁷	take	*ta?ɨ	etage
	*kat'	-ikketi	-kudo-	katˢege	-gete
	-e?ne³³		iani		
	ton⁴⁸	tana	itaño	tanani¹⁹	tontan¹⁸
epan	ãebn	penawa	ebuño	*e-pona¹⁹	pan-⁵⁸
kuni	kiane		koni	kouni	kuni
čakon		sik'imara			
tˢiktˢi³⁷	šaga	čiki	sɨkɨi	e-jikidi³⁷	tˢĩpe³⁷
	kob	kããp	okoma⁶⁰		kap/kã
		usī	usu	yius³²	iši
	poi³⁶	buɨš			beia³⁵
jaku	okõa	ako	woku⁴⁶	uaka	waka⁴⁶
	temba³⁰	-timbeu³¹	tapasej	tome³¹	
		andu	itua⁴⁴	isu³¹	
	ñãka	onak			
takun⁴⁵		dikexe⁴⁵			deku²²
suma	-čemači⁵⁰	-tˢiama⁵⁰		utsama	
	asikẽ⁴¹	sikia⁶¹	tuku-⁴¹	tuxlin⁶¹	*tɨk⁴¹
		kuču-			*keč
malq'a³⁹		mirko⁶²	e?mōkï		
tet²⁴		tiji			-čir
wilʲe²⁷	wála⁶⁴		uri-²⁸		wenní²⁸
-wen-	w'ãn²⁵	awani		wo-	-va

³²'urinate,' ³³'vulva,' ³⁴'niece,' ³⁵'rain,' ³⁶'to wet,' ³⁷'bat,' ³⁸'chew food,' ³⁹'throat,' ⁴⁰'green,' ⁴¹'black,' ⁴²'river,' ⁴³'from water,' ⁴⁴'forest,' ⁴⁵'dress,' ⁴⁶'drink' (n.), ⁴⁷'foot,' ⁴⁸'daughter,' ⁴⁹'girl,' ⁵⁰'beautiful,' ⁵¹'what?,' ⁵²'when?,' ⁵³'both,' ⁵⁴'chew,' ⁵⁵'bite,' ⁵⁶'look at,' ⁵⁷'sister,' ⁵⁸'sister-in-law,' ⁵⁹'coral snake,' ⁶⁰'wasp,' ⁶¹'night,' ⁶²'drink,' ⁶³'to spy,' ⁶⁴'talk.'

hesitate to give a genetic explanation for this distribution. Nor did Edward Sapir, when he became aware (independently) of the broad distribution of the two American pronouns. In 1918, in a personal letter to a friend, he wrote: "How in the Hell are you going to explain general American *n*- 'I' except genetically?" (quoted in Ruhlen 1987). Franz Boas, who preferred to attribute linguistic similarites such as these to diffusion rather than to common origin, was himself troubled by the broad distribution of *n*- and *m*- in the Americas, but for an explanation he could do no better than to suggest that "the frequent occurrence of similar sounds for expressing related ideas (like the personal pronouns) may be due to obscure psychological causes rather than to genetic relationship." In 1954 Morris Swadesh posited the *n*-/*m*- pronominal pattern for his Penutoid family, which included languages from both North and South America. Finally, Greenberg has shown in his recent book on Amerind that the *n*-/*m*- pattern is attested in all of his eleven Amerind subgroups.

Still, today, new and even more fanciful explanations are offered—without evidence—in attempts to do away with the "problem" of the Amerind pronouns. Sarah Thomason (1988) has recently proposed that "too many of the inherited shared features in the very distantly related languages are going to be unmarked, stable features [like *n*- 'I' and *m*- 'you'] that could just as easily be relics of parallel but historically unconnected attrition processes in unrelated languages." This is an empirical claim that can be tested, and in order to do so I collected the first- and second-person pronouns for all of the world's major linguistic families to see just how common the Amerind pattern really is (see Chapter 12). I did not find a single family anywhere else in the world that shares the Amerind pattern, which turns out not only to *define* the Amerind family, but at the same time to *differentiate* it from the world's other language families.

Amerind is a well-defined linguistic taxon, notwithstanding the clamor of certain experts. Not simply the pronominal pattern discussed above, but a wealth of other grammatical and lexical similarities, a few of which are given in Table 3, guarantee its validity. Table 3 presents some representative Amerind forms from different Amerind subgroups, most of them taken from Greenberg (1981, 1987; many additional cognate forms may be found in these two sources).

DENE-CAUCASIAN

Soon after Edward Sapir proposed the Na-Dene family in 1915, he became aware that this family shared many striking parallels with the Sino-Tibetan languages of East Asia. In a letter to Alfred Kroeber in 1920 he wrote: "I do *not* feel that Na-Dene belongs to the other American languages. . . . Do not think me an ass if I am seriously entertaining the notion of an old Indo-Chinese offshoot into N.W. America. . . . At least I know that Déné's a long shot nearer to Tibetan than to Siouan" (quoted in Golla 1984: 350). A year later he wrote again to Kroeber on the same subject, this time more convinced than ever of a genetic affinity between Na-Dene and Sino-Tibetan: "If the morphological and lexical accord which I find on every hand between Na-Dene and Indo-Chinese is 'accidental,' then every analogy on God's earth is an accident. It is all so powerfully cumulative and integrated that when you tumble to one point a lot of others fall into line" (Golla 1984: 374). For reasons not known, Sapir never published any of the evidence he had assembled in support of the genetic affinity of Na-Dene and Sino-Tibetan. Perhaps the hostile reception accorded Na-Dene itself by Pliny Goddard, following soon after the equally hostile attack on Sapir's Algonquian-Ritwan proposal by Truman Michelson, convinced Sapir that even more distant proposals would not be considered at all, no matter what the evidence. In any event, Sapir's Na-Dene–Sino-Tibetan proposal fell into disrepute as yet another longshot that failed to convince, despite the efforts of a few supporters (Shafer 1952, 1957; Swadesh 1952).

During the 1980's, however, Sapir's idea was revived and extended by Russian scholars, albeit in a somewhat circuitous manner. First, in 1984, Sergei Starostin proposed a family including (North) Caucasian, Sino-Tibetan, and Yeniseian, which he named Sino-Caucasian. The following year V. A. Chirikba presented evidence connecting Basque with (North) Caucasian, an idea that had already been suggested with considerable supporting evidence by Trombetti in 1926. In 1986 Starostin's colleague Sergei Nikolaev offered evidence connecting Na-Dene with (North) Caucasian, thus constituting a larger family that is now usually called Dene-Caucasian. In this Russian work Sapir's original idea of a connection between Na-Dene and Sino-Tibetan is supported by the transitivity of genetic affinity (that is, if language A is known to be related to language B, and language B is known to be related to language C, then language C must be related to language A), even though the Russians have yet to compare Na-Dene with Sino-Tibetan, as Sapir did.

More recently John Bengtson (1991a,b) has taken the first multilateral look at all of Dene-Caucasian, and has proposed a significant amount of new evidence for this family, which in his view also includes Basque, Burushaski, and Sumerian. I have compared Starostin's Yeniseian reconstructions (Starostin 1982; see also Chapter 4) with Na-Dene etymologies (see Chapter 5), as well as with Nahali, and have discovered additional Dene-Caucasian cognates (see Chapter 4). It should be noted, as well, that Claude Boisson (1989) has compared Sumerian with both Dene-Caucasian (where Bengtson places it) and

TABLE 4 Dene-Caucasian Cognates

Word	Basque	(North) Caucasian	Burushaski	Sumerian	Nahali
I		*z^wo	ǰa/ǰe		ǰuo
we	-t[15]	*it^l'i[16]			tē-ku[45]
thou$_1$		*we[18]	ū-ŋ		
thou$_2$	-k	*Gu	gu-		
thou$_3$					nā-ko[23]
who?$_1$	ze-	*sa			
who?$_2$	no-	*nV		ana[40]	nāni
tongue	mili-[8]	*mēlt$^{s'}$i	-melǯ[9]	-me	lãy
paw	hatz	*k^{w}ač'e	qʌš[34]	kiš-ib[79]	
pupil (of eye)	-nini-	*nănV	nʌna[39]		
head		*sqa[18]	-sk-īl[44]	sag̃	
cheek	gal-tzar[80]	*-G^{w}ə̃ɫ^{w}V[54]			
back	bi-zka-r	a-zk^{w}a[46]	-sqa[22]		
blood	o-dol		del[50]		
elbow	u-kondo	*q'^{w}ʌntV			
vagina					
penis		*k'əlč'V[67]	-ɣūš[69]		
father		*b^{w}ab^{w}ʌjʌ	bʌba	ab.ba	aba
child		*kənt$^{s'}$V			giṭa[28]
otter	ur-txakur				
squirrel	sagu[10]	*t^{s}arku[11]	čʰərge[31]		
frog	i-gel	*q'^{w}VrV-q'V	gʊr-qut^s		
water	i-toi[61]	*tujV[62]	thī-š[61]		
tree/wood					
day(light)	e-gun	*-GɨnV	gōn[4]	gùn[5]	
star	i-zar	*-d^{zw}ᵃ'ärʕi	čʰār[52]	-sar[51]	
river					
ice	-tzig-[70]	t^{s}iq̄[71]	čʰʌɣ-[72]	šeg[70]	
cold			thātine	ten	
yellow		*t^{s}ak^{w}V[24]	šɪk-ʌrk	sig[77]	
hungry	gose	*ḡašī			
spit	to	*tŭk'	thū		ṭhuk-
sleep			gʊč-[58]		
bite		*qát^{s}ᵢ[59]			

Notes: Adapted from Starostin (1984), Nikolaev (1986), Bengtson (1991a,b), Ruhlen (1992e), and Starostin and Ruhlen (1992). [1]Newari, [2]'ocean,' [3]'creek, stream,' [4]'dawn,' [5]'bright,' [6]Old Chinese, [7]'sun,' [8]'lick' (cf. also *mihi* 'tongue'), [9]'jaw,' [10]'rat, mouse,' [11]'marten,' [12]Carrier 'chipmunk,' [13]Kato, [14]'self,' [15]'I,' [16]'we in-clusive,' [17]'us,' [18]Proto-Northwest Caucasian, [19]'you,' [20]'what?,' [21]Old Chinese 'what?,' [22]'on one's back,' [23]'you-2,' [24]'yellow, white,' [25]'urinate,' [26]'green,' [27]Tanaina, [28]'younger brother or sister,' [29]'children,' [30]Navajo 'son,' [31]'flying squir-rel,' [32]'knee,' [33]Sarsi 'knee, elbow,' [34]'arm length from elbow to fingertips,' [35]'foot,'

Sino-Tibetan	Yeniseian	Haida	Tlingit	Eyak	Athabaskan
ji[1]	*ʔad[z]			chuu	*šī
		īt[b17]			*-ī'd
	*ʔu		weh		
*kʷVj	*kV-		ɣi[19]		-hʷī[73]
*naŋ					nan[38]
	*ʔas-		ah-sa		
ʔan[21]	*ʔan-				
*mlay					
	*kiʔs[35]			-kaša[37]	*-keč'[36]
-sko[47]	*tˢɨ̃ʔG-	-ǰi	si[48]	-tˢiʔ[48]	*-tˢɨ̃ʔ
*qālH[55]	*χol-			l-quhɬ	
		skwai			
				deɬ	*deɬ
	*gid			Guhd	gūd[33]
*dźuk[67]		čúu			dzū́z[68]
	*gʌns-			guč	ɣīd[ẓ]á̃ʔ[68]
*bwa	*ʔob				-ba[41]
	*gʌʔt[29]	gyīt'	git'a	qēč'	ɣèʔ[30]
	*täχʌr				
*srǎiŋ	*saʔqa	-tˢ'ākʷ	tˢʌlk	tˢaɬk'	tˢolq-[12]
	*xiʔr-			čiaɬq	č'ʷal[49]
*twiy		sū[63]			*tū
*siŋ		tˢan-			tˢin[43]
*kʷāŋ[6]	*gəʔn[5]	kūŋ[7]	-gan[7]	ǰah	ǰanih[56]
tśar[53]					
	*ses	sī(s)[2]		šī[3]	sis-kãã[2]
-tˢik[74]	*tiχ[75]		t'iq'	t'itˢ'	tʰitˢ'[76]
					*tʰen[64]
*tsyak[42]	*täk-[78]	tˢɛgɛñ[25]	sūhw[26]	tˢeʔq	tˢək[27]
kʰusší[65]					gas[66]
*(m-)tuk	*tuk		tuχ	tux	šek'[13]
	*xus-				ɣʷoš[60]
		q'us-gat	kʷač[57]	q'ətˢ'	gətˢ[13]

[36]'claw,' [37]'(finger-)nail,' [38]Galice, [39]'eyeball,' [40]'what?,' [41]Carrier, seemingly isolated within Na-Dene, [42]'gold, red,' [43]Navajo, [44]'face,' [45]'we-2,' [46]Abkhaz, [47]Tibetan, [48]'neck,' [49]Hupa, [50]'oil,' [51]'new moon,' [52]'morning star,' [53]'sun, moon, star,' [54]'side,' [55]'back, cheek,' [56]Tanaina, [57]'swallow,' [58]'lie sleeping,' [59]Proto-East Caucasian, [60]Coquille, [61]'a drop,' [62]'spit' (n.), [63]'lake,' [64]'ice,' [65]Hruso, [66]Galice 'become hungry,' [67]'vulva,' [68]Sarsi, [69]'vagina,' [70]'frost,' [71]Avar 'sleet,' [72]'cold,' [73]San Carlos Apache 'you,' [74]Garo 'cold,' [75]'snow,' [76]Hupa, [77]'yellow, green,' [78]'white,' [79]'hand,' [80]'side of body, flank.'

Nostratic, but because he leans toward a stronger affinity with the latter, the question of the affiliation of Sumerian is yet to be definitively settled. In Table 4 I have given a representative sample of some of the Dene-Caucasian etymologies proposed in the works enumerated above. As can be seen in the table, the basic pronouns are quite distinct from those of both Eurasiatic and Amerind, but form many connections among themselves. The additional grammatical and lexical evidence, only a very small fraction of which is given here, convinces me that these families—those constituting Dene-Caucasian— share a common origin, and that Sapir's long-neglected proposal was essentially correct, if incomplete.

THE MONOGENESIS OF HUMAN LANGUAGE

If we accept the proposals outlined above for Eurasiatic, Amerind, and Dene-Caucasian, as well as those for Austric (Austronesian, Daic, Miao-Yao, Austroasiatic), then the world's languages can be classified into as few as a dozen families, as shown in Figure 3. The question thus arises whether these larger families in turn share cognates, or whether they are "independent," with no visible connections. In the preceding discussion, we encountered several of the more crippling myths of historical linguistics, but we have arrived now at a more formidable linguistic taboo, the monogenesis of human language. Any mention of this topic was banned by the Société de Linguistique de Paris in 1866, and discussion of this question has been decidedly rare throughout the twentieth century. The reason of course is that if one accepts the myth that Indo-European is unrelated to any other family, then the question of monogenesis becomes moot. If the best-known family in the world cannot be shown to be related to any other family, then what would be the point of trying to proceed even beyond that notion? Thus in order to approach the question of monogenesis one must first shake loose from these all but universal myths. Several scholars have in fact done so, with Trombetti (1905) and Swadesh (1971) perhaps the two best-known supporters of monogenesis.

Less well known is the fact that the twentieth century's two great taxonomists, Sapir and Greenberg, also were inclined toward the hypothesis of monogenesis. In a letter to Kroeber in 1924 Sapir wrote, regarding Trombetti's theory of monogenesis, "There is much excellent material and good sense in Trombetti in spite of his being a frenzied monogenist. I am not so sure that his standpoint is less sound than the usual 'conservative' one" (quoted in Golla 1984: 420). In his book on Amerind, Greenberg defined the "ultimate goal" of genetic linguistics as "a comprehensive classification of what is very likely a single language family" (Greenberg 1987: 337).

1. Khoisan
2. Niger-Kordofanian:
   a. Kordofanian
   b. Niger-Congo
3. Nilo-Saharan
4. Australian
5. Indo-Pacific
6. Austric:
   a. Austroasiatic
   b. Miao-Yao
   c. Daic
   d. Austronesian
7. Dene-Caucasian:
   a. Basque
   b. (North) Caucasian
   c. Burushaski
   d. Nahali
   e. Sino-Tibetan
   f. Yeniseian
   g. Na-Dene
8. Afro-Asiatic
9. Kartvelian
10. Dravidian
11. Eurasiatic:
    a. Indo-European
    b. Uralic-Yukaghir
    c. Altaic
    d. Korean-Japanese-Ainu
    e. Gilyak
    f. Chukchi-Kamchatkan
    g. Eskimo-Aleut
12. Amerind

Figure 3. The World's Language Families

During the past decade the question of monogenesis has arisen once again, in the work of scholars who have eschewed the myth of Indo-European independence. The Russian Nostraticists, much maligned in this country, must be recognized as having taken important initial steps in proving monogenesis. By connecting Indo-European beyond any doubt with other families, their work broke down that dike against all long-range comparison and allowed the question of monogenesis to be broached once again. Once Starostin and Nikolaev had postulated Dene-Caucasian, a logical next step was to compare this family with Nostratic, and in undertaking that comparison, Starostin (1989) has shown many convincing connections between the two groups. Ilja Pejros (1989) has in turn presented evidence linking Austric (Austroasiatic, Miao-Yao, Daic, Austronesian) with both Nostratic and Dene-Caucasian, and Vitaly Shevoroshkin (1989a) has noted similarities between Nostratic, Dene-Caucasian, Amerind, Australian, and Indo-Pacific. Moving equally far afield, Mark Kaiser and Shevoroshkin (1988) have suggested (as noted above) that Niger-Kordofanian and Nilo-Saharan should be added to Nostratic as well. Clearly, if we pause long enough to concatenate these various proposals we are not far from monogenesis itself.

Toward that end, and independently of the Russian work, John Bengtson and I, operating in the Greenbergian tradition of multilateral comparison, have proposed 27 etymologies connecting all of the world's language families (see Chapter 14), and these represent the merest fraction of what could be brought to bear on the question if all documented materials were duly assembled.

But all of these efforts—so intuitively reasonable and so methodologically sound—continue to be assailed by the conservative Indo-Europeanists and their followers. It has been fashionable among such critics of long-range comparison to claim that "unsystematic similarities [between language families] are *not* sufficient [to prove genetic affinity] because—as many people have pointed out—unsystematic similarities can be found for *any* pair, or set, of languages" (Thomason 1988). In a similar vein Ives Goddard (1979: 376) remarks "how easy it is to find lexical resemblances between groupings of large numbers of poorly recorded languages." And James Matisoff (1990: 112) specifically criticizes the very robust TIK etymology, given in Chapter 14, as "wildly fantastical."

What is characteristic of the claims that one can find *whatever* one looks for is that they are never supported by *evidence*. If the correlations between TIK and 'finger,' and PAL and 'two,' documented in Chapter 14, are simply artifacts of the analysis, as claimed by Thomason, Goddard, and Matisoff, rather than historically connected forms, as we maintain, then Thomason, Goddard, or Matisoff should offer alternative etymologies in which TIK is connected with 'two,' and PAL with 'finger.' Unless they do this, their claims of what one can do should not be taken seriously.

Militating against the position advocated by Greenberg's critics is the fact that if the TIK and PAL etymologies represent simply a clever sifting of the evidence, then one should be able to do the same thing with 'three' and higher numbers. In our survey of the world's linguistic literature, however,

Bengtson and I have found no other widespread numerals except 'one' and 'two.' There is, of course, a simple explanation for this observation. In many hunter-gatherer societies—which included all of mankind until about 12,000 years ago—numerals are limited to 'one,' 'two,' and 'many,' a trait preserved by Australian languages to the present day. Thus the fact that there are no widespread numerals higher than 'two' is not altogether unexpected, and their absence tends more to support our etymologies than to refute them.

THE BIOLOGICAL TAXONOMY OF MODERN HUMANS

Quite unexpectedly the debate on long-range comparison in linguistics was buffeted by a signal event of the late 1980's, the discovery by human geneticists that the biological classification of the human species closely parallels the linguistic classifications postulated by long-range comparison, not only for low-level families like Indo-European and Bantu, but even for families such as Niger-Kordofanian, Khoisan, Nilo-Saharan, Afro-Asiatic, Indo-Pacific, and Amerind, groupings often considered little more than "guesses" by Indo-Europeanists (Hopper 1989).

In 1986 Greenberg, together with the anthropologist Christy Turner and the biologist Stephen Zegura, pointed out a general congruence between Greenberg's linguistic classification of New World populations and the classifications of Turner, based on dental evidence, and Zegura, based on traditional genetic markers such as blood groups (Greenberg, Turner, and Zegura 1986; it is worth noting that the three had initially reached their conclusions quite independently, unaware of the work of the others). A similar finding, based on more substantial genetic evidence, was reported by L. L. Cavalli-Sforza and colleagues two years later (Cavalli-Sforza et al. 1988).

In 1987 Laurent Excoffier and his colleagues found, in a study of human genetics in sub-Saharan Africa, that "genetic differentiation clearly parallels the clustering of major linguistic families. . . . A rather clear distinction may . . . be made between Bantu and West Africans. As a matter of fact, they seem to form two overlapping but different clusters. . . . Concerning East Africans, the genetic data support quite clearly the main ethnic groupings defined by the linguistic approach. . . . Genetic results also completely concur with two other specific ethnic distinctions inside Africa, commonly known as Pygmies and Khoisan" (Excoffier et al. 1987: 151, 166–67). Excoffier and his colleagues concluded from their study that "most of the genetic peculiarities concerning present populations can be explained, when confronted with historical and linguistic sources, rather than being considered as examples of founder effects, random genetic drift, or frequency convergence. . . . Most of the time, genetic specificities correspond to linguistic differentiations"

(p. 185). In a study of the island of Sardinia, Alberto Piazza and colleagues (1992) compared the geographic distributions of human genes, linguistic traits (in the form of lexical items), and surnames. They found a high degree of correlation among all three, concluding that "languages and genes have a similar geographical distribution even at a microareal level."

In 1989 Guido Barbujani, Neal Oden, and Robert Sokal proposed a new method (which they called "wombling") of identifying biological boundaries, that is, "areas where the rates of change of biological variables across space are particularly high" (p. 376). Such boundaries may correspond either to "steep ecological gradients" (such as mountains or oceans) or "regions of limited admixture among demes" (such as that resulting from linguistic differences among populations). One of the examples of their application of this new technique concerns the Yanomami Indians of northern South America. Here, the authors found "that both at the level of variation among dialect groups as well as within such groups the regions of rapid genetic change agree with observable linguistic differences. These findings support conclusions from other studies on the relation of genetics and language" (Barbujani, Oden, and Sokal 1989: 386). This same technique has been applied to Europe by Barbujani and Sokal, who found a similarly high degree of correlation between genetic and linguistic distributions. They report that "of the 33 gene-frequency boundaries discovered . . . , 31 are coincident with linguistic boundaries marking contiguous regions of different language families, languages, or dialects. . . . The congruence of the discovered boundaries with linguistic boundaries is far too strong to be due to chance" (Barbujani and Sokal 1990: 1816–18).

Finally, Luca Cavalli-Sforza and colleagues published in 1988 a brief summary of their findings concerning the geographical distribution of human genes on a worldwide scale (see Figure 4). The complete results of this investigation are reported in a book now in press (Cavalli-Sforza, Piazza, and Menozzi 1994). Already the short article by Cavalli-Sforza and colleagues (1988) has stirred up a furor among those opposed to long-range comparison (O'Grady et al. 1989, Bateman et al. 1990, Hopper 1989), for the simple reason that these human geneticists have found biological clusters in the human population that are the same as or similar to the linguistic families identified by linguists. For the opponents of Greenberg's classification of the languages of the New World, the results of this study were dismaying indeed, for Cavalli-Sforza and colleagues found that, on the basis of human genetics, the populations of the Americas fall into the same three groups that Greenberg had posited a year earlier on the basis of language. Elsewhere in the biological phylogenetic tree can be found clusters corresponding to such linguistic groups as Australian, Indo-Pacific, and Austric.

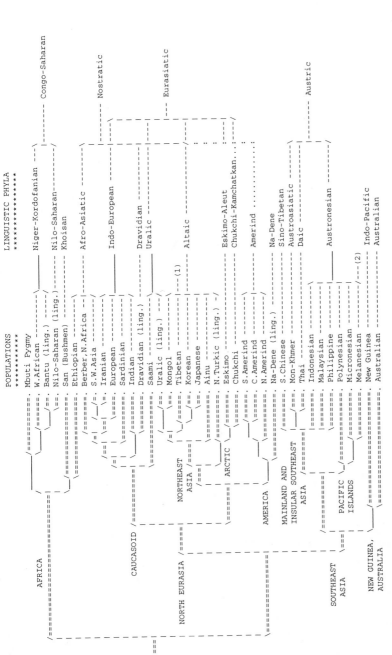

Figure 4. Comparison of the Genetic Tree with the Linguistic Phyla

Notes: (ling.) indicates populations pooled on the basis of linguistic classification. (1) Tibetans are associated genetically with the Northeast Asian cluster, but linguistically with the Sino-Tibetan phylum. (2) Melanesians speak, in part, Indo-Pacific languages. Genetic data are not currently available for Kartvelian or (North) Caucasian populations. (Adapted from [Cavalli-Sforza et al. 1988])

There are of course cases where genes and languages are not congruent. Black Americans speak American English, not a Black African language. But cases such as these, which for the most part have known historical causes, are the exception, not the rule. Cavalli-Sforza and colleagues conclude that although "gene flow and language replacement . . . may blur the genetic and the linguistic picture, . . . they do not obscure it entirely" (Cavalli-Sforza et al. 1990: 18).

Since Cavalli-Sforza and colleagues provide a comprehensive tree for the entire human family—something linguists have so far been unable to do—it is interesting to consider their higher-level findings for those areas where linguistic taxonomy has so far been unsuccessful. As one can see in Figure 4, the first branching in the human tree separates Black Africans, including Pygmies and the Khoisan, from the remainder of human populations. (Edgar Gregersen [1972] has proposed linguistic evidence connecting Niger-Kordofanian with Nilo-Saharan.) The Khoisan appear to be an admixture of roughly 50 percent Black African genes and 50 percent non-African genes, with the admixture having taken place more than 20,000 years ago. Ethiopians represent a much later admixture of the same two populations. Pygmies speak languages belonging to either Niger-Kordofanian or Nilo-Saharan, having presumably lost their original language(s).

The second branching in the genetic tree separates the populations of Southeast Asia and Oceania from the remainder; in linguistic terms this second branching includes Austric, Indo-Pacific, and Australian, with the last two groups closer to each other than either is to Austric. What remains after these first two branchings from the biological tree is a population that corresponds to Nostratic/Eurasiatic + Amerind. (Linguistic evidence supporting such a group is given in Chapter 10.) Within this vast gene-based grouping, which stretches from North Africa, across northern Eurasia, and throughout the Americas, there are three basic clusters: (1) Afro-Asiatic, Indo-European, Dravidian, (2) Uralic, Altaic, Chukchi-Kamchatkan, and Eskimo-Aleut, and (3) Amerind and Na-Dene. Very likely, Na-Dene falls together with Amerind in that third group because the two have experienced substantial genetic (but not linguistic) admixture. Conspicuously absent from this biological tree are most of the Dene-Caucasian populations, for which genetic data are largely lacking.

CONCLUSIONS

I have argued here that the "conservative" view of genetic linguistic classification, which sees Indo-European as unrelated to any other family, the New World inhabited by dozens of different families with no genetic connections, and no known genetic links existing between language families of the Old and New Worlds, is for the most part a collection of myths which, while still fervently believed by most linguists, are not borne out by the linguistic evidence. Rather, Indo-European is intimately connected with language families spread across northern Eurasia, and the New World contains just three stocks, each with a different Asian origin (Ruhlen 1990). Furthermore, evidence for monogenesis, far from being totally lacking as is widely contended, is in fact abundant. The real problem is not that there are "no nonuniversal markers of remote genetic relationship," but rather that there are so many it is difficult to determine the precise distribution of each. When all of the relevant materials are collected and analyzed, we may perhaps be able to construct a comprehensive linguistic tree to compare with that developed by human geneticists. At least that should be the goal of genetic linguistics.

REFERENCES

Barbujani, Guido, Neal L. Oden, and Robert R. Sokal. 1989. "Detecting Regions of Abrupt Change in Maps of Biological Variables," *Systematic Zoology* 38: 376–89.

Barbujani, Guido, and Robert R. Sokal. 1990. "Zones of Sharp Genetic Change in Europe Are Also Linguistic Boundaries," *Proceedings of the National Academy of Sciences* 87: 1816–19.

Bateman, Richard, Ives Goddard, Richard O'Grady, V. A. Funk, Rich Mooi, W. John Kress, and Peter Cannell. 1990. "Speaking of Forked Tongues: The Feasibility of Reconciling Human Phylogeny and the the History of Language," *Current Anthropology* 31: 1–24.

Bengtson, John D. 1991a. "Notes on Sino-Caucasian," in Vitaly Shevoroshkin, ed., 1991: 67–129.

———. 1991b. "Some Macro-Caucasian Etymologies," in Vitaly Shevoroshkin, ed., 1991: 130–41.

Bengtson, John D., and Merritt Ruhlen. 1994. "Global Etymologies," Chapter 14 of this volume.

Boisson, Claude. 1989. "Sumerian/Nostratic/Sino-Caucasian Isoglosses," ms.

Callaghan, Catherine A. 1990. "Comment," in Bateman et al. 1990: 15–16.

Campbell, Lyle, and Marianne Mithun, eds. 1979. *The Languages of Native America*. Austin, Tex.

Cavalli-Sforza, L. L., Alberto Piazza, and Paolo Menozzi. 1994. *History and Geography of Human Genes*. Princeton, N.J.

Cavalli-Sforza, L. L., Alberto Piazza, Paolo Menozzi, and Joanna Mountain. 1988. "Reconstruction of Human Evolution: Bringing Together Genetic, Archeological and Linguistic Data," *Proceedings of the National Academy of Sciences* 85: 6002–6.

———. 1990. "Comment," in Bateman et al. 1990: 16–18.

Chirikba, V. A. 1985. "Baskskij i severokavkazskie jazyki," *Drevnjaja Anatolija.* Moscow, 95–105.

Dolgopolsky, Aron. 1964. "Gipoteza drevnejšego rodstva jazykovyx semei severnoj Eurasii s verojatnostnoj točki zrenija," *Voprosy Jazykoznanija* 2: 53–63. [English translation in Vitalij V. Shevoroshkin and T. L. Markey, eds., *Typology, Relationship and Time,* 1986. Ann Arbor, Mich., 27–50.]

———. 1984. "On Personal Pronouns in the Nostratic Languages," in Otto Gschwantler, Károly Rédei, and Hermann Reichert, eds., *Linguistica et Philologica.* Vienna, 65–112.

Excoffier, Laurent, Béatrice Pellegrini, Alicia Sanchez-Mazas, Christian Simon, and André Langaney. 1987. "Genetics and History of Sub-Saharan Africa," *Yearbook of Physical Anthropology* 30: 151–94.

Goddard, Ives. 1979. "The Languages of South Texas and the Lower Rio Grande," in Campbell and Mithun, eds., 1979: 355–89.

Golla, Victor, ed. 1984. *The Sapir-Kroeber Correspondence.* Berkeley, Calif.

Greenberg, Joseph H. 1963. *The Languages of Africa.* Bloomington, Ind.

———. 1971. "The Indo-Pacific Hypothesis," in Thomas A. Sebeok, ed., *Current Trends in Linguistics,* Volume 8. The Hague, 807–71.

———. 1981. "Comparative Amerindian Notebooks," 23 vols. Mss. on file, Green Library, Stanford University, Stanford, Calif.

———. 1987. *Language in the Americas.* Stanford, Calif.

———. To appear. *Indo-European and Its Closest Relatives: The Eurasiatic Language Family.* Stanford, Calif.

Greenberg, Joseph H., Christy G. Turner II, and Stephen L. Zegura. 1986. "The Settlement of the Americas: A Comparison of Linguistic, Dental, and Genetic Evidence," *Current Anthropology* 27: 477–97.

Gregersen, Edgar A. 1972. "Kongo-Saharan," *Journal of African Languages* 11: 69–89.

Hopper, Paul. 1989. Review of *Language Contact, Creolization, and Genetic Linguistics,* by Sarah Grey Thomason and Terrence Kaufman, *American Anthropologist* 91: 817–18.

Illich-Svitych, Vladislav M. 1965 [1967]. "Materialy k sravnitel'nomu slovarju nostratičeskix jazykov," *Etimologija* (Moscow): 321–96. [English translation in Shevoroshkin, ed., 1989c: 125–76.]

———. 1971–84. *Opyt sravnenija nostratičeskix jazykov,* 3 volumes. Moscow. [English translation of the reconstructions, and a semantic index to them, in Shevoroshkin, ed., 1990: 138–67.]

Kaiser, Mark, and Vitaly Shevoroshkin. 1988. "Nostratic," *Annual Review of Anthropology* 17: 309–29.

Kaufman, Terrence. 1990. "Language History in South America: What We Know and How to Know More," in Doris L. Payne, ed., *Amazonian Linguistics: Studies in Lowland South American Languages.* Austin, Tex., 13–73.

Matisoff, James A. 1990. "On Megalocomparison," *Language* 66: 106–20.

Nikolaev, Sergei L. 1986. "Sino-kavkazkie jazyki v Amerike," ms. [English translation in Shevoroshkin, ed., 1991: 42–66.]

O'Grady, R. T., I. Goddard, R. M. Bateman, W. A. Dimichele, V. A. Funk, W. J. Kress, R. Mooi, and P. F. Cannell. 1989. "Genes and Tongues," *Science* 243: 1651.

Pejros, Ilja I. 1989. "Dopolnenie k gipoteze S. A. Starostina o rodstve nostratičeskix i sinokavkazskix jazykov," *Lingvističeskaja rekonstruktsija i drevnejšaja istorija vostoka.* Moscow, 125–30.

Piazza, A., R. Griffo, N. Cappello, M. Grassini, E.. Olivetti, S. Rendine, and G. Zei. 1992. "Genetic Structure and Lexical Differentiation in Sardinia," ms.

Robins, R. H. 1968. *A Short History of Linguistics.* Bloomington, Ind.

Ruhlen, Merritt. 1987. *A Guide to the World's Languages,* Volume 1: Classification. Stanford, Calif.

———. 1990. "Phylogenetic Relations of Native American Languages," in Takeru Akazawa, ed., *Prehistoric Mongoloid Dispersals* (Tokyo) 7: 75–96.

———. 1994a. "The Origin of Language: Retrospective and Prospective," Chapter 13 of this volume. [Russian translation in *Voprosy Jazykoznanija* 1 (1991): 5–19.]

———. 1994b. "Is Algonquian Amerind?," Chapter 6 of this volume.

———. 1994c. "Additional Amerind Etymologies," Chapter 8 of this volume.

———. 1994d. "First- and Second-Person Pronouns in the World's Languages," Chapter 12 of this volume.

———. 1994e. "Na-Dene Etymologies," Chapter 5 of this volume.

———. 1994f. "Linguistic Origins of Native Americans," Chapter 10 of this volume.

Sapir, Edward. 1915. "The Na-dene Languages: A Preliminary Report," *American Anthropologist* 17: 534–58.

Shafer, Robert. 1952. "Athabascan and Sino-Tibetan," *International Journal of American Linguistics* 18: 12–19.

———. 1957. "Note on Athabascan and Sino-Tibetan," *International Journal of American Linguistics* 23: 116–17.

Shevoroshkin, Vitaly. 1989a. "Methods in Interphyletic Comparisons," *Ural-Altaische Jahrbücher* 61: 1–26.

———, ed. 1989b. *Explorations in Language Macrofamilies.* Bochum, Germany.

———, ed. 1989c. *Reconstructing Languages and Cultures.* Bochum.

———, ed. 1990. *Proto-Languages and Proto-Cultures.* Bochum.

———, ed. 1991. *Dene-Sino-Caucasian Languages.* Bochum.

Starostin, Sergei A. 1982. "Prajenisejskaja rekonstruktsija i vnešnie svjazi enisejskix jazykov," *Ketskij sbornik.* Leningrad, 144–237.

———. 1984. "Gipoteza o genetičeskix svjazjax sinotibetskix jazykov s enisejskimi i severnokavkazskimi jazykami," *Lingvističeskaja rekonstruktsija i drevnejšaja istorija vostoka* 4. Moscow, 19–38. [English translation in Shevoroshkin, ed., 1991: 12–41.]

———. 1989. "Nostratic and Sino-Caucasian," in Shevoroshkin, 1989b.

Starostin, Sergei A., and Merritt Ruhlen. 1994. "Proto-Yeniseian Reconstructions, with Extra-Yeniseian Comparisons," Chapter 4 of this volume.

Swadesh, Morris. 1952. Review of "Athapaskan and Sino-Tibetan," by Robert Shafer, *International Journal of American Linguistics* 18: 178–81.

———. 1954. "Perspectives and Problems of Amerindian Comparative Linguistics," *Word* 10: 306–32.

———. 1971. *The Origin and Diversification of Language.* Chicago.

Thomason, Sarah Grey. 1988. "Greenberg's Classifications: Africa vs. the Americas," ms.

Trombetti, Alfredo. 1905. *L'unità d'origine del linguaggio.* Bologna.

———. 1926. *Le origini della lingua basca.* Bologna.

2

The Basis of Linguistic Classification

How do linguists classify languages into families, and these families in turn into higher-level families?* In this regard, linguistics is no different from any other field: the comparative method begins with a listing of the entities to be classified, a listing that excludes entities obviously foreign to the list (e.g. birds are removed from a listing of fishes), but excludes none that are remotely possible members (tadpoles are listed, if only to be deleted in the first weeding), and then proceeds with a detailed comparison of the entities being classified. As Ernst Mayr (1988: 268) aptly put it, "From the earliest days, organisms were grouped into classes by their outward appearance, into grasses, birds, butterflies, snails, and others. Such grouping 'by inspection' is the expressly stated or unspoken starting point of virtually all systems of classification." What is compared in linguistics are words in different languages, or, more precisely, *lexical* items like 'hand, water, walk' and *grammatical* items like first person, past tense, and plural (see Greenberg 1957). It is the search for words that are similar in sound *and* meaning that forms the initial step in linguistic classification.

Once one has identified words in different languages that are similar in both sound and meaning, one must then determine the origin of these similarities, and here there are essentially three possibilities: convergence, borrowing, and common origin.

---

* This essay is a revised version of a talk given at the Cold Spring Harbor Centennial Symposium on Evolution: From Molecules to Culture (September 1990). The second half of the paper, similar in content to Chapter 1, is here omitted.

CONVERGENCE

In biology, *convergence* is more often than not motivated by the environment, or by other factors: it is not by accident that bats resemble birds, or dolphins, fish. But convergence in linguistics differs sharply from convergence in biology, for the simple reason that in linguistics convergence is almost always *unmotivated*: resemblance in such circumstances is almost always an accident. That linguistic convergence is almost always unmotivated is a direct consequence of the fundamental property of all human languages, namely, that language is based on the principle that a word is an *arbitrary* association of sound and meaning. For example, in English we use the sounds [hand] to represent a 'hand,' whereas other languages use entirely different sounds to represent the same meaning, for example Spanish [mano], Russian [ruka], and Japanese [te]. There is, thus, no reason to expect any particular meaning to be associated with any particular set of sounds. Accordingly, the probability that different languages would *independently* come to represent the meaning 'hand' by the sounds [mano] decreases rapidly as the number of languages possessing this word increases.

But how do we know that certain similarities are accidental, while others are historically related? In fact, we recognize accidental similarities only *after* we have arrived at a classification of the languages involved. Let us consider a specific example. The English word 'bad' is virtually identical in both sound and meaning with Persian *bad.* English 'bad,' however, is not found elsewhere in Germanic, the branch of Indo-European to which English belongs, and Persian *bad* is not found elsewhere in Indo-Iranian, the branch of Indo-European to which Persian belongs. Nor is this word found in any other branch of Indo-European. There is thus a formidable presumption that these two forms are not genetically related, despite their similarity in sound and meaning, and despite the fact that the languages in which they are found, English and Persian, are known to be related. What is important to note is that the accidental nature of this resemblance stands out *only against the background* of an already-defined Indo-European family.

To be sure, there are a few exceptions to the arbitrary nature of the sound/meaning relationship, the most obvious being *onomatopoeic* words such as 'buzz' and 'murmur.' Since such words constitute a very small percentage of a language's vocabulary, and can only be a source of dispute, they may be safely ignored by taxonomists.

A second alleged source of nonarbitrary sound/meaning relationships is nursery words like *mama* for 'mother' and *papa* for 'father.' It had long been noted that such forms were frequently shared by supposedly "unrelated" families when Roman Jakobson proposed, in 1960, to explain such similarities on the basis of the order of acquisition of sounds in child language, for [m] and [p] are among the first sounds produced by the child and hence could naturally come to represent the basic semantic meanings of 'mother' and 'father,' which for a child are obviously among its most important concepts. Though I would not deny that there may be an element of truth in Jakobson's proposal, I believe it was so readily accepted because it explained similarities which, for want of a better explanation, would have to have been attributed to common origin, thus undermining the supposed independence of many language families. Were *mama* and *papa* the only such widespread kinship terms, one might be able to accept Jakobson's explanation, but there are many others for which Jakobson's explanation seems far less viable, for example the kinship term based on the consonant [k], with forms such as *aka, kaka, kaki,* and the like, where the meaning is typically 'older male relative, uncle, older brother' (see Table 2 in Chapter 1). It is difficult to imagine that human society could be so finely organized that older brothers or uncles would show up at the baby's crib just when the child is learning velar consonants like [k]. Many other such examples (e.g. AJA 'mother' in Chapter 14) lead me to believe that the supposedly independent development of kinship terms like *mama* and *papa* in the world's languages has been greatly exaggerated; in most such cases we are probably dealing with historically connected forms rather than independent creations.

A final alleged source of nonarbitrary sound/meaning relationships involves pronouns, which are known to be among the most stable meanings in language. As with the kinship terms just discussed, the "problem" is that certain pronominal patterns connect families that have been declared unrelated by conservative taxonomists. An example is the vast Amerind family, covering most of North and all of South America, which is characterized by the pronominal pattern *n-* 'I' and *m-* 'you' (sg.). The prevalence of this pattern in the Americas—and its virtual absence elsewhere in the world—has been noted since early in this century and has required some explanation. Taxonomists like Alfredo Trombetti, Edward Sapir, and Joseph Greenberg, who were willing to weigh the evidence without preconception, have argued that this pattern can only be explained genetically. Franz Boas, however, attributed this pronominal pattern to "obscure psychological causes," and recent critics of Greenberg have invented equally fanciful explanations to explain away the problem of the Amerind pronouns.

An analogous situation has arisen in the Old World with regard to the Indo-European pronoun system. No description of the Indo-European family has ever failed to note the pronominal pattern *m-* 'I' and *t-* 'you' (sg.), as in English 'me, thee,' French *moi, toi,* Russian *menja, ty,* etc. The problem for Indo-Europeanists is that the same *m-/t-* pattern also characterizes other language families, such as Uralic, Altaic, Chukchi-Kamchatkan, and Eskimo-Aleut (see Table 2 in Chapter 1), and throughout this century Indo-Europeanists have pretended, for reasons having little to do with the actual evidence, that these families are unrelated to Indo-European. Trombetti (1905: 44) criticized this inconsistency of reasoning among Indo-Europeanists in the following terms: "It is clear that in and of itself the comparison of Finno-Ugric *me* 'I,' *te* 'you' with Indo-European *me-* and *te-* [with the same meaning] is worth just as much as any comparison one might make between the corresponding pronominal forms in the Indo-European languages. The only difference is that the common origin of the Indo-European languages is accepted, whereas the connection between Indo-European and Finno-Ugric is denied." As we have seen in the case of Amerind, it is the unwillingness to follow the comparative method to its logical conclusion—not the absence of evidence—that leads to the imaginary and willful isolation of Indo-European.

In summary, because convergence in linguistic taxonomy is almost always accidental, it constitutes only a very minor problem, and its manifestations are easily weeded out of the taxonomic process. Claims of convergence in pronoun systems are not supported by the worldwide evidence (see Chapter 12) and are to be rejected.

BORROWING

A second source of similarities in sound and meaning between words in two different languages is *borrowing*. Because almost all languages have borrowed some of their words from other languages, the possibility of borrowing must always be kept in mind. Two factors, however, make borrowing only a modest impediment to taxonomy. First, only certain kinds of words are particularly susceptible to borrowing, especially the words for previously unknown items like coffee, tobacco, and television, where the word is borrowed along with the item. Most of the basic vocabulary of a language is fairly resistant to borrowing; pronouns, body parts, and other fundamental vocabulary are seldom borrowed. Second, borrowing takes place only under special circumstances, almost always where the two languages in question are in intimate daily contact, as were English and French following the Norman invasion. For these reasons attempts to explain similarities among numerous languages over enormous geographical distances by means of borrowing are not to be taken seriously. Throughout this century such a diffusional approach to linguistic similarities, usually associated with Boas, has nevertheless opposed the genetic explanation of common origin preferred by Trombetti, Sapir, Swadesh, and Greenberg. Writing with regard to all of anthropology, not linguistics alone, William Durham (1992: 334–35) has recently objected that "in all four main subfields of anthropology . . . descent has rarely been given its due, in part because of the demanding nature of the necessary data, comparative and/or diachronic, but also because of a prejudice widely held since Boas . . . that diffusion reliably 'swamps' all traces of phylogeny." Perhaps the time has come for linguists to shed once and for all this long-held prejudice.

An example of how genuine borrowing may be detected would perhaps be instructive here. It was long thought that the Thai language was a member of the Sino-Tibetan family, which includes Chinese, Tibetan, Burmese, and other languages. But, in 1942, Paul Benedict showed that the Thai similarities to Sino-Tibetan were in fact borrowings from Chinese, and that Thai was to be classified in a different family, which Benedict called Kadai (= Daic). Two factors revealed the true affiliation of Thai: first, the Thai words resembling Sino-Tibetan tended to be words for items that are easily borrowed; and second (and more important), whenever Thai resembles Sino-Tibetan it always resembles Chinese, never one of the other branches. Were Thai really a branch of Sino-Tibetan, it should show some measure of independence within the family, manifesting its similarities *all around* the family, just as do all the branches of Indo-European, with respect to one another. Similarly, we could show that English has borrowed numerous words from French—and did not derive them independently from the same common origin— even if we did not have the historical records that demonstrate this to be the case.

In sum, borrowing can in almost all cases be detected, and therefore does not constitute a serious impediment to linguistic classification. Claims that masses of resemblances in the fundamental vocabulary of numerous languages separated by great distances are due to borrowing must be rejected.

COMMON ORIGIN

If, then, we find a mass of resemblances between different languages, resemblances that are not onomatopoeic in nature and do not appear to be borrowings, we must conclude that the similarities are the result of *common origin,* followed by descent with modification in the daughter languages. Similar words in different languages that are presumed to derive from a common source are called *cognates,* and the set of all related cognates for an individual word in different languages is known as the *etymology* for that word. Cognates thus play the same role in linguistics that homologies play in biology.

The process of linguistic classification, having at its heart the idea of common origin, may seem straightforward and uncontroversial, at least to biologists. Yet it is poorly understood within the linguistic community, where "reconstruction" and "sound correspondences" are usually deemed to play a crucial role in discovering genetic relationships: "The ultimate proof of genetic relationship, and to many linguists' minds the only real proof, lies in a successful reconstruction of the ancestral forms from which the systematically corresponding cognates can be derived. . . . It is through the procedure of comparative reconstruction, then, that we can establish *language families,* such as those of Indo-European, Uralic, Dravidian, Altaic, Sino-Tibetan, Malayo-Polynesian, Bantu, Semitic, or Uto-Aztecan" (Hock 1986: 567). I believe it would be virtually impossible to find an evolutionary biologist who would express similar views with regard to biological taxonomy. That reconstruction is a *secondary level* of investigation in historical linguistics, upon which taxonomy does not depend, was eloquently explained by Greenberg (1957: 45) long ago: "Reconstruction of an original sound system has the status of an explanatory theory to account for *etymologies already strong on other grounds* [my italics]. Between the **vaida* of Bopp and the **γwoidxe* of Sturtevant lie more than a hundred years of intensive development of Indo-European phonological reconstruction. What has remained constant has been the validity of the etymologic relationship among Sanskrit *veda,* Greek *woida,* Gothic *wait,* all meaning 'I know,' and many other unshakable etymologies both of root and non-root morphemes *recognized at the outset* [my italics]."

REFERENCES

Benedict, Paul K. 1942. "Thai, Kadai, and Indonesian: A New Alignment in Southeastern Asia," *American Anthropologist* 44: 576–601.

Durham, William H. 1992. "Applications of Evolutionary Culture Theory," *Annual Review of Anthropology* 21: 331–53.

Greenberg, Joseph H. 1957. "Genetic Relationship among Languages," in Joseph H. Greenberg, *Essays in Linguistics.* Chicago, 35–45.

Hock, Hans Henrich. 1986. *Principles of Historical Linguistics.* Berlin.

Jakobson, Roman. 1960. "Why Mama and Papa?," in Bernard Kaplan and Seymour Wapner, eds., *Perspectives in Psychological Theory.* New York, 21–29.

Mayr, Ernst. 1988. *Toward a New Philosophy of Biology.* Cambridge, Mass.

Trombetti, Alfredo. 1905. *L'unità d'origine del linguaggio.* Bologna.

3

Khoisan Etymologies

The Khoisan languages, now restricted for the most part to southern Africa (from southern Angola to South Africa), are renowned for their use of clicks as ordinary consonants (see below). It is thought that the Khoisan family was formerly much more widespread in subequatorial Africa, but that it was largely replaced by the Bantu expansion in the past two and a half millennia. The Khoisan etymologies given below are intended to supplement the 116 lexical etymologies cited in Greenberg (1963), and for that reason they begin with No. 117.* In Greenberg's work, Khoisan etymologies were proposed only when they involved Hadza and/or Sandawe, the two most divergent members of the family, which are spoken in northern Tanzania, several thousand miles from the rest of the extant Khoisan languages. There are, in addition, a substantial number of apparent cognates between the three Khoisan subgroups that make up the rest of the family, namely, the Northern (Zhu), Central (Khoe), and Southern (!Kwi) branches. It is hoped that this larger etymological base will facilitate the comparison of the Khoisan family with the world's other language families, and that it will lead to further discovery of whatever genetic links there may be at that level. To my mind, the position of the Khoisan family in the classification of the world's languages is the most important unresolved problem in linguistic taxonomy. Although there is some evidence that Khoisan is related to other language families (see Chapter 14), the origin

---

* I would like to thank Christopher Ehret for constructive criticism of an earlier version of this study.

of the Khoisan clicks—and their relationship to ordinary consonants in other families—remains unresolved.

The etymologies suggested below are based on the work of Dorothea Bleek (1929), which gives data for a dozen Khoisan languages. Six belong to the Southern branch (/Kham [S1], //Ng-!'e [S2], //Khegwi [S3], /'Auni [S4], Khakhea [S5], /Nu-//'e [S6]); three to the Central branch (Tati [C1], Naron [C2], Nama [C3]); and three to the Northern branch (//Kh'au-//'e [N1], !Kung [N2], !'O-!Kung [N3]). Bleek designated each language with a code, so that language S1 was language number one of the southern branch of Khoisan, /Kham. I have added these codes after the language names in this chapter for two reasons. First, they show at a glance which of the three Khoisan branches are involved; and second, they separate the language name and the word in that language, which otherwise are difficult to distinguish visually.

Other etymologies, sometimes overlapping with those given below, have been proposed by other scholars. Of particular interest for those who wish to pursue the study of the Khoisan family in more detail are Bleek (1956), Ehret (1986), Fleming (1986), Köhler (1973–74, 1981), and Ladefoged and Traill (1984).

Bleek's system of transcribing clicks is followed here. Five basic varieties of clicks are distinguished: dental / (English tsk tsk), palatal ≠, alveolar ! (cork popping), lateral //, and bilabial ⊙ (kiss). Each click may have a variety of releases. The bilabial click may be followed by g, k, kh, x or kx, h, ʔ, or any vowel. Thus, //gwa is to be interpreted as a CV syllable with an initial labialized lateral click with voiced release followed by the vowel a. For the most part, clicks are restricted to word-initial position, though reduplication sometimes puts them in medial position. They never occur word-finally.

Long vowels are marked with ⁻ above the vowel, e.g. ā. High tone is marked with an acute accent over the vowel, e.g. á; low tone, by a grave accent, e.g. è. Mid tone is unmarked.

The proposed etymologies follow:

117 ACHE (v.) /Kham (S1) taŋ, //Ng-!'e (S2) taŋ, Naron (C2) tū, Nama (C3) tsū.

118 AFTERNOON //Ng-!'e (S2) !kwiŋki, //Kh'au-//'e (N1) !gwằká, Naron (C2) !gwằká.

119 AFTERWARDS Khakhea (S5) //nằa, //Kh'au-//'e (N1) //na, Naron (C2) //naūa 'later.'

120 ALSO /Kham (S1) kɔa, !'O-!Kung (N3) (ne)kwe, Tati (C1) (če)koha.

121 AND₁ /'Auni (S4) e, Khakhea (S5) e, //Kh'au-//'e (N1) e, Naron (C2) e, Nama (C3) e.

122 AND₂ //Ng-!'e (S2) /na, //Kh'au-//'e (N1) na, !'O-!Kung (N3) na, Naron (C2) na.

123 ANGRY, TO BE /Kham (S1) !k"wein ~ !kwằ, //Kh'au-//'e (N1) kwákwá, Tati (C1) kxai, Naron (C2) //kxwằ.

124 ANKLE₁ Khakhea (S5) //guru, /Nu-//'e (S6) !guru, Tati (C1) //golo.

125 ANKLE₂ /Kham (S1) !xɔ̃ãm, //Kh'au-//'e (N1) !kum (tsisi), !Kung (N2) //khum, !'O-!Kung (N3) //ʔum.

126 ANT₁ /Nu-//'e (S6) //kamate, !Kung (N2) //k'am (//kari), Naron (C2) !kwama-!kwama.

127 ANT₂ /Kham (S1) /xweĩn/xweĩn, //Ng-!'e (S2) kwēn, Khakhea (S5) /gān, //Kh'au-//'e (N1) /gāĩ/gāĩ, Naron (C2) k'aniša.

128 ANTEATER /'Auni (S4) //kɔm, Tati (C1) //xamee.

129 APRON //Ng-!'e (S2) !kai, /'Auni (S4) !kai, /Nu-//'e (S6) !gai, Naron (C2) !kái.

130 ARM /Kham (S1) //kũ, Naron (C2) //k'õã, Nama (C3) //õab.

131 ARRIVE Khakhea (S5) //ka//ka ~ //kɑ̀ alə, !'O-!Kung (N3) //ka//kalə.

132 ARROWHEAD (IRON) //Kh'au-//'e (N1) /kum /na, Naron (C2) /kum //na.

133 ARROWHEAD (BONE) //Kh'au-//'e (N1) //kaba, Naron (C2) //gaba.

134 ASK Khakhea (S5) ti, //Kh'au-//'e (N1) tẽ, !'O-!Kung (N3) titi, Naron (C2) tĩ, Nama (C3) tẽ.

135 AT /'Auni (S4) ke, Khakhea (S5) ke ~ ka, //Kh'au-//'e (N1) ke ~ ka, !Kung (N2) ká 'to,' !'O-!Kung (N3) ká 'to,' Tati (C1) ka, Naron (C2) ka.

136 AWAY (TO GO AWAY) /Kham (S1) xū ~ ū, //Khegwi (S3) ū, //Kh'au-//'e (N1) ú, !Kung (N2) ṹ, !'O-!Kung (N3) ú, Naron (C2) xū, Nama (C3) xū ~ u.

137 AXE !'O-!Kung (N3) bɔ, Tati (C1) boo, Naron (C2) bɔ̃ša.

138 BABOON₁ /Nu-//'e (S6) /gɔri, //Kh'au-//'e (N1) //gɔra, Naron (C2) /gɔraba.

139 BABOON₂ /'Auni (S4) /nera, Nama (C3) /nérab.

140 BACKBONE /Kham (S1) /kəri, /'Auni (S4) !xuri, Naron (C2) !kɔri (/õã), Nama (C3) !huoríb.

141 BAD //Kh'au-//'e (N1) /k'au, !Kung (N2) /k'aó, Tati (C1) /kxau (čo).

142 BAG (= QUIVER) /'Auni (S4) !gɔru, /Nu-//'e (S6) !kɔru, //Kh'au-//'e (N1) !kuru, !Kung (N2) !kuru, Tati (C1) //gárus.

143 BAG (ROUND)₁ /Kham (S1) //hó, //Ng-!'e (S2) //ho, //Khegwi (S3) //kō, /'Auni (S4) //hō, Nama (C3) //hób.

144 BAG (ROUND)$_2$ /Nu-//'e (S6) ≠gɔbe, Naron (C2) ≠gɔbeša.

145 BAKE //Kh'au-//'e (N1) šou, !Kung (N2) sau, !'O-!Kung (N3) šau ~ sau, Tati (C1) čoo.

146 BARK (v.) !Kung (N2) //gṹ, Nama (C3) //hṹ.

147 BARTER !Kung (N2) //ama, Nama (C3) //ama(-!kuni).

148 BE$_1$ /Kham (S1) e, //Ng-!'e (S2) e, //Khegwi (S3) e, /'Auni (S4) e, Khakhea (S5) e, /Nu-//'e (S6) e, //Kh'au-//'e (N1) e, !Kung (N2) e, !'O-!Kung (N3) e, Tati (C1) je, Naron (C2) e.

149 BE$_2$ /Kham (S1) ā, //Ng-!'e (S2) ā, /'Auni (S4) ha, Khakhea (S5) ha, /Nu-//'e (S6) hà ~ a, //Kh'au-//'e (N1) ā, Naron (C2) hὰ ~ ā, Nama (C3) a.

150 BE, NOT TO //Kh'au-//'e (N1) kὰ, Naron (C2) kä́, Nama (C3) gā.

151 BEAD /Nu-//'e (S6) !am, //Kh'au-//'e (N1) !ʌ́m, Nama (C3) !àms.

152 BEAD (OSTRICH EGGSHELL) //Kh'au-//'e (N1) !kɔrə, Naron (C2) !xɔriba ~ !kɔriba.

153 BEAR (GIVE BIRTH TO)$_1$ //Ng-!'e (S2) !naia, //Kh'au-//'e (N1) !nai.

154 BEAR (GIVE BIRTH TO)$_2$!'O-!Kung (N3) //k'am, Naron (C2) //k'ʌm.

155 BEARD /Kham (S1) /num, /Nu-//'e (S6) /nūm, Naron (C2) /numša, Nama (C3) /nomgu.

156 BEAT //Kh'au-//'e (N1) //ám, Tati (C1) //gam, Naron (C2) //kʌm.

157 BECAUSE //Kh'au-//'e (N1) kama ~ ka, Tati (C1) ka, Naron (C2) kama.

158 BECOME //Kh'au-//'e (N1) ké, !'O-!Kung (N3) ki, Nama (C3) géi.

159 BEETLE$_1$ /Kham (S1) !nu!nurusi, !Kung (N2) !no!nonohe.

160 BEETLE$_2$ //Kh'au-//'e (N1) /kama (ču), Tati (C1) !kam ~ //kama, Naron (C2) /kama, Nama (C3) (/kunutsi-)//koma.

161 BEHIND Khakhea (S5) /u, //Kh'au-//'e (N1) /ō.

162 BERRY /Nu-//'e (S6) !num, !Kung (N2) !núm.

163 BIND$_1$ /Kham (S1) ≠kʌm, !Kung (N2) ≠kʌm, !'O-!Kung (N3) ≠kʌ́m.

164 BIND$_2$ //Ng-!'e (S2) !kai, Khakhea (S5) //kai, Tati (C1) /kae.

165 BIND$_3$ //Kh'au-//'e (N1) ≠ũ, Naron (C2) ≠ū.

166 BIRD /Kham (S1) k" af̃i, Khakhea (S5) /k'arika, /Nu-//'e (S6) ≠kariron, !Kung (N2) k"ani.

167 BLACK //Kh'au-//'e (N1) žɔ̃, !Kung (N2) ǧɔ, !'O-!Kung (N3) ǧɔ, Tati (C1) ǧunje.

168 BLACK MAN //Kh'au-//'e (N1) dama, Naron (C2) damaba, Nama (C3) (berin) dama 'Kafir.'

169 BLUE (PALE) /Kham (S1) /kainja, !Kung (N2) /kaŋ, !'O-!Kung (N3) /gã.

170 BODY /'Auni (S4) sɔru, Nama (C3) sorob.

171 BOIL /Kham (S1) /kū̧, //Ng-!'e (S2) /kɔ̃, /Nu-//'e (S6) /kū, //Kh'au-//'e (N1) /kū, !Kung (N2) /kɔ̧, !'O-!Kung (N3) /kɔnu, Nama (C3) /gū.

172 BONE /Kham (S1) !kwa, //Khegwi (S3) !kā, //Kh'au-//'e (N1) !kū̧, !'O-!Kung (N3) !ʔū̧.

173 BOWELS /Kham (S1) /kwíŋ/kwíŋ, Nama (C3) /guib.

174 BOWSTRING !Kung (N2) //abā, Naron (C2) //āba.

175 BOY /Nu-//'e (S6) //gàmama, //Kh'au-//'e (N1) !gōma, !Kung (N2) //gɔmã, !'O-!Kung (N3) //gɔma.

176 BRACELET /'Auni (S4) !kāū̧, /Nu-//'e (S6) !kanate, !'O-!Kung (N3) !kanu, Nama (C3) !ganus.

177 BRAINS /Kham (S1) !kun, !Kung (N2) ≠xu≠xunu, Nama (C3) ≠kūs.

178 BRANCH /Nu-//'e (S6) //kan, !Kung (N2) //kāū̧.

179 BREAK /Kham (S1) !kwā ~ !gwa, Khakhea (S5) !kau, //Kh'au-//'e (N1) !kwà, Naron (C2) kõa, Nama (C3) //goa.

180 BREATHE //Ng-!'e (S2) /ʌmsa, Nama (C3) /òm.

181 BRIGHT /Kham (S1) ≠xī, Khakhea (S5) //kī, !Kung (N2) ≠k'ī.

182 BUCHU (an herb) /Kham (S1) sā, //Ng-!'e (S2) sāŋ, /Nu-//'e (S6) tsẽ, //Kh'au-//'e (N1) čā, Naron (C2) tsā, Nama (C3) sāb.

183 BUILD //Kh'au-//'e (N1) !nūe, Naron (C2) !nū̧, Nama (C3) ≠nuwi.

184 BULB /Kham (S1) !kaui, //Kh'au-//'e (N1) !gau.

185 BURN /Kham (S1) //ke ~ //ka, //Ng-!'e (S2) //ke ~ //ka, //Khegwi (S3) kha, /'Auni (S4) !xa(u), Khakhea (S5) //ko, /Nu-//'e (S6) //kā, !Kung (N2) //ke, Tati (C1) ŋ//gai.

186 BURY /Kham (S1) !naū, //Kh'au-//'e (N1) /nàu.

187 BUT₁ /Kham (S1) ta, !Kung (N2) ta, !'O-!Kung (N3) ta.

188 BUT₂ //Kh'au-//'e (N1) xabe, Nama (C3) xawe.

189 BUTTERFLY /Kham (S1) dadábaši, //Kh'au-//'e (N1) tátaba, !Kung (N2) tátaba.

190 BUY₁ //Ng-!'e (S2) //wā, !'O-!Kung (N3) //wã.

191 BUY₂ //Kh'au-//'e (N1) //ama 'buy, sell,' !Kung (N2) //ama, Naron (C2) //ama, Nama (C3) //amá, //ama(-bē) 'sell.'

192 CALF /Nu-//'e (S6) tsau(-ma), !Kung (N2) zāū̧, Nama (C3) tsãub.

193 CALL₁ //Khegwi (S3) //kài, Khakhea (S5) //kaī, /Nu-//'e (S6) //kai, Naron (C2) //k'ē.

194 CALL₂ !'O-!Kung (N3) !ʔau, Nama (C3) !hǎo.

195 CANNOT /Kham (S1) k"ɔ́α ~ /kōwa, //Ng-!'e (S2) kwã, //Khegwi (S3) //kwe, Khakhea (S5) //kwa(ba), Nama (C3) //oa.

196 CAP₁ /Nu-//'e (S6) //gai ~ //kari, //Kh'au-//'e (N1) //gã̀ ~ //kā.

197 CAP₂ Khakhea (S5) túru, Tati (C1) t'oro.

198 CARRY (IN HAND) /Kham (S1) !khei, //Khegwi (S3) //ke, Khakhea (S5) !ke, //Kh'au-//'e (N1) //kē, !Kung (N2) !ke, !'O-!Kung (N3) //kē.

199 CARRY (IN THE KAROSS)₁ !Kung (N2) !gámi, Nama (C3) !nami.

200 CARRY (IN THE KAROSS)₂ !'O-!Kung (N3) //naia, Naron (C2) /nài.

201 CARRY (IN A BAG) //Khegwi (S3) //gōa, Naron (C2) !gwē, Nama (C3) //gowe.

202 CAT (RED) /Nu-//'e (S6) (/ka)≠wi, //Kh'au-//'e (N1) ≠wī, Tati (C1) ue.

203 CAT (WILD) //Ng-!'e (S2) ⊙mwa, /'Auni (S4) ⊙pōo, Khakhea (S5) ⊙pō, /Nu-//'e (S6) ⊙ō, //Kh'au-//'e (N1) /nwà, !Kung (N2) /nuā, !'O-!Kung (N3) ≠noɛ, Naron (C2) /nwaba, Nama (C3) /hõas.

204 CATCH₁ /Kham (S1) /kē ~ /ki, Khakhea (S5) /kai, //Kh'au-//'e (N1) //kai 'seize,' !'O-!Kung (N3) //kei, Naron (C2) ≠kái.

205 CATCH₂ Tati (C1) xoo ~ kxoo, Naron (C2) !xōo, Nama (C3) !khō.

206 CHEEK BONES /Kham (S1) !kweitn!kweitn, //Ng-!'e (S2) ≠kwike, /'Auni (S4) ≠uī≠uīte, Nama (C3) ≠ui≠uira.

207 CHEST /Nu-//'e (S6) /gu, !'O-!Kung (N3) (t'oa) /ʔõ, Tati (C1) /huu, Nama (C3) /ub.

208 CHILD /Kham (S1) ⊙pwa 'small,' //Khegwi (S3) ⊙pwo, Khakhea (S5) ⊙pwā, ⊙pwāni 'children,' /Nu-//'e (S6) ⊙pwā, Tati (C1) /gwa, /gware 'children,' Naron (C2) /kwa, /kwāne 'children,' Nama (C3) /gõai, /gõan 'children.'

209 CHIN //Kh'au-//'e (N1) //gã̀, !Kung (N2) //gaŋ, !'O-!Kung (N3) !gã̄ŋ, Naron (C2) !gani, Nama (C3) !gàni.

210 CHOP₁ /Kham (S1) //k'au, Tati (C1) //kau, Naron (C2) //kau.

211 CHOP₂ Khakhea (S5) //kū, //Kh'au-//'e (N1) //gum, !Kung (N2) //kum, !'O-!Kung (N3) //kùm.

212 CLAP HANDS //Kh'au-//'e (N1) //amka, Naron (C2) //ʌm, Nama (C3) //am.

213 CLAY //Kh'au-//'e (N1) !kà, !Kung (N2) ≠ka, !'O-!Kung (N3) /kāo, Tati (C1) /khā.

214 CLEAN (v.) /Kham (S1) t'à́ɔ, !'O-!Kung (N3) ča.

215 CLIMB //Kh'au-//'e (N1) /k'abe, !Kung (N2) !kaba, Tati (C1) abo, Naron (C2) !aba, Nama (C3) !áwa.

216 CLOUD //Ng-!'e (S2) !gum, !'O-!Kung (N3) !kɔm, Tati (C1) ≠kom.

217 COLD, TO BE₁ /Kham (S1) *k"òo*, !'O-!Kung (N3) /*k'au* ~ *k'xau*, Khakhea (S5) /*k"au* (n.), //Kh'au-//'e (N1) /*káū*.

218 COLD, TO BE₂ //Kh'au-//'e (N1) ≠*xi*, Naron (C2) ≠*xei*, Nama (C3) !*kèi*.

219 COME BACK Khakhea (S5) //*k'ʌm ši*, //Kh'au-//'e (N1) //*kamtsí*.

220 COOK //Ng-!'e (S2) !*xame*, //Kh'au-//'e (N1) ≠*xame*, Naron (C2) //*xām*.

221 COVER (v.) /Kham (S1) *tum*, Khakhea (S5) *tum* 'to wrap up,' Nama (C3) *tami* 'to wrap up.'

222 CRUNCH /Kham (S1) *k"aun*, //Kh'au-//'e (N1) *k"ɔ*, Naron (C2) *xaunša kɔ̀*.

223 CUCUMBER₁ //Kh'au-//'e (N1) *tõa*, Naron (C2) *tõa*.

224 CUCUMBER₂ //Ng-!'e (S2) /*gɔrusi*, Naron (C2) /*gerisa*.

225 CUT /Kham (S1) /*kau*, Tati (C1) //*kau*, Naron (C2) //*kau*, Khakhea (S5) !*kau* 'to cut off,' !'O-!Kung (N3) //*káu* 'to cut off.'

226 DANCE₁ Khakhea (S5) /*nʌm*, //Kh'au-//'e (N1) /*nʌm*, Naron (C2) /*nʌm*.

227 DANCE₂ //Kh'au-//'e (N1) *čane*, !Kung (N2) *čxane*, Naron (C2) *čàne*.

228 DANCE₃ //Kh'au-//'e (N1) *čxai*, !'O-!Kung (N3) *čxē̃*, Naron (C2) *čxái*.

229 DAWN //Kh'au-//'e (N1) !*ūká*, Naron (C2) !*ūka*.

230 DAY //Kh'au-//'e (N1) /*kʌm*, !Kung (N2) /*kʌm*, !'O-!Kung (N3) /*kʌm*, Tati (C1) /*kam*, Naron (C2) /*kamsa*.

231 DECAY //Kh'au-//'e (N1) *čoū*, Tati (C1) *čoro*, Naron (C2) *č'ɔ* ~ *čǔ*, Nama (C3) *tsowá*.

232 DICE //Kh'au-//'e (N1) /*xừsi*, !Kung (N2) /*xu*, !'O-!Kung (N3) /*xō*, Tati (C1) /*kxou*, Naron (C2) /*xūji*.

233 DIG /Nu-//'e (S6) *xaro*, Nama (C3) *xoro*.

234 DIG UP WATER Khakhea (S5) //*ybi*, !'O-!Kung (N3) //*gàba*, Naron (C2) //*gwəbe*.

235 DISH //Ng-!'e (S2) !*kɔrë̃*, /Nu-//'e (S6) !*ɔre*, Naron (C2) !*kɔre*, Nama (C3) !*ores*.

236 DO /Kham (S1) *dī*, Khakhea (S5) *ti*, !Kung (N2) *di*, Nama (C3) *dì*.

237 DOWN, TO GET; TO FALL //Khegwi (S3) //*koā*, //Kh'au-//'e (N1) //*gwà*, Naron (C2) //*gwã*, Nama (C3) //*gőa*.

238 DREAM /Kham (S1) //*khabo*, Nama (C3) //*kawő*.

239 DRINK /Kham (S1) *k"wã* ~ *k"wẽ*, //Ng-!'e (S2) *k"ã* ~ *k"eĩ*, //Khegwi (S3) *k"ã* ~ *k"ẽ*, /'Auni (S4) *k"āa*, Khakhea (S5) *k"ã*, /Nu-//'e (S6) *k"ã*, !Kung (N2) *k"ã*, Naron (C2) *k"ā*.

240　DRIVE₁　Khakhea (S5) *!xai*, //Kh'au-//'e (N1) *!xãĩ*, Naron (C2) *!kaiï* 'to drive on,' Nama (C3) *!hài-xu*.

241　DRIVE₂　!'O-!Kung (N3) *!kxwe*, Naron (C2) *!xwē* 'to drive away.'

242　DRY　/Kham (S1) //*k̀ɔ*, //Ng-!'e (S2) //*k̀ɔ*, !Kung (N2) //*kāo*, Naron (C2) //*kóë*.

243　DUIKER BUCK (a kind of antelope)　/Kham (S1) /*nau*, //Kh'au-//'e (N1) /*óu*, !Kung (N2) /*óu*, !'O-!Kung (N3) /*áu*, Naron (C2) /*nouša*.

244　DWELL₁　/'Auni (S4) //*an* 'hut,' Nama (C3) //*àŋ* 'to live.'

245　DWELL₂　/Kham (S1) //*ɛn*, //*nei* 'hut,' //*neiŋ* 'hut,' //Ng-!'e (S2) //*nei* 'hut,' //Khegwi (S3) //*neiŋ* 'hut,' Khakhea (S5) //*nai* 'hut,' //*hain* 'to stay,' /Nu-//'e (S6) //*nei*, Naron (C2) //*ēĩ* 'to dwell, stay.'

246　EARLY　/Nu-//'e (S6) *kɔbe (k"au)*, !'O-!Kung (N3) *kɔvə*.

247　EARRING　/'Auni (S4) *!kãũnu*, !Kung (N2) *!kãnuma*, !'O-!Kung (N3) *!kã*.

248　EAT　/Kham (S1) /*ũŋ* 'to eat marrow,' *!kũŋ* 'to eat fat,' Tati (C1) ≠*ũ* 'to eat vegetable food,' Nama (C3) ≠*ũ*.

249　EGG　Naron (C2) ≠*ybi*, //Kh'au-//'e (N1) ≠*ybi* 'eggshell.'

250　ELAND (a kind of antelope)　Khakhea (S5) *dũ*, Tati (C1) *du*, Naron (C2) *dùba*.

251　ELBOW　/Nu-//'e (S6) ≠*guni*, //Kh'au-//'e (N1) ≠*ɔni*, !Kung (N2) ≠*kwɔ́ni*, !'O-!Kung (N3) ≠*kuni*, Tati (C1) *čuni*, Naron (C2) ≠*huni*.

252　EMBERS　//Kh'au-//'e (N1) *dà !nūsi* (literally, "fire stones"), Naron (C2) *!numsa*.

253　ENTER　/Kham (S1) /*ē* ~ /*e/ē*, //Ng-!'e (S2) /*ē*, !Kung (N2) /*gē*.

254　EVENING　Khakhea (S5) *!gwā*, //Kh'au-//'e (N1) *!gwà*, Naron (C2) *!gwàká*.

255　EYE　//Khegwi (S3) *tsãĩ*, *tsãĩn* 'eyes,' Tati (C1) *čaĩ*.

256　FACE　/Kham (S1) *xū*, //Ng-!'e (S2) *xū*, //Khegwi (S3) *xū*, /'Auni (S4) /*ka*, //Kh'au-//'e (N1) /*khó*, !Kung (N2) /*khó*, !'O-!Kung (N3) /*kō*, Tati (C1) ≠*kxuu*.

257　FAR　Khakhea (S5) *!ã́*, //Kh'au-//'e (N1) *!xã̄* ~ /*ká̃*, !Kung (N2) ≠*xã́*, !'O-!Kung (N3) ≠*xa*.

258　FASTEN　//Kh'au-//'e (N1) *!kam*, Naron (C2) *!ama*.

259　FAT (n.)　//Kh'au-//'e (N1) /*nī*, !Kung (N2) //*nwī*, !'O-!Kung (N3) /*ní* ~ *ní*, Naron (C2) //*nwība*, Nama (C3) //*nuib*.

260　FATHER₁　/Kham (S1) *bobo*, //Khegwi (S3) *bāba*, //Kh'au-//'e (N1) *ba*, !Kung (N2) *ba*, !'O-!Kung (N3) *ba*, *pá* (vocative), Tati (C1) *bae*, Naron (C2) *auba*, *aba* (vocative).

261　FATHER₂　/Kham (S1) *tata*, /Nu-//'e (S6) *tata*, Nama (C3) *dadắb*.

262　FEEL₁　/Kham (S1) *tutŭim* 'to feel with the feet,' !Kung (N2) (//*ke*) *tu* 'to feel about,' Tati (C1) *čom*.

263 FEEL₂ /Kham (S1) tā̃ ~ ta, //Ng-!'e (S2) taŋ, !Kung (N2) saä,
Nama (C3) tsã.

264 FEMALE //Ng-!'e (S2) /gaiki, Khakhea (S5) //gai, /Nu-//'e (S6)
//gaite, Tati (C1) //gai, Naron (C2) //gai.

265 FETCH /Nu-//'e (S6) šō, !Kung (N2) šá, Naron (C2) šε ~ sε.

266 FETCH WATER Khakhea (S5) hɔle, /Nu-//'e (S6) hare, //Kh'au-
//'e (N1) hǝre, Naron (C2) hòre, Nama (C3) harě.

267 FETCH WOOD //Kh'au-//'e (N1) gū, Naron (C2) gū.

268 FEVER //Kh'au-//'e (N1) !gĩ̀, Naron (C2) !gī(ša).

269 FIGHT (v.) /Kham (S1) /ā, //Kh'au-//'e (N1) //ā, !Kung (N2) //ã,
Tati (C1) //gaa, Naron (C2) //ã̄, Nama (C3) //äë.

270 FILL₁ /Nu-//'e (S6) !gum, !Kung (N2) !kum.

271 FILL₂ //Kh'au-//'e (N1) /ú, !'O-!Kung (N3) /o, Nama (C3) /òa/òa.

272 FIND //Kh'au-//'e (N1) hō, !Kung (N2) ō, Naron (C2) hɔ̄, Nama
(C3) hò̃.

273 FINGER/TOE /Nu-//'e (S6) /kɔnu, //Kh'au-//'e (N1) (!gou)/kɔne,
Naron (C2) (čou) /khɔ̀nu, Nama (C3) /kunub.

274 FINISH /Nu-//'e (S6) toä, //Kh'au-//'e (N1) tòa, !Kung (N2) toá,
!'O-!Kung (N3) tɔa, Nama (C3) tŏa.

275 FIVE₁ /Nu-//'e (S6) kɔro, Naron (C2) kɔro, Nama (C3) goro.

276 FIVE₂ !Kung (N2) ču, Tati (C1) (e)čowe (a hand), Naron (C2) čou.

277 FLOW //Kh'au-//'e (N1) čū, Tati (C1) ĵoo.

278 FLUTTER //Kh'au-//'e (N1) //gani, Nama (C3) //kana.

279 FLY₁ (n.) Khakhea (S5) žóĩ (v.), žù̃ žwē 'to fly away,' //Kh'au-//'e
(N1) žwažwa, !Kung (N2) ĵɔãĵɔã, !'O-!Kung (N3) dzwãdzwã.

280 FLY₂ (n.) /'Auni (S4) ≠gam, !Kung (N2) //gama (v.).

281 FOLLOW //Kh'au-//'e (N1) //xam, !Kung (N2) //xam, !'O-!Kung
(N3) //xam, Tati (C1) kamaa, Nama (C3) /hamã.

282 FOOT //Khegwi (S3) /k'e, /'Auni (S4) !k'ai, //Kh'au-//'e (N1) /kē,
!Kung (N2) /k'i, !'O-!Kung (N3) /k'ε.

283 FOR₁ /Kham (S1) tā, !Kung (N2) ta.

284 FOR₂ //Kh'au-//'e (N1) kama, Naron (C2) kama.

285 FORBID //Kh'au-//'e (N1) !khau, Nama (C3) !khãi.

286 FOREHEAD /Kham (S1) xū, //Kh'au-//'e (N1) /khó, !Kung (N2)
/khó, !'O-!Kung (N3) /kō, Tati (C1) ≠kxuu.

287 FORGET /Kham (S1) /urūwá, !Kung (N2) /uru, Tati (C1) ŋ/xuru,
Naron (C2) /uru, Nama (C3) /uru.

288 FOUR Khakhea (S5) //ke, //Kh'au-//'e (N1) //kéi, Naron (C2) //xē.

289 FRIEND /Kham (S1) /kē̃ŋ, Naron (C2) !kēn.

290 FROM Khakhea (S5) ke, //Kh'au-//'e (N1) kwé, !Kung (N2) kwe,
Naron (C2) kwé.

291 FULL /Kham (S1) !kauŋ-a, //Ng-!'e (S2) !xaŋ, //Kh'au-//'e (N1)
!kau.

292 GATHER /Kham (S1) /k'wā̃, !'O-!Kung (N3) /ʔhã.

293 GEMSBOK₁ (a kind of antelope) /Kham (S1) !kwi, //Kh'au-//'e
(N1) !gwé̃.

294 GEMSBOK₂ /'Auni (S4) /xa, Naron (C2) /xɔba.

295 GET DOWN /Kham (S1) //kóë, Tati (C1) //kwaho.

296 GHOST //Kh'au-//'e (N1) //gã́ũa, !Kung (N2) //gãũa, !'O-!Kung
(N3) //gãũã, Naron (C2) //gãũa, Nama (C3) //gãũa 'evil spirit.'

297 GIRAFFE Khakhea (S5) /xuä, //Kh'au-//'e (N1) ≠koä, !Kung (N2)
≠koä́.

298 GIVE₁ //Kh'au-//'e (N1) aū, Naron (C2) aū.

299 GIVE₂ /Kham (S1) /kā ∼ ā, //Ng-!'e (S2) ā, Khakhea (S5) /a,
//Kh'au-//'e (N1) /ā, !Kung (N2) /ká ∼ /ã́ ∼ ā, !'O-!Kung (N3) /kā.

300 GNAW Khakhea (S5) /kɑa, //Kh'au-//'e (N1) kai, Naron (C2) //kaī.

301 GO /Kham (S1) !ũ 'to go out,' /'Auni (S4) !kuŋ, /Nu-//'e (S6) //kū
'to go away,' //Kh'au-//'e (N1) !kū, !Kung (N2) !kú, Naron (C2) !kū,
Nama (C3) !gūŋ.

302 GOOD //Ng-!'e (S2) !hãīja, //Kh'au-//'e (N1) !kāī, !Kung (N2) kaiä,
Naron (C2) !kāī, Nama (C3) !gāī.

303 GRANDCHILD /Kham (S1) ⊙pwa⊙pwaidi, Tati (C1) /gwa/gwa.

304 GRANDFATHER //Kh'au-//'e (N1) mama 'grandfather, grandmother,' Tati (C1) mae 'grandmother,' Naron (C2) mamai 'grandfather, grandson.'

305 GRASS //Khegwi (S3) gā̃, /Nu-//'e (S6) //gã, Naron (C2) /gã̃ša,
Nama (C3) /gãb.

306 GREEN/YELLOW /Kham (S1) /kainja, //Kh'au-//'e (N1) /kãũ,
!Kung (N2) /kaŋ, !'O-!Kung (N3) /kãŋ.

307 GROUND Khakhea (S5) //khūm, /Nu-//'e (S6) ≠gùm, Naron (C2)
xumša, Nama (C3) xùb.

308 GROW /Kham (S1) kí, //Kh'au-//'e (N1) kéia, Naron (C2) kéia,
Nama (C3) géi.

309 HAIR /Kham (S1) /kɯ, //Ng-!'e (S2) /kɯ, //Khegwi (S3) /ku,
/'Auni (S4) /ko, Khakhea (S5) /kwāni, /Nu-//'e (S6) /kɯnte, Tati
(C1) /hoo, Naron (C2) /ū, Nama (C3) /ū̃.

310 HARE /Kham (S1) !nãū, //Ng-!'e (S2) !nau, //Kh'au-//'e (N1) !nɑ̀u,
!'O-!Kung (N3) !nau.

311 HAVE /Kham (S1) /ki, //Ng-!'e (S2) /ki ∼ /ka, //Khegwi (S3) /ge,
/'Auni (S4) /kēi, Khakhea (S5) //ke, !Kung (N2) //ke, !'O-!Kung (N3)
//kai.

312 HE/SHE/IT /Kham (S1) *ha*, //Ng-!'e (S2) *ha*, //Khegwi (S3) *ha*,
Khakhea (S5) *ha*, //Kh'au-//'e (N1) *ha*, !Kung (N2) *ha*, !'O-!Kung
(N3) *ha*.

313 HEAD /Kham (S1) /*nā*, //Ng-!'e (S2) /*nā*, //Khegwi (S3) /*nā*,
/'Auni (S4) /*nā*, Khakhea (S5) /*nā*, /Nu-//'e (S6) /*na* ~ /*ni*, //Kh'au-
//'e (N1) /*né* ~ /*ní*, !Kung (N2) /*ne*, !'O-!Kung (N3) /*né*.

314 HEAR /Kham (S1) *tum*, Tati (C1) *čom*.

315 HEART /'Auni (S4) ≠*k?a*, //Kh'au-//'e (N1) *!kā*, !Kung (N2) *!k'á*,
!'O-!Kung (N3) *k'a*, Naron (C2) *!gausa*, Nama (C3) ≠*gaob*.

316 HEEL /Kham (S1) *!kú*, //Ng-!'e (S2) *!kɔra*, !Kung (N2) (/*ke*) *!gōa*,
!'O-!Kung (N3) *!gɔ̱*.

317 HEMP //Kh'au-//'e (N1) /*hī*, Nama (C3) /*hĩ́*.

318 HERE₁ //Ng-!'e (S2) *kí*, //Khegwi (S3) /*ki*, Khakhea (S5) /*ki*, Nama
(C3) (*ne*) /*i*.

319 HERE₂ /Kham (S1) *tí*, /'Auni (S4) *ti*, Khakhea (S5) *ši*, /Nu-//'e
(S6) *tí*, //Kh'au-//'e (N1) *tsīke* ~ *čī*.

320 HIDE /Kham (S1) *!náū*, Nama (C3) *!nava*.

321 HILL Khakhea (S5) *!gɔm*, Nama (C3) *!nomis*.

322 HOLD //Khegwi (S3) //*ke*, //Kh'au-//'e (N1) //*kái*, !Kung (N2) //*ke*,
!'O-!Kung (N3) //*ke* ~ //*kai*, Tati (C1) //*ka*.

323 HOLD UP !Kung (N2) //*kʌm*, Nama (C3) //*kam*.

324 HOLE₁ /Kham (S1) *tū*, //Ng-!'e (S2) *tū*, Khakhea (S5) *ǰu*, /Nu-//'e
(S6) *žɔ̃e*, //Kh'au-//'e (N1) *ču*.

325 HOLE₂ /Kham (S1) *!kɔrro* 'to be hollow,' /*huru* 'hole,' /*ūru* 'anus,'
/'Auni (S4) *!kuru* 'quiver,' //Kh'au-//'e (N1) *!kuru* ~ *!koro* 'hole,
grave,' !'O-!Kung (N3) *kɔlɔ* 'hollow,' Tati (C1) *koro* 'hole in tree,'
(*čui*) *kxolo* 'nostrils' (literally, "nose hole").

326 HOT, TO BE /'Auni (S4) /*kʌm*, Nama (C3) /*gam*.

327 HUNGRY, TO BE Khakhea (S5) //*k'aba*(//*kau*), //Kh'au-//'e (N1)
//*kabe*, Naron (C2) //*kɑba* 'hunger, to be hungry,' Tati (C1) //*kaba*
'hunger.'

328 HUNT /'Auni (S4) ≠*kai* (*ho*), Khakhea (S5) //*kãĩ*, //Kh'au-//'e (N1)
!kɔ̀i ~ *!gɔ̀i*, Naron (C2) *kɔ̀i* ~ *!xãĩ*, Nama (C3) *!hài*.

329 HURT /Kham (S1) //*kã́ĩ*, Khakhea (S5) //*kõĩ*, //Kh'au-//'e (N1)
//*kãũ*, !Kung (N2) //*gáni*-//*gáni*.

330 HUSBAND /Kham (S1) /*ha*, //Khegwi (S3) /*ha*, /Nu-//'e (S6) /*ha*,
!'O-!Kung (N3) /*gā*.

331 HUT //Kh'au-//'e (N1) *čū*, !Kung (N2) *ču*, !'O-!Kung (N3) *ču* (*!ní*),
Tati (C1) *ǰu*.

332 HYENA (SPOTTED) //Kh'au-//'e (N1) *!káu*, !'O-!Kung (N3) *!k"ãũ*,
Naron (C2) *!gau*.

333   I_1 /Kham (S1) ŋ ~ n, //Ng-!'e (S2) ŋ ~ n ~ ni, //Khegwi (S3) ŋ ~ aŋ, /'Auni (S4) ŋ, Khakhea (S5) ŋ ~ na, /Nu-//'e (S6) ŋ ~ na, !Kung (N2) ŋ ~ na.

334   I_2 /Kham (S1) m, //Ng-!'e (S2) m, //Khegwi (S3) am, Khakhea (S5) m, /Nu-//'e (S6) m, //Kh'au-//'e (N1) m ~ mi, !Kung (N2) m ~ mi, !'O-!Kung (N3) mi ~ ma.

335   ILL, TO BE   //Khegwi (S3) /a, Khakhea (S5) //kai, //Kh'au-//'e (N1) /kei, Nama (C3) /ai.

336   IN   /Kham (S1) /ē, //Ng-!'e (S2) /ē, //Khegwi (S3) /ē, /Nu-//'e (S6) /ē, !'O-!Kung (N3) /ē.

337   INSIDE   /Kham (S1) //kaīe, //Ng-!'e (S2) //kaīe, //Khegwi (S3) //xē, !'O-!Kung (N3) //gàī.

338   INTERROGATIVE PARTICLE$_1$ /Kham (S1) xa, //Kh'au-//'e (N1) xa.

339   INTERROGATIVE PARTICLE$_2$ /Nu-//'e (S6) ba, //Kh'au-//'e (N1) ba.

340   INTERROGATIVE PARTICLE$_3$ /Kham (S1) dε, //Ng-!'e (S2) djε, //Kh'au-//'e (N1) dε, !Kung (N2) de, Naron (C2) dī.

341   JUMP   /Kham (S1) ≠hau ~ ≠kōú, //Ng-!'e (S2) !kaú, //Kh'au-//'e (N1) !hãū.

342   KAROSS (SMALL)   /Kham (S1) !kʔousi, //Ng-!'e (S2) !ko, //Kh'au-//'e (N1) !gū, !Kung (N2) !kū, !'O-!Kung (N3) !gō, Naron (C2) !gūša, Nama (C3) !gús̄.

343   KIDNEY   //Kh'au-//'e (N1) !nē, Naron (C2) !nēi, Nama (C3) !néis.

344   KILL$_1$ /Kham (S1) /ā, //Ng-!'e (S2) /ā, Khakhea (S5) //ā, Nama (C3) ≠ā́.

345   KILL$_2$ //Kh'au-//'e (N1) !kũ, !Kung (N2) !kũ ~ !kuŋ, !'O-!Kung (N3) !kɔ̃, Naron (C2) /kũ.

346   KNOCK   //Kh'au-//'e (N1) ≠k'ʌm, !'O-!Kung (N3) //kʌ́, Tati (C1) //kam, Naron (C2) //kama.

347   KNOW   /Kham (S1) ≠en ~ ≠ená, //Kh'au-//'e (N1) ≠ā̄ ~ ≠kã, Tati (C1) aa ~ an, Naron (C2) ≠ãna, Nama (C3) ≠an.

348   KNOW, NOT TO   /Kham (S1) /uru, //Kh'au-//'e (N1) /ū, !Kung (N2) /uru, Nama (C3) /uru.

349   KORHAAN BRANDKOP (a kind of rooster)   /Nu-//'e (S6) //āba, Khakhea (S5) //gaba 'korhaan vaal,' Naron (C2) //gàba 'korhaan vaal.'

350   KUDU (an African hoofed mammal)   //Ng-!'e (S2) k'āī, /'Auni (S4) xai, /Nu-//'e (S6) xain, Naron (C2) xeiba, Nama (C3) xaib.

351   LANGUAGE   //Kh'au-//'e (N1) k'wi, !Kung (N2) ok'wi, !'O-!Kung (N3) ok'wí, Tati (C1) kwio, Naron (C2) k'wīša.

352 LARGE //Ng-!'e (S2) !na, //Kh'au-//'e (N1) !naa, !'O-!Kung (N3) //nāa.

353 LAUGH₁ /Kham (S1) k"wē-ī, //Ng-!'e (S2) k'ãi̯-ã, Nama (C3) ãi̯.

354 LAUGH₂ Khakhea (S5) //kēi̯, //kxài 'to laugh at,' Naron (C2) //kxe 'to laugh at.'

355 LAY EGGS /Kham (S1) //kain, /Nu-//'e (S6) //gãi̯, !'O-!Kung (N3) ka.

356 LEAD (v.) /Kham (S1) //gwēi̯tən, Khakhea (S5) /kwē, Nama (C3) ≠gui.

357 LEAF /Nu-//'e (S6) /nabu, //Kh'au-//'e (N1) /nɔbu, !Kung (N2) /nɔ̀bu, !'O-!Kung (N3) //gɔba.

358 LEAVE₁ /Kham (S1) (xū) tu 'to leave off,' toä 'to leave for,' //Kh'au-//'e (N1) toa 'to leave off,' Naron (C2) tōε 'to leave off,' Nama (C3) toa 'to leave off.'

359 LEAVE₂ /Kham (S1) xū ūi, xū u 'to leave for,' !Kung (N2) xun, Tati (C1) huu, Naron (C2) xū, Nama (C3) xú.

360 LEAVE₃ //Kh'au-//'e (N1) //nā, !Kung (N2) //nā, Nama (C3) //ná.

361 LEG //Ng-!'e (S2) !kōgən, !Kung (N2) !kō, !'O-!Kung (N3) !kō.

362 LET₁ /Kham (S1) ā, Khakhea (S5) a, Nama (C3) a.

363 LET₂ /Kham (S1) /na, //Kh'au-//'e (N1) //na, !Kung (N2) /na, !'O-!Kung (N3) //na, Nama (C3) //nà.

364 LIE (n.) !Kung (N2) tjǘa, Naron (C2) čuša.

365 LIGHT₁ (NOT HEAVY) !Kung (N2) šwi, Naron (C2) ču, Nama (C3) sùi̯.

366 LIGHT₂ (BRIGHT) /Kham (S1) ≠xī, //Kh'au-//'e (N1) ≠i.

367 LIGHT₃ (BRIGHT) //Ng-!'e (S2) !kā, !'O-!Kung (N3) !gã̀, Nama (C3) !nã̀ ~ !ga.

368 LIGHTNING !'O-!Kung (N3) //gãūa tala, Tati (C1) //kxau.

369 LIKE, TO BE₁ /Kham (S1) //ke//kē, !Kung (N2) //ke//ke.

370 LIKE, TO BE₂ /Kham (S1) k'waŋ, !'O-!Kung (N3) kwã.

371 LIMP !'O-!Kung (N3) //kēa, Naron (C2) //k'ēa.

372 LION /Nu-//'e (S6) xam, //Kh'au-//'e (N1) xam, !Kung (N2) xam, Tati (C1) kxam ~ hōm, Naron (C2) xamba, Nama (C3) xami.

373 LIP Khakhea (S5) /kōši, /Nu-//'e (S6) /gōši (!nʌm), //Kh'au-//'e (N1) tsī /ō, !Kung (N2) si /ō, !'O-!Kung (N3) tsī /nɔ.

374 LISTEN !Kung (N2) !kã, Nama (C3) !gã.

375 LIVER //Kh'au-//'e (N1) čī, !Kung (N2) čiŋ, !'O-!Kung (N3) čī, Tati (C1) če.

376 LOCUST /Kham (S1) !hau, //Kh'au-//'e (N1) !hàu, !Kung (N2) !gãū.

377   LOINCLOTH   /Kham (S1) //kɔro, //Kh'au-//'e (N1) //go, !Kung
      (N2) //ko, !'O-!Kung (N3) //gò̃.
378   LOVE   /Kham (S1) /kòɳ-a, //Ng-!'e (S2) //aŋ, Nama (C3) //ã́.
379   LYNX   //Kh'au-//'e (N1) !gàu, Naron (C2) !kãũba.
380   MAKE₁   //Kh'au-//'e (N1) kuru, !Kung (N2) kuru, Naron (C2) kúru,
      Nama (C3) guru.
381   MAKE₂   /Kham (S1) taba, Khakhea (S5) tabi 'work,' !Kung (N2)
      taba.
382   MAKE₃   /Kham (S1) di, /'Auni (S4) ti, Nama (C3) dì.
383   MALE₁ (adj.)   //Ng-!'e (S2) !gō, //Khegwi (S3) //kɔ̄, /Nu-//'e (S6)
      //gɔ̄, //Kh'au-//'e (N1) //gɔ̄, !Kung (N2) //gɔ̄, //go (n.), !'O-!Kung
      (N3) //gɔ̄, //gɔ̀ (n.), Tati (C1) //kxowe.
384   MALE₂ (adj.)   //Kh'au-//'e (N1) k'au (n.), !'O-!Kung (N3) k'au (n.),
      Naron (C2) k'au ~ //k'au.
385   MAN (MALE)   /Kham (S1) !ku 'person,' !Kung (N2) !kũ, !'O-!Kung
      (N3) !kũ, Tati (C1) čo.
386   MAN (PERSON)   Khakhea (S5) tu 'person,' /Nu-//'e (S6) tu ~ du
      'person,' //Kh'au-//'e (N1) žū, !Kung (N2) jū ~ žū, !'O-!Kung (N3) jū
      ~ žū.
387   MANE   /Kham (S1) /keri-(ta /kɯkən), Khakhea (S5) //kari, !Kung
      (N2) /kere ~ /kare, Tati (C1) tsere, Naron (C2) /gare-ba.
388   MANY   //Kh'au-//'e (N1) ≠khî́, !Kung (N2) ≠khî́, !'O-!Kung (N3)
      ≠khî́, Naron (C2) kéi, Nama (C3) ≠gű̃i.
389   MASTER (n.)   /Kham (S1) /hũ, //Ng-!'e (S2) /hu, /Nu-//'e (S6)
      /hũ(!kwã), //Kh'au-//'e (N1) /hũ, Naron (C2) /hũba.
390   MAT (GRASS)   //Kh'au-//'e (N1) /xari, !Kung (N2) /xeru, Naron
      (C2) /xɔruŋ 'sieve,' Nama (C3) /karub.
391   MEDICINE   /Kham (S1) šo /óä, !'O-!Kung (N3) čɔ̄, Naron (C2) čɔ̄,
      Nama (C3) sò̃ /õab.
392   MEDICINE MAN   /Kham (S1) !gɛi-tən, //Kh'au-//'e (N1) !gei-xa,
      Nama (C3) !géi-aob.
393   MEET   //Kh'au-//'e (N1) //kaiä, Tati (C1) !kxaio, Naron (C2) //kái,
      Nama (C3) //ai.
394   MELON   /Nu-//'e (S6) tʌm, //Kh'au-//'e (N1) tàma, Tati (C1)
      tsama.
395   MIDDAY   /Kham (S1) //kwɔř̃a, //Kh'au-//'e (N1) //gɔreká.
396   MILK (v.)   /Nu-//'e (S6) /au, //Kh'au-//'e (N1) /k'au, !Kung (N2)
      /k'aó, Naron (C2) /k'au, Nama (C3) /ào.
397   MILKY WAY   !Kung (N2) /gu ≠ɔroko, Nama (C3) xam ≠khara-kha.
398   MIMOSA   /Nu-//'e (S6) //kũ, //Kh'au-//'e (N1) !gũ, Naron (C2)
      !gõba.

399 MIX /Kham (S1) (*hweitən*) //*kõïtẽ*, Tati (C1) //*kai*//*kai*.

400 MOISTEN Khakhea (S5) *čā* 'pour,' //Kh'au-//'e (N1) *čà* 'pour,'
!Kung (N2) *ča*, !'O-!Kung (N3) *čā* 'pour,' Tati (C1) *ča*.

401 MOO (v.) //Ng-!'e (S2) *k"ā*, Khakhea (S5) //*k"ā*, /Nu-//'e (S6) *k"ā*,
Naron (C2) *k"ai*.

402 MOON /Kham (S1) !*ka*!*karo*, //Ng-!'e (S2) !*kɔro*, //Khegwi (S3)
klolo, Khakhea (S5) !*xʌn*, /Nu-//'e (S6) !*xān*, //Kh'au-//'e (N1)
!*ka*!*kani*, !'O-!Kung (N3) !*ka*!*karī* (*še*), Nama (C3) ≠*kani* 'new moon.'

403 MORNING₁ /Nu-//'e (S6) !*kobe*, !'O-!Kung (N3) *kɔvəkɔvə*.

404 MORNING₂ Khakhea (S5) *kɔ̄ma*, //Kh'au-//'e (N1) *kɔ̄ma*, !Kung
(N2) /*kʌm*(/*gi*).

405 MORTAR (WOODEN) Khakhea (S5) !*kai*, !Kung (N2) !*ke*, !'O-
!Kung (N3) !*kei*, Tati (C1) !*koe*.

406 MOTHER /Kham (S1) *mama*, /Nu-//'e (S6) *mama*, Nama (C3) *ma-
mas*.

407 MOTHER-IN-LAW //Kh'au-//'e (N1) /*wi dzou*, !Kung (N2) /*wīso*
(!*nāa*), Naron (C2) /*wīsa*, Nama (C3) /*ùis*.

408 MOUNTAIN Khakhea (S5) /*num*, /Nu-//'e (S6) !*gum*, //Kh'au-//'e
(N1) !*num*, !Kung (N2) !*num*.

409 NAIL (FINGER-) /Kham (S1) //*kuru*, //Ng-!'e (S2) //*kuri*, //Khegwi
(S3) //*kɔla*, /'Auni (S4) //*kɔra*, //Kh'au-//'e (N1) //*kuru*, !Kung (N2)
//*kuru*, !'O-!Kung (N3) //*kulu*, Naron (C2) //*k'ɔro*, Nama (C3) //*goros*.

410 NAVEL //Kh'au-//'e (N1) !*num*, !Kung (N2) !*num*, Tati (C1) !*kom*,
Naron (C2) !*num*.

411 NEAR //Kh'au-//'e (N1) /*kū* 'to be near,' Tati (C1) /*ku*, Naron
(C2) /*kū*, Nama (C3) /*gu*.

412 NECKLACE //Kh'au-//'e (N1) //*kale* !*àm*, Tati (C1) //*kaie*.

413 NEEDLE /Kham (S1) //*kẽīŋ*, //Ng-!'e (S2) //*kẽnja*, !'O-!Kung (N3)
//*ēīsi*.

414 NET /Kham (S1) /*ũï*, //Kh'au-//'e (N1) /*wí*, Naron (C2) /*wīsiba*,
Nama (C3) /*uis*.

415 NICE /Kham (S1) *twai-i*, //Ng-!'e (S2) *tsaī*, //Kh'au-//'e (N1) *tãī*,
Naron (C2) *tõī*.

416 NO Khakhea (S5) *ŋ́ŋ́*, /Nu-//'e (S6) *ŋ́ŋ́*, //Kh'au-//'e (N1) *ŋ́ŋ́*, !Kung
(N2) *ŋ́ŋ́*, Naron (C2) *ŋ́ŋ́*.

417 NO/NOT₁ //Khegwi (S3) *ka*, //Kh'au-//'e (N1) *ká*, Naron (C2) *káa*,
Nama (C3) *ga*.

418 NO/NOT₂ //Khegwi (S3) /*kēwa*, /'Auni (S4) /*ka*, /Nu-//'e (S6)
/*kwa*, //Kh'au-//'e (N1) /*kwá* ~ /*ká*, !Kung (N2) /*kũä*, !'O-!Kung
(N3) /*kwa*.

419 NOSE   //Kh'au-//'e (N1) č'ũ, !Kung (N2) ts'ú̃, !'O-!Kung (N3) tsn ~
čn.

420 OLD₁   //Ng-!'e (S2) !naiŋ, //Kh'au-//'e (N1) !nā, !'O-!Kung (N3)
//nāa.

421 OLD₂   Khakhea (S5) //xau, //Kh'au-//'e (N1) /gò, !'O-!Kung (N3)
//gāa, Tati (C1) //gao.

422 ONION (WILD)   /Kham (S1) !kauï, //Ng-!'e (S2) !õũ, //Kh'au-//'e
(N1) !gau.

423 OSTRICH   /'Auni (S4) kō, /Nu-//'e (S6) koi, //Kh'au-//'e (N1) !gò,
!Kung (N2) !kúi, !'O-!Kung (N3) !gòe.

424 OTHER   //Kh'au-//'e (N1) !nwí, !'O-!Kung (N3) /nwí, Nama (C3)
/ni.

425 PACK UP   //Kh'au-//'e (N1) !nau, Nama (C3) !nao.

426 PASS   Khakhea (S5) //kwai 'to pass behind,' //Kh'au-//'e (N1) //kai
'to pass in front,' !'O-!Kung (N3) //ki.

427 PATH   Khakhea (S5) dau, /Nu-//'e (S6) dau, //Kh'au-//'e (N1)
dàusa, Tati (C1) dhau, Naron (C2) dauba, Nama (C3) daob.

428 PAUW (a kind of peacock)   /Kham (S1) !kú̃, //Ng-!'e (S2) !kú̃,
//Kh'au-//'e (N1) !gwi, !'O-!Kung (N3) /gwi, Nama (C3) !huib.

429 PICK   //Ng-!'e (S2) //kā 'to pick up,' /Nu-//'e (S6) //kai, //Kh'au-
//'e (N1) //géi.

430 PIERCE   //Kh'au-//'e (N1) dɔro, Naron (C2) dɔro, Nama (C3) doro.

431 PIG   //Kh'au-//'e (N1) gàri, Nama (C3) girib.

432 PLACE (n.)   /Kham (S1) ti, /'Auni (S4) ti (su), !Kung (N2) si.

433 PLAY THE BOW   //Kh'au-//'e (N1) /nʌm, !Kung (N2) ≠neʌm̃, !'O-
!Kung (N3) /nʌm ~ ≠naʌm, Nama (C3) ≠nam.

434 PLEASE (IF YOU —)   Khakhea (S5) !nā, !Kung (N2) /nāa.

435 PLUCK₁   /Kham (S1) thuru, Naron (C2) čxɔro, Nama (C3) tsuru.

436 PLUCK₂   //Kh'au-//'e (N1) šwe, !Kung (N2) swà, !'O-!Kung (N3)
swà ~ šwa, Tati (C1) čwako, Naron (C2) čwī.

437 PLUNGE INTO   /Kham (S1) !kum (/ē), //Kh'au-//'e (N1) !gɔm.

438 POOR   //Kh'au-//'e (N1) /gā̃, Tati (C1) kaa, Naron (C2) /kāna,
Nama (C3) /gá̃.

439 PORCUPINE   //Ng-!'e (S2) /kwī, Tati (C1) gwee.

440 POSSESS   /Kham (S1) //ēi, Nama (C3) //èī.

441 POSSESSIVE PARTICLE   /Nu-//'e (S6) -ti, Naron (C2) -di.

442 POT₁   /Kham (S1) !kõã, //Ng-!'e (S2) !kɔ̃ã, !'O-!Kung (N3) !k'á.

443 POT₂   /'Auni (S4) ≠am, Tati (C1) ama.

444 POT₃   //Khegwi (S3) ču, Naron (C2) šūba 'clay pot,' šū ša 'iron pot,'
Nama (C3) sús.

445 POUND   /Kham (S1) /kum, Tati (C1) /kom.

446 POUR Khakhea (S5) //ko, Nama (C3) //hò.

447 PRAY //Kh'au-//'e (N1) /gɔre, Naron (C2) /gɔre *(ma šɛ)*, Nama (C3) /gɔre.

448 PUFF-ADDER /'Auni (S4) *(!ka)* !gãĩ, Tati (C1) gaii, Nama (C3) !gèis.

449 PUT /Kham (S1) /ē /ē 'to put in,' //Ng-!'e (S2) /ē 'to put in,' //Kh'au-//'e (N1) /ē 'to put in,' Tati (C1) /ge 'to put in.'

450 PYTHON /Kham (S1) //kē(tən), !Kung (N2) *(!na)*//kē.

451 QUIET, TO BE₁ /Kham (S1) kwē, !Kung (N2) kwē.

452 QUIET, TO BE₂ /Kham (S1) ≠gou, Tati (C1) goo.

453 QUIVER //Ng-!'e (S2) !gɔru, /'Auni (S4) !kɔru, //Kh'au-//'e (N1) !kuru, !Kung (N2) !kuru, Nama (C3) !gurus.

454 RAIN (n.) //Ng-!'e (S2) !khã̀, /'Auni (S4) //khã̀, Khakhea (S5) //ka, //Kh'au-//'e (N1) !gà, !Kung (N2) //gã, !'O-!Kung (N3) //gã́.

455 RAIN (v.) /Kham (S1) kã́ũ, //Ng-!'e (S2) kãũ, !'O-!Kung (N3) kãũ.

456 RAIN TIME !'O-!Kung (N3) bɑla, Tati (C1) bara.

457 RAM //Kh'au-//'e (N1) gū(//gɔ̀ɔ̈), !Kung (N2) gū(//gɔ̀ɔ̈), Tati (C1) ǰu, Naron (C2) gūba, Nama (C3) gùb.

458 RAW /Kham (S1) /kã̀, //Ng-!'e (S2) /xã, !Kung (N2) /kãŋ.

459 RED Khakhea (S5) /kanja, /Nu-//'e (S6) /gàne, //Kh'au-//'e (N1) !gã, !Kung (N2) !gã, !'O-!Kung (N3) !gai, Nama (C3) //gani.

460 REED /Kham (S1) !nwā, //Kh'au-//'e (N1) !nwā, !Kung (N2) //nɔa.

461 RESEMBLE /Kham (S1) //kei//kei, !Kung (N2) //ke//ke.

462 RETURN //Kh'au-//'e (N1) débi, !Kung (N2) débi, !'O-!Kung (N3) dəbi ~ dibi, Naron (C2) débi.

463 RHINOCEROS₁ //Kh'au-//'e (N1) /xī, !Kung (N2) /khí, Tati (C1) kxii.

464 RHINOCEROS₂ Khakhea (S5) !gɔba, //Kh'au-//'e (N1) !naba, !Kung (N2) !naba, Tati (C1) gaba, Naron (C2) !naba, Nama (C3) !nàvas.

465 RIDE /Kham (S1) !kabi, //Kh'au-//'e (N1) ≠kʌbi, !Kung (N2) !kabi, Naron (C2) !kabe, Nama (C3) !gavi.

466 RISE /Kham (S1) !kwai, Naron (C2) !kwã.

467 RIVERBED /Nu-//'e (S6) dum, //Kh'au-//'e (N1) dùm, Naron (C2) dùmba.

468 ROAST₁ //Kh'au-//'e (N1) s'ó̃ ~ šou, !Kung (N2) sou ~ sau, !'O-!Kung (N3) šau, Tati (C1) čoo.

469 ROAST₂ !'O-!Kung (N3) /kũ, Naron (C2) ≠kũ.

470 ROLL₁ Khakhea (S5) //nai, !Kung (N2) //nai *(gangani)*.

471 ROLL₂ !'O-!Kung (N3) galə, Nama (C3) gari.

472 ROOT /Nu-//'e (S6) //kani 'root fibre,' //Kh'au-//'e (N1) //kari 'root fibre,' !Kung (N2) //keri 'root fibre,' !'O-!Kung (N3) //kari.

473 ROPE   //Kh'au-//'e (N1) *!kwí*, Tati (C1) *gwii*, Naron (C2) *!gwīša*.

474 RUB₁   Khakhea (S5) *!kum*, Naron (C2) *!kū*.

475 RUB₂   //Ng-!'e (S2) *(/kuna) /ē*, //Kh'au-//'e (N1) */xē*, Naron (C2) */xēi*.

476 RUB₃   Khakhea (S5) *šoa*, //Kh'au-//'e (N1) *šõã*.

477 RUN   /'Auni (S4) *!kuŋ*, Naron (C2) *!kū*.

478 SALT   //Kh'au-//'e (N1) *dabe*, Tati (C1) *debe*, Naron (C2) *dabe*.

479 SAY   /Kham (S1) *kūi*, //Kh'au-//'e (N1) *k'wí*, !Kung (N2) *k'wí*, !'O-!Kung (N3) *k'wi*, Naron (C2) *k'wí* 'speak.'

480 SCORPION   /Nu-//'e (S6) *//kaī*, Tati (C1) *//kadi*.

481 SCRAPE   /Kham (S1) *≠nai (turu)*, !Kung (N2) *≠nwāī*.

482 SCRATCH   Khakhea (S5) *čali*, !Kung (N2) *čxane*, !'O-!Kung (N3) *čxɔ*.

483 SCREAM   !Kung (N2) *!kóu*, Nama (C3) *!hao*.

484 SEE₁   /Kham (S1) */nī*, //Ng-!'e (S2) */nī*, //Khegwi (S3) */nē*, Khakhea (S5) */ne*, /Nu-//'e (S6) */nē*, !'O-!Kung (N3) */ne*.

485 SEE₂   /Kham (S1) *mu (≠en)* 'recognize' (literally, "see know"), Tati (C1) *moo*, Naron (C2) *mū*, Nama (C3) *m̆u*.

486 SEEDS₁   //Kh'au-//'e (N1) */nōsi*, !Kung (N2) */nēsiŋ*, Naron (C2) */ne /kēsi*.

487 SEEDS₂   !'O-!Kung (N3) *!kɔ́*, Nama (C3) *!komi*.

488 SEEK   //Kh'au-//'e (N1) *k'aru*, !Kung (N2) *k'aru ~ k'atu*, !'O-!Kung (N3) *kwātu*, Naron (C2) *k'ātu*.

489 SETTLE (birds)   Khakhea (S5) *//khá*, //Kh'au-//'e (N1) *//kauwa*, !Kung (N2) *//kūwa*, !'O-!Kung (N3) */nàua*.

490 SEW   //Kh'au-//'e (N1) *!gé*, !Kung (N2) *!géi*, !'O-!Kung (N3) *!gèi*, Naron (C2) *!gãī*.

491 SHADE₁   //Ng-!'e (S2) *//ʌhã́ŋ*, !Kung (N2) *//kɔhã ~ //khõã*.

492 SHADE₂   /Kham (S1) *!ɔ̀n*, !'O-!Kung (N3) *!kána*.

493 SHADE₃   /'Auni (S4) *sɔm*, Khakhea (S5) *šum*, /Nu-//'e (S6) *šɔm*, Tati (C1) *šom*, Nama (C3) *somi*.

494 SHADE₄   //Kh'au-//'e (N1) *!karise*, Tati (C1) */karaise*, Nama (C3) *!àris*.

495 SHAKE₁   Khakhea (S5) *!nɔpəm*, !Kung (N2) *//nabuä*, !'O-!Kung (N3) *//nabi//nabi*.

496 SHAKE₂   //Kh'au-//'e (N1) *//kai*, Naron (C2) *//kaijɑ*.

497 SHAVE   //Kh'au-//'e (N1) *//nau*, Naron (C2) *//nau*.

498 SHEEP   Khakhea (S5) *gū ~ kū*, //Kh'au-//'e (N1) *gū*, !Kung (N2) *gū*, !'O-!Kung (N3) *ğu*, Tati (C1) *ju*, Naron (C2) *ğuša*, Nama (C3) *ğus*.

499 SHELL₁   /Kham (S1) *tū*, !Kung (N2) *čum*.

500 SHELL₂ /Kham (S1) hɔro 'eggshell,' Nama (C3) soros.

501 SHINE /Kham (S1) ≠xī, !Kung (N2) ≠xi.

502 SHOE /'Auni (S4) //abo, Tati (C1) //kabo, Naron (C2) //nabo.

503 SHOOT //Ng-!'e (S2) //kaũ, Naron (C2) //xaũ.

504 SHOOT (with a gun) //Ng-!'e (S2) !nwā, /'Auni (S4) ≠nɔa, /Nu-//'e (S6) !nwā, //Kh'au-//'e (N1) !nwā, Naron (C2) !nwā̀, Nama (C3) ≠noá.

505 SHORT₁ !Kung (N2) !kōma, Tati (C1) //komnje, Naron (C2) !gum ~ //kum.

506 SHORT₂ //Kh'au-//'e (N1) !gɔ̄, !'O-!Kung (N3) !kō ~ !ko!ko, Tati (C1) !kxo (kadi).

507 SHOULDER //Kh'au-//'e (N1) !kɔma, Naron (C2) //kum.

508 SHOULDERBLADE /Kham (S1) //gài, //Ng-!'e (S2) //gài, Khakhea (S5) //gãī, /Nu-//'e (S6) //gɔre, //Kh'au-//'e (N1) !nɔru, !Kung (N2) //nūuru, Naron (C2) //nara, Nama (C3) //garàb.

509 SHOW (v.) /Kham (S1) //nēja, Nama (C3) //nai.

510 SHUT /Kham (S1) /kʌm, Khakhea (S5) /kū, //Kh'au-//'e (N1) /ú 'shut eyes,' !Kung (N2) /ú 'shut eyes,' Tati (C1) /kum, Naron (C2) !kʌm, /ūm 'shut eyes,' Nama (C3) /óm 'shut eyes.'

511 SING //Ng-!'e (S2) /nē, Khakhea (S5) //nai, //Kh'au-//'e (N1) //nai, Naron (C2) //nei, Nama (C3) //nài.

512 SINK Khakhea (S5) //kwā, Naron (C2) //gwā.

513 SIT /Kham (S1) s'ō ~ š'ō, //Ng-!'e (S2) s'ɔ̄ ~ s'o, //Khegwi (S3) šō, Khakhea (S5) tsū́, čū (/ki) 'to sit down,' /Nu-//'e (S6) šu ~ ču, //Kh'au-//'e (N1) šú 'to sit down.'

514 SKY /Nu-//'e (S6) !nari (sa), Naron (C2) !nérība.

515 SLOWLY /Nu-//'e (S6) !kwoisa, //Kh'au-//'e (N1) //k'wēsi, Naron (C2) //kwè̄še.

516 SMEAR //Kh'au-//'e (N1) /xauä, !'O-!Kung (N3) //kauwa, Nama (C3) kóu.

517 SMOKE₁ (v.) !'O-!Kung (N3) !gùm, Tati (C1) gom.

518 SMOKE₂ (v.) //Kh'au-//'e (N1) /kɔ̄ɔ̄, !'O-!Kung (N3) /kɔ̄, Naron (C2) /kɔ̄ɔ̄.

519 SMOOTH, TO BE !Kung (N2) tó, Naron (C2) tó.

520 SNAKE //Ng-!'e (S2) /k'au, /'Auni (S4) (si) /k'au, !'O-!Kung (N3) /kaũ, Tati (C1) /gauo, Naron (C2) /kaūba, Nama (C3) /àob.

521 SNORE /Kham (S1) !hɔ̀in, Nama (C3) !khaun.

522 SO, TO BE /Kham (S1) /kwēú, !'O-!Kung (N3) kwē.

523 SOON /Kham (S1) /kɔ̀ti, Nama (C3) /āse.

524 SPARROW //Kh'au-//'e (N1) //áru, Naron (C2) //áruba.

525 SPOON₁ //Ng-!'e (S2) /xame, Khakhea (S5) /gʌm, /Nu-//'e (S6) ≠gʌm, !Kung (N2) ≠kʌm.

526 SPOON₂ /Nu-//'e (S6) //goa, //Kh'au-//'e (N1) /gwã, Naron (C2) //gwāba, Nama (C3) //goàb.

527 SPOOR₁ //Kh'au-//'e (N1) !gǒ, !'O-!Kung (N3) //gō, Naron (C2) //kōša.

528 SPOOR₂ //Kh'au-//'e (N1) dàusa, Naron (C2) dàuša, Nama (C3) daob.

529 SPRING (season) /Kham (S1) !káuä, /Nu-//'e (S6) //hau, //Kh'au-//'e (N1) !kā, !'O-!Kung (N3) !kǒa, Naron (C2) !xōba, Nama (C3) !aváb.

530 SPRINGBOK₁ (a kind of antelope) //Khegwi (S3) !kõã, //Kh'au-//'e (N1) !kõ.

531 SPRINGBOK₂ //Ng-!'e (S2) !gai, Naron (C2) !gàiba, Nama (C3) !hãeb.

532 STALK (n.) /Kham (S1) !kwã̄, !'O-!Kung (N3) !ʔã.

533 STAMP₁ (v.) /Kham (S1) !um, Khakhea (S5) !um, Nama (C3) !hũ.

534 STAMP₂ (v.) /Kham (S1) /kum, Tati (C1) /kom.

535 STAR //Kh'au-//'e (N1) ≠gõe, !Kung (N2) ≠kõ, Tati (C1) ≠kxaine, Nama (C3) ≠kani.

536 STAY /Nu-//'e (S6) ha, Naron (C2) hà, Nama (C3) hã̀.

537 STEAL //Kh'au-//'e (N1) č'ā, !Kung (N2) ča, !'O-!Kung (N3) č'á, Tati (C1) tsaa, Naron (C2) čã̀ ~ tsã.

538 STEENBOK (a kind of antelope) Khakhea (S5) /gai, /Nu-//'e (S6) /gī, Tati (C1) gaie, Naron (C2) !gèiba.

539 STICK₁ (n.) //Khegwi (S3) ⊙ho, /'Auni (S4) ⊙hő̃ä, Nama (C3) !hõas.

540 STICK₂ (n.) //Kh'au-//'e (N1) //abi, Naron (C2) //abi.

541 STILL (adv.) /Kham (S1) !kar̃a, //Kh'au-//'e (N1) //keire, Naron (C2) !kane ~ //kàra.

542 STIR //Ng-!'e (S2) hɔrí̃, Naron (C2) hɜrí.

543 STONE /Nu-//'e (S6) !um, //Kh'au-//'e (N1) !num, !Kung (N2) !num, !'O-!Kung (N3) !num.

544 STOP /Kham (S1) /kum 'stop up,' Khakhea (S5) //kũ, /Nu-//'e (S6) //kū ~ //u, Nama (C3) /ũ.

545 STORK /Nu-//'e (S6) //nɔbe, !Kung (N2) !nɔbo.

546 STRETCH₁ /Kham (S1) !gouwa, //Kh'au-//'e (N1) !gõ.

547 STRETCH₂ /Kham (S1) //kau, Naron (C2) //xauë.

548 STUPID //Kh'au-//'e (N1) kàra, Nama (C3) gãre.

549 SUCK /Kham (S1) /ómi, //Kh'au-//'e (N1) /num, !Kung (N2) /kum, Naron (C2) /kum, Nama (C3) /góm.

550 SUMMER₁ /Kham (S1) //kwána, Nama (C3) //kunab.

551 SUMMER₂ Khakhea (S5) !nwā, //Kh'au-//'e (N1) !nau, Naron (C2) //nauba.

552 SUN //Kh'au-//'e (N1) /kʌm, !Kung (N2) /kʌm, !'O-!Kung (N3) /kʌm, Tati (C1) /kam, Naron (C2) /kʌmša.

553 SWALLOW (v.) //Kh'au-//'e (N1) tum, Tati (C1) t'om, Naron (C2) tùm.

554 SWEET₁ /Kham (S1) t'waĩ, //Kh'au-//'e (N1) t'õĩ.

555 SWEET₂ //Ng-!'e (S2) t'jaŋ, !Kung (N2) táŋ.

556 SWELL /Kham (S1) xẽ, Naron (C2) xãĩ, Nama (C3) xài.

557 SWING (v.) !Kung (N2) //nabu, Naron (C2) //abi.

558 TAIL /Kham (S1) !khwi, //Kh'au-//'e (N1) !khwí, !Kung (N2) //khwe, !'O-!Kung (N3) //kwé.

559 TAKE /Kham (S1) ≠nī 'take away,' Nama (C3) ≠nei.

560 TATTOO₁ (v.) /Nu-//'e (S6) //ka, !'O-!Kung (N3) //kɔ.

561 TATTOO₂ (v.) //Kh'au-//'e (N1) /k'ɔre, /'Auni (S4) /kɔre (sa) (n.), Naron (C2) /kɔre (n.).

562 TEACH //Ng-!'e (S2) //xa//xa-ā, //Kh'au-//'e (N1) //ka//ka, Naron (C2) //xa//xa, Nama (C3) //khā//khā.

563 TEAR (n., "rip") /Kham (S1) twī, Khakhea (S5) čwe, Tati (C1) twi.

564 THAT₁ (dem. adj.) Khakhea (S5) ti, /Nu-//'e (S6) ti, //Kh'au-//'e (N1) či, !Kung (N2) ši.

565 THAT₂ (dem. adj.) /Kham (S1) ha, //Ng-!'e (S2) a, //Khegwi (S3) ha, Khakhea (S5) a, Tati (C1) a ~ ho.

566 THAT₃ (dem. adj.) /Kham (S1) /kēá, //Ng-!'e (S2) /neá, Naron (C2) /ne.

567 THAT (rel.) /Kham (S1) ē, //Ng-!'e (S2) ē, !Kung (N2) e, Naron (C2) ē.

568 THAT (conj.) /Kham (S1) ti (ē), Tati (C1) či.

569 THERE /Kham (S1) //na, //Ng-!'e (S2) //na, Khakhea (S5) //na, /Nu-//'e (S6) //na, !'O-!Kung (N3) ≠na, Naron (C2) //na, Nama (C3) //naba.

570 THEY /'Auni (S4) sa 'them,' //Kh'au-//'e (N1) sa, !Kung (N2) sa, !'O-!Kung (N3) sa.

571 THIGH /Kham (S1) tẽ, //Khegwi (S3) tẽ, /Nu-//'e (S6) tẽ, Tati (C1) tee, Naron (C2) tẽša, Nama (C3) tẽs.

572 THING /Kham (S1) ti ~ ts'a, /'Auni (S4) ča, Khakhea (S5) ča, //Kh'au-//'e (N1) či ~ ča, !Kung (N2) či ~ ši, !'O-!Kung (N3) či.

573 THINK /Kham (S1) ≠ẽ ~ ĩ, //Ng-!'e (S2) ≠ẽ ~ ĩ, //Kh'au-//'e (N1) ≠ẽ, !Kung (N2) ≠ĩŋ, Naron (C2) ≠ĩ, Nama (C3) ≠ẽĩ.

574　THIS₁　Khakhea (S5) *te(a)* ~ *ti (a)*, //Kh'au-//'e (N1) *či* ~ *tsi*, !'O-
!Kung (N3) *či*.

575　THIS₂　/Kham (S1) *ēá*, //Ng-!'e (S2) a, !Kung (N2) *e* ~ *ēa* ~ *ēja*,
Tati (C1) *e*.

576　THIS₃　//Kh'au-//'e (N1) /*ni*, Naron (C2) /*ní* ~ /*ne*.

577　THONG　/Kham (S1) *!hāū*, //Kh'au-//'e (N1) *!nou*, Naron (C2)
!nàuba, Nama (C3) *!hōūb*.

578　THORN　Khakhea (S5) //*kaba*, /Nu-//'e (S6) //*kaba*, Tati (C1)
//*kam*, Naron (C2) //*gama*, Nama (C3) //*khāb*.

579　THOU　/Kham (S1) a, //Ng-!'e (S2) a, //Khegwi (S3) a, /'Auni (S4)
a, Khakhea (S5) a, /Nu-//'e (S6) a, //Kh'au-//'e (N1) a, !Kung (N2) *ā*
'thee,' !'O-!Kung (N3) a.

580　THREE　/Kham (S1) *!nwɔna*, //Ng-!'e (S2) *!nwana*, //Khegwi (S3)
khɔana, /'Auni (S4) *!nwɔna*, //Kh'au-//'e (N1) *!naní*, Tati (C1) *ngo-
nawe*, Naron (C2) *!nwɔna*, Nama (C3) *!nona*.

581　THROAT　/Kham (S1) *dom*, //Kh'au-//'e (N1) *dɔm*, !Kung (N2)
dɔm, !'O-!Kung (N3) *dɔm*, Tati (C1) *dham (/kwia)*, Naron (C2) *dɔm*,
Nama (C3) *domi*.

582　THROW₁　Khakhea (S5) //*gʌm*, Tati (C1) //*gama* 'to throw away.'

583　THROW₂　//Kh'au-//'e (N1) /*namú* 'to throw away,' Naron (C2)
/*name* 'to throw down,' Nama (C3) /*nami* 'to throw down.'

584　THUNDER　/Nu-//'e (S6) *(!xwē še) tana*, !'O-!Kung (N3) *(//gā ne)
tala*.

585　TIE (v.)　/Kham (S1) //*hiŋ*, //Ng-!'e (S2) //*ế* ~ //*kēīn* 'sew,' Khakhea
(S5) //*hē*, //Kh'au-//'e (N1) //*ēī* ~ //*ī*, !Kung (N2) //*īŋ*, !'O-!Kung
(N3) //*ēī*, Nama (C3) ≠*hì̃*.

586　TIME　//Kh'au-//'e (N1) //*aiä*, Nama (C3) //*aib*.

587　TINDERBOX　/Kham (S1) (//*kau*) *dɔro*, /'Auni (S4) *dɔro* (≠*nantá*),
//Kh'au-//'e (N1) *dari*, !Kung (N2) *(ši) tɔroha*, Naron (C2) *dɔroša*,
Nama (C3) *doros*.

588　TIRED　/Kham (S1) //*kű*, //Kh'au-//'e (N1) //*kwĩ*, Naron (C2)
//*k'wiã*.

589　TOGETHER　/Kham (S1) //*k'ɛ̄*, //Kh'au-//'e (N1) //*kai*, Tati (C1)
//*kae*, Naron (C2) //*kaiä*, Nama (C3) //*ai*.

590　TOMORROW　Khakhea (S5) *kɔ̀ma*, //Kh'au-//'e (N1) *!nwe kɔma* ~
kɔmaká, !'O-!Kung (N3) *kɔmakɔma*.

591　TORTOISE₁　/Nu-//'e (S6) //*néisi*, !'O-!Kung (N3) //*nēša*.

592　TORTOISE₂　/Kham (S1) //*gō*, //Ng-!'e (S2) //*gō*, //Kh'au-//'e (N1)
//*gwā*, !Kung (N2) //*kɔā*, Naron (C2) //*gwēba*.

593　TOUCH　/Kham (S1) *tā̃tā̃*, Nama (C3) *tsā (/kha)*.

594 TRAP (n.) //Kh'au-//'e (N1) !*gwi*, !Kung (N2) !*gwi*, Naron (C2) !*gwíša*.

595 TRAVEL (v.) !Kung (N2) //*k'ʌm*, Naron (C2) //*kʌm*.

596 TROT /Nu-//'e (S6) !*gaba*, !Kung (N2) !*kaba*.

597 TURN !Kung (N2) *gabi*, Tati (C1) *gabi*, Naron (C2) *gàbi (ši)*, Naron (C2) *khabi*.

598 TWIST //Kh'au-//'e (N1) *tɔro*, Tati (C1) *tsonoo*, Naron (C2) *tɔ́rnu*, *dɔro* 'twirl.'

599 TWO /'Auni (S4) /*kʌm*, Tati (C1) /*kamnje*, Naron (C2) /*kʌm*, Nama (C3) /*gam*.

600 UNTIE /Kham (S1) *kwəre*, !Kung (N2) *kwara*, Nama (C3) *kore*.

601 VELD /Kham (S1) !*kauxu*, //Ng-!'e (S2) !*aũ tsĩ*, Tati (C1) *kaoo*, Nama (C3) !*oúb*.

602 VISIT (v.) //Kh'au-//'e (N1) //*gãĩ*, !Kung (N2) //*ga*, Tati (C1) //*gaie*, Naron (C2) /*gã̀*.

603 VOCATIVE /Kham (S1) -*wɛ*, //Ng-!'e (S2) -*bɛ*, Khakhea (S5) -*bɛ*, !Kung (N2) -*we*.

604 WAIT₁ /Kham (S1) !*kā* ~ !*kã*, !Kung (N2) !*ka* ~ !*kã*, Naron (C2) !*kã*.

605 WAIT₂ //Ng-!'e (S2) //*nʌm*, Nama (C3) //*nàm*.

606 WALK Khakhea (S5) !*hũ*, Naron (C2) !*kũ*, Nama (C3) !*gũŋ*.

607 WALL Khakhea (S5) !*ani*, Nama (C3) !*anìb*.

608 WANT /'Auni (S4) /*kau/kau*, //Kh'au-//'e (N1) ≠*kau*, Naron (C2) ≠*kau*, Nama (C3) ≠*gao*.

609 WARM //Khegwi (S3) *kuruwa*, Naron (C2) *kuruša*.

610 WASH //Kh'au-//'e (N1) //*k'a*, !Kung (N2) //*ka*, !'O-!Kung (N3) //*k'a*, Naron (C2) //*k'ā*, Nama (C3) //*ā*.

611 WASP₁ /Kham (S1) !*khóu*, !Kung (N2) !*gãũ*!*gãũa*.

612 WASP₂ //Kh'au-//'e (N1) *gáu*, Naron (C2) *gwãgwã*.

613 WASP₃ //Kh'au-//'e (N1) /*gəru*, Naron (C2) /*garuba*, Nama (C3) /*gerub*.

614 WATER (v.) Naron (C2) /*nã* ~ /*kã/kã*, Nama (C3) /*ã-/ã*.

615 WATERHOLE /Kham (S1) *xwara*, Tati (C1) *hwere*.

616 WE (inc.) /Kham (S1) *i*, //Ng-!'e (S2) *i* ~ *e*, //Khegwi (S3) *i*, /'Auni (S4) *e*, Khakhea (S5) *i*, /Nu-//'e (S6) *i*, //Kh'au-//'e (N1) *e* (!*ka*) 'we masc.,' *e(he)* 'we fem.,' !Kung (N2) *i*, !'O-!Kung (N3) *i* ~ *e* 'we.'

617 WE (ex.) /Kham (S1) *si*, //Ng-!'e (S2) *si*, //Khegwi (S3) *si*, /'Auni (S4) *si*, Khakhea (S5) *ši*, /Nu-//'e (S6) *si*, !Kung (N2) *šiši*, Naron (C2) *ši(-//kei)* 'we masc.,' *ši(-ta)* 'we fem.,' *ši(-si)* 'we common,' Nama (C3) *si(-gje)* 'we masc.,' *si(-se)* 'we fem.,' *si(-da)* 'we common.'

618 WHAT₁ (inter.) /Kham (S1) *ts'a-dɛ*, !Kung (N2) *tsa-de*.
619 WHAT₂ (inter.) /Kham (S1) *ts'a-ba*, //Kh'au-//'e (N1) *če-ba*.
620 WHAT₃ (inter.) /Kham (S1) *-ba*, //Kh'au-//'e (N1) *-ba*.
621 WHEN (rel.) //Kh'au-//'e (N1) *kama*, Tati (C1) /*kam*, Naron (C2) *kama*.
622 WHERE (inter.) /Nu-//'e (S6) *maba*, Nama (C3) *mába*.
623 WHICH (rel.) /Kham (S1) *ē ~ he* (pl.), //Ng-!'e (S2) *he* (pl.), //Kh'au-//'e (N1) *e*, !Kung (N2) *e*.
624 WHIP (n.) /'Auni (S4) *tsami*, Khakhea (S5) *seme*, !Kung (N2) *tsàme*.
625 WHISTLE //Kh'au-//'e (N1) /*nʌm*, Nama (C3) *≠nam*.
626 WHO (inter.) /Kham (S1) *!ku-dɛ (xa)*, !Kung (N2) *!kū-de*.
627 WHO (rel.) /Kham (S1) *ē ~ hē*, //Ng-!'e (S2) *e ~ he*, //Kh'au-//'e (N1) *e*, !Kung (N2) *e*, Naron (C2) *e*, Nama (C3) *i*.
628 WILDEBEEST (BLUE) //Ng-!'e (S2) *!gā*, //Kh'au-//'e (N1) *!gḛ̀*, !Kung (N2) *!gi*, !'O-!Kung (N3) *!gēi*.
629 WIND (n.) //Kh'au-//'e (N1) *≠á̰*, !Kung (N2) *≠á̰*, Naron (C2) *≠āba*, Nama (C3) *≠oáb*.
630 WIND (v.) /Kham (S1) *≠kʌm (//kho)*, //Kh'au-//'e (N1) *≠kam*.
631 WINGS /Nu-//'e (S6) //*kabuxāte*, //Kh'au-//'e (N1) *!nabusi*, Tati (C1) //*kabaa*, Naron (C2) //*kabuži*, Nama (C3) //*gavòkha*.
632 WITH //Kh'au-//'e (N1) /*kwa*, !Kung (N2) *kwe*, !'O-!Kung (N3) *kwe*, Naron (C2) *-kwe ~* /*kwa*, Nama (C3) /*kà*.
633 WOOD /Kham (S1) ⊙*hō*, //Khegwi (S3) ⊙*hō*, Tati (C1) /*hoo*.
634 WORK //Ng-!'e (S2) *sēsē ~ siŋsiŋ*, /Nu-//'e (S6) *sīsī*, //Kh'au-//'e (N1) *sīsī*, Naron (C2) *sēsē*, Nama (C3) *sīsen*.
635 WOUND (v.) /Kham (S1) *twī*, Khakhea (S5) *twī*, Nama (C3) *tswi*.
636 WRITE₁ Khakhea (S5) *kwala*, Tati (C1) *kola*.
637 WRITE₂ /Kham (S1) *xő̃ä*, //Ng-!'e (S2) *xwa*, !Kung (N2) *xő̃ä*, Naron (C2) *xaua*, Nama (C3) *xoa*.
638 YAWN (v.) /Kham (S1) *!gõägən*, //Kh'au-//'e (N1) *!õã*, !Kung (N2) *!kõã*.
639 YES₁ //Ng-!'e (S2) *jē*, /Nu-//'e (S6) *ɛ̄*, //Kh'au-//'e (N1) *ɛ̄*, Tati (C1) *je*, Naron (C2) *ɛ̄*.
640 YES₂ Khakhea (S5) *ŋ́ŋ*, !Kung (N2) *ŋ́ŋ*.
641 YOU₁ /Kham (S1) *u*, //Ng-!'e (S2) *u*, /'Auni (S4) *u*, Khakhea (S5) *u*, !'O-!Kung (N3) *u*.
642 YOU₂ /'Auni (S4) *i*, Khakhea (S5) *i*, /Nu-//'e (S6) *i*, //Kh'au-//'e (N1) *i*, !Kung (N2) *i*, !'O-!Kung (N3) *i*.
643 YOUNG₁ /Kham (S1) *-⊙pwa*, //Ng-!'e (S2) *-⊙pwa*, Naron (C2) /*kwa*.

644   YOUNG$_2$ /Nu-//'e (S6) -ma, //Kh'au-//'e (N1) -ma, !Kung (N2)
      -ma, !'O-!Kung (N3) -ma.
645   ZEBRA   !Kung (N2) *!kwɔre*, Nama (C3) *!goreb*.

REFERENCES

Bleek, Dorothea F. 1929. *Comparative Vocabularies of Bushman Languages*.
Cambridge, Eng.

——. 1956. *A Bushman Dictionary*. New Haven, Conn.

Ehret, Christopher. 1986. "Proposals on Khoisan Reconstruction," *Sprache und Geschichte in Afrika* 7.2: 105–30.

Fleming, Harold C. 1986. "Hadza and Sandawe Genetic Relations," *Sprache und Geschichte in Afrika* 7.2: 157–87.

Greenberg, Joseph H. 1963. *The Languages of Africa*. Bloomington, Ind.

Köhler, Oswin. 1973–74. "Neuere Ergebnisse und Hypothesen der Sprachforschung in ihrer Bedeutung für die Geschichte Afrikas," *Paideuma* 19/20: 162–99.

——. 1981. "Les langues khoisan," in Jean Perrot, ed., *Les langues dans le monde ancien et moderne*. Paris, 455–615.

Ladefoged, Peter, and Anthony Traill. 1984. "Linguistic Phonetic Descriptions of Clicks," *Language* 60: 1–20.

Traill, Anthony. 1973. "'N4 or S7?': Another Bushman Language," *African Studies* 32: 25–32.

——. 1974. "Westphal on 'N4 or S7?': A Reply," *African Studies* 33: 249–55.

Westphal, E. O. J. 1974. "Notes on A. Traill: 'N4 or S7,'" *African Studies* 33: 243–47.

4

Proto-Yeniseian Reconstructions, with Extra-Yeniseian Comparisons

Sergei A. Starostin and Merritt Ruhlen

The small Yeniseian family of central Siberia—now reduced to a single extant language, Ket—has traditionally been considered an isolate.* Though less famous than the well-known European isolate, Basque, its genetic affinity has been considered no less mysterious. Even information on this family has not been easy to come by for those wishing to compare it with the world's other language families. Starostin (1982), however, has fundamentally changed this state of affairs. In this pivotal paper he not only reconstructed Proto-Yeniseian—and the sound laws that connect its several languages—but also sought to show its genetic connections with the Sino-Tibetan and (North) Caucasian families, and even the genetic connections of this larger family with the Nostratic family. The external connections of the Yeniseian family were further elaborated in Starostin (1984), which posited a Sino-Caucasian family (uniting Yeniseian, Sino-Tibetan, and (North) Caucasian), and Starostin (1989a) addressed the question of the relationship between Nostratic and Sino-Caucasian. Additional work by Bengtson (1991a,b), Chirikba

---

* We would like to thank John Bengtson for numerous suggestions on an earlier version of this chapter. Many of his suggestions have been incorporated, with citation, in this chapter.

(1985), and Nikolaev (1991) has led to the replacement of the name Sino-Caucasian by Dene-Caucasian (see Chapter 1). It should be noted that the higher-level comparisons between Proto-Yeniseian, Proto-Sino-Tibetan, and Proto-(North) Caucasian are based on the first author's reconstructions of all three families (Starostin 1989b, Nikolaev and Starostin 1992)—with due acknowledgment of previous work.

This chapter, an abridged version of Starostin (1982), gives the Proto-Yeniseian reconstructions and their reflexes in the various Yeniseian languages (again, of these, only Ket is extant). Also given are the extra-Yeniseian comparisons suggested by Starostin. My role, as second author, has been limited to translating Starostin's work from the original Russian, with the hope of making it accessible to a larger audience, and to adding a few extra-Yeniseian comparisons with Basque, Burushaski, Nahali, and Na-Dene. Since the appearance of Starostin's original article in 1982, additional proposed cognates have been suggested by John Bengtson, Václav Blažek, Sergei Nikolaev, and Starostin himself. Some of these are indicated at the ends of the etymologies thus supplemented.

Each entry is arranged alphabetically according to the semantic gloss, which is followed by the Proto-Yeniseian reconstruction and its reflexes in the six Yeniseian languages: Ket, †Yug, †Kott, †Arin, †Pumpokol, and †Assan. This information is followed by extra-Yeniseian comparisons with Old Chinese, Proto-Andi, Proto-Abkhaz-Adyg, Proto-Abkhaz-Tapant, Proto-Dagestanian, Proto-Indo-European, Proto-Kartvelian, Proto-Lezghian, Proto-Nax, Proto-Tsez, Proto-(North) Caucasian, Proto-Tibeto-Burman, and Proto-Sino-Tibetan, all taken from Starostin's article. The comparisons with Basque, Burushaski, Nahali, and Na-Dene are mine. The Na-Dene forms come from Greenberg (1981; see Chapter 5 herein); Burushaski forms, from Lorimer (1938); and Nahali forms, from Kuiper (1962).

For the most part the phonemic transcription follows that of Starostin's article. Thus, for example, *c* represents t^s, and *I* indicates pharyngealization of the preceding consonant. I have, however, used normal IPA symbols for the lateral fricatives and affricates, instead of the idiosyncratic Russian symbols; the effect is that what appear as *x̌*, *γ̃*, *k̃*, and *ǧ* in the original article are here transcribed as *ɬ*, *ɮ*, *tˡ*, and *dˡ*. In addition, *í* and *ń* are represented by *ʎ* and *ñ*, respectively, and *dᶻ* is used in place of *ʒ*. Furthermore, *ʌ* represents a lower-mid unrounded central vowel in the Yeniseian languages and in Burushaski, but a vowel of indeterminate timbre in the reconstructions. The meanings of all forms are the same as those of the Proto-Yeniseian reconstruction, unless specified otherwise.

Starostin's reconstructions follow:

1   ADJECTIVE SUFFIX   *-se*, Ket -*ś*, Yug -*s*, Kott -*še*. Cf. Proto-Dagestanian *-*s̄ʌ*-, Proto-Andi *-*s̄ʌ*-, Proto-Tsez *-*s̄(ʌ)*.

2   ALIVE   **?e?te*, Ket *eäte*, Yug *eät*, Kott *ēti*, Arin *atie* ~ *ätie*, Pumpokol *atodu*, Assan *editu* ~ *etutu*.

3   ANGRY (TO BE)   **χəjbʌč*, Yug *xʌjbɛt'*, Kott *haipičaŋ* 'angry, cross.'

4   ARM   **xɨre*, Ket *ɨʎ(i)*, Arin *karam-*. Cf. Proto-(North) Caucasian **q̄ʷIełʌ*.

5   ARMFUL   **kʌm-*, Kott *hamal*. Cf. Proto-Dagestanian **k'ʌmʌ*, Proto-Lezghian **k'em*.

6   ARMPIT   **qoʎ-*, Ket *qɔʎ-*, Yug *xɔl-*. Cf. Proto-(North) Caucasian **q̄ʷ(I)ʌt̄ˡ'i*, Proto-Tibeto-Burman **k(a)li*, Burushaski -*qʌt*, Nahali *kaṭhla*. According to Kuiper (1962: 83), the Nahali form is borrowed from Kurku (Munda).

7   AUTUMN   **χogde*, Ket *qɔgdi*, Yug *xɔgdi*, Kott *hōri*, Arin *kute*.

8   AWL   **du?t*, Ket *du?t*, Yug *du?t*, Kott *tūt*. Cf. Proto-Abkhaz-Adyg **d́ʷəd́ʷə*, Proto-Abkhaz-Tapant **d́ᶻad́ᶻə*, Old Chinese **tuj* (n.).

9   BACK (n.)   **χɔb-*, Ket *qɔb-* ~ *qɔv-*, Kott *hap-*, Arin *qop*, Pumpokol *kolpar*.

10 BACK (adv.)   **suga*, Ket *śuga*, Yug *sugej*, Kott *šūka*, Pumpokol *tuk*. Cf. Burushaski -*sqa* 'on one's back.' Bengtson (1991a: 92) compares these forms with Basque *bi-zka-r*, Abkhaz (Caucasian) *a-zkʷa*, and Haida (Na-Dene) *sku*.

11 BADGER   **χas*, Kott *hāš*. Cf. Proto-Dagestanian **χʷIʌŕʎ* 'squirrel, marten,' Proto-Nax **χešt* 'otter,' Basque *hartz* 'bear,' *azkonar* (< **harz-konH-*) 'badger'; for the second element of this latter form, see the Proto-Yeniseian word for WOLVERINE₁ below.

12 BALD/NAKED   **tɔtpʌl-*, Ket *tɔtpuʎ*, Kott *tʰapalō*.

13 BE   **hʌs-*, Ket *uśaŋ*, Yug *ūsɛ*, Kott *hičōga*. Cf. Basque *i-za-n*.

14 BEAK   **kup*, Ket *kūp*, Yug *kup*. Cf. Proto-Dagestanian **qʷIepʌ*.

15 BEAR (n.)   **čajaŋ*, Kott *šajaŋ*, Pumpokol *xanki*. Cf. Proto-(North) Caucasian **cʰʷä?nʌ*, Proto-Tibeto-Burman **s-wam*, Old Chinese **wəm*, Burushaski *yə̄*.

16 BEARD   **kuʎe(p)*, Ket *kūʎe*, Yug *kūʎ*, Kott *hulup*, Arin *korolep*, Pumpokol *xlep-uk*, Assan *xulūp*.

17 BELT₁   **hʌqtʌ*, Yug *axtaŋ* ~ *ɛxtaŋ*, Kott *hītēg*, Arin *ittä*.

18 BELT₂   **gu?da*, Ket *ku?t*, Kott *kūra* 'cord, belt,' Assan *kura* 'rope.'

19 BERRY   **sulpe-*, Kott *šulpi*, Arin *šulpä*.

20 BIG   **χe?*, Ket *qɛ?*, Yug *xɛ?*, Pumpokol *xää-se*, Kott *hī-*. Cf. Proto-(North) Caucasian *-aχ(I)i*.

21 BILE/BITTER *qʌqʌr, Ket qʌ́ʎ 'bile,' qōlɨŋ 'bitter,' Yug xʌxul
'bile,' xʌxɨʎaŋ 'bitter,' Kott ogar 'bile,' ?Pumpokol leō-xoxar 'bladder' (?< 'gall bladder'). Cf. Proto-(North) Caucasian *q'eq'ʌ ~
*-eq'ʌ- 'bitter,' Proto-Tibeto-Burman *ka 'bitter,' Old Chinese
*qāʔ, Burushaski γāqʌy(um). Bengtson (1991a: 110) adds Basque
kharr-atx 'bitter, sour' and Werchikwar (a Burushaski dialect)
qʌqaa-m 'bitter, sour.'

22 BIRCH BARK *χɨʔw-, Ket qɨʔj, Yug xɨʔj, Kott hīpal.

23 BIRCH TREE *xūsa, Ket ūśə, Yug ūʰs, Kott ūča, Arin kus, Pumpokol uta.

24 BIRD *duma, Ket dūm, Yug dɨl-tɨm, Kott al-tūma. Cf. Proto-
(North) Caucasian *t'ɨmHʌ.

25 BLOOD *sur, Ket śūʎ, Yug sur, Kott šur, Arin sur. Cf. Nahali
corṭo. Kuiper (1962: 67) suggests the Nahali form is borrowed from
Dravidian.

26 BOAT₁ *tʌχʌ-, Ket tī, Yug tī, Arin taj, Pumpokol tɨg, Assan ul-
tēj 'vessel.' Cf. Proto-(North) Caucasian *t'aqʌ 'vessel.'

27 BOAT₂ *qä(ʔ)p, Yug xa(ʔ)p, Kott xep. Cf. Proto-(North) Caucasian *q̄ʷap'a, Old Chinese *qhāp 'wooden cup, vessel.'

28 BOIL (v.) *ʔəqan, Ket ʌn, Yug ʌxan, Kott auganaŋ 'cook.' Cf. Na-
Dene: Haida k'untˡ'daa 'burn,' Tlingit ɢan 'burn,' Eyak d-q'a 'burn,'
Kato k'an 'burn.'

29 BONE *ʔaʔd, Ket aʔt, Yug aʔt. Cf. Proto-Dagestanian *hIəmdʌ,
Proto-Tsez *Hod̄, Proto-Lezghian > Tsax ad.

30 BOW (n.) *χɨʔj̄, Ket qɨʔt, Yug qɨʔt', Kott hī, Arin qoj, Pumpokol
kaj.

31 BRAID (OF HAIR) *sug-, Kott šugai ~ šukai. Cf. Proto-(North)
Caucasian *śakʰʷa ~ *kʰʷaśa.

32 BRANCH *ʔəqe, Ket ə̄Rə, Yug ə̄x, Kott ōge, Pumpokol kediŋ
jaxi 'bough' (kediŋ = 'root').

33 BREAST *təga, Ket tʌga, Yug tʌga, Pumpokol tike. Cf. Proto-
(North) Caucasian *jerk'ʷi ~ *rek'ʷi 'heart,' Proto-Tibeto-Burman
*raŋ, Old Chinese *ʔ(r)ək, Burushaski tshʌγur 'chest,' Na-Dene:
Haida tek'o-go 'heart,' Tlingit tek' 'heart,' Kutchin t'agu, Tahltan t'ódž-e, Hare t'oy, Mattole tˢ'ooʔ. The Haida and Tlingit forms
were added by Bengtson and Blažek (1992).

34 BREATH *ʔir₁- ~ *ʔir̄-, Ket īl, Yug īr. Cf. Proto-Dagestanian
*hʌ Ɉʎʌ, Proto-Andi > Tindi hā 'exhalation, steam,' Proto-Nax *ʕi
'exhalation, steam,' Proto-Lezghian *hel- 'exhalation, steam, respi-
ration.' Nikolaev (1991: 55) compares these forms with Eyak xahɬ
'hot-house, bath-house.'

35 BROTHER **bis*, Ket *biś-ɛʔp*, Yug *bis-ɛʔp*, Kott *popēš, popēča* 'sister,' Pumpokol *bič*. Cf. Proto-(North) Caucasian **w-ɨ́čʰwi*, ?Proto-Tibeto-Burman **dzar* 'man's sister,' ?Old Chinese **ćəj?* 'older sister.' Bengtson (1991b: 135) adds Basque *a-hiz-pa* 'sister' and Burushaski *-ačo* ~ *-aču* 'brother, sister'; and Nikolaev (1991: 49) adds Proto-Eyak-Athabaskan **wuǰ* 'older brother.'

36 BUD **bajbʌl*, Ket *bajbuʎ*, Yug *baibɨl*, Kott *koipala*. Cf. Basque *pipil*.

37 BURN/FIRE **χɔt*, Yug *xɔtn*, Kott *hat*, Arin *kōt* ~ *qot*. Cf. Nahali *oṭṭi*.

38 CEDAR **päʔj*, Ket *haʔj*, Yug *faʔj*, Kott *fei*, Arin *im-pʰaj, pʰaj-dʼa* 'fir tree,' Pumpokol *pɨ*, Assan *pej*.

39 CHEEK **χol-*, Ket *qɔʎet*, Yug *xɔlat*, Kott *hol*, Arin *bɨ-qoʎoŋ* 'my cheek,' Assan *holan* 'cheeks.' Cf. Proto-Sino-Tibetan **qālH* 'back, cheek,' Na-Dene: Eyak *l-quhɬ*.

40 CHILD₁ **pʌl-* ~ **pʌɨ́-* ~ **pʌrɨ-*, Arin *al-polat*, Pumpokol *phalla* 'boy, son.' Cf. Proto-Dagestanian **paHadˡʌ* 'boy, youngster,' Old Chinese **bōk* 'servant,' Burushaski *pɨlpɨli*, Nahali *palco* 'son.' Kuiper (1962: 96) suggests the Nahali word may be a borrowing from "pre-Dravidian."

41 CHILD₂ **dᶻʌl*, Ket *dɨ́ʎ*, Yug *dɨl*, Ket *dʼal, dʼaleä* 'girl,' Arin *bi-kal* 'boy, son,' *bi-kála* 'daughter,' Pumpokol *pi-kola* 'children, daughter,' Assan *jali* 'children, boy.' Cf. Nahali *eǰer* 'boy.'

42 CHILDREN **gəʔt*, Ket *kʌʔt, kitej* 'young,' Yug *kʌʔt, kitej* 'young,' Kott *kat*. Cf. Proto-(North) Caucasian **kʰwerčʼi* 'youngster,' Nahali *giṭa* 'younger brother,' Na-Dene: Haida *gyīt'* 'child,' *gít* 'son,' Tlingit *git'a* 'child,' *git* 'son,' Eyak *qēč* 'child,' *qē* 'son,' Navajo *ɣèʔ* 'son.'

43 CLAY **tuʔw-*, Ket *tuʔ*, Arin *tʼuburun*, Pumpokol *tu-*, Assan *tʼu* ~ *tʰʸu*. Cf. Na-Dene: Haida *tow-ge* 'earth.'

44 CLAY/DIRT **təq-*, Ket *tuɣit* 'smear with clay,' *tagar* 'clay,' Yug *təx* 'clay,' *tɨx-kɛtʼ* 'smear with clay,' Kott *tʰagar* 'dirt,' As *tagar* 'clay,' *tʰagan* ~ *tʰakan* 'sand,' Arin *tanen* 'sand.' Cf. Basque *toska* 'clay,' Burushaski *tīk* 'earth,' Nahali *tˢikal* 'earth,' Na-Dene: Haida *tˡig* 'earth,' Tlingit *tˡiak-ū* ~ *tˡit-tik* 'earth,' Eyak *tzatlkh* 'earth,' Navajo *ɬe* 'earth.' Kuiper (1962: 67) considers the Nahali word a borrowing from Kurku (Munda).

45 CLEAN (adj.) **tur-* ~ **tul-*, Yug *tul-en*. Cf. Proto-(North) Caucasian **dᶻʌnʃu*, Proto-Tibeto-Burman **tsyaŋ*, Old Chinese **cheŋ*. Bengtson and Blažek (1992) add Basque *šanhu*.

46 CLEAN (v.) *-pʌx-, Yug fɔgət, Kott ō-pajaŋ. Cf. Burushaski pāk (adj.).

47 CLEAR (about weather) *puʔr, Ket hiʔʎ, Yug fiʔr, Kott pʰur ~ fur.

48 CLOTHES *χäʔdᶻ, Ket qaʔt, Yug xaʔt, Kott hei 'fur coat, outer garment,' Arin qaj, Assan hejaŋ.

49 CLOUD *(ʔas-)pʌr, Ket aś-puʎ, Yug as-fil, Kott aš-par, Arin ejš-paraŋ ~ es-peraŋ. Cf. Burushaski burūnč̣.

50 COLD/FROST *jʌr₁ ~ *jʌl, Kott čal 'cold' (n. & adj.), Arin solo-ŋa 'frost.' Cf. Proto-(North) Caucasian *reč̌'ü 'cold,' Na-Dene: ?Beaver tsíl 'snowdrift.'

51 COMB *tuxʌ-ñ, Ket tuɣuñ, Yug tugin, Kott thun, Arin ten. Cf. Proto-(North) Caucasian *hirīḡʷʌ.

52 COPPER *tiʔn, Ket tiʔn, Yug tiʔn, Pumpokol a-tin.

53 COPPER/ORE *čur-, Ket tuʎä, Assan šur. Cf. Proto-(North) Caucasian *corʌ ~ *rocʌ 'copper.'

54 COUGH *χaqtʌm, Ket qaqtəm, Yug xaxtem, Kott hatam.

55 COW *tiχa, Kott tʰiʔä ~ tʰigä, Arin t'ūja, Assan tig ~ tik.

56 CRANE (bird) *xime, Assan imi, Arin kem.

57 CRY (tears) *-ʌjʌ(n)-, Yug d-īd'ä, Kott d-äčēnaŋ, Arin äšiñaŋ 'I cry,' Pumpokol čiin-du 'I cry.'

58 CRY/SHOUT *(h)uxʌ-, Ket d-ūɣə, Kott hujei.

59 CUT *pak-, Ket haɣej, Yug fagej, Arin it-päkuju 'I cut.' Cf. Basque ebaki ~ ebagi.

60 DAUGHTER/SON *puʔ-n 'daughter,' *puʔ-b 'son,' Ket huʔn 'daughter,' hiʔp 'son,' Yug fuʔn 'daughter,' fiʔp 'son,' Kott fun 'daughter,' fup 'son.' Cf. Proto-Abkhaz-Tapant *pa 'son,' Proto-Abkhaz-Adyg *pə-χʷʌ 'daughter.' Bengtson (pers. comm.) compares these forms with Basque -pa ~ -ba in forms such as alha-ba 'daughter,' a-hiz-pa 'sister,' ne-ba 'brother.'

61 DAY *xi(ʔ)ɢ, Ket iʔ, Yug īh, Kott īg ~ īx, Arin ji, Pumpokol ha, Assan i ~ i.

62 DAY(TIME) *χōŋ, Ket qɔŋ, Yug xɔʰŋ, Kott hōnaŋ 'recently,' Pumpokol xaŋ-ga-cedin. Bengtson (1991a: 98) adds Basque e-gun, Proto-(North) Caucasian *ɢʷem-tʌ, Burushaski gōn 'dawn,' and Proto-Athabaskan *dlʷen.

63 DEEP *pōqe, Ket hɔR(u), Yug fɔʰx, Kott fōge ~ pʰōge.

64 DEER *sēr₁e, Ket śēʎə, Yug sēr, Kott šeli ~ šele, Arin sin (< *sil(ʌ)n), Pumpokol salat. Cf. Proto-(North) Caucasian *wʌnsʷirʌ 'deer, aurochs,' Na-Dene: Galice silii ~ selii 'doe.'

65 DIE/DEATH   *qɔ-, Ket qɔ-deŋ, Yug xɔ-dəŋ, Kott xa ~ kʰa
    'death,' Arin in-qo 'dead,' Pumpokol ka-doŋdu 'dead.' Cf. Na-Dene:
    Haida k'ut'ahl ~ koo-tulh 'die, dead,' Eyak kous 'dies.'
66 DIRT   *dʌr-, Kott taran. Cf. Proto-Dagestanian *tʰərʌ, Burushaski
    thɛr 'dirty.'
67 DO   *wʌ-, Ket bēri, Yug bēʰt', Kott ba-ttaŋ, Arin ša-pi-te 'I do.'
    Cf. Na-Dene: Haida 'waa 'do so,' wa 'do,' Eyak wau-gung 'do.'
68 DOG   *čip ~ *čib, Ket tīp, Yug čip, Kott al-šip, Arin il-čap.
    Cf. Proto-Dagestanian *čʰirpʌ 'bitch,' Proto-Andi *čiba.
69 DOOR₁   *ʔerk-, Ket ɛllə, Yug ɛrfɔx, Pumpokol elxan.
70 DOOR₂   *ʔajtol, Kott atʰol, Arin ejtol, Assan atol.
71 DRY   *qʌj-, Ket tɔ-Rai-ŋ, Yug tɔ-xɔiŋ, Kott xuj-ga, Arin qoija,
    Pumpokol ič-koj-ŋa, Assan xuj-ga. Cf. Na-Dene: Haida k'a.
72 DUCK₁ (n.)   *tɔq, Ket tɔRə, Yug tɔʰx 'golden-eye,' Kott al-tʰax
    'a kind of duck.'
73 DUCK₂ (n.)   *ʔalg-, Ket aʎgə, Kott agaŋa 'mallard.'
74 EAGLE   *dʌʔɢ-, Ket diʔ, Yug diʔ, Kott tage. Cf. Proto-(North)
    Caucasian *leq'ʷIa 'name of a large bird,' Proto-Tibeto-Burman *laŋ
    ~ *lak 'falcon, hawk,' Old Chinese *laŋ ~ tˡaŋ 'hawk.' Bengtson
    (pers. comm.) adds Na-Dene: Haida lɢo 'heron' and Tlingit lɑq'
    'heron, crane.'
75 EAR   *ʔɔqtʌ ~ *ʔɔgde, Ket ɔgde, ɔqtən 'ear-rings,' Yug ɔxtɨŋ,
    ɔgdɔnɨŋ 'ear-rings,' Arin utkenoŋ, Pumpokol atkin. Cf. Proto-Andi
    *han-k'it'a ~ *han-t'ik'a, Na-Dene: Tlingit ʔaχ 'hear.'
76 EARTH   *baʔŋ, Ket baʔŋ, Yug baʔŋ, Kott paŋ, Arin peŋ, Pumpo-
    kol biŋ.
77 EAT   *siɢ-, Ket śī, Yug sī, Kott šig 'food,' Arin ša-n, Pumpokol
    sogo. Starostin (1984: 23) compared the Proto-Yeniseian form with
    Proto-Sino-Tibetan *dᶻhăH and later (1989a: 64) added Proto-
    (North) Caucasian *dᶻaHV 'drink.' Bengtson and Blažek (1992)
    compare these forms with Burushaski ši-.
78 EGG/FISH EGGS   *jeŋ ~ *jɔŋ, Ket ɔŋ-diś 'fish eggs,' ēŋ 'eggs,'
    Yug ɔŋ-dis 'fish eggs,' eŋ 'egg,' Kott d'anan 'fish eggs,' Arin ujnun
    'fish eggs,' aŋ 'egg,' Pumpokol tañaŋ 'egg,' Assan anaŋ 'fish eggs.'
    Bengtson and Blažek (1992) compare the Proto-Yeniseian form with
    Proto-(North) Caucasian *dˡiŋgwV 'roe,' Burushaski tiŋ 'egg,' and
    Proto-Sino-Tibetan *di 'egg.'
79 ELBOW/JOINT   *gid, Ket uʎ-git, Yug uʎ-git, Assan kenar-xat-
    ken 'elbow,' pul-gat-ken 'tibia.' Cf. Proto-Dagestanian *q'ʷIʌntʰʌ
    'elbow, knee,' Basque ukondo 'elbow,' Na-Dene: Eyak ɢuhd 'knee,'
    Sarsi gūd 'knee, elbow,' Kutchin -gwod 'knee,' Coquille gʷad 'knee,'
    Hupa got' 'knee,' Navajo gòd 'knee.'

80 ELK *ɢʌ̄ja, Ket qājə, Yug xāʰj, Kott kōja, Arin o-q̇aj-ši, Pumpokol xaju, Assan koja 'deer.'

81 EMPTY *ɢūj, Ket qūjə, Yug xūʰj, Kott koi.

82 ERMINE *kulʌp, Ket kuʎep, Yug kulɛp, Kott hulup, Arin kulep.

83 EVENING *bis, Ket bīś, Yug bis, Kott pīs, Arin pis, Pumpokol bič-idin, Assan pijaga. Cf. Proto-(North) Caucasian *bʌsʌ 'night, evening,' Ingush bijsa 'night,' Ubykh zʷa-psə 'evening.' Bengtson and Blažek (1992) add Burushaski basa 'halting for the night; night or day (as a measure of time).'

84 EXCREMENT/DIRT *poʔq, Ket hɔʔq, Yug fɔʔq, Kott phōk ~ fōk 'excrement,' phago ~ fago 'dirt.' Cf. Proto-Dagestanian *pʰɨHɨ lχʷʌ 'diarrhea, feces.'

85 EYE *de-s, Ket dēś, Yug des, Kott tīś, Assan teš, Arin tieŋ, Pumpokol dat. Cf. Proto-(North) Caucasian *ʔʷilhi, Na-Dene: Kutchin ə-nde, Hare e-dʲa, Galice -daai, Chiricahua ⁿdáà.

86 FACE *bat(t)-, Ket bāt ~ battat, Yug bāt ~ battat. Cf. Proto-Dagestanian *mət'ʌ.

87 FACE/CHIN *bunč-, Kott punjol ~ punčol 'chin,' Arin pinjal 'chin,' Assan punčola 'cheek.'

88 FAT (n.) *gɨʔd, Ket kɨʔt, Yug kɨʔt, Kott kīr, Arin ki. Cf. Basque gizen.

89 FATHER *ʔob, Ket ōp, Yug op, Kott ōp, Arin iṕa, Pumpokol ab. Cf. Proto-(North) Caucasian *ʔopʌ-, Proto-Tibeto-Burman *ba, Old Chinese *ba, Burushaski bʌba 'father (in royal circles),' Nahali aba ~ ba. Kuiper (1962: 58) regards the Nahali form as a borrowing from Kurku (Munda).

90 FATHOM (2.13 meters) *χän, Ket qāñ, Yug xan, Kott hen.

91 FIELD *kʌb-, Ket ɔ-ɣup, Kott hīp-ēg, Arin kaba ~ q̇abi.

92 FIR/SPRUCE *dɨñe, Ket dɨ̄ñ, Yug dɨn, Kott tīni, Arin tin, Pumpokol dɨñe, Assan tin. Bengtson and Blažek (1992) compare the Yeniseian forms with Burushaski thōn 'coriander' and Proto-Sino-Tibetan *taŋ 'pine.'

93 FIRE *boʔk, Ket bɔʔk, Yug bɔʔk, Pumpokol buč. Cf. Burushaski pfu, Nahali āpo.

94 FISH TRAP *dōb-, Ket dɔ̄və ~ dɔ̄bə. Cf. Proto-Lezghian *t'ap'.

95 FIST *kʌ̄ŋq-, Ket kɔ̄Rə ~ kɔq, Yug kūʰx, Kott haŋkan. Cf. Proto-Dagestanian *χink'ʷɨ. Bengtson (pers. comm.) adds Eyak guʔk'.

96 FIVE *qäka, Ket qāk, Yug xak, Kott kʰēgä, Arin qaga, Pumpokol xej-laŋ. Bengtson (pers. comm.) compares these forms with Eyak q'əq 'fist.'

97 FLEE *čaq-, Ket tɔq-tət, Yug čattat, Kott čagantʰak.

98   FLOUR₁   *talkʌn, Ket *tallɨn*, Assan *talkan*.

99   FLOUR₂   *qʌ(ʔ)rʹ ~ *qʌ(ʔ)j, Kott *u-xēi*. Cf. Proto-Dagestanian
     *χ̄ʷɪ̄ərʌ, Proto-Nax *Hor-.

100 FLY/GNAT   *tɨt-, Ket *tɪ̄t*, Yug *tɨt*, Kott *al-thītega* 'ant.' Cf. Proto-
     Dagestanian *t'əmt'o, Proto-Nax *t'ot'.

101 FOG   *qʌʔŋ-, Yug *xoaŋ*. Cf. Proto-(North) Caucasian *k̄ʷɨm(h)ʌ
     ~ *mɨk̄ʷʌ 'cloud, fog,' Proto-Tibeto-Burman *mūk, Old Chinese
     *mōk 'drizzle.'

102 FOOT₁   *kiʔs, Ket *kiʔś*, Yug *kiʔs*. Cf. Proto-(North) Caucasian
     *kʷʌc̓'a 'foot, paw,' Na-Dene: Tlingit *k'os* ~ *q'os*, Eyak *q'aš* ~ *kuš*,
     Sarsi *kàʔ*, Carrier *-ke*, Galice *-kiʔ*, Navajo *-kèèʔ*, Kiowa Apache *-kìì*.

103 FOOT₂   *bul, Ket *būʎ*, Yug *bul*, Kott *pul*, Arin *pil*. Cf. Proto-
     (North) Caucasian *mäHätˡʰə '(toe-)nail, hoof,' Sino-Tibetan: Ti-
     betan *bol* 'upper part of the leg,' Old Chinese *bəj (< *bəl) 'calf of
     the leg.'

104 FOUR   *sika, Ket *śīk*, Yug *sik*, Kott *šēgä*, Arin *šaga*, Pumpokol
     cia-ŋ.

105 FOX   *kəqʌn, Ket *kʌ̄n*, Yug *kʌxɨn*, Kott *agan*.

106 FROG   *xɨʔr-, Ket *ʌʔl*, Yug *ʌʔl*, Arin *kere*. Cf. Basque *igel*, Proto-
     (North) Caucasian *q'ʷʌrʌq'ʌ, Burushaski *gur-quts* ~ *ɣur-kun*.

107 FULL   *ʔute, Yug *ūt*, Kott *ūti*. Cf. Proto-(North) Caucasian
     *-oc'a.

108 GIVE   *qəj-, Ket *qʌdəm*, Yug *xʌd'iŋ-fɨt' 'give back,' Arin *koja-
     pelä* 'I give.' Cf. Na-Dene: Haida *gijuu* 'give away.'

109 GLUE   *piʔt, Ket *hiʔt*, Yug *fiʔt*, Ket *fɨt*. Cf. Proto-Dagestanian
     *pʰinc̄ʷʌ 'resin, tar,' Proto-Nax > Chechen *mutta* 'sap.'

110 GO   *hejʌŋ, Ket *ējeŋ*, Yug *ejiŋ*, Kott *hejaŋ*. Cf. Basque *j-oan*.
     Starostin (1984: 25) compares the Yeniseian forms with Proto-East
     Caucasian *ʔʌʔwʌ-n- and Proto-Sino-Tibetan *ʔʷă(ŋ), Old Chinese
     *w(h)áŋ.

111 GOOD   *haq-, Ket *aq-ta*, Yug *ax-ta*, Kott *hag-ši*, Arin *bergar-ɨktu*.

112 GOODS (furs)   *rʹəq-, Ket *lə̄q*, Yug *ləx*.

113 GOOSE   *čem-, Ket *tēm*, Yug *čem*, Kott *šame*, Arin *sam*, Pumpo-
     kol *xam*, Assan *šame*.

114 GRASS   *gʌre, Kott *keri*. Cf. Proto-(North) Caucasian *q'ʌɬʌ ~
     *q'Iʌɬʌ, Nahali *jhara*. According to Kuiper (1962: 81), the Nahali
     form is borrowed from Kurku (Munda).

115 GUEST   *ja-ŋ, Kott *čaŋ*. Cf. Proto-(North) Caucasian *c̄ʷʌ(Hʌ).

116 GUTS   *piʔiʎ, Ket *hɪ̄ʎ*, Yug *fɪ̄ʎ*, Arin *p̓hor-ga* 'belly.' Cf. Proto-
     Dagestanian *peHertˡ'ʌ, Proto-Nax *bʕara, Proto-Tibeto-Burman
     *pik 'entrails, guts.'

117 HAIL *barbʌd, Ket baʎbɛt, Kott kojpat, Arin polpieŋ. Cf. Na-
Dene: Mattole bad.

118 HAIR *cəŋe, Ket tə̄ŋə, Yug čə̄ŋ, Kott heŋai, Arin q̇agaŋ, Pumpokol xɨŋa. Cf. Proto-Dagestanian *c'em(H)ʌ 'eyebrow,' Proto-
Tibeto-Burman *tsam, Old Chinese *srām (< *r-sām).

119 HALF₁ *su-, Yug sū-, Kott šu-, Pumpokol tu. Cf. Proto-(North)
Caucasian *hamc'ü.

120 HALF₂ *ʔa(ʔ)l, Ket a(ʔ)ʎ, Yug a(ʔ)l, Kott āl-īx 'noon, midday.'
Cf. Proto-(North) Caucasian *-etˡ'i, Proto-Tibeto-Burman *lāy
'center, middle.' Bengtson and Blažek (1992) add Basque erdi 'half,
middle,' Proto-Sino-Tibetan *tˡay 'center,' Burushaski ālto 'two,'
and Eyak laʔd 'two.'

121 HAND *pʌg-, Ket hʌŋn, Arin pʰiaga. Cf. Burushaski bʌɣu 'double armful,' Nahali bok(k)o.

122 HE *dʌ, Ket da- ~ di-, Yug da- ~ di-. Cf. Proto-Dagestanian *tʰʌ
'that,' Tibeto-Burman: Burmese thəw 'this,' Old Chinese *tə 'this,
he,' Nahali eṭe(y) ~ eta-re 'he,' Na-Dene: Haida dei 'just that way,'
Tlingit de 'now,' Slave ti 'this,' Chiricahua dí 'this thing.'

123 HE/SHE *wʌ, Ket bū, Yug bu, Assan ba-ri 'he,' Arin au 'he.'
Cf. Proto-(North) Caucasian *mʌ 'this, that,' Na-Dene: Haida wūn-
a-sa 'he,' wa- 'that,' Tlingit ū 'he,' we 'that,' Chasta Costa yū 'that
one.'

124 HEAD₁ *cɨʔɢ-, Ket tɨʔ, Yug čɨʔ, Kott takai, Arin ke-dake.
Cf. Proto-Abkhaz-Adyg *sq̇la, Na-Dene: Tanaina tsiʔ, Beaver tsiiʔ,
Galice -siiʔ, Navajo -tˢìiʔ.

125 HEAD₂ *kərga-, Ket kʌjga, Arin kolká, Pumpokol kolka.
Cf. Proto-Lezghian *k̄urk̄ 'skull,' Lak k̄ʷark 'top, head.'

126 HEART *pu-, Ket hū, Yug fu, Kott pʰui ~ fui 'insides,' Pumpokol
pfu.

127 HEAVY *səɢ-, Ket śʌ̄, Yug sə̄ ~ səu, Kott šīk-ŋ, Arin šoga, Assan šuoga.

128 HEEL *sʌɢʌ(-dᶻʌ), Ket śʌ̄t, Yug sə̄t ~ səut, Kott šugaiči, Arin
i-žege-n. Cf. Proto-Dagestanian *s̄olq̄'ʷIʌ ~ *q'ʷIolš̄ʌ 'heel, foot.'
Bengtson (1991a: 92) adds Burushaski šoq 'sole (of boot).'

129 HIGH *tɨŋgɨr-, Ket tɨŋ(g)əʎ, Yug tɨŋgɨl, Pumpokol tokar-du.

130 HOLE *χuχ, Ket qūk, Yug xuk, Kott huk. Cf. Na-Dene: Haida
k'yu 'door,' Tlingit k'úqʷ.

131 HORN *χɔʔ, Ket qɔʔ, Yug xɔʔŋ. Cf. Proto-(North) Caucasian
*qʰʷä(hʌ), Proto-Tibeto-Burman *kruw, Old Chinese *qrō-k.

132 HORSE   *kuʔs, Ket kuʔś 'cow,' Yug kuʔs, Kott huš, Arin kus,
     Pumpokol kut. Cf. Proto-Dagestanian *kʷačʷʌ 'mare.'

133 HOUSE/TENT   *χuʔs, Ket quʔś, Yug xuʔs 'tent,' Kott hūš 'tent,'
     Arin kus, Pumpokol hu-kut. Cf. Proto-(North) Caucasian *qʼʷIʌrcʌ
     'house, dwelling.'

134 HUNDRED   *jus, Arin jus, Pumpokol uta-msa.

135 HUNGER   *ɢɔɢant, Ket qɔ̄t, Yug xɔxat, Kott kajante, Arin q̇ogat
     'hungry.'

136 HUSBAND   *cʌ(n)t-, Ket tēt, Yug čet, Kott hat-kīt, Arin kintej,
     Pumpokol ils-et (< *ils-xet).

137 I   *ʔadᶻ, Ket āt, Yug at, Kott ai, Arin aj, Pumpokol ad. Cf. Proto-
     (North) Caucasian *zo, Burushaski jɛ ~ ja, Nahali jō ~ jŭō.

138 IDOL   *guʔus, Ket kūs, Yug kūs. Cf. Proto-Dagestanian *kʰʷi̯čʰʌ
     'form, appearance, look,' Proto-Nax *kust 'figure, appearance.'

139 INTERROGATIVE PRONOUN ROOT   *wir₁, Ket biʎa 'how,'
     biʎɛś 'where,' Yug birɛ 'how,' birɛs 'where,' Kott biʎäŋ 'what,' bili
     'where.' Cf. Proto-Dagestanian *mʌ and Proto-Nax *mʌ. Bengtson
     and Blažek (1992) add Burushaski men 'who,' a-min 'which.'

140 INTESTINE (SMALL)   *tūʎ, Ket tuʎi, Yug tūʰʎ, Kott tʰutul,
     Arin šodoroŋ.

141 IRON   *ʔeχʌ, Ket ē, Yug ej, Pumpokol ag. Cf. Proto-(North) Cau-
     casian *ritˡʰʷʌ 'name of a metal.'

142 JAW   *piŋkadᶻ, Ket hiɣat, Yug figači, Arin piŋaiŋ 'lip,' Pumpokol
     pinet 'chin, cheek.'

143 KNEAD   *loŋ-, Ket ʎɔŋ-dǝŋ, Yug ʎɔŋ-dʼaŋ.

144 KNEE   *bat-, Ket bat-puʎ, Yug bat-pɨl, Assan pul-patap 'metatar-
     sus,' Arin patas. Cf. Proto-Dagestanian *porčʰʌ 'thigh, paw,' Proto-
     Tibeto-Burman *put(s), Old Chinese *pǝt ~ *pit 'knee-cap.'

145 KNIFE   *dɔʔn, Ket dɔʔn, Yug dɔʔn Kott ton, Arin ton. Cf. Proto-
     (North) Caucasian *wʌsünʌ.

146 LAKE   *deʔɢ, Ket dɛʔ, Yug dɛʔ, Kott ūr-tēg, Arin kur-tük, Pum-
     pokol danniŋ. Cf. Na-Dene: Tlingit da 'to flood,' Eyak taʔ 'into wa-
     ter.'

147 LAND/SOIL   *su, Kott šu. Cf. Proto-(North) Caucasian *Hʷenšʷi
     'land, clay.'

148 LARCH   *seʔs, Ket śɛʔś, Yug sɛʔs, Kott šēt, Arin čit, Pumpokol
     tag. Cf. Proto-(North) Caucasian *cacʌ 'thorn, burr.' Bengtson
     (1991b: 133) adds Basque sasi 'bramble, thicket' and Burushaski
     čhʌš 'thornbush, thorns.'

149 LAUGH   *jāqʌ-, Ket dāRǝ, Yug dʼāʰx, Kott čake, Arin soja-keaŋ 'I
     laugh,' Pumpokol jai-či-du 'I laugh.'

150 LEAF *jə̄pe, Ket ӆ, Yug ӆp, Kott d'ipi, Arin ipoŋ, Pumpokol
(xogon-)dɨpun. Cf. Proto-(North) Caucasian *tˡ'epi, Proto-Tibeto-
Burman *lap, Old Chinese *lap. Bengtson (pers. comm.) adds Burushaski tap (< *ltap(V), preserved in du-ltap-as 'wither').

151 LIGHT (adj. & n.) *gəʔn-, Ket kʌʔn, Yug kʌʔn, Kott kanaŋ-
ičiban 'lightning.' Cf. Proto-Dagestanian *(HA)kʰʷenʌ, Old Chinese
*kʷāŋ.

152 LIGHT/CHEAP *tor-, Ket tōʎ-git 'cheap,' Kott tʰui 'light, cheap,'
Arin tütelä 'light.'

153 LIP *ron, Ket ʎōn, Yug lon, Kott d'an, Arin e-tan, Assan anag
(< *anaŋ).

154 LIVER *seŋ, Ket śēŋ, Yug seŋ, Arin šin-trun 'entrails.' Cf. Proto-
(North) Caucasian *cʷämʔi 'bile, anger,' Proto-Tibeto-Burman *m-
sin, Old Chinese *sin 'bitter.' Bengtson (1991b: 131) adds Basque
be-ha-zun 'bile, gall,' Burushaski čhɛmɪ-liŋ 'bitter, poisonous,' and
suggests that possibly Eyak -saʰt and Proto-Athabaskan *-səd? belong here as well.

155 LOG *bäk, Ket bā̆ɣə, Yug bāk, Kott pēg. Cf. Proto-(North) Caucasian *pənᴳ(I)u 'pole, stick, stake, post,' Old Chinese *pāk 'pole,
post, column.'

156 LONG *ʔux-, Ket ug-də, Yug ug-də, Kott ui, Arin u-ta. Cf. Proto-
(North) Caucasian *-uqʰ(I)a(-nʌ) 'long, big, tall,' Old Chinese *kāw
'tall,' Tibeto-Burman: Burmese khau-h 'protrude.'

157 LOW *pitʌm-, Ket hītim, Yug fitim, Pumpokol fidam-du.

158 LOW/BELOW *kan-, Kott hāna 'down,' hānal 'below, low,' Arin
xamartu 'low.' Cf. Proto-(North) Caucasian *ʔotˡ'onu 'bottom.'

159 LUNGS *sisa(l)-, Kott šičātn, Arin šišali. Cf. Proto-(North) Caucasian *ćʌćʌ 'kidney.'

160 MALE *iχ(ʌ), Ket ӻ 'male deer,' Yug iʔk 'male, male polecat,'
Kott ig 'little man,' Arin au 'male.'

161 MAN₁ *keʔt, Ket kɛʔt, Yug kɛʔt, Kott het ~ hit, Arin kit, Pumpokol kit, Assan hit. Cf. Proto-Andi *kʷint'a 'man, husband, male,'
Proto-Nax *k'anat 'boy, lad,' Na-Dene: Tlingit qah ~ kah 'man,'
Eyak qaʔ ~ kha 'husband.' Bengtson (pers. comm.) suggests that
perhaps Nahali kalto belongs here.

162 MAN₂ *pixe, Ket hīɣə, Yug fik, Kott fī, Arin pa-nalikip.

163 MEADOW *ʔoᴳ-, Ket ū, Yug ou, Kott ōx, Arin jujuŋ 'grass.'
Cf. Proto-Dagestanian *ʔenqʰʷIʌ 'meadow, plot of land.'

164 MEAT *ʔise, Ket īś, Yug īs, Kott īči, Arin is. Cf. Proto-(North)
Caucasian *jəmcʰo 'bull, ox.'

165   MILK/NIPPLE   *de(ʔ)n, Kott ten 'nipple,' Arin teŋul 'milk,' Pumpokol den. Cf. Proto-(North) Caucasian *s̄inwʌ 'milk, udder.' Bengtson (pers. comm.) adds Basque esne 'milk.'

166   MITTEN   *bɔq-, Ket bōq, Yug bɔxɔn, Kott pagan.

167   MOON   *(ʔʌ)suj, Kott šui, Arin ešuj, Pumpokol tuj. Cf. Proto-(North) Caucasian *wəmc̄'o 'moon, month,' Old Chinese *ŋʷat 'moon.'

168   MORNING   *pʌk-, Ket higem, Pumpokol cɨl-paga. Cf. Proto-Dagestanian *pəkʌ 'morning, dawn, dusk.' Bengtson (pers. comm.) adds Basque bigar 'tomorrow.'

169   MOTHER   *ʔama, Ket ām, Yug am, Kott āma, Arin amä, b́-ama 'my mother,' Pumpokol am, Assan ama. Cf. Basque ama, Burushaski māma, Nahali māy, Na-Dene: Eyak amma, Navajo má. The Nahali form is considered by Kuiper (1962: 90) a borrowing from Kurku (Munda).

170   MOUNTAIN₁   *ŕɨʔj, Ket ʌ́ɨʔt, Yug lɨʔt', Kott d'ī, Assan jii.

171   MOUNTAIN₂ (WOODED)   *qäʔj, Ket qaʔj, Yug xaʔj 'wooded mountain,' Kott xē-lēx 'mountain ridge,' Arin (ena-)haj 'forest,' Pumpokol ko-nnoŋ. Cf. Proto-Lezghian *x̄ʷaʔ 'mountain,' Proto-Nax *Hawχē 'shady slope of a mountain,' Old Chinese *khʷə 'hill.'

172   MOUSE   *jūta, Ket ūt, Yug ūt, Kott d'ūta, Pumpokol ute. Cf. Proto-(North) Caucasian *jʌcʰʷe 'squirrel, badger, mouse,' Old Chinese *lu-s (< *ju-s) 'weasel,' Tibetan jos 'hare.'

173   MOUTH   *χowe, Ket qō, Yug xo, Kott hōpi, Assan xoboj. Starostin (1984: 24) compares the Yeniseian forms with Proto-Sino-Tibetan *Khō(w)H and Proto-(North) Caucasian k'ʷēɫʔV. Bengtson and Blažek (1992) add Basque a-ho.

174   MUSHROOM   *borba, Ket bɔʌ́ba, Yug bɔlba, Arin penbe-tu.

175   MY   *b- ~ *ʔab-, Ket āp ~ ābə, ba- ~ bo- (first-person marker on verbs). Cf. Proto-Dagestanian *nʌ 'I,' Proto-Tibeto-Burman *ŋa 'I,' Old Chinese *ŋa 'I.'

176   NAME   *ʔiɢ, Ket ī, Yug i, Kott ix, Pumpokol i. Cf. Burushaski -ík. Bengtson and Blažek (1992) add Chipewyan (Athabaskan) -yeʔ ~ -yiʔ 'to be named.'

177   NAVEL   *tɨr- ~ *tɨl-, Ket tɨʌ́, Yug tɨl. Cf. Proto-Dagestanian *d̄ᶻonHu, Proto-Nax *c'an-k'u, Old Chinese *dᶻəj.

178   NECK₁   *pujm-, Kott fuimur ~ pʰuimur, Arin pemä. Cf. Burushaski būi 'shoulder-blade.'

179   NECK₂   *kəqənt-, Ket kə̄qtɨ, Yug kəxtɨ, Kott agantan 'collar, neck.' Cf. Basque kokot.

180 NEEDLE *ʔiʔn, Ket iʔn, Yug iʔn, Kott in ~ īn, Arin in. Cf. Proto-Dagestanian *ʕima 'awl.'

181 NET *pəʔŋ, Ket hʌʔŋ, Yug fʌʔŋ, Kott fuŋ, Arin pen.

182 NETTLE *kita, Ket kītn, Yug kitn 'nettle, hemp,' Kott hīta 'hemp.' Cf. Proto-(North) Caucasian *q̄ʰIüč̌ʰu 'nettle, grass.'

183 NEW *tur- ~ *tul, Yug tul-im. Cf. Proto-(North) Caucasian *c'änhʌ, Proto-Tibeto-Burman *siŋ, Old Chinese *sin. Alternatively, the Proto-Yeniseian form might be compared with Proto-Tibeto-Burman *sar 'new, fresh' and Old Chinese *sar 'fresh.'

184 NIGHT *siɢ, Ket s̄ī, Yug si, Kott s̄īg, Arin saj, Pumpokol teč. Cf. also Proto-Yeniseian *sʌm- 'sleep' below.

185 NIGHT (SPEND THE —) *saɢar₁, Ket sāl, Yug sāʰr, Kott šagal 'spending the night,' ha-čāgal 'spend the night,' Pumpokol tōl 'night.' Cf. Basque gau 'night,' Na-Dene: Haida ɢal 'night,' Eyak χətlʾ 'night,' Carrier ɣeɫ 'night,' Kato kaɫʰ 'night passes,' Chipewyan xiɫ 'darkness,' Navajo di-ɫ-xiɫ 'black.'

186 NINE *jum-, Kott čum-nāga. Cf. Proto-(North) Caucasian *ʕʌrć'ʷʌm-.

187 NIT *jog- ~ *jok, Ket (ʌɣin-)ɔk, Yug (etiŋ-)ʌ̄k, Kott d'oga. Cf. Proto-Dagestanian *q'ʌ(I)jʌ > Dargwa q'i.

188 NO/NOT₁ *wə-, Ket bə-n, Yug bə-ń, Kott mo-n (< *bo-n), Arin bo-n, Pumpokol a-mu-t (< *a-wu-n-t). Cf. Proto-(North) Caucasian *mʌ, Proto-Tibeto-Burman *ma, Old Chinese *ma, ?Burushaski bɛ, ?Nahali beko 'no,' beṭe 'not,' biji 'not.' The Nahali form is considered by Kuiper (1962: 62) a borrowing from Kurku (Munda).

189 NO/NOT₂ *ʔat ~ *ta-, Ket āt 'not,' tāŋ 'no,' Yug ata 'not,' tāŋə bə̄ś 'not at all.' Cf. Proto-Dagestanian *tʌ, Proto-Tibeto-Burman *ta (prohibitive particle), Nahali hoṭ (used with the past tense). Kuiper (1962: 77) suggests that the Nahali form is a Munda borrowing.

190 NOSE₁ *ʔolk-, Ket ɔlin, Arin arquj.

191 NOSE₂ *xaŋ, Kott aŋ, Pumpokol haŋ.

192 NUT *im, Ket īm, Yug im, Kott īm, Arin im.

193 OLD/DECREPIT *sin, Ket śin, Yug sin. Cf. Proto-(North) Caucasian *śüno 'year,' Proto-Tibeto-Burman *sniŋ 'year,' Old Chinese *nīn (< *(s)nīŋ) 'year,' Na-Dene: Tlingit šàn 'old person,' Tlatskanai sen 'old man,' Navajo sání 'old man.' Bengtson (pers. comm.) adds Burushaski šini 'summer.'

194 ONE *χu-sa, Ket qū̄ś (inan.), Yug xus (inan.), Kott hūča, Arin khuzej ~ qusej ~ kusa, Pumpokol xuta. Cf. Proto-(North) Caucasian *cʰə, Proto-Tibeto-Burman *it, *kat (< *qac), Old Chinese *ʔit (< *ʔic).

195 ONION   *guwurkʌn-, Kott kuburgenaŋ, Arin kuburgan, Assan
kabɨrgina.

196 OTTER   *täχʌr, Ket tāʎ, Yug tār, Kott thēgär. Cf. Proto-Dagestanian *tendˉˡʷʌ ~ *tengˉʷʌ 'weasel, marten,' Basque urtxakur.

197 OUTSIDE   *hərₗ-, Ket ʌʎa, Yug ʌrej, Kott hili. Cf. Burushaski
hōlum, Nahali bahare. Kuiper (1962: 61) consideres the Nahali
word a borrowing from Kurku (Munda).

198 OWL/HAWK   *kʌg-, Kott hikei-še 'owl,' Arin kak 'hawk,' Pumpokol xagam-kolka 'owl.'

199 PALM   *battɔp ~ *pattɔp, Ket battop, Ko fatap ~ pʰatap.

200 PATH/ROAD   *qoʔt, Ket qɔʔt, Yug xɔʔt 'path,' Arin kat ~ kut,
Pumpokol koat 'road.' Cf. Proto-Dagestanian *ʁ̄ʷat'ʌ 'street, pas-
sage.' Nikolaev (1991: 54) compares these forms with Proto-Eyak-
Athabaskan *ged 'road,' Hare -giér-eʔ 'road.'

201 PENIS/TESTICLES   *gʌns-, Kott kančal 'testicles,' Pumpokol
kutte 'penis.' Cf. Proto-Dagestanian *k'əlč'ʌ 'penis, vulva,' Burushaski -ɣūš 'vagina,' Na-Dene: Eyak guč, Sarsi ɣīdzáʔ.

202 PEOPLE   *jeʔ-ŋ, Ket dɛʔŋ, Yug d'ɛʔŋ, Kott čeäŋ. Cf. Proto-
(North) Caucasian *č̣ʰiw(i) 'person, man,' Na-Dene: Haida e-tliñga
'man,' Tlingit tˡ'inkit 'people.'

203 PERCH (fish)   *təʔɢ-, Ket tʌʔ, Yug tʌʔ, Pumpokol tou, Assan
tuga.

204 PIKE   *χūja, Ket qūri, Yug xūʰt', Kott hūja, Arin quj, Pumpokol
kod'u, Assan huja.

205 PINE TREE   *ʔej-, Ket ēj, Yug ej, Kott ei, Arin aja, Assan ej.

206 PLURAL SUFFIX₁   *-ŋ, Ket -ŋ, Yug -ŋ, Kott -ŋ. Cf. Proto-Dagestanian *-mʌ.

207 PLURAL SUFFIX₂   *-nʌ, Ket -n ~ -ñ, Yug -n, Kott -n. Cf. Proto-
Dagestanian *-nʌ, Proto-Tibeto-Burman *-n (collective plural).

208 POINT   *saʔrₗ, Ket śaʔʎ, Yug saʔr, Kott šal. Cf. Proto-(North)
Caucasian *č'əwlɨ 'arrow, point,' Burushaski išāra ɛt 'point out.'

209 POLE (of a tent)   *həgʌne, Ket ʌŋn, Yug ʌŋńiŋ, Kott hagīni.

210 PRINCE   *χɨj(e), Ket qɨj, Kott hīji, Arin bi-khej. Cf. Proto-
Abkhaz-Adyg *(a)χ́ə.

211 RABBIT   *ʔaχ ~ *ʔak, Yug ak 'jumping hare.' Cf. Proto-(North)
Caucasian *rʌgˉʷʌ 'squirrel, marten, weasel, mouse,' Proto-Tibeto-
Burman *rwak 'rat,' Na-Dene: Eyak ɢəχ, Slave gah, Tsetsaut qax,
Navajo gaʔ.

212 RAIN   *xur ~ *xur-es, Ket uʎeś, Yug ures, Kott ur, Arin kur,
Pumpokol ur-ait. Cf. Basque euri, Burushaski hərālt.

213 REINS/BRIDLE *kūnd-, Ket kūndaŋɨn 'reins,' Arin qonda 'bridle.'

214 RELATIVE ADJECTIVE SUFFIX *-tu-, Ket -tu-, Yug -tu-.
Cf. Proto-(North) Caucasian *-tʷɨ (adjective suffix).

215 RIB *ʔuʎadᶻ, Ket uʎet, Yug uʎat, Kott ulai.

216 RIVER *ses, Ket śēś, Yug ses, Kott šēt, Arin sat, Pumpokol tataŋ, Assan šet. Cf. Na-Dene: Haida sī(s) 'ocean,' Eyak šī 'creek, stream,' Galice siskãã 'ocean.'

217 ROAD *χɨχ, Ket qɨ̄k, Yug xɨk, Kott hek.

218 ROOT₁ *čɨ̄j-, Ket tɨ̄ri, Yug tɨʰt', Pumpokol kediŋ, Assan i-čičan. Cf. Burushaski tshirɨš.

219 ROOT₂ *tempʌl, Kott tʰempul, Arin t'ēmbirgaŋ ∼ tenbir.

220 ROPE₁ *ʔāŋ-, Ket āŋə, Yug āŋ, Kott anaŋ 'small strap.'
Cf. Proto-Dagestanian *Hʷʌmʔʌ.

221 ROPE₂ *tiʔ, Ket tiʔ. Cf. Proto-Dagestanian *rʌʕʷʌ, Burushaski ʈʌk 'string (of choga),' Na-Dene: Tlingit t'ix'.

222 SABLE *xēja, Ket ēri ∼ ēdə ∼ ēʰt', Kott ija, Pumpokol hiju, Assan ija.

223 SALIVA₁ *duk ∼ duq, Kott tuk. Cf. Proto-Nax *tug ∼ *tuk', Proto-Tibeto-Burman *tūk 'saliva, spit (v.),' Basque to egin 'spit' (v.), Burushaski thū ɛt 'spit' (v.), Nahali ṭhuk 'spit' (v.), Na-Dene: Tlingit tuχ 'spit' (v.), Eyak tux, Sarsi zák'àʔ, Kato šek', Navajo šééʔ.

224 SALIVA₂ *huʎʌŋ, Ket uʎəŋ, urɨŋ, Kott hujuŋ. Cf. Proto-Yeniseian WATER below.

225 SALT *čəʔ, Ket tʌʔ, Yug čʌʔ, Kott ši-. Cf. Proto-Abkhaz-Adyg *čə ∼ *ȷ̌ə, Proto-Tibeto-Burman *(m)tśi. Bengtson (1991b: 132) adds Basque itsaso 'sea' and Burushaski šau 'oversalted (of food).'

226 SAND *pənʌŋ, Ket hʌnəŋ, Kott fenaŋ ∼ pʰenaŋ, Arin fiñaŋ ∼ pʰiñaŋ, Pumpokol pinniŋ.

227 SEVEN *ʔoʔn, Ket ɔʔn, Arin una ∼ ɨña, Pumpokol oñaŋ.

228 SHAMAN *sen, Ket śen-əŋ, Yug sɛnəŋ, Kott šēnaŋ 'shamanism,' šēnaŋ hit. Cf. Proto-(North) Caucasian *nɨwcʰʷa 'prince, God'; a metathesized form, according to Starostin.

229 SHARP *ʔete, Ket ēti, Yug ēt, Kott ēti. Cf. Proto-Dagestanian *-ʌč'ʌ.

230 SHOE/BOOT *cēse, Ket tēśi, Yug čēʰs, Kott hēči, Arin qisɨŋ 'shoes.'

231 SHOULDER *ken-, Ket kɛn-tə-buʎ 'shoulder joint,' Kott hēnar, Arin qínaŋ ∼ xinaŋ 'shoulder, arm.' Cf. Proto-(North) Caucasian *ḡʷIɨnʌ ∼ *nɨḡʷIʌ 'shoulder, arm,' Old Chinese *qēn, Nahali

khaṇḍa, Na-Dene: Ingalik *-gòn* 'arm,' Tanana *gan* 'arm,' Tlatskanai *okane* 'arm,' Navajo *gaan* 'arm.' According to Kuiper (1962: 85), the Nahali form is borrowed from Kurku (Munda).

232 SIX **ʔaχʌ,* Ket *ā,* Yug *ā,* Arin *ögga* ~ *ɨga,* Pumpokol *aggiaŋ.* Cf. Proto-(North) Caucasian **ʔäränt^{lh(w)}ɨ,* Proto-Tibeto-Burman **(d)ruk,* Old Chinese **ruk.*

233 (ANIMAL) SKIN **sās,* Ket *śāśi,* Yug *sā^hs,* Kott *šēt.* Bengtson (pers. comm.) adds the following Na-Dene forms: Tlingit *d^zas,* Hupa *sit^s* 'bark, skin,' Galice *-saas,* Navajo *sìs.*

234 SKY/GOD **ʔes,* Ket *ēś,* Yug *es,* Kott *ēš,* Arin *es,* Pumpokol *eč.* Cf. Proto-Dagestanian **ʔamⱺʌ* 'sky, cloud; dignity, conscience,' ?Na-Dene: Haida *q^wēs,* Tlingit *kuts,* Eyak *koas.*

235 SLAVE/SERVANT **har-,* Kott *haran-get* 'slave, servant,' Arin *ar(a)* 'self name of the Arin.' Cf. ?Nahali *halk* 'servant.' Kuiper (1962: 75) derives the Nahali form from Indo-Aryan **hālk.*

236 SLED **soʔol,* Ket *śūʎ,* Yug *sōl* ~ *soul,* Kott *fun-čol* 'little sled,' Arin *šal,* Pumpokol *cel.*

237 SLEEP₁ (v.) **xus,* Ket *uśen,* Yug *usan,* Kott *uča* 'sleep' (n.), *učākŋ* 'sleep' (v.), Arin *kus,* Pumpokol *utu.* Cf. Burushaski *gučhaiyʌs* 'to lie sleeping,' *ʌgučaiyʌs* 'put to sleep,' Na-Dene: Chipewyan *γùs* 'snore,' Coquille *γ^woš,* Navajo *-γòš.*

238 SLEEP₂ (n.) **sʌm-,* Kott *šame.* Cf. Proto-Dagestanian **Hič^winⱺ* ~ **Hinič^wⱺ* 'night, sleep.' According to Starostin, the Yeniseian form is in all likelihood related to Proto-Yeniseian **siɢ* 'night,' which Starostin derives from an earlier **sim-ɢ.* Starostin (1989a: 64) adds Proto-Sino-Tibetan **chen* 'night, darkness.' Bengtson and Blažek (1992) compare these forms with Basque *a-mets* 'dream' (with metathesis), Tlingit *čun* 'dream,' and Eyak *t^sī̃-d^z* 'dream.'

239 SLY/DECEIVE **ʔaru-,* Ket *aʎ-bet,* Yug *ar-bet'* 'deceive,' Kott *āru* 'sly,' *āru-pi* 'deceit.' Cf. Basque *ero* 'stupid, fatuous.'

240 SMOKE (n.) **duʔχ-,* Ket *duʔ,* Yug *duʔ,* Kott *tu(g),* Arin *t'u,* Pumpokol *dukar,* Assan *tu.* Bengtson (pers. comm.) compares the Yeniseian forms with Burushaski *tux* 'steam, mist,' Tibetan *du-ba,* Sarsi (Athabaskan) *-t'uʔ,* and Navajo *-t'ooh* 'smoke' (v.).

241 SNAKE/FISH **cīk,* Ket *tīγⱺ* ~ *tiγ* 'snake,' Yug *čīk* 'snake,' Kott *tēg* ~ *tēx* 'fish,' Arin *il-ti* 'fish,' Pumpokol *cič* 'meat.' Cf. Proto-Lezghian **č'ek'-* 'fish, lizard,' ?Basque *suge* 'snake,' ?Na-Dene: Haida *si-guh* ~ *si-ga* 'snake.'

242 SNOW₁ **tiχ,* Ket *tīk,* Yug *tik,* Kott *thīk,* Arin *tē,* Pumpokol *tɨg.* Cf. Proto-(North) Caucasian **diχ^wIʌ* 'snow, precipitation,' Na-Dene: Tlingit *t'iq'* ~ *t'ix'* ~ *tix* 'snow, ice, hard,' Eyak *t'it^s* 'snow, ice,' Hupa *t^l'it^s* 'hard,' Navajo *t^l'ìz* 'hard.'

243 SNOW₂ *beʔč 'snow,' Ket bɛʔt, Yug bɛʔt', Pumpokol beč. Bengtson (pers. comm.) compares these forms with Eyak wehs 'soft snow,
tundra.'

244 SNOW CRUST *čaɢ ~ čak, Kott sāk 'icy crust on the snow.'
Cf. Proto-(North) Caucasian *čʰowq̄ʰIʌ 'drizzle, sleet, frost, gran-
ular snow.' Bengtson (1991a: 102) adds Burushaski čhʌγ(-ūrʋm)
'cold' (adj.).

245 SOFT *puɢʌm-, Ket hɔm-iʎəŋ, Yug fɔm-iʎiŋ, Kott pʰūgam ~
fūgam, Arin puma.

246 SOLE *kassad, Ket kassat, Kott hačar. Cf. Proto-(North) Caucasian *kʷarč'ʌ ~ *k'ʷarčʰʌ 'heel, foot.'

247 SON-IN-LAW/BROTHER-IN-LAW *ʔēñe, Ket ɛñ ~ ēne, Yug
ɛ̄ʰñ, Kott ani ~ añe, Arin b-än 'my son-in-law.'

248 SOON *ʔäʔc, Ket aʔt, Yug aʔt', Kott et-paŋ, Arin ati.

249 SOUP *ʔuʔχ ~ *xuʔk, Ket uʔk, Yug uʔk, Kott uk. Cf. Proto-
Dagestanian *herenq'u (> Proto-Andi *ʔoq'ʌ, Proto-Tsez *jɔq'u,
Proto-Lezghian *riq'), ?Basque zuku.

250 SPOON *kalp, Kott xalpen, Arin kilpʰan, Pumpokol hapi. Cf. Burushaski khʌpʋn.

251 SPRING (season) *xɨ̄je, Ket ɨdə ~ ɨ́ri, Yug ɨ̄ʰt', Kott ɨ̄ji, Arin kej.

252 SPRING/WATERHOLE IN THE ICE *sin-, Ket śinʎ, Yug sinɨr,
Kott šinaŋ. Cf. Proto-Dagestanian *ʔʷin(i)čʰʌ, Old Chinese *ceŋ?
'well.' Bengtson (1991b: 133) adds Basque hosin 'well, pool.'

253 SQUIRREL *saʔqa, Ket saʔq, Yug saʔx ~ saʔq, Kott šaga, Arin
sava, Pumpokol tak, Assan šaga. Cf. Na-Dene: Haida gaɬtˢ'aakʷ,
Tlingit tˢʌlk, Eyak tˢətʲk, Galice salas.

254 STAR *qɔ̄qa, Ket qɔR, Yug xɔ̄ʰx, Kott alaga (< *al-xaga), Arin
il-koj ~ il-xok, Pumpokol kaken. Cf. Na-Dene: Haida kūng 'sun,'
Tlingit kuk-kan ~ k'akan ~ ɢagan 'sun.'

255 STERLET (kind of fish) *ʔok, Ket ōk, Yug ok, Pumpokol ot.

256 STOCKING *bulor, Ket buʎɔʎ, Yug bulɔl, Arin proroŋ 'stock-
ings.'

257 STONE *čɨʔs, Ket tɨʔś, Yug čɨʔs, Kott śɨ̄š, Arin kes, Pumpokol
kit, Assan šiš. Bengtson (pers. comm.) compares the Yeniseian
forms with Burushaski čiṣ 'mountain, hill' and Eyak čiiš 'beach,
sand bank, gravel bank, sand, gravel.'

258 STRAIGHT *tat(aŋ), Ket tatəŋ, Yug tatɨŋ, Arin tedenga.
Cf. ?Basque zuzen, ?Burushaski tshʌn.

259 (SKI-)STRAP *ʔēs-, Ket ɛ̄śe, Yug ēs. Cf. Proto-(North) Caucasian *ʔIarš̄ʷa '(leather) cord, strap, thong.'

260 (BOW) STRING   *cu(ʔ) ~ *cuc, Yug tut' (< *t'ut'), Assan gij-
     tu, Arin kej-tu. Cf. Proto-(North) Caucasian *ćʌʔʌ 'bow, arrow,'
     Burushaski čhukus 'bow string.'

261 STRONG₁   *bɨd-, Ket bɨt, Yug bɨt ~ bɨdam. Cf. Proto-(North)
     Caucasian *pʌtʰʌ 'strong, dense, firm.' Bengtson and Blažek (1992)
     add Basque bethe 'full,' i-phete 'thick, fat' and Burushaski buṭ
     'much, very.'

262 STRONG₂   *ʎa(ʔ), Yug ʎāŋ 'strong, firm,' Kott d'aʔ-ut 'fasten-
     ing,' d'oʔ-ūtaŋ 'fasten, strengthen.' Cf. Na-Dene: Haida tlaats'gaa,
     Tlingit litsin, Eyak atliahŭkh, Galice tˡ'aʔs, Kato lətˢ.

263 STUMP   *sʌŋgʌl-, Ket śuŋuʎt, Kott šagali.

264 SUMMER   *sir₁-, Ket śīʎi, Yug sīr, Kott šil-paŋ, Arin šil.
     Cf. Proto-(North) Caucasian *cʰowilHʌ ~ *c̄ʰiwolHʌ 'fall (season),'
     Old Chinese *ćhiw 'fall (season).'

265 SUN   *xiɢa, Ket ī, Yug i, Kott ēga, Arin ega, Pumpokol hixem.
     Cf. ?Na-Dene: Haida xai 'sunshine,' Tlingit -xaa-tˢ' 'be cloudless,'
     Proto-Eyak-Athabaskan *xwaa 'sun.'

266 SWAMP/LAKE   *täk-, Ket taɣ-ɔ '(large) swamp,' Kott ol-tēg ~
     ol-tēx 'swamp,' Assan ol-tegan 'lake.' Cf. Proto-Lezghian *t̄akar
     'pond, lake, swamp.'

267 SWAN   *čike, Ket tīɣə, Yug čik, Kott šīgi.

268 SWEET   *pir₁-, Ket hīʎ 'sweet mass under the crust of a birch
     tree,' hiʎaŋ 'sweet,' Yug fiʔr 'sweet mass under the crust of a birch
     tree,' fɔran 'sweet,' Kott fil 'sap of a tree,' pʰalaŋ ~ falaŋ, Arin
     kulun-pala.

269 TAIL   *puɢaj, Ket hūt, Yug fūt, Kott pʰugai ~ fugai, Arin p̓ʰugaj,
     Assan pugaj. Cf. Nahali pago.

270 TEN₁   *χɔɢa, Ket qō, Yug xo, Kott hāga, Arin hioga ~ qoa ~
     kova, Pumpokol xajaŋ. Bengtson and Blažek (1992) compare these
     forms with Basque hogoi '20,' Proto-(North) Caucasian *ɢə '20,'
     and, in Na-Dene, Tlingit -qa '20,' and Eyak ɢā '10.' The Caucasian–
     Na-Dene comparison was first suggested by Nikolaev (1991: 55).

271 TEN₂   *tuʔ-ŋ, Kott -thukŋ, Arin -thūn. Cf. Proto-(North) Cau-
     casian *w-enc'ɨ, Proto-Tibeto-Burman *tsiy ~ *ts(y)ay. Bengtson
     (pers. comm.) compares these forms with Basque -tzi (as in bedera-
     tzi '9,' zor-tzi '8').

272 TENT   *χuʔs, Ket quʔś, Yug xuʔs, Kott hūš, Arin kus, Pumpokol
     hu-kut.

273 THAT   *ka-, Ket ka-śaŋ 'there,' Yug kā-t, ka-ñ 'there,' Arin xa-tu
     'he.' Cf. Proto-Dagestanian *gʌ 'that (below the speaker),' Sino-
     Tibetan: Tibetan kho 'he, she,' Old Chinese *kə-s 'this, that,' *gə
     'his, her.'

274 THIGH *päp-, Ket hāp, Yug fap, Kott phēpar ~ fēpar. Cf. Proto-Lezghian *piImp 'knee,' Proto-Tibeto-Burman *bop 'leg, calf of the leg.'

275 THIN *paksʌm, Ket hakśem, Yug faksim, Kott pʰačam ~ fačam. Cf. ?Nahali basi 'small.'

276 THIS *tu-, Ket tūdə, tuna 'these,' Yug tūt, tuña 'these,' Arin itaŋ 'they.' Cf. Proto-(North) Caucasian *tʌ- 'this, that,' Proto-Tibeto-Burman *day 'this, that,' Old Chinese *deʔ 'this.'

277 THOU *ʔaw ~ ʔu, Ket ū, Yug u, Kott au, Arin au, Pumpokol ue. Cf. Proto-(North) Caucasian *wo-, Burushaski ūŋ ~ um, Na-Dene: Tlingit weh.

278 THOU/YOU *kʌ- ~ *ʔʌk-, Ket k- ~ ku- (second-person singular personal prefix), kɛŋ (second-person plural personal prefix), ɔ̄k(ŋ) 'you,' ūk 'thy,' Yug k- ~ ku- (second-person singular personal prefix), kɛŋ (second-person plural personal prefix), (k)əkŋ 'you,' uk 'thy,' Pumpokol ajaŋ 'you.' Cf. Proto-Dagestanian *Ru ~ *ʔʌR- 'thou,' Proto-Nax *Ho ~ *ʔah 'thou,' Proto-Tibeto-Burman *k(w)ʌj 'thou.'

279 THREE *doʔŋa, Ket dɔʔŋ ~ dōŋ, Yug dɔʔŋ ~ doŋ, Kott tōŋa, Arin tūŋa, Pumpokol doŋa. Cf. Proto-Dagestanian *s̄ʷimHʌ, Proto-Tibeto-Burman *g-sum, Old Chinese *sɔ̄m.

280 THROAT *kərʌd ~ *gərʌd, Ket kʌʎit, Yug kʌlat, Arin u-kurii. Cf. Nahali garḍan, Na-Dene: Haida haɬ ~ χil 'neck,' Tlingit kaɬ-dukh 'neck.' Kuiper (1962: 73) compares the Nahali form with a similar Hindi word.

281 TONGUE *ʔej, Ket ēj, Yug ej, Kott ei 'voice, sound,' Pumpokol aj. Cf. Nahali lãy.

282 TWENTY *ʔeʔχ, Ket ɛʔk, Yug ɛʔk. Cf. Proto-Dagestanian *ɢ̄ə, Proto-Tibeto-Burman *(m)kul.

283 TWO *xi-na, Ket in, Yug in, Kott īna, Arin kina, Pumpokol hineaŋ. Cf. Proto-(North) Caucasian *q'ʷIä, Proto-Tibeto-Burman *g-ni-s, Old Chinese *nij-s.

284 UNMARRIED *ʔəpʌl, Ket ʌ̄l, Yug ʌfil, Kott ipal 'free.' Cf. Proto-(North) Caucasian *ʔʌpʌj 'orphan,' Proto-Kartvelian *obol- 'orphan,' Proto-Indo-European *orbho- 'orphan.'

285 UTENSIL *siʔχ 'trough for dough,' Ket śiʔk, Yug siʔk. Cf. Proto-(North) Caucasian *c̄'äq'ʷa 'spoon, scoop, wooden vessel.' Starostin (1984: 32) added Proto-Sino-Tibetan *čekʷ 'to draw, to ladle.' Nikolaev (1991: 53) adds Proto-Na-Dene *c'ãg(w) 'basket, bowl, dish,' Eyak c'āk-ɬ 'dipper,' Navajo c'aaʔ 'plate.' Bengtson and Blažek (1992) add Burushaski čuq 'a measure of grain,' Werchikwar (a Burushaski dialect) čhiq 'sifting tray.'

286 VULVA₁   *ŕɔs, Ket ʌōś, Yug los, Pumpokol lat. Cf. Proto-Dagestanian *rɔcʷʌ 'anus,' Proto-Tibeto-Burman *ryes 'hind part, back,
seat, posterior.'

287 VULVA₂   *gar, Kott kar, Assan kar, Arin ken (< *ker-(ʌ)n).
Cf. Proto-Dagestanian *kʰʷəru 'hole,' Proto-Nax *kor 'window'
(< 'hole'), Proto-Tibeto-Burman *kor 'hole.'

288 WAR   *kār₁e, Ket kāʌi, Yug kār, Kott hali, Arin kel 'army.'
Cf. Proto-Dagestanian *ḏⁱełʌ, Proto-Tibeto-Burman *rāl (< *lāl)
'war, fight.'

289 WARM   *xus- ∼ *xuʔus, Ket ūś, Yug ūs, Arin kuši 'hot,' Pumpokol
uttɨ-čidin 'hot.'

290 WATER   *xur₁, Ket ūʎ, Yug ur, Kott ūl, Arin kul, Pumpokol ul.
Cf. Proto-Dagestanian *x̄änʔɨ, Proto-Nax *χi, Old Chinese *łujʔ,
Proto-Tibeto-Burman *lwi(y) 'flow, river,' Cf. also the Proto-
Yeniseian words for WET and RAIN, herein. Starostin (1984: 26)
added Proto-Sino-Tibetan *ḫu-s 'moisture.' Nikolaev (1991: 53)
compares the Caucasian forms with Proto-Na-Dene *xanʔ 'water,
river,' Haida ɢan-dl 'fresh water,' Tlingit hin 'fresh water, river,'
Proto-Athabaskan *xanʔe 'river,' Tutchone xanʔe 'river,' Hupa
hanʔ 'river,' Kutchin han 'river,' Kwalhioqua xonee 'river.' Bengtson (1991a: 101) adds Basque i-hin-tz 'dew' and Burushaski huu-ṣ
'moisture.'

291 WET   *xura, Ket uʎ-tu, Yug ul, Kott ūra 'wet, rainy,' Arin kur,
Pumpokol ur-ga.

292 WHERE   *wir₁, Ket biʎeś, biʎa 'how,' Yug birɛs, birɛ 'how,' Kott
bili, biʎäŋ 'what.' Cf. WHO₁ below.

293 WHITE   *täk- ∼ *täkam, Ket taɣam, Yug tig-bēʰs, Kott tʰēgam
∼ tʰēkam, Arin tāma, Pumpokol tam-xo, Assan tegama ∼ tiekama.
Cf. Na-Dene: Eyak tˢeʔq 'yellow,' Tanaina tsɔk 'yellow,' Galice tˢ'oh
'yellow,' Navajo tˢò 'yellow.'

294 WHO₁   *wi- ∼ *we-, Ket bi-śśe (masc.), bɛ-śa (fem.), bi-ʎa 'how,'
bi-ʎeś 'where,' Yug bɛ-tta, bi-rɛ 'how,' bi-rɛs 'where,' Kott bi-li
'where,' bi-ʎäŋ 'what.' Bengtson and Blažek (1992) compare the
Yeniseian forms with Caucasian forms such as Archi ba-sa 'when'
and Godoberi e-bu 'what,' with Burushaski be 'what,' be-se 'why,'
and with Sino-Tibetan forms such as Burmese ba 'what' and Karen
bei 'what, how.'

295 WHO₂   *ʔan-, Ket anej ∼ ana, Yug anet. Cf. Proto-(North) Caucasian *nʌ (interrogative pronoun base), Sino-Tibetan: Old Chinese
*nāj 'how, what,' Tibetan na 'when,' Khamti an-nan 'what,' Nahali
nāni, nān 'what.' Bengtson (pers. comm.) adds Basque no-r.

296 WHO₃ *ʔas- ~ *sʌ-, Ket aśeś 'what,' aś-ka 'when,' Yug asera, asejs 'what,' ās-kej 'when,' as-sa 'what,' Kott ašix 'what, how,' ši-na 'what.' Cf. Proto-(North) Caucasian *s̄ʌ (interrogative pronoun base), *s̄ʌ (interrogative pronoun base), Proto-Tibeto-Burman *su, Basque zer 'what,' zein 'which,' Na-Dene: ?Tlingit ah-sa.

297 WIDE *χiɢʌʎ, Ket qīʎ, Yug xēʎ, Kott hīgal. Cf. Proto-(North) Caucasian *-ʌrq'ü ~ *q'ʌrq'ü.

298 WIDOW *bəs, Ket bʌssem, bʌśśəʎ-git 'widower,' Yug bʌssem, Kott paš-ūp-še 'orphan, widow, widower,' Assan pašup jali 'step-son,' Arin pas 'slave,' bi-pašša 'my servant.' Cf. Proto-(North) Cau-casian *p'ʌs̄i 'orphan, relative from a second marriage.'

299 WILLOW *dəʎe, Ket dʌʎ-okś, Yug dəʎ-git, Kott tīli 'thicket of willows,' Arin tal-set.

300 WIND *bej, Ket bej, Yug bej, Kott pēi, Arin paj, Pumpokol baj ~ bej. Cf. Proto-(North) Caucasian *mɨwHʌ 'smell.'

301 WINTER *gəte, Ket kətə, Yug kət, Kott kēti. Cf. Proto-Lezghian *q'Iorī(a).

302 WITCH/SHE-DEVIL *qos, Ket qɔśɛd-ɛm, Yug xɔsed-ɛm. Cf. Proto-Lezghian *qʷarc 'brownie (a small sprite),' Proto-Abkhaz-Adyg *Rʷəsət 'devil,' Burushaski gus- 'she-, woman.'

303 WOLVERINE₁ *kūñ, Ket kūñe, Yug kūʰn, Pumpokol kun. Bengt-son (pers. comm.) compares these forms with Basque *-konH in harz-koin 'badger'; for the first element in this compound, see the Proto-Yeniseian word for BADGER above.

304 WOLVERINE₂ *pestap, Kott feštap ~ pʰeštap, Arin ṕʰjastap, Assan pestap. Starostin (1984: 29) compares the first syllable of the Proto-Yeniseian reconstruction with Proto-(North) Caucasian *běHěrc'i 'wolf' and with Old Chinese *prāt-s 'mythical predator.' Bengtson (1991a: 103) adds Basque potzo 'wolf, big dog.'

305 WOMAN₁ *qʌm-, Ket qīm, Yug xim ~ xem, Arin bi-qamal 'my wife,' kemelä 'woman,' Pumpokol ils-em (< *ils-qem) 'wife.' Cf. Proto-Dagestanian *qʰʌmʌ. Bengtson (1991a: 114) adds Basque ema-kume and Burushaski quma 'concubine.'

306 WOMAN₂ *ʔalit ~ *ʔar₁it, Kott alit, Arin alte. Cf. Proto-Dages-tanian *ɨ̄rdʌ.

307 WOOD₁ *ʔɔkse, Ket ōkś, Yug oksɨ, Kott atči, Arin ošče ~ otši, Assan ač(i).

308 WOOD₂ *xaʔq, Ket aʔq, Yug aʔx ~ aʔq 'trees, firewood,' Kott āx ~ ag, Arin oo 'firewood,' Pumpokol hoxon 'wood, forest.' Cf. Na-Dene: Haida q'aw, Tlingit χaw 'log,' Eyak q'aʔ 'bushes.'

309 WOOD₃ (ROTTEN) *tulaq, Ket tulaq, Yug tulax, Kott tʰalak.

310   WORD   *qä(ʔ)ɢ, Ket qaʔ, Yug xā, Kott xēg ~ kʰēg. Cf. Na-Dene: Tlingit qa 'say.'

311   YEAR   *sīɢa, Ket śī, Yug sī, Kott šēga, Arin šʰej, Pumpokol ciku.

312   YELLOW   *suŕ-, Ket sulemam, Kott šui, Pumpokol tul-si. Bengtson (1991a: 111) compares the Yeniseian forms with Basque zuri 'white' and Proto-(North) Caucasian *hʷö-čʷörʌ 'gray, yellow.'

313   YESTERDAY   *kʌns-, Yug kisɔŋ, Kott honč-ig, Arin kanji, Assan xonji. Bengtson (pers. comm.) compares the Yeniseian forms with Burushaski gunc 'day.'

REFERENCES

Bengtson, John D. 1991a. "Notes on Sino-Caucasian," in Shevoroshkin, ed., 1991: 67–129.

———. 1991b. "Some Macro-Caucasian Etymologies," in Shevoroshkin, ed., 1991: 130–41.

Bengtson, John D., and Václav Blažek. 1992. "Macro-Caucasica and Dene-Caucasica," ms.

Chirikba, V. A. 1985. "Baskskij i severokavkazskie jazyki," *Drevnjaja Anatolija.* Moscow, Nauka, 95–105.

Greenberg, Joseph H. 1981. "Comparative Na-Dene Notebook," ms.

Kuiper, F. B. J. 1962. *Nahali: A Comparative Study.* Amsterdam.

Lorimer, D. L. R. 1938. *The Burushaski Language.* Oslo.

Nikolaev, Sergei L. 1991. "Sino-Caucasian Languages in America," in Shevoroshkin, ed., 1991: 42–66.

Nikolaev, Sergei L., and Sergei A. Starostin. 1992. "A Caucasian Etymological Dictionary," ms.

Ruhlen, Merritt. 1992. "Na-Dene Etymologies," Chapter 5 of this volume.

Shevoroshkin, Vitaly, ed. 1991. *Dene-Sino-Caucasian Languages.* Bochum, Germany.

Starostin, Sergei A. 1982. "Prajenisejskaja rekonstruktsija i vnešnie svjazi enisejskix jazykov," *Ketskij sbornik.* Leningrad, 144–237.

———. 1984. "Gipoteza o genetičeskix svjazjax sinotibetskix jazykov s enisejskimi i severnokavkazskimi jazykami," *Lingvističeskaja rekonstruktsija i drevnejšaja istorija vostoka* 4, Moscow, 19–38. [English translation in Shevoroshkin, ed., 1991: 12–41.]

———. 1989a. "Nostratic and Sino-Caucasian," in Vitaly Shevoroshkin, ed., *Explorations in Language Macrofamilies.* Bochum, Germany, 42–66.

———. 1989b. *Rekonstruktsija drevnekitaiskoi fonologicheskoi sistemy.* Moscow.

5

Na-Dene Etymologies

Particularly controversial in linguistic taxonomy during the 1980's was the so-called "Na-Dene Problem." The problem was whether Haida, a language spoken on the Queen Charlotte Islands off the western coast of Canada, was a member of the Na-Dene family, as Edward Sapir had originally claimed in 1915, or was, rather, unrelated to the other branches of Na-Dene (i.e. Tlingit, Eyak, and Athabaskan). When Sapir's Na-Dene family was attacked by Pliny Goddard (1920), a leading Athabaskanist of his day, Sapir, weary and disgusted by a similar taxonomic dispute with the Algonquianist Truman Michelson (see Chapter 6), chose not to respond to Goddard's criticism.

This controversy was renewed in the 1960's and 1970's in a dispute between Heinz-Jürgen Pinnow, who maintained, with evidence even more abundant than that in Sapir's original material, that Haida was indeed a member of Na-Dene, and Michael Krauss, who argued that Haida had not been shown to be related to the Na-Dene family (for references to this dispute, see Pinnow 1990). In 1979 Robert D. Levine claimed that "the evidence offered in support of the 'classical' Na-Dene hypothesis (i.e., as set up by Sapir in his 1915 statement) is spurious, and that there is currently no empirical basis for including Haida in the Na-Dene grouping" (Levine 1979: 157). That same year Krauss (1979) also maintained that "there is no detectable genetic relationship between Haida and the others in the group, Tlingit and Athabaskan-Eyak" (p. 838) and thanked Levine "for debunking once and for all the claim that Haida has been demonstrated to be genetically related to Tlingit, etc." (p. 841).

Other scholars who have examined the evidence, however, have tended to side with Sapir and Pinnow rather than with Krauss and Levine. Sergei Nikolaev (1991: 43) noted that "certain doubts have been expressed regarding the inclusion of Haida in the Na-Dene family, but they should be considered unsubstantiated." In his book on the classification of New World languages, Joseph Greenberg (1987: 321–30) devoted an entire chapter to the "Na-Dene Problem," arguing that Levine's method of dismantling Na-Dene could just as easily be turned against Indo-European. Even if one were to ignore the new evidence adduced by Pinnow, and even accepting Levine's mostly erroneous strictures on methodology, Greenberg showed that Sapir's original evidence connecting Haida with the rest of Na-Dene was more than sufficient: "Even after Levine's unreasonable attack (1979), what survives is a body of evidence superior to that which could be adduced under similar restrictions for the affinity of Albanian, Celtic, and Armenian, all three universally recognized as valid members of the Indo-European family of languages" (p. 331).

During the data-gathering stage, in preparation for his work on the classification of New World languages, Greenberg assembled a Na-Dene comparative wordlist (Greenberg 1981). These data, however, were not used in *Language in the Americas* (1987), where Greenberg simply defended Sapir's original evidence. The present study is intended to show that had Greenberg chosen to use his Na-Dene wordlists, he could easily have strengthened Sapir's case, and in fact, as the etymologies given below indicate, the "Na-Dene Problem" was based on a misunderstanding of methodology, not on a lack of evidence. Can anyone really believe that Haida shares as many, or as precise, similarities with the Khoisan family (or any other family) as it does with the other Na-Dene languages? The etymologies in this chapter, based on my interpretation of Greenberg's Na-Dene notebook (a copy of which may be found in Stanford University's Green Library), argue to the contrary.

It should be noted that Greenberg's notebook includes information from 16 different Haida sources, 11 different Tlingit sources, and six different Eyak sources. Consequently, there is a certain fluctuation in the transcriptions for words in these languages that reflects dialectal differences, differing transcriptional abilities on the part of the linguists who produced the various works, and different systems of phonetic transcription. With a few exceptions I have not sought to impose uniformity on the varying transcriptions, which would be a daunting and not wholly feasible task. I have, however, consistently rendered [c] as [t^s], and glottalized consonants are always indicated by a following apostrophe (e.g. p', t', k'). Furthermore, all morphological boundaries cited in these etymologies are actually posited in the sources, as shown in Greenberg's notebook. Quite often, however, morphologically unanalyzed forms are compared, where a certain morphological break is implicit in the comparison. Usually the portion of unanalyzed words being compared is clear, even without the specification of morpheme boundaries.

After assembling the set of Na-Dene etymologies on the basis of Greenberg's notebook, I compared these etymologies with those originally suggested by Sapir in 1915. In cases of overlap (roughly 25 examples), I have indicated the number of the Sapir etymology at the end of the etymology (e.g. [S44]). The other Sapir etymologies were then added to the list, again with an indication of their number in each case. Finally, some Na-Dene etymologies from a letter of Heinz-Jürgen Pinnow (pers. comm.) were added to the list; they, too, are identified at the ends of the appropriate etymologies (e.g. [P18]).

The etymologies follow:

1   ABOVE   Haida *k'wa-ji* ~ *gī*, Tlingit *k'e* 'upward,' *kí* 'top,' Proto-Athabaskan *χa-* 'up, out of.' [S82]

2   AGAIN   Tlingit *ts'u*, Proto-Athabaskan *ts'i*. [S76]

3   ALL   Haida *tlōqan*, Eyak *tunhlokh*, Athabaskan: Tlatskanai -*wēɬ$^\alpha$q*.

4   AMONG   Haida *t'a-oan* 'alongside of,' Tlingit -*t'a:-k^w* 'in the middle of,' Proto-Athabaskan *-*t'a*. [S60]

5   ANKLE   Tlingit *kakaushitl'*, Athabaskan: Tsetsaut *ɛkyagɔ*.

6   ARROW$_1$ Tlingit *tax'aɬ'* 'needle,' Eyak *takl* ~ *teklj* ~ *t'ik'-ɬ* ~ *t'ek'*.

7   ARROW$_2$ Haida *s-q'a* 'stick,' *q'a* 'harpoon,' Proto-Athabaskan *q'aʔ*, Navajo *k'aaʔ*. [P19]

8   ASK   Eyak *qeʔd*, Athabaskan: Chipewyan *kɔr*, Hupa *xid*, Mattole *kid* ~ *kɔt*, Navajo *kìd*.

9   AUNT   Tlingit *'át'*, Athabaskan: Mattole -*a:tsiʔ*. [S2]

10   BACK   Haida *ts'awii* ~ *ts'ak'ii*, Tlingit *t'á* ~ *déχ'*, Eyak *t'aʔ-q'* 'in back of,' Athabaskan: Slave *t'ä̃ʔ* 'backwards,' Tututni *t'an* 'backwards.' [S69]

11   BE   Haida *ʃit*, Tlingit *hitɬ* ~ *(s-)ti*, Athabaskan: Tsetsaut *t'ɛ*, Tututni *ti*, Navajo *zí:d* 'become.'

12   BEAR$_1$ Haida *xúuts* 'brown bear,' Tlingit *xúts* 'brown bear,' Athabaskan: Tsetsaut *xɔ* 'grizzly bear.'

13   BEAR$_2$ Tlingit *s'ik* ~ *seek* ~ *tzeek* 'black bear,' Eyak *tziū* ~ *ts'iyu* 'black bear.'

14   BEAVER   Haida *ts'ang*, Athabaskan: Tahltan *čā*, Chipewyan *tsa'*, Hare *tsáʔ*, Navajo *čā'*.

15   BECAUSE OF   Haida -*t'a*, Proto-Athabaskan *-*t'a*. [S67]

16   BELLY   Tlingit *q'oɬ'* 'stomach,' Eyak *ku:l*.

17   BITE   Tlingit *t'ax'*, Athabaskan: Chipewyan *tθàih* ~ *tθày*, Kato *t'ōγ*, Mattole *t'o* 'sting.'

18 BLACK   Tlingit *t'ùč'* 'black, coal,' Eyak *t'uʔč'*, Athabaskan: Sarsi
    t'ès 'charcoal,' Chipewyan *t'és* 'charcoal,' Tlatskanai *tês*, Wailaki
    t'es 'charcoal,' Navajo *tèèš* 'charcoal.'

19 BLOOD$_1$ Eyak *deɬ*, Athabaskan: Sarsi *-dīt^l-*, Chipewyan *dèɬ*,
    Tsetsaut *a-dila*, Tututni *dəɬ*, Navajo *dìɬ*.

20 BLOOD$_2$ Haida *ɢai* ~ *ɢáy*, *s-ɢi-t* 'be red,' Tlingit *-ɢee* 'be bright,'
    Proto-Athabaskan *-ɢay* 'be white,' Navajo *-gai* 'be white.' [P20]

21 BLOW   Haida *ux*, Tlingit *'úx*.

22 BLUE$_1$ Haida *ʃu-ɬaɬ*, Tlingit *khatɬeh*, Eyak *khatl* 'green.'

23 BLUE$_2$ Haida *t^l'ánt^s'uut* 'bluejay,' Eyak *tɬãt*.

24 BODY   Haida *k'ōt* 'corpse,' Eyak *ɢeʔt*.

25 BONE   Tlingit *s'a:q*, Proto-Athabaskan *-ts'ĕn*. [S75]

26 BOW   Haida *tl-kīt*, Tlingit *i-i-elte*, Athabaskan: Chipewyan *iɬtī*,
    Navajo *aɬtī*.

27 BROTHER$_1$ Tlingit *hunx* 'man's elder brother,' Proto-Athabaskan
    -onaɣ(e) 'older brother.' [S56]

28 BROTHER$_2$ Haida *qā* 'mother's brother,' *(ti-)ka(-gha)* 'older
    brother,' Tlingit *akh-keek* 'younger brother,' *kak* 'mother's brother.'

29 BUILD   Tlingit *yeχ* 'build, make,' Athabaskan: Mattole *yih*.

30 BURN$_1$ Haida *da:dj* ~ *das* 'live coals,' Proto-Athabaskan *-das*.
    [S9]

31 BURN$_2$ Haida *go* ~ *k'untl'daa*, Tlingit *ɢАn* ~ *gan'*, Eyak *d-q'a*,
    Athabaskan: Ingalik *k'á(n)*, Carrier *-k'en*, Hare *k'ō*, Kato *k'an*,
    Navajo *k'ããh*, Jicarilla *k'ã*. [S35] [Cf. FIRE below.]

32 BUTTOCKS$_1$ Eyak *t^l'iǰ*, Athabaskan: Sarsi *-tɬ'āʔ*, Kato *t^l'a*, Mat-
    tole *t^l'aʔ*. [S44]

33 BUTTOCKS$_2$ Tlingit *k'í*, Athabaskan: Kato *kīʔ*.

34 CEDAR   Haida *čju*, Proto-Athabaskan *č'o* 'fir, spruce.' [S80]

35 CHEEK   Tlingit *wàš*, Athabaskan: Coquille *ni-paš*. [S47]

36 CHEW   Haida *haljang*, Eyak *ʔaʔt^l'*, Athabaskan: Chipewyan *ʔaɬ*
    'bite,' Dogrib *ʔaɬ* 'bite,' Mattole *ʔaɬ*.

37 CHILD   Haida *gyīt'*, Tlingit *git'a*, Eyak *qēč'*. [Cf. SON below.]

38 CLAY   Tlingit *s'ā*, Eyak *t^s'aʔ*.

39 CLOUD$_1$ Haida *yai-en* ~ *yēn* ~ *yáan* 'cloud,' Eyak *jaa* 'heaven,'
    Proto-Athabaskan *yaa* 'heaven, sky,' Tanaina *yo-k'*, Koyukon *yo*,
    Hare *yà-k'è*, Kato *ya*, Navajo *yá*. [P11]

40 CLOUD$_2$ Haida *qwii*, Tlingit *gus'*, *qo-gas'* 'fog,' *gwas'* 'be foggy,'
    Eyak *q'ahs*, Athabaskan: Sarsi *nàk'uś*, Carrier *k'wes*, Hare *k'o*,
    Navajo *k'òs*.

41 COLD$_1$ Haida *χwi* ~ *xwi*, Tlingit *kūsa*, Athabaskan: Sarsi *k'ás*,
    Carrier *k'wez*, Hupa *k'at^s'*, Mattole *k'at^s_e*, Navajo *k'àz*, Lipan *k'às*.

42 COLD₂ Haida *t'at*, Tlingit *t'a:dj*, Proto-Athabaskan **t'e* 'be cold,' *t'ĕn* 'ice.' [S64]

43 COUGH Haida *q'usáang*, Athabaskan: Chipewyan *kwòθ*, Kato *kōs*.

44 COUNT Tlingit *t'uw*, Athabaskan: Sarsi *tà:i*, Chipewyan *tá*, Tututni *-tuk*, Mattole *ta'x*, Navajo *tàʔ*.

45 COVER Tlingit *kèt* (n.), Eyak *kaač* 'blanket.'

46 CRANE Haida *dilɑ*, Tlingit *du:ł*, Proto-Athabaskan *deł. [S11]

47 CRY Haida *sqa-yetl* ~ *sga-ił*, Athabaskan: Tanaina *tsax*, Beaver *tšûg*, Chipewyan *tsàγ*, Kato *čeγ*, Navajo *tsééh* ~ *tsà*.

48 CUT Haida *-(t')at*, Athabaskan: Tsetsaut *t'a*, Kato *t'atˢ* ~ *t'as*, Mattole *t'ās*, Navajo *-t'ās*.

49 DANCE Tlingit *atl'ekh* ~ *ł'eχ*, Athabaskan: Tsetsaut *dlɛ*, Tututni *daš*, Mattole *dāx*.

50 DARK Haida *ʕaalgaa*, Eyak *khalhetetiutu*, Athabaskan: Chipewyan *xɛł* ~ *xíł*.

51 DAUGHTER Tlingit *sik* ~ *sí* ~ *si-k'ʷ*, Eyak *tsī(y)*, Athabaskan: Sarsi *-ts'ɑh*, Galice *-siiʔee*, Mattole *-tsī(y)*, Navajo *-tsiʔ*.

52 DAWN Tlingit *qea*, Eyak *qa* (v.).

53 DAY Haida *sɛn* ~ *siŋ* ~ *shang* ~ *sung*, Athabaskan: Tanaina *džanih*, Beaver *dzene*, Hare *dzíné*, Galice *sinis*, Mattole *džiŋ*, Navajo *jí*.

54 DECAY Haida *gu:na* 'decayed,' Proto-Athabaskan **-gaŋ* 'be mouldy.' [S15]

55 DEER Haida *k'áat*, Athabaskan: Tsetsaut *xadzinɛ* 'male deer.'

56 DIE Tlingit *na*, Proto-Athabaskan **-na*. [S49]

57 DIG Eyak *ša*, *šiyah* 'dig for,' Athabaskan: Galice *sīʔ* 'dig a hole,' Kato *šīʔ*, Mattole *čiʔ*.

58 DIRT Haida *sq'íl*, Eyak *tˢ'ətˡ'*, Athabaskan: Tsetsaut *kwuł'*.

59 DISH Haida *ts'a-* (classifier for dishes), Tlingit *s'ix'*, Proto-Eyak-Athabaskan **ts'aa'k'*, Eyak *ts'aag-ł* 'basket,' Athabaskan: Navajo *ts'ààʔ* 'shallow basket,' Kiowa Apache *ʔi-ts'eeh* 'plate.' [S74, P13]

60 DIVE₁ Haida *ji:*, Proto-Athabaskan **-jid* ~ *yid*. [S17]

61 DIVE₂ Tlingit *tsis*, Athabaskan: Tututni *sił*.

62 DOG Haida *χa* ~ *hā* ~ *ħa*, Eyak *hava* ~ *xəwa*.

63 DREAM Tlingit *čun* ~ *jun*, Eyak *tsī:dz*.

64 DRINK₁ Tlingit *autenah* ~ *katana* ~ *na*, Athabaskan: Tlatskanai *tatɛna*, Chipewyan *-dằ*, Kato *-nan*, Navajo *-tˡằ*. [S8, S50]

65 DRINK₂ Haida *χutˡ'ʌ*, Eyak *khatilia*.

66 DURATIVE Tlingit *s-* (modal prefix), Proto-Athabaskan **s-*. [S57]

67 DUST Tlingit s'ix, Athabaskan: Carrier xeɬ-tˢ'ih 'ashes,' Galice
č'as 'ashes,' Navajo lèèš-č'ìih 'ashes.'

68 EAR Haida gyū ~ kiū ~ gēu, Tlingit gūk ~ ka-kūk, Eyak kha-
khikh ~ ka-čech ~ ǰehχ, Athabaskan: Tanaina džaɣoh, Koyukon
dzaɣa, Beaver džûgeʔ, Kato -č'əgeʔ, Navajo -ǰààʔ.

69 EARTH₁ Haida tlig ~ tˡga ~ klik, Tlingit tliak-ū ~ klatk ~ tlit-
tik, Eyak tzatlkh, Athabaskan: Navajo ɬe.

70 EARTH₂ Eyak an ~ 'ã ~ a, Athabaskan: Kutchin nən, Hare ne,
Hupa nin, Navajo nìʔ.

71 EAT₁ Tlingit yaːn, Proto-Athabaskan *yan. [S88]

72 EAT₂ Haida táa ~ -t'áang ~ kul-tah, Athabaskan: Chipewyan -tĩ̀,
Kato tan, Navajo -t'āh. [S62]

73 EAT₃ Haida ɬ-da-naaw 'mealtime' (EAT + DRINK), Tlingit -da-naa
'drink,' Proto-Eyak-Athabaskan *-naam 'drink,' Proto-Athabaskan
*de-naam 'drink,' Navajo -dlá̃ 'drink.' [P16]

74 EDGE Tlingit wɑn, Proto-Athabaskan *man. [S46]

75 EGG Haida k'ao 'salmon egg,' kow ~ kaua, Tlingit kwɑt' ~ k'ʷʌ́t'
~ kwūt, Eyak k'udə-ʔuhdg ~ kota-ut, Athabaskan: Ingalik k'úw-
k'una 'fish egg,' Chipewyan k'ūn-έ 'fish egg.'

76 ELBOW Haida hie-tsi-kwe ~ çī-tsɛguī, Tlingit t'íy ~ t'iyšu, Eyak
-čiǰ, Athabaskan: Sarsi -ts'ìs, Chipewyan ts'úz, Navajo -č'ōžlā'.

77 ELK Haida tsish-ku ~ čišku ~ wut-tsish, Tlingit tiskh ~ wutzekh,
Athabaskan: Tlatskanai čisčex, Galice disčoh, Navajo dᶻéːh.

78 END Haida tɬan, Proto-Athabaskan *-ɬad. [S42]

79 FALL Haida -'wii ~ ɢwi, Athabaskan: Sarsi gùh ~ gùùì, Navajo
gèèh ~ gòʔ.

80 FAT Haida ʕáay, Tlingit ēqē, 'eχ 'fish oil,' íχ 'oil,' Eyak q'əχ,
Athabaskan: Beaver k'a, Carrier -k'a, Chipewyan k'à, Hare e-ɣe,
Tsetsaut eχɛ, Galice k'ah, Wailaki k'ah, Navajo k'àh, Jicarilla xéh.
[S20]

81 FATHER₁ Haida ħáat ~ hadáa, Eyak ata, Athabaskan: Sarsi -tàʔ,
Chipewyan -t'à, Tsetsaut tä', Tututni taʔ, Galice taʔ, Chiricahua
-tàà.

82 FATHER₂ Tlingit ak'ish ~ 'ìš ~ īš, Athabaskan: Lipan -ʔààší.

83 FEAR Haida χetˡ ~ ɢēd ~ ʕíit'ang 'be ashamed,' xált'as 'fear-
ful,' Tlingit χetˡ 'afraid,' Athabaskan: Tanaina git, Ahtena ged,
Beaver dzid, Sarsi ǰìʔ(d), Kutchin ǰed, Chipewyan ǰɛ̀r, Tututni dzít
'frighten,' Hupa gʲid, Kato git, Mattole ǰid, Navajo ǰìd, Chiricahua
ǰìʔ.

84 FEATHER Haida t'aw ~ t'a-ɢun, Tlingit t'áw, Eyak t'ātɬ 'feather,
leaf,' Proto-Athabaskan *t'aan' 'leaf,' Sarsi t'àh, Kutchin -t'e, a-

t'an 'leaf,' Carrier *-t'a*, *-t'an* 'leaf,' Hare *t'a*, *īt'õ* 'leaf,' Tututni *t'a*, Tlatskanai *tan* 'leaf,' Galice *t'aiʔ*, *t'āāĩ* ~ *t'āʔ* 'leaf,' Navajo *-t'àʔ*, *-t'ǎàʔ* 'leaf.' [S68, P22]

85 FIRE Haida *č'ānu* ~ *tˢ'anu*, Tlingit *k'ān* ~ *q'ān*, Athabaskan: Beaver *konʔ*, Sarsi *kùnàʔ*, Han *kwon*, Chipewyan *kún*, Tlatskanai *kwen*, Coquille *xʷan*, Galice *kwan*, Mattole *koŋ'*, Navajo *kò̰*, Lipan *kõõʔ*. [Cf. BURN₂ above.]

86 FIREWOOD Haida *kūk* ~ *kuk*, Eyak *kug-ɬ*, Proto-Athabaskan *kwegw*, Beaver *čûč*, Ahtena *čeč*, Hupa *čʷiž*, Mattole *čiš*, Navajo *čìž*, Lipan *čìš*. [P5]

87 FISH₁ Haida *χao* 'fish' (v.), Proto-Athabaskan *-k'a(n)* 'fish with a net.' [S29]

88 FISH₂ Tlingit *ɬ'uku'* 'salmon,' Athabaskan: Sarsi *tˡúk'á*, Ingalik *tɬúk'àʔ*, Han *ɬugu*, Tsetsaut *ɬoʔ*, Galice *ɬuuk'e*, Navajo *ɬóóʔ*, Jicarilla *ɬógèè*. [S43]

89 FLOAT Eyak *ɬə-dux*, Athabaskan: Galice *t'uh* 'swim.'

90 FLY₁ (v.) Haida *χīt* ~ *xit*, Eyak *k'aʔt'*, Athabaskan: Mattole *kād*.

91 FLY₂ (v.) Tlingit *t'atɬ* 'fly, flap wings,' Athabaskan: Sarsi *t'áh*, Carrier *-t'ah*, Hare *t'a*, Galice *t'ah*, Hupa *t'aw*, Mattole *t'ah*, Navajo *t'á*, Lipan *t'áh*.

92 FOAM Tlingit *xeɬ* ~ *χeɬ* ~ *χel* ~ *χeš*, Athabaskan: Chipewyan *-γʷòs*.

93 FOLLOW Tlingit *k'e*, *k'en* 'to trace,' Athabaskan: Tututni *-k'eh* 'following.'

94 FOOD Haida *dáayang*, Athabaskan: Sarsi *dání*, Galice *s-taane*, Navajo *dãã*.

95 FOOT Tlingit *k'os* ~ *ka-kūs* ~ *q'os* ~ *χ'us*, Eyak *q'āš* ~ *k'ahš* ~ *kuš*, Athabaskan: Sarsi *γùs*, Kato *-woos*.

96 FOR₁ Haida *ɢa* 'to,' *ɢan* 'for,' Tlingit *ɢa* 'for,' Proto-Athabaskan *-γa* 'for,' *-γan* 'to.' [S18]

97 FOR₂ Tlingit *-χɑ-n* 'to,' Proto-Athabaskan *-χa*. [S81]

98 FORT Tlingit *nu*, Proto-Athabaskan *no* 'place of retreat, island.' [S55]

99 FRIEND Tlingit *χo:n*, Proto-Athabaskan *k'ene*. [S32]

100 FROG Eyak *čiaɬq*, Athabaskan: Tsetsaut *tˢ'alɛ*, Tlatskanai *swax-alxɛl*, Hupa *čʷ'al*, Kato *č'ahɑl*, Navajo *č'aɬ*.

101 FUTURE Haida *-sa-ŋ*, Proto-Athabaskan *tˢa-ŋ*. [S3]

102 GIRL₁ Haida *jada-kudso* ~ *i-adda-hudsu* ~ *ntzahtahutzo*, Tlingit *shaa-kutsku* ~ *shatkakuatsku*, Eyak *gelikutzkuki*, *khetzkisaha* 'daughter.'

103   GIRL$_2$ Eyak *keël*, Athabaskan: Mattole *či?ɬ*.

104   GIVE   Tlingit *'ek* 'give a potlatch,' Athabaskan: Tsetsaut *'a* 'give a feast.'

105   GO$_1$ Haida *qa*, Tlingit *ha* ~ *nuk-koh*, Eyak *qah*, Athabaskan: Dogrib *γa*, Tsetsaut *-ga*. [S19]

106   GO$_2$ Haida *daal* ~ *dal*, Athabaskan: Chipewyan *dɛɬ*, Kato *dəɬ* ~ *del?*. [S7, S10]

107   GOOD   Haida *lah-gung* ~ *lā-gung*, Tlingit *gú* 'happy,' Eyak *d^{z}u*, Athabaskan: Koyukon *zun*, Tanaina *žin*, Chipewyan *zù*, Hare *zù*, Kato *šōŋ*, Mattole *xwoŋ*, Navajo *žǫ́*.

108   GOOSE   Haida *χaha* 'mallard,' Proto-Athabaskan *$χ$a'*. [S83]

109   GRANDCHILD   Haida *t'ak'an*, Tlingit *čxank'*, Athabaskan: Sarsi *-šiγá*, Tsetsaut *isča*, Tlatskanai *ōtsɛnee*, Kato *-čai*, Navajo *čyai*.

110   GRANDFATHER   Haida *č'ɪn*, Proto-Athabaskan *-č'i*. [S77]

111   GRANDMOTHER   Haida *nān* ~ *náan*, Athabaskan: Sarsi *ná* 'mother,' Chipewyan *né* 'mother,' Tsetsaut *na* 'mother,' Kato *nan* 'mother,' Mattole *-an-* 'mother.'

112   GRASS$_1$ Eyak *t^l'ihχ*, Athabaskan: Sarsi *gù-t^l'òwú*, Kutchin *t^l'o*, Chipewyan *t^l'òγ*, Dogrib *t^l'ó?*, Tlatskanai *t^{l}okwa*, Galice *t^l'uu*, Mattole *t^{l}oh*, Navajo *t^l'òh*.

113   GRASS$_2$ Haida *q'ɑn*, Proto-Athabaskan *k'ëŋ* 'withes.' [S34]

114   GREEN   Tlingit *s'ùw*, souk 'grass,' Athabaskan: Tututni *soh* 'blue,' Chasta Costa *ɬ-θo* 'blue,' Hupa *t^{s}ow'*, Mattole *-t^{s}ow*, Kato *-t^{s}oo*.

115   GUTS$_1$ Haida *qasan-ts'ang* 'brains' (= head-guts), Athabaskan: Sarsi *čá(n)*, Ingalik *-cání*, Galice *sāā* 'brains.'

116   GUTS$_2$ Haida *k'íits* 'belly,' *kēs*, Athabaskan: Kutchin *e-t^s'ig*, Carrier *-t^s'i*, Tsetsaut *ɛ-t^s'ē?*, Galice *č'iič'e?*, Hupa *č'eek^j'e?*, Navajo *č'íí?*.

117   HAIR   Haida *kow*, Tlingit *χàw*, Eyak *χu?* 'body hair,' Athabaskan: Tahltan *-γa?*, Chipewyan *-γá*, Tsetsaut *axa*, Galice *-wa?* ~ *-γaa*, Hupa *-wa?*, Kato *-ga?*, Navajo *-γàà?*, Lipan *-γàà*.

118   HAND   Haida *stlai* ~ *st^l'a* ~ *stlaih* ~ *slai*, Tlingit *tl'eeq* 'finger,' Athabaskan: Sarsi *-là?*, Tsetsaut *aɬa(?)*, Galice *-la?*, Navajo *-í-là?*. [P9]

119   HAT   Tlingit *sja:x^w*, Proto-Athabaskan *č'a*. [S79]

120   HE   Tlingit *iūtah* ~ *ū*, Athabaskan: Chasta Costa *yū* 'that one,' Mattole *yī*. [S27]

121   HEAD   Haida *ša*, Eyak *shi-shage* ~ *šāw*.

122   HEAR   Haida *gudáng* ~ *gūdɛñ*, Athabaskan: Sarsi *-t^s'á(n)*, Kutchin *tθ'eg*, Carrier *t^s'ai*, Hupa *-t^s'in*, Kato *-t^s'eg*, Navajo *t^s''íih*, *t^s'aŋ* 'listen,' Lipan *-t^s'àh*.

123 HEART Haida *tee-kuk* ~ *tek'ogo* ~ *k'úuk* ~ *kook*, Tlingit *téχ'* ~ *tēk'* ~ *teh-uk'h*, Athabaskan: Sarsi *dᶻàɣàní*, Kutchin *-dᶻⁱi*, Carrier *-dᶻi*, Galice *-siiyiʔ*, Kato *-jiiʔ*, Navajo *-jéí*, Lipan *-jíí*.

124 HEAVEN Haida *qwēs* ~ *kweeskun* ~ *kwai*, Tlingit *kuts* ~ *'haatz* ~ *kohs*, Eyak *koas*.

125 HEAVY Tlingit *dáɬ* ~ *dal*, Eyak *dās*, Athabaskan: Chipewyan *dáδ*, Tututni *das*, Hupa *das*, Navajo *ṅdāz*.

126 HEW Haida *tshool-tao* 'axe,' Tlingit *s'uw*, Athabaskan: Slave *tθéɬ*, Navajo *tˢēɬ* 'chop.'

127 HIDE₁ (v.) Haida *sʕál*, Tlingit *č'aɬ*.

128 HIDE₂ (v.) Tlingit *sīn*, Athabaskan: Galice *sīī*, Hupa *sən*. [S58]

129 HIT Haida *kwa*, Tlingit *gwaɬ*, Athabaskan: Hupa *waɬ*, Mattole *gāɬ*, Navajo *ɣàɬ* 'hit with a stick.'

130 HORTATORY Haida *-dja-ŋ*, Proto-Athabaskan *-dja*. [S13]

131 HOUSE Eyak *yahd*, Athabaskan: Ingalik *yax*, Chipewyan *yὲ*, Kato *ye*.

132 I Tlingit *hutt* ~ *khŭt*, Eyak *hŭtak*.

133 ICE₁ Haida *qaɬ* 'freeze,' *qalk* ~ *ɢal(ga)*, Tlingit *xatˡ* 'iceberg,' Athabaskan: Tlatskanai *kolo*.

134 ICE₂ Tlingit *t'iq'* ~ *t'ix'* 'ice, hard,' *t'ik* 'stiffen,' Eyak *t'itˢ'*, Athabaskan: Beaver *tsíl* 'snowdrift,' Hupa *tˡ'itˢ'*, Navajo *tˡ'ìz*, Kiowa Apache *tˡ'ìs*.

135 IN Haida *ɢei* 'into,' Tlingit *-ɢe:* 'inside of,' *-ɣi-k* 'inside,' Proto-Athabaskan *-ye*. [S93]

136 INSIDE Tlingit *daq* 'inland, shoreward,' Athabaskan: Slave *-t'á*, Dogrib *t'ah*.

137 INTRANSITIVIZER Haida *ta-*, Tlingit *da-*, Eyak *da-*, Proto-Athabaskan *-de-* (passive prefix). [P2]

138 ISLAND Tlingit *χ'at'* ~ *kat'h* ~ *gat-te*, Eyak *qāt* ~ *k'āt'*.

139 JUMP₁ Tlingit *t'àn*, Athabaskan: Tututni *-təm'*, Kato *tōŋ'*.

140 JUMP₂ Haida *tɬa*: 'dive,' Proto-Athabaskan *-ɬa*. [S41]

141 KICK Haida *tl'aa*, Tlingit *tseχ*, Eyak *taʔtˡ'*, Athabaskan: Tsetsaut *txa*.

142 KIDNEY Haida *čaē* ~ *cháay*, Athabaskan: Sarsi *ts'ùzá*, Chipewyan *εts'ɑsε*, Navajo *-časkazí*.

143 KILL₁ Tlingit *'in*, Athabaskan: Carrier *-ɣe*, Hare *-xe*, Galice *gīī*, Kato *gīŋ*, Mattole *giin*, Navajo *-ɣé*. [S23]

144 KILL₂ Tlingit *chŭkh* ~ *yeh-achuk*, Eyak *khŭkūvasheh*.

145 KNEE Eyak *ɢuhd*, Athabaskan: Sarsi *gūd* 'knee, elbow,' Kutchin *-gwod*, Chipewyan *tˢa-gwór-*, Tlatskanai *o'kwît*, Coquille *gʷad*, Hupa *got'*, Mattole *-gwoʔɬ*, Navajo *gòd*.

146   KNOW₁   Haida *'un-sēda* ~ *ʔun-sʔʌd*, Tlingit *k'ú* ~ *k'ven*, Athabaskan: Dogrib *žó*, Hare *žū̀*.

147   KNOW₂   Haida *'un-sēda* ~ *ʔun-sʔʌd*, Athabaskan: Galice *-tˢ'id*, Kato *tsət*, Mattole *ts'id*.

148   LAKE   Eyak *maa*, Athabaskan: Tsetsaut *mmē*.

149   LEFT   Tlingit *s'át'*, Athabaskan: Tsetsaut *xuts'ede'*.

150   LIE DOWN₁   Haida *wu-daa*, Proto-Athabaskan **daa*, Navajo *-dá* 'sit.' [P15]

151   LIE DOWN₂   Haida *tai* ~ *tay* ~ *tī*, Tlingit *t'a*, *-tii*, Proto-Eyak-Athabaskan **tee-ng*, Eyak *te*, Athabaskan: Sarsi *tí(n)*, Kutchin *či*, Carrier *ti*, Chipewyan *tì̃*, Hare *ti*, Galice *tī*, Kato *teen*, Wailaki *tiŋ*, Navajo *tí̃*. [S65, P14]

152   LIQUID   Haida *χao*, Proto-Athabaskan **-k'a* (liquid has position). [S28]

153   LIVER₁   Haida *tl'ak'ul*, Tlingit *tl'úɢù*, Athabaskan: Tsetsaut *aɬ'ɔq'*.

154   LIVER₂   Eyak *-sahd*, Athabaskan: Tanaina *zit'*, Tahltan *zid*, Beaver *zût'*, Sarsi *-zì̃ʔ*, Kutchin *ðàd*, Hupa *sit'*, Navajo *zìd*.

155   LONG   Haida *dzíng*, Proto-Athabaskan **ngee's*, Navajo *-neez*. [P7]

156   LOOK₁   Tlingit *t'iʔn* 'see,' Proto-Athabaskan **-t'e* 'look for,' **t'an* 'look.' [S63]

157   LOOK₂   Haida *qyahtsgat* 'look at,' Athabaskan: Galice *gaš*, Kato *gets* ~ *guš* 'look, see.'

158   LUNGS   Haida *kāgᴇn*, Tlingit *kyēgú̃* ~ *kègú*.

159   MAKE   Tlingit *sī*, Athabaskan: Tanaina *čin*, Koyukon *tsi(n)*, Ingalik *-tse(n)*, Chipewyan *-tsì* ~ *-tsī*, Hare *sì̃*, Chasta Costa *sī*, Mattole *čī*, Navajo *čí̃* ~ *čí*.

160   MAN₁   Haida *e-tliñga* ~ *i-ɬiŋa*, Tlingit *tl'inkit* 'people.'

161   MAN₂   Haida *tlal* ~ *t'al* ~ *tláal* ~ *tee-tlalh* 'husband,' Eyak *ɬilāʔ* ~ *lilia*.

162   MAN₃   Tlingit *qáh* ~ *qá* ~ *kah* ~ *ka*, Eyak *qaʔ* ~ *kha* 'husband.'

163   MANY   Haida *hlangáa* 'be plenty,' Tlingit *atlēn*, Athabaskan: Sarsi *-tˡā(n)*, Han *lē̃*, Carrier *ɬanɛ*, Tlatskanai *ɬán*, Kato *-ɬaŋ*, Navajo *lān*, Kiowa Apache *ɬá̃*.

164   MOSQUITO   Haida *tshī-kul-di-gwa* ~ *tsi-kul-toon*, Eyak *tˢ'iyux*, Athabaskan: Sarsi *tˢ'í*, Dogrib *tθ'íh*, Tsetsaut *tˢ'esdja*, Tlatskanai *tzīz* 'wasp,' Navajo *tˢ'í̃'ī*.

165   MOTHER₁   Eyak *amma*, Athabaskan: Navajo *má*, Kiowa Apache *má*.

166   MOTHER₂   Haida *ʔaw* ~ *aw* ~ *ao* ~ *āo* ~ *ow*, Eyak *-ʔehd* 'wife,' Athabaskan: Tlatskanai *o'át*, Galice *ʔah*, Navajo *-a'ā́d* 'wife.'

167 MOTHER₃ Tlingit *at-tlhee* ~ *ak'tlia* ~ *tˡa*, Athabaskan: Beaver *-łí* 'co-wife.'

168 MOTHER-IN-LAW Haida *djo:n*, Tlingit *č'a:n*, Proto-Athabaskan **-č'oŋ*. [S78]

169 MOUSE₁ Haida *kagan*, Tlingit *kαgαk'* ~ *kuGʌk*.

170 MOUSE₂ Eyak *tłútiyas*, Athabaskan: Sarsi *tˡòòná*, Chipewyan *tˡúnè*, Tsetsaut *łōná*, Hupa *lo?n*, Kato *łoon* 'rodent.'

171 MOUTH Eyak *sa?-d*, Athabaskan: Tanaina *zah*, Sarsi *-zò?*, Ingalik *-δod*, Kutchin *šεd*, Tsetsaut *asa?*, Hupa *-sa?*, Navajo *-zéé?*, Lipan *-zí?*.

172 MUCH Haida *łangáa* 'be much,' Proto-Athabaskan **łaang*, Navajo *łá*. [P6]

173 MUD₁ Haida *čān*, Eyak *tˢ'a?*, Athabaskan: Chipewyan *dzā̃* 'sediment,' Kato *djāŋ*, Navajo *čā̄'í* 'muddy.' [S14]

174 MUD₂ Haida *hlq'ut'uu* 'slime,' Tlingit *qótl'kw* ~ *k'otˡk'* ~ *χetˡ'* 'slime.'

175 NAIL Haida *kun* ~ *kwun* ~ *gun*, Athabaskan: Sarsi *-gán*, Chipewyan *-gànέ*, Hare *-gone*, Galice *-gwan-yu*, Navajo *-s-gàan*.

176 NAME Tlingit *sa* ~ *sα*, *sen* (v.), Eyak *vahsheh*, Athabaskan: Ahtena *zä*, Tahltan *u-zii*, Sarsi *í-zì?*, Slave *se-źi?*, Galice *-ši?*, Hupa *-uu-ši?*, Navajo *yí-ží*, Lipan *í-żìì?*.

177 NAPE Haida *ts'ekyē*, Athabaskan: Tsetsaut *ats'īχa* (borrowing?).

178 NARROW Eyak *tˢidᶻ*, Athabaskan: Chipewyan *č'ùδὲ*, Kato *sōs*, Navajo *ts'òs*.

179 NEAR Haida *aχan*, Tlingit *χan* 'proximity.'

180 NECK Haida *halh* ~ *χil* ~ *ħil* ~ *hil*, Tlingit *kahl-dukh* ~ *kalyatik*.

181 NEST Haida *hltálk*, Athabaskan: Sarsi *i-t'ú*, Chipewyan *εt'ok*, Tsetsaut *at'ɔ*, Navajo *t'oh*.

182 NEW Haida *tˡāga*, Tlingit *tˡakʷ*.

183 NIGHT₁ Haida *Gaał-gaa* 'be dark,' *ł-Gał* 'black,' Tlingit *Giit* 'become dark,' Eyak *χətˡ'*, Athabaskan: Sarsi *wīł*, Carrier *γeł*, Hupa *xātˡ'e*, Kato *kał'* 'night passes,' Chipewyan *xíł* 'darkness,' Navajo *di-ł-xił* 'black.' [S22, P21]

184 NIGHT₂ Tlingit *tāt* ~ *t'at'* ~ *tat* ~ *taht*, Athabaskan: Kutchin *taδ*, Chipewyan *təδ-ὲ*. [S66]

185 NOT Tlingit *ł*, Proto-Athabaskan **ł-* ~ *ła*. [S39]

186 OLD Tlingit *šàn* 'old person,' Athabaskan: Tlatskanai *sen* 'old man,' Navajo *sání* 'old' ("seems to be applied to men mostly."), *są̄* 'old age.' [S85]

187 ON₁ Tlingit *-k'a*, Proto-Athabaskan **k'a*. [S30]

188 ON₂ Tlingit *-q'* 'at,' Proto-Athabaskan **-k'e*. [S36]

189   ONE   Tlingit *tlex'* ~ *tlek* 'one,' Eyak *tleki* ~ *łíhɢ* ~ *tikhi*, Athabaskan: Kutchin *(ī-)łagə*, Tsetsaut *(ī-)łege*, Hupa *ła?*, Kiowa
Apache *łà?*. [S40]

190   PAIN   Eyak *k'ahd* ~ *k'a?d*, Athabaskan: Mattole *č'a-h* ~ *č'a-d*.

191   PAINT   Haida *k'otlaño* ~ *k'udlan* (v.), Tlingit *gwαł'*.

192   PENIS   Eyak *γə́čàq'* ~ *guč*, Athabaskan: Sarsi *γídzà?*, Galice
-iise?, Mattole *-ītse?*.

193   PERFECT   Haida *wu-* (perfect prefix), Tlingit *wu-* (perfect prefix).
[P15]

194   PERSON₁   Haida *na* 'live, house,' Tlingit *na* 'people,' Proto-Athabaskan *-ne* ~ *-n* 'person, people.' [S51]

195   PERSON₂   Haida *tōwī* 'people,' Eyak *tahūiū* 'people.'

196   PLAY   Haida *naŋ*, Proto-Athabaskan *-ne*. [S53]

197   PLURAL₁   Haida *-χa* (distributive suffix), Tlingit *-nα-χ* (distributive numeral suffix), Proto-Athabaskan *-k'e* (personal noun plural).
[S31]

198   PLURAL₂   Tlingit *-γε-n* (plural of kinship terms), Proto-Athabaskan *-yĕ* (personal noun plural). [S91]

199   PLURAL₃   Haida *-ɢu* ~ *-ɢo* ~ *-da-ɢu*, Tlingit *da-ɢa-*, Athabaskan:
Chiricahua *daa-* ~ *-gó* ~ *daa-gó*. [P1]

200   POSTPOSITION   Haida *-n* ~ *-ŋ*, Tlingit *-n* 'with,' Proto-Athabaskan *-n* ~ *-ŋ*. [S48]

201   POUND   Haida *taq'it*, Tlingit *t'εχ'*, *t'aq'* 'hit,' *tʌqł* 'hammer,'
Eyak *deq'* 'smack.'

202   PULL   Tlingit *yiš*, Athabaskan: Kato *yōs* 'lead, drag.'

203   PUS   Tlingit *qit'*, Eyak *χəs*, Athabaskan: Sarsi *γíz*, Navajo *xis*.

204   PUSH   Haida *-q'aa* 'push over,' Athabaskan: Tsetsaut *-qa* 'push
with a stick.'

205   QUICKLY   Haida *xao* 'do a thing quickly,' Proto-Athabaskan *χa-
ŋ*. [S84]

206   RABBIT   Eyak *ɢəχ*, Athabaskan: Slave *gah*, Tsetsaut *qax*, Tlatskanai *sqεx*, Navajo *ga?*.

207   RAW   Haida *taaw* 'raw food,' Eyak *t'ə̄-ɢ* 'raw,' Athabaskan: Chipewyan *t'ε*, Mattole *t'eeγ* 'raw meat,' Navajo *t'ǎ*.

208   RED₁   Tlingit *x'àn* ~ *k'han* ~ *kaan*, Eyak *q'a*, Athabaskan: Carrier *deł-k'en*.

209   RED₂   Eyak *č'ē?* 'turn red,' Athabaskan: Tlatskanai *ttsīs*, Wailaki
čii?, Mattole *-čiiĵ*, Navajo *-číí?*, Lipan *čís*.

210   RELATIVE CLAUSE SUFFIX   Tlingit *-γi*, Proto-Athabaskan *-ye*.
[S94]

211   RETURN   Haida *sdiihl*, Athabaskan: Galice *dał*.

212 RIB Tlingit *ts'oq* ~ *s'úkʷ* ~ *s'úgù*, Athabaskan: Beaver *čoñgɛʔ*, Chipewyan *ɛčã*, Tlatskanai *čãqe*, Navajo *-tsā̃*.

213 RING Haida *st'a* 'ring-shaped object,' Proto-Athabaskan **tsa* 'ring-like object.' [S73]

214 RIVER Tlingit *wat* 'mouth of river,' Athabaskan: Kato *kwōt* 'stream.'

215 ROAD Tlingit *dè*, Eyak *tā*, Athabaskan: Ingalik *tìnà*, Carrier *ti*, Tlatskanai *tɛn'é*, Coquille *tanee*, Hupa *tin*, Navajo *ʔà-tììn*.

216 ROAST Haida *kits'aá* 'roast on a stick,' Eyak *gis*.

217 RUB₁ Tlingit *t'us*, Proto-Athabaskan **-t'od*. [S72]

218 RUB₂ Haida *gūš* 'wipe,' Tlingit *x'ut'* ~ *x'aś* ~ *xas'* 'scratch, scrape,' Athabaskan: Wailaki *guts* ~ *gãs* 'scrape.'

219 RUN Haida *Ga:t*, Proto-Athabaskan **-ɣed*. [S21]

220 SALIVA Tlingit *tuχ* 'spit' (v.), Eyak *tux*, Athabaskan: Sarsi *zák'àʔ*, Kutchin *e-zʲig*, Umpqua *seek'eʔ*, Kato *šek'*, Navajo *šééʔ*.

221 SAY Tlingit *q'a*, Proto-Athabaskan **-'a* 'tell, sing,' Tutuni *ʔa* 'talk.' [S97]

222 SEA Haida *sī(s)* 'ocean,' Eyak *šī* 'creek, stream,' Athabaskan: Galice *siskãã* 'ocean.'

223 SEE Haida *qiŋ* ~ *qiñ* ~ *kain*, *qɛn* 'look,' Tlingit *Gen* ~ *Gin* 'look,' Athabaskan: Sarsi *ʔí(n)*, Han *ʔin*, Carrier *-ʔen*, Slave *-ʔì̃*, Galice *ʔī*, Hupa *-ʔiŋ*, Navajo *ʔí̃*. [S98]

224 SEW Haida *ħay* 'knit,' Tlingit *qa* ~ *q'a*, Athabaskan: Sarsi *kà̃ʔ(d)*, Galice *-kaʔ*, Kato *gat*, Mattole *kàʔɬ* ~ *kaʔd*, Navajo *kàd*, Jicarilla *kàʔ*, Kiowa Apache *kà*.

225 SHARPEN Haida *k'aa*, Tlingit *k'ats'* 'be sharp,' Athabaskan: Chipewyan *k'à* ~ *k'ã̃* ~ *k'a*, Chiricahua *kaš*. [S33]

226 SHIN Tlingit *χis'*, Eyak *xiʔtˢ'*.

227 SHOOT Tlingit *t'uk*, Proto-Athabaskan **-t'o*. [S71]

228 SHORE Tlingit *yàχ* ~ *'éq* 'beach,' Eyak *yəqt*.

229 SHORT Eyak *dik'* ~ *dək*, Athabaskan: Tututni *dəgʷ*.

230 SING₁ Haida *k'aju* ~ *k'atsao*, Eyak *kutzgi*.

231 SING₂ Tlingit *ší* ~ *sī* ~ *ši(n)* 'sing, song,' Eyak *tˢĩ*, Athabaskan: Tanaina *šen*, Galice *šan* 'song,' Navajo *sin*, Lipan *sĩ̀*. [S86]

232 SIT Eyak *da*, Athabaskan: Sarsi *dá*, Carrier *da*, Tsetsaut *da*, Galice *da*, Mattole *-daa*, Navajo *dá*.

233 SKIN Haida *q'aɬ*, Tlingit *χas'* ~ *xás'* 'fish scales,' Athabaskan: Sarsi *-kàɬ* 'hide,' Navajo *'akaɬ* 'leather.' [P17]

234 SMALL Haida *kut-soo* ~ *hūdzū*, Tlingit *k'atsku* ~ *akwatsku*, Eyak *kutˢ'* ~ *kuč'*, Athabaskan: Mattole *-k'ow'*.

235 SMELL   Haida sánjuu, Tlingit čαn 'stench,' Eyak čăh ~ čắʔ 'smell, stink,' Athabaskan: Galice šan ~ šắã̄, Kato čən, Mattole č'a, Navajo -č'ắ: 'stench.'

236 SMOKE   Eyak tɬắ't ~ ɬắhd, Athabaskan: Sarsi tɬʲī̆, Kutchin lade, Carrier ɬed, Hare lere, Tlatskanai ɬit, Tututni ɬəd, Galice ɬad, Navajo ɬìd.

237 SNAKE   Haida si-guh ~ si-ga, Athabaskan: Tsetsaut goʔ, Jicarilla gó.

238 SON   Haida gît ~ keet ~ kete, Tlingit git ~ geeth ~ yít' ~ yitik, Eyak qē, Athabaskan: Sarsi γá, Navajo γèʔ. [Cf. CHILD above.]

239 SON-IN-LAW   Haida qunaa ~ qone, Athabaskan: Galice -gandaa, Tlatskanai oxontáne.

240 SPEAK   Haida sota 'speak to,' -soot- ~ shoo, Tlingit sʌ̀tú 'voice,' Athabaskan: Navajo sād 'word.'

241 SPIDER   Haida q'utlsiaŋ, Tlingit qasist'an.

242 SPIRIT₁   Tlingit yék' ~ γe:k 'spirit, spirit helper,' 'iχt' 'shaman,' Proto-Athabaskan *ye 'supernatural being,' *-yĕn 'to practice shamanism,' Galice -yiiʔs 'spirit, breath.' [S92]

243 SPIRIT₂   Haida ɢan-aa 'be taboo,' s-ɢáan 'supernatural being,' Tlingit da-ɢan-qú 'hereafter,' Athabaskan: West Apache gaan 'supernatural being,' Chiricahua gã́-hé. [P18]

244 SQUIRREL   Haida gahlts'aakw ~ gɛtltsak, Tlingit tsʌlk, Eyak tsətɬk, Athabaskan: Galice salas, Kato slús 'ground squirrel,' Mattole čalis.

245 STAND   Haida gya ~ gyaraŋ ~ gyáa'ang, Tlingit gya, Athabaskan: Galice -giʔ, Mattole ge' 'get up.' [S87]

246 STEAL   Haida q'otlta ~ q'uhldáa ~ kolt ~ kwōl, Eyak č'uʔ, Athabaskan: Hupa čōt ~ čōl, Mattole čōd ~ čōh.

247 STEAM   Haida sil 'steam' (v.), Tlingit si:t 'cook' (v.), Proto-Athabaskan *sil 'steam' (n. & v.). [S59]

248 STEP (v.)   Haida t'a, Proto-Athabaskan *-t'es. [S70]

249 STICK   Haida t'asq' 'shaman's baton,' Tlingit t'ah ~ t'á 'board.'

250 STONE   Haida t'ees 'rock, ledge,' Tlingit teh ~ t'ɛ ~ tɛ́ 'rock, stone,' Eyak tˢā, Athabaskan: Tahltan tsê, Beaver tseh, Kutchin či, Carrier tθe, Tsetsaut tsɛ', Hupa tˢee, Navajo tˢé.

251 STRONG   Haida tlaats'gaa, Tlingit litsin, Eyak atliahŭkh, Athabaskan: Chipewyan tɬʲéδ, Galice -tɬʲaʔs, Kato ləts 'strong, rough.'

252 SUCK   Haida tl'án, Tlingit l'a.

253 SUN₁   Haida xai 'sunshine,' Tlingit -xaa-ts' 'be cloudless,' Proto-Eyak-Athabaskan *xwaa, Navajo shá. [P12]

254 SUN₂   Haida kūng, Tlingit kuk-kan ~ kakan ~ ɢagan ~ k'akan.

255 SWALLOW   Tlingit *kwač*, Athabaskan: Kato *kət*, Mattole *ked* ~ *keʻ*.

256 SWEEP   Haida *hlk'yaawdaa*, Athabaskan: Galice *tˢ'ad*.

257 SWIM₁   Haida *x'ak* 'swim under water,' Tlingit *q'aq* 'swim (of fish),' Athabaskan: Navajo *-kóóh*, Jicarilla *-kóh*.

258 SWIM₂   Eyak *we*, Athabaskan: Kutchin *-vi*, Carrier *-bih*, Tsetsaut *bɛ*, Kato *-be*, Mattole *-bee*.

259 TAIL   Haida *sk'yaaw*, Tlingit *kuwú* 'bird's tail,' Eyak *k'ugutˡ'ah*.

260 TAKE   Haida *sáldaa* 'borrow,' Tlingit *šɑt'*. [S4]

261 TEAR (v.)   Tlingit *s'eɬ'*, Athabaskan: Tsetsaut *ts'ɛ* ~ *tsɛ*.

262 TELL   Tlingit *nîk* ~ *nikʻ*, Athabaskan: Kato *nək* 'relate,' Navajo *-nih*. [S52]

263 TESTICLE   Eyak *dl-tsā*, Athabaskan: Hupa *-šaoʔ*, Wailaki *čōk*, Navajo *-čo'*.

264 THAT₁   Haida *hao*, Tlingit *he* 'this,' Proto-Athabaskan *hai*. [S25]

265 THAT₂   Haida *wa-*, Tlingit *we*, Proto-Athabaskan *mĕ* 'he, it.' [S45]

266 THAT₃   Haida *gu* 'there,' Tlingit *yu* 'that yonder,' Proto-Athabaskan *yo* 'that yonder.' [S95]

267 THEY   Tlingit *hass* ~ *ass*, Eyak *ashanū*. [S26]

268 THIGH   Haida *tíl*, Tlingit *ts'ēyu* 'calf,' Athabaskan: Sarsi *-tì* 'calf.'

269 THIN₁   Haida *t'ɑmdju*, Athabaskan: Chipewyan *t'ànɛ̀*, Navajo *t'āhi*.

270 THIN₂   Haida *ts'iyaa* 'thin person,' Athabaskan: Chipewyan *ts'ɛ̀*, Mattole *č'ix*.

271 THINK   Tlingit *ji*, Athabaskan: Sarsi *zìin*, Chipewyan *δī*, Coquille *san*, Hupa *siŋ(ʔ)*, Mattole *sii(ʔ)n*, Navajo *zìn*.

272 THIS₁   Haida *a-*, Tlingit *a-*, Proto-Athabaskan *a-*. [S1]

273 THIS₂   Haida *dei* 'just that way,' Tlingit *de* 'now,' Proto-Athabaskan *di*. [S12]

274 THIS₃   Haida *gai* 'this, that, the,' Tlingit *ya*, Proto-Athabaskan *ye-* 'that,' *y-* 'he.' [S89]

275 THORN   Eyak *χūʔš* 'thorns, sliver,' Athabaskan: Sarsi *xūs*, Chipewyan *xòs*, Navajo *xòš*.

276 THREAD   Haida *gy'etlao*, Eyak *q'əǰ* 'ribbon.'

277 THUMB   Haida *sli-k'use*, Tlingit *ka-kūsh* ~ *guš*.

278 THUNDER   Haida *hii-lang* ~ *hī-ling-a* ~ *he-lun*, Tlingit *xetˡ* ~ *heh'tl*, Athabaskan: Mattole *leʻ* ~ *liɣ*.

279 TIE₁   Haida *tˢ'atˢ'as'*, Athabaskan: Koyukon *sos* 'knot,' Chipewyan *šás* 'knot,' Hare *šáʔ* 'knot,' Navajo *-žaš*.

280 TIE₂   Eyak *χehɬ* 'tie up,' Athabaskan: Galice *geɬ* 'tie up.'

281 TIE₃ Eyak *tˡ'i*, Athabaskan: Chiricahua *tˡ'ó*.

282 TIE₄ Haida *tˢ'u*, Proto-Athabaskan *-tˢ'os* ~ *-tˢ'es*. [S37]

283 TO Haida *-da*, Tlingit *-t* ~ *-dε*, Proto-Athabaskan *-d* ~ *-dĕ*. [S5]

284 TOMORROW Tlingit *suk-kan* ~ *seh-kann*, Athabaskan: Chipewyan *k'ǎní*.

285 TOOTH Haida *q'u-* 'with the teeth,' Tlingit *'úx* ~ *ka-ogh* ~ *ka-
och*, Eyak *χuu-ɬ*, Proto-Athabaskan *χwuu'*, Tahltan *γuʔ*, Sarsi
-γòòʔ, Carrier *-γu*, Tsetsaut *εxoʔ*, Tlatskanai *o'o*, Hupa *-woʔ*, Mattole *-γwoʔ*, Navajo *-γòòʔ*. [S24, P10]

286 TOUCH Tlingit *ni* 'put,' Proto-Athabaskan *-ni*. [S54]

287 TOWARD Haida *gua* ~ *gui*, Proto-Athabaskan *-go*. [S16]

288 TREE Haida *qíit*, *qēt* 'spruce,' Tlingit *k'ε* 'log.'

289 TURN Tlingit *t'ix'* 'twist,' Eyak *taʔk'* 'twist.'

290 UMBILICAL₁ Haida *χil'* ~ *sgíl* ~ *skil*, Tlingit *kóutl* ~ *kùɬ*.

291 UMBILICAL₂ Tlingit *t'an* ~ *tànu*, Eyak *ts'a'* ~ *tˢ'āʔ*, Athabaskan:
Sarsi *ts'ak'àʔ*, Hupa *ts'eek*, Navajo *ts'ééʔ*.

292 UNDER Tlingit *yì*, Athabaskan: Kato *-ye*. [S90]

293 URINE Haida *tsεgεñ* 'urinate,' Eyak *tˢeʔq'*.

294 VAGINA Haida *čúu*, Athabaskan: Sarsi *dzŭz*, Tsetsaut *εdju*
'vulva,' Galice *ǰoš*, Navajo *ǰóž*.

295 VEIN₁ Haida *kassu*, Eyak *k'uʔt'* 'vein, tendon, sinew,' Athabaskan:
Hupa *ky'ots'* 'sinew,' Navajo *ts'òòs* 'vein, nerve.'

296 VEIN₂ Tlingit *tít'i*, Athabaskan: Tahltan *-č'ide*, Hare *č'íré*, Navajo
tˢ'ìd 'sinew.'

297 WALK Haida *qáa* ~ *qa*, Athabaskan: Kato *qal* ~ *qaɬ*. [S96]

298 WASP Haida *sral*, Athabaskan: Tsetsaut *tsrāmaʔ*.

299 WATER₁ Haida *sū* ~ *súu* ~ *shoo* 'lake,' Athabaskan: Sarsi *tú*,
Carrier *tuu*, Slave *tuʔ*, Tlatskanai *tū*, Galice *tuu*, Hupa *too*, Mattole
toʔ, Navajo *tó*.

300 WATER₂ Haida *ʃan-tˡ* 'water, river,' Tlingit *hain* ~ *hin* 'water,
river,' Eyak *ʔā̃* 'river.'

301 WATER₃ Haida *tʌñ* 'sea water,' Eyak *tã* ~ *t'ã* 'waves,' Athabaskan: Galice *ta-*. [S61]

302 WAX₁ Haida *gyáa* 'tallow,' Tlingit *k'uχu* 'pitch,' Eyak *gahɢ*
'pitch.'

303 WAX₂ Eyak *sīhχ* 'resin,' Athabaskan: Sarsi *dzàh* 'pitch,' Chipewyan *dzέ* 'gum,' Tsetsaut *tsε'* 'pitch,' Galice *seh* 'pitch, gum,'
Hupa *džeh* 'pitch,' Navajo *ǰēh* 'pitch.'

304 WE₁ Tlingit *gigwann* ~ *yehwenn* 'you,' Eyak *khūinkhan*, Athabaskan: Tanana *xweni*, Hare *naxeni*, Tsetsaut *daxɔne*, Wailaki *nehiŋ*,
Lipan *nàhí*.

305 WE₂ Haida *iitl'* 'us,' Proto-Athabaskan *-ii'd* (< *-iit'*), Navajo *-iid-*. [P4]

306 WET₁ Haida *tl'akdaa* 'soak,' Tlingit *tˡ'ak'*, Eyak *ɬq'ú* 'become damp.'

307 WET₂ Haida *t'iɬ* 'wet on surface,' Athabaskan: Kato *čəl* ~ *čəɬ*, Mattole *čil* ~ *čēl*.

308 WHAT₁ Haida *gōsu* ~ *guus*, Tlingit *kusu* ~ *gùsú* ~ *gù*.

309 WHAT₂ Tlingit *da:*, Proto-Athabaskan *da*. [S6]

310 WHEN Haida *dlu*, Athabaskan: Slave *ʔɛdláú*.

311 WHERE Haida *tl'aan*, Athabaskan: Chipewyan *ʔɛdlīni*.

312 WIND Eyak *k'uy*, Athabaskan: Ahtena *ɬ-ts'ih*, Sarsi *-tˢ'ī*, Kato *-čii*, Navajo *ńɬ-č'ī*.

313 WISH Haida *sdahláa* ~ *sdaɬʌ* 'wish, want,' Athabaskan: Galice *taɬ*.

314 WITH Haida *-eeɬ* ~ *-áɬ* ~ *-ɬ*, Tlingit *-(ii)n*, Proto-Athabaskan *-ɬ*, Navajo *-(i)ɬ*. [S38, P3]

315 WOLF Haida *ʕúuts* ~ *hūts* ~ *hōdz*, Tlingit *kūtsh* ~ *k'utsch* ~ *kūdsh*, Eyak *kuutschi*.

316 WOMAN Haida *jáadaa* ~ *jat*, Tlingit *šát* 'wife,' Eyak *syet* ~ *syot*, Athabaskan: Navajo *'as-dzání*. [P8]

317 WOOD₁ Haida *q'aw*, Tlingit *χaw* 'log,' Eyak *q'aʔ* 'bushes.'

318 WOOD₂ Haida *tsan-oo* ~ *tshano*, Athabaskan: Kutchin *də-čan*, Chipewyan *dɛ̀-čìn*, Galice *čan*, Mattole *čʲiŋ*, Navajo *tˢìn*, Lipan *-tˢīī*.

319 WORM Haida *k'áam* 'bug,' Eyak *ɢəma*.

320 YELLOW Haida *kun-tlulh* ~ *q'an-hlahliaa*, Tlingit *tˡ'atˡ'*.

321 YESTERDAY₁ Haida *ta-gha*, Tlingit *tʌtgέ* ~ *tat-keh*.

322 YESTERDAY₂ Haida *utahl* ~ *adahl* ~ *tahtla-lees-ta*, Eyak *tlehatl*.

323 YOU Haida *dalɛñ* ~ *daláng*, *t'alɛñgua* 'we,' Athabaskan: Tlatskanai *ɬan*.

324 YOUNG Tlingit *yís*, Athabaskan: Kato *yašts*.

REFERENCES

Goddard, Pliny E. 1920. "Has Tlingit a Genetic Relation to Athapaskan?," *International Journal of American Linguistics* 1: 266–79.

Greenberg, Joseph H. 1981. "Comparative Na-Dene Notebook," ms.

———. 1987. *Language in the Americas*. Stanford, Calif.

Krauss, Michael E. 1979. "Na-Dene and Eskimo-Aleut," in Lyle Campbell and Marianne Mithun, eds., *The Languages of Native America*. Austin, Tex., 803–901.

Levine, Robert D. 1979. "Haida and Na-Dene: A New Look at the Evidence," *International Journal of American Linguistics* 45: 157–70.

Nikolaev, Sergei L. 1991. "Sino-Caucasian Languages in America," in Shevoroshkin, ed., 1991: 42–66.

Pinnow, Heinz-Jürgen. 1990. *Die Na-Dene-Sprachen im Lichte der Greenberg-Klassifikation*. Nortorf, Germany.

Sapir, Edward. 1915. "The Na-Dene Languages: A Preliminary Report," *American Anthropologist* 17: 534–58.

Shevoroshkin, Vitaly, ed. 1991. *Dene-Sino-Caucasian Languages*. Bochum, Germany.

6

Is Algonquian Amerind?

*It seemed and still seems to me that
the general cumulative evidence presented
is so strong and that many of the specific
elements compared are so startlingly similar
that no reasonable doubt could be entertained
of the validity of the claim.*

—Edward Sapir (1915)

When Edward Sapir, in 1913, announced his brilliant discovery that Wiyot
and Yurok—two seemingly isolated languages on the Northern California
coast—were related to the widespread Algonquian family that extended from
the Great Plains to the Atlantic seaboard, he initiated a debate that is as
fiercely argued today as it was then. The central question was *how* one could
prove that a group of languages (or language families) were related, that they
shared a common ancestor. In support of his hypothesis Sapir presented a
fairly extensive list of grammatical and lexical similarities, including his *pièce
de résistance*, virtual identity in the pronominal prefixes used to indicate the
first-person, second-person, third-person, and indefinite possessor (i.e. 'somebody's, a').[1] After laying out the evidence for these four prefixes in Algonquian, Wiyot, and Yurok, Sapir concluded: "I fail to see how any ingenuities
of mere 'accident' could bring about such perfect accord in use and form of
possessive pronominal elements" (1913: 622). Sapir's colleague and friend Alfred Kroeber, who had himself earlier in the year discovered (with Roland
Dixon) the Penutian and Hokan families, was equally impressed with Sapir's
evidence, writing him on July 30, 1913: "The pronouns turn the trick, alone,

---

[1] These are presently reconstructed for Proto-Algonquian as *ne- 'my,' *ke- 'your,' *we-
'his,' *me- 'a' (see Goddard 1975: 251).

but the rest looks good" (quoted in Golla 1984: 112). The material available on Wiyot and Yurok at this time was scanty, and Sapir did not expect that every etymological connection he proposed would stand up to scrutiny; he did, however, firmly believe that he had proved his case: "I am well aware of the probability that a considerable number of my lexical and morphological parallels will, on maturer knowledge, have to be thrown out of court; I cannot hope to have always hit the nail on the head. However, even if we eliminate fifty per cent. of our cognates as errors of judgment (doubtless far too great a sacrifice to caution) we are still confronted with no fewer than one hundred or more reasonably close analogies in stems and morphological elements" (1913: 639).

THE ATTACK ON SAPIR

The task of judging the validity of Sapir's hypothesis fell to the leading Algonquianist of the day, Truman Michelson, the son of the first American Nobel Laureate, Albert A. Michelson, who received the Nobel prize in physics in 1907. After receiving a Ph.D. in Indo-European philology from Harvard in 1904, Michelson spent the rest of his life studying the Algonquian family. Michelson could hardly avoid expressing an opinion on this quite unexpected, and seemingly improbable, relationship, and indeed he recognized that "the importance of this discovery, if valid, can hardly be overestimated" (1914: 362). Nevertheless, he dismissed Sapir's putative cognates as "fancied lexicographical similarities"; he criticized Sapir for comparing "different morphological elements"; he asserted that what few resemblances remained were simply "accidental"; and he concluded that "[e]nough has been said to show the utter folly of haphazard comparisons unless we have a thorough knowledge of the morphological structure of the languages concerned" (1914: 362, 365, 366, 367). His conclusion was so harsh and "invidious" (Haas 1958: 161) that the Algonquian-Ritwan relationship (Ritwan = Wiyot + Yurok) came to be considered, by the academic community at large, an unresolved taxonomic puzzle.

Sapir and Kroeber never wavered in their conviction that Wiyot and Yurok were indeed cousins of Algonquian. In an exchange of letters following the appearance of Michelson's rebuttal (Golla 1984: 151–54), Sapir wrote to Kroeber: "His [Michelson's] narrowness of outlook . . . is quite apparent . . . I am particularly surprised to see that he makes such an excessive use of what I would consider purely negative evidence." Kroeber was even less impressed with Michelson's arguments: "Michelson's review strikes me as puritanical. I have never had any doubt of the validity of your union of Wiyot and Yurok with Algonkin. . . . I hardly consider it worth while seriously to refute

Michelson. His attitude speaks for itself as hypercritical and negative. . . . I regard the case in point so one-sided as to be already conclusively settled." As other, similar disputes over genetic affinity arose (e.g. Hokan, Penutian, Na-Dene), there quickly developed two opposing camps. On the one side were scholars such as Kroeber and Sapir who interpreted lexical and grammatical similarities as evidence of genetic relationship. On the other side were men such as Michelson, Pliny Goddard, and Franz Boas who attributed these perceived resemblances to misanalysis, borrowing, and chance. We might call the former Geneticists and the latter Diffusionists. Both camps survive to the present day.

A MODERN PERSPECTIVE

When one reads the Sapir-Michelson confrontation today, one can hardly fail to be struck by two things. First, the case that Sapir presented was simply overwhelming. And second, whatever talents Michelson may have had as an Algonquianist—and these apparently were considerable—he had little understanding of basic taxonomic principles, and the vast majority of his objections to Sapir's hypothesis were irrelevant. In fact, most of his rebuttal was taken up with listing ways in which Wiyot and Yurok differed from Algonquian, as if this negative evidence could somehow offset the positive evidence that Sapir had offered! Nonetheless, Michelson's reputation was such that his denial alone was sufficient to prevent the general acceptance of Sapir's proposal. There can be no doubt that had Michelson given his approval *there would never have been a controversy at all.* But in the face of his vigorous, if ill-conceived, dissent, outsiders were understandably hesitant to question him, loath to overrule an expert on his home ground.

There the question stood until, in the early 1950's, Joseph Greenberg, fresh from his landmark classification of African languages, reexamined the controversy. He found that the real puzzle was not whether Wiyot and Yurok were related to Algonquian, but why there was any doubt about it: "[E]ven a cursory investigation of the celebrated 'disputed' cases, such as Athabaskan-Tlingit-Haida and Algonkin-Wiyot-Yurok, indicates that these relationships are not very distant ones and, indeed, are evident on inspection" (1953: 283). In 1958, with new fieldwork on both Wiyot and Yurok at her disposal, Mary Haas examined the alleged relationship, and pronounced herself "in agreement with Greenberg's remarks about this relationship."[2] Thus, by the end of the

---

[2] Haas 1958: 160. This article is often incorrectly interpreted as the conclusive proof that Sapir was right about Algonquian-Ritwan: cf. Campbell and Mithun (1979: 26): "a relationship controversial at the time, but subsequently demonstrated" and Goddard (1975: 249): "At present, however, largely as a result of new data provided by recent fieldwork on Wiyot and Yurok, scholars are in general agreement that the daring hypothesis of Sapir

1950's, with all the experts now on one side of the debate—Sapir's side—
the rest of the linguistic community was quite willing to let this pseudo-
controversy die the quiet death it had for so long deserved.

But if this particular dispute was resolved, the underlying disagreement between the Geneticists and the Diffusionists remained practically untouched.
And, ironically, it was the Diffusionists who came to dominate Amerindian linguistics, Sapir's successes in argumentation notwithstanding. The one scholar
who might have counterbalanced this unfortunate swing of the pendulum,
Morris Swadesh (a brilliant linguist and student of Sapir), was effectively
banished to Mexico for political reasons, where he died in 1967. With the
Diffusionists firmly in control of the Amerindian establishment, a series of
conferences was held at which the proposed higher-level groupings of Kroeber
and Sapir were dismantled, one by one, until the list of independent families
in North America approached what it had been at the start of this century.
Seen from this perspective (see Campbell and Mithun 1979), Sapir's lone sur-
viving success would be the Algonquian-Ritwan grouping. Almost all of his
other proposals were abandoned, and the field settled into a great array of
specialist preoccupations.

THE ATTACK ON GREENBERG

The calm was broken in 1987 by the appearance of Greenberg's classification of New World languages, the result of some thirty years of research
and the compilation of the most extensive Native American wordlists ever
assembled. Greenberg's proposal that all the languages of the Western Hemisphere belonged to one of three phyla (Eskimo-Aleut, Na-Dene, or Amerind)
was so at variance with the prevailing Diffusionist climate that it immediately
provoked a firestorm of criticism from one Diffusionist after another, each
reminiscent of Michelson's attack on Sapir. Even before Greenberg's book
was published—and without seeing the evidence it contained—Lyle Campbell called for Greenberg's classification to be "shouted down" (1986: 488).
A year later Campbell wrote: "In light of this disregard for the work in the
American field, it is indeed surprising that a publisher of the calibre of Stanford Press agreed to publish [*Language in the Americas*]; it is tempting to
speculate that this would not have been possible if the book did not bear

---

is, indeed, correct." Haas herself, by seconding Greenberg's conclusion on the obvious
nature of the relationship, shows that she considered the matter to have been already
settled—presumably by Sapir in 1913. Moreover, she explicitly states that "my purpose in
preparing the present paper is to give the evidence not given by others in support of the
Algonquian-Ritwan affiliation" (p. 160). See also Haas (1966) for further discussion of the
Sapir-Michelson controversy.

G[reenberg]'s name. A scholar of lesser renown would not have been permitted to slight the canons of scholarship in this way" (1987; quoted from *Mother Tongue* 5: 22). Terrence Kaufman criticized Greenberg for "comparing words whose morphemic make-up he does not understand," for not "hold[ing] back on the task until accurate and extensive data are available," and for "avowed values [that] are subversive and should be explicitly argued against."[3] Wallace Chafe saw Greenberg's "book as a random collection of chance resemblances and resemblances due to diffusion indiscriminately mixed with some that do reflect the common origins of some subsets of these languages" (1987: 653). Victor Golla, after first endorsing the accuracy and usefulness of Greenberg's book,[4] changed his mind a year later, for reasons unknown. In a thoroughly negative review Golla concluded that "[v]ery little of this [Greenberg's classification] will be taken seriously by most scholars in the field" (1988: 435), primarily because Greenberg's proposed etymologies do not observe regular phonological correspondences. That Greenberg devoted the first chapter of his book to just this question Golla fails to mention. William Bright warned potential readers of the book that "most scholars in native American comparative linguistics regard Greenberg's methodology as unsound" (1988: 440). Finally, Ives Goddard, like Michelson an Algonquianist with a Ph.D. from Harvard and effectively holding Michelson's "chair" at the Smithsonian Institution,[5] dismissed Greenberg's book as a worthless conglomeration of "[e]rrors in the Algonquian data, . . . incorrect or unsupported meanings, . . . incorrect analyses, . . . chance [resemblances], . . . [and] unacknowledged segmentations. . . . [Greenberg's] technique excludes historical linguistic analysis . . . [and] is so flawed that the equations it generates do not require any historical explanation, and his data are unreliable as a basis for further work" (1987a: 656–57). Worse, Goddard attributed Greenberg's errors not simply to carelessness, haste, or incompetence, but to dishonesty: "Greenberg makes often unacknowledged segmentations that are not based on grammatical analysis but merely serve to make the forms being equated seem more similar than they really are. . . . Such distortions are an integral part of Greenberg's technique" (1987a: 657). Thus, the charges leveled against Green-

---

[3] Kaufman 1990: 16, 63. Inasmuch as Greenberg was almost 72 at the time his book was published—over three decades after he had first announced his classification—one can only wonder just how long Kaufman expected Greenberg to "hold back."

[4] "I do not mean to challenge its fundamental accuracy. Greenberg has provided us with a useful survey of lexical similarities among the languages of the Americas on a scale far beyond anything previously attempted. His identification of common 'Amerind' elements uniting all American Indian languages with the exclusion of Na-Dene and Eskimo-Aleut will be a lasting contribution to American Indian linguistics" (Golla 1987: 658).

[5] Michelson worked for the Bureau of American Ethnology in Washington, D.C.

berg's Amerind hypothesis are effectively a resurrection of those directed at Sapir's Algonquian-Ritwan hypothesis: misanalysis, undetected borrowings, and chance resemblances, with a dose of *ad hominem* invective in the bargain.

AN ANALYSIS OF THE ATTACK ON GREENBERG

Whatever its virtues or failings, an assault of this breadth and character carries an air of verisimilitude, and history demands that its particulars be examined. As one of the principal instruments in the assault, Goddard's two-page review of *Language in the Americas* bears closer scrutiny. One of his charges is that because Greenberg's work is based on linguistic data from *contemporary* languages,[6] it cannot tell us anything about linguistic prehistory; the resemblances Greenberg notes are just as likely to result from accidental convergence as from common origin. Goddard also claims that "[i]n a proper etymology every divergence must be explained by a postulated change consistent with a complete historical hypothesis" (1987a: 657) and, furthermore, "[w]here grammatical elements are etymologized it is necessary to present an hypothesis about the system of which they are a part in its entirety" (1975: 255). This pronouncement (already doubtful, on its face) did not, however, prevent Goddard from "etymologizing" an intercalated *-t-* for Proto-Algonquian-Ritwan with no hypothesis whatsoever about its historical source: "In Algonquian and Wiyot vowel-initial non-dependent nouns insert a -t- after the [pronominal] prefixes: Fox *ahkohkwa* 'kettle,' *netahkohkwa* 'my kettle'" (with *ne-* plus *-t-*); Wiyot *íʔl* 'intestines,' *dutíʔl* 'my intestines' (with *du-* and *-t-*)" (1975: 252).

Now if one artificially limits one's perspective to the Algonquian-Ritwan family, then the historical source of this mysterious *-t-* is indeed obscure. And it is precisely in such cases that the broader context of the Amerind phylum, with its greater chronological depth, can clarify unresolved issues. In his extensive discussion of the origin and development of the Amerind pronominal system Greenberg adduces evidence from eight of Amerind's eleven basic subgroups for a demonstrative/third-person pronoun whose original form was probably **ti* or **ta* (1987: 44-48, 281-83). From the perspective of his already classic study of the origin of gender markers (1978: 47-82), Greenberg then surveys the development of this demonstrative element throughout the Amerind family. In some branches the original demonstrative meaning is preserved, either exclusively (e.g. Macro-Tucanoan) or in part (e.g. Andean, Macro-Carib, Macro-Panoan). In other branches the demonstrative has developed into a third-person pronoun (e.g. Macro-Panoan, Macro-Ge,

---

[6] This is not true. Greenberg also used reconstructed forms, where they exist; the sources of these are listed on p. 181 of his book.

Andean, Penutian) or relative pronoun (e.g. Macro-Panoan). In Macro-Ge
and Macro-Panoan it has also developed into a marker of the masculine gender. Finally, in its semantically most eroded form, it occurs in Hokan and
Algonquian-Ritwan reduced to a Stage III article, that is, a mere marker of
nominality. What is particularly striking is that in Hokan and Macro-Carib,
as in Algonquian-Ritwan, this element occurs only before stems beginning
with a vowel (e.g., in Carib, Pemon *i-paruči* 'his, her sister' vs. *i-t-enna* 'his,
her hand'). Greenberg explains this apparent anomaly as a consequence of an
originally ergative pronoun system in Amerind. Proto-Amerind contained two
sets of pronouns, an *ergative* set used as the subject of a transitive verb (and
in nominal possession, e.g. 'my foot'), and an *objective* set used as the subject
of an intransitive verb or object of a transitive verb (and in nominal predica-
tion, e.g. 'I am a man'). In Proto-Amerind the ergative third-person pronoun
was *t, while the objective third-person pronoun was *i.[7] In a number of
cases, when the ergative system broke down, what had originally been morphologically conditioned variants of an ergative system became phonologically
conditioned. At a later date this irregularity was ironed out by the addition
of the "regular" pronoun *i to all stems, leading to the anomalous distribution of *t* in the Pemon example above. From the deeper perspective of the
Amerind phylum, idiosyncratic—and synchronically unmotivated—elements
such as the mysterious Algonquian intercalated *-t- can be explained by the
action of well-attested diachronic processes. Such integration of typological
pattern with diachronic process is one of Greenberg's many contributions to
general linguistics.

Goddard's reluctance to consider the broader Amerind context should come
as no surprise, since he has already shown a predilection for maintaining
the status quo against historical reality, even within the Algonquian family.
When Leonard Bloomfield reconstructed Proto-Algonquian in 1925 he posited
a proto-segment *θ to account for an alternation between *t* and *n* in the four
languages he considered. In a later work (1946: 87), Bloomfield gave the enig-
matic gloss "an unvoiced interdental or lateral?" to describe this segment.
But in his survey of comparative Algonquian, Goddard concluded that "[i]t
is hard to see what testable consequences the assumption of one or the other
phonetic value for *θ would have . . . and this small point of uncertainty may
be allowed to remain" (1979: 73). Other Algonquianists,[8] however, have argued persuasively that there *are* testable consequences, and that both internal
and external evidence points to an original voiceless lateral fricative *ł, not
the totally improbable *θ. This is but one example of the narrow-mindedness

---

[7] The extensive distribution of this formative in the Amerind phylum is discussed by
Greenberg on pp. 279-81.

[8] Siebert 1975, Picard 1984, Proulx 1984.

that has characterized Algonquianists from Michelson to Goddard, and that has been duly criticized by Paul Proulx:

Some reluctance to revise PA [Proto-Algonquian] reconstructions on the basis of Algic data is understandable: PA is familiar territory and generally seems securely reconstructed. In contrast, Proto-Algic is very unfamiliar and may seem speculative. But all linguistic reconstructions, including PA, are biased toward the present. It is precisely archaic features in the protolanguage which are the most difficult to reconstruct, and it is here that a deeper time level is invaluable. The reluctance to use Proto-Algic in Algonquian studies must be overcome, for many of the most recalcitrant problems of Algonquian will be understood in no other way. [1984: 205]

But far from using Greenberg's book to inform his own field of study, Goddard's sole purpose, both in his review and in his public lecture (1987a,b), has been to attempt to discredit Greenberg's tripartite classification of the languages of the New World, and in particular to deny that the Algic family (Algonquian + Wiyot + Yurok) has any known relatives. The claim is thus the same as Michelson's, except that Goddard is willing to accept another two languages, Wiyot and Yurok, into the family. Goddard attacks Greenberg's classification by a series of criteria, each of which supposedly "invalidates" a certain number of the 2,000 etymologies Greenberg offered in support of Amerind and its subgroups. He restricts his attention to the 142 lexical etymologies in which Algonquian forms are cited; the *grammatical* support for Amerind—to which Greenberg devotes an entire chapter—is not mentioned. In light of Goddard's claim that "it is virtually impossible to prove a distant genetic relationship on the basis of lexical comparisons alone" (1975: 255), it is puzzling that he should choose to examine the evidence he finds least persuasive, and to totally ignore the grammatical evidence on which he puts so much weight. In any event, of the 142 lexical cognate sets involving Algonquian, Goddard is able to invalidate, by his criteria, all but 35. The significance of the remaining 35 etymologies, which stand up to Goddard's most rigorous methodology (but are not explicitly identified), is not discussed. But it is in fact more illuminating to examine those etymologies that Goddard claims to have invalidated, that we might better understand how his techniques work.

According to Goddard, errors in the Algonquian data invalidate 93 of the etymologies, the largest source of disqualification (34) being cases where Greenberg has cited unrelated Algonquian forms. Goddard gives four examples of etymologies he eliminates by this criterion, and examining one of the four here should prove instructive. In Amerind etymology No. 238 (SMELL$_1$), Greenberg includes three of Bloomfield's Proto-Central Algonquian reconstructions: *mat*, *mat^{s}i* 'smell'; *mi:s*, *mit* 'excrement'; and *mači* 'bad.' Goddard objects that *mat* 'bad' and *mi:t* 'defecate' are etymologically unrelated, and hence the Amerind etymology is invalid. But if Bloomfield's three roots *are* etymologically distinct, then Greenberg has simply mixed together two distinct roots, in which case the etymology should be broken up into two separate etymologies, not done away with altogether. (*Croisement de racines* is not exactly an unknown phenomenon in etymological dictionaries!) In the case at hand the etymology is apparently restricted to the three branches of Northern Amerind—Almosan-Keresiouan, Penutian, and Hokan—and thus constitutes one of the pieces of evidence for this higher-level grouping. The original meaning, SMELL BAD/STINK, is preserved either exclusively or in part in all three subgroups of Northern Amerind. In Hokan the meaning is uniformly STINK or SMELL; in Penutian and Almosan-Keresiouan, forms with the meanings DIRTY and BAD are cited alongside others meaning STINK or SMELL. All three branches suggest an original form containing three consonants, *M-T-K, the second of which has been assibilated to t^s, č, s, or š in quite a few languages, no doubt under the influence of a following palatal vowel that is preserved in some of the languages. Thus a form such as *MATIK would constitute a reasonable hypothesis for the original phonetic shape, and such a form is virtually identical with the attested Shasta form *(ku-)matik'(-ik)* 'it stinks.' The presence of either a glottal stop or glottalized consonant is also characteristic of the root in question, but its original locus is hard to pinpoint. Taken all in all, the thirty forms cited in the etymology are sufficiently similar in sound and meaning that few linguists would be so rash as to reject the entire etymology. One may quibble over certain parts of an etymology, but such loose ends, particularly in a pioneering work like Greenberg's, hardly invalidate the core of the etymology.

Goddard's second criterion invalidates 21 etymologies that involve Blackfoot but no other Algonquian language. By his lights, such roots cannot be reconstructed for Proto-Algonquian and hence are not available for comparison further afield. In fact Blackfoot is, by Goddard's own admission, the most divergent Algonquian language, and the fact that it should have preserved certain roots that have been lost in the rest of the family is therefore not only not surprising, but exactly what one should expect. From *within* Algonquian, of course, it is impossible to tell which of these Blackfoot roots are innovations that serve to define Blackfoot as a distinct genetic group, and which are inheritances from Proto-Algonquian that have been lost elsewhere in the family. That distinction cannot be made without considering Algonquian *in a wider context,* as Greenberg has done, using the method known in biological taxonomy as out-group comparison. But instead of recognizing that Greenberg's methodology of multilateral comparison has revealed certain Blackfoot roots that must also have existed in Proto-Algonquian, even though they have left no trace elsewhere in the family, Goddard uses the isolated nature of the Blackfoot form to dismiss the entire etymology. A more egregious *non sequitur* one can scarcely imagine.

Just how silly Goddard's "methodology" is can be demonstrated by another example. One of the pieces of evidence that Sapir adduced in 1913 to connect Algonquian with Wiyot and Yurok was the resemblance of Blackfoot *(mo-)kíts(-is)* 'finger' and Wiyot *(mo-)kèc* 'fingers.' Sapir was so impressed by this correspondence that he mentioned it in a letter to Kroeber even before his article had appeared, with the comment: "Are these 'accidents'? Fiddlesticks!" (Golla 1984: 120). To Sapir's comparison Greenberg added the Yurok form *(cey-)ketew* '(little) finger,' as well as Salish forms such as Squamish *čis* 'hand.' Goddard rejects the entire etymology, and many other cogent etymologies, simply because the form in question cannot be reconstructed for Proto-Algonquian. For Goddard, such striking lexical resemblances are mere coincidences not requiring historical explanation. But were we to accept his methodology, we could no longer compare even Wiyot *kƚæl-* 'to ask' with Kutenai *akƚeƚ* 'to ask,' because the former cannot be reconstructed for Proto-Algic. For Goddard, then, Greenberg's book is simply one remarkable coincidence after another, all without historical import. Also coincidental must be the high degree of correlation between linguistic taxa and biological taxa, including an Amerind group distinct from the rest of the world's populations.[9] Perhaps coincidental as well is the fact that a statistical analysis of the distribution of Greenberg's Amerind etymologies produces a subgrouping and mapping of the eleven Amerind subgroups that are highly plausible on geographical grounds (see Ruhlen 1991).

The example above is symptomatic of the many erroneous methodological pronouncements that Goddard proffers in his review of Greenberg's book. He also instructs us that "even stricter guidelines are obviously necessary in proposing comparisons between languages whose relationship is in question" (1987a: 657). Again, he claims that "[h]istorical method requires that the facts of each subgroup or family be established separately before being compared with each other. Hence, while Algonquian **neθk-* ['arm, hand'] and Northern Iroquoian *nētsh* ['arm'] may properly be compared, if desired, forms descended from these may not" (1987: 657). First, this proclamation is not true; and second, it violates the very point that Goddard is trying to make. Surely he does not believe that each branch of Indo-European was established separately before being compared with other branches. And why is he comparing *Northern* Iroquoian with *Algonquian*? Both of these are intermediate nodes (Algonquian under Algic and Northern Iroquoian under Iroquoian), precisely the sort of elements he claims cannot be compared! Had he claimed that only

---

[9] See Cavalli-Sforza et al. 1988. The Diffusionist position has always been associated with the belief, expressed by Campbell (1986: 488), that "there is no deterministic connection between language and gene pools." Geneticists, such as Trombetti (1905: 55), have long realized that "agreement between language and race is the rule. Disagreement is the exception."

Algic can be compared with Iroquoian, at least the illustration of his principle would have been aptly selected, even if the principle itself were not. How
he *should* be proceeding has been lucidly explained by Proulx: "When both
PA [Proto-Algonquian] and Proto-Algic forms are reconstructed from a single
pair of cognates (e.g. Menominee and Yurok), the PA reconstruction is *not*
logically prior to the Proto-Algic one. The attested forms are constants, the
reconstructed ones interdependent variables. . . . [T]he reconstructed forms
are not evidence for each other; both depend on the attested ones. The data
are scantier in such cases than in most, but this is only a matter of degree"
(1984: 167).

Goddard dismisses other etymologies in *Language in the Americas* for a
variety of reasons, some as trivial as the misidentification of a language. No
doubt he has uncovered some flaws in Greenberg's Algonquian data, as any
specialist would in a work of this breadth, but in no case can these imper-
fections alone be taken as invalidating an entire etymology. An interesting
example is Amerind etymology No. 85 (DIRTY), which Goddard rejects for
its "looseness" under the criterion of semantic similarity. The meanings he
cites from this etymology—'excrement', 'night,' and 'grass'—do seem an unusual combination, and their conjunction provoked a tittering in the audience
at his lecture. But an examination of the whole etymology reveals quite a
different story. First of all we find, contrary to Goddard's semantic character-
ization, that this etymology is not about feces, but about color, specifically the
area of the spectrum encompassing black and green. In Almosan the meaning is uniformly BLACK and, as we shall see, the distribution of the various
meanings throughout North and South America suggests that this was the
original meaning. Keresiouan shows both DARK IN COLOR (Iroquoian) and
GREEN (Keresan). In Penutian the meaning has shifted completely to GREEN
and its close semantic connections GRASS and BLUE; the original meaning of
BLACK/DARK is not attested. In South America, Macro-Tucanoan preserves
the original meaning of BLACK in Proto-Ge *tɨk, but in Cayapo and Chiquito the meaning has shifted to DIRTY. Finally, in the Equatorial group the
meaning is uniformly EXCREMENT. Phonetically, the original form was probably similar to Chiquito *tuki*, though Penutian and Almosan forms raise the
possibility that one of the consonants was originally an ejective. Paralleling
Penutian's semantic divergence (BLACK > GREEN) is the presence of a reduplicated stem in the Plateau, California, and Mexican subgroups (e.g. North
Sahaptin *tˢəktˢək*, Rumsien *čuktuk*, Zoque *tˢuhtˢuh*.[10]

---

[10] Campbell (1988: 600) also criticizes Greenberg's etymologies as "quite permissive in
semantic latitude. Semantic equations such as the following are not convincing: 'excrement/
night/grass,' . . . . And these are only some of G[reenberg]'s unconvincing semantic
equations."

We can see now how Goddard's analysis proceeds. By failing to mention the fundamental meaning of an etymology, and citing only semantic extensions from this unnamed core, he makes it appear that Greenberg has combined meanings in an arbitrary and capricious fashion. When the whole etymology is examined, however, Goddard's shabby trick is revealed, and the semantic cohesiveness of the entire etymology can hardly be doubted. In resorting to such tactics, Goddard simply reveals the weakness of his own position.

THE VERDICT

In many respects the Diffusionist critique has remained constant from Michelson to Goddard, its chief ingredients being a list of errors (real or imagined), an allusion to accidental resemblances and borrowings, a willful disregard of the most convincing positive points, a dose of taxonomic non-sense, and often an appeal to authority. The current crop of Diffusionists seldom fails to mention "how far outside the mainstream Greenberg's work lies" (Golla 1988: 434) or that "most scholars in native American comparative linguistics regard Greenberg's methodology as unsound" (Bright 1988: 440). Both statements are of course true, but that they *are* true is irrelevant to the truth or falsity of Greenberg's claims. When his work in African classification appeared, almost four decades ago, it was just as far outside the mainstream. And in retrospect it should not be surprising that the foremost Bantuist of the day, Malcolm Guthrie, vehemently rejected Greenberg's proposal that the Bantu family was a relatively minor branch in a larger Niger-Congo family. Though an expert in some family would seem to be in the best position to judge whether or not that family is related to some other family, in practice such experts are often the least receptive to new relationships, as the examples of Michelson, Guthrie, and Goddard demonstrate. Similarly, Indo-Europeanists (with a few notable exceptions) are notorious for their dogmatic denial that Indo-European has any known relatives, a position held despite the overwhelming evidence to the contrary adduced by the Nostratic school and others. At the turn of the century Henry Sweet characterized the narrow-mindedness of Indo-Europeanists in terms that apply equally well to today's Diffusionists:

In philology, as in all branches of knowledge, it is the specialist who most strenuously opposes any attempt to widen the field of his methods. Hence the advocate of affinity between the Aryan [= Indo-European] and the Finnish [= Finno-Ugric] languages need not be alarmed when he hears that the majority of Aryan philologists reject the hypothesis. In many cases this rejection merely means that our specialist has his hands full already, and shrinks from learning a new set of languages. . . . Even when this passively agnostic attitude develops into aggressive antagonism, it is generally little more than the expression of mere prejudice against dethroning

Aryan from its proud isolation and affiliating it to the languages of yellow races; or want of imagination and power of realizing an earlier morphological stage of Aryan; or, lastly, that conservatism and caution which would rather miss a brilliant discovery than run the risk of having mistakes exposed. [1901: *vi*]

The most telling datum favoring the Amerind phylum was discovered independently by several different scholars, including Trombetti, Sapir, Swadesh, and Greenberg.[11] They all noticed that first-person *n-* and second-person *m-* seemed to characterize American Indian languages from Canada to the tip of South America. Since these two pronouns are known to be among the most stable items in language (see Dolgopolsky 1964), and are rarely borrowed, their broad distribution throughout the New World, as impossible to overlook as a herd of buffalo, has always constituted an inescapable problem for the Diffusionists. Boas attributed the prevalence of these two pronouns in Amerindian languages to "obscure psychological causes"; today's Diffusionists call them "Pan-Americanisms."[12] Both terms are simply euphemisms for the proscribed word "cognate"; for the Diffusionists, cognates exist only within homogeneous low-level groups like Algonquian, Siouan, and Salish. For apparent cognates between distantly related groups, almost any explanation, no matter how implausible, is seemingly to be preferred to the simple and obvious explanation of common origin.[13] Thus, Bright proposes that "Pan-Americanisms" arose in Asia through borrowing among different Amerind groups *before these distinct groups migrated to the New World:*

I would not be opposed to a hypothesis that the majority of the recognized genetic families of American Indian languages must have had relationships of multilingualism and intense linguistic diffusion during a remote period of time, perhaps in the age when they were crossing the Bering Straits from Siberia to Alaska. We can imagine that the so-called pan-Americanisms in American Indian languages, which have attracted so much attention from "super-groupers" like Greenberg, may have originated in that period. [1984: 25]

Such a scenario would have required a traffic controller at the Bering land bridge, checking the would-be immigrants for the proper "Pan-Americanisms" before admitting them to the New World.

In sum, the evidence that Greenberg adduces for the Amerind phylum is at least as strong as that offered by Sapir for Algonquian-Ritwan, and consid-

---

[11] See Ruhlen 1987 for a discussion of this point.

[12] They really should be called "Pan-Amerindisms" since they usually exclude Na-Dene and Eskimo-Aleut. The fact that the Amerind phylum occupies so much of North and South America has so far permitted the Diffusionists to perpetrate this linguistic sleight of hand unchallenged.

[13] Cf. Campbell (1988: 597): "those similarities which may *possibly* [my emphasis] have an explanation other than common ancestry must be set aside."

erably stronger than the evidence Greenberg presented for his African classification, *now universally accepted.* The Amerind phylum is well-defined and
amply supported; its validity as a linguistic taxon is firmly established; and in
time *Language in the Americas* will be hailed as a monumental achievement.
The outrageously vituperative attack on the Amerind phylum by the Diffusionists reflects their blind prejudice, their basic ignorance of the fundamental
principles of genetic classification, and perhaps, understandably, an apprehen-
sion of redirected research. Appeals to authority and group solidarity cannot
save the Diffusionist position, which, after almost a century of dominance in
Amerindian comparative linguistics, is finally fading into the night.

REFERENCES

Bloomfield, Leonard. 1946. "Algonquian," in Harry Hoijer, ed., *Linguistic
Structures of Native America.* New York, 85–129.

Bright, William. 1984. *American Indian Linguistics and Literature.* Berlin.

———. 1988. Review of *Language in the Americas*, by Joseph H. Greenberg,
American Reference Books Annual 23: 440.

Campbell, Lyle. 1986. "Comment," on an article by Joseph H. Greenberg,
Christy G. Turner, and Stephen L. Zegura, *Current Anthropology* 27: 488.

———. 1987. Public lecture at Stanford University, July 30.

———. 1988. Review of *Language in the Americas*, by Joseph H. Greenberg,
Language 64: 591–615.

Campbell, Lyle, and Marianne Mithun, eds. 1979. *The Languages of Native
America.* Austin, Tex.

———. 1988. Letter to *Mother Tongue* 5: 21–23.

Cavalli-Sforza, L. L., Alberto Piazza, Paolo Menozzi, and Joanna Mountain.
1988. "Reconstruction of Human Evolution: Bringing Together Genetic,
Archeological and Linguistic Data," *Proceedings of the National Academy
of Sciences* 85: 6002–6.

Chafe, Wallace. 1987. Review of *Language in the Americas*, by Joseph H.
Greenberg, *Current Anthropology* 28: 652–53.

Dolgopolsky, Aron B. 1964. "Gipoteza drevnejšego rodstva jazykovyx semei
severnoj Eurasii s verojatnostnoj točki zrenija," *Voprosy Jazykoznanija* 2:
53–63. [English translation in Vitalij V. Shevoroshkin and T. L. Markey,
eds., *Typology, Relationship and Time*, 1986. Ann Arbor, Mich., 27–50]

Goddard, Ives. 1975. "Algonquian, Wiyot, and Yurok: Proving a Distant
Genetic Relationship," in M. Dale Kinkade, Kenneth L. Hale, and Oswald
Werner, eds., *Linguistics and Anthropology: In Honor of C. F. Voegelin.*
Lisse, Netherlands, 249–62.

——. 1979. "Comparative Algonquian," in Lyle Campbell and Marianne Mithun, eds., *The Languages of Native America*. Austin, Tex., 70–132.

——. 1987a. Review of *Language in the Americas*, by Joseph H. Greenberg, *Current Anthropology* 28: 656–57.

——. 1987b. Public lecture at Stanford University, July 30.

Golla, Victor, ed. 1984. *The Sapir-Kroeber Correspondence*. Berkeley, Calif.

——. 1987. Review of *Language in the Americas*, by Joseph H. Greenberg, *Current Anthropology* 28: 657–59.

——. 1988. Review of *Language in the Americas*, by Joseph H. Greenberg, *American Anthropologist* 90: 434–35.

Greenberg, Joseph H. 1953. "Historical Linguistics and Unwritten Languages," in A. L. Kroeber, ed., *Anthropology Today*. Chicago, 265–86.

——. 1978. "How Does a Language Acquire Gender Markers?," in Joseph H. Greenberg, Charles A. Ferguson, and Edith Moravcsik, eds., *Universals of Human Language*. Stanford, Calif., Volume 3: 47–82.

——. 1987. *Language in the Americas*. Stanford, Calif.

Haas, Mary R. 1958. "Algonkian-Ritwan: The End of a Controversy," *International Journal of American Linguistics* 24: 159–73.

——. 1966. "Wiyot-Yurok-Algonkian and Problems of Comparative Algonkian," *International Journal of American Linguistics* 32: 101–7.

Kaufman, Terrence. 1990. "Language History in South America: What We Know and How to Know More," in Doris L. Payne, ed., *Amazonian Linguistics*. Austin, Tex., 13–73.

Michelson, Truman. 1914. "Two Alleged Algonquian Languages of California," *American Anthropologist* 16: 361–67.

Picard, Marc. 1984. "On the Naturalness of Algonquian *ɬ*," *International Journal of American Linguistics* 50: 424–37.

Proulx, Paul. 1984. "Proto-Algic I: Phonological Sketch," *International Journal of American Linguistics* 50: 165–207.

Ruhlen, Merritt. 1987. *A Guide to the World's Languages*, Vol. 1: Classification. Stanford, Calif.

——. 1991. "The Amerind Phylum and the Prehistory of the New World," in Sydney M. Lamb and E. Douglas Mitchell, eds., *Sprung from Some Common Source: Investigations into the Prehistory of Languages*. Stanford, Calif., 328–50.

——. 1992. "The Origin of Language: Retrospective and Prospective," Chapter 13 of this volume. [Russian version in *Voprosy Jazykoznanija* 1 (1991): 5–19.]

Sapir, Edward. 1913. "Wiyot and Yurok, Algonkin Languages of California," *American Anthropologist* 15: 617–646.

———. 1915. "Algonkin Languages of California: A Reply," *American Anthropologist* 17: 188–94.

Siebert, Frank T., Jr. 1975. "Resurrecting Virginia Algonquian from the Dead: The Reconstituted and Historical Phonology of Powhatan," in James M. Crawford, ed., *Studies in Southeastern Indian Languages.* Athens, Georgia, 285–453.

Sweet, Henry. 1901. *The History of Language.* London.

Trombetti, Alfredo. 1905. *L'unità d'origine del linguaggio.* Bologna.

7

A Semantic Index to Greenberg's Amerind Etymologies

In *Language in the Americas* (1987) Joseph Greenberg presented over 2,000 etymologies in support of the Amerind family and its eleven subgroups. Each etymology was identified by an English gloss, but no comparable phonetic gloss was given. Since it is useful to have both a semantic gloss and a phonetic gloss in identifying an etymology, I first added phonetic glosses to all the etymologies and then alphabetized this semantic index. The index allows one to see at a glance which phonetic shapes are associated with which meanings in the Amerind family. Consideration of this list has led me to conclude that in a fair number of cases Greenberg should have combined etymologies from different Amerind subgroups into additional, more comprehensive Amerind etymologies (see Chapter 8 of the present volume).

This chapter presents, then, a complete semantic index to the 2,003 Amerind etymologies contained in Greenberg's book. Each entry consists of (1) a semantic gloss, (2) a phonetic gloss, and (3) the etymology number. For grammatical etymologies the distribution of the etymology is also indicated. In addition, some suggestions of possible overlap or further consolidation are indicated after certain etymology numbers. The following abbreviations are used: A: Amerind, AK: Almosan-Keresiouan, P: Penutian, H: Hokan, CA: Central Amerind, CP: Chibchan-Paezan, AN: Andean, E: Equatorial, MT: Macro-Tucanoan, MG: Macro-Ge, MP: Macro-Panoan, MC: Macro-Carib, G: grammar section (in Chapter 5 of Greenberg). For Amerind etymologies (i.e.

those etymologies that include at least two Amerind subgroups) the semantic gloss is given in boldface type; etymologies restricted to one Amerind subgroup are given in plain roman type. For example, "ASK *kɫal* AK10" means that Greenberg's tenth Almosan-Keresiouan etymology associates the meaning 'ask' with the phonetic form *kɫal*; "**ANGRY** *iri* A4" indicates that Amerind etymology No. 4 associates the meaning 'angry' with the phonetic form *iri*; and "AUNT *pan* AN9; =CA1; =MP63" means that Andean etymology No. 9 associates the meaning 'aunt' with the phonetic form *pan*, and furthermore that this particular sound/meaning relationship is similar to that posited by Greenberg for Central Amerind etymology No. 1 and Macro-Panoan etymology No. 63. Finally, "ACCUSATIVE *s* G42 [P]" means that Greenberg's grammatical etymology No. 42 (in his Chapter 5) is an accusative marker *s* that appears to be restricted to the Penutian branch of Amerind. The subscripts on the meaning glosses may seem, at first sight, confusing. For example, for the gloss DANCE, two entries have no subscript, three have the subscript 1, and three have the subscript 2. This is, however, simply a reflection of the fact that different branches of Amerind have different words for DANCE, and some branches have more than one.

The index follows:

ABLE, TO BE   *nako*   AK1
ABLE, TO BE   *tama*   P1
ABLE, TO BE   *wan*   MP1
ABOVE   *hawi*   H1
ABOVE   *kalu*   CP1; =A147
ABOVE   *lal*   P2
ABOVE   *meme*   E1; =A148
ABOVE₁   *itai*   A1
ABOVE₂   *apak*   A2; cf. MT66
ABOVE₃   *araka*   A3
ACCUSATIVE   *s*   G42 [P]
ADJECTIVAL   *ki*   G66 [A]
ADJECTIVAL   *m*   G67 [H]
ALL   *pota*   MG1; =E78
ALL   *pu*   H2; =E79
ALL₁   *kape*   AK2
ALL₁   *kuš*   P3; cf. AK4
ALL₁   *pilo*   AN1
ALL₁   *tina*   E2
ALL₂   *auk^w*   AK3
ALL₂   *muma*   P4

ALL₂   *pa*   AN2; cf. P86
ALL₂   *taki*   E3
ALL₃   *k^wet*   AK4; cf. P3
ALL₃   *mal*   P5
ALLATIVE   *be*   G50 [MP]
ALLATIVE   *ki*   G45 [A]
ALLATIVE   *le*   G51 [MP]
ANGRY   *ka?*   P6
ANGRY   *iri*   A4
ANGRY   *xut*   AN3
ANIMAL   *aka*   H3
ANIMAL   *sikok*   MP2
ANSWER   *kama*   MP3
ANSWER   *nek*   AK5
ANT   *bohu*   CP2
ANT   *putu*   MG2
ANT   *tenu*   MC1
ANT₁   *tai*   A5
ANT₁   *tapu*   E4
ANT₂   *mani*   E5
ANT₂   *tˢakon*   A6

ANUS *kote* AN4; =CP3
ANUS *kut^{s}o* CP3; =AN4
ANUS *wexa* MP4
ARM *kwala* CP4; cf. H5
ARM *nanu* E6
ARM *pala* AN5
ARM *take* MT1
ARM *wasi* P7; =AN53
ARM₁ *kin* AK6
ARM₁ *lak* H4
ARM₁ *pok* A7; =MT46; =P214
ARM₂ *galu* H5; cf. CP4
ARM₂ *nak* AK7; =A8
ARM₂ *nok'o* A8; =AK7
ARMPIT *dama* H6
ARRIVE *nes* AK8
ARRIVE *pi* A9; =CP34; =MC24; =MG115
ARRIVE *wal* P8; =H49
ARROW *kani* CP5
ARROW *kawi* AK9
ARROW *mã* A10
ARROW *nuk* P9; =E113
ARROW *pan* MG3
ARROW *sawa* H7
ARROW₁ *ajaku* AN6
ARROW₂ *el* AN7
ASHES *auxe* AN8; =H61
ASHES *nuka* MT2
ASHES *pot* P10
ASHES *puli/pok* A11; =P58
ASHES *tap* H8
ASK *kɫal* AK10
ASK₁ *mat^{s}a* A12
ASK₂ *tempa* A13
AUNT *(i)nan* A14; =MP46
AUNT *manku* CP6
AUNT *mut* H9
AUNT *pan* AN9; =CA1; =MP63
AUNT *pan* CA1; =AN9; =MP63

AUNT *teke* MT3
AUNT *toje* MG4
AWAKE *nom* MP5
AWAKE₁ *tenga* CP7
AWAKE₂ *kup* CP8
AXE *boko* CP9
BACK *išak* AN10
BACK *pani* MG5; =CP14
BACK *puka* MP6
BACK *wak* P11
BACK *čepa* E7
BACK₁ *čom* H10
BACK₁ (n.) *iki* A15
BACK₂ *maki* H11; =CP190
BACK₂.(n.) *kana* A16; =AK6; =CP4
BACK (N.) *tan* CA2
BAD *ašia* AK11
BAD *boxe* E8
BAD *kat* P12
BAD *pat^s* CP10
BAD *čepa* AN11
BAD *čoj* MP7
BAD₁ *kalen* A17
BAD₂ *čaka* A18
BARK (SKIN) *ko* CA3
BARK (SKIN) *kuri* MT4
BARK (SKIN) *pai* MG6; =AN102
BARK (SKIN) *pel* A19
BARK (SKIN) *šu* P13; =H130; =MT81
BAT *jo* MT5
BAT *kasi* MP8; =A190; =AK130
BAT *t^{s}ikt^{s}ik* AN12; cf. AK22
BATHE *ama* AN13
BATHE *oka* CP11; =P269
BATHE *puk* A20; =H157; =MP59; =AK77
BATHE *wã* AK12
BE *hi* MP9; cf. AK13

BE   *ke*   AN14; =H128; =AK171;
  cf. P217
BE   *ʔi*   AK13; cf. MP9
BE₁   *upi*   A21
BE₂   *(a)t'a*   A22
BEAR₁ (N.)   *maki*   AK15
BEAR₂ (N.)   *nume*   AK16
BEAR (V.)   *kat*   H12
BEAR (V.)   *koj*   MP10
BEAR (V.)   *mate*   E9
BEAR (V.)   *to*   CP12
BEAR (V.)   *wij*   AK14
BEAR (v.)   *ʔa*   A23
BEARD   *amu*   AN15
BEARD₁   *p'oti*   A24; =A108;
  =CA45; =E42
BEARD₂   *tuk*   A25
BEAT   *pok*   P14; =CA47
BEAUTIFUL   *k'ača*   AN16; =AN48
BEAUTIFUL   *kali*   P15; =MC2;
  =AK88; =H75
BEAUTIFUL   *kule*   MC2; =P15;
  =AK88; =H75
BEAUTIFUL   *noa*   MT6
BEAUTIFUL₁   *pai*   MG7; =CP86
BEAUTIFUL₂   *pati*   MG8
BEAVER   *mek*   AK17
BEE   *iko*   MT7
BEE   *wali*   CP13
BEE₁   *pana*   A26
BEE₂   *mumu*   A27; =MG117;
  cf. AK79
BEFORE   *nahi*   MP11
BEGIN   *ka*   AK18
BEHIND   *(a)pi*   A28
BEHIND   *ino*   AK19; =E110
BEHIND   *mina*   H13
BEHIND   *mow*   MC3
BEHIND   *pene*   CP14; =MG5
BELLY   *bi*   CP15; =CA9

BELLY   *kuax*   H14
BELLY   *nion*   MG9; =MT18
BELLY   *sehi*   CA4; =AK33
BELLY₁   *kata*   E10; =A29
BELLY₁   *kate*   A29; =E10
BELLY₁   *taʔča*   AK20; =A59;
  =H24
BELLY₂   *ika*   E11
BELLY₂   *naki*   AK21
BELLY₂   *palin*   A30; =AK43
BELLY₃   *mat*   A31
BELLY₄   *to*   A32
BIRD   *kaču*   AN17
BIRD   *tˢuri*   CP16
BIRD   *tu*   CA5
BIRD₁   *mila*   MT8
BIRD₁   *tˢitˢipe*   AK22; cf. AN12
BIRD₂   *iki*   MT9; cf. P84
BIRD₂   *riʔt*   AK23
BITE   *era*   CP17
BITE   *esa*   E12
BITE   *k'am*   AK24
BITE   *kašʌt*   P16
BITE   *pro*   MG10
BITE₁   *kua*   A33
BITE₂   *tak*   A34
BITTER   *koro*   MG11
BITTER   *saken*   AK25
BITTER₁   *paska*   A35; =MP58
BITTER₂   *tˢah*   A36
BLACK   *him*   MG12
BLACK   *kata*   P17; cf. A200;
  cf. AN27
BLACK   *mai*   H15
BLACK   *mekoro*   MC4
BLACK   *tuni*   MT10; cf. CP19
BLACK₁   *pol*   A37; =CP18
BLACK₁   *pola*   CP18; =A37
BLACK₁   *sinka*   E13
BLACK₂   *k'ara*   A38

BLACK₂ *ko* E14
BLACK₂ *turi* CP19; cf. MT10
BLACK₃ *sakua* E15; =A85
BLACK₃ *tu* A39; ?=A85
BLADDER *koro* E16
BLOOD *akuat* H16
BLOOD *aru* CP20
BLOOD *ku* MG13
BLOOD *unaka* AN18
BLOOD *wo* MP12; =E18
BLOOD₁ *ira* E17
BLOOD₁ *konia* MT11
BLOOD₁ *pile* A40
BLOOD₁ *potˢik* P18; =AK157
BLOOD₂ *deu* MT12
BLOOD₂ *meʔi* A41
BLOOD₂ *wi* E18; =MP12
BLOOD₂ *ʔati* P19
BLOOM *pak* P20; =AK78
BLOW *pusuk* H17; =A42; =AK26
BLOW *puti* A42; =AK26; =H17
BLOW *pōta* AK26; =A42; =H17
BODY *jaʔ* AK27
BODY *kakua* CP21
BODY *mata* H18; =A185
BODY *tap* MP13
BODY *wal* P21
BODY₁ *piʔ* A43; =MT13
BODY₁ *upi* MT13; =A43
BODY₂ *ime* A44
BODY₂ *paka* MT14
BOIL *ise* CP22
BOIL *mokʷ* AK28; =A73
BOIL *saʔ* CA6
BOIL *tˡok* A45; =AK206
BOIL₁ *mul* H19; =H26
BOIL₁ *šoxt* P22
BOIL₂ *kok* P23; =MT23
BOIL₂ *pot* H20
BONE *ija* H21

BONE *kuk* MG14
BONE *t'umak* AK29
BONE *ta(n)ku* E19
BONE *uino* MT15
BONE₁ *tui* A46; cf. MG58
BONE₁ *čote* CP23
BONE₂ *dita* CP24
BONE₂ *tiaki* A47
BONE₃ *ipi* A48
BOW (N.) *poko* MT16; =A157
BOW (N.) *taku* MC5
BOY *očo* CP25
BOY *puč* P24
BOY *tu* CA7
BOY *wila* AN19
BRANCH *polo* MC6
BREAD₁ *čene* H22
BREAD₂ *las* H23
BREAK *k'at'i* A49; =MP20;
  =MG70
BREAK *peto* E20
BREAK *pok* MP14
BREAK *tʰa* CA8
BREAK₁ *tepa* AK30
BREAK₂ *tak* AK31; =A149
BREAST *k'amin* A50
BREAST *maku* AN20
BREAST *mana* MC7
BREAST *neme* MP15
BREAST *pin* CA9; =MT17;
  =CP15
BREAST₁ *atˢiki* H24; =A59;
  =AK20
BREAST₁ *puen* MT17; =CA9;
  =CP15
BREAST₁ *tali* AK32; =CP30;
  =CP131
BREAST₁ *ču* P25; =H25; =P107;
  =CP98
BREAST₂ *muš* P26

BREAST₂ *nano* MT18; =MG9
BREAST₂ *ʔiču* H25; =P25;
　=P107; =CP98
BREAST₂ *si* AK33; =CA4
BREATHE *ake* MG15
BRING *mana* MT19
BRING *tuk* A51
BRING₁ *u* P27
BRING₂ *mah* P28
BRING₃ *iki* P29
BROAD *paki* AK34
BROAD *patˡa* A52
BROAD *tape* P30
BROAD *wanka* E21
BROTHER *azot* AN21
BROTHER *kani* MP16; =AN101
BROTHER *pali* E22
BROTHER *papi* A53
BROTHER *sin* CP26
BROTHER *tat* AK35
BROTHER₁ *ton* MG16
BROTHER₂ *kejak* MG17
BROTHER (OLDER) *akti* P31
BUFFALO *kun* CA10
BURN *huli* P32; =P78
BURN *hõi* MT20
BURN *konia* AN22
BURN *koʔ* CA11; =AK37
BURN *pok* MG18; =CP105;
　=CP109
BURN *tuke* A54; =A251;
　=AK108; cf. P285
BURN₁ *mali* H26; =H19
BURN₁ *tapi* E23
BURN₁ *ton* AK36
BURN₁ *tuli* CP27
BURN₂ *k'o* AK37; =CA11
BURN₂ *kara* E24
BURN₂ *pi* H27
BURN₂ *čipa* CP28

BURY *ake* CP29
BURY *ja* CA12
BURY *muke* P33
BUTTOCKS *teli* MC8
BUTTOCKS₁ *tuxki* AK38
BUTTOCKS₂ *ũse* AK39
BUY *taw* AK40; =CA13
BUY *te* CA13; =AK40
CALF *ila* E25
CALL *jat* AK41
CALL *kai* MG19
CALL₁ *(a)nik* A55
CALL₂ *pai* A56
CARRY *neku* AK42
CARRY₁ *apa* A57
CARRY₂ *ko(n)* A58
CAUSATIVE *atu* G92 [A]
CAUSATIVE *ma* G93 [A]
CAUSATIVE *n* G95 [P]
CAUSATIVE *s* G94 [AK]
CHEEK *al* P34
CHEEK *mone* MT21
CHEEK *pako* MC9; =H28
CHEEK *poke* H28; =MC9
CHEST *p'ala* AK43; =A30
CHEST *pekua* MC10; cf. CP170
CHEST *tala* CP30; =CP131;
　=AK32
CHEST *tomin* P35
CHEST *tuki* A59; =H24; =AK20
CHEW *kan* A60
CHEW *peki* CP31
CHIEF *peru* E26
CHILD *ksi* AK44; =P88; =H29;
　=A281
CHILD *kuto* H29; =P88; =AK44;
　=A281
CHILD₁ *(a)nu* A61; =MP57
CHILD₁ *saka* P36
CHILD₂ *kil* P37˙

CHILD₂   *makin*   A62
CHILD₃   *ka*   P38
CHILD₃   *pan*   A63
CHILD₄   *ʔali*   A64
CHIN   *taki*   CP32
CLASSIFIER (ROUND OBJECTS)   *kwa*   G40[CP]
CLASSIFIERS   *aʔ/he/o*   G107 [AK]
CLEAN   *kurin*   MG20
CLEAN (v.)   *tˢ'uk'ʷa*   A65
CLIMB   *man*   H30
CLOSE₁ (V.)   *je*   CA14
CLOSE₂ (V.)   *ku*   CA15; cf. P109
CLOSE (V.)   *apu*   MC11
CLOSE (V.)   *bi*   MT22
CLOSE (v.)   *k'ap'a*   A66
CLOSE (V.)   *kaska*   AK45
CLOSE (V.)   *pan*   P39; =MP17
CLOSE (V.)   *pone*   MP17; =P39
CLOUD   *kuma*   CP33
CLOUD   *poʔtit*   P40; cf. E59
CLOUD₁   *anek̄ʷa*   AK46
CLOUD₁   *talu*   A67
CLOUD₂   *pa(n)k*   A68
CLOUD₂   *waʔn*   AK47
COLD   *kere*   MG21
COLD   *tˢtaje*   AK48
COLD   *tal*   AN23
COLD   *tatu*   P41
COLD₁   *duha*   E27; cf. CA18
COLD₁   *kʷi*   CA16; =MP19
COLD₁   *mati*   MP18
COLD₁   *tˢanik*   A69
COLD₂   *it'ak'*   A70
COLD₂   *koi*   MP19; =CA16
COLD₂   *tˢia*   CA17; =E28
COLD₂   *čiwa*   E28; =CA17
COLD₃   *hipe*   E29
COLD₃   *katˢa*   A71; =AN44
COLD₃   *to*   CA18; cf. E27

COME   *antoi*   P42
COME   *kem*   CA19
COME   *nani*   A72
COME₁   *akwa*   AN24; cf. P187
COME₁   *ape*   CP34; =A9; =MC24; =MG115
COME₁   *how*   AK49; =CP37
COME₂   *pusa*   AN25
COME₂   *ta*   CP35; =H74
COME₂   *wa*   AK50; =E48; =H72
COME₃   *taka*   CP36; cf. P189
COME₄   *hau*   CP37; =AK49
CONTINUATIVE   *ala*   G76 [P]
CONTINUATIVE   *is*   G70 [A]
COOK   *kako*   MT23; =P23
COOK   *kino*   E30
COOK   *maki*   A73; =AK28
COOK   *siqa*   AK51
COOK₁   *jok*   P43
COOK₁   *nina*   CP38
COOK₂   *hari*   CP39
COOK₂   *om*   P44
COOK₃   *hona*   P45
COUNT   *pe*   CA20
COVER   *iti*   P46
COVER   *mi*   MG22
COVER₁   *tˢiko*   H31; =CP40; =H58; =MG31
COVER₂   *sape*   H32; cf. CP73
COVER (V.)   *ma*   CA21
COVER (V.)   *taku*   CP40; =H31; =H58; MG31
COVER (v.)   *tumpa*   A74; =A80; =CP83; =MP30
CROCODILE   *lampa*   CP41
CROCODILE₁   *min*   MG23
CROCODILE₂   *ai*   MG24
CROOKED   *kotun*   AK52; =P62; =P63; =CP61
CROOKED   *ton*   MG25

CRUSH   *ju*   CA22

CRY   *poa*   MG26; =H34

CRY   *wuni*   A75

CRY_1 *mika*   H33

CRY_1 *waka*   P47

CRY_2 *jau*   P48

CRY_2 *ʔipia*   H34; =MG26

CUT   *ki*   MG27

CUT   *t'an*   CA23

CUT   *četa*   MP20; =MG70; =A49

CUT_1 *pala*   P49

CUT_2 *top*   P50

DANCE   *nan*   CA24

DANCE   *taki*   AN26

$DANCE_1$ *bak*   MT24

$DANCE_1$ *para*   CP42

$DANCE_1$ *wehte*   P51

$DANCE_2$ *bit*   P52

$DANCE_2$ *tara*   MT25; =CP43

$DANCE_2$ *telake*   CP43; MT25

DARK   *kaši*   AN27; =A200; cf. P17

DARK   *pe*   MP21

DARK   *t'umak*   A76

DATIVE   *ja*   G44 [CP]

DATIVE   *taki*   G43 [AN]

DAUGHTER   *pača*   CP44

DAY   *ibi*   H35

DAY   *jua*   CP45

DAY   *pine*   E31

DAY   *tū*   MG28; =H141

DEEP   *ka*   MT26

DEER   *ao*   H36

DEER   *jama*   MT27

DEER   *kotu*   MC12; cf. H41

DEER   *mana*   CP46; cf. AN60

DEER   *tek*   AK53; =CA25; A78

$DEER_1$ *sula*   A77

$DEER_1$ *te*   CA25; =AK53; =A78

$DEER_2$ *pa*   CA26

$DEER_2$ *taʔ*   A78; =AK53;

     =CA25

DEFECATE   *iku*   MG29

DENT (V.)   *kol*   H37

DESIDERATIVE   *he*   G82 [A]

DESIDERATIVE   *no*   G83; =AN125 [MP]

DESIDERATIVE   *čili*   G85 [H]

DIE   *kama*   H38

DIE   *pe*   CA27; =A155; =P14; =MG69; cf. AK54

DIE_1 *koli*   AN28

DIE_1 *maki*   A79

DIE_1 *otaw*   P53

DIE_1 *up*   AK54; =CA27;cf. A155; cf. P14; cf. MG69

DIE_2 *hen*   P54

DIE_2 *lakatu*   AN29

DIE_2 *nep*   AK55

DIE_2 *tampa*   A80; ?=A74; =CP83; =MP30

DIE_3 *tˢok*   P55; =P129

DIE_3 *ti*   A81

DIG   *mena*   CP47

DIG   *po*   H39

DIG   *tiho*   MP22

DIG   *ʔuhu*   MT28

DIG_1 *(o)kua*   A82

DIG_2 *tik*   A83

DIG_3 *wali*   A84

DIRTY   *pel*   H40; =CP58

DIRTY   *tuki*   A85; ?=A39; =E15

$DIRTY_1$ *toaken*   CP48

$DIRTY_2$ *uli*   CP49; =A94

DIVE   *mučix*   P56

DOG   *(a)k'uan*   A86

DOG   *ba*   MG30

DOG   *haju*   MT29

DOG   *hoko*   MC13

DOG   *kuču*   H41; cf. CA28; cf. MC12

DOG *nuk* MP23
DOG *sa* P57
DOG *tˢu* CA28; cf. H41
DOG *tija* AK56
DOG *wera* CP50
DOOR *tˢiki* MP24
DREAM *neka* MC14
DREAM₁ (V.) *maka* H42
DREAM₂ (V.) *xada* H43
DRESS *taku* MG31; =CP40; =H31; =H58
DRESS (V.) *ira* E32
DRESS (V.) *tula* MP25
DRINK *ʔitˢi* H44; =P272; =MT100
DRINK₁ *aquna* A87; =MG118; =AK185
DRINK₁ *kuti* CP51; =MG33; =AN121; =E64
DRINK₁ *čop* MG32
DRINK₂ *asi* CP52
DRINK₂ *kotu* MG33; =CP51; =AN121; =E64
DRINK₂ *ula* A88
DRINK₃ *me* A89; =CP211; =E125
DRINK₃ *to* CP53
DRY *amo* MT30
DRY *jim* MP26; =MP27
DRY₁ *paki* A90
DRY₂ *ana* A91
DUAL *si* G29 [A]
DURATIVE *ke* G72 [C]
DURATIVE/PUNCTUAL *a/i* G73 [A]
DUST *api* H45; =A92; =CP76
DUST *pe* A92; =H45; =CP76
DUST *pol* P58; =A11
EAGLE *kawi* E33
EAR *bia* MG34

EAR *kamo* A93
EAR *kuñi* E34; cf. P106
EAR *mat* P59
EAR₁ *jam* CP54
EAR₁ *t'eni* AK57; =A146
EAR₂ *apa* AK58; =MG61
EAR₂ *kuru* CP55
EAR₃ *kukati* CP56
EARTH *fe* MG35
EARTH *ki* ÇA29
EARTH *ñohe* MC15
EARTH₁ *bate* MT31; =AN32
EARTH₁ *ila* A94; =CP49
EARTH₁ *katˢi* CP57
EARTH₁ *wiši* AN30
EARTH₂ *kake* MT32; =CP59
EARTH₂ *pile* CP58; =H40
EARTH₂ *tali* AN31
EARTH₂ *tampi* A95
EARTH₃ *ama* A96
EARTH₃ *koka* CP59; =MT32
EARTH₃ *putˢa* AN32; =MT31
EARTH₄ *nanu* A97
EARTH₄ *tui* CP60
EAT *am* AK59; =H46; cf. AK131
EAT *ama* H46; =AK59; cf. AK131
EAT *itoʔ* P60
EAT *miku* AN33; =A252
EAT₁ *hura* E35
EAT₁ *pa* A98
EAT₂ *iu* E36; =A191
EAT₂ *kuri* A99
EAT₃ *añe* E37
EGG *dia* MT33
EGG *tini* E38
EGG *wa* CA30
EGG *čika* MG36
EGG₁ *na* A100
EGG₁ *nakʷika* AK60
EGG₁ *piʔe* H47; cf. A253

EGG₂   lak   AK61
EGG₂   tompa   A101
EGG₂   ʔuruh   H48
ELBOW   kuika   CP61; =P62;
   =P63; =AK52
ELBOW₁   tema   P61
ELBOW₂   čuk   P62; cf. CP61;
   cf. P63; =AK52
ELBOW₃   koče   P63; =P62;
   =CP61; =AK52
EMPTY   jim   MP27; =MP26
ENTER   eta   MC16
ENTER   wul   H49; =P8
ENTER   ʔoku   P64; =H73
EVENING   kebo   CP62
EVENING   najo   MC17
EVENING   nakʷa   AK62
EXCREMENT   ami   CP63
EXCREMENT   name   MC18
EXCREMENT   tin   P65
EXCREMENT   waki   H50
EXCREMENT₁   pa   A102
EXCREMENT₂   (i)ta(h)   A103
EXTINGUISH   čap   H51
EYE   (i)to(?)   A104; =MG38
EYE   hutˢi   P66
EYE   kepi   CP64
EYE   nimi   MC19
EYE   qali   AK63
EYE   tel   AN34; =CP159; =P150
EYE   tuki   E39; =MT34
EYE₁   keto   MG37
EYE₁   toke   MT34; =E39
EYE₂   into   MG38; =A104
EYE₂   tum   MT35
EYE₃   iku   MT36; =AK163
FACE   paka   CP65
FACE   sia   MT37
FALL   kote   MG39
FALL   mana   H52

FALL   tik   A105; cf. P68
FALL   wen   CA31
FALL₁   peta   P67
FALL₂   tˢe   P68; cf. A105
FALL₃   tot   P69; =P124
FAR   jo   CP66; =P70
FAR   lu   AK64
FAR   pali   A106
FAR₁   ja   P70; =CP66
FAR₂   wajat   P71
FAT   ji   CA32
FAT   pak   H53
FAT   sẽ   AK65; cf. MG78
FAT   tomp   MG40
FAT₁ (N.)   tota   CP67
FAT₁ (N.)   ñandi   E40; =A184
FAT₂ (N.)   kio   CP68; MC20
FAT₂ (N.)   mika   E41
FAT (N.)   kehi   MC20; CP68
FAT (N.)   minan   MT38
FATHER   koko   H54; =A178
FATHER   kuti   AN35; =P92; MT61
FATHER   main   MT39
FATHER   pais   P72
FATHER   ta   CA33
FEAR   kʷaiʔ   AK66
FEAR   kul   A107
FEAR₁   mole   P73
FEAR₁ (V.)   nowa   MP28
FEAR₂   b'uk   P74; cf. MP34
FEAR₂ (V.)   lako   MP29
FEAR (V.)   mu   MT40
FEAR (V.)   pe   CA34
FEATHER   kʷan   AK67
FEATHER   lia   P75; =AN52;
   =MG57
FEATHER   pi   CA35; =A109
FEATHER   poti   E42; =A108;
   =A24; =CA45
FEATHER₁   isak   H55

FEATHER₁ *ja* CP69
FEATHER₁ *pal* A108; =A24; =CA45; =E42
FEATHER₂ *kui* CP70
FEATHER₂ *pi* A109; =CA35
FEATHER₂ *pomi* H56
FEEL *pes* AK68
FELLOW *wit* G56 [AL]
FEMALE *marin* CP71
FEMALE *tonton* MG41; =A125
FEW *kre* MG42
FIELD *sepa?* P76
FIELD *?atˢa* AK69
FIGHT *polo* H57
FIGHT₁ *kaj* AN36
FIGHT₂ *tok* AN37; =P110; =AK153
FINGER *krai* MG43
FINGER *pal* CP72
FINGER₁ *tik* A110
FINGER₂ *itˢi* A111
FINISH *hujo* AK70
FINISH *sop* CP73; cf. H32
FINISH *tump* MP30; =A74; =A80; =CP83
FINISH₁ *toka* H58; =H31; =CP40; =MG31
FINISH₂ *mama* H59
FIRE *iso* E43; =AK73
FIRE *kata* CP74; =A113
FIRE *pa* CA36; =AK72
FIRE₁ *(i)ta* A112
FIRE₁ *jim* P77
FIRE₁ *man* H60; =A114
FIRE₁ *qʷap* AK71
FIRE₂ *hel* P78; =P32
FIRE₂ *kuti* A113; =CP74
FIRE₂ *paj* AK72; =CA36
FIRE₂ *?auho* H61; =AN8
FIRE₃ *huk* P79

FIRE₃ *is* AK73; =E43
FIRE₃ *ma* A114; =H60
FIREWOOD *aina* MT41
FIREWOOD *apali* A115
FIRST *is* AK74
FISH *kami* MT42; =AN38; =E44
FISH *mak* P80
FISH *suma* AN38; =MT42; =E44
FISH *top* MG44
FISH *čima* E44; =MT42; =AN38
FISH₁ *mema* AK75
FISH₂ *k'atˢi* AK76
FLAT *pa* MG45
FLAT *pana* AN39
FLEA *mak'in* A116
FLEA *tˢat* P81
FLEA *?epel* H62
FLEA *čuka* CP75
FLEA₁ *nane* E45
FLEA₂ *kutipa* E46
FLOAT *pukʷa* AK77; =A20; =H157; =MP59
FLOUR *hui* MT43
FLOUR *koni* MG46
FLOUR *tu* CA37
FLOUR₁ *apu* CP76; =A92; =H45
FLOUR₂ *kač* CP77
FLOWER *pak* AK78; =P20
FLOWER *se* CA38
FLOWER *tutu* CP78; =AN40
FLOWER₁ *čukčuk* AN40; =CP78
FLOWER₂ *akeše* AN41
FLY₁ (n.) *k'umpa* A118
FLY₁ (V.) *paš* P82
FLY₂ (n.) *mulu* A119; ?=A189
FLY₂ (V.) *kaj* P83
FLY₃ (V.) *jaka* P84; cf. MT9
FLY (N.) *matˢok* AK79
FLY (N.) *moka* MT44
FLY (N.) *usi* CP79; =MT99

FLY (V.)   *he?*   CP80
FLY (V.)   *lapa*   AN42
FLY (V.)   *naj*   MP31
FLY (v.)   *t'a*   A117
FOG   *mol*   H63
FOG   *piu*   AK80
FOLLOW   *note*   AK81
FOOD   *sok*   AN43
FOOT   *kin*   AK82
FOOT   *kot^{s}a*   CP81
FOOT   *tapu*   MC21
FOOT$_1$ *emi*   H64
FOOT$_1$ *peti*   A120; =MC66
FOOT$_2$ *asi?*   A121
FOOT$_2$ *pel*   H65
FOREHEAD   *imi*   MC22
FOREHEAD   *pali*   H66
FOREHEAD$_1$ *pe*   A122
FOREHEAD$_2$ *koa*   A123
FOREST   *anta*   MG47
FOREST   *rampa*   E47; =MT95;
   =MC71; =P235
FORGET   *xama*   H67
FREEZE   *kosek*   AN44; =A71
FRIEND   *meti*   MG48
FROG   *wala*   AN45
FROG$_1$ *peri*   MG49
FROG$_2$ *ru*   MG50
FRONT   *kan*   CP82
FRUIT   *elaw*   P85
FRUIT   *ta*   MG51
FRUIT   *teka*   A124
FRUIT   *tu*   CA39
FULL   *tompa*   CP83; =A74;
   =MP30; =A80
FULL$_1$ *pa*   P86; cf. AN2
FULL$_1$ *paka*   H68
FULL$_1$ *pana*   AK83; =H69
FULL$_2$ *mok*   AK84
FULL$_2$ *patki*   P87

FULL$_2$ *pena*   H69; =AK83
FUTURE (TENSE)   *sa?*   G84 [H]
FUTURE (TENSE)   *ta*   G81 [A]
GALL   *hipa*   AN46
GATHER   *t^{s}upi*   CA40
GIRL   *kič*   P88; =H29; =AK44;
   =A281
GIRL   *kuma*   CP84
GIRL   *t'una*   A125; =E129;
   =MG41
GIVE   *i*   MC23
GIVE   *pe*   CP85
GIVE$_1$ *kuč*   P89; =AK93; =CP92
GIVE$_1$ *?eka*   H70
GIVE$_1$ *?u*   AK85
GIVE$_2$ *aja*   H71
GIVE$_2$ *nak*   AK86
GIVE$_2$ *taut*   P90
GO   *le*   AK87
GO   *po*   MC24; =A9; =CP34;
   =MG115
GO   *wai*   E48; =H72; =AK50;
   =P267
GO$_1$ *(a)mina*   A126
GO$_1$ *wa*   H72; =E48; =AK50;
   =P267
GO$_2$ *tem*   A127
GO$_2$ *?ax*   H73; =P64
GO$_3$ *ja?*   A128
GO$_4$ *ko*   A129
GO DOWN   *kax*   P91
GO OUT   *pore*   E49; cf. MG92
GO OUT   *ta*   H74; =CP35
GO UP   *kea*   AN47
GOOD   *ajo*   E50
GOOD   *kenax*   H75; =AK88; =P15;
   =MC2
GOOD$_1$ *it^{s}i*   A130
GOOD$_1$ *k'ača*   AN48; =AN16
GOOD$_1$ *kani*   AK88; =H75; =P15;

=MC2

GOOD$_1$ *meka* MG52

GOOD$_1$ *pui* CP86; =MG7

GOOD$_2$ *ko* MG53

GOOD$_2$ *lap* AN49

GOOD$_2$ *t^{s}aki* AK89

GOOD$_2$ *t^{s}umpa* A131

GOOD$_2$ *uwa* CP87

GOOD$_3$ *malin* A132

GRANDFATHER *apita* MC25; =AK90

GRANDFATHER *bai* AN50

GRANDFATHER *toi* MG54

GRANDFATHER$_1$ *pit^{s}omas* AK90; =MC25

GRANDFATHER$_2$ *ikani* AK91; =P263

GRANDMOTHER *kota* P92; =AN35; =MT61

GRANDMOTHER *su* CA41; =A273

GRANDMOTHER *čeče* E51; =H100

GRASS *are* MG55

GRASS *kuli* A133

GRASS *numpa* E52

GRASS *peu* CP88; =P93

GRASS *pu* P93; =CP88

GREEN *zawa* MP32

GRIND *kuri* P94

GRIND *su* CA42

GRIND *ʔiknu* H76

GROW *ja* CA43

GUM *nok* P95

GUTS *akai* P96

GUTS *dodi* AN51

GUTS *he* E53

GUTS *suku* CP89

GUTS *t'impe* AK92

GUTS$_1$ *epokul* A134

GUTS$_2$ *kul* A135

HAIR *ali* AN52; =MG57; =P75

HAIR *ii* MT45

HAIR *sa* CP90

HAIR *t^{s}ume* A136; =E54

HAIR$_1$ *kai* MG56

HAIR$_1$ *kueš* P97

HAIR$_1$ *t^{s}oni* CA44; =E55

HAIR$_1$ *čuma* E54; =A136

HAIR$_2$ *ari* MG57; =AN52; =P75

HAIR$_2$ *it^{s}i* P98

HAIR$_2$ *po* CA45; =A24; =A108; E42

HAIR$_2$ *tuna* E55; CA44

HALF *keri* CP91

HAND *još* AN53; =P7

HAND *kepi* E56

HAND *nitale* MC26

HAND *poto* P99; =AK203

HAND$_1$ *kite* AK93; =CP92; =P89

HAND$_1$ *kuse* CP92; =AK93; =P89

HAND$_1$ *makan* A137

HAND$_1$ *pake* MT46; =A7; =P214

HAND$_1$ *tani* H77; =E126

HAND$_2$ *limpa* MT47

HAND$_2$ *mut* H78

HAND$_2$ *saka* CP93; =AK94

HAND$_2$ *saki* AK94; =CP93

HAND$_2$ *ʔani* A138

HAND$_3$ *atu* A139

HANG *pani* MP33

HARD *nako* AN54

HARD *ni* AK95

HARD *t'ara* CP94

HARD *taio* MG58; cf. A46; cf. MC63

HARD$_1$ *k^{w}ele* A140

HARD$_1$ *āl* P100

HARD$_2$ *k'at^{s}i* A141; =P102; =CP184

HARD$_2$ *tiʔ* P101

HARD$_3$ *k'ati* P102; =A141;

=CP184

HATE   pak   MP34; cf. P74

HATE   pul   A142

HAVE   iči   P103

HE   na   G15 [A]; cf. G23

HE   s   G18 [AK]

HE   ʔi   G12 [A]

HEAD   kitan   MG59

HEAD   koati   MT48

HEAD   toliš   P104

HEAD   tope   E57

HEAD$_1$ lax   H79

HEAD$_1$ pusu   CP95

HEAD$_1$ puta   A143

HEAD$_1$ sako   AK96; =CP96

HEAD$_2$ hiba   H80

HEAD$_2$ pa(ksu)   AK97

HEAD$_2$ saku   CP96; =AK96

HEAD$_2$ take   A144

HEAR   aina   MT49

HEAR   koe   H81

HEAR   nan   CA46

HEAR   opisa   E58

HEAR$_1$ mar   MG60

HEAR$_1$ naka   A145

HEAR$_1$ pok   P105

HEAR$_2$ kan   P106; =E34

HEAR$_2$ pa   MG61; =AK58

HEAR$_2$ tine   A146; =AK57

HEART   t^{s}ukul   H82; =CP107

HEART   te   AK98

HEART   tu   P107; =P25; =H25;
   =CP98

HEART$_1$ ia   CP97

HEART$_2$ iso   CP98; =P25; =P107;
   =H25

HEAVEN   kutu   AN55

HEAVEN   nano   CP99

HEAVEN   poto   E59; cf. P40

HEAVEN$_1$ kali   A147; =CP1

HEAVEN$_2$ ema   A148; =E1

HEAVY   meʔe   MC27

HEAVY   mita   H83

HEAVY   nake   AK99

HEAVY   nul   CP100

HEAVY   pali   E60

HERE   kre   MG62

HERE   tih   MT50

HIDE   disu   CP101

HIDE$_1$ (V.)   łoma   P108

HIDE$_2$ (V.)   ʔikoj   P109; cf. CA15

HILL   wasa   H84

HIT   hol   H85

HIT   kora   MG63

HIT   moka   AK100

HIT   pa   CA47; =P14

HIT   taki   A149; =AK31

HIT   toh   P110; =AK153; =AN37

HOLD   kun   AK101

HOLE   jata   AK102

HOLE$_1$ hop   P111

HOLE$_1$ kre   MG64

HOLE$_1$ paka   CP102

HOLE$_1$ t^s"imak   A150

HOLE$_2$ doro   MG65; cf. P115

HOLE$_2$ mu   A151

HOLE$_2$ palo   CP103

HOLE$_2$ łapu   P112

HOLE$_3$ tuk   P113

HOLE$_4$ hol   P114

HOLE$_5$ talok   P115; cf. MG65

HONEY   belu   MT51

HONEY$_1$ mapa   E61

HONEY$_2$ kote   E62

HORN   kaču   CP104

HORN   kin   A152

HORN   taš   MP35

HORN   wesu   H86

HORTATIVE   pa   G86 [A]

HOT   kerank   MG66

HOT *k'ʷetˢ* AK103

HOT *pači* CP105; =CP109; =MG18

HOT *uka* MC28

HOT₁ *haji* P116

HOT₂ *lahp* P117

HOT₃ *tˢa* P118

HOUSE *ama* H87

HOUSE *ika* MC29; =CA48

HOUSE *ja* CP106; =H96

HOUSE *ka* CA48; =MC29

HOUSE *men* MT52

HOUSE *pā* MG67

HOUSE *toh* A153

HOUSE₁ *han* P119; cf. AK118

HOUSE₂ *keli* P120

HOW MANY? *tan* MG68; cf. G106

HUNGER *mača* AN56

HUNGRY *kaʔ* P121

HUNT *ore* AK104

HURT₁ *kama* AN57

HURT₂ *ke* AN58

HUSBAND *mano* A154

HUSBAND₁ *nau* P122; =MC31

HUSBAND₁ *wano* MC30; =P179

HUSBAND₂ *haja* P123

HUSBAND₂ *ino* MC31; =P122

I *ma* G3 [A]

I *na(ʔ)* G1 [A]

I *ʔi* G2 [A]

ICE *kʷami* AK105

IMPERATIVE *ka* G90 [H]

IMPERATIVE *la* G89 [H]

IMPERATIVE *u* G87 [CP]

IMPERATIVE *ʔi* G88 [H]; =G91

IMPERATIVE *ʔi* G91 [K]; =G88

INSIDE *huk* AK106

INSIDE *man* AN59

INTERROGATIVE *kin* G102 [A]

INTERROGATIVE *min* G103 [A]

INTERROGATIVE *na* G104 [MC]

INTERROGATIVE *pi* G105 [C]

INTERROGATIVE *tin* G106 [P]; cf. MG68

ITERATIVE *te* G74 [A]

JAGUAR *mana* AN60; cf. CP46

JAGUAR *puti* MT53

JUMP *tˢat* P124; =P69

KEEP *pal* P125

KIDNEY *soka* CP107; =H82

KILL *keče* AN61

KILL *pa* A155; =P14; =CA27; =AK54; =MG69

KILL *pata* CP108

KILL *pi* MG69; =A155; =P14; =CA27; cf. AK54

KILL₁ *tʲe* P126

KILL₂ *nim* P127

KILL₃ *lap* P128

KILL₄ *tˢxa* P129; =P55

KILL₅ *oks* P130

KINDLE *patˢe* CP109; =CP105; =MG18

KINDLE₁ *ũ* AK107

KINDLE₂ *tˢuku* AK108; =A54; =A251; =P285

KISS *muča* AN62

KNEAD *pon* MP36

KNEE *k'ʷalenk* P131

KNEE *nopui* E63

KNEE *pulutˢ* H88

KNEE *tula* AN63

KNEE₁ *kati* A156

KNEE₂ *puku* A157; =MT16

KNIFE *keti* MG70; =MP20; =A49

KNOW *hona* MP37

KNOW *kom* A158

KNOW₁ *hoto* P132

KNOW₂ *joki* P133
LAKE *kuače* E64; =AN121;
　=CP51; =MG33
LAKE *re* AK109; =CP212
LARGE *bui* CP110; =H89
LARGE *kuttu* AK110
LARGE *mara* MT54
LARGE *mono* MC32; =AN64
LARGE *mwi* CA49
LARGE *uman* AN64; =MC32
LARGE₁ *hot* P134
LARGE₁ *po* H89; =CP110
LARGE₁ *tak* A159
LARGE₂ *kwaku* H90
LARGE₂ *mek'ati* A160
LARGE₂ *ʔate* P135
LARGE₃ *pane* H91
LAUGH *alu* CP111
LAUGH *beči* E65
LAUGH *kali* A161; =AN65
LAUGH *kolka* AN65; =A161
LAUGH *lik* H92
LAUGH₁ *amas* P136
LAUGH₂ *haja* P137
LEAF *awa* MP38
LEAF *ji* MT55
LEAF *lapi* AN66
LEAF *maso* CP112
LEAF *p'aqʷ* AK111
LEAF *tala* H93
LEAF₁ *ene* A162
LEAF₁ *osi* P138
LEAF₂ *pane* A163
LEAF₂ *t'apa* P139
LEAF₃ *imi* A164
LEAVE *jane* MP39
LEFT (SIDE) *mwenik* AN67
LEFT (SIDE) *ketˢ* AK112; =MG71
LEFT (SIDE) *keč* MG71; =AK112
LEFT (SIDE) *kuli* H94

LEG *inoa* MT56
LEG *kela* AN68; =H122; =MC56;
　cf. CP155
LEG *ku* CA50
LEG *kumpa* E66
LEG *tˢaka* AK113; ?=A165;
　cf. CP167
LEG *ta(k)* A165; ?=AK113;
　cf. CP167
LEG₁ *mal* P140
LEG₁ *moka* CP113
LEG₁ *tia* MC33
LEG₂ *lul* P141
LEG₂ *mana* MC34
LEG₂ *sona* CP114
LICK *me* MC35
LICK *tumpe* MG72
LIE₁ (TELL A) *mal* P143
LIE₂ (TELL A) *holabi* P144
LIE (TELL A) *pe* AK114
LIE (TELL A) *upati* E67
LIE (TELL A) *win* MG73
LIE DOWN *jok* P142
LIE DOWN *ko* CA51; cf. AN103
LIE DOWN *pas* CP115
LIE DOWN₁ *tˢek* AK115
LIE DOWN₂ *jã* AK116
LIGHT *k'i* P145
LIGHT (n.) *mea* A166
LIGHTNING *meru* MC36
LIGHTNING *met* H95
LIGHTNING *wilep'* P146
LIP *jape* A167
LIP *no* MT57
LIP *skʷa* AK117
LIVE *ha* AK118; cf. P119
LIVE₁ (V.) *lak* P147
LIVE₂ (V.) *nom* P148
LIVE (V.) *ia* H96; =CP106
LIVE (V.) *si* CP116

LIVER *apati* A168; =E69
LIVER *kʷani* AK119
LIVER *k'otˢel* P149
LIVER *pa* MG74
LIVER₁ *kepa* E68
LIVER₂ *pita* E69; =A168
LIZARD *tare* MT58
LIZARD *ten* CA52
LIZARD *uli* A169; cf. CP179
LOCATIVE *ma* G46 [A]
LOCATIVE *ni* G47 [A]
LOCATIVE *pa* G48 [A]
LOCATIVE *te* G49 [A]
LONG *mahe* MT59
LONG *sin* AN69
LONG *tuku* E70
LONG₁ *ali* A170
LONG₂ *kule* A171
LOOK *pon* CA53
LOOK *čola* MP40
LOOK₁ *t'en* P150; =CP159;
  =AN34
LOOK₂ *pe* P151; =A222;
  =AK162
LOSE *manu* MP41
LOUSE *pepe* MG75
LOUSE *tami* MT60
LOUSE₁ *koma* E71
LOUSE₁ *mu* CP117
LOUSE₁ *ti* A172
LOUSE₂ *tina* A173
LOUSE₂ *tuma* CP118
LOUSE₂ *wi* E72
LOUSE₃ *ik'e* A174
LOUSE₃ *kwapi* E73
LOVE *iČo* E74
LOVE *luna* CP119
MAKE *make* CP120
MAKE *ne* MC37
MAKE *wa* MP42

MAKE₁ *japo* E75
MAKE₁ *kami* P152
MAKE₁ *taʔ* A175
MAKE₂ *ju* A176
MAKE₂ *nino* E76; =CP224
MAKE₂ *ʔiča* P153
MALE *alak* AN70; =E77
MAN *luku* E77; =AN70
MAN *non* AN71
MAN *pek* AK120
MAN *sin* CA54
MAN *tai* MG76
MAN *tima* MC38; cf. CP138
MAN₁ *ači* A177
MAN₁ *kote* MT61; =AN35; =P92
MAN₁ *ʔel* CP121
MAN₂ *kak* A178; =H54
MAN₂ *mia* MT62
MAN₂ *muki* CP122
MAN₃ *ipa* A179
MAN₃ *porki* MT63
MAN (OLD) *amu* E91
MAN (OLD) *tompa* CP138;
  cf. MC38
MANY *lama* MP43
MANY *paka* MT64
MANY *pelak* H97
MANY *tite* MG77
MANY₁ *ali* A180; =AK121;
  =P162
MANY₁ *hila* AK121; =P162;
  =A180
MANY₁ *putˢa* E78; =MG1
MANY₂ *kali* AK122
MANY₂ *poj* E79; =H2
MANY₂ *tol* A181
MANY₃ *isa* AK123
MANY₃ *moni* A182
MASCULINE/FEMININE *i/u*
  G39 [A]

MASCULINE/FEMININE *t/s*
G38 [A]

MEAT   *kal* AN72

MEAT   *nak* AK124; =MP44

MEAT   *noha* MP44; =AK124

MEAT   *tin* MG78; cf. AK65

MEAT₁   *lau* A183

MEAT₁   *sami* P154

MEAT₂   *anena* A184; =E40

MEAT₂   *nope* P155

MEAT₃   *mati* A185; =H18

MEAT₄   *ati* A186

MIDDLE   *mak* H98

MIDDLE   *sena* AK125

MONKEY   *kukoi* MG79; =E80

MONKEY   *kučiro* E80; =MG79

MONKEY₁   *nome* MC39

MONKEY₂   *homa* MC40

MOON   *nunti* AK126; =MC42

MOON   *pina* MG80

MOON   *tˢopi* E81; =A188;
   =AN109

MOON   *tel* AN73

MOON₁   *malan* MC41

MOON₁   *poto* A187

MOON₂   *nuna* MC42; =AK126

MOON₂   *tamp* A188; =E81;
   =AN109

MORNING   *tuki* P156; =A251

MORNING   *tuna* E82

MOSQUITO   *ija* MP45

MOSQUITO   *koka* MG81

MOSQUITO   *polunk* A189;
   ?=A119

MOSQUITO   *tˢampa* AK127

MOSQUITO   *tˢele* H99

MOSQUITO   *tinu* CP123

MOTHER   *ja* CA55

MOTHER   *nana* MP46; =A14

MOTHER   *tati* H100; =E51

MOTHER   *ʔukasima* AK128

MOUNTAIN   *awaj* H101; cf. MT65

MOUNTAIN   *kompa* CP124

MOUNTAIN   *neko* AK129

MOUNTAIN   *pian* CA56

MOUNTAIN   *tampo* E83

MOUNTAIN₁   *nani* P157

MOUNTAIN₁   *waiku* MT65;
   cf. H101

MOUNTAIN₂   *kot* P158

MOUNTAIN₂   *poχa* MT66; cf. A2

MOUSE   *kʷasi* AK130; =A190;
   =MP8

MOUSE   *kusi* A190; =AK130;
   =MP8

MOUSE   *meka* MP47

MOUSE   *pote* E84

MOUSE   *tˢampa* P159

MOUTH   *intako* MG82

MOUTH   *kala* H102; =AN75;
   cf. MT67

MOUTH   *kana* MT67; cf. H102;
   cf. AN75

MOUTH   *kopo* E85

MOUTH   *ma* AK131; cf. AK59;
   cf. H46

MOUTH   *mata* MC43

MOUTH   *sapa* CP125

MOUTH   *či* P160

MOUTH₁   *jauʔ* A191; =E36

MOUTH₁   *lal* AN74

MOUTH₂   *kolo* AN75; =H102;
   cf. MT67

MOUTH₂   *kua* A192

MUCH₁   *la* P161

MUCH₁   *ʔana* AK132

MUCH₂   *aʔte* AK133

MUCH₂   *hele* P162; =AK121;
   =A180

MUCH₃   *wi* P163

NAIL *ape* E86

NAIL *ki* CP126

NAIL *su* CA57

NAIL *tak* P164

NAIL₁ *pati* MT68

NAIL₂ *peko* MT69

NAME *ako* CP127

NAME *ire* E87

NAME₁ *senok* AK134

NAME₂ *wew* AK135

NARROW *tⁱⁱan* A193

NAVEL *kupu* AN76

NAVEL *lapu* H103

NAVEL *tok* P165

NAVEL *tompa* A194

NEAR *kama* A195

NEAR *kata* AK136

NEAR *kole* CP128

NEAR *maku* H104

NEAR₁ *haja* P166

NEAR₂ *nakak* P167

NECK *aru* AN77; =E115

NECK *k'oe* A196

NECK *kak* AK137; =CP129

NECK *pok* H105; =CP130

NECK *tou* MG83

NECK₁ *guaka* CP129; =AK137

NECK₁ *tetˢ* MP48

NECK₂ *paka* CP130; =H105

NECK₂ *u* MP49

NECK₃ *tala* CP131; =CP30;
 =A228; =MC59

NEGATIVE *ama* G101 [MP]

NEGATIVE *kua* G100 [A]

NEPHEW *paito* MC44

NET *wana* CA58

NEW *eli* CP132

NEW *iti* P168; cf. CA63

NEW *mako* AN78

NEW *oron* MG84

NEW *pala* H106

NEW *wask* AK138

NIGHT *pitun* E88

NIGHT₁ *jam* A197

NIGHT₁ *nak* P169

NIGHT₂ *mok* A198

NIGHT₂ *tuwa* P170

NIGHT₃ *sepi/pasi* A199

NIGHT₄ *kači* A200; =AN27;
 cf. P17

NOMINALIZER *an* G65 [A]

NOMINALIZER *kar* G63 [AN]

NOMINALIZER *na* G61 [A]

NOMINALIZER *ri* G60 [A]

NOMINALIZER *s* G64 [P]

NOMINALIZER *sti* G59 [K]

NOMINALIZER *wa* G62 [CA]

NOMINALIZER *we* G58 [AN]

NOSE *kane* MT70

NOSE *nampi* E89

NOSE *nari* MC45

NOSE *netik* A201

NOSE *nine* MG85

NOSE *ʔapi* H107

NOSE *čuna* AN79; =A79;
 =AK175

NOSE₁ *aču* CP133; =AN106

NOSE₁ *kosa* AK139

NOSE₂ *jas* AK140

NOSE₂ *kimpu* CP134

NOW *eroma* MC46; =CP135;
 =MG112

NOW *wa* AK141

NOW₁ *ira* CP135; =MC46;
 =MG112

NOW₂ *aman* CP136

OLD *ano* A202

OLD *ača* AN80

OLD *hʷasi* P171

OLD *keri* MG86

OLD   *kã* AK142

OLD   *patu* H108

OLD   *san* E90

OLD   *seri* MP50

OLD   *tare* CP137

ONE   *suk* AN81; =AK143

ONE₁   *iska* AK143; =AN81

ONE₁   *paka* H109

ONE₁   *pes* CP139

ONE₁   *tama* A203

ONE₂   *ba* CP140

ONE₂   *kela* A204

ONE₂   *kot* AK144

ONE₂   *pani* H110

ONE₃   *ato* CP141

ONE₄   *nekui* CP142

ONION   *si* CA59

OPEN₁   *hakin* P172

OPEN₁   *ken* AK145; =P173

OPEN₂   *kune* P173; =AK145

OPEN₂   *ta* AK146

OPEN₃   *pai* P174; =CP143

OPEN   *pai* CP143; =P174

OTHER   *non* MG87

OTHER₁   *kaku* AN82; =H153

OTHER₂   *wah* AN83

OUT   *manà* MC47

PAIN   *(n)ana* A205

PAIN   *punuk* AN84

PAIN   *sala* CP144

PAIN   *taka* AK147

PAIN   *uri* MG88

PARTICIPIAL   *ma* G68 [E]

PARTICIPIAL   *na* G69 [CP]

PAST (TENSE)   *ipa* G80 [H]

PAST (TENSE)   *ite* G78 [MP]

PAST (TENSE)   *na* G77 [A]

PAST (TENSE)   *weči* G98 [MC]

PAST (TENSE)   *š* G79 [C]

PENIS   *jot* P175

PENIS   *ko* A206

PENIS   *laka* AN85

PENIS   *nol* H111

PENIS   *pen* MC48

PENIS   *sako* AK148

PENIS   *tuka* MT71

PEOPLE   *oni* P176

PERSON   *kaja* A207

PERSON   *komo* MC49

PERSON   *tali* CP145

PERSON₁   *kala* P177

PERSON₁   *onkʷe* AK149

PERSON₂   *amai* P178

PERSON₂   *nik* AK150

PERSON₃   *hajanu* AK151

PERSON₃   *wintu* P179; =MC30

PIERCE   *oko* AN86

PIERCE   *pe* MC50

PLACE   *awa* P180

PLACE   *pa* E92

PLANT (V.)   *ke* AK152

PLAY   *leuk* P181

PLAY   *maki* AN87

PLURAL   *aki* G32 [A]

PLURAL   *bo* G35 [MP]

PLURAL   *ele* G33 [A]

PLURAL   *ma* G31 [A]

PLURAL   *na* G30 [A]

PLURAL   *to* G34 [MP]

PLURAL   *wa* G36 [H]

PLURAL   *ʔał* G37 [AL]

POUND   *taʔ* AK153; =P110; =AN37

POUR   *sik* AK154

PRESENT (TENSE)   *i* G71 [A]

PRESENT (TENSE)   *na* G75 [AN]

PRESS   *tom* MG89

PULL   *hoka* E93

PULL   *jun* H112

PULL   *mana* MT72

PULL₁ *čal* P182

PULL₂ *taku* P183

PULL OFF *pil* H113

PULL OUT *pu* MT73

PUSH *paka* CP146

PUT *ne* MG90

PUT₁ *poli* P184

PUT₂ *mačg* P185

RABBIT *kuni* H114

RABBIT *pa* CA60

RAIN *akwi* H115

RAIN *lulu* MT74

RAIN *na* A208

RAIN *sta* AK155

RAIN *toma* MC51; =E94

RAIN *tompa* E94; =MC51

RAIN₁ *nusa* CP147

RAIN₁ *pala* AN88

RAIN₂ *sebu* CP148

RAIN₂ *uxla* AN89

RAIN₃ *man* CP149

RAIN₃ *ten* AN90

RAISE *sa* CA61

RAT *pi* CA62

RAW *kašu* H116

RAW *tˢana* CP150

RECIPROCAL *po* G27 [P]

RED *kapen* AN91

RED *kike* P186

RED *pe* A209

RED *tek* MP51; =AK156

RED *tipo* MC52

RED₁ *tˢakʷa* AK156; =MP51

RED₂ *matˢkʷi* AK157; =P18

REFLEXIVE *ki* G96 [MP]

REFLEXIVE *m* G97 [AN]

REFLEXIVE *ti* G25 [A]

RETURN *kuti* AN92

RETURN₁ *joke* P187; cf. AN24

RETURN₂ *malo* P188

RETURN₃ *tok* P189; cf. CP36

RIB *kora* MC53

RIB *mana* MP52

RIB *nokʷak* AK158

RIB *pani* AN93

RIB *wexut* P190

RIPE *nako* H117

RIPE *te* CA63; cf. P168

RIVER *buitˢu* E95

RIVER *waro* MG91; =CP151

RIVER₁ *pel* A210

RIVER₁ *wala* CP151; =MG91

RIVER₂ *kuna* CP152; =A87;
     =AK185; =MG118

RIVER₂ *tia* A211

ROAD *kampa* H118

ROAD *miku* P191

ROAD *poro* MG92; cf. E49

ROAD *tewa* MT75

ROAD₁ *nama* A212

ROAD₂ *p'en* A213

ROAST *k'ʷali* AK159

ROAST *rui* MC54

ROAST *sil* H119

ROAST *tau* P192

ROOT *tap* A214

ROOT *ʔima* H120

ROOT₁ *ti* MT76

ROOT₁ *łakʷi* P193

ROOT₂ *bil* P194

ROOT₂ *neko* MT77

ROPE *ampa* MT78

ROPE *asul* H121

ROPE *kapu* MC55

ROPE *tˢ'ak* P195

ROPE *čita* CP153

ROTTEN *pate* CP154

ROTTEN *poko* MP53

ROTTEN *tokun* AN94

ROTTEN *īs* P196

ROUND *molok* A215

RUB *sepa* CA64

RUN *gali* H122; =MC56;
  cf. CP155; =AN68

RUN *kane* MC56; =H122;
  cf. CP155; =AN68

RUN *kuri* CP155; cf. H122;
  cf. MC56; =AN68

RUN *pi* E96

RUN *pron* MG93

RUN *t'ik'a* AN95; =P198

RUN₁ *pala* P197

RUN₂ *taka* P198; =AN95

RUN₃ *wele* P199

SALIVA *išo* MG94; cf. P272;
  cf. H44; cf. MT100

SALIVA *ole* A216

SALIVA *tuku* P200; =AK161

SALIVA₁ *čupa* AK160

SALIVA₂ *tak* AK161; =P200

SALT *akai* H123

SALT *nanku* CP156

SALT *tin* CA65

SAND *se* CA66

SAY *aj* CP157; =P202; cf. P204

SAY *ana* AN96; =P201

SAY₁ *ene* P201; =AN96

SAY₁ *ti* A217; =CA74

SAY₂ *hai* P202; =CP157; cf. P204

SAY₂ *kʷela* A218

SAY₃ *koʔe* A219; =P246

SAY₃ *wali* P203; =MT90; =MC60

SAY₄ *ʔa* P204; cf. CP157;
  cf. P202

SCRATCH *bur* CP158

SEA *amum* AN97; =A89;
  =CP211; =E125

SEE *de* MT79

SEE *ma* CA67; =CP160

SEE₁ *neu* A220

SEE₁ *p'a* AK162; =A222; =P151

SEE₁ *ruk* AN98

SEE₁ *tene* CP159; =AN34;
  =P150

SEE₁ *ʔaʔo* H124

SEE₂ *iʎa* AN99

SEE₂ *k'a* AK163; =MT36

SEE₂ *maki* H125

SEE₂ *mi* CP160; =CA67

SEE₂ *win* A221

SEE₃ *manitˢ* AN100

SEE₃ *pi* A222; =AK162; =P151

SEED *koi* MT80

SEED *tan* CA68

SEED₁ *mak* A223

SEED₁ *ñin* CP161

SEED₂ *itˢu* A224

SEED₂ *uba* CP162

SEEK *kʷat* AK164

SEEK *peno* A225

SEEK₁ *hojo* P205

SEEK₁ *kap* CP163

SEEK₂ *paka* CP164

SEEK₂ *wana* P206

SELL *jik* P207

SEVEN *te* CA69

SEW *ketˢ* CP165

SEW *pik* P208; =H159

SHADOW *itka* P209

SHADOW *kajo* E97

SHADOW *mani* MC57; =CP166

SHADOW *manis* CP166; =MC57

SHADOW *nokʷak* AK165

SHARP (TASTE) *are* MG95

SHARPEN *angro* MG96

SHIN *pesi* E98

SHIN *sagua* CP167; cf. AK113

SHINE *lemp* A226

SHINE *mak* AK166

SHINE *waxa* P210

SHOOT   na   H126

SHOOT   t'ux^we   P213

SHOOT   teja   CP168

SHORT   kunek   A227; =E101

SHORT   taputi   MC58

SHORT   te   CA70

SHORT₁   mink   P211

SHORT₂   pok   P212

SHOULDER   (mo-)tali   MC59; =A228; =CP30; =CP131

SHOULDER   pak   P214; =A7; =CP219; =MT46

SHOULDER   tala   A228; =MC59; ?=CP30; =CP131

SHOULDER₁   pala   CP169

SHOULDER₂   peču   CP170; cf. MC10

SHOUT   tˢeja   MP54

SHOUT (V.)   pai   CP171

SHOW   kima   P215

SIBLING   wa   CA71

SICK   mao   MG97

SIDE   aji   MP55

SIDE   kati   CP172

SIDE   mal   AK167

SINEW   ipam   H127

SING   angrin   MG98

SING   namake   CP173

SING   sija   A229

SING₁   kam   AK168

SING₂   kan   AK169

SING₃   wã   AK170

SISTER   kañi   AN101; =MP16

SIT   moin   MG99

SIT   ča?u   CP174

SIT₁   ik   H128; =AK171; =AN14; cf. P217

SIT₁   k'u   AK171; =H128; =AN14; cf. P217

SIT₁   ni   A230

SIT₁   t'ok^w   P216; =A232

SIT₂   ikel   H129

SIT₂   met   AK172

SIT₂   uwa   A231

SIT₂   čai   P217; cf. AK171; cf. H128; cf. AN14

SIT₃   tak   A232; =P216

SKIN   api   AN102; =MG6

SKIN   kat   MG100; =CP175

SKIN   k'ʷati   CP175; =MG100

SKIN   som   H130; =P13; =MT81

SKIN   čimo   MT81; =P13; =H130

SKIN₁   talik   P218

SKIN₁   toke   A233

SKIN₂   pakti   A234

SKIN₂   ?uk   P219

SKY   epalu   P220; =H155

SLEEP   aka   AN103; cf. CA51

SLEEP   t'e   AK173

SLEEP   weha   MT82

SLEEP₁   ino   A235

SLEEP₁   pa   CP176

SLEEP₁   simak   H131

SLEEP₂   apok   H132

SLEEP₂   kampa   CP177

SLEEP₂   kana   A236

SMALL   es   AK174

SMALL   man   A237

SMALL   piči   AN104

SMALL   rog   MG101

SMALL   sin   CA72

SMALL   taku   H133; MP56

SMALL   tika   MP56; H133

SMALL₁   nuksti   P221

SMALL₁   papi   E99

SMALL₂   isel   P222

SMALL₂   ku   E100

SMALL₃   kunič   E101; =A227

SMELL   k'uk^wi   A239

SMELL   senok   AK175; =CP133;

=A79

SMELL　*ume*　E102

SMELL₁　*matik'*　A238

SMELL₁　*moka*　AN105

SMELL₂　*asi*　AN106; =CP133

SMOKE　*kale*　P223

SMOKE　*kum*　MG102

SMOKE　*tˢaka*　H134; =AK176

SMOKE　*tˢ'eqa*　AK176; =H134

SMOKE (N.)　*kiepo*　E103

SMOKE (V.)　*t'oi*　CP178

SMOOTH　*hin*　P224

SMOOTH　*lak'*　H135

SNAKE　*nat*　AK177

SNAKE　*paj*　P225

SNAKE　*peno*　MT83

SNAKE₁　*kan*　A240

SNAKE₁　*angia*　E104

SNAKE₁　*jora*　CP179; cf. A169

SNAKE₂　*huhi*　CP180

SNAKE₂　*manu*　E105

SNAKE₂　*tompa*　A241; =E131

SNOW₁　*nija*　AK178

SNOW₁　*pen*　P226

SNOW₁　*ʔiju*　H136

SNOW₂　*kuwila*　P227

SNOW₂　*maʔ*　AK179

SNOW₂　*poj*　H137

SOCIATIVE　*ja*　G57 [MP]

SOCIATIVE　*kan*　G54 [P]

SOCIATIVE　*mane*　G52 [A]

SOCIATIVE　*maɬ*　G55 [AL]

SOCIATIVE　*na*　G26 [CA]

SOCIATIVE　*pi*　G53 [CP]

SOFT　*apoi*　AN107

SOFT　*to*　CA73

SON　*ina*　MP57; =A61

SOUR　*kai*　A242

SOUR　*patˢi*　MP58; =A35

SPEAK　*tu*　CA74; =A217

SPEAK　*ura*　MC60; =P203;
　　=MT90

SPIDER　*lom*　P228

SPIDER　*toti*　MC61

SQUIRREL　*hiɬu*　P229

STAND　*kara*　MT84

STAND　*taʔ*　AK180; =P233

STAND　*wine*　CA75

STAND₁　*tala*　P230

STAND₂　*tak*　P231

STAND UP₁　*juko*　P232

STAND UP₂　*to*　P233; =AK180

STAR　*upa*　CP181

STAR₁　*(a)sin*　A243

STAR₁　*pole*　AN108

STAR₂　*metˢa*　A244

STAR₂　*čup*　AN109; =A188; =E81

STEAL　*kemoti*　AK181

STEAL　*meri*　MC62; =CP183

STEAL　*w'ilu*　P234

STEAL₁　*ise*　CP182

STEAL₂　*mer*　CP183; =MC62

STICK　*muli*　AK182

STICK　*tomaj*　P235; =MT95;
　　=MC71; =E47

STICK　*čapa*　MT85

STONE　*k'atu*　CP184; =A141;
　　=P102

STONE　*kena*　MG103; cf. A245

STONE　*pote*　E106

STONE　*ta*　CA76; cf. MC63;
　　cf. MG58; cf. A46

STONE　*taho*　MC63; cf. CA76;
　　cf. MG58; cf. A46

STONE₁　*kela*　A245; cf. MG103

STONE₁　*mēj*　AK183

STONE₁　*nota*　MT86

STONE₁　*pak*　H138

STONE₁　*ʔoa*　P236

STONE₂　*kape*　H139

STONE₂ *tape* MT87
STONE₂ *tiak* A246
STONE₂ *tola* P237
STONE₂ *čane* AK184
STONE₃ *aki* MT88
STRING *nu* MT89; =H140
STRING *nulu* H140; =MT89
STRONG *pale* A247
STRONG₁ *tae* CP185
STRONG₂ *tar* CP186
SUN *hena* AN110
SUN *wani* MC64
SUN₁ *ali* A248
SUN₁ *kati* CP187; =E109
SUN₁ *kuman* E107
SUN₁ *tˢual* H141; =MG28
SUN₂ *koli* A249
SUN₂ *lako* H142
SUN₂ *lan* CP188
SUN₂ *masiku* E108
SUN₃ *kati* E109; =CP187
SUN₃ *pali* A250
SUN₄ *toki* A251; =P156
SWALLOW *kot* MG104
SWALLOW *mik'o* A252; =AN33
SWALLOW *q'one* AK185; =A87;
 =MG118; =CP152
SWALLOW₁ *lak* P238
SWALLOW₂ *milq* P239
SWAMP *ikali* MC65
SWEAT *astuk* H143
SWEEP *pas* P240
SWEET *anite* AK186
SWEET *jali* AN111
SWELL *peos* AK187
SWIM *begi* MP59; =A20; =H157;
 =AK77
SWIM *kate* H144
SWIM *naq'* AK188
SWIM *topi* MG105

SWIM₁ *mil* P241
SWIM₂ *me* P242
TAIL₁ *ine* E110; =AK19
TAIL₁ *teta* CP189
TAIL₂ *kari* E111
TAIL₂ *mex* CP190; =H11
TAKE *pita* P243
TAKE *uwa* CP191
TAKE OUT *ke* MG106
TALK *mala* CP192; =P247
TASTE *latˢa* P244
TASTE *p'akatˢi* AK189
TEAR (DROP) *kako* MG107
TELL *rake* AK190
TELL *ware* MT90; =P203;
 =MC60
TELL₁ *wič* P245
TELL₂ *ka* P246; =A219
TELL₃ *mal* P247; =CP192
TEN *maku* P248
TEN *te* CA77
TESTICLE *katu* MT91
TESTICLE *mak'in* AK191
TESTICLE *paki* A253; ?=H47
TESTICLE *tˢolo* H145; =P249
TESTICLE *talo* P249; =H145
THAT *a* G17 [CP]
THAT *ha* G24 [MP]
THAT *mo* G14 [A]
THAT *pa* G16 [A]
THAT *ti* G13 [A]
THICK *kapa* AK192
THIGH *pate* MC66; =A120
THIGH *teta* E112
THIN *aru* MG108
THIN *k'ut'i* A254
THIN *kam* MP60
THIN *paka* P250
THIS *ki* G22 [A]
THIS *ni* G23 [A]; cf. G15

THORN   *meč*   AN112
THORN   *nuk*   E113; =P9
THORN   *tat*   H146
THORN$_1$ *pu*   CP193
THORN$_2$ *sikali*   CP194
THOU   *a*   G7 [A]
THOU   *i*   G9 [E]
THOU   *ki*   G10 [A]; ?=G19; ?=G28
THOU   *kuma*   G8 [AN]
THOU   *ma*   G6 [A]
THOU   *so*   G11 [AK]
THREAD   *wia*   CA78
THREE   *kala*   AN113
THREE   *mai*   CP195
THREE   *pai*   CA79
THROAT   *nuk'*   A255
THROAT$_1$ *kolo*   E114
THROAT$_2$ *jari*   E115; =AN77
THROW   *aha*   AN114; =H149
THROW   *ame*   MG109
THROW$_1$ *pil*   P251
THROW$_1$ *tampi*   H147
THROW$_2$ *pat*   H148
THROW$_2$ *wit*   P252
THROW$_3$ *aka*   H149; =AN114
THROW$_4$ *sum*   H150
THUNDER   *mukak*   AK193
THUNDER   *pia*   CP196
THUNDER   *tim*   P253
THUS   *han*   MG110
TIE   *mai*   MC67
TIE   *pu*   CA80
TIE$_1$ *ola*   P254
TIE$_1$ *taka*   CP197
TIE$_2$ *koja*   CP198
TIE$_2$ *tep*   P255
TIRED   *kare*   MG111
TODAY   *nepi*   MC68
TODAY   *nokoa*   MT92

TODAY   *ore*   MG112; =CP135; =MC46
TOMORROW   *bauna*   AN115
TOMORROW   *koro*   MC69
TOMORROW   *tan*   CA81
TOMORROW   *čiki*   CP199
TONGUE   *jen*   CA82
TONGUE   *ʔipali*   H151
TONGUE$_1$ *ala*   P256
TONGUE$_1$ *nik*   A256
TONGUE$_1$ *sona*   CP200
TONGUE$_2$ *otu*   A257; =CP201
TONGUE$_2$ *tu*   CP201; =A257
TONGUE$_2$ *tulak*   P257
TONGUE$_3$ *nene*   A258
TOOTH   *it^{s}au*   H152; =E117; =CA83; =MG113
TOOTH   *je*   MC70
TOOTH   *onen*   AK194; =CP202
TOOTH   *pe*   MT93
TOOTH   *te*   CA83; =H152; =E117; =MG113
TOOTH   *tio*   MG113; =H152; =CA83; =E117
TOOTH$_1$ *nai*   E116
TOOTH$_1$ *nene*   CP202; =AK194
TOOTH$_1$ *t'ik*   P258
TOOTH$_2$ *ati*   E117; =H152; =CA83; =MG113
TOOTH$_2$ *kita*   CP203
TOOTH$_2$ *teli*   P259
TOPICALIZER   *te*   G41 [CP]
TORTOISE   *katu*   MG114
TOUCH   *kata*   CP204
TOUCH   *pit*   P260
TOWARD/AWAY   *m/k*   G99 [H]
TREE   *apa*   P261; =E118
TREE   *awa*   E118; =P261
TREE   *naku*   AN116
TREE   *topa*   MC71; =MT95; =E47;

=P235
TREE₁ *juka* MT94
TREE₁ *ko* CA84; =A275
TREE₁ *mis* AK195
TREE₁ *tua* A259
TREE₂ *lat* AK196
TREE₂ *nana* A260
TREE₂ *so* CA85
TREE₂ *tamba* MT95; =MC71;
    =E47; =P235
TREE₃ *kan* A261
TRUNK *kurku* AN117
TURN *k'ot* P262
TURTLE₁ *niwot* AK197
TURTLE₂ *kis* AK198
TWO *ačui* AK199
TWO *hoka* H153; =AN82
TWO *mena* MC72
TWO *pal* A262
TWO *soki* AN118
TWO *wi* CA86
UGLY *mane* E119
UGLY *po* CA87
UNCLE *kan* P263; =AK91
UNCLE *nari* AN119
UNDER *iti* H154
UNDER *kama* CP205
UNDER *papo* MC73
UNTIE *lauk* CP206
UP *apala* H155; =P220
UPON *wina* H156
URINE *jiso* MP61; =P264;
    =CP208
URINE *kane* MT96
URINE *saka* AK200; =E120
URINE *tˢako* E120; =AK200
URINE *wuš* P264; =CP208;
    =MP61
URINE₁ *tˢipi* CP207
URINE₂ *wisi* CP208; =P264;

=MP61
VAGINA *eni* MC74; =MT97;
    =P265
VAGINA *nes* P265; =MT97;
    =MC74
VAGINA *petu* A263; =E121
VAGINA *susi* CP209
VAGINA *tˢupote* E121; =A263
VEIN *pala* E122
VEIN *pok* P266
VEIN *tau* CP210
VOMIT *čuña* AN120
VULVA₁ *jaʔne* MT97; =MC74;
    =P265
VULVA₂ *de* MT98
WAIT *moki* MC75
WALK *pa* MG115; =A9; =CP34;
    =MC24
WALK *wi(n)* P267; =AK50;
    =H72; =E48
WASH *kupe* MG116
WASH *ʔo* CA88
WASH₁ *paki* H157; =A20;
    =MP59; =AK77
WASH₁ *tˢo* P268
WASH₂ *huka* P269; =CP11
WASH₂ *pola* H158
WASH₃ *jok* P270
WASP *botˢ* AK201
WASP *miu* MG117; =A27; =AK79
WASP *uti* MT99; =CP79
WASP *šušu* P271
WATER *ide* MT100; =P272;
    =H44
WATER *iše* P272; =H44;
    =MT100; cf. MG94
WATER *kota* AN121; =CP51;
    =MG33; =E64
WATER *kuŋ* MG118; =A87;
    =AK185; =CP152

WATER₁   *ma*   CP211; =A89;
=E125; AN97

WATER₁   *mani*   A264

WATER₁   *uni*   E123

WATER₂   *hija*   E124

WATER₂   *li*   CP212; =AK109

WATER₂   *poi*   A265

WATER₃   *jume*   E125; =A89;
=CP211; =AN97

WAX   *koma*   MT101

WAX   *mobi*   CP213

WAX   *moro*   MC76

WE   *sun*   G4 [MP]

WE   *to*   G5 [MT]

WE INCLUSIVE   *s*   G21 [A]

WE 2   *ko*   G28 [MC]; ?=G10;
?=G19

WE 2 INCLUSIVE   *ki*   G19 [A];
?=G10; ?=G28

WE 2 INCLUSIVE   *õ*   G20 [K]

WEAK   *jel*   MP62

WEAK   *ñiña*   MG119

WEAVE   *vik*   H159; =P208

WET   *paku*   CP214; =P273

WET₁   *pak*   P273; =CP214

WET₂   *lokak*   P274

WHITE   *jurak*   AN122

WHITE   *kel*   P275

WHITE   *matal*   H160

WHITE   *mone*   MC77

WHITE   *ta?*   CA89

WHITE₁   *pole*   A266

WHITE₁   *tara*   CP215; =MG120

WHITE₁   *tora*   MG120; =CP215

WHITE₂   *kuatˢa*   CP216

WHITE₂   *oka*   MG121

WHITE₂   *pek*   A267

WIFE   *ta*   H161; cf. MG123

WIND₁   *kela*   AN123; =P276

WIND₁   *wani*   MT102

WIND₁   (N.)   *kuli*   P276; =AN123

WIND₂   *fik*   AN124

WIND₂   *owa*   MT103

WIND₂   (N.)   *pantˢ*   P277

WIND   (N.)   *?aja*   H162

WIND (n.)   *kuki*   A268

WIND   (N.)   *laq*   AK202

WIND   (N.)   *puluk*   CP217

WING   *kampi*   A269

WING   *peto*   AK203; =P99

WING   *tana*   E126; =H77

WING₁   *keka*   CP218

WING₁   *li*   P278

WING₂   *pako*   CP219; =P214;
=MT46; =A7

WING₂   *tap*   P279

WISH   *ina*   AN125; =G83

WISH   *k'uni*   H163

WISH   *mena*   A270

WISH   *naq*   AK204

WISH   *pea*   CP220

WISH   *rani*   MC78

WISH   *taku*   MT104

WISH₁   *hata*   E127

WISH₁   *saka*   P280

WISH₂   *ea*   E128

WISH₂   *san*   P281

WISH₃   *kau*   P282

WOLF   *kua*   CA90; =A86

WOMAN   *kana*   P283; =A272;
=H164

WOMAN   *pen*   MP63; =CA1; =AN9

WOMAN   *wato*   MC79

WOMAN   *ĩhõ*   AK205

WOMAN₁   *kapa*   MT105

WOMAN₁   *kuan*   H164; =A272;
=P283

WOMAN₁   *pako*   MG122

WOMAN₁   *tom*   A271

WOMAN₁   *tuna*   E129; =A125;

=MT106; =MG41

WOMAN₁ *wale* CP221

WOMAN₂ *kame* E130

WOMAN₂ *keko* H165

WOMAN₂ *kuna* A272; =P283; =H164

WOMAN₂ *suna* CP222; =A273; =CA41

WOMAN₂ *tain* MT106; =A125; =E129; =MG41

WOMAN₂ *ti* MG123; cf. H161

WOMAN₃ *mati* H166

WOMAN₃ *sun* A273; =CA41; =CP222

WOOD *lak* AK206; =A45

WOOD₁ *ije* A274

WOOD₁ *kauk* P284

WOOD₂ *ake* A275; =CA84

WOOD₂ *tok* P285; cf. A54; cf. A251; cf. AK108

WORK₁ (V.) *kampa* CP223

WORK₁ (v.) *kua* A276

WORK₂ (V.) *noni* CP224; =E76

WORK₂ (v.) *pi* A277

WORM *kesi* CP225

WORM *laua* AN126

WORM *moka* H167

WORM₁ *tˢumpo* E131; =A241

WORM₁ *čuwi* AK207

WORM₂ *jakʷe* AK208

WORM₂ *niñi* E132

YELLOW *jalu* H168

YELLOW *kas* P286

YELLOW *putˢia* MT107

YELLOW *sunga* CP226

YELLOW *tal* AN127

YELLOW *teka* AK209; ?=A279

YELLOW *čaken* E133

YELLOW₁ *tampa* A278

YELLOW₂ *tˢi* A279

YESTERDAY *ija* AN128

YESTERDAY *kani* A280

YOUNG *kuta* A281; =H29; =AK44; =P88

YOUNG *mani* AN129

YOUNG₁ *mu* P287

YOUNG₂ *čumat* P288

8

Additional Amerind Etymologies

A further sifting of the 2,003 etymologies contained in Joseph Greenberg's *Language in the Americas* (1987, Stanford) suggests that some of the etymologies presented in support of one or another of the eleven Amerind subgroups should, rather, be combined to form an etymology supporting the Amerind family itself. The following list indicates such possible consolidations. The forms given in the etymologies are only those sufficient to suggest that the etymologies should in fact be combined. For all of the additional forms the reader should consult Greenberg's book. Some of these proposed consolidations seem wholly defensible; future research must show whether others, of a more tentative nature, should be corroborated or rejected. In addition to these new Amerind etymologies, there are also cases where an etymology for an Amerind subgroup should be combined with an already existing Amerind etymology. Such possible cases are listed at the end of the chapter. Finally, there are a few cases of consolidation within Amerind subgroups; these too are listed at the end of the chapter.

ADDITIONAL AMERIND ETYMOLOGIES

The numbering of these proposed etymologies begins at 282 to indicate that they are supplementary to the 281 Amerind (lexical) etymologies contained in *Language in the Americas*. The number of the etymology in Greenberg's book is given after the Amerind subgroup. Thus "PENUTIAN [3]" refers to Greenberg's third Penutian etymology. Where no number follows the Amerind subgroup, the forms cited have been taken from Greenberg's unpublished Amerindian notebooks (1981) or other sources. Forms without glosses have the same meaning as that given for the respective Amerind subgroup.

282 ALL

ALMOSAN-KERESIOUAN [4] ALL.   Wiyot *qat^s* 'be many,' Thompson *hwet*, Kitsai *akwat^s*.

PENUTIAN [3] ALL.   Coos *gōs*, Atakapa *kuš*, Tzeltal *k'aš* 'very,' Quiché *k'is* 'finish.'

283 ANUS

CHIBCHAN-PAEZAN [3] ANUS.   Paez *kuts*, Bintucua *gase*, Borunca *kas* 'ravine.'

ANDEAN [4] ANUS.   Qawashqar *kioot-pe*, Gennaken *oqoti*, Yamana *guta* 'hole.'

284 ARM

HOKAN [5] ARM.   Yana *galu*, Southeast Pomo *xal*.

CHIBCHAN-PAEZAN [4] ARM.   Guamaca *gula*, Gualaca *kula* 'hand,' Guambiana *kwal*.

285 ARRIVE

PENUTIAN [8] ARRIVE.   Bodega *wila* 'come!,' Kekchí *uli*, Yakonan *wīl*.

HOKAN [49] ENTER.   Achomawi *uilu*, Yahi *wul* 'entering.'

286 AUNT

CENTRAL AMERIND [1] AUNT.   Proto-Uto-Aztecan **pa*, Proto-Oto-Manguean **k^{w}a(H)(n)*.

ANDEAN [9] AUNT.   Tehuelche *epan*, Cholona *pan* 'mother.'

MACRO-PANOAN [63] WOMAN.   Moseten *pen*, Proto-Tacanan **e-pona*.

287 BACK

HOKAN [11] BACK.   Yana *mak'i*, Comecrudo *wamak* 'behind.'

CHIBCHAN-PAEZAN [190] TAIL.   Colorado *meh*, Ulua *umax-ka*.

288 BACK

CHIBCHAN-PAEZAN [14] BEHIND.   Allentiac *punak*, Colorado *bene*.

MACRO-GE [5] BACK.   Guato *ipana* 'tail,' Apucarana *pani*, Bororo *i-puru*.

289 BE

ALMOSAN-KERESIOUAN [13] BE.   Wichita *ʔi*, Cherokee *i*.
MACRO-PANOAN [9] BE.   Mataco *hi*, Mascoy *h-*.

290 BEHIND

ALMOSAN-KERESIOUAN [19] BEHIND.   Yurok *hinoj*, Cherokee *ōni*, Kutenai *iɬ*.
EQUATORIAL [110] TAIL.   Cayuvava *eñe*, Paresi *inihu*, Saliba *inea*.

291 BELLY

ALMOSAN-KERESIOUAN [33] BREAST.   Acoma *(ka-)si*, Hidatsa *at^si* (< **a-si*).
CENTRAL AMERIND [4] BELLY.   Tewa *sī*, Proto-Oto-Manguean **(n)(ʔ)se(h)(n)*, Mono *sihi* 'intestines,' Opata *siwa-t*.

292 BIRD

ALMOSAN-KERESIOUAN [22] BIRD.   Proto-Central Algonquian **s̄īs̄īpa*, Bella Bella *t^sit^sipe*.
ANDEAN [12] BAT.   Quechua *t^sikt^si*, Gennaken *čexčux*.

293 BLACK

CHIBCHAN-PAEZAN [19] BLACK.   Borunca *turinat*, Tarascan *tuli*, Chami *tauri* 'shadow.'
MACRO-TUCANOAN [10] BLACK.   Mobima *tuni*, Southern Nambikwara *t'un*.

294 BLOOD

ALMOSAN-KERESIOUAN [157] RED.   Proto-Algonquian **meçkwi*, Santa Ana *mʔaʔat^s'i*, Bella Bella *muk^w*.
PENUTIAN [18] BLOOD.   Tsimshian *misk* 'red,' Atakapa *pošk*, Yokuts *pajčikin*.

295 BLOOD

EQUATORIAL [18] BLOOD.   Tora *wi*, Santa Rosa *xue*, Proto-Tupi **uwɨ*.
MACRO-PANOAN [12] BLOOD.   Lule *ewe*, Chunupi *woi*, Chama *woʔo* 'red.'

296 BREAST

MACRO-TUCANOAN [18] BREAST.   Capixana *njãnõ* 'bosom,' Huari *nini*, Ticuna *nonnon*.
MACRO-GE [9] BELLY.   Kradaho *i-nioŋu*, Mashakali *inioñ*.

297 BREAST

CENTRAL AMERIND [9] BREAST.   Tewa pĩ, Proto-Oto-Manguean
*kʷi(ʔ)(n), Proto-Uto-Aztecan *pi.
CHIBCHAN-PAEZAN [15] BELLY.   Tucura bi, Colorado bi 'inside,' Matagalpa pu.
MACRO-TUCANOAN [17] BREAST.   Wanana peno, Hubde pwun, Kaliana
wi.

298 BREAST

PENUTIAN [25] BREAST.   Chorti ču, Tunica ʔuču.
PENUTIAN [107] HEART.   Atakapa šo, Yuki t'u 'belly,' Zuni tˢu 'stomach.'
HOKAN [25] BREAST.   Washo šū, Chumash s-čwø, Karok ʔūčič.
CHIBCHAN-PAEZAN [98] HEART.   Dobocubi iši 'belly,' Ulua asung 'liver,'
Sambu izo.

299 BROTHER

ANDEAN [101] SISTER.   Culli kañi, Cholona akiñiu.
MACRO-PANOAN [16] BROTHER.   Lule kani, Choroti kiini.

300 BURN

CHIBCHAN-PAEZAN [105] HOT.   Paez bač 'become hot,' Dobocubi bočon
'heat.'
CHIBCHAN-PAEZAN [109] KINDLE.   Bribri patˢe, Paez apaz 'burn,' Paya
pas.
MACRO-GE [18] BURN.   Botocudo pek, Karaho puk, Erikbatsa
okpog(-maha).

301 BURN

ALMOSAN-KERESIOUAN [37] BURN.   Santa Ana hā-k'a-ni 'fire,' Kutenai
ko.
CENTRAL AMERIND [11] BURN.   Proto-Oto-Manguean *ka, Proto-Uto-
Aztecan *ku, koʔ 'fire,' Taos xa 'roast.'

302 BURN

ALMOSAN-KERESIOUAN COOK.   Proto-Salish *wəɬqʷ 'cook, boil,' Upper
Chehalis wλqʷ 'cook.'
PENUTIAN BURN.   Tsimshian māʔlk, Nass meɬ, Takelma meʔl, Siuslaw
maɬč, Nisenan molmol 'boil,' Patwin māɬa 'cook.'
HOKAN [19, 26] BURN.   Yana maʔlak 'bake,' South Pomo māli, Washo
meli 'make a fire,' Jicaque myolko 'boil.'

CENTRAL AMERIND BOIL.   Zacapoaxtla *momoluca*.

303 BUY

ALMOSAN-KERESIOUAN [40] BUY.   Shuswap *tew*, Kwakiutl *da* 'take.'
CENTRAL AMERIND [13] BUY.   Proto-Oto-Manguean **te*, Proto-Aztec-
Tanoan **ty*.

304 CHEEK

HOKAN [28] CHEEK.   Jicaque *pʰok*, Tequistlatec *bege*.
MACRO-CARIB [9] CHEEK.   Motilon *ipæpok*, Ocaina *faʔxon*.

305 CLOSE

PENUTIAN [109] HIDE.   Yakima *ik*, Central Sierra Miwok *ʔokoj* 'cover,'
Chitimacha *ʔiki*, Quiché *k'uj*.
CENTRAL AMERIND [15] CLOSE.   Proto-Oto-Manguean **ku* 'close, cover,'
Taos *kʷi-l*.

306 CLOSE

PENUTIAN [39] CLOSE.   Atakapa *pan*, Wappo *pɔn*, Maidu *ban* 'cover.'
MACRO-PANOAN [17] CLOSE.   Choroti *pone*, Cavineña *pene*.

307 COLD

CENTRAL AMERIND [18] COLD.   Kiowa *t'o* 'be cold,' Proto-Oto-Manguean
*tome.
EQUATORIAL [27] COLD.   Saliba *duha*, Toyeri *dohina*.

308 COLD

CENTRAL AMERIND [16] COLD.   Taos *k'o*, Proto-Oto-Manguean **kʷi(n)*,
Proto-Uto-Aztecan **kʷi*.
MACRO-PANOAN [19] COLD.   Chunupi *kui*, Lule *kei*.

309 COLD

CENTRAL AMERIND [17] COLD.   Taos *tˢia*, Proto-Aztec-Tanoan **tˢija*,
Proto-Uto-Aztecan **sep*.
EQUATORIAL [28] COLD.   Yaruro *čiwah*, Taruma *siwa*.

310 COME

HOKAN [74] GO OUT.   Tonkawa *ta*, Atsugewi *-ta* 'out of,' Chimariko *tap*
'out of.'
CHIBCHAN-PAEZAN [35] COME.   Cuna *-ta-* 'go,' Xinca *taa*, Itonama *t'o*.

311 COME

PENUTIAN [189] RETURN.   Nez Perce *toq*, Tsimshian *adək* 'turn back.'
CHIBCHAN-PAEZAN [36] COME.   Cuna *taka*, Paya *tek*.

312 COME

PENUTIAN [187] RETURN.   Proto-Maidu *joʔkʰe*, Tunica *jaka*.
ANDEAN [24] COME.   Araucanian *aku* 'arrive,' Kahuapana *kwa*, Zaparo
ikwa 'go.'
Cf. No. 347 below.

313 COME

ALMOSAN-KERESIOUAN [49] COME.   Wiyot *how*, Cheyenne *ho*, Proto-
Siouan **hu* 'arrive.'
CHIBCHAN-PAEZAN [37] COME.   Atakama *hau*, Cayapa *ha*.

314 COOK

PENUTIAN [23] BOIL.   Wappo *kʰohkʰoh*, Atakapa *uk*.
MACRO-TUCANOAN [23] COOK.   Siona *kwako*, Puinave *a-kag*.

315 CLOUD

PENUTIAN [40] CLOUD.   Coast Yuki *poʔtit*, Yakima *pasčit* 'fog.'
EQUATORIAL [59] HEAVEN.   Ebidoso *pod*, Guayabero *fato*, Timote *ki-
veuč* 'cloud.'

316 COVER

HOKAN [31] COVER.   Washo *ītsʼig* 'close,' Northeast Pomo *šīkʼo* 'blanket,' Karok *-čak* 'closing up.'
HOKAN [58] FINISH.   North Yana *dikʼau*, Tonkawa *tōxa*.
CHIBCHAN-PAEZAN [40] COVER.   Tarascan *šuku-ta-hpe-ni*, Tunebo *teka-
ra* 'poncho,' Cuna *tukusii* 'be hidden.'
MACRO-GE [31] DRESS.   Botocudo *atak*, Caraja *taku* 'clothing,' Caraja
deku 'woman's shirt.'

317 COVER

HOKAN [32] COVER.   Karok *sap* 'close,' Mohave *sapet* 'close,' Yurumangui *sipa-na* 'hat.'
CHIBCHAN-PAEZAN [73] FINISH.   Itonama *soʔp*, Eten *siaip*.

318 CRY

HOKAN [34] CRY.   Washo *iʔb*, Jicaque *pija*, Karok *ʔivūr* 'weep for.'

MACRO-GE [26] CRY.   Chiquito *ipu*, Tibagi *fua*, Mashakali *opo* 'he cries.'

319 DANCE

CHIBCHAN-PAEZAN [43] DANCE.   Itonama *tuluke*, Colorado *terake-de*.
MACRO-TUCANOAN [25] DANCE.   Yuri *tarøhene*, Mobima *telo*.

320 DEER

CHIBCHAN-PAEZAN [46] DEER.   Cayapa *mana*, Barira *maana* 'meat.'
ANDEAN [60] JAGUAR.   Jebero *amana*, Auca *mēnē*.

321 DOG

HOKAN [41] DOG.   Washo *gušu*, San Antonio *xuč*, Coahuilteco *keš*.
CENTRAL AMERIND [28] DOG.   Proto-Uto-Aztecan *t^su, Piro *t^sue*.
MACRO-CARIB [12] DEER.   Miranya *göhsu*, Witoto *kyto*, Bakairí *kxose-ka*.

322 EAR

PENUTIAN [106] HEAR.   Choctaw *ikhana* 'hear,' Yuki *hāl* 'hear.'
EQUATORIAL [34] EAR.   Moxo *nu-kiña*, Uro *kuñi*.

323 EAR

ALMOSAN-KERESIOUAN [58] EAR.   Santa Ana *s'-īpe* 'my ear,' Hidatsa *apa* 'animal's ear.'
MACRO-GE [61] HEAR.   Botocudo *apa*, Karaho *pa*.

324 EARTH

ANDEAN [32] EARTH.   Quechua *pat^sa* 'ground,' Hivito *put^s*.
MACRO-TUCANOAN [31] EARTH.   Iranshe *bata*, Puinave *(m)baγtçi*.

325 EARTH

CHIBCHAN-PAEZAN [59] EARTH.   Paya *kuka*, Borunca *kak*, Manare *kakka* 'world.'
MACRO-TUCANOAN [32] EARTH.   Auixiri *okake*, Capixana *kekeke*, Dou *čax*.

326 EARTH

HOKAN [40] DIRTY.   Tipai *xpił* 'dirty,' Comecrudo *papeleple* 'dirty.'
CHIBCHAN-PAEZAN [58] EARTH.   Cuaiquer *piʎ*, Timucua *pile* 'field,' Guambiana *pire*.

327 EAT

ALMOSAN-KERESIOUAN [59] EAT. Proto-Central Algonquian *-am- 'eat small inanimate object,' Kalispel ʔem 'feed.'
ALMOSAN-KERESIOUAN [131] MOUTH. Chippewa -am 'by mouth,' Nootka m'a 'hold in mouth.'
HOKAN [46] EAT. Achomawi ām, Chimariko -ama-, Esselen am, Quinigua ama 'eat fish,' Yana ma, Yuma ama.

328 ELBOW

ALMOSAN-KERESIOUAN [52] CROOKED. Mohawk aʔktu, Shawnee kotekwi 'turn,' Squamish k'ʷutˢun, Yuchi kota.
PENUTIAN [63] ELBOW. Yaudanchi kʰošoji, Creek ekučē, North Sahaptin k'ašinu, Sierra Popoluca kōsu 'knee.'

329 ELBOW

PENUTIAN [62] ELBOW. Atakapa šuk, Uspantec čuk.
CHIBCHAN-PAEZAN [61] ELBOW. Tarascan kukui-si, Paya kokisa 'knee,' Sinsiga kuika.

330 EYE

PENUTIAN [150] LOOK. Maidu tˢ'en 'look,' Zoque tuʔn 'look at,' Takelma tˢ'elei, Zuni tuna.
CHIBCHAN-PAEZAN [159] SEE. Millcayac tene(-kina), Norteño teen, Xinca tili.
ANDEAN [34] EYE. Qawashqar teɬ, Yamana tella.

331 EYE

ALMOSAN-KERESIOUAN [163] SEE. Mohawk kã, Hidatsa ika, Yuchi k'a 'watch.'
MACRO-TUCANOAN [36] EYE. Capixana i-kaẽ, Proto-Nambikwara *eika, Bendiapa iku.

332 EYE

MACRO-TUCANOAN [34] EYE. Canichana tokhe, Auixiri atuka.
EQUATORIAL [39] EYE. Itene tok, Santa Rosa tuxua, Caranga čukˣi.

333 EYE

ALMOSAN-KERESIOUAN [63] EYE. Nitinat qaliʔ, Pentlatch kəlom, Nisqualli kalob, Tillamook -gāɬ-, Kutenai -qɬiɬ, Quileute -qaɬ 'look at,' Wiyot tu-kɬ 'watch,' Yurok kʷəɬ 'image,' Kwakiutl qwāxwa 'see,' Proto-North

Iroquoian *kakáhraʔ 'eyes,' Mohawk okà̃raʔ 'eyes,' Oneida okà̃laʔ 'eyes,' Pawnee kirīku 'eye, look at,' Wichita kirik'a.

PENUTIAN EYE.   Tfalatik kwallak, Coos xwalxwal, North Sahaptin wal 'by sight,' Atakapa wōl, Coast Yuki hul, Wintun ʔat-ma 'look,' Chinook kəl 'see,' Huastec wal, Tzotzil k'alel 'look.'

HOKAN SEE.   East Pomo kār-, Yana kel 'peer,' Cochimi gir, ʔTonkawa helʔeya 'look.'

CHIBCHAN-PAEZAN EYE.   Itonama uj-k'ururu, Cayapa querā- 'appear,' Colorado kiriasa 'see.'

ANDEAN LOOK.   Qawashqar qualeona, Zaparo karīyā.

MACRO-TUCANOAN EYE.   Bahukīwa djakoli, Cubeo yakoli ~ yakori.

EQUATORIAL EYE.   Manao nu-kurika, Itene ikirikira 'look,' Callahuaya khura-na 'see.'

MACRO-PANOAN EYE.   Caduveo oge-kuře, Opaye či-gareye.

MACRO-GE EYE.   Mashubi akari.

334 FAR

PENUTIAN [70] FAR.   Atakapa ja, Zoque jaʔaj.

CHIBCHAN-PAEZAN [66] FAR.   Cuitlatec jaj-, Tarascan io- 'high, long.'

335 FAT

CHIBCHAN-PAEZAN [68] FAT.   Cuitlatec kuji, Timucua uke, Tirub kio.

MACRO-CARIB [20] FAT.   Nonuya kwi, Andoke kehə.

336 FEAR

PENUTIAN [74] FEAR.   Yaudanchi bax, Chol bʔuknian.

MACRO-PANOAN [34] HATE.   Abipone n-paak 'hated,' Moseten fakoj.

337 FIRE

ALMOSAN-KERESIOUAN [73] FIRE.   Proto-Central Algonquian *-su 'by heat,' Northern Arapaho isei, Squamish tm-iʔis 'summer' (tm = 'season').

EQUATORIAL [43] FIRE.   Chapacura ise, Guahibo iso, Kamaru isu, Amuesha soʔ.

338 FIRE

HOKAN [61] FIRE.   Karok ʔāha, Kashaya ʔoho, San Antonio ṭ-aʔauh, Kiliwa ʔaau.

ANDEAN [8] ASHES.   Yamana øxwa, Tsoneka ahe, Itucale auxe 'charcoal.'

339 FIRE

ALMOSAN-KERESIOUAN [72] FIRE.   Acoma *baja* 'make fire,' Osage *poe* 'flames.'

CENTRAL AMERIND [36] FIRE.   Piro *faje*, Isleta *pʰāi-de*, Proto-Oto-Manguean *(n)(h)kʷa* 'hot.'

340 FISH

ANDEAN [38] FISH.   Sechura *šuma*, Jebero *samer*.

MACRO-TUCANOAN [42] FISH.   Pankaruru *kami(-jo)*, Tiquie *homp*.

EQUATORIAL [44] FISH.   Piro *čima*, Chapacura *ĩšuam*, Tora *hoam*.

341 FLOWER

CHIBCHAN-PAEZAN [78] FLOWER.   Cuitlatec *tuxtu*, Cuna *tutu*.

ANDEAN [40] FLOWER.   Catacao *čukču(m)*, Culli *čuču*.

342 FLOWER

ALMOSAN-KERESIOUAN [78] FLOWER.   Proto-Central Algonquian *paQk*, Twana *s-p'q'ab*.

PENUTIAN [20] BLOOM.   Proto-Muskogean *pak* 'bloom,' Tetontepec *puk*, Huave *mbah*.

343 FLY (v.)

PENUTIAN [84] FLY.   Hitchiti *jaka*, Wappo *jɔkkɔ*.

MACRO-TUCANOAN [9] BIRD.   Proto-Nambikwara *ʔaik'* 'bird,' Iranshe *itˢi* 'bird,' Ticuna *goe*.

344 FLY (n.)

CHIBCHAN-PAEZAN [79] FLY.   Yupultepec *usu* 'fly, wasp,' Cuitlatec *øɫi*.

MACRO-TUCANOAN [99] WASP.   Uasona *utia*, Iranshe *ači*.

345 FULL

PENUTIAN [86] FULL.   Coos *paa* 'to fill,' Maidu *pe*, Atakapa *pū*.

ANDEAN [2] ALL.   Auca *baa*, Kahuapana *ipa* 'enough.'

346 FULL

ALMOSAN-KERESIOUAN [83] FULL.   Quapaw *panã* 'all,' Proto-Salish *p'ər* 'overflow.'

HOKAN [69] FULL.   North Yana *baʔni* 'be full,' Yurumangui *pini-ta* 'empty' (*-ta* is negative.).

347 GO

PENUTIAN [64] ENTER.   Mutsun *akku*, Tunica *ʔaka* 'come in,' Central
Sierra Miwok *ʔūk*, Kakchiquel *ok*.
HOKAN [73] GO.   Cocopa *ʔax*, North Yana *ha* 'woman goes,' Chimariko a.
Cf. No. 312 above.

348 GO

ALMOSAN-KERESIOUAN [50] COME.   Wiyot *wa* 'go,' Yuchi *wi*, Kutenai w-
'arrive.'
PENUTIAN [267] WALK.   Plains Miwok *wən*, Atakapa *wang*, Takelma *wī*
'go about.'
HOKAN [72] GO.   East Pomo *wa-*, Quinigua *wan*, Tequistlatec *wa*.
EQUATORIAL [48] GO.   Coche *wajo* 'walk,' Dzubucua *wa*, Saliba *wa*.

349 GO

EQUATORIAL [49] GO OUT.   Cayuvava *βɔrɔ*, Yuracare *porere*.
MACRO-GE [92] ROAD.   Botocudo *mporõ*, Proto-Ge **prɨ*.

350 GOOD

ALMOSAN-KERESIOUAN [88] GOOD.   Proto-Algonquian **kan* 'beautiful,'
Mohawk *akarite* 'be healthy,' Catawba *kəri*, Tillamook *k'unək* 'beauti-
ful.'
PENUTIAN [15] BEAUTIFUL.   Central Sierra Miwok *kəlli* 'healthy,' North
Wintu *čal*, Jacaltec *č'ul*.
HOKAN [75] GOOD.   Cotoname *kenax*, Akwa'ala *xan*.
MACRO-CARIB [2] BEAUTIFUL.   Proto-Carib **kuule* 'good,' Ocaina *xa-
rooga*.

351 GOOD

CHIBCHAN-PAEZAN [86] GOOD.   Dobocubi *baj*, Chiripo *bui*.
MACRO-GE [7] BEAUTIFUL.   Krenje *pej* 'beautiful, good,' Mashakali
epai, Malali *epoi*.

352 GRANDFATHER

ALMOSAN-KERESIOUAN [90] GRANDFATHER.   Yurok *pitˢowas*, Ojibwa
ne-miššomis 'my grandfather.'
MACRO-CARIB [25] GRANDFATHER.   Nahugua *apitˢi*, Andoke *japitah*.

353 GRANDFATHER

ALMOSAN-KERESIOUAN [91] GRANDFATHER.   Pawnee *ikani*, Biloxi *ikoni.*

PENUTIAN [263] UNCLE. Chitimacha *kan* 'paternal uncle,' Quiché *ikan* 'uncle.'

354 GRASS

PENUTIAN [93] GRASS. Proto-California Penutian **pu*, Chitimacha *po*, Zuni *pe.*
CHIBCHAN-PAEZAN [88] GRASS. Chimu *pe*, Cuitlatec *bejoʔo*, Guambiana *pu.*

355 HAIR

CENTRAL AMERIND [44] HAIR. Proto-Uto-Aztecan **tˢoni* 'body hair,' Proto-Oto-Manguean **(Y)su(n).*
EQUATORIAL [55] HAIR. Tora *tuni*, Piapoco *čona.*

356 HAIR

PENUTIAN [75] FEATHER. Atakapa *li* 'feather,' Tsimshian *li* 'feather,' Zuni *la* 'feather.'
ANDEAN [52] HAIR. Ona *aal*, Yamana *ali* 'feather.'
MACRO-GE [57] HAIR. Erikbatsa *ka-ari*, Fulnio *li*, Krenje *ara* 'down.'

357 HAND

PENUTIAN [7] ARM. Atakapa *wiš*, Natchez *ʔīs* 'arm, hand,' Huave *owiš*, Yuki *hyss*, Mutsun *isu* 'hand.'
ANDEAN [53] HAND. Yamana *još*, Tehuelche *oš.*

358 HAND

ALMOSAN-KERESIOUAN [93] HAND. Blackfoot *-kitˢ-* 'finger,' Squamish *čis.*
PENUTIAN [89] GIVE. Natchez *kus*, Quiché *koč* 'gift.'
CHIBCHAN-PAEZAN [92] HAND. Norteño *kuse*, Move *kise*, Paez *kose*, Borunca *i-kus(-kua)* 'finger.'

359 HAND

HOKAN [77] HAND. Chimariko *-teni*, South Pomo *tʰāna.*
EQUATORIAL [126] WING. Urupa *tiñi*, Bare *dana* 'arm.'

360 HAND

ALMOSAN-KERESIOUAN [203] WING. Proto-Algonquian **na-xpeto-ni*, Pawnee *pīd*, Bella Bella *p'ətˡ-am.*

PENUTIAN [99] HAND.   Yokuts *pʰutʰɔng*, Chinook *pote* 'arm,' Kalapuya *putukwi* 'arm.'

PENUTIAN [243] TAKE.   Alabama *pota*, Wappo *pita*.

PENUTIAN [260] TOUCH.   Proto-Muskogean **put* 'touch,' Wappo *pito* 'touch.'

361 HAND

ALMOSAN-KERESIOUAN [94] HAND.   Proto-Siouan **šaki*, Caddo *sik*.

CHIBCHAN-PAEZAN [93] HAND.   Andaqui *saka-a*, Chibcha *yta-saka*, Tiribi *sak-wo* 'finger.'

362 HEAD

ALMOSAN-KERESIOUAN [96] HEAD.   Cherokee *u-sko-li*, Kwakiutl *sɘq'a* 'over,' Tutelo *sako* 'above.'

CHIBCHAN-PAEZAN [96] HEAD.   Betoi *ro-saka*, Bintucua *saku-ku* 'skull,' Cuna *sakla*, Jutiapa *usaxle*.

363 HEART

HOKAN [82] HEART.   East Pomo *tˢukun*, North Yana *dᶻugutˢ'i*, San Antonio *šk'oʔil* 'lungs.'

CHIBCHAN-PAEZAN [107] KIDNEY.   Cabecar *sokko*, Paya *sakka* 'spleen.'

364 HIT

ALMOSAN-KERESIOUAN [153] POUND.   Coeur d'Alene *tiʔ*, Caddo *daʔ* 'pound corn,' Kutenai *t'ā-* 'knock.'

PENUTIAN [110] HIT.   Coos *tōh*, Wappo *tɔh*, Natchez *ta*.

ANDEAN [37] FIGHT.   Qawashqar *toks*, Aymara *tok'e* 'quarrel.'

365 HIT

PENUTIAN [14] BEAT.   Atakapa *pak*, Maidu *bok-*.

CENTRAL AMERIND [47] HIT.   Proto-Uto-Aztecan **pa*, Proto-Oto-Manguean **(n)(h)kʷa(h)*.

366 HOLE

PENUTIAN [115] HOLE.   Lake Miwok *talokʰ*, Atakapa *tol* 'anus,' Takelma *telkan* 'buttocks.'

MACRO-GE [65] HOLE.   Kaingan *doro*, Coroado *dore* 'cave.'

367 HOUSE

CENTRAL AMERIND [48] HOUSE.   Proto-Oto-Manguean **(n)ka(H)(n)*,

Proto-Uto-Aztecan *ki.
MACRO-CARIB [29] HOUSE.   Muinane *ixa*, Taulipang *kə* 'stay.'

368 HUSBAND

PENUTIAN [122] HUSBAND.   Huchnom *i-na*, Cayuse *inaiu*, Tepehua *noh*.
MACRO-CARIB [31] HUSBAND.   Proto-Carib *ino*, Witoto *inuj*.

369 IMPERATIVE

G88 [Hokan] IMPERATIVE.   Yana *-ʔi*, Karok *-i*, Salinan *-i-*, Yurumangui
-i.
G91 [Keresiouan] IMPERATIVE.   Wichita *hi-*, Keres *ʔi*.

370 INTERROGATIVE

G106 [Penutian] WHAT?   Central Sierra Miwok *tinnə*, North Sahaptin
tunn, Siuslaw *tɔn*, Chinook *tan*, Totonac *tu*.
MACRO-GE [68] HOW MANY?   Botocudo *tan*, Palmas *ndena*.

371 LARGE

HOKAN [89] LARGE.   Jicaque *-po* (augmentative), Subtiaba *-mba* (augmentative).
CHIBCHAN-PAEZAN [110] LARGE.   Duit *oba*, Itonama *bɨ*, Chilanga *buj*.

372 LARGE

ANDEAN [64] LARGE.   Leco *umun*, Iquito *uumaana*.
MACRO-CARIB [32] LARGE.   Proto-Carib *moonomi*, Ocaina *aamon*
'grow.'

373 LEFT (SIDE)

ALMOSAN-KERESIOUAN [112] LEFT.   Nootka *qatˢ*, Proto-Salish *tˢʼiqʷ*,
Yurok *kes(-omewet)*.
MACRO-GE [71] LEFT.   Proto-Ge *kɛč*, Mashakali *čač*.

374 LEG

ALMOSAN-KERESIOUAN [113] LEG.   Fox *-ska-* 'with the foot,' Yurok *tˢka*
'foot,' Kutenai *saqʼ*.
CHIBCHAN-PAEZAN [167] SHIN.   Andaqui *sa-sagua-na* 'tibia,' Chibcha *tsa-
sagua-ne* 'kneecap.'

375 LIVE

ALMOSAN-KERESIOUAN [118] LIVE.   Mohawk *ha*, Yuchi *ha*.

PENUTIAN [119] HOUSE.   Chitimacha *hana*, Yuki *han*.

376 LIVE

HOKAN [96] LIVE.   Subtiaba *ja*, Seri *-i?*, Yana *jai* 'stay.'
CHIBCHAN-PAEZAN [106] HOUSE.   Cayapa *ja*, Panikita *ja*, Paya *uja* 'nest.'

377 MAN

CHIBCHAN-PAEZAN [138] OLD MAN.   Tarascan *tama-pu*, Warrau *idamo*,
Miskito *dama* 'grandfather.'
MACRO-CARIB [38] MAN.   Miranya *thimae*, Motilon *tama* 'boy.'

378 MAN

ANDEAN [70] MALE.   Yanacocha *oloqo* 'husband,' Quechua *orqo* 'husband,' Araucanian *alka*, Qawashqar *arak*.
EQUATORIAL [77] MAN.   Arawak *lukku*, Uro *luku*.

379 MAN

PENUTIAN [92] GRANDMOTHER.   Maidu *koto*, Zuni *hotta*, Yakima *katla*.
ANDEAN [35] FATHER.   Iquito *kati*, Sechura *kuč*, Itucale *kiča*, Hivito
kotk.
MACRO-TUCANOAN [61] MAN.   Canichana *kohti* 'husband,' Gamella *katu*,
Curiariai *xot* 'person.'

380 MANY

HOKAN [2] ALL.   Subtiaba *bā*, Waicuri *pu*.
EQUATORIAL [79] MANY.   Cofan *bu*, Piaroa *buio* 'large,' Sanamaika *pui*
'large.'

381 MANY

EQUATORIAL [78] MANY.   Coche *but^{s}a* 'large,' Kariri *pečo*, Yuracare *puče*
'surpass.'
MACRO-GE [1] ALL.   Botocudo *pota*, Caraja *ibote*, Masacara *pautzöh*.

382 MEAT

ALMOSAN-KERESIOUAN [65] FAT.   Proto-Siouan **šī* 'fat,' Seneca *sē* 'be
fat.'
MACRO-GE [78] MEAT.   Botocudo *čin*, Came *tini*.

383 MEAT

ALMOSAN-KERESIOUAN [124] MEAT.   Nisqualli *nq?* 'animal,' Kutenai *łak*

($ɨ < n$).

MACRO-PANOAN [44] MEAT.   Huarayo *noči*, Pilaga *niiak* 'fish,' Lengua *nohak* 'wild animal.'

384 MONKEY

EQUATORIAL [80] MONKEY.   Campa *kočiro*, Uro *kusiʎo*.
MACRO-GE [79] MONKEY.   Patasho *kuki*, Proto-Ge **kukəz*.

385 MOON

ALMOSAN-KERESIOUAN [126] MOON.   Catawba *nunti* 'sun, moon,' Cherokee *nãto* 'sun, moon.'
MACRO-CARIB [42] MOON.   Proto-Carib **nuuna*, Ocaina *nəhna*.

386 MOTHER

HOKAN [100] MOTHER.   Yavapai *titi*, Achomawi *tatʰi*, Karok *tat*, Seri *ʔita*.
EQUATORIAL [51] GRANDMOTHER.   Cayuvava *tætæ*, Bare *čeče*, Chapacura *čiči*, Uro *ačiči*.

387 MOUNTAIN

HOKAN [101] MOUNTAIN.   Comecrudo *waj*, Cocopa *wi* 'mountain, rock.'
MACRO-TUCANOAN [65] MOUNTAIN.   Kaliana *ũaĩkũ*, Maku *wike*.

388 MOUTH

HOKAN [102] MOUTH.   Karok *-kara* 'into the mouth,' Tonkawa *kala*.
ANDEAN [75] MOUTH.   Leco *kollo*, Sechura *bo-korua*.
MACRO-TUCANOAN [67] MOUTH.   Mobima *kuana*, Huari *kan* 'beak.'

389 NECK

ANDEAN [77] NECK.   Lupaca *aru* 'voice, speech,' Culli *uro*.
EQUATORIAL [115] THROAT.   Toyeri *ari*, Proto-Tupi **ajur*.

390 NECK

ALMOSAN-KERESIOUAN [137] NECK.   Proto-Central Algonquian **-hkweeka-ni*, Kutenai *-ōkak*.
CHIBCHAN-PAEZAN [129] NECK.   Andaqui *san-guaka*, Chibcha *guikin*.

391 NECK

HOKAN [105] NECK.   Chumash *paktamus*, Seri *k-iphk* 'hang on neck,' Tlappanec *apuh*.

CHIBCHAN-PAEZAN [130] NECK.   Itonama *pakas-* 'front of . . . ,' Gayon *apaxiguo.*

392 NEW

PENUTIAN [168] NEW.   Monterey *iiti*, Huastec *it*, Maidu *di* 'young.'
CENTRAL AMERIND [63] RIPE.   Proto-Oto-Manguean **(n)(?)te(n)* 'ripe, cooked,' San Juan *t^si* 'be cooked,' Kiowa *ta* 'be ripe, cooked.'

393 NOSE

CHIBCHAN-PAEZAN [133] NOSE.   Cuna *asu*, Paez *asa* 'stink,' Warrau *aha* 'smell.'
ANDEAN [106] SMELL.   Itucale *asi*, Patagon *os*, Quechua *asia* 'stink.'

394 NOW

CHIBCHAN-PAEZAN [135] NOW.   Terraba *eri* 'now, today,' Cacaopera *ira* 'today.'
MACRO-CARIB [46] NOW.   Galibi *ereme*, Yameo *errama*.
MACRO-GE [112] TODAY.   Tibagi *ori*, Coropo *hora*, Fulnio *łe* 'now.'

395 ONE

ALMOSAN-KERESIOUAN [143] ONE.   Pawnee *asku*, Seneca *ska*, Acoma *ʔiska*.
ANDEAN [81] ONE.   Lamisto *sok*, Jebero *saka* 'only.'

396 OPEN

ALMOSAN-KERESIOUAN [145] OPEN.   Kutenai *uk'un*, Yurok *kæn*, Arapaho *kãne*.
PENUTIAN [173] OPEN.   Wappo *k'ine*, Lower Umpqua *qunh*.

397 OPEN

PENUTIAN [174] OPEN.   Atakapa *pai*, Nisenan *pe*.
CHIBCHAN-PAEZAN [143] OPEN.   Atacama *pai* 'uncover,' Catio *ebaja*.

398 PEOPLE

ALMOSAN-KERESIOUAN [151] PERSON.   Proto-Keresan **hanu* 'people,' Caddo *hajānuʔ*.
PENUTIAN [176] PEOPLE.   Wappo *oni*, Tunica *ʔoni*.

399 RIVER

CHIBCHAN-PAEZAN [151] RIVER.   Cuna *ti-wala*, Guajiquero *wara*, Miskito *awala.*

MACRO-GE [91] RIVER. Otuke *ouru*, Caraja *bero*, Palmas *war* 'swamp.'

400 RUN

HOKAN [122] RUN. Yuma *kono*, Coahuilteco *kuino*, Washo *igelu.*
CHIBCHAN-PAEZAN [155] RUN. Dobocubi *kuri* 'flee,' Sumu *kiri.*
ANDEAN [68] LEG. Qawashqar *kal* 'leg,' Aymara *čara* 'leg,' Tsoneka *kel* 'foot.'
MACRO-CARIB [56] RUN. Roucouyenne *ta-kane*, Witoto *ekain-ite* 'walk fast.'

401 RUN

PENUTIAN [198] RUN. Plains Miwok *taige*, Nisenan *dok*, Tunica *taka* 'chase.'
ANDEAN [95] RUN. Aymara *t'ikta*, Jebero *tək'k'a.*

402 SALIVA

ALMOSAN-KERESIOUAN [161] SALIVA. Nootka *tāxʷ* 'to spit,' Quileute *tux-al* 'to spit,' Osage *tatoxe.*
PENUTIAN [200] SALIVA. Marin Miwok *tuka* 'to spit,' Proto-Muskogean *tuxʷ*, Sayula *tˢux*, Yakonan *tˢak.*

403 SAY

PENUTIAN [203] SAY. Yokuts *wili*, Natchez *weł* 'speak,' Tunica *wali* 'call,' Chitimacha *wan* 'speech,' Totonac *wan.*
MACRO-TUCANOAN [90] TELL. Iranshe *wala* 'talk,' Tucano *uere.*
MACRO-CARIB [60] SPEAK. Carib *ura*, Witoto *uʔurii.*

404 SAY

PENUTIAN [202] SAY. Wappo *hai*, *ha*, Tsimshian *he*, Natchez *hi.*
PENUTIAN [204] SAY. Maidu *ʔa*, Koasati *a.*
CHIBCHAN-PAEZAN [157] SAY. Tarascan *aj* 'tell,' Chilanga *aj (-on)*, Cuitlatec *e.*

405 SAY

PENUTIAN [201] SAY. Bodega Miwok *ʔona*, Coos *na*, Alabama *ni.*
ANDEAN [96] SAY. Zaparo *ana*, Sabela *ã*, Quechua *ni.*

406 SEE

CENTRAL AMERIND [67] SEE. Proto-Uto-Aztecan *mai*, Taos *mũ.*

CHIBCHAN-PAEZAN [160] SEE.   Tarascan *mi, miu*, Yanomama *mɨ*, Cayapa *mi*, Atacama *mini*.

407 SEW

PENUTIAN [208] SEW.   Zuni *pik(-ɫa)*, Natchez *bōx*.
HOKAN [159] WEAVE.   Karok *vik*, Yana *waga-* 'twine a basket.'

408 SHADOW

CHIBCHAN-PAEZAN [166] SHADOW.   Itonama *manis-* 'be in the shadow,' Atacama *minas*.
MACRO-CARIB [57] SHADOW.   Witoto *manaide*, Trio *amali-li*.

409 SHOULDER

CHIBCHAN-PAEZAN [170] SHOULDER.   Itonama *pačĔu-kaka*, Tarascan *pešo*, Colorado *behči* 'back.'
MACRO-CARIB [10] CHEST.   Yagua *upeko* 'neck,' Faii *mex-pikua*, Ocaina *bagooʔja*.

410 SIT

ALMOSAN-KERESIOUAN [171] SIT.   Yuchi *k'u* 'dwell,' Proto-Siouan **amã-ki* 'sit on ground' (**amã* = 'ground'), Arikara *ku*, Kutenai *qa* 'be.'
PENUTIAN [217] SIT.   Klamath *či, ča*, Yuki *šai* 'live,' Chinook *š-* 'be,' Cakchiquel *ša* 'be.'
HOKAN [128] SIT.   Seri *-ix-*, Subtiaba *-iʔiguʔ*.
ANDEAN [14] BE.   Iquito *iikii*, Ona *ke*, Quechua *ka*.

411 SKIN

PENUTIAN [13] BARK.   Yuki *ol-šo* (*ol* = 'tree'), Chitimacha *suʔu* 'bark, skin,' Totonac *šuwaʔ*.
HOKAN [130] SKIN.   Tonkawa *-som-*, Tequistlatec *l-išmi*.
MACRO-TUCANOAN [81] SKIN.   Maku *čimo*, Ticuna *čame*.

412 SKIN

CHIBCHAN-PAEZAN [175] SKIN.   Atacama *k'ati*, Cuitlatec *kuti*, Move *kuata*, Cacaopera *k'uta*, Paez *kati*, Timucua *ukwata* 'body, flesh,' Yanomamï *kasi* 'lip.'
MACRO-GE [100] SKIN.   Botocudo *kat*, Mashubi *či-kati* 'lip.'

413 SKIN

ANDEAN [102] SKIN.   Mayna *-pa*, Yamana *api*, Jebero *pi* 'body.'
MACRO-GE [6] BARK.   Coroado *pe*, Guato *i-fai*.

414 SKY

PENUTIAN [220] SKY.   Tunica ʔaparu 'heaven,' Tzotzil -bail 'above,' Huastec ebal 'above.'

HOKAN [155] UP.   Yahi -bal- 'up from the ground,' Karok ʔipan 'top,' Comecrudo apel 'above, heaven.'

415 SLEEP

CENTRAL AMERIND [51] LIE DOWN.   Proto-Uto-Aztecan *ka 'sit down,' Taos k'uo.

ANDEAN [103] SLEEP.   Yamana aka, Aymara iki.

416 SMALL

HOKAN [133] SMALL.   Shasta at'uk, Jicaque tˢikwaj, Subtiaba taxū.

MACRO-PANOAN [56] SMALL.   Culino tukuča 'short,' Suhin tika, Towothli taake 'short.'

417 SMOKE

ALMOSAN-KERESIOUAN [176] SMOKE.   Proto-Keresan *tˢ'ekə 'to smoke,' Abenaki ahsokʷ 'cloud,' Upper Chehalis šq 'cloud.'

HOKAN [134] SMOKE.   North Yana tˢ'ēk'au, Southeast Pomo tˢaxa, Esselen čaxa, Subtiaba na-sīxa 'to smoke.'

418 STAND

ALMOSAN-KERESIOUAN [180] STAND.   Mohawk taʔ 'stand up,' Yuchi ta.

PENUTIAN [233] STAND UP.   Maidu ʔoto, Tunica to.

419 STEAL

CHIBCHAN-PAEZAN [183] STEAL.   Catio mera, Chimu omor 'thief.'

MACRO-CARIB [62] STEAL.   Muinane meri-de, Ocaina muuro, Yabarana mərə 'take!'

420 STRING

HOKAN [140] STRING.   Subtiaba -ūñulū, Tequistlatec -ajnuɬ 'fiber.'

MACRO-TUCANOAN [89] STRING.   Proto-Nambikwara *nu, Masaka nai.

421 SUN

HOKAN [141] SUN.   Achomawi tˢul, Shasta tˢ'uwar.

MACRO-GE [28] DAY.   Chiquito tˢuu 'day, sun,' Caraja tiuu 'day, sun,' Guato ma-čuo.

422 SUN

CHIBCHAN-PAEZAN [187] SUN.   Miskito *kati* 'moon,' Tarascan *kut^ssi*
'moon,' Guajiquero *kaši*, Eten *kæss*.
EQUATORIAL [109] SUN.   Guahibo *ikatia*, Goajiro *kači* 'moon,' Cuica *kuči*
'day,' Digüt *gati* 'moon.'

423 TALK

PENUTIAN [247] TELL.   Tsimshian *mał*, Takelma *malg^j*.
CHIBCHAN-PAEZAN [192] TALK.   Intibucat *malmal*, Cuitlatec *oxmele*
'chat.'

424 TESTICLE

PENUTIAN [249] TESTICLE.   Nez Perce *tālo*, Tunica *-htolu*.
HOKAN [145] TESTICLE.   Tonkawa *t^sāl*, San Antonio *solo*.

425 THIS

G15 [Andean, Equatorial] HE.   Quechua *-n* 'his,' Zaparo *no*, Jebero *nana*
'that,' Amuesha *ña*, Chiriana *ne*, Chipaya *ni*, Huambisa *nu* 'that.'
G23 [Chibchan-Paezan, Macro-Carib, Macro-Panoan, Macro-Ge] THIS.
Paez *ana*, Colorado *ne* 'he,' Choco *nan* 'that,' Hishcariana *en*, Chacobo
naa, Suya *ni*.

426 THORN

PENUTIAN [9] ARROW.   Natchez *onoxk* 'thorn,' Maidu *nok'o*, Kalapuya
enuk, Proto-Mayan **lah* 'nettle.'
EQUATORIAL [113] THORN.   Guaranoco *onak*, Cofan *nuxa*.

427 THROW

HOKAN [149] THROW.   Comecrudo *aka*, Tonkawa *kā*.
ANDEAN [114] THROW.   Aymara *aha*, Zaparo *aha*.

428 TOOTH

HOKAN [152] TOOTH.   Atsugewi *i?t^saw*, Chimariko *h-ut^s'u*, Shasta *it^sau*,
Yahi *ki-t^s'au-na*.
CENTRAL AMERIND [83] TOOTH.   Proto-Uto-Aztecan **tam*, Proto-Oto-
Manguean **(n)te(n)* 'chew.'
EQUATORIAL [117] TOOTH.   Yaru *iti(-či)*, Achagua *esi*, Uro *atse*, Calla-
huaya *iti* 'bite.'
MACRO-GE [113] TOOTH.   Otuke *itio*, Chiquito *t^soo*, Proto-Ge **t^swa*,
Macuni *tsioi*, Caraja *tju*.

429 TOOTH

ALMOSAN-KERESIOUAN [194] TOOTH. Kutenai *unān*, Cheyenne *-onen* 'toothed.'

CHIBCHAN-PAEZAN [202] TOOTH. Cacaopera *nini*, Atacama *enne*, Ulua *ana*.

430 TREE

PENUTIAN [235] STICK. Lake Miwok *tumaj* 'stick, wood,' Atakapa *t^{s}om*, Quiché *čamij* 'staff.'

MACRO-TUCANOAN [95] TREE. Tiquie *temba* 'firewood,' Kaliana *taba*.

EQUATORIAL [47] FOREST. Toyeri *nemba*, Saliba *rampo*, Zamuco *ẽrãp*.

MACRO-CARIB [71] TREE. Andoke *doapa* 'forest,' Peba *tapasej*.

431 TREE

PENUTIAN [261] TREE. Hitchiti *abi*, Natchez *pa* 'plant,' Ḧuchnom *ipo*.

EQUATORIAL [118] TREE. Culino *awa*, Yavitero *awa-bo* 'forest,' Uro *wa*.

432 TWO

HOKAN [153] TWO. Achomawi *haq*, Chimariko *xoku*, Karok *ʔaxak*, San Antonio *kakšu*, Tequistlatec *kook^h*, Tonkawa *haikia*, Cocopa *xawak*.

ANDEAN [82] OTHER. Yamana *hakū*, Tehuelche *kajuko*, Araucanian *ka* 'other.'

433 TWO

CENTRAL AMERIND [86] TWO. Proto-Oto-Manguean **(h)wi(n)* 'two, twins,' Proto-Uto-Aztecan **wo/wa*, Taos *wi-*.

ANDEAN [83] OTHER. Quechua *wah*, Auca *wa*.

434 URINE

ALMOSAN-KERESIOUAN [200] URINE. Proto-Central Algonquian **šeki*, Musquam *səχ^{w}a* 'urinate.'

EQUATORIAL [120] URINE. Kamaru *t^{s}ako* 'urinate,' Shuara *šiki*, Piaroa *t^{s}axkuelia*.

435 URINE

PENUTIAN [264] URINE. Chinook *wiuš*, Yuki *aš* 'urinate,' Yucatec *iš*.

CHIBCHAN-PAEZAN [208] URINE. Kagaba *wisi*, Cuitlatec *wiłi* 'urinate,' Manare *jisa*, Borunca *wiš(-ku)*, Ulua *usu*.

MACRO-PANOAN [61] URINE. Lengua *jis(-weji)* 'urinate,' Lule *ys* 'urinate,' Suhin *juł*, Churupi *yius* 'urinate,' Proto-Panoan **isõ*.

436 VAGINA

PENUTIAN [265] VAGINA.   Chitimacha *neʔēs*, Quiché *nus*.
MACRO-TUCANOAN [97] VULVA.   Maku *ts-eʔne*, Yahuna *jaʔna*.
MACRO-CARIB [74] VAGINA.   Witoto *iani*, Proto-Carib **eni* 'vase.'

437 VAGINA

ALMOSAN-KERESIOUAN VAGINA.   Nitinat *ʔaʔot^s*, Blackfoot *-ats-*, Arapaho
hehéč, Wichita *ʔāhas* 'urine,' Seneca *-heohsa-* 'urine.'
PENUTIAN VAGINA.   Zuni *ʔašo*, Koasati *hasiʔ*, Quiché *(a)šiš*.
HOKAN VAGINA.   Seri *ʔasit*.
CHIBCHAN-PAEZAN [209] VAGINA.   Cuna *sisi*, Matagalpa *su*, Lenca
shusho, Chibcha *sihi*, Binticua *sisi* 'vulva,' Cayapa *su*, Dobocubi *ču*.
ANDEAN VAGINA.   Patagon *isse*, Kahuapana *sišila*.

438 WASH

PENUTIAN [269] WASH.   Yuki *hukol*, Southern Sierra Miwok *heka*.
CHIBCHAN-PAEZAN [11] BATHE.   Cuna *oka*, Paya *ok(-ka)*, Bribri *uk*.

439 WATER

ALMOSAN-KERESIOUAN [109] LAKE.   Proto-Siouan **re*, Seneca *(njota)-re*.
CHIBCHAN-PAEZAN [212] WATER.   Bintucua *ria* 'liquid,' Atacama *(pu-)ri*,
Tegria *ria*, Move *-ri* 'liquid,' Rama *ari* 'liquid,' Tarascan *p^{h}i-ri* 'a small
amount of liquid.'

440 WATER

PENUTIAN [272] WATER.   Tunica *wiši*, Wappo *isɛ* 'dig for water.'
HOKAN [44] DRINK.   Achomawi *iss*, Karok *ʔis*, Seri *isī*, North Yana *sii*,
Yurumangui *si*.
MACRO-GE [94] SALIVA.   Kadurukre *išu* 'saliva,' Kamakan *jašo*.

441 WATER

CHIBCHAN-PAEZAN [51] DRINK.   Colorado *kuči*, Cuaiquer *kuase*, Itonama
kasi(-ʔna), Timucua *okut*.
ANDEAN [121] WATER.   Cholona *kot*, Hivito *kači*, Sechura *xoto*.
EQUATORIAL [64] LAKE.   Kitemoka *su-huaiše*, Itene *huče* 'swamp,' Uro
koasi.
MACRO-GE [33] DRINK.   Umotina *i-kotu*, Fulnio *i-kote*.

442 WE-2

G10 [Chibchan-Paezan, Macro-Tucanoan, Macro-Ge] THOU.   Allentiac
ka, Xinca *ka-* 'thy,' Tarascan *-ke(-ni)* 'first-person singular acts on second-

person singular,' Kaliana *ka(-be)*, Auake *kai(-kiete)*, Erikbatsa *ikia*, Bororo *aki*, Coroado *ga*.

G19 [Almosan-Keresiouan, Penutian, Hokan, Central Amerind, Macro-Carib, Andean] WE-2 INC.   Proto-Algic **k-* 'thou,' Wyandot *kj*, Yokuts *ma-k'*, Maratino *ko* 'we inc.,' San Antonio *kak* 'we,' South Pame *kakh* 'we inc.,' Taos *ki-* 'our,' Proto-Carib **ki-*, Mayna *-ke* 'let us,' Cholona *ki* 'our.'

G28 [Macro-Carib] TWO.   Witoto *-ko* (dual), Surinam *oko*, Hishcariana *asa-ko*.

443 WET

PENUTIAN [273] WET.   Tsimshian *p'ak^{h}p'ak^h* 'wash,' Kekchi *puč'* 'wash,' Huastec *pakul* 'wash,' Atakapa *pat^s* 'wash,' Natchez *pat^{s}ak*.

CHIBCHAN-PAEZAN [214] WET.   Terraba *puk*, Tucura *bek(-eai)* 'to water,' Betoi *ofaku* 'rain.'

444 WHITE

CHIBCHAN-PAEZAN [215] WHITE.   Tucura *torro*, Atacama *tara*.

MACRO-GE [120] WHITE.   Caraja *dora*, Chiquito *turasi*.

445 WIND (n.)

PENUTIAN [276] WIND.   Chinook *ikxala*, Yakima *xuli*, Takelma *kwalt*.

ANDEAN [123] WIND.   Iquito *akira*, Qawashqar *kel*.

446 WISH

ANDEAN [125] WISH.   Leco *era*, Jebero *?ina* (desiderative), Quechua *-naa* (desiderative), Yamana *jana*.

G83 [Macro-Panoan] DESIDERATIVE.   Chacobo *-no*, Lule *-no*.

447 WOMAN

HOKAN [161] WIFE.   Achomawi *ta*, Esselen *ta*, East Pomo *da*, Yurumangui *ita(-asa)*.

MACRO-GE [123] WOMAN.   Fulnio *de*, Krenje *jiti*, Capoxo *ti*.

448 WORK

CHIBCHAN-PAEZAN [224] WORK.   Bintucua *nina* 'activity,' Guaymi *noaine* 'do,' Timucua *inoni*, Rama *uni* 'make.'

EQUATORIAL [76] MAKE.   Dzubucua *niño*, Kandoshi *ina*, Aguaruna *na-*.

ADDITIONAL SUPPORT FOR AMERIND ETYMOLOGIES

Some of the etymologies offered in support of one of the 11 Amerind subgroups in Chapter 3 of *Language in the Americas* appear to belong instead to one of the Amerind etymologies in Chapter 4. The following is a list of such possibilities.

A2 = MT66
A7 = P214 = CP219 = MT46
A8 = AK7
A9 = CP34 = MC24 = MG115
A11 = P58
A14 = MP46
A16 = AK6 = CP4
A20 = AK77 = H157 = MP59
A24 = A108 = CA45 = E42
A27 = AK79 = MG117
A29 = E10
A30 = AK43
A35 = MP58
A37 = CP18
A39 = A85 = E15
A42 = AK26 = H17
A43 = MT13
A45 = AK206
A46 = CA76 = MC63 = MG58
A49 = MP20 = MG70
A54 = A251 [CP] = AK108 = P285
A59 = AK20 = H24
A61 = MP57
A71 = AN44
A73 = AK28
A74 = A80 = CP83 = MP30
A78 = AK53 = CA25
A79 = AK175 = AN79 = CP133
A85 = E15
A86 = CA90
A87 = AK185 = CP152 = MG118
A89 = CP211 = AN97 = E125
A92 = H45 = CP76

A94 = CP49
A104 = MG38
A105 = P68
A109 = CA35
A113 = CP74
A114 = H60
A119 = A189
A120 = MC66
A125 = E129 = MT106 = MG41
A136 = E54
A141 = P102 = CP184
A146 = AK57
A147 = CP1
A148 = E1
A149 = AK31 = AK153 = P110 = AN37
A155 = AK54 = P14 = CA27 = MG69
A157 = MT16
A161 = AN65
A165 = AK113 = CP167
A168 = E69
A169 = CP179
A178 = H54
A180 = AK121 = P162
A184 = E40
A185 = H18
A188 = AN109 = E81
A190 = AK130 = MP8
A191 = E36
A196 = E114
A200 = P17 = AN27
A217 = CA74
A219 = P246
A222 = AK162 = P151
A227 = E101
A228 = CP30 = CP131 = MC59
A232 = P216
A241 = E131
A245 = MG103
A251 [P] = P156
A252 = AN33
A253 = H47

A257 = CP201
A263 = E121
A272 = P283 = H164
A273 = CA41 = CP222
A275 = CA84
A279 = AK209
A281 = AK44 = P88 = H29

CONSOLIDATION WITHIN AMERIND SUBGROUPS

In at least six instances different etymologies within an Amerind subgroup should be combined as a single etymology: P32 and P78; P55 and P129; P69 and P124; H19 and H26; AN16 and AN48; and MP26 and MP27.

REFERENCES

Greenberg, Joseph H. 1981. "Comparative Amerindian Notebooks," 23 vols. Mss. on file, Green Library, Stanford University, Stanford, Calif.
———. 1987. *Language in the Americas.* Stanford, Calif.

9

Amerind T'APNA 'Child, Sibling'

It has recently been claimed (proclaimed may be more accurate) that the comparative method in linguistics is inherently limited to some arbitrary date variously placed at 5,000 to 10,000 years before the present.* *After* this magical date we may delineate families (i.e. valid linguistic taxa) and even reconstruct large and intricate portions of the various proto-languages, often involving subtle and complex sound correspondences among the constituent families or languages. *Before* this mystical date we suddenly and abruptly encounter a black hole, as it were, devoid of any useful linguistic information whatever. We are thus doomed, according to this view, to be forever incapable of investigating linguistic relationships deeper in the past than 10,000 years.

According to Terrence Kaufman (1990: 23), "a temporal ceiling of 7,000 to 8,000 years is inherent in the methods of comparative linguistic reconstruction. We can recover genetic relationships that are that old, but probably no earlier than that. The methods possibly will be expanded, but for the moment we have to operate within that limit in drawing inferences." Kaufman then argues that, since the Americas are *known* to have been inhabited longer than the alleged limits of the comparative method, "the proof of a common origin for the indigenous languages of this hemisphere is not accessible to the comparative method as we know it" (p. 26). In a similar vein, Johanna Nichols

* I would like to thank John Bengtson, William Croft, William Jacobsen, and Joseph Greenberg for criticism of an earlier version of this chapter.

(1990: 477) defines a *stock* as "the oldest grouping reachable by application of the standard comparative method. . . . Most of these are in the vicinity of 6,000 years old since their own internal breakups." She also claims that "genetic unity for 'Amerind' is incompatible with the chronology demanded by the lingustic facts" (p. 475), though one must hasten to add that what Nichols considers "linguistic facts" is not a catalogue of cognate words but "typological diversity."

In this chapter I will try to show, by examining the interaction of a single Amerind lexical item with a number of morphological processes and affixes, that Amerind, as set forth by Joseph Greenberg (1987), is a well-defined linguistic taxon, with all eleven subgroups connected by the lexical item in question. Furthermore, the constellation of forms that will be shown to connect all branches of Amerind does not exist, to the best of my knowledge, in any other linguistic taxon—at any level—in the world. It follows that if Amerind is a well-defined genetic unit, as I will argue, then the supposed time limits of the comparative method should perhaps be reconsidered.

THE ROOT *TANA* 'CHILD, SIBLING'

One of the lexical items posited by Greenberg in support of the Amerind family was a word whose general meaning is 'child, sibling,' and whose general phonetic shape is *tana* or the like (Greenberg 1987: 225). Although Greenberg cited only a few forms—all from North America—the root in question is in fact widespread throughout both North and South America and is found in every branch of the Amerind family. As such, it represents a diagnostic trait of Amerind comparable in value to the Amerind pronominal pattern *na* 'I'/*ma* 'thou,' whose importance Greenberg and others have stressed.

As a first approximation, one might reconstruct the root in question as **t'ana* 'child, sibling' for Proto-Amerind. North American reflexes of this root include forms such as Nootka *t'an'a* 'child.' The Haida form reported by Sapir (1923b: 149), *t'á'na'* 'child,' is in all likelihood a borrowing of this Nootka word. Sapir himself had documented the borrowing of a Haida kinship term by the Tsimshian through mixed marriages (Sapir 1921). In the present case we seem to have borrowing going in the opposite direction, from the Amerind Nootka to the Na-Dene Haida. The biological consequences of these mixed marriages between peoples of quite distinct ethnic groups, Amerind and Na-Dene, are reported in Cavalli-Sforza et al. (1994). Other North American reflexes of the root **t'ana* 'child, sibling' include Kwakwala *t'ana* 'blood relative,' Yurok *tˢān-ūk-s* 'child,' Tsimshian *ɬuk-taēn*[1] 'grandchild,' Cayuse

---

[1] Throughout this paper I have added morpheme boundaries at points where I believe they are *historically* justified, even though there is often no longer any synchronic motivation for them in the modern languages. For example, I suspect that Tsimshian *ɬuk-taēn*

i-tsaŋu 'young,' Totonac *t'ána-t* 'grandchild,' Achomawi *-tsan* (diminutive), Washo *t'ánu* 'person,' Santa Barbara Chumash *taniw* 'little, child,' Coahuilteco *t'an-pam* 'child,' *kuan-t'an* 'grandchild,' Proto-Uto-Aztecan **tana* 'son, daughter,' Varahio *taná* 'son, daughter,' Proto-Oto-Manguean **ʔntan* 'child,' Popoloca *tˢhjān* 'child, son,' Proto-Oto-Manguean **taʔn* 'sibling,' Mixtec *tãʔã* 'sibling,' and Miskito *tuk-tan* 'child, boy.' South American examples of this root include Shiriana *tasém-taiina* 'child,' Urubu-Kaapor *taʔin* 'child,' Wapishana *dan* 'child, son,' and Atoroi *dan* 'baby, son.' (The genetic classification of all languages cited is given in the final section of this chapter.)

All of the forms that I believe (with varying degrees of conviction) to be cognate with those just enumerated are given at the end of this chapter. Those cited above represent what might be considered the original form and meaning. There are quite naturally many items that diverge, often by a single step, from either the original meaning or the original phonetic shape. Let us turn now to these slightly modified forms, first with regard to meaning, and then with regard to form. If we begin with the meaning 'child, sibling,' the simplest, and most expected, shifts would be to 'son, daughter' for the first term, and to 'brother, sister' for the second. In fact, within the context of Algic, Sapir (1923a: 41) noted precisely these semantic developments for the lexical item discussed here: "Proto-Algonquian **-tan-* must be presumed to have originally meant 'child' . . . and to have become specialized in its significance either to 'son' (Wiyot) or 'daughter' (Algonkin proper), while in Yurok its close relative *-ta-tˢ* ['child'] preserved a more primary genetic significance."

Within the larger Amerind context, Greenberg also noticed the connection between the basic meaning of 'child' and that of 'daughter, sister,' but he overlooked a parallel connection with masculine forms such as 'son, brother,' probably because the latter forms tend to be phonologically more deviant, as we shall see below. Let us consider first a sample of some of the related feminine forms. For Almosan one may point to Proto-Algonquian **ne-tān(-ehsa)*

'grandchild,' Chol *čok-tuiun* 'boy' (cf. Chol *aluš-čok* 'girl'), Miskito *tuk-tan* 'child,' Tibagi *tog-tan* 'girl,' and Chapacura *a-čoke-tunia* 'girl' are all cognate in both their parts, representing an Amerind compound of two words for child, as discussed below. The fact remains, however, that as far as I can tell there is no *synchronic* motivation for a bimorphemic analysis of the stem in either Tsimshian or Miskito, nor perhaps is there in the South American languages. It is only in the context of the broad analysis proposed here that these apparently monomorphemic stems can be given their proper etymological explanation. The morpheme boundaries proposed are thus a part of the overall hypothesis (and I am likely to be wrong about some of them), but they are *not* an attempt to deceive the reader into thinking that each boundary is still synchronically motivated, an unrealistic expectation for a family older than 12,000 years. Similarly, most of the hypothesized proto-forms given in parentheses (e.g. < **tenten*) are intended merely to represent *my* hypothesis, usually fairly transparent, of an earlier form of the word in question.

‘my daughter,’ _*ne-tān-kwa_ ‘my sister-in-law,’ Kutenai _ga’-t^{sw}ɪn_ ‘daughter,’ _tsu_ ‘sister,’ Coeur d’Alene _tune_ ‘niece,’ and Pentlatch _tan_ ‘mother.’ Examples from Keresiouan include Proto-Siouan _*i-thã́-ki_ ‘man’s sister (older or younger),’ _*i-thã́-ka_ ‘woman’s younger sister,’ _*thṹ-wĩ_ ‘paternal aunt,’ Yuchi _t^{s}’one_ ‘daughter,’ Caddo _tan-arha_ ‘wife,’ Arikara _i-tahni_ ‘his sister,’ Mohawk _-a-thũ-wisə̃_ ‘woman,’ and Keres _t’aona_ ‘sister.’ In Penutian we find Takelma _t‘a-wā_ ‘younger sister,’ North Sahaptin _kw-tən_ ‘daughter of a female,’ Wintun _o-tun-_ ‘older sister,’ _to-q-_ ‘sister-in-law,’ Saclan _tune_ ‘daughter,’ Central Sierra Miwok _tūne-_ ‘daughter,’ Ohlone _tana-n_ ‘older sister,’ Atakapa _ten-sa_ ‘niece,’ Tunica _htóna-yi_ ‘wife,’ Huastec _t^{s}anū-b_ ‘aunt,’ Ixil _i-t^{s}’an_ ‘aunt,’ and Pocomam _iš-tan_ ‘girl.’ Examples from Hokan are Shasta _a-ču-gwi_ ‘younger sister, younger female cousin’ (< _*a-tun-kwi_), Achomawi _a-tā-wi_ ‘daughter,’ Washo _wi-t^{s}’u-k_ ‘younger sister’ (< _*wi-t’un-ki_), Southeast Pomo _wi-m-t’a-q_ ‘younger sister,’ East Pomo _tuts_ ‘mother’s older sister’ (< _*tuntun_), Esselen _tano-č_ ‘woman,’ Salinan _a-ton_ ‘younger sister,’ Coahuilteco _ya-t’ān_ ‘sister,’ and Yurumangui _tintin_ ‘woman.’ Feminine forms from Central Amerind include Taos _t’út’ina_ ‘older sister’ (< _*t’unt’una_), _si-tona_ ‘wife,’ _kle-tuna_ ‘woman,’ Proto-Central Otomi _*t^{s}ũ_ ‘female,’ Mazatec _č^{h}ũ_ ‘woman,’ _ču-kwhã_ ‘aunt,’ Proto-Oto-Manguean _*ntaHn_ ‘mother,’ and Mixtec _táʔnù iʔšá_ ‘younger sister.’ For the Chibchan branch of Amerind, probable examples include Xinca _u-tan_ ‘mother,’ Lenca _tuntu-rusko_ ‘younger sister,’ Sumu _i-tanni_ ‘mother,’ Cuna _tuttu_ ‘woman’ (< _*tuntun_), Guamaca _a-tena-šina_ ‘old woman,’ and Motilon _diani_ ‘wife.’ In the Paezan branch there is Citara _tana_ ‘mother,’ Cayapa _t^{s}uh-ki_ ‘sister’ (< _*tun-ki_), Colorado _sona-_ ‘woman,’ Eten _čan-ka_ ‘sister,’ and Chimu _čuŋ_ ‘sister’ (< _*tun-ki_). Andean examples include Ona _thaun_ ‘sister’ and Tsoneka _ke-tun_ ‘sister.’ In Macro-Tucanoan, feminine forms are well attested: Kaliana _tone_ ‘mother-in-law,’ Tiquie _ton_ ‘daughter,’ Papury _toŋ_ ‘daughter,’ _tein_ ‘wife,’ Ubde-Nehern _tëtón_ ‘niece,’ Parawa _iš-tano_ ‘woman,’ Canichana _eu-tana_ ‘mother,’ Masaca _tani-mai_ ‘sister,’ Tagnani _tana-nde_ ‘mother,’ Mamainde-Tarunde _denō_ ‘woman,’ Coreguaje _čĩio_ ‘daughter,’ _aʔ-čo_ ‘elder sister,’ and _čoʔ-jeo_ ‘younger sister.’ Feminine forms also abound in Equatorial languages: Mocochi _nak-tun_ ‘woman,’ Esmeralda _tin_ ‘woman,’ _tini-usa_ ‘daughter,’ Guamo _tua_ ‘daughter,’ Paumari _a-thon-i_ ‘granddaughter,’ Uru _thun_ ‘wife,’ Chipaya _t’uana_ ‘woman,’ Chapacura _tana-muy_ ‘daughter,’ Abitana _tana_ ‘woman,’ Wapishana _u-dan-rin_ ‘daughter,’ Palicur _tino_ ‘woman,’ Yaulapiti _tine-ru-tsu_ ‘girl,’ Arawak _o-tu_ ‘daughter,’ and Manao _y-tuna-lo_ ‘woman.’ In Macro-Carib we find such feminine forms as Macusi _taŋ-sa_ ‘girl,’ Witoto _i-taño_ ‘girl,’ and Nonuya _om(w)ŭ̈-tona_ ‘sister.’ Macro-Panoan examples include Mascoy _tanni-yap_ ‘sister-in-law,’ Mataco _čina_ ‘younger sister,’ Towithli _tuna-ni_ ‘woman,’ Suhin _tino-iče_ ‘young woman,’ Mayoruna _čuču_ ‘older sister’ (< _*tuntun_), and Tacana _-tóna_ ‘younger sister.' Finally, we may cite feminine forms from Macro-Ge such as Oti *dondu-ede* 'woman' (< *tuntun-ede*), Botocudo *giku-taŋ* 'sister,' *tontan* 'wife,' Macuni *a-tina-n* 'girl, daughter,' Palmas *tantã* 'female,' Coropo *ek-tan* 'mother,' Mashakali *etia-tün* 'woman,' Patasho *a-tön* 'mother,' Apucarana *wey-tytan* 'younger sister,' Tibagi *tog-tan* 'girl,' *tantö* 'woman,' Apinaye *i-tõ-dy* 'sister,' Cayapo *torri-tuŋ* 'old woman,' *tun-ĵuo* 'girl,' Aponegicran *i-thon-ghi* 'sister,' Caraho *a-ton-ka* 'younger sister,' *tõ-i* '(older?) sister,' Krẽye *-tõ-ue* 'sister,' and Piokobyé *a-tõn* 'older sister,' *a-tõn-kä* 'younger sister.'

Masculine forms are no less abundant, but they offer the additional complication that some of them overlap with those of the widespread root *tata* 'father,' whose global distribution has long been recognized. Still, in most cases I believe it is possible to distinguish the two roots. Almosan preserves traces of the masculine forms in Cheyenne *tatan-* 'older brother,' Arapaho *na-tseno-ta* 'my nephew,' Yurok *tˢin* 'young man,' and possibly Kutenai *tsiya* 'younger brother' and *tat'* 'older brother.' In Keresiouan there are a number of masculine forms, including Proto-Siouan **thũ-kã* 'grandfather,' Biloxi *tan-do* 'woman's brother,' Quapaw *ĩ-do-ke* 'male,' Biloxi *i-to* 'male, man,' Yuchi *tane* 'brother,' *-tˢ'one* 'woman's son,' *go-t'ɛ* 'man, father,' *tu-kã* 'grandfather,' Caddo *dono* 'male,' Pawnee *ti-ki* 'boy, son,' Cherokee *a-tsã* 'male of animals,' *a-tsutsu* 'boy' (< **a-tuntun*), and Mohawk *-ʔtsin* 'boy, male.' Probable Penutian cognates include Takelma *t'ĩ^ĵ* 'man, male,' Siuslaw *t'āt* 'nephew,' Molale *pam-tin* 'nephew,' Cayuse *puna-taŋ* 'younger brother,' Proto-Maiduan **týn* 'younger brother,' Yaudanchi *bu-tson* 'son,' Lake Miwok *ʔa-táa* 'older brother,' Central Sierra Miwok *ta-či* 'older brother,' *a-te* 'younger brother,' San Francisco Costanoan *šen-is-muk* 'boy,' Mutsun *šin-ie-mk* 'boy,' Natchez *hi-dzina* '(man's) nephew,' Atakapa *ten-s* 'nephew,' Kakchiquel *a-čin* 'man,' Sierra Popoluca *hā-thuŋ* 'father,' and Texistepec *tene(-ĩap)* 'man.' In Hokan we find Achomawi *ā-tũn* 'younger brother,' Konomihu *ču-ka* 'boy,' Northeast Pomo *tono* 'brother-in-law,' Eastern Pomo *tsets* 'mother's brother' (< **tenten*), Washo *ʔã-t'u* 'older brother,' Chumash *(ma-k-)ič-tuʔn* '(my) son,' Santa Cruz Chumash *tunne-č* 'boy,' *huk-tana-hu* 'my son,' Yuma *an-tˢen* 'older brother,' Coahuilteco *t'āna-gē* 'father,' and *ku-t'an* 'uncle.' Central Amerind examples include Proto-Uto-Aztecan **tu* 'boy,' Northern Paiute *tua* 'son,' Mono *tuwa* 'son,' *tˢu-ku* 'old man,' Tübatulabal *tena* 'man,' Kawaiisu *tuwaa-na* 'son,' *to-go* 'maternal grandfather,' Pipil *pil-tsin* 'boy, son,' Tewa *sēŋ* 'man, male,' Mazahua *t'i-ʔi* 'boy,' Otomi *ʔi-dã́* 'woman's brother,' Cuicatec *ʔdĩ́nó* 'brother,' and Zapotec *p-taʔn* 'woman's brother.' Masculine forms in the Chibchan branch include Cuitlatec *ču* 'boy,' Rama *ⁿdu-tuŋ* 'younger brother,' *i-tũŋ* 'father,' Move *nge-dan* 'brother-in-law,' and Motilon *a-te-gwa* 'nephew' (< **a-ten-kwa*). Paezan examples are *ne-tson* 'brother-in-law,' Cayapa *tˢāna* 'son,' Chimu *čaŋ* 'younger brother,' and Millcayac *tzhœng* 'son.' In Andean we have Simacu *kax-ðana* 'maternal uncle,' Araucanian *tˢoñi* 'woman's son,' Tehuelche *den* 'brother,' Manekenkn *ie-tog-te* 'brother,' and Ona *tane-ngh* 'maternal uncle.' In Macro-Tucanoan there are also numerous examples: Auake *toto* 'older brother' (< **tonton*), Tiquie *ten* 'son,' Ubde-Nehern *têain* 'boy,' *ten* 'son,' *tën-do* 'maternal uncle,' Capishana *miatuna* 'older brother,' *totoi* 'brother-in-law' (< **tonton-i*), Tagnani *ui-tono-re* 'son,' Amaguaje *tˢin* 'boy,' *ye-tˢen-ke* 'son,' Coreguaje *čĩi̱* 'son,' *aꞀ-či̱* 'elder brother,' *čoꞀ-jei̱* 'younger brother,' Yupua *tsīn-geē* 'boy,' and Tucano *ti-kã* 'son-in-law' (< **tin-kan*). Masculine forms are also widespread in Equatorial: Cayuvava *tete* 'uncle' (< **tenten*), Mocochi *tin-gua* 'son, boy' (< **tin-kwa*), Cofan *tzándey-dése* 'boy,' *tõꞀtõ* 'uncle' (< **tonton*), Yaruro *to-kwī* 'small boy' (< **ton-kwi*), Tembe *tỹ-kỹhỹr* 'older brother,' *ty-h̃uhỹr* 'younger brother,' *coai-tỹ* 'brother-in-law,' *a-tiu* 'father-in-law,' Arikem *u-taua* 'brother,' Aweti *a-tu* 'grandfather,' Uruku *toto* 'grandfather' (< **tonton*), Guahibo *ā-tō* 'elder brother,' Uru *(t)soñi* 'man,' Wapishana *douani* 'lad,' *i-dini-re* 'son-in-law,' *teti* 'maternal uncle' (< **tintin*), Uainuma *at-tsiu* 'uncle' (< **aꞀ-tyu*), Custenau *a-tu* 'grandfather,' Uirina *a-tina-re* 'man,' Mehinacu *a-to* 'grandfather,' Manao *no-tany* 'my son,' Atoroi *dani-Ꞁinai* 'son,' *a-tidn* 'younger brother,' and Goajiro *čon* 'son,' *tan-či* 'brother-in-law' (< **tan-ki*). Macro-Carib examples include Yameo *a-tin* 'man,' Galibi *tun* 'father,' Pavishana *tane* 'my son,' *tutu* 'grandfather' (< **tuntun*), Bakairi *i-tano* 'grandfather,' Imihita *tãã-ti* 'grandfather,' and Muinane *i-to* 'paternal uncle.' In Macro-Panoan we find masculine forms such as Kaskiha *an-tū-ye* 'woman's son,' Moseten *čuñe* 'brother-in-law,' Sotsiayay *taão-kla* 'boy,' Mayoruna *tsana* 'man,' Culino *hatu* 'brother,' Huarayo *toto* 'man's brother' (< **tonton*), Arasa *dodo* 'brother' (< **tonton*), and Chama *toto* 'uncle' (< **tonton*). Finally, in Macro-Ge we have examples such as Guato *čina* 'older brother,' Caraja *wa-θana* 'uncle,' Umotina *in-dondo* 'maternal son-in-law' (< **in-tonton*), Cotoxo *či-ton* 'brother,' Meniens *a-to* 'brother,' Puri *ek-ton* 'son,' *makaša-tane* 'brother,' Patasho *eke-tannay* 'brother,' Apucarana *ti* 'man,' Apinaye *i-tõ* 'brother,' *tu'-ká* 'paternal uncle, son-in-law' (< **tun-ko*), *tu'-ka-ya* 'maternal grandfather,' *tu'-ka-tí* 'brother-in-law, son-in-law,' Cayapo *i-ton* 'brother,' Krẽye *tana-mni* 'boy,' *tõ* 'younger brother,' Caraho *tõ* 'brother,' *ton-ko* 'older brother,' and Piokobyé *tõn-ko* 'older brother,' *ha-tõn* 'younger brother.'

Let us turn now to the question of form. The evidence from languages such as Nootka, Kwakwala, Keres, Takelma, Siuslaw, Yuki, Atakapa, Ixil, Pokomchi, Tzeltal, Tzotzil, Chontal, Totonac, Yana, Yahi, Southern Pomo, Washo, Coahuilteco, Mazahua, and perhaps Chipaya indicates that the initial consonant was probably a glottalized *t*'; the second consonant was *n*. (Chipaya is the only South American language I have found that appears to retain the original glottalization.) There are indications in a number of languages that the root-initial vowel was originally followed by a glottal stop (cf. Nez Perce *pi-t'í?n* 'girl,' Chumash *(ma-k-)ič-tu?n* '(my) son,' Proto-Oto-Manguean **ta?n* 'sibling,' Mixtec *tá?nù i?šá* 'younger sister,' Zapotec *p-ta?n* 'woman's brother,' Proto-Oto-Manguean **si(?)(n)* 'youngster,' Isthmus Zapotec *ži?iñi?* 'son,' Southern Nambikwara *tyū?n* 'small,' Urubu-Kaapor *ta?in* 'child,' and Erikbatsa *tsi?n-kärar* 'small'). In many languages the original glottal stop was lost, with compensatory lengthening of the preceding vowel (e.g. Proto-Algonquian **ne-tāna* 'my daughter,' Lillooet *s-tūnə-q* 'niece,' North Sahaptin *p-t'īn-ik-s* 'girl,' Central Sierra Miwok *tūne-* 'daughter,' Achomawi *a-tūn* 'younger brother,' Coahuilteco *ya-t'ān* 'sister,' Cuicatec *?díínó* 'brother,' Rama *i-tūŋ* 'father,' Cayapa *t^sāna* 'son,' Yupua *tsīn-geē* 'boy,' and Yagua *dēnu* 'male child').

The vowel situation is far less clear, with a superficial appearance of complete heterogeneity. Nevertheless, I would like to suggest that these diverse forms have all evolved from a system that consisted of three terms in Proto-Amerind: **t'i?na* 'son, brother,' **t'u?na* 'daughter, sister,' and **t'a?na* 'child, sibling.' From these terms, the working of analogy (in various directions in various languages), the addition of affixes to modulate the meaning, and both regular and sporadic sound changes have produced the multiplicity of forms enumerated in the final section of this chapter. From time to time a few linguists have noticed seemingly related forms that differ in their initial vowel and meaning, but within the context of a single language the origin of these differences has remained mysterious. Thus, for example, Berman (1986: 421) concludes that Yurok "*t^sān-* 'young' is related to *t^sin* 'young man' cited above. I believe that one of these is an old changed form of the other, but I do not know which is which." If one considers only Yurok, then no explanation of these forms is possible. However, when Yurok is placed in the wider context of Amerind, the source of these related forms is a trivial consequence of the Proto-Amerind system of gender ablaut outlined in this chapter.

Greenberg pointed out the presence of an opposition between masculine *i* and feminine *u* in the Equatorial and Macro-Tucanoan branches of Amerind, but considered it an innovation restricted to these two groups (Greenberg 1987: 296–98). The evidence outlined above shows, I believe, that this alternation was already present in Proto-Amerind and involved a third term as well, sex-neutral a.[2] No presently extant Amerind language preserves all

---

[2] The same alternation is found in another Amerind word for child (Greenberg, pp. 203–4), Proto-Amerind **makV* 'child,' Nez Perce *méqe?* 'paternal uncle,' Washo *mēhu* 'boy,' Chimariko *meku* 'brother-in-law,' Southeast Pomo *i-mek* 'father,' Walapai *mik* 'boy,' Tequistlatec *(ł a-)mihkano* 'boy,' Pamigua *mekve* 'boy,' Waikina *mehino* 'boy,' Yawelmani *moki* 'wife,' *mokoi* 'maternal aunt,' Gashowu *mokheta* 'girl,' Santa Cruz Costanoan *mux-aš* 'girl,' Shiriana *moko* 'girl,' Pavishana *mu'gi* 'daughter,' Waikina *maxkē* 'child,' Ticuna *mākan* 'child.'

three grades with the original vowel and meaning, but several preserve two
of the three, and even more preserve one of the three variants essentially
unchanged. One of the clearest examples occurs in Tiquie, a member of the
Puinave group of Macro-Tucanoan, where we find *ton* 'daughter' and *ten* 'son.'
A closely related language, Nadobo, has *tata* 'child,' perhaps derived from an
original **tantan*. In the Tucanoan branch of Macro-Tucanoan, Coreguaje has
čïï 'son' opposed to *čïïo* 'daughter,' and *aʔ-čï* 'elder brother' opposed to *aʔ-čo*
'elder sister.' Elsewhere in South America, in the Arawakan branch of Equatorial, we find Atoroi *dan* 'baby' and *a-tidn* 'younger brother,' the latter form
probably deriving from original **a-tin*. Another Arawakan language, Ipurina,
contrasts *ni-tari* 'my brother' with *ni-taru* 'my sister,' showing that the *i/u* opposition has been grammaticized in both the Equatorial and Macro-Tucanoan
branches of Amerind. In the Timote branch of Equatorial, Mocochi contrasts
tin-gua 'son, boy' with *nak-tun* 'woman.' At the southern tip of South America, in two closely related languages of the Andean family, we find Tehuelche
den 'brother' and Tsoneka *ke-tun* 'sister.' Chimu, in the Paezan branch, almost preserves the original forms in *čuŋ* 'sister' contrasting with *čaŋ* 'younger
brother.'

In North America, the Yurok language of California, a member of Almosan,
contrasts *tˢān-ūk-s* 'child' with *tˢin* 'young man.' In California Penutian
*-tŏ 'grandmother' and **téh* 'child, son' have been reconstructed for Proto-
Maiduan. Elsewhere in California Penutian we find Wintun *te-* 'son, daughter'
and *o-tun-* 'older sister.' In the Pomo branch of Hokan, also in California, East
Pomo contrasts *tuts* 'mother's older sister' with *tsets* 'mother's brother'; the
first form presumably derives from **tuntun*, the latter, from **tenten*. Siouan
languages preserve the gender contrast in Proto-Siouan **yǐ-ki* 'son' and **yǔ-
ki* 'daughter.' Furthermore, according to Matthews, internal reconstruction
points to Pre-Siouan **sǐ-ki* 'son' and **sǔ-ki* 'daughter' (Matthews 1959: 273).
It seems likely that these forms, in turn, derive from earlier **thin-ki* and
*thun-ki, respectively, thus exemplifying not only the gender-induced vowel
alternation, but even the root under discussion in this chapter. If this is correct, then perhaps the source of Siouan aspiration lies in Amerind ejectives.
Unexplained for the moment is the differential treatment of initial **thun-* in
the words for 'daughter' and 'paternal aunt.' Possibly the "normal" sound
change *thi* > *ši* in the word for 'son' was analogically extended to the morphologically similar word for 'daughter.' It would appear that Biloxi has preserved
the vowel contrast in *as-tõ-ki* 'daughter' and *as-tǐ-ki* 'boy.' In the Tanoan
branch of Central Amerind we have Tewa *sēŋ* 'man, male' (< **ten*) contrasting with Taos *t'út'ina* 'older sister' (< **t'unt'una*). In Mexico, Proto-Oto-
Manguean contrasted **sehn* 'male' with **suhn* 'female,' and the similarity of
Proto-Central Otomi **sǔ-tˢi* 'girl' with both Tewa (Tanoan) *sūn-tsi* 'intimate

friend, chum' and Pre-Siouan *sŭ-ki 'daughter' is striking. In Mayan, Pokom-chi contrasts ī-tsʲin- 'younger sibling' with i-tsan-naʔ 'aunt,' while Kakchiquel has a-čin 'man' and iš-tan 'señorita.' On the East Coast of North America, Mohawk has a-thŭ-wisã 'woman' contrasting with -ʔtsin 'male, boy,' while Yuchi opposes *tane* 'brother' and -tsʲone 'daughter.'

MORPHOLOGICAL AFFIXES AND PROCESSES

As the observant reader will have already noticed, it is not just the root *t'aʔna* 'child, sibling' that connects the various forms given in the preceding section. There are, in addition to the root itself, a number of affixes and morphological processes that show up in various Amerind subgroups in conjunction with the root.

The Gender Ablaut System. The interaction of the stem with the process of gender-induced vowel alternation was discussed above. Additional examples are provided in the final section of this chapter.

The Age-Differential System. One of the primary factors leading to "incorrect vowels"—from the point of view of the gender ablaut system—was the development of a competing system, based on age, in which the -i- vowel was reinterpreted as meaning 'young child, regardless of sex,' and/or the vowel -u- was reinterpreted as 'older relative, regardless of sex.' Examples of the -i- vowel reinterpreted in this manner include Yurok tsits 'younger sibling' (< *tintin), Kutenai tiʔte 'granddaughter,' Mohawk -a-ten-oʔsã- 'brothers and sisters, to be siblings,' Nez Perce pi-t'íʔn 'girl,' Wintun te- 'son, daughter,' Proto-Maiduan *téh 'child, son,' Natchez tsitsī 'infant,' Proto-Tzeltal-Tzotzil *ʔih-tsʲin 'man's younger brother, woman's younger sibling,' Yahi t'i'nī-si 'child, son, daughter,' Southern Pomo t'i-ki 'younger sibling,' San Buenaventura Chumash u-tinai 'infant,' Proto-Oto-Manguean *si(ʔ)(n) 'youngster,' Pehuenche čeče 'grandchild' (< *tenten), Alakaluf se-kwai 'grandchild,' Maku tenu-'pa 'son, daughter,' Tiquie tenten 'grandchild,' Yehupde tẽ 'child,' Kamaru te-ke 'nephew, niece,' Marawa tino 'small child,' Bare hana-tina-pe 'child,' Arara enru-te-po 'small child,' and Suhin tino-iče 'young woman.' Examples where the -u- vowel has been reinterpreted as a marker of the parent's or grandparent's generation include Northeast Pomo tono 'brother-in-law,' Tewa t'ūnu 'maternal uncle,' possibly Caddo dono 'male,' Corobisi tun 'man,' Move dun 'father,' Kagaba du-we 'elder brother,' Paez ne-tson 'brother-in-law,' Capishana mia-tuna 'older brother,' Iranshe šūna 'father-in-law,' Yuracare suñe 'man,' Cofan tõʔtõ 'uncle' (< *tonton), Aweti a-tu 'grandfather,' Manaže tutý 'paternal uncle,' Paumeri ā-θu 'paternal uncle,' Caranga čuñi-l 'brother-in-law,' Galibi tun 'father,' Pavishana tutu 'grandfather,' Moseten čuñe 'brother-in-law, paternal son-in-law,' Culino mu-tun 'old man,' Tacana *e-du-e* 'older brother,' Chama *toto* 'uncle' (< **tonton*), Botocudo *gy-ǰune* 'brother-in-law,' Opaye *o-čobn* 'man,' and Cayapo *ǰuno* 'father.'

Reduplication. Many of the forms show reduplication, a common process for Amerind kinship terms. I have shown elsewhere (see Chapter 10 herein) that Proto-Amerind contrasted **p'oj* 'younger brother' with a reduplicated form **p'ojp'oj* 'older brother.' A similar process can be seen with the forms discussed in this chapter, where the reduplicated form represents someone older than that represented by the non-reduplicated form. Thus, Proto-Amerind constrasted **tin* '(younger) brother, son' with **tintin* 'older brother, uncle, grandfather' (e.g. Eastern Pomo *tsets* 'mother's brother,' Nisenan *ʔi-tīti* 'cousin,' Cayuvava *tete* 'uncle,' Wapishana *teti* 'maternal uncle'), as well as **tun* '(younger) sister, daughter' with **tuntun* 'older sister, aunt, grandmother' (e.g. Wintun *tūtuh* 'mother,' Tzeltal *čučuʔ* 'grandmother,' Eastern Pomo *tuts* 'mother's older sister,' Esselen *tutsu* 'niece,' Taos *-t'út'ina* 'older sister,' Tarascan *tˢutˢu* 'grandmother,' Cuna *tuttu* 'woman,' Colorado *sonasona* 'woman,' Mayoruna *čuču* 'older sister'). Other reduplicated forms show the same pattern, though with a vowel different from that predicted by the gender system (e.g. Cherokee *e-dudu* 'grandfather,' Central Sierra Miwok *tete* 'older sister,' Yurumangui *tintin* 'woman,' Sumu *titin-ki* 'grandmother,' Auake *toto* 'older brother,' Ubde-Nehern *tetein* 'wife,' Capishana *totoi* 'brother-in-law,' Cofan *tõʔtõ* 'uncle,' Uruku *toto* 'grandfather,' Manaže *tuty* 'paternal uncle,' Wapishana *teti* 'maternal uncle,' Pavishana *tutu* 'grandfather,' Azumara *toto* 'man,' Huarayo *toto* 'man's brother,' Puri *titiña-*'grandmother'). In some cases the reduplicated form represents a younger generation (e.g. Kutenai *tiʔte* 'granddaughter,' Tiquie *tenten* 'grandchild,' Caranga *tuto* 'grandchild'). This may be the result of a reciprocal system of kinship terminology in which there is a single term for both 'grandchild' and 'grandparent.'

First-Person **na-*. Since kinship terms are necessarily preceded by a pronominal suffix in many Amerind languages (and probably in Proto-Amerind as well), it is not surprising that we often find the ubiquitous first-person **na-* 'my' preceding the root in question. Examples include Proto-Algonquian **ne-tāna* 'my daughter,' **ne-tān-kwa* 'my sister-in-law,' Nez Perce *ʔin-tˢi-k'ī-wn* 'my wife's brother,' Kiowa *nɔ:-tɔ:* 'my brother,' Taos *añ-t'út'ina* 'my older sister,' Cahuilla *ne-suŋa-mah* 'my daughter,' Paez *ne-tson* 'my brother-in-law,' Manao *no-tany* 'my son,' Yavitero *nu-tani-mi* 'my daughter,' Baniva *no-tani* 'my son,' and Ipurina *ni-tari* 'my brother.'

Diminutive **-ihsa*. The Proto-Algonquian diminutive suffix **-ehsa* is in fact of Amerind origin, appearing widely in both North and South America with this and other roots. L. S. Freeland (1931: 32) called attention to its presence in both Penutian and Hokan languages: "This Penutian *-si diminutive is characteristic, it would seem, as contrasted with its undoubtedly cognate Hokan *-tsi (*-'tsi)." For the root in question one may cite Proto-Algonquian *ne-tān-ehsa 'my daughter,' Yurok tˢān-ūk-s 'young child,' Nootka t'an'ē-ʔis 'child,' Chumash ma-k-ič-tuʔn 'my son' (literally, "the-my-diminutive-son"), Koasati tˢika-si 'younger son,' ắto-si 'infant child,' Mixtec táʔnù iʔšá 'younger sister' (iʔšá = 'child'), Esmeralda tini-usa 'daughter,' Macusi taŋ-sa 'girl,' and Suhin tino-iče 'young woman.' Other examples of this diminutive suffix include Cayuse kwun-asa 'girl,' Paez kuen-as 'young woman,' Cahuapana willa-ša 'boy, girl,' Amuesha koy-an-ešaʔ 'girl,' and Chama e-gʷan-asi 'woman.'

Diminutive *-mai. Another diminutive suffix that is widespread within Amerind is *-mai, exemplified in Luiseño tuʔ-mai 'woman's daughter's child,' Cahuilla ne-suŋa-mah 'my daughter,' Masaca tani-mai 'younger sister,' Chapacura tana-muy 'daughter,' Itene tana-muy 'girl,' and Yavitero nu-tani-mi 'my daughter.'

*-kwa '. . .-in-law'. The Proto-Algonquian suffix *-kwa '. . .-in-law' is likely cognate with the corresponding suffix in Columbian ti-kʷa 'father's sister,' Flathead tití-kʷe 'woman's brother's daughter,' Yuki -tˢí-hwa 'husband's brother,' -tˢí-hwa-pi 'husband's sister, wife's sister,' Iowa tá-gwa 'son-in-law,' Northern Paiute taŋ-ʔwa 'man,' Shasta a-ču-gwi 'younger female cousin,' Jicaque tsi-kway 'boy, child,' Mazatec ču-kwhã 'aunt,' Trique du-ʔwe 'aunt,' Kagaba tu-gwa 'grandchild,' Mixtec du-ʔwi 'aunt,' Motilon a-te-gwa 'nephew,' Paez anš-tsun-kue 'grandchild,' Tucano ti-kã 'son-in-law,' Yaruro hia-to-kwi 'maternal grandson,' Alakaluf se-kwai 'grandchild,' Surinam Carib tī-ʔwo 'brother-in-law,' and Tacana u-tse-kwa 'grandchild,' as well as with other roots (e.g. Yurok ne-kwa 'my mother/father-in-law,' Proto-Mixtecan *kuʔn-gwi 'woman's sister,' Cahuapana kaik-kwa 'sister-in-law,' Krenye pan-çwö 'sister-in-law').

Demonstrative *i-. The prefix i- found on many forms (e.g. Proto-Siouan, Pokomchi, Chontal, Ulua, Sumu, Guambiana, Manao, Witoto, Apinage, Aponegicran, Capaxo) was probably originally a demonstrative pronoun.

*ʔa- 'Elder'. Many of the forms show traces of a prefix whose original form and meaning appear to have been *ʔa- 'elder.' Examples include Wintun o-tun-če 'older sister,' Proto-Miwok *ʔá-ta 'older brother,' Lake Miwok ʔa-táa 'older brother,' Yuki ʔā-ṭ'át 'man,' Kakchiquel a-čin 'man,' Sierra Popoluca hā-thuŋ 'father,' Mixe a-ts 'elder brother,' Shasta ʔá-ču 'older sister,' Achomawi a-tūn 'younger brother,' Washo -ʔá-t'u 'older brother,' Northern Paiute a-tsi 'maternal uncle,' Coreguaje aʔ-čɨ 'elder brother,' aʔ-čo 'elder sister,' Aweti a-tu 'grandfather,' Guahibo ā-tō 'elder brother,' Paumari ā-dyu 'older brother,' Uainuma a-ttsiu 'uncle,' Custenau a-tu 'grandfather,' Yameo a-tin 'man,' and

Piokobyé *ha-tõn* 'younger brother.' This prefix may also be found in Proto-Maipuran **ahšeni* 'man, person,' which could reflect an earlier **ʔa-teni*.

*-ko 'Elder'. The suffix **-ko* also modulates the root with the meaning 'elder.' Its clearest attestation is in Macro-Ge forms such as Caraho *ton-ko* 'older brother,' Piokobyé *tõn-ko* 'older brother,' Umotina *žu-ko* 'paternal father-in-law' (< **tun-ko*), Apinaye *tu'-ká* 'paternal uncle, son-in-law,' *tu'-ka-ya* 'maternal grandfather,' *tu'-ka-tí* 'brother-in-law, son-in-law.' Outside of Macro-Ge, possible reflexes include Proto-Siouan **thų́-kã* 'grandfather,' Assiniboine *tū-gã́* 'maternal grandfather,' Santee *thū-kã́* 'maternal grandfather,' Biloxi *tú-kã* 'maternal uncle,' Tfalti *čaŋ-ko* 'man,' Zuni *tač-ču* 'father' (if this derives from **tan-ko*), Mixe *tsu-gu* 'aunt,' Northern Paiute *to-go'o* 'maternal grandfather,' Mono *tˢu-ku* 'old man,' Tübatulabal *tu-gu* 'brother's wife,' Kawaiisu *to-go* 'maternal grandfather,' and Yuri *čo-ko* 'man.'

*-win 'Female'. The similarity between Proto-Siouan **thų́-wĩ* 'paternal aunt,' Yurok *ne-ts-iwin* 'my mother-in-law,' Southeast Pomo *wi-kwi* 'sister' (< **win-kwi*), and Nez Perce *ʔin-tˢi-k'ĩ-wn* 'my wife's brother' suggests a Proto-Amerind formative **win* 'female.' Whether Tlappanec *ada-tāh-wĩʔ* 'child' is related to these forms is unclear.

*wis- 'Older Female'. The comparison of Mohawk *-a-thū-wisɔ̃* 'woman,' Proto-Tzeltal-Tzotzil **wiš-* 'older sister,' Cogui *wežu* 'older female,' Guayabero *wišʲ* 'female,' and Churuya *-viči* 'female' suggests that Proto-Amerind had a formative **wis-* 'older female,' preserved in Mohawk as a fossilized affix on the root this chapter discusses.

*iš- 'Female'. This prefix is perhaps related to the preceding. Examples include Pocomam *iš-tan* 'girl,' Kakchiquel *iš-tan* 'señorita,' Yaruro *išĩ-to-hwĩ* 'small girl' (cf. *to-kwĩ* 'small boy'), and Parawa *iš-tano* 'woman.'

Reciprocal *-ki/-ka. In his classic study of Proto-Siouan kinship terminology G. H. Matthews noted that "there are two suffixes, **-ki* and **-ka*, which were probably productive in Proto-Siouan, but which, in the daughter languages, are nonproductive, or, in the case of **-ki* in some languages, semiproductive. Reflexes of these suffixes are now best treated as a part of the stems they follow, with the result that a stem in one language will sometimes be cognate with all but the last syllable of a stem in another language, this last syllable being a reflex of one of these Proto-Siouan suffixes" (Matthews 1959: 254–55). It seems likely that the Proto-Siouan suffix **-ki* is cognate with the Yanan suffix **-si* that Sapir noted in forms such as Yahi *t'i'nī-si* 'child, son, daughter.' Regarding this suffix, Sapir wrote that it "is used in several . . . terms indicating relations to one of a younger generation" (Sapir 1918: 156). It would appear that Proto-Amerind had at least two reciprocal suffixes used to denote certain kinship relationships: *-ki* and *-ka*. Possibly the diachronic source of the first affix, and perhaps of both, is the Proto-Amerind suffix *-ki* 'we-2 inclusive,' discussed by Greenberg (1987: 287–89) in detail. Examples of the *-ki* suffix include Proto-Siouan *i-thã-ki* 'man's sister (older or younger),' Proto-Siouan *yĭ-ki* 'son,' Proto-Siouan *yŭ-ki* 'daughter,' possibly Wiyot *čĭ-k* 'child' (if this derives from *tin-ki*), Southern Sierra Miwok *tá-čiʔ* 'older brother,' Biloxi *as-tĭ-ki* 'boy,' Yuchi *wi-ta-ki* 'young man,' Pawnee *ti-ki* 'boy, son,' Yahi *t'i'nī-si* 'child, son, daughter,' Southern Pomo *t'i-ki* 'younger sibling,' Mazahua *t'i-ʔi* 'boy,' Tewa *sũn-tsi* 'intimate friend, chum' (< *tun-ki*), Proto-Central Otomi *šũ-tˢi* 'girl' (< *tun-ki*), Cayapà *tˢuh-ki* 'sister,' Kaliana *tai-ge* 'brother,' Amaguaje *ye-tsen-ke* 'son' (cf. *tˢin* 'boy'), Yupua *tsīn-geē* 'boy,' Kamaru *te-ke* 'nephew, niece,' Goajiro *tan-či* 'brother-in-law,' Taulipang *a-tˢi-ke* 'older brother,' and Aponegicran *i-thon-ghi* 'sister.'

The following are probably reflexes of the *-ka* suffix: Proto-Siouan *i-thã-ka* 'woman's younger sister,' San Juan Bautista *ta-ka* 'older brother,' Rumsen *tá-ka* 'older brother,' Konomihu *ču-ka* 'boy,' Binticua *ču-ka* 'grandchild,' *a-ta-ka* 'old woman,' Tegria *su-ka* 'sister,' Eten *čan-ka* 'sister,' Iquito *i-ta-ka* 'girl,' Caraho *a-ton-ka* 'younger sister,' and Piokobyé *a-tõn-kä* 'younger sister.'

*tˡuk- 'Child'. Several forms appear to represent the remnants of a Proto-Amerind compound **tˡuk-t'aʔna*, both of whose constitutents originally meant 'child.' Putative examples of this compound include Tsimshian *ɬuk-taēn* 'grandchild,' Chontal *čox-to* 'young,' Chol *čok-tuiun* 'boy' (cf. *aluš–čok* 'girl'), Miskito *tuk-tan* 'child, boy,' Manekenkn *ie-tog-te* 'brother,' Tibagi *tog-tan* 'girl,' and Chapacura *a-čoke-tunia* 'girl.' It seems likely that Santa Cruz Chumash *huk-tana-hu* 'my son' and Yurok *tˢān-ūk-s* 'young child' (< **tˢān-hūk-s*) exhibit the same compound.

*pam 'Child'. Both Penutian and Hokan languages show a compound consisting of **pam* 'child' and the root discussed in this chapter. In the Plateau branch of Penutian we find Molale *pam-tin* 'nephew,' Proto-Sahaptian **pámt* 'nephew' (woman's brother's son), North Sahaptin *pám-ta* 'nephew,' Nez Perce *pám-tin* 'nephew.' Coahuilteco, a Hokan language, appears to show the same compound in *t'an-pam* 'child,' though with a different grade of the Amerind root and with a different ordering of the constituents.

Demonstrative *mV. There is a final element that is found sporadically with the root under discussion in this chapter. In synchronic grammars it is usually described as an intercalated *-m-* that appears, somewhat mysteriously, between a possessive prefix and a kinship term. Its meaning, if any is specified, is usually vague. Moshinsky (1974: 102) reports that in Southeastern Pomo, a member of the Hokan branch of Amerind, "the *-m-* prefix occurs on the non-vocative forms of all kinship terms" (with a few exceptions) in forms such as *Pi-m-sen* 'maternal uncle,' *Pi-m-tˢe-x* 'paternal uncle,' *Pi-m-tˢen* 'maternal grandfather,' *wi-m-t'a-q* 'younger sister.' This latter form is suspiciously similar to Washo *wi-tˢ'u-k* 'younger sister,' which appears to lack the intercalated *-m-* and to involve a different grade of the Amerind root, and also resembles Yuchi *wi-ta-ki* 'young man.' It should be emphasized that the Washo form is synchronically monomorphemic, whereas in the Southeastern Pomo form the final morpheme boundary is not synchronically motivated. In both languages the reciprocal *-ki* ~ *-ka* has become fossilized on the stem, as in Siouan languages. In Washo the archaic first-person singular pronoun *wi-* has also become fossilized in the word for 'younger sister,' but in Southeastern Pomo both the first-person singular pronoun *wi-* and the intercalated *-m-* are synchronically motivated.

In the Plateau branch of Penutian we find a similar intercalated *-m-* in both Nez Perce and Northern Sahaptin. For most Nez Perce kinship terms the first-person possessed form is simply the first-person prefix followed by the root, as in *naP–tót* 'my father,' *Pim'–tót* 'thy father.' In four of the terms, however, an intercalated *-m-* appears in the first-person term, but not in the second-person form: *Pin-m'-ásqap* 'man's younger brother,' *Pin-ím-qanis* 'man's younger sister,' *Pin–m'-átˢip* 'woman's younger sister,' *Pin-m'-ít-x* 'woman's sister's child.' In Northern Sahaptin we find the following forms: *in-m-išt* 'my son,' *in-ma-awit'ał* 'my brother-in-law,' *in-m-ač* 'my sister-in-law,' *in-əm-am* 'my husband,' *in-m-ašam* 'my wife.' With regard to this *-m-*, Jacobs (1931: 235) concluded that "there is some doubt concerning *m*; it may be possessive *-mi* or *inmi* vestigially prefixed before a front vowel."

In South America, a similar intercalated *-m-* appears in Itonama, a Paezan language of Bolivia, as reported in Rivet (1921: 175). Rivet noted this prefix, between first-person *š-* and the root in the following forms: *š-me-tíka* 'my mother,' *š-mi-múka* 'my father,' *š-máy-yamăšne* 'my father-in-law,' *š-ma-yamăšne-ka* 'my mother-in-law,' *š-mi-yama* 'son-in-law,' and *š-mey-mapi-ni* 'my husband.' (First-person *š-* is perhaps cognate with the first-person suffix *-(a)š* in Sahaptin.)

It seems likely that this intercalated *-m-*, for which no meaning is usually specified, represents a fossilized article that has become part of the stem synchronically. The diachronic source of this element is in all probability the Proto-Amerind demonstrative **mV-* posited by Greenberg (1987: 283–84). Greenberg noted that the original demonstrative meaning has been eroded in many languages, appearing fossilized on nouns as a Stage III article in Guato, as the impersonal possessor in Algic, as the third-person reflexive pronoun in Uto-Aztecan, and as a body-part prefix in Salish.

AMERIND *T'AʔNA* 'CHILD, SIBLING'

Here I present the evidence I have found for *t'aʔna* 'child, sibling,' and its masculine and feminine grades, within Amerind. For expository purposes only I list Almosan, Keresiouan, Chibchan, and Paezan separately, though the first two form one branch of Amerind, and the latter two, another. Many of these forms are taken from Greenberg's unpublished Amerind notebooks (Greenberg 1981), whose data originally suggested to me the analysis presented in this chapter. Subsequently, I added many additional items as the result of my own library research. During this research I often came upon the same forms that Greenberg had included in his notebooks. Since it has recently been alleged that his notebooks are untrustworthy and filled with errors, I must take this opportunity to report that I have found the claim to be wholly unwarranted. The notebooks do faithfully reflect the linguistic literature upon which they are based. The few errors that were introduced in the various stages of the production of his book can hardly be taken to invalidate Greenberg's basic classification of Native American languages, any more than errors in his African data invalidated his African classification, or, for that matter, any more than the numerous errors in the standard etymological dictionary of Indo-European (Pokorny 1959) invalidate the Indo-European family. We are, after all, not dealing with a mathematical proof that can be invalidated by a single false step. We are dealing rather with the *preponderance of evidence,* which does not rest on any single datum. Furthermore, if one wishes to find out whether a particular sound/meaning association exists in Native American languages, there is at present no other place to find such information except in Greenberg's notebooks.

As mentioned in footnote 1, I have added many morpheme boundaries that do not appear in the original sources, either on the basis of indicated morpheme boundaries in other related languages, or according to the analysis proposed in this chapter. Many of these suffixes are no longer synchronically motivated in the modern languages, representing fossilized elements that have lost their meaning. No doubt some of my proposed morpheme boundaries will turn out to be erroneous, and obviously not all of the proposed cognates have equal probabilities of being correct. Though many forms are virtually certain to be cognate (and it is these that guarantee the validity of the etymology), others can only be included with varying degrees of confidence, owing to semantic and/or phonological anomalies. It would of course be a miracle if every form cited below were genuinely cognate. But it would, in my opinion, be even more miraculous if the *vast majority* of these forms were *not* cognate, and the few random errors that inevitably creep into a work of this scope are not likely to affect the general conclusions drawn.

ALMOSAN: Proto-Algonquian *ne-tāna* 'my daughter,' Proto-Central Algonquian *-tāna- 'daughter,' Blackfoot *ni-tána* 'my daughter,' Menomini *ni-tān* 'my daughter,' Cheyenne *nah-tōnna* 'my daughter,' Arapaho *na-tane* 'my daughter,' Atsina *na-tan* 'my daughter,' Proto-Algonquian *ne-tān-ehsa* 'my daughter,' Cree *ni-tān-is* 'my daughter,' Ojibwa *nen-tān-iss* 'my daughter,' Potawatomi *n-tan-əs* 'my daughter,' Fox *ne-tān-esa* 'my daughter,' Shawnee *ni-tān-e?θa* 'my daughter,' Proto-Algonquian *ne-tān-kwa* 'my sister-in-law,' Ojibwa *nen-tān-kwe* 'my sister-in-law,' Fox *ni-tā-kwa* 'my sister-in-law'; ?Proto-Algonquian *nī?-tā-wa* 'my brother-in-law (man speaking),' Abenaki *na-dɔ-kw* 'my brother-in-law, my sister-in-law,' Cheyenne *?tatan-* 'older brother' (< *tantan*), Blackfoot *tsi-ki* 'boy' (< *tin-ki*), Arapaho *na-tsenota* 'my nephew'; Ritwan: Wiyot *(yi)-dān* ~ *(yi)-dār* '(my) son, father,' *tse-k* ~ *čī-k* ~ *tsa-k* 'child'(< *tin-ki*), Yurok *ne-ta-tˢ* 'my child,' *tˢān-ūk-s* 'young child,' *tˢin* 'young man,' *tˢitˢ* (Robins) 'younger sibling' (< *tintin* or perhaps < *tin-ki*), *čič* (Gifford) 'very young sibling, very young child'; Kutenai *ga'-tˢʷɪn* 'daughter' (cf. Yuchi *go-t'o* 'child' [*go-* = 'human being'], *go-t'e* 'man'), *tsu* 'sister (of a girl),' *tat'* 'older brother,' *tsā* ~ *tsiya* 'younger brother,' *ti?te* 'granddaughter' (< *tintin*); Chimakuan: Chemakum *činni-s* 'sister,' Salish: Flathead *sín-tˢe?* 'younger brother (man speaking),' *tún-š* 'sister's children,' *tití-kʷe* 'woman's brother's daughter,' Lillooet *s-tūnə-q* 'niece,' Coeur d'Alene *tune* 'niece,' Columbian *šín-ča* 'younger brother,' *ti-kʷa* 'father's sister,' *tūn-x* 'man's sister's child,' Spokane *tūn-š* 'man's sister's child,' *łuwɛs-tɪn* 'deceased parent's sibling,' Lower Fraser *tān* 'mother,' Pentlatch *tan* 'mother,' *tet* 'boy,' Lkungen *nə-tan* 'mother'; Wakashan: Nootka *t'an'a* 'child,' *t'an'ē-?is* 'child,' Kwakwala *t'ana* 'blood relative,' Oowekyala *tān'i-ǧui-ł* 'to be closely related to one's spouse.'

KERESIOUAN: Siouan: Proto-Siouan *i-thá̃-ki* 'man's sister (younger or older),' Dakota *taŋ-ke* 'man's older sister,' Santee *mi-tān-ke* 'my sister,' Osage *i-tõ-ge* 'elder sister,' Quapaw *tã-ki* 'younger sister,' Kansa *wi-tõ-ge* 'younger sister,' Chiwere *taŋ-e* 'sister,' Biloxi *tã-ki* 'elder sister,' Tutelo *tahāk* 'sister,' Proto-Siouan *i-thá̃-ka* 'woman's younger sister,' Mandan *tã-ka* 'younger sister,' Dakota *taŋ-ka* 'woman's younger sister,' Proto-Siouan *yí-ki* 'son' (< Pre-Siouan *ší-ki* < *thin-ki?*), Assiniboine *tˢī-k-ši* 'son,' Teton *tshī-k-ši* 'son,' Omaha *ží-ge* 'son,' Biloxi *as-tĭ-ki* 'boy,' Proto-Siouan *yú-ki* 'daughter' (< Pre-Siouan *šú-ki* < *thun-ki?*), Assiniboine *tˢũ-k-ší* 'daughter,' Santee *tshũ-k-ší* 'daughter,' Osage *žǒ-ge* 'daughter,' Biloxi *as-tõ-ki* 'girl,' Proto-Siouan *thú-wĩ* 'paternal aunt,' Dakota *toŋ-wiŋ* 'aunt,' Santee *tõ-wĩ* 'aunt,' Winnebago *čũ-wi* 'paternal aunt,' Biloxi *tõn-i* 'paternal aunt, son-in-law,' Proto-Siouan *thú-ká̃* 'grandfather,' Assiniboine *tũ-gá̃* 'maternal grandfather,' Santee *thũ-ká̃* 'maternal grandfather,' Biloxi *tú-ka̍* 'maternal uncle,' *tan-do* 'woman's younger brother,' *a-di* 'father,' Quapaw *ĩ-do-ke* 'male,' Biloxi *i-to* 'male, man,' Mandan *i-se-k* 'male,' Iowa *tá-gwa* 'son-in-law'; Yuchi *-tˢ'one* 'son, daughter (woman speaking),' *-tane* 'brother,' *-s'anɛ* 'man's son,' *go-t'ɛ̃* 'man, father,' *go-t'o* 'child,' *tu-kã* 'grandfather,' *wi-ta-ki* 'young man'; Caddoan: Caddo *tan-arha* 'wife,' *dadin* 'his sister,' *dono* 'male,' Pawnee *i-tahri* 'his sister,' *ti-ki* 'boy, son' (< **tin-ki*), Arikara *i-tahni* 'his sister,' Adai *hã-siŋ* 'man'; Iroquoian: Cherokee *a-tsɔ̃* 'male of animals,' *ã-t'ɔn'ɔ̃ⁿ* 'young woman,' *a-tsutsu* 'boy,' *e-dudu* 'grandfather,' Seneca *-a-tẽn-ɔ̃te-* 'to be siblings,' *-tẽno-ɔ̃?-* 'to be parents-in-law,' *-a-tyoh* 'sibling-in-law,' Onandaga *ho-tonia* 'baby,' Cayuga *htsi?* 'older sibling,' *-a-tẽhn-õtē?* 'to be siblings,' Mohawk *-?tsin* 'male, boy,' *-a-ten-o?sɔ̃-* 'brothers and sisters, to be siblings,' *-a-tyo-* 'brother-in-law,' *thɔ̃-th-* 'aunt,' *-a-thũ-wisɔ̃* 'woman,' *?-tsi-* 'older sibling,' *?-a-te-re-* 'grandchild'; Keresan: Keres *-t'aona* 'sister.'

PENUTIAN: Tsimshian *ɬuk-taēn* 'grandchild,' ?Gitksan *dii-kw* 'daughter, sister (woman speaking)'; Oregon: Takelma *t'ī ʲ-* 'man, male, husband,' *t'ī-(t'kʲ)* '(my) husband,' *tˢ'a-* 'woman's brother's child, man's sister's child,' Tfalti *čaŋ-ko* 'man,' Coos *teᵘ* 'nephew,' Siuslaw *tīl* 'niece,' *t'āt* 'nephew' (< **t'an-t'an*); Plateau: North Sahaptin *p-t'īn-ik-s* 'girl' (cf. the Yurok form for 'young child' cited above), *p-ta-χ* 'son's child,' *pi-tə-χ* 'maternal uncle,' *pám-ta* 'woman's brother's son,' Nez Perce *pi-t'í?n* 'girl,' *?in-tˢi-k'ī-wn* 'my wife's brother' (literally, "my-brother-reciprocal-wife"), *pám-tin* 'woman's brother's son,' *?tá-qa?* 'maternal uncle,' Molale *pam-tin* 'nephew,' Cayuse *pnē-t'iŋ* 'my brother,' *i-tsaŋu* 'young'; Proto-California Penutian **tač* 'father' (< **tan-ki*), Wintun *te-* 'son, daughter,' *o-tun-če* 'older sister,' *tan-(če)* 'father, paternal uncle,' *tai-* 'nephew, niece, grandchild,' *tũtuh* 'mother' (< **tuntun*), *to-q-* 'sister-in-law,' Northwest Wintun *bi-čen* 'daughter'; Maiduan: Proto-Maiduan **týn* 'younger brother,' Nisenan *tyne* 'younger brother,' *?i-tīti* 'cousin' (< **?i-tintin*), *teᵃ naj* 'boy,' Proto-Maiduan **téh* 'child,' Maidu *té* 'son,' Proto-Maiduan **-tó* 'grandmother'; Yokuts: Yaundanchi *bu-tson* 'son,' *ṭaaṭi* 'man,' *t'uta* 'maternal grandmother' (< **t'untan*); Miwok: Proto-Miwok **?á-ta* 'older brother,' Saclan *tune* 'daughter,' Lake Miwok *?a-táa* 'older brother,' Plains Miwok *tī-ka* 'sister, elder sister,' *?ā-ti-* 'younger brother or sister,' *?a-ta-tˢi* 'older brother' (< **?a-tan-ki*), *tūne-* 'daughter,' *tete* 'mother's younger sister,' *tete-či* 'mother's brother's daughter, father's sister's daughter'(< **tenten-ki*), Southern Sierra Miwok *tune-* 'daughter,' *tá-či?* 'older brother,' Central Sierra Miwok *ṭūni* 'small, young,' *-tūne* 'daughter,' *tá-či* 'older brother,' *a-če* 'grandchild,' *a-te* 'younger brother, younger sister,' *téte* 'older sister'; Costanoan: San Francisco *ta-ka* 'brother,' *šen-is-muk* 'boy' (MALE-DIMINUTIVE-CHILD?), Ohlone *tanan* 'older sister,' *tˢinin* 'daughter, child,' *ta-ka-m* 'older brother,' Santa Cruz *tānan* 'older brother,' *ū-te-k* 'younger sibling,' *sinsin* 'nephew,' Rumsen *-tān* 'older sister,' San Juan Bautista *ta-ka* 'older brother,' Rumsen *tana* 'older sister,' *tá-ka* 'older brother,' Mutsun *šin-ie-mk* 'boy,' *ṭuta* 'young man,' *ta-ka* 'older brother,' *tit*^s*-tan* 'daughter-in-law'; Zuni *tač-ču* 'father' (< **tan-ku*); Gulf: Yuki *ʔā-ṭʼát* 'man,' -*t*^sʼína 'daughter's husband,' -*t*^sʼí-hwa 'husband's brother,' -*t*^sʼí-hwa-pi 'wife's sister, husband's sister,' Wappo *taʔa* 'mother's younger brother,' Coast Yuki *di-ke* 'older sibling,' Natchez *tsitsī* 'infant' (< **tintin*), *hi-dzina* 'nephew,' Chitimacha *tāt'in* 'younger brother or sister,' *ʔa-si* 'male,' Atakapa *t*^s*on* 'small, young,' *ten-s* 'nephew,' *ten-sa* 'niece,' *teñ* 'mother,' Tunica *šī* 'male,' *htóna-yi* 'wife,' Koasati *t*^s*i-ka* 'elder son,' *ā-ti* 'person,' *t*^s*i-ka-si* 'younger son,' *ā-to-si* 'infant child'; Mexican: Mayan: Yucatec *a-tan* 'wife,' Lacandon *i-tsin* 'younger brother,' Chorti (*w-*)*ih-tān* 'sibling,' (*w-*)*ih-t*^sʼ*in* 'younger sibling,' Cholti *i-tan* 'sister,' Proto-Cholan (Fox) **ih-tan* 'man's older sister, man's older female cousin,' Chol *ih-tiʔan* 'man's sister,' *čok-tuiun* 'boy,' Huastec *t*^s*anū-b* 'aunt,' Ixil *i-t*^sʼ*an* 'aunt,' Pokomchi *ī-t*^sʼ*in-* 'younger sibling,' *i-t*^s*an-naʔ* 'aunt,' Pocomam *iš-tan* 'girl' (*iš* = female), Kakchiquel *iš-tan* 'señorita,' *a-čin* 'man,' Proto-Tzeltal-Tzotzil **ʔih-t*^sʼ*in* 'man's younger brother, woman's younger sibling,' **ʔi-čan* 'maternal uncle,' Tzeltal *čučuʔ* 'grandmother,' Aguacatec *ču* 'grandmother,' Ixil *t*^sʼ*uy* 'grandmother,' Kekchi *naʔ-čin* 'grandmother,' Mam *ču* 'mother,' Ixil *čuč* 'mother,' Quiché *ču* 'mother,' Chontal *i-t*^sʼ*in* 'younger sibling,' *i-čan* 'father-in-law,' *čič* 'older sister'; Mixe-Zoque: Sierra Popoluca *hā-thuŋ* 'father,' Sayula *čuʔ-naʔ* 'father-in-law,' Texistepec *tene-īap* 'man,' Mixe *tat* 'father,' *ta-gh* 'mother,' *ats* 'elder brother,' *ïts* 'younger brother,' *uts* 'younger sister,' *tsyö* 'elder sister,' *tsu-gu* 'aunt,' Totonac *t'ána-t* 'grandchild.'

HOKAN: Proto-Hokan (Kaufman) **(ā)t'u(n)* 'brother,' **-č'i* (diminutive) (< **-t'in*?), Karok *tunuè-ič* 'small,' Arra-arra *atit*^s (< **a-tin-ki*) 'grandson, paternal grandparent'; Shasta: Shasta *ʔá-ču* 'older sister,' *a-ču-gwi* 'younger sister, younger female cousin,' Konomihu *ču-ka* 'boy'; Palaihnihan: Achomawi *a-tūn* 'younger brother,' *a-tā(-wi)* 'daughter,' *ōt'* 'daughter-in-law,' *čini* 'maternal uncle,' *-tsan* (diminutive); Yanan: Northern Yana *t'inī* 'to be little,' *t'inī-si* 'child, son, daughter,' Yahi *t'i'nī-si* 'child, son, daughter'; Pomo: Proto-Pomo (McLendon) **t*^s*u-t*^sʼ*i* ~ **t*^s*e-t*^sʼ*i* 'mother's brother,' **ṭʼá-qi* 'younger sibling,' **ṭ*^h*ūt*^sʼ 'mother's older sister,' Southern Pomo *ṭ'i-ki* 'younger sibling,' *aba-tsin* 'father's older brother,' *amu-tsin* 'father's sister,' Northeast Pomo *ṭ'i-ki* 'younger sibling,' *čunū-š* 'child' (cf. Chemakum *činni-s* 'sister'), *ti-ki-dai* 'older sister,' *tono* 'brother-in-law,' *tā'-č'i* 'maternal grandfather,' Central Pomo *de-ki* 'older sister,' *de-ki-dai* 'younger sister,' Eastern Pomo *tsets* 'mother's brother,' *tuts* 'mother's older sister,' Southeast Pomo *ʔi-m-sen* 'maternal uncle,' *ʔi-m-t*^s*e-x* 'paternal uncle,' *ʔi-m-t*^s*en* 'maternal grandfather,' *χá-t*^sʼ*in* 'sister's child,' *wi-m-t'a-q* 'younger sister,' (*du-*)*ṭ'a-q* 'younger brother,' Southwest Pomo *ṭ'i-ki* 'brother's son'; Washo -*ʔá-t'u* 'older brother,' *wi-ts'u-k* 'younger sister,' *t'ánu* 'person'; Salinan-Chumash: Chumash: Ynezeño *tuʔn* 'son, daughter,' (*ma-k-*)*ič-tuʔn* '(my) son,' *čiči* 'boy,' Santa Barbara *taniw* 'little, child,' San Buenaventura *u-tinai* 'infant,' Santa Cruz *tunne-č* 'boy,' *huk-tana-hu* 'my son'; Esselen *tano-č* 'woman,' *tutsu* 'niece'; Salinan *a-t'on* ~ *a-tʰon* 'younger sister,' *tani-l* 'granddaughter,' *ta-k* 'nephew, niece'; Yuman: Mohave *n-tai-k* 'mother,' *in-čien-k* 'older brother,' *n-athi-k* 'mother's older sister,' Yuma *an-tˢen* 'older brother,' Kamia *in-ča-čun* 'my older sister,' Havasupai *θa-wa* 'woman's sister' (< **tan-kwa*?); Coahuiltecan: Coahuilteco *ya-t'ān* 'sister,' *t'an-pam* 'child,' *t'āna-gē* 'father,' *ma-t'ān* 'paternal grandchild,' *tza-t'an* 'maternal grandchild,' *kuan-t'ān* 'grandchild,' *ku-t'an* 'uncle,' *maki-t'ān* 'aunt,' *ʔt'atā-l* 'brother,' *tˢan* 'small, young' (cf. Achomawi *-tsan* [diminutive]); Tlappanec *ada-tāh-wīʔ* 'child'; Jicaque *tsi-kway* 'boy, child'; Yurumangui *ki-tina* ~ *tintin* 'woman,' *a-ta-isa* (< **a-tan-isa*) 'sister.'

CENTRAL AMERIND: Uto-Aztecan: Proto-Uto-Aztecan **tana* 'daughter, son,' Varahio *taná* 'son, daughter,' Tarahumara *rana* 'son, daughter,' Proto-Uto-Aztecan **tu* 'boy,' ?Proto-Uto-Aztecan **sun* ~ **son* 'woman,' Northern Paiute *tua* 'son,' *a-tsi* 'maternal uncle,' *to-go'o* 'maternal grandfather,' ?*taŋ-ʔwa* 'man,' Southern Paiute *tua* 'son'(< **tona-*, according to Sapir), *tˢinA-nI* 'mother's younger brother,' Mono *tuwa* 'son,' *tˢu-ku* 'old man,' Tübatulabal *tena* 'man,' ?*tôhan* 'father's younger brother,' *u-tsu* 'maternal grandmother,' *tu-gu* 'brother's wife,' Kawaiisu *tuwaana* 'son,' *to-go* 'maternal grandfather,' *šinu* 'maternal uncle,' Northern Diegueño *e-čun* 'paternal uncle's daughter, maternal aunt's daughter,' Luiseño *tuʔ* 'maternal grandmother,' *tuʔ-mai* 'woman's daughter's child' (*-mai*=diminutive), *šuŋáa* 'woman,' Cahuilla *ne-suŋa-mah* 'my daughter,' Serrano *-suŋ* 'daughter,' *čič* 'woman's sister's son-in-law' (< **tintin*), Pipil *-tsin* (diminutive), *pil-tsin* 'boy, son' (cf. Tewa *ebile* 'child'), Nahuatl *ten-tzo* 'younger brother,' *tzin* (diminutive), *min-ton-tli* 'great grandson'; Tanoan: Kiowa *tā̃ʔ* 'sister, brother,' *nɔ-tɔ̃:* 'my brother,' Hano *tutu'uŋ* 'paternal uncle,' *t'ete* 'maternal grandfather,' Tewa *ti'u* 'younger sibling,' *t'ūnu* 'maternal uncle,' *t'et'e* 'maternal grandfather,' *tũʔɛ* 'nephew, niece' (< **tun-ke*), *sēŋ* 'man, male,' *sūn-tsi* 'intimate friend, chum,' Taos *añ-t'út'ina* 'my older sister,' *ñɬi-tona* 'wife,' *añ-tāna* 'kin of wife,' San Ildefonso *-tiu* 'younger sibling,' Isleta *tiyū* 'younger sister'; Oto-Manguean: Proto-Oto-Manguean **sehn* 'male,' **suhn* 'female,' Proto-Central Otomi **šū-tˢi* 'girl' (< **t'un-ki*?), **tˢū* 'female,' Chichimec *-čõ* 'female,' Mazahua *t'i-ʔi* 'boy' (< **t'in-ki*), Otomi *t'i-xū̃* 'daughter,' *ʔi-dā̃* 'woman's brother,' Mazatec *čʰū* 'woman,' *ču-kwhã* 'aunt,' *in-ta* 'son,' Chatina *tˢunõ-hõ* 'woman,' Proto-Oto-Manguean **ntaHn* 'mother,' **ʔntan* 'child,' **taʔn* 'sibling,' Mixtec *tā̃ʔã* 'sibling,' *táʔnù i?šá* 'younger sister' (*i?šá* = 'child'; cf. Proto-Algonquian **-tān-ehsa* 'daughter'), *du-ʔwi* 'aunt,' Trique *du-ʔwe̞* 'aunt,' Cuicatec *ʔdíínó* 'brother,' Popoloca *tˢhjān* 'child, son,' Chinantec *tsañi-h* 'man,' Zapotec *p-taʔn* 'woman's brother,' Proto-Oto-Manguean **si(ʔ)(n)* 'youngster,' Popoloca *čin-ka* 'little (of animals),' Proto-Otomi **tˢi* 'small (of animals and humans),' Proto-Chatino **šiñVʔ* 'son,' Isthmus Zapotec *žiʔiñiʔ* 'son,' Proto-Chinantecan **sīʔ* 'child.'

CHIBCHAN: Tarascan *tsutsu* 'grandmother' (< **tuntun*), Cuitlatec *ču* 'boy,' *čanu-i* 'my wife,' Xinca *u-tan* 'mother,' *tatan* 'father,' Lenca *tuntu-rusko* 'younger sister,' *ū-t'áne* 'father,' Sumu *i-tanni* 'mother,' *ti-tin-ki* ∼ *ti-tan-ki* 'my grandmother,' Miskito *tuk-tan* 'child, boy,' *tah-ti-ki* 'my maternal uncle (woman speaking),' Corobisi *tun* 'man,' Rama *ⁿdu-tuŋ* 'younger brother,' *i-tūŋ* 'father,' *tau* 'baby,' Changuena *sin* 'brother,' Move *nge-dan* 'brother-in-law,' *dun* 'father,' *ni-dan* 'male,' Sanema *ul-dwīn* 'child,' *ur-dwīn* 'boy,' *haš-twín* 'grandfather,' *píiši-dwīn* 'mother-in-law,' Shiriana *tasém-taiina* 'child,' Ulua *i-taŋ* 'mother,' Cuna *tuttu* 'woman,' *toto* 'small girl,' Atanque *ah-töna* 'old, old man, old woman,' Guamaca *tana* ∼ *tena* 'old,' *terrua-töna* 'old man,' *mona-töna* 'old woman,' Kagaba *tu-gua* 'grandchild,' *?suk-kua* 'son,' *?du-we* 'elder brother,' Chimila *tún-gva* 'friend,' Binticua *ču-ka* 'grandchild,' *a-ta-ka* 'old woman,' Guamaca *a-tena-šina* 'old woman,' Motilon *diani* 'wife,' *a-te-gwa* 'nephew,' Dobokubi *a-te-ki* 'father,' *ti-kwa* 'young man,' Chibcha *čune* 'grandchild,' Muyska *te-kua* 'boy, young man,' Tegria *su-ka* 'sister.'

PAEZAN: Citara *tana* 'mother,' Tucura *dana* 'mother,' Warrau *dani-jota* 'mother's older sister,' *dani-katida* 'mother's younger sister,' Chami *tana* 'mother,' ?Guambiana *i-ču* 'woman, wife,' Paez *ne-čī-k* 'son' (< **ne-tin-ki*), *ne-tson* 'brother-in-law,' *n-duh* 'son-in-law,' *anš-tsun-kue* 'grandchild,' ?Totoro *i-šu-k* 'wife,' ?Nonoma *doana* 'son-in-law,' Cayapa *tsuh-ki* 'sister' (< **tun-ki*), Colorado *sona(-sona)* 'woman,' *suna-lat-suna* 'wife,' *so-ke* 'sister,' Eten *čan-ka* 'sister,' *sonä-ŋ* ' wife,' Chimu *čaŋ* 'younger brother, nephew,' *čuŋ* 'sister,' Millcayac *tzhœng* 'son.'

ANDEAN: Simacu *kax-ðana* 'maternal uncle,' Iquito *i-ta-ka* 'girl,' Araucanian *tsoñi* 'woman's son' (cf. Yuchi *ts'one* 'woman's son'), Aymara *tayna* 'first-born of either sex,' *t'ini* 'a woman near to her delivery,' Tehuelche *den* 'brother,' Patagon *čen* 'brother,' Pehuenche *a-tsena* 'brother,' *čeče* 'grandchild,' Manekenkn *ie-tog-te* 'brother,' Ona *tane-ngh* 'maternal uncle,' Tehuelche *thaun* 'sister,' Tsoneka *ke-tun* 'sister,' Alakaluf *se-kwai* 'grandchild,' *se-kway-ok* 'grandmother,' *esna-tun* 'mother.'

MACRO-TUCANOAN: Iranshe *šūna* 'father-in-law,' *señu-p* 'man'; Kaliana-Maku: Kaliana *tone* 'mother-in-law,' *tai-ge* 'brother,' Auake *toto* 'older brother,' Maku *tenu-'pa* ∼ *tenu-ba* 'son, daughter'; Puinave: Puinave *a-tíi* 'my son,' *tēĩ-ūaĩ* 'brother,' *a-tõaĩ* 'cousin,' *ali-tan* 'father-in-law, grandfather,' Tiquie *ton* 'daughter,' *ten* 'son,' *tenten* 'grandchild,' Yehupde *tẽ* 'child,' Nadobo *tata* 'child,' Dou *tute* 'child,' Papury *toŋ* 'daughter,' *ten* 'son,' *tein* 'wife,' *tong-teip* 'son-in-law,' Ubde-Nehern *têain* 'boy,' *ten* 'son,' *tetein* 'wife,' *tëteté* 'grandchild,' *tën-do* 'maternal uncle' (cf. Biloxi *tan-do* 'woman's younger brother'), *tëtón* 'niece'; Catuquinan: Bendiapa *iš-tano* 'woman,' Parawa *iš-tano* 'woman'; Canichana *eu-tana* 'mother'; Huari: Huari *tān* 'mother,' Masaca *tani-mai* 'younger sister'; Capishana *mia-tuna* 'older brother,' *totoi* 'brother-

in-law,' ña-tō-küi 'older sister,' a-ta? 'aunt'; Nambikwara: Mamainde-Tarunde
denō 'woman,' čōnē 'grandfather,' (t)oán-osu 'older sister,' Southern Nambikwara tyū?n 'small,' Tagnani tana-nde 'mother,' teno-re 'woman,' ui-tono-re
'son'; Ticuna-Yuri: Yuri čo-ko 'man'; Tucanoan: Amaguaje tˢin 'boy,' ye-tsen-
ke 'son,' Coreguaje čīi̱ 'son,' čīio 'daughter,' a?-či̱ 'elder brother,' a?-čo 'elder sister,' čo?-jei̱ 'younger brother,' čo?-jeo 'younger sister,' Siona tˢijn 'son,'
Yupua tsīn-geē 'boy,' a-čane 'man,' Tucano ti-kã 'son-in-law,' Tatuyo teñë
'brother-in-law.'

EQUATORIAL: Trumai tain 'younger sister (man speaking),' ta-kwai 'younger
brother (woman speaking),' Cayuvava tete 'uncle,' tena-ni 'woman,' Taruma
a-či 'sister,' Yuracare suñe 'man,' Timote: Cuica tin-gua 'son, boy,' Mocochi
tin-gua 'son, boy,' nak-tun 'woman'; Zamucoan: Morotoko a-tune-sas 'girl'; Piaroa tsehãū 'brother,' tsēã'nã 'grandfather,' čōno 'grandfather,' tsēãnã 'grandmother'; Jivaroan: Cofan tzán-dey-dése 'boy,' tsan-deye 'man,' tō?tō 'uncle,'
Esmeralda tin ~ tīon 'woman,' tini-usa 'daughter,' Yaruro to-kwī 'small boy,'
iší-to-hwī 'small girl,' ieyī-to-kwī 'young woman,' hia-to-kwi 'maternal grandson,' hada-to-kwi 'paternal granddaughter,' Kariri: Dzubucua to 'grandfather,' Kamaru te-ke 'nephew, niece,' Kariri to 'grandfather,' Tupi: Guayaki
tuty 'paternal uncle, sister's son,' Digüt ðánǫǎ 'younger sister,' Ramarama
i-te 'brother,' Amniape o-ta 'daughter,' Kamayura u-tu 'grandmother,' Sheta
kuña-tai 'young woman,' Canoeiro kuña-tain 'small girl,' Tapirape ã-tãi 'female infant,' kot-ãtãi 'young girl,' Urubu-Kaapor ta?in 'child,' Tembe tỹ-
kỹhỹr 'older brother,' ty-h̃uhỹr 'younger brother,' coai-tỹ 'brother-in-law,'
a-tiu 'father-in-law,' Emerillon tsitsi? 'younger sister,' dzadza 'older sister,'
Arikem u-taua 'brother,' Cocama i̱kra-tsüng-ra 'child,' Guarani tatyu 'maternal father-in-law,' tuty 'uncle,' Aweti a-tu 'grandfather,' Uruku toto 'grandfather,' Manaže tutý 'paternal uncle,' Oyampi tu-ku 'younger brother'; Gua-
hiban: Guahibo ā-tō 'elder brother'; Guamo tua 'daughter'; Coche tan-gua
'old man'; Arawan: Deni tu 'daughter,' da?u 'son,' Paumari a-thon-i 'granddaughter,' ā-dyu 'older brother'; Chipayan: Uru thun 'wife,' (t)soñi 'man,'
Chipaya thun 'wife,' t'uana ~ txuna 'woman,' t'uñi ~ tsuñi 'brother's wife
(man talking),' Caranga tʰun 'wife,' čuñi-l 'brother-in-law,' tuto 'grandchild';
Chapacuran: Chapacura tana-muy 'daughter,' a-čoke-tunia 'girl,' Itene tana
'woman,' tana-muy 'girl,' tana-man 'woman,' Abitana tana 'woman,' Kumana
tana-man 'woman'; Maipuran: Proto-Maipuran *ahšeni 'man' (< *a?-teni?),
Amuesha ah-šēñ-ō(š) 'male,' Ignaciano a-čane 'person,' Asheninca a-šeni-nka
'fellow countryman,' Marawa tino 'small child,' tana-n 'woman,' Wapishana
iǐ-dan(e) 'child, son, daughter' u-dan-rin 'daughter,' ī-dan-karo 'nephew,' ī-
dan-kearo 'niece,' douani 'lad,' i-dĭni-re 'son-in-law,' i-dĭni-ru 'daughter-in-
law,' teti 'maternal uncle,' Uainuma a-ttsiu 'uncle,' Moxo a-ču(-ko) 'grandfather,' Proto-Maipuran *čina-ru 'woman,' Baure e-tón 'woman,' Palicur

te 'younger brother,' *tino* 'woman,' *tana-n* 'woman,' Karipura *tina-gubari* 'woman,' Custenau *tine-ru* 'woman,' *a-tu* 'grandfather,' Uirina *a-tina-re* 'man,' Yaulapiti *tine-ru-tsu* 'girl,' *tina-u* 'woman,' Yavitero *nu-tani-mi* 'my daughter,' *no-taịn-tani* 'my son,' Baniva *no-tani* 'my son,' Mehinacu *tene-ru* 'woman,' *a-to* 'grandfather,' Waura *tine-ru-ta* 'girl,' *tiné-šu* 'woman,' Arawak *o-tu* 'daughter,' *a-daün-ti* 'maternal uncle,' Manao *no-tany* 'my son,' *y-tuna-lo* 'woman,' Campa *tˢina-ni* 'woman,' *a-ten-dari* 'man,' Tuyoneri *ua-tone* 'old man, old woman,' Atoroi *dan* 'baby, son,' *dani-ʔinai* 'son,' *tidn* 'younger brother,' Goajiro *čon* 'son,' *tan-či* 'brother-in-law,' Bare *hana-tina-pe* 'child,' Ipurina *nu-tani-ri* 'my husband,' *ni-tari* 'my brother,' *ni-taru* 'my sister,' *n-atu-kiri* 'my grandfather.'

MACRO-CARIB: Andoke *tīna* 'a woman,' *tihi* 'mother, female child' (< **tin-ki*), Peba-Yaguan: Yagua *dēnu* 'male child,' Yameo *a-tin* 'man'; Carib: Surinam *tī-ʔwo* 'brother-in-law,' Macusi *taŋ-sa* 'girl' (cf. Atakapa *ten-sa* 'niece'), *ake-ton* 'old man,' Arara *enru-ten-po* 'small child,' Taulipang *a-tˢi-ke* 'older brother,' *aeke-toŋ* 'old person,' Galibi *tun* 'father,' Pavishana *tane* 'my son,' *tutu* 'grandfather,' Azumara *toto* 'man,' Bakairi *i-tano* 'grandfather'; Boran: Imihita *tãã-ti* 'grandfather,' Muinane *i-to* 'paternal uncle'; Witotoan: Witoto *i-taño* 'girl,' *o-suño* 'aunt,' *i-su* 'paternal uncle,' Witoto-Kaimö *iu-suna* 'aunt, grandmother,' Nonuya *om(w)ŭ̃-tona* 'sister.'

MACRO-PANOAN: Mascoian: Mascoy *tanni-yap* 'sister-in-law,' Kaskiha *an-tũ-ye* 'woman's son,' Lengua *tawin* 'grandchild,' *a-tai* 'my grandfather'; Moseten: Moseten *čuñe* 'brother-in-law, paternal son-in-law,' Mataco: Sotsiayay *taão-kla* 'boy,' Mataco *čina* 'younger sister,' Vejoz *činna* 'younger sister,' Churupi *čin-jo* 'younger sister,' Towithli *tuna-ni* 'woman,' Suhin *tino-iče* 'young woman,' *suña* 'younger sister'; Panoan: Cashibo *ṭanu* 'woman,' Cashibo *toa* 'child,' *didan* 'mother,' Shipibo *sanu* 'grandmother,' *tita* 'mother,' *sun-taku* 'young woman,' Sensi *čina-n* 'woman,' Panobo *ṭon-tako* 'girl,' Arazaire *čina-ni* 'wife,' Mayoruna *šanu* 'grandmother,' *nso-ton* 'child,' *čuču* 'older sister,' *tsana* 'man,' Culino *ha-tu* 'brother,' *a-tsi* 'sister,' *mu-tun* 'old man,' Nocaman *tano* 'woman, wife'; Tacanan: Huarayo *čina-ni* 'woman,' Tacana *-tóna* 'younger sister,' *dúdu* 'older sister,' *u-tse-kwa* 'grandchild,' Huarayo *toto* 'man's brother,' Arasa *deana-wa* 'son,' *dodo* 'brother,' Chama *toto* 'uncle,' *čina-ni* 'wife,' Tiatinagua *čina-ni* 'wife.'

MACRO-GE: Erikbatsa *tsiʔn-kärar* 'small'; Oti *dondu-ede* 'woman'; ?Fulnio *efone-don-kia* 'wife'; Guato *čina* 'older brother'; Caraja *wa-θana* 'uncle'; Bororo: Bororo *i-tuna-regede* 'child,' Umotina *yúto* ~ *in-dondo* 'maternal son-in-law,' *žu-ko* 'paternal father-in-law' (< **tun-ko*); Botocudo *giku-taŋ* 'sister,' *tontan* 'wife,' *gy-ĵune* 'brother-in-law'; Macuni *a-tina-n* 'girl, daughter,' Palmas *tantã* 'female,' *tanti* 'woman'; Kamakan: Cotoxo *či-ton* 'brother,' Kamakan *totsöhn-tan* 'mother,' Meniens *a-to* 'brother,' *as-čun* 'woman'; Puri: Puri *ek-ton* 'son,' *makaša-tane* 'brother,' *titiña-n* 'grandmother,' Coroado *mokaša-tane* 'brother,' Coropo *ek-tan* 'mother'; Mashakali: Mashakali *etia-tün* 'woman,' Malali *niop-tan-piteknan* 'woman,' *tana-tämon* 'father,' Patasho *eke-tannay* 'brother,' *a-tön* 'mother,' Capoxo *asče-tan* 'wife'; Kaingang: Apu-carana *wey-tytan* 'younger sister,' *ti* 'man,' *un-tantan* 'woman,' ?Came *tata* 'woman,' Catarina *tata* 'young woman, young man, young,' Guarapuava *tetan* 'girl,' *un-tantan* 'woman,' Tibagi *tog-tan* 'girl,' *tantö* 'woman'; Ge: Timbira *tõ* 'older brother,' Apinaye *i-tõ* 'brother,' *i-tõ-dy* 'sister,' *tuʔ-ká* 'paternal uncle, son-in-law,' *tuʔ-ka-ya* 'maternal grandfather,' *tuʔ-ka-tí* 'brother-in-law, son-in-law,' Cayapo *i-ton* 'brother,' *i-ton-ǰuö* 'cousin,' *torri-tuŋ* 'old woman,' *tun-ǰuo* 'girl,' *ǰūno* 'father,' Aponegicran *i-thon-ghi* 'sister,' *i-thon-g* 'brother,' Krẽye *tana-mni* 'boy,' *tõ* 'younger brother,' *-tõ-ue* 'sister,' *n-čõ* 'father,' *n-čū* 'paternal uncle,' Caraho *a-ton-ka* 'younger sister,' *tõ-i* 'sister,' *tõ* 'brother,' *ton-ko* 'older brother,' *n-čon* 'father,' *in-t⁵un* 'uncle,' Krahó *ĩ-čū* 'father,' *ĩ-če* 'mother,' *i-tõ* 'brother,' *i-tõ-i* 'sister,' Canella *i-nču* 'my father,' *i-nčeʔ* 'my mother,' *i-to* 'older sibling,' Parkateye *a-ton* 'brother,' *a-ton-kâ* 'older brother,' *a-ton-re* 'younger brother,' *a-toin* 'sister,' *a-toin-kâ* 'older sister,' *a-toin-re* 'younger sister,' Piokobyé *a-tõn* 'older sister,' *a-tõn-kä* 'younger sister,' *tõn-ko* 'older brother,' *ha-tõn* 'younger brother.'

REFERENCES

Aoki, Haruo. 1966. "Nez Perce and Proto-Sahaptin Kinship Terms," *International Journal of American Linguistics* 32: 357–68.

Berman, Howard. 1986. "A Note on the Yurok Diminutive," *International Journal of American Linguistics* 52: 419–21.

Cavalli-Sforza, L. L., Alberto Piazza, and Paolo Menozzi. 1994. *History and Geography of Human Genes.* Princeton, N.J.

Fox, James A. 1985. "Kinship Terminology and Social Process: Two Mayan Etymologies," *International Journal of American Linguistics* 51: 405–7.

Freeland, L. S. 1931. "The Relationship of Mixe to the Penutian Family," *International Journal of American Linguistics* 6: 28–33.

Greenberg, Joseph H. 1981. "Comparative Amerindian Notebooks," 23 vols. Mss. on file, Green Library, Stanford University, Stanford, Calif.

———. 1987. *Language in the Americas.* Stanford, Calif.

Jacobs, Melville. 1931. "A Sketch of Northern Sahaptin Grammar," *University of Washington Publications in Anthropology* 4: 85–292.

Kaufman, Terrence. 1988. "A Research Program for Reconstructing Proto-Hokan: First Gropings," in Scott DeLancey, ed., *Papers from the 1988 Hokan-Penutian Languages Workshop.* Eugene, Oregon, 50–168.

————. 1990. "Language History in South America: What We Know and How to Know More," in Doris L. Payne, ed., *Amazonian Linguistics*. Austin, Tex., 13–73.

Matthews, G. H. 1959. "Proto-Siouan Kinship Terminology," *American Anthropologist* 61: 252–78.

McLendon, Sally. 1973. *Proto Pomo*. Berkeley, Calif.

Moshinsky, Julius. 1974. *A Grammar of Southeastern Pomo*. Berkeley, Calif.

Nichols, Johanna. 1990. "Linguistic Diversity and the First Settling of the New World," *Language* 66: 475–521.

Pokorny, Julius. 1959. *Indogermanisches etymologisches Wörterbuch*. Bern.

Rivet, Paul. 1921. "Nouvelle contribution à l'étude de la langue itonama," *Journal de la Société des Américanistes de Paris* 13: 173–95.

Rude, Noel. 1989. "The Grammar of Kinship Terms in Sahaptin," in Scott DeLancey, ed., *Papers from the 1989 Hokan-Penutian Languages Workshop*. Eugene, Oregon, 87–95.

Ruhlen, Merritt. 1992. "Linguistic Origins of Native Americans," Chapter 10 of this volume.

Sapir, Edward. 1918. "Yana Terms of Relationship," *University of California Publications in American Archaeology and Ethnology* 13: 153–73.

————. 1921. "A Haida Kinship Term among the Tsimshian," *American Anthropologist* 23: 233–34.

————. 1923a. "The Algonkin Affinity of Yurok and Wiyot Kinship Terms," *Journal de la Société des Américanistes de Paris* 15: 36–74.

————. 1923b. "The Phonetics of Haida," *International Journal of American Linguistics* 2: 143–59.

10

The Linguistic Origins of
Native Americans

Ever since European explorers stumbled upon the Americas 500 years ago—
and discovered a continent already populated by myriad ethnic groups, speaking hundreds of distinct languages—the question of the origin of the indigenous Americans has puzzled scientist and layman alike.* When it became
known in the late eighteenth century that language could be used to trace
the origins and migrations of different peoples, it was hoped that these techniques could be applied to Native American languages, first, to classify New
World languages into some number of linguistic families comparable to Indo-
European, and, second, to find relatives for these groups in the Old World.
Thomas Jefferson had a well-known interest in such matters throughout his
life. A little over 200 years ago (January 12, 1789) he wrote James Madison,
"I endeavor to collect all the vocabularies I can, of American Indians, as of

* An earlier version of this chapter was presented at the International Conference on
Language and Prehistory, University of Michigan, November 10, 1988, and was published
as Ruhlen (1989). I would like to thank Joseph H. Greenberg for graciously allowing me
to use material from his Eurasiatic notebooks. As the proposed etymologies attest, this
material often strengthens and extends Nostratic etymologies and in many cases provides
evidence for new etymologies. It was, in fact, Greenberg who first suggested a "special
relationship" between Eurasiatic and Amerind, in a private conversation in 1985. I would
also like to thank John Bengtson, Allan Bomhard, Dell Hymes, and Vitaly Shevoroshkin
for critical suggestions, not all of which I have heeded.

those of Asia, persuaded, that if they ever had a common parentage, it will appear in their languages" (Jefferson 1904: 267). But although the process of classifying the languages of the Americas proceeded with demonstrable progress during the succeeding two centuries—especially at the lower levels of classification—the problem of finding Old World relatives has until recently had little success. According to William Bright (1974: 208), "attempts to relate native American languages to Asian languages have not gained general acceptance." In a recent comparative treatment of North American languages (Campbell and Mithun 1979), a possible genetic relationship between Eskimo-Aleut and Chukchi-Kamchatkan is deemed "the only proposal of connections between New World and Old World languages which at present appears to be worthy of attention" (p. 39).

In recent decades, the results of three major research programs have allowed us to attack the problem of the origin of Native Americans in a new light. The first of these programs is the Russian Nostratic school, which has published over 600 etymologies connecting six Old World families (Illich-Svitych 1967, 1971–84). The second is Greenberg's classification of New World languages (Greenberg 1987). The third, Greenberg (to appear) is a book on a language family he calls Eurasiatic, which corresponds to a considerable degree with Nostratic (for differences between the two, see below). What follows will make extensive use of all these materials.

I will begin by examining earlier efforts to connect Old and New World languages genetically and will indicate why they were generally unsuccessful. I will then discuss the general congruence between biological classifications and linguistic classifications that has recently been noted by human geneticists studying the structure of the human population on the basis of genetic polymorphisms (Excoffier et al. 1987, Cavalli-Sforza et al. 1988, Barbujani and Sokal 1990). Finally, I will present evidence connecting the Amerind family with the Eurasiatic family. It should be pointed out that additional connections between Amerind and Eurasiatic are given in Chapter 14 herein. The etymologies given there, however, connect both Amerind and Eurasiatic with other other language families. The etymologies adduced in this chapter have a narrower domain, each apparently being restricted to the Eurasiatic/Nostratic-Amerind group.

NOSTRATIC AND EURASIATIC

The belief that Indo-European is a "family isolate," that is, a family with no known relatives, is one of the most cherished myths of twentieth-century linguistics. Yet at the beginning of this century many linguists had already determined that Indo-European was clearly affiliated with other language families. The English phonetician Henry Sweet wrote in 1901 that "if all these and many other resemblances that might be adduced do not prove the common origin of Aryan [Indo-European] and Ugrian [Finno-Ugric] . . . , then the whole fabric of comparative philology falls to the ground, and we are no longer justified in inferring from the similarity of the inflections in Greek, Latin and Sanskrit that these languages have a common origin" (p. 120). The Italian linguist Alfredo Trombetti expressed the same view four years later: "It is clear that in and of itself the comparison of Finno-Ugric *me* 'I,' *te* 'you' with Indo-European *me-* and *te-* [with the same meaning] is worth just as much as any comparison one might make between the corresponding pronominal forms in the Indo-European languages. The only difference is that the common origin of the Indo-European languages is accepted, whereas the connection between Indo-European and Finno-Ugric is denied" (p. 44). By mid-century such dissenting views had largely fallen silent.[1]

But in the late 1950's two Russian linguists, Vladislav Illich-Svitych and Aron Dolgopolsky—at first independently and unknown to each other—began a new attack on the problem of demonstrating that Indo-European did indeed have relatives. By comparing reconstructed forms from half a dozen different families of North Africa, Europe, and Asia (Afro-Asiatic, Kartvelian, Indo-European, Uralic, Dravidian, Altaic)[2] these two linguists proposed over 600 etymologies connecting all six of the families in a higher-level family. Some of these etymologies had previously been noted, at least in part, by other linguists, but many were new. Adopting Holger Pedersen's term, this even larger family came to be called Nostratic (Dolgopolsky originally used the name Sibero-European). At the time of Illich-Svitych's tragic death in 1966 none of his etymological studies had yet appeared in print. Through the persistent efforts of his friend and colleague Vladimir Dybo, and with the assistence of Dolgopolsky, the work that Illich-Svitych had completed in manuscript form at the time of his death has now been published (Illich-Svitych 1967, 1971–84). Several articles by Dolgopolsky (1964, 1969, 1971, 1972, 1974, 1984) contain additional Nostratic etymologies. Recently the American linguist Allan Bomhard (1984, 1991) has begun investigating the Nostratic family, employing a set of sound correspondences—based on the Glottalic theory of Indo-European—slightly different from those postulated by Illich-Svitych and Dolgopolsky.

In his classification of New World languages Greenberg assigns the Eskimo-Aleut family to a Eurasiatic stock that also includes Indo-European, Uralic-Yukaghir, Altaic, Korean-Japanese-Ainu, Gilyak, and Chukchi-Kamchatkan,

---

[1] Commendable exceptions include Karl Menges, Bjorn Collinder, and Nicholas Poppe.

[2] Dolgopolsky originally included Chukchi-Kamchatkan and Sumerian, but not Kartvelian or Dravidian, in his comparisons.

and in his book on the Eurasiatic family (to appear), he presents over 500 etymologies. As can be seen, the Nostratic and Eurasiatic families overlap. Indo-European, Uralic, Altaic, and Korean belong to both, but the two families differ in that Eurasiatic includes additional groups in East Asia (Japanese, Ainu, Gilyak, Chukchi-Kamchatkan, Eskimo-Aleut), while Nostratic includes not these, but additional groups in Southwest Asia (Dravidian, Kartvelian, Afro-Asiatic). As might be anticipated, there is also considerable overlap in the etymologies supporting these two families.

What are we to make of the different constituencies of the Nostratic and Eurasiatic families? Two different aspects of the question must be clearly distinguished, and the frequent confusing of the two by scholars has led to a certain amount of misunderstanding in discussions of distant relationship. The first is whether the languages within Nostratic, or those within Eurasiatic, have been shown to be genetically related; the second is whether Nostratic and/or Eurasiatic are valid taxa. Concerning the first question, there is really no difference between the Nostraticists' views and those of Greenberg, who readily admits that Kartvelian, Dravidian, and Afro-Asiatic are related to Eurasiatic. The three are not, however, in his view, as *closely* related to the Eurasiatic languages as the Eurasiatic languages are to each other. Thus Eurasiatic might be thought of as a subgroup of an even larger Nostratic stock, and both Eurasiatic and Nostratic might be valid taxa.

But it is also possible that neither Eurasiatic nor Nostratic is a valid taxon. It is possible that Kartvelian should be included in Eurasiatic, with which it shares the characteristic first- and second-person pronouns, m and t/s. And as regards Nostratic, we can say with certainty that the classical definition of Nostratic—as subsuming the six families enumerated above—is not a valid taxon. This is not surprising, since during the development of Nostratic the choice of the six families was determined in part simply by the availability of reconstructed proto-forms, which eliminated certain families from consideration. In any event, the Nostraticists never intended to exclude the addition of other families to Nostratic as better historical materials became available. In fact, all of Greenberg's eastern extensions have at one time or another been included in the work of Nostraticists. At the western end of Nostratic the situation is less clear, in the sense that certain families, such as Khoisan and Nilo-Saharan, have been excluded from consideration by the Nostraticists primarily because there are no reconstructed proto-forms.

The essential difference, then, between the work of the Nostraticists and that of Greenberg, is that Greenberg, as in all his taxonomic work from Africa to the Americas, has sought to *classify* the world's languages. He has never attempted to prove that *A* is related to *B*; relationships, whether close or distant, are merely the consequences of classification. Nostraticists, on the other hand, have never been primarily concerned with classification, but rather with the attempt to prove that Indo-European is related to other families. Indeed the Nostratic family is *defined* as consisting of those families that are related to Indo-European. This is not, however, a permissible way to define a taxon on any level, in biology or in linguistics. The stubborn insistence of so many linguists on according Indo-European special status cannot be defended; it is simply one family among many to be classified—nothing more, nothing less.

Another difference between the Nostraticists and the Greenberg camp is that Nostraticists place great emphasis on reconstruction and sound correspondences, which in Greenberg's methodology—and in biological taxonomy— play no essential role (see Chapter 14 herein). Recently some Nostraticists have begun to recognize the importance of classification itself. Thus, Sergei Starostin (1989) now considers Afro-Asiatic related to Nostratic at greater remove, rather than being simply a member of it, and he goes on to say: "I have no reason at all to suppose a closer genetic link between Nostratic and Sino-Caucasian than, e.g., between Nostratic and Afro-Asiatic or Afro-Asiatic and Sino-Caucasian" (p. 49).

So what, then, has all this to do with Amerind? If we combine the work of the Nostraticists with Greenberg's work on Eurasiatic, we have a rich collection of close to 1,000 etymologies defining a vast family of the Old World. And although the edges of that vast family remain somewhat fuzzy, it offers ample evidence to compare with the corresponding data provided for the Amerind family by Greenberg (1987), and thus to identify genetic relationships between Amerind and Nostratic/Eurasiatic.

AMERIND

The long and tumultuous history of the classification of Native American languages is reviewed in Ruhlen (1987: 205–27). For our purposes here it suffices to note that Greenberg (1987) presented evidence that the indigenous languages of the Americas fall into three distinct genetic groups: (1) Eskimo-Aleut, (2) Na-Dene, and (3) Amerind. Since the first two groups had long been recognized and accepted, it was the inclusion of all other aboriginal languages in a single family that set Greenberg's classification apart from previous attempts. Greenberg presented over 2,000 etymologies in support of Amerind and its eleven subfamilies, 329 of which connect at least two subgroups of Amerind. Closer scrutiny of the etymologies defining individual Amerind subgroups (e.g. Penutian, Hokan, Andean) indicates that an additional 160 Amerind etymologies can be discerned in Greenberg's data (see Chapter 8 herein), raising the total number of Amerind etymologies to almost 500. Just as first-person *m* and second-person *t/s* characterize the Eurasiatic family, the

Amerind family is characterized by first-person n and second-person m, both of which are attested in every Amerind subfamily. In addition, there are lexical items that permeate every nook and cranny of the Amerind family, while being apparently absent elsewhere in the world (see Chapter 9 herein). We might note that Greenberg's classification of New World languages has been greeted with disbelief and incredulity by many Amerindian linguists, just as his African classification provoked controversy among Africanists some four decades ago. For discussion of the current debate on the classification of American languages, see Chapter 6 herein and Greenberg (1989).

Greenberg's tripartite classification of American languages has obvious implications for the peopling of the Americas, for it suggests that there were *at most* three migrations from Asia that have left a trace in the linguistic record. Of course there could have been a single migration, with subsequent diversification into Greenberg's three families, and two migrations is also a theoretical possibility. But in fact the number of distinct migrations can only be determined by the larger—non-American—context. Three distinct migrations can only be supported by showing that each of Greenberg's three New World families is more closely related to an Old World family—and in each case a *different* Old World family—than any two of the New World families are to each other. And indeed this appears to be the case.

The genetic affinity of the Eskimo-Aleut family with languages of Northern Eurasia was already recognized by Rasmus Rask in the early nineteenth century, and since that time numerous scholars have noted the connection, though usually in terms of binary comparisons that made the relationship less apparent than it would be in a multilateral comparison. Greenberg includes Eskimo-Aleut in his Eurasiatic family, and Dolgopolsky (1984) included it in Nostratic. Even the relatively small amount of material I will offer here leaves little doubt that Eskimo-Aleut is an integral part of the Eurasiatic family, and archaeological evidence supports a very recent arrival of the ancestors of Eskimos and Aleuts in the New World.

It is well known that Edward Sapir, in the early part of this century, proposed a genetic affinity between Na-Dene and Sino-Tibetan. On the question of the Na-Dene–Sino-Tibetan relationship Sapir was blunt: "If the morphological and lexical accord which I find on every hand between Na-Dene and Indo-Chinese is 'accidental,' then every analogy on God's earth is an accident. It is all so powerfully cumulative and integrated that when you tumble to one point a lot of others fall into line. I am now so thoroughly accustomed to the idea that it no longer startles me" (quoted in Golla 1984: 374). Recently Campbell (1988: 593) has ridiculed this proposal: "Needless to say, no specialist today embraces this claim." In fact, however, Sapir's proposed connection has recently been supported by both Russian scholars (Starostin

1984, Nikolaev 1991) and American scholars (Bengtson 1991a,b, Ruhlen 1990 and Chapter 4 of this volume); both groups now place Na-Dene in a proposed Dene-Caucasian family that also includes Sino-Tibetan, Yeniseian, and North Caucasian (see Chapter 1 herein). It thus appears that Na-Dene is related to a different Old World language family (Dene-Caucasian) than is Eskimo-Aleut (Eurasiatic), which implies that each represents a distinct migration from Asia, just as Sapir suspected in 1920: "I do *not* feel that Na-Dene belongs to the other American languages. I feel it as a great intrusive band that has perhaps ruptured an old Eskimo-Wakashan-Algonquian continuity. . . . Do not think me an ass if I am seriously entertaining the notion of an old Indo-Chinese offshoot into N.W. America" (Golla 1984: 350).

So what, then, of Amerind? It is the aim of this chapter to provide linguistic evidence that the Amerind family reflects a third migration from the Old World, almost certainly the first of the three. This evidence concludes the chapter, and the etymologies assembled there indicate that the Amerind family is more closely related to the Eurasiatic/Nostratic family in the Old World than to any other Old World family. But whereas Eskimo-Aleut is a *member* of Eurasiatic, Amerind is simply *related to* Eurasiatic, at greater remove, and Na-Dene belongs to a different family altogether, Dene-Caucasian.

In light of the now substantial archaeological, biological, and linguistic evidence, the following scenario for the peopling of the Americas seems most likely. The initial migration into the New World, some time before 12,000 BP (before present), gave rise to the Amerind family, whose vast geographic spread and great linguistic diversity are indicative of its early arrival. Just how early that arrival may have been is a bone of contention among archaeologists. Many maintain that humans did not reach the Americas until the Clovis culture appears in the archaeological record around 12,000 years ago, and they dismiss alleged earlier dates as spurious. There are, however, other archaeologists who claim to have evidence of earlier human habitation in the Americas, with dates ranging from 13,000 BP (the Monte Verde site in Chile), to 16,000 BP (the Meadowcroft site in Pennsylvania) to over 40,000 BP (the Pedra Furada site in Brazil). I tend to share the views recently expressed by Jared Diamond (1992: 345): "How could people have gotten from Alaska to Pennsylvania or Chile, as if by helicopter, without leaving good evidence of their presence in all the intervening territory? For these reasons, I find it more plausible that the dates given for Meadowcroft and Monte Verde are somehow wrong than that they are correct. The Clovis-first interpretation makes good sense; the pre-Clovis interpretation just doesn't make sense to me." Unfortunately, linguistic evidence, which is notoriously poor at providing absolute dates, cannot resolve this controversy. Nor, so far, have studies of blood types, gene pools, and such.

The precise date of the second migration is also uncertain, but we might estimate 7,000 BP for the migration that brought the Na-Dene family into the Americas. Finally, perhaps 4,000 years ago, a third migration gave rise to the Eskimo-Aleut family, whose lesser linguistic divergence and marginal position on the Northern periphery of the Americas both indicate late arrival.

DISTANT RELATIONSHIP

Over the years there has been no shortage of attempts to find genetic links between New and Old World languages. The vast majority of such attempts have suffered from a fatal flaw: they invariably sought to show that some specific language (or language family) in the New World was related to some language (or language family) in the Old World. For example, Karl Bouda (1960–64) tried to show that Quechua (South America) was related to Tungus (East Asia). Such binary comparisons, usually chosen by happenstance, have been the bane of long-range comparison. There is very little likelihood that a language spoken in one part of the world is *directly* related to some language spoken on the other side of the world. Tungus is clearly most closely related to the other Altaic languages, which in turn are but one subfamily of Nostratic/Eurasiatic. Quechua, on the other hand, is just as obviously most closely related to other Andean languages in South America, which themselves form but one branch of the vast Amerind family. So to compare one member of Nostratic/Eurasiatic with one member of Amerind, ignoring the evidence of other, more closely related languages on each side of the equation, is methodologically unsound and can hardly be expected to provide useful results. Nonetheless, in the United States, in recent decades, such ad hoc binary comparisons became a substitute for classification, and serious taxonomic work ground to a halt.

But for those who sought Old World relatives for American Indian languages, there was at the time no way out of the dilemma, since the basic classificatory work had simply not yet been done on American languages. And in the Old World, prior to the rise of the Russian Nostratic school, most comparisons between Old World families were themselves more often than not of a binary nature. Greenberg's classification of American languages, with hundreds of etymologies defining the vast Amerind family, has for the first time provided the wherewithal for comparisons with similar material from Old World language families to which Amerind might in fact be directly related. In the same way, Nostratic and Eurasiatic etymologies define a comparable family in the Old World, providing the wherewithal for the other half of the comparison.

There is of course no a priori reason why the Amerind family should be genetically closer to Nostratic/Eurasiatic than to some other Old World group. Where the relationships fall, in the scheme of things, is strictly an empirical question, to be decided by comparative research. Nor have I chosen to compare Amerind with Nostratic/Eurasiatic simply because the detailed materials on the two are now available. Rather, a comprehensive comparison of these two families with the world's other language families has led me to conclude that the vast Amerind family is genetically closest to Nostratic/Eurasiatic, among all of the world's families. Though I consider it unlikely, it is of course possible that future research will find that Amerind is closer to some other Old World family. And I recognize that the still higher-level family comprising Nostratic/Eurasiatic *and* Amerind languages is genetically related to *other* high-level language families. Some of the evidence of these further genetic connections is given in Chapter 14 herein, and Starostin (1989) presents convincing evidence linking Nostratic and Dene-Caucasian.

Though the problems at this level of classification are formally the same as those of classifying languages at the lowest level, they are often treated as if they were somehow different. The point is not merely to show that *A* is related to *B,* but rather to specify the *degrees* of relationship among all relevant language families (*A, B, C, . . .*) in the form of a hierarchy of relationships that is customarily represented by a tree diagram. Trees of this sort are of course just what zoologists and botanists have been constructing and reconstructing for centuries.

One other scholar whose interhemispheric comparisons did not suffer from the fatal flaw of binary comparison was Morris Swadesh. Following the earlier pioneering efforts of Alfredo Trombetti (1905), Swadesh sought to show that all the world's languages are related in one large family. "On Interhemispheric Linguistic Connections" (1960) is perhaps his most explicit presentation of evidence connecting Old World and New World languages. He wrote there, for example, that "recent research seems to show that the great bulk of American languages form a single genetic phylum going far back in time. . . . Eskimo-Aleutian and Nadenean seem to stand apart, and may therefore represent later waves of migration" (p. 896). Some of the etymologies I will present below overlap with some of Swadesh's, and I recognize that his case for interhemispheric connections was not without merit. Nevertheless, many of his etymologies are not convincing, and frequently even his valid etymologies contain many forms that I believe are spurious. In my opinion, Swadesh permitted excessive semantic liberty in his etymologies—the etymologies given below, I believe, are more tightly constrained, both semantically and phonologically—and in his later work he seemed to lose sight of the importance of a hierarchical classification, preferring instead a less explicit global network. This is not to minimize his contribution, for he himself recognized that "all published theories of interhemisphere relations, along with the present one, are not yet adequately supported, but they reaffirm the need for, and perhaps show the feasibility of, this kind of study. In time we will surely see satisfactory proof of these or other theories of interhemisphere linguistic relations" (pp. 895–96). It is my hope that the materials presented here will take us one step further along the path that Swadesh pioneered.

BIOLOGICAL AND LINGUISTIC CLASSIFICATIONS

If the genetic isolation of Indo-European is no more than a cherished myth of contemporary linguistics, the notion that biological and linguistic classifications of the human population show little correlation is another. As Campbell (1986: 488) puts it, "repetition of the obvious seems required: there is no deterministic connection between language and gene pools or culture." Recently, however, biologists studying the structure of the human population on the basis of genetic markers have discovered that there is in fact a very high degree of correlation between biological and linguistic classifications, confirming Trombetti's observation at the beginning of this century that "agreement between language and race is the rule. Disagreement is the exception" (Trombetti 1905: 55).

During the past decade Trombetti's insight has been rediscovered by a number of human biologists (see Chapter 1 herein). For the Americas the correlation between language and genes has proved to be remarkably and unexpectedly close. A year before the publication of *Language in the Americas,* Greenberg, Christy Turner, and Stephen Zegura (1986) discovered that classifications of Native Americans based on either dental traits or genetic traits (such as blood groups) both arrive at the same tripartite classification proposed by Greenberg on the basis of language. A similar conclusion was reached by Luca Cavalli-Sforza and colleagues (1988, 1994), who, in the most detailed study to date of human genetics among aboriginal American populations, found that Native Americans fall into precisely Greenberg's three families. Furthermore, the Cavalli-Sforza group found that the population that appears closest to Amerind (disregarding Na-Dene, whose biological closeness to Amerind is probably due to millennia of admixture) is the population that is spread across northern Eurasia, the group known linguistically as Eurasiatic or Nostratic: "A link of Nostratic with Amerind . . . was recently suggested by Shevoroshkin. It is most striking that the union of Eurasiatic and Nostratic, with the Amerind extension, includes all, and only, the languages spoken in our major Northeurasian cluster, with the exception of Na-Dene, the origin of which is less clear" (Cavalli-Sforza et al. 1988: 6005). It is for this vast grouping—stretching all the way from northern Africa, across Eurasia, and throughout both North and South America—that linguistic evidence of affinity is adduced in the present chapter.

Biologists have long recognized the fundamental importance of classification as a means of providing diachronic insight. As Stephen Jay Gould (1989) recently put it, "the reconstruction of the human family tree—its branching order, its timing, and its geography—may be within our grasp. Since this tree is the basic datum of history, hardly anything in intellectual life could be more important" (p. 22). Many linguists, on the other hand, have developed the quaint notion that the only use for classification is in reconstruction and the discovery of regular sound correspondences. As Sarah Thomason (to appear) has put it: "If we want to say, with Greenberg, that demonstrating genetic relationship does not require showing that reconstruction is possible, then I think it's appropriate to ask what the purpose of our classification is. If it is merely a way of bringing some order into a long list of languages . . . , then historical linguists will have no quarrel with the enterprise as long as it's not called genetic classification." Theodora Bynon (1977: 272) renders a similar assessment of Greenberg's methods: "It is clear that, as far as the historical linguist is concerned, it [multilateral comparison] can in no way serve as a substitute for reconstruction, for to him the mere fact of relationship is of little interest in itself." Though such views are not unusual among linguists, it would be difficult, if not impossible, to find a biologist who would subscribe to them.

NOSTRATIC/EURASIATIC–AMERIND ETYMOLOGIES

There is no a priori reason why Nostratic/Eurasiatic and Amerind should share numerous and detailed similarities. Indeed, were it true, as many linguists believe, that evidence of genetic affinity disappears through constant phonetic and semantic erosion after just 6,000 years, then there should be no similar roots at all between Nostratic/Eurasiatic and Amerind—whose time of separation must be considerably greater than 12,000 years—save those arising from sheer accident. I believe that the detailed similarities presented below, frequently so precise as to exhibit the same glottalized consonant in the root in both Nostratic and Amerind, can only be the result of common origin. Such intimate analogies cannot realistically be ascribed to anything else.

In the following etymologies the general order, from one etymology to the next, is alphabetical either by Nostratic reconstruction (e.g. *bälʌ in No. 3), or, where the Nostratic reconstruction is lacking, by a Eurasiatic phonetic gloss of my own creation (e.g. *aka in No. 1). In each etymology the Nostratic or Eurasiatic forms are listed first, followed by the Amerind forms. Within the Nostratic-Eurasiatic complex the ordering of the constituent subfamilies generally proceeds from west to east, while the Amerind subfamilies generally follow a north-south progression. Sources of the information are given in brackets at the ends of the etymologies, with the Nostratic, Eurasiatic, and Amerind sources separated by a semicolon. For Nostratic (N), one will find either the etymology number from the Nostratic dictionary (N 232), the page number in Volume 1, where many unnumbered etymologies are given (N I:7), or the page number in Illich-Svitych's 1967 article (IS 335). For the Eurasiatic (E) etymologies, drawn from Greenberg (to appear), either the number of the grammar section (E G15) or the semantic gloss (E SPEAK) is given. For Amerind (A), drawn chiefly from Greenberg (1981, 1987), the etymology number (A 218, MP 30) or the number of the grammar section (A G12) is cited. The following abbreviations are used to identify the relevant sections of Greenberg's book: AK: Almosan-Keresiouan, P: Penutian, H: Hokan, CA: Central Amerind, CP: Chibchan-Paezan, AN: Andean, EQ: Equatorial, MT: Macro-Tucanoan, MC: Macro-Carib, MP: Macro-Panoan, MG: Macro-Ge. In addition to the Amerind forms cited in Greenberg's book, I have added many additional Amerind forms from Greenberg's unpublished Amerind notebooks (Greenberg 1981).

1. EURASIATIC *aka* 'older brother,' Yukaghir *aka* 'older brother,' Proto-Turkic *āka* 'older brother,' Mongolian *aqa* 'older brother,' Tungus *akā* 'brother,' Ryukyuan *aka* 'older brother,' Ainu *ak/aki* 'younger brother,' Gilyak *ikin* 'older brother' = AMERIND *(k)aka* 'older brother, older sister,' Nisqualli *kukh* 'older brother,' Okanagan *kīka* 'older sister,' Shuswap *kix* 'older sister,' Kalispel *qaxe* 'maternal aunt,' Kutenai *kokt* 'maternal aunt,' Seneca *-hak* 'aunt,' Tuscarora *gus-xahg* 'paternal aunt,' Adai *ahhi* 'aunt,' Hidatsa *ika* 'aunt,' Alsea *hāʔt* 'older brother,' Bodega Miwok *kaaka* 'uncle,' Southern Sierra Miwok *kaka* 'uncle,' Yuki *kīk-an* 'maternal uncle,' Tfalatik *kaka* 'aunt,' Zuni *kaka* 'maternal uncle,' Natchez *kāka* 'older brother,' Mixe *ahč* 'older brother,' Sayula *axč* 'older brother, uncle,' Kekchí *as* 'older brother,' Zoque *ʔatˢi* 'older brother,' Totonac *kuku* 'uncle,' Achomawi *kex* 'uncle,' East Pomo *kēq* 'uncle,' North Pomo *-ki-* 'older brother,' Kashaya *-ki-* 'older brother,' Salinan *kaai* 'older brother,' Karok *xukam* 'uncle,' Jicaque *kokam* 'uncle,' Tewa *koʔō* 'aunt,' Varohio *kukuri* 'paternal uncle,' *ka'ká* 'maternal aunt,' Ixcatec *kwaʔa* 'aunt,' Tirub *kega* 'uncle,' *kak* 'aunt,' Matagalpa *kuku-ke* 'uncle,' Paya *uku* 'uncle,' Kagaba *kukui* 'aunt, niece,' Ona *kakan* 'paternal aunt,' Yeba *kako* 'uncle,' Masaca *kokomai* 'uncle,' Waraicu *ghuk* 'uncle,' Manao *ghooko* 'maternal uncle,' Sammaika *koko* 'uncle,' Mashco *kokoa* 'uncle,' Kushichineri *koko* 'uncle,' Cuniba *kuku* 'uncle,' Bare *koko* 'aunt,' Canamarim *ghughu* 'un-

cle,' Piro *koko* 'uncle,' Apiaca *koko* 'uncle,' Bakairi *kxuɣu* 'uncle,' Pimenteira *kuckú* 'uncle,' Cavineña *ekoko* 'uncle,' Panobo *kuka* 'uncle,' Pacawara *kuko* 'uncle,' Palmas *kẽke-* 'older sibling,' Apucarana *kanki* 'older brother,' Oti *koaka* 'brother.' [E BROTHER; A 178, P 31, H 54]

2. EURASIATIC **ana* 'mother, grandmother, old woman,' Proto-Indo-European **an-* 'grandmother, mother,' Hittite *annas* 'mother,' *ḫannas* 'grandmother,' Lycian *xãna* 'grandmother,' Armenian *han* 'grandmother,' Proto-Turkic **äñä* 'mother,' Tungus *ĕñī̆/ĕñē̆* 'mother,' Korean *ĕñi* 'mother,' Yupik *aana* 'mother,' Labrador *anāna* 'mother,' Greenlandic *ānak* 'grandmother' = AMERIND **nani* 'mother, aunt,' Blackfoot *naʔa* 'mother,' Gros Ventre *-inã* 'mother,' Caddo *ʔi-naʔ* 'my mother,' Huron *anan* 'aunt,' Osage *ina* 'aunt,' Proto-Oto-Manguean **(n)(ʔ)na(h)(n)* 'mother, woman,' Proto-Uto-Aztecan **na* 'mother,' Catuquina *inai* 'aunt,' Kaliana *ĩnoĩ* 'grandmother,' Puinave *aiña* 'aunt,' Ticuna *niai* 'woman,' Yuri *aino* 'female,' Guahibo *ena* 'mother,' Kariri *aña* 'aunt,' Kandoshi *aniari* 'mother,' Proto-Tacanan **nene* 'aunt,' Macca *nana* 'mother,' Vilela *ɛnana* 'aunt,' *nane* 'mother.' [E GRANDMOTHER & MOTHER; A 14, MP 46]

3. NOSTRATIC **bälʌ* 'light,' Proto-Afro-Asiatic **bl-* 'light, shine,' Proto-Indo-European **bhel-* 'white, light,' Proto-Altaic **bäli* 'light, pale' = AMERIND **pala* 'white,' Yakonan *λpāal-* 'white,' Lutuami *palpal* 'white,' Mixe *põʔp* 'white,' Zoque *popo* 'white,' Washo *dal-popoi* 'white,' Santa Cruz Chumash *pupu* 'white,' Qawashqar *palihhl* 'white,' Canichana *bala/bara* 'white,' Chiranga *bole* 'white,' Särä *boro* 'white,' Catuquina *parany* 'white,' Bare *balini* 'white,' Wapishana *barak* 'white,' Yuracare *bolo-* 'white,' Chamacoco *poro* 'white,' Cayuvava *-pora-* 'white,' Turaha *põr̃ã* 'white,' Achagua *paray* 'white,' Towothli *apol-* 'white,' Vilela *po* 'white,' Vejoz *pelaj* 'white,' Lule *pop* 'white.' [IS 363; A 266]

4. NOSTRATIC **bišʌ* 'bile,' Proto-Indo-European **bis-(t)lʌ* 'bile,' Proto-Uralic **pyša* 'bile, yellow, green' = AMERIND **patˢi* 'liver,' Proto-Algonquian **wīswi* 'gall,' Montagnais *uiši-* 'bitter,' Hidatsa *apiša* 'liver,' Wichita *wass* 'bitter,' Crow *išīa* 'bitter,' Yuchi *w'asdá* 'sour' (v.), Cherokee *uyəsdi* 'bitter,' Nez Perce *pisakas* 'bitter,' Atakapa *añpats* 'sour,' Atsugewi *õpsi* 'liver,' Karok *vafis* 'liver,' Shasta *ʔepsi* 'liver,' Mohave *hipasa* 'liver,' Cocopa *č-iposo* 'liver,' Akwa'ala *čuposi* 'liver,' Rama *i-psa* 'liver,' Cuitlatec *bahči* 'sour,' Paez *pos* 'sour,' Guajiquero *pasa* 'bitter,' Manare *pasi-gui* 'sweet' (*-gui* = 'not'), Guambiana *patˢe* 'liver,' Cayapa *basu* 'human liver,' Chimu *počak* 'liver,' Zaparo *hipatˢka* 'gall,' Yamana *hīpa* 'liver,' Quechua *p'ošqo* 'sour,' Nadobo *böčihign* 'sour,' Yuracare *ipasa* 'liver,' Candoshi *šipič* 'liver,' Caranga *paxč* 'liver,' Proto-Tacanan **patˢe* 'bitter,' Tacana *patˢeda* 'bitter,' Huarayo *pase* 'bitter,' Moseten *bitˢtˢa* 'bitter,' Chiquito *piča-ka-s* 'bitter.' [IS 340; A 35 & 168, MP 58]

5. NOSTRATIC *č'ik'ʌ 'cut,' Proto-Kartvelian *č'eč'k'- 'cut (finely),' Proto-Altaic *čikʌ- 'cut, chop,' Evenki čikā- 'cut, chop,' Even čiki- 'chop' = AMERIND *t'ik'ʷa/*t'ak'ʷi 'hit, cut, break,' Proto-Salish *t'aqʲʷ 'break,' Snohomish tˢaq' 'hit,' Lillooet tˢikən 'beat, whip,' Seshault tˢ'iqʷət 'hit,' Shuswap tˢíkən 'hit,' Squamish t'əq'ʷ 'break,' Nootka tˢ'oqʷ 'hit,' Quileute tˢex 'hit,' Kutenai tˢik' 'destroy,' Proto-Central Algonquian *šākw- 'break,' Kowilth tik 'cut through,' Yurok tik'ʷohs 'break, cut,' Wichita tīkʷi/takʷi 'hit,' Ofo diki 'hit,' Tsimshian t'āʔ 'slap,' Chinook t'āk ~ tsəx 'break,' North Sahaptin šaχ 'cut through,' Coos tōh 'hit,' Wappo ṭ'ak'iʔ 'cut,' Mixe tsuk 'cut,' Sayula tsuk 'cut,' Huastec t'ak'iyal 'cut,' Proto-Mayan *sak 'hit,' Quiché tˢ'ax 'hit,' Jacaltec tsok'o 'chop,' Shasta kʷannitīk 'he chopped it,' East Pomo t'es 'cut off,' Salinan šāko 'chop,' Maricopa tˢikʲet 'cut,' Jicaque t'ɨ- 'cut,' Hopi tïïkï 'cut,' Nahua -teki 'cut,' Pipil tegi 'cut,' Zacapoaxtla teki 'cut,' Tewa tˢ'áʔ 'sever with a knife,' Popoloca t'iče 'break,' Cuna čike 'cut,' Move tikeko 'cut,' Sanema tiiksaki 'a blow,' Yamana ačikam 'cut,' Ticuna tīčei 'cut,' Cofan čičiku 'knife,' Cocoma tsaki-ta 'cut,' Paumari siiki 'cut.' [IS 361, N 55; A 149, AK 31, P 110, AN 37]

6. NOSTRATIC *da (locative), Proto-Afro-Asiatic *d (locative), Proto-Kartvelian *-da (allative), Proto-Indo-European *-D/-eD (ablative), Proto-Dravidian *-ṭṭ/-tt(ʌ) (locative, ablative), Proto-Uralic *-δa/-δä (ablative), Yukaghir -da (locative), Proto-Altaic *-da (locative), Korean it-te 'now' (= demonstrative + locative), te 'place,' Japanese -ta (locative), Ainu -ta/-te (locative), Koryak ti-te 'when,' Aliutor ti-ta 'when' = AMERIND *te ~ *ta (locative), Maidu di 'in,' Klamath di 'place of,' Catio -de (locative), Move -te 'in,' Lule ta- 'through, in.' [N 59; E G32; A G49]

7. NOSTRATIC *gät'i/käčʌ 'hand,' Proto-Afro-Asiatic *kt̠ 'hand,' Proto-Western Cushitic *kč' 'hand,' Proto-Indo-European *ĝhes- 'hand,' Proto-Uralic *käte 'hand,' Proto-Dravidian *kac- 'hand,' Korean kaci (< kati) 'branch, bough,' Kamchadal hk'ec 'hand' = AMERIND *kitˢe/kutˢe 'hand,' Blackfoot -kitˢ- 'finger,' Wiyot kisan 'finger,' ?Yurok -ketew 'little finger,' Nootka qātˢ- 'give present,' Squamish čis 'hand,' Lower Fraser aqus 'give,' Kalispel xʷiṭˢ 'give,' Pawnee skitsik 'finger,' Wichita iškitsa 'finger,' Tutelo -ksa 'hand,' Chinook ōkši 'finger,' Wishram wa-kšən 'finger,' Natchez kus 'give,' Quiché koč 'gift,' Shasta akhusik 'finger,' Santa Ynez Chumash ikš 'give,' Santa Barbara Chumash xiks 'give,' Penomeño kuse ~ kise 'hand,' Norteño kuse 'hand,' Move kusegra 'finger,' Borunca i-kūs(-kwa) 'finger, hand,' Kagaba guaša 'give,' Paez kuse 'hand, finger,' Ayoman a-kosi-kega 'finger,' Panikita kuse 'hand,' Moguex koze 'hand,' Betoi ru-m-okosi 'hand,' Qawashqar kisiaol 'give me!,' Andoa ku-agwaši 'hand,' Coche kukuač 'hand,' Chipaya k'as 'give me!,' Kokoz toai-ikisu 'hand,' Anunze ua-kize 'hand,' Tauite toai-kize 'hand,' Suya nikasi 'finger,' Oti ikese 'finger,' Erikbatsa kašuisa 'hand.' [IS 362, N 80; E HAND₂; AK 93, P 89, CP 92]

8. NOSTRATIC *goHjʌ 'sunlight, dawn,' Proto-Indo-European *(s)kāi 'clear, light,' Proto-Uralic *kojʌ 'dawn, sun,' Yakut kujaš 'dawn,' Mongolian gei 'shine,' Dagur gei 'become light,' Orok gewa 'dawn,' Korean hay 'sun,' Japanese -ka 'day,' Ainu ko 'day,' Gilyak ku 'day,' Chukchi kivkiv 'day,' Inuit qau 'day, daylight' = AMERIND *q'ʷai 'sun, day, dawn, daylight,' Kwakwala q'ʷəʔla 'be bright,' Chemakum qal- 'sun,' Nootsack skʷayl 'day,' Upper Chehalis -qʷ 'day,' Lkungen sqʷəqʷə 'sun,' Snohomish qəq 'sunshine,' Yurok kekeʔy- 'shine,' Seneca kē-hkwā 'sun, moon,' Cherokee iga 'day, light,' Yuchi aga 'day, east,' Siuslaw qaī 'dawn' (v.), Yakonan qaī 'be light,' Coos k'ʷiʔi-s 'light,' North Sahaptin quiχ 'dawn, light,' Maidu ʔeki 'day,' San Juan Bautista Costanoan ake 'day,' Proto-Mayan *q'īxʲ 'day, sun,' Mam kih 'sun, day,' Ixil k'ix 'day,' Kakchiquel q'ih 'day,' Quiché q'ih 'sun, day,' Seri kkwáaʔ-ka 'light,' Comecrudo xi 'light,' Tlappanec ā'kaʔ 'sun,' Kiowa khiH 'day,' Tewa ki 'be daylight,' Isleta koʔ 'light,' Chatina quīh 'light,' Trique gwi 'sun, day,' Isthmus Zapotec gui 'light,' Mazatec tˢ'ui 'sun,' Norteño kowe 'day,' Binticua gei 'light,' Guamaca kuaka 'shine,' Borunca kak 'sun,' Paez kwikkwi 'light, be light,' Andaqui kaki 'sun,' Jebero köki 'sun,' Cahuapana kogua 'sun,' Ticuna iake 'sun,' Kapishana kuikae 'sun,' Dzubucua ukie 'day, sun,' Uru uxi 'light,' Goajiro kaʔi 'sun,' Muinane kúuxé 'day,' Jaricuna xi 'sun,' Taruma hwa 'sun.' [IS 342, N 85; E DAWN, DAY₁ & LIGHT₃; P 145]

• Many of the forms appear to show reduplication of the stem.

9. NOSTRATIC *gurʌ 'swallow, throat,' Proto-Afro-Asiatic *g(w)r 'swallow, throat,' Proto-Kartvelian *q'orq'- 'throat,' Proto-Indo-European *gʷer(H)- 'swallow,' Proto-Uralic *kürke 'throat,' Proto-Dravidian *kurʌ- 'throat, voice,' Proto-Altaic *gürä 'neck,' Korean kālki 'mane,' Gilyak qorqr 'throat' = AMERIND *k'ora 'neck,' ?Yurok ʔekeʔr 'necklace,' Yuchi k'o 'throat,' Proto-Maiduan *k'uji 'neck,' Proto-Muskogean *kwalak 'swallow,' Chitimacha k'e 'neck,' Atakapa kol ~ kul 'swallow,' Proto-Mayan *qul 'neck,' Quiché qul 'neck, throat,' Uspantec k'ul 'neck,' ?Achomawi hāllōq 'neck,' Isleta k'ôa 'neck,' Kiowa k'ou-l 'neck,' Proto-Uto-Aztecan *ku 'neck,' Southern Paiute qura 'neck,' Tübatulabal kulā 'neck,' Atanque göla 'neck,' Binticua güergüero 'neck,' Guatuso kolosi 'neck,' Warrau korá 'swallow,' Catio okarra 'throat,' Macu tse-kolo 'throat,' Esmeralda kola 'neck,' Uro k'ora 'neck,' Caranga kˣora 'throat,' Emerillon e-kurukawe 'throat,' Yaruro goro 'neck,' Zamuco potogoro 'throat,' Bare nu-kurateka 'throat,' Galibi kororo 'neck,' Bakairi kiu-ɣoro-l 'throat.' [IS 335, N 91; E THROAT₂; A 196, EQ 114]

10. NOSTRATIC *ɣʌmʌ 'darkness, night,' Proto-Afro-Asiatic *ǵm 'dark,' Arabic ǵammā 'darkness,' Proto-Kartvelian *ɣam-(e) 'night,' Georgian ɣame-'night,' Chan ɣoma(n) 'yesterday,' Megrelian ɣuma 'last night' = AMERIND *xama 'night, dark, black,' Bodega Miwok ʔume 'evening,' Lake Miwok ʔúme 'night,' Chitimacha žima 'night,' Chontal umi 'black,' Karankawa ma 'black,'

Chimariko *hime* 'night,' San Luis Obispo Chumash *č-xime* 'night,' Yurumangui *mai-sa* 'night,' Mazatec *hma* 'black,' Mazahua *xômü* 'night,' Warrau *ima-
jana* 'night, dark,' Allentiac *hom-hom-niag* 'black,' Itonama *yumani* 'night,'
Guambiana *yem* 'night,' Warrau *ima* 'night,' Matanawi *yamāru* 'night,' Colorado *āma* 'shadow,' Manekenkn *mai* 'black,' Pehuelche *yema* 'black,' Siona
aījammas 'black,' Yahuna *yamia* 'night,' Cubeo *yami* 'night,' Tsöla *yami*
'night,' Tucano *yami* 'night,' Waikina *yami* 'night,' Wanana *yami* 'night,'
Movima *imai* 'night,' Itene *mana* 'night,' Arikem *emα* 'black,' Bakairi *yama*
'become dark,' Moseten *iomo* 'night,' *yomoi* 'spend the night,' Proto-Panoan
jamɨ 'night,' Panobo *yamuo* 'night,' Shipibo *yamui* 'night,' Arazaire *ya-
muiki* 'night,' Botocudo *him(e)* 'dark, black,' Chavante *maia* 'night,' Camacan
hamani 'night.' [IS 368, N 99; A 197, H 15, MG 12]

11. NOSTRATIC *Hok'ʌ/HuK'a* 'eye, see,' Proto-Indo-European *hʷekʷ-/okʷ-*
'eye, see,' Proto-Dravidian *akʌ* 'understand, know,' Proto-Altaic *uka* 'notice, understand' = AMERIND *ʔuk'a* ~ *ʔik'a* 'eye, see,' Cheyenne -*exa* 'eyed,'
maʔ-exa 'eye,' Cherokee *ha-ga-ta* 'look,' Seneca -*kā-* 'eye,' *kɛ-* 'see,' Tuscarora
-*ghoh-* 'eye,' Yuchi *k'a* 'watch,' Santa Ana Keres *ga* 'look,' Hidatsa *ika* 'see,
look,' Crow *ikya* 'look,' Nass *gáa* 'see,' Yokuts *ʔek'a* 'see,' Yaudanchi *öka*
'see,' Atsugewi *iʔʔɨ* 'look,' Washo *iki* 'see,' Havasupai *ʔūka* 'see,' Walapai *ʔūk*
'see,' Yurumangui -*ikui-* 'see,' Tarascan *exe-ni* 'look, see,' Terraba *ik* 'see,'
Changuena *uku* 'eye,' Chumulu *oko* 'eye,' Norteño *okua* 'eye,' Move *ogua*
'eye,' Paya *guā* 'eye,' Colorado *kaka* 'eye,' Catio *akai* 'see,' Quechua *qā* 'see,'
Mapudungu *ghe* 'eye,' Pehuenche *ge* 'eye,' Parawa *iku* 'eye,' Capishana *i-kīi*
'eye,' Maku *ku* 'see,' Proto-Nambikwara *eika* 'eye,' Guahibo *eka* 'look,' Ipurina *n-oke* 'eye,' Taruma *gugwa* 'watch,' Ocaina *xā* 'see,' Kokoz *toai-ikiki-su*
'eye,' Bororo *yoko* 'my eye.' [IS 333, N 118; AK 163, MT 36]

12. NOSTRATIC *jamʌ* 'water, sea,' Proto-Afro-Asiatic *jam* 'water, sea,'
Proto-Uralic *jamʌ* 'sea,' Proto-Dravidian *am(m)* 'water' = AMERIND *jume*
'water,' Nootsack *huem* 'water,' Cherokee *ama* 'water,' Laurentian *ame* 'water,' Wyandot *amẽ* 'water,' Wappo *méy* 'water,' Zuni *ăm* 'drink,' Atsugewi *jume* 'river,' Achomawi *ajūmā* 'river,' San Buenaventura Chumash *ma*
'river,' Esselen *imi-la* 'sea,' Washo *ime* 'drink,' Tonkawa *yōmʔa* 'rain,' Coahuilteco *xama* 'wet,' *yaman* 'drink,' Cuitlatec *ʔumʌ* 'water,' Yurumangui *č-uma*
'drink,' Tewa *ʔomū* 'wet,' Chinantec *jmë* 'rain,' Ixcatec *ʔuhme* 'wash,' Tarascan -*ma-* (action in water), Cabecar *mo* 'rain,' Shiriana *mau* 'water,' Jaqaru
uma 'water, drink,' Aymara *uma* 'water, drink,' Zaparo *moo* 'water,' Colan
amum 'sea,' Cholona *omium* 'wave,' Macu *mi* 'drink,' Curiariai *mõ* 'lake,'
Waikina *maa* 'river,' Uasona *ma* 'river,' Querari *mã* 'water,' *uẹmẽ* 'river,'
Proto-Nambikwara *hamə̄i* 'rain,' Aguaruna *jumi* 'water, rain,' *um-* 'drink,'
Yuracare *jumijumi* 'rain,' Guamo *jum* 'lake,' Shuara *umu-* 'drink,' *yumi* 'rain,'
Guahibo *ema* 'rain,' Tuyoneri *meei* 'water,' *ja-mai* 'drink,' Achual *yumi* 'wa-

ter,' Gualaquiza *yumi* 'water,' Guarani *ama* 'rain,' Yukuna *oõo* 'river,' Pilaga *yum* 'drink,' Toba-Guazu *yom* 'drink,' Komlek *yomyi* 'drink,' Vilela *ma* 'water,' Botocudo *himo-hum* 'wash,' *muniă* 'water, rain.' [IS 349, N 144; A 89, CP 211, AN 97, EQ 125]

13. NOSTRATIC **k'äćä* 'cut, break,' Proto-Afro-Asiatic **qs* 'cut, beat, break,' Proto-Kartvelian **k'ac₁-* 'cut, chop,' Svan *k'č-* 'chop,' Proto-Indo-European **k̂es-* 'cut,' Proto-Uralic **käćʌ/kećä* 'knife, edge, point,' Proto-Dravidian **kacc-* 'bite, sting,' Proto-Altaic **k'äsä-* 'cut' = AMERIND **k'atˢi* 'cut, break,' Proto-Central Algonquian **kīšk-* 'cut through, sever,' Quileute *k'i* 'cut,' Tutelo *kitse-* 'break,' Santee *ksa* 'break,' Wichita *ʔikatski* 'cut off,' Dakota *kašda* 'cut off,' Biloxi *utkusi* 'cut,' Pawnee *akakatˢk'* 'cut,' Nez Perce *kas* 'cut,' Nomlaki *kači* 'slice,' Patwin *k'osa* 'knife,' Central Sierra Miwok *kiče* 'arrowhead,' Natchez *kets* 'cut,' Koasati *kōs* 'cut,' Wappo *k'ɛše* 'cut,' *lil-kus* 'knife,' Huchnom *wai-kūči* 'knife,' Creek *koče* 'break,' Tzotzil *k'as* 'break,' Yana *kaʔča* 'knife,' Kashaya *kača* 'knife,' East Pomo *katsa* 'knife,' Seri *kišix* 'cut,' Cochimi *čisili* 'knife,' Tonkawa *kesʔatˢe* 'be broken,' Karankawa *kusila* 'knife,' Papago *híkutˢi* 'cut,' Zapotec *kuča'* 'break sticks,' Ixcatec *ʔučʰe* 'break,' Miskito *kisuru* 'knife,' Quechua *kʰuču* 'cut,' Aymara *kʰuču* 'cut,' Ticuna *kiči* 'knife,' Movima *kačiru* 'knife,' Taparita *gače* 'cut,' Chamacoco *kēčērēha* 'knife' (cf. Palmella *rexe* 'knife'), Guahibo *kučiaba* 'knife,' Guajajara *kitˢi* 'cut,' Oyampi *kəsi* 'cut,' Kamayura *kiči* 'cut,' Siriono *kise* 'cut,' Guarani *kɨče* 'knife,' Cocoma *kɨči* 'knife,' Maue *kese* 'knife,' Munduruku *kise* 'knife,' Caranga *kˣač-* 'cut,' Yagua *kiči* 'knife,' Fulnio *kʰeči* 'divide,' Camican *keča* 'knife,' Kaingan *kiče* 'knife.' [N 196; A 49, MP 20, MG 70]

14. NOSTRATIC **k'aćʌ* 'man, youth,' Proto-Kartvelian **k'ac₁-* 'man, youth,' Proto-Uralic **kaĆʌ* 'youth, man' = AMERIND **k'ači* 'boy, child,' Proto-Salish **qetˢk* 'older brother,' Lillooet *käčih* 'older brother,' Siletz *suq'eʔs* 'older brother,' Kalispel *qetˢč* 'older brother,' Kutenai *qask'o* 'male,' Chemakum *katˢ'a-pat* 'girl,' Proto-Algonquian **ne-kwiʔsa* 'my son,' Ojibwa *nen-kwiss* 'my son,' Menomini *ne-kīʔs* 'my son,' Proto-Siouan **kši* 'boy,' Ofo *wakasik* 'child,' Mohawk *-ksa-* 'child,' Chinook *-k'asks* 'child,' Miluk *kwič'-* 'child,' Coos *kwēs* 'girl,' Molale *kus-asa* 'child,' San Jose Costanoan *kočo* 'boy,' Southern Sierra Miwok *kotˢo* 'son,' Zuni *katsi-k'i* 'girl, daughter,' Huchnom *-k'ič* 'older brother,' Chitimacha *kiča* 'girl,' Atakapa *kiš* 'girl,' Mixe *kīs* 'girl,' Sayula *kiʔčway* 'boy,' Tzeltal *ač'iiš* 'girl,' Karok *kač* 'son,' Arra-arra *akitˢ* 'brother,' Konomihu *kwičekh* 'girl,' Achomawi *qəsāwi* 'man,' East Pomo *qus* 'baby,' Santa Cruz Chumash *kučo* 'child,' Santa Inez Chumash *kiči* 'infant,' Cochimi *kača* 'brother, sister,' Cocopa *ksa* 'older brother,' Maricopa *ačis* 'daughter,' Comecrudo *kišaχ* 'boy, girl,' Zacapoaxtla *ukič* 'man,' Terraba *kwazir* 'boy,' Boncota *ohutˢ-kašo* 'girl,' Pehuelche *akač* 'son, daughter,' Genneken *agačke* 'son, daughter,' Simacu *kiča* 'man,' Mocochi *kašim* 'brother,'

Cuica *kašik* 'brother, sister,' Trumai *axos* 'young, child,' Murato *kīša* 'girl,' Timote *kušik-neum* 'my sister,' Miranya *kossá* 'daughter,' Mocoa *čišik* 'female child,' Motilon *šwkāš* 'little son,' Botocudo *kižak* 'brother, sister,' Tibagi *akoči* 'son,' Guarapuava *koši* 'son,' Krenye *i-kasü-ye* 'daughter.' [N 191; A 281, AK 44, P 88, H 29, MT 61]

15. NOSTRATIC **K'älHä* 'tongue, talk,' Proto-Indo-European **k(ʌ)lē/kel* 'call,' Proto-Uralic **kēle* 'tongue,' Proto-Altaic **k'älä-* 'tongue, speak,' Gilyak *qlai* 'converse,' Chukchi *qulit* 'voice,' Kamchadal *kel* 'shout,' Yuit *qalaʁtuq* 'talk, speak,' Kuskokwim *kaligaa* 'calls' = AMERIND **q'ʷal* ~ **q'ʷel* 'say, speak,' Proto-Algonquian **kelaw* 'speak,' Shawnee *kala* 'talk,' Micmac *kelusit* 'he speaks,' Kutenai *ʔaqaɫcxa-* 'tell,' Squamish *qʷal* 'speak,' Kalispel *qʷel* 'speak,' Pentlatch *kwal* 'say,' Lkungen *qʷɛl* 'say,' Nootsack *sq'ʷuqʷal* 'speak,' Coeur d'Alene *qwaʔqʷel* 'speak,' Kwakwala *-(k)ʔāla* 'say,' Nootka *-wā(ɬ)* 'say,' Bella Bella *wālaq'wāla* 'speak,' Oneida *-kalatu-* 'tell a story,' Chinook *kʷtˡ* 'tell,' North Sahaptin *Wal* 'converse,' Coos *γāla* 'speak,' Siuslaw *haɫ* 'shout,' Yakonan *qalx* 'shout,' Takelma *sgelew* 'shout,' Bodega Miwok *ʔākal* 'tell,' Wappo *ʔokál'iʔ* 'talk,' Zuni *ʔikʷa* 'say,' Natchez *weɫ* 'speak,' Totonac *kiɫwan* 'say,' Santa Cruz Chumash *kalala* 'shout,' Salinan *k'ok'ol'še* 'speak,' Cocopa *kʷarkʷar* 'speak,' Shoshone *ʔekʷa* 'tongue,' Ona *kal* 'tongue,' Qawashqar *kalaktas* 'tongue,' Quechua *qallu* 'tongue,' Yahgan *galana* 'shout,' Iranshe *wala* 'talk,' Masaca *walu* 'tongue.' [N 221; E SPEAK₁; A 218]

16. NOSTRATIC **K'ap'a* 'cover, close,' Proto-Afro-Asiatic **kp-/qp-* 'close, cover,' Proto-Uralic **kopa* 'bark,' Kamassian *kuba* 'skin, hide,' Estonian *kõba* 'fir bark,' Cheremiss *kuwo* 'shell, hull, husk,' Proto-Dravidian **kapp-/kavʌ-* 'to close,' Proto-Altaic **k'apa-* 'cover,' Middle Korean *këpcil* 'bark,' Japanese *kabur-* 'put on, cover,' *kapá* 'bark,' Ainu *sik-kap* 'eyelid,' Gilyak *xip* 'birch bark,' Greenlandic *qapuk* 'scum, froth' = AMERIND **q'ap'a* 'cover, close,' Squamish *qəp'* 'close,' ?Kalispel *čep* 'lock a door,' Kwakwala *qāpōtəla* 'close,' Chemakum *hap'ilii* 'cover,' Oowekyala *kapa* 'to lift a lid, blanket,' Haisla *kàpa* 'covered with frost,' Proto-Central Algonquian **kep* 'close,' Shawnee *kip-* 'covered, closed up,' Ojibwa *-kopy* 'bark,' Wiyot *kʷapɫ* 'be covered,' Dakota *akaxpa* 'close,' Santee *akaxpa* 'cover,' Catawba *kəpa* 'close,' Tutelo *kəpa* 'cover,' ?Nass *hāp* 'cover,' Takelma *k'ūb-i* 'skin,' Molala *qeps* 'skin,' Maidu *kápú* 'bark,' Wintu *χap-la* 'bark,' Nomlaki *kapala* 'bark,' Zuni *k'apa* 'be broad,' Quiché *q'op* 'close,' Kekchi *ts'ap* 'close,' Mixe *kip-ak* 'bark,' Southern Pomo *kʰawa* 'bark,' Northeast Pomo *kʰawa* 'bark,' East Pomo *xāWal* 'bark,' Southeast Pomo *χwal* 'bark,' Salinan *awuɫ* 'bark,' Tonkawa *-kapa* 'shut,' Tlappanec *hwapa* 'broad,' Jicaque *kupal-pone* 'broad,' Tewa *k'owa* 'skin,' San Ildefonso *kʰowa* 'bark,' Cuna *akapa* 'close one's eyes,' Tarascan *hupr-ku* 'cover,' Chimila *akopron* 'cover,' Binticua *auan-kaba* 'broad,' Atacama *k'aba* 'hide,' Aymara *khopi-* 'cover,' Iranshe *kap* 'cover,' Tuyoneri *ua-kipe* 'scale,' Itene

kapi-ye 'skin,' Amniape *koapa* 'skin,' Arawak *kabburan* 'be broad,' Waraquena *kēpili* 'broad,' Mascoy *kjab* 'cover,' Panobo *kepui* 'close,' Shipibo *kepu* 'close,' Coroado *kapo-em* 'to close,' Krenye *kapi* 'to bolt,' Botocudo *unkupa* 'broad.' [N 212; E SKIN; A 66]

• Illich-Svitych (1967: 356) gave the reconstruction **k'ap'ʌ*.

17. NOSTRATIC **K'ara* 'hearth, burn,' Proto-Afro-Asiatic **k'rr* 'burn,' Proto-Kartvelian **k'era* 'hearth,' Proto-Indo-European **ker-* 'burn, fry, fire,' Proto-Uralic **kor-pe-* 'singe, burn,' Proto-Dravidian **kar(ʌ)-* 'burn, be scorched' = AMERIND **qʷala* 'burn,' Proto-Salish **qʷəl* 'cook, roast,' Shuswap *qʷl-* 'roast,' Twana *qʷələb* 'cook,' Nootsack *kʷl* 'cook,' Squamish *qʷəl-t* 'cook,' Pentlatch *kwolaš* 'roast, cook,' Seshault *kʷəl* 'cook,' Lower Fraser *qʷələm* 'cook,' Chemakum *qʷałili* 'roast,' Mohawk *karis* 'cook,' Tsimshian *gwalk* 'burn,' Takelma *kʷalay* 'fire,' Coos *kwił* 'cook, boil, burn,' Tarascan *kharhipa* 'roast,' Sanema *kwarag'e* 'fire,' Colorado *guaranae* 'boil,' Warrau *koré-* 'boil,' Eten *karrm* 'cook, boil,' Nonama *kura* 'fireplace,' Qawashqar *isgura* 'cook,' Tschaawi *kalu* 'cook,' Cahuapana *kalota-* 'cook,' Siona *kuara* 'boil,' Kandoshi *kora* 'burn,' Wapishana *karimet* 'roast,' Arawak *akkurran* 'bake,' Kozarini *kera* 'burn,' Saliba *igara* 'burn, fire,' Yuracare *kula* 'cook,' Siriono *kwarokwara* 'boil,' Yuruna *karigon* 'cook,' Tacana *kwarara* 'boil,' Cayapo *kūrü* 'fire,' Bororo *goriddo* 'roast.' [IS 353, N 215; EQ 24]

18. NOSTRATIC **K'arä* 'black, dark,' Proto-Afro-Asiatic **k'r/kr* 'black,' Proto-Indo-European **ker-/ker-s* 'black, dark,' Proto-Dravidian **kar̲/kār/kār̲* 'black, dark,' Proto-Altaic **Karä* 'black,' Mongol *küreŋ* 'dark brown,' Manchu *kuri* 'dark brown,' Korean *kɨrɨnca* 'shadow,' Japanese *kuro-i* 'black,' Ainu *ekurok* 'black,' *kuru* 'shadow,' Gilyak *i·γr-* 'black,' Eskimo *qirniq* 'black' = AMERIND **k'ara* 'black,' Wichita *kārʔi* 'black,' Mohawk *-akaraʔ-* 'to darken,' Tutelo *ikare* 'dark,' Rumsen *karsist* 'black,' Karok *ikxaram* 'night,' Atacameño *kirikiri* 'black,' Ona *kar* 'charcoal,' Qawashqar *ha-kar* 'dark, black,' Araucanian *kuru* 'black,' Saliba *igarri* 'become dark,' Shuara *kiar* 'become dark,' Upano *kerama* 'dark,' Mekens *koärap* 'black,' Surinam *kārai* 'black,' Mocoa *karanka* 'paint the face black,' *korošik* 'black,' Galibi *mekoro* 'black,' Opaie *kõra* 'black.' [IS 372, N 213; E BLACK₁; A 38, MC 4]

19. NOSTRATIC **K'Eč'a* 'summer heat,' Proto-Afro-Asiatic **q(j)t̲* 'summer, heat,' Proto-Uralic **kEČa* 'summer heat, summer' = AMERIND **k'etˢ* ~ **k'atˢ* 'hot, heat, sun, summer,' Proto-Central Algonquian **kešj* 'hot,' Shawnee *kiš* 'hot,' Cree *kis-* 'hot,' Fox *kišesw* 'sun,' Passemaquody *kīsus* 'sun,' Yurok *ketˢoyn-hego* 'sun,' Proto-Salish **kʷas* 'hot, scorch,' Nootsack *kʷas* 'hot,' Pentlatch *kwas* 'hot,' Columbian *skwats* 'hot,' Wichita *kišɔ* 'sun,' Acoma *kásâıtı* 'summer, year,' Natchez *haši* 'sun,' Choctaw *haši* 'sun,' Huastec *kʔīčā* 'sun,' Tzeltal *kʔišin* 'heat,' Arra-arra *kišen* 'summer,' Santa Ynez Chumash *kɨs-si* 'sun,' Seri *kkošiŋ* 'be hot,' Utah *kʷučíi* 'hot,' Mixtec *kači* 'warm, damp,'

Popoloca *kusuwa* 'heat,' Lenca *kaši* 'sun,' Miskito *kisni-sa* 'heat,' Yahgan *kisi*
'summer,' Koaia *kasa* 'sun,' Opaye *hečŏ-ata* 'summer' (*ata* = 'hot'), Choroti
a-kus 'hot,' Suhin *kus* 'hot.' [N 224; AK 103]

20. EURASIATIC **ki* '2, dual,' Armenian *-kʻ* (plural), *me-kʻ* 'we,' Turkish *iki*
'2,' Yukaghir *ki* '2,' Proto-Finno-Ugric **-me-k* 'we' (cf. **-te-k* 'thou'), Hungarian *-k* (plural), Saami *-k* (plural), Ostyak *-k(-an)* (dual), Yenisei Ostyak
k(-an) ~ *k(-ai)* (dual), Selkup *-qi* (dual), Yukaghir *tkit* '2,' Turkish *äkir̆* '2,'
Mongolian *ikire* 'twins,' *iki* '2,' Gilyak *me-gi* 'we 2' (cf. *me-r* 'we inc.'), *-ki*
'and,' Chukchi *-mA-k* 'we,' *-tA-k* 'you' (verb suffixes), Proto-Eskimo-Aleut
*-mi-k 'we 2,' **-ti-k* 'you 2,' Eskimo *-k* (dual), Aleut *-k* (dual) = AMERIND
*ki 'we 2 inc.,' Proto-Algonquian **ke-* 'thy,' Potawatomi *kin* 'thou,' *kin-an* 'we
inc.' (cf. *nin-an* 'we ex.'), *kin-wa* 'you,' Yurok *-k'* 'I,' Wiyot *-ak* 'I,' Iroquois
k- 'I,' Wyandot *kj-* 'we 2 inc.,' *kw-* 'we inc.,' Pawnee *k-* 'I,' Yokuts *ma-k'*
'we 2 inc.' (cf. *ma-i* 'we inc.'), Rumsien *ma-k* 'we,' Chitimacha *-ki-* 'me,' Pa-
pantla *ki-t* 'I,' *ki-n* 'we,' Maratino *ko* 'we inc.,' Pomo *ke-* 'my,' Karok *ki-n*
'we,' Taos *ki-* 'we,' South Pame *kakh* 'we inc.,' Xinca *ka-* 'thou,' Millcayac *ka*
'thou,' Tarascan *-ke(-ni)* 'first-person singular acts on second-person singular,'
Kaliana *ka(-be)* 'thou,' Proto-Ge **ka* 'thou,' Carib *k-* 'we 2 inc.,' Uitoto *koko*
'we 2,' *-ko* (dual), Galibi *oko* '2,' Hishcariana *asa-ko* '2,' Cholona *ok* 'I,' *ki-*
'our,' Gennaken *ki-* 'my,' *kia* 'I,' Mayna *-ke* 'let us,' Andoa *kua* 'I,' Zaparo *kui*
'I,' *ko-* 'my,' *ka(-na)* 'we exc.' [E TWO₂ & G14; A G10, G19 & G28]

21. EURASIATIC **ku* ~ **ko* 'this,' Japanese *ko-no* 'this,' Ryukyuan *ku-ni*
'this,' Ainu *ku-ri* 'this,' Gilyak *ku* 'that,' Chuvash *ku* 'this,' Southern Uighur
ko 'this,' Korean *ko* 'that,' Hittite *kā* 'this,' *kūn* 'this' (acc.), *kūs* 'these'
(nom./acc.) = AMERIND **ko* ~ **ki* 'this,' Chumash *kaki* 'this,' Subtiaba *kagi*
'this,' Cochimi *khu* 'this,' Jicaque *kone* 'this,' *kiʔa* 'here,' Auake *kiʔa* 'this,'
Guarani *ko* 'this,' Puquina *ko* 'this, that,' Caraja *kua* 'this,' Kamakan *kue*
'that,' Cherente *kua* 'he.' [E G10; A G22]

22. NOSTRATIC **k'utʌ* 'small,' Proto-Afro-Asiatic **k'(w)t* 'small,' Proto-
Kartvelian **k'ut'-* 'small,' Proto-Dravidian **kuḍḍ-* 'small,' Turkish *küčük*
'small,' Uighur *kičik* 'small,' Evenki *köčaken* 'small,' Ryukyuan *kūt-ēng* 'be
small,' Kamchadal *kižg* 'fine, small,' Kuskokwim *kituq* 'be small,' Inuit *-kuči*
(diminutive) = AMERIND **k'ut'i* 'small, thin, narrow,' Chemakum *k'utin*
'small,' Quileute *k'udī* 'small,' Laguna *k'ïčï* 'tight,' Santa Ana *k'ičï* 'tight,'
Wishram *k'aitˢ* 'small,' Nez Perce *kutskuts* 'small,' Molala *kutˢa* 'small,' Klamath *k'ečča* 'small,' Modoc *ketsa* 'thin,' Proto-California Penutian **kut* 'little,' Patwin *kuči* 'small,' San Jose Costanoan *kuču-wis* 'small,' Wappo *kut'ija*
'small,' *hutˢ'íw'is* 'thin,' Zuni *k'usa* 'become thin,' Quiché *č'uti-k* 'be small,'
Huave *kičeeč* 'small,' Pokomchi *k'isa* 'small,' Totonac *aktzú* 'small,' Santa
Cruz Chumash *kučo* 'child,' Santa Ynez Chumash *kiči* 'infant,' ?Salinan
k'oškwetop 'thin,' Seri *kísił* 'small,' *koosot* 'narrow,' Kiliwa *ket* 'small,' Wala-

pai ḳētˢ 'small,' Yavapai ḳitˢi 'small,' Tequistlatec guʔušu 'narrow,' ?Kiowa kā't'-syãn 'narrow,' Mazahua xũt'ü 'thin,' Tehuelche kutr 'thin, narrow,' Qawashqar ikot 'small,' Macu kudi 'small,' Canamari kuduta 'small,' Quitemo kuči 'thin,' Amuesha kitˢke 'narrow,' Piaroa kikiče 'small,' Tuyoneri -ket 'small,' Caranga kos 'thin,' Maquiritare akede 'thin,' Toba-Guaza quoti 'small,' Angaite ketsoo 'small,' Lengua kutˢk 'small,' Choroti a-kisa 'thin,' Botocudo kuji 'small,' Ingain kutui 'small,' Krenye akod. [IS 348, N 205; E SMALL3; A 254]

23. NOSTRATIC *K'ʌ (allative), Proto-Afro-Asiatic *k (allative), Proto-Uralic *-kkʌ/-kʌ (allative), Yukaghir -ge/-go (allative), Proto-Dravidian *-kkʌ/-kʌ (dative, allative), Proto-Altaic *-kʌ (dative, allative), Gilyak -ak (dative, allative), Aliutor -ka (allative), Chukchi -ki (locative), -kjit (direction of), mi-k 'where,' Greenlandic -k (locative), na-k-it 'whence' = AMERIND *k(')i (allative), Wiyot okʷ 'in,' Yurok -ik 'in,' Seneca -keh 'in,' Maidu -k 'toward,' Alsea k- (locative), Yuki k'il 'toward,' Totonac k- 'in,' Yana -ki 'hither,' Washo -uk 'toward,' Atsugewi -k (allative), Chimu -ek 'to,' Cuna ki- 'in, at, by.' [N 245; E G26; A G45]

24. NOSTRATIC *-la (collective), Proto-Uralic *-la (collective), Proto-Dravidian *-l (plural), Proto-Altaic *-l(a) (collective), Kamchadal -al (collective) = AMERIND *-le ~ *-la (plural), Mataco -el (plural), Lule mi-l 'you' (cf. mi 'thou'), -l (personal plural, e.g. kwe-l 'children'), Mocovi le- (plural, cf. i-tā 'his father' and le-tā 'their father'), Guambiana -ele (noun plural), Colorado -la (plural of nouns and pronouns), Xinca -li (plural of nouns and pronouns), Murire -re (pronoun plural), Bribri -r (noun plural), Paya -ri (plural verb subj.). [N 246; E G20; A G33]

25. NOSTRATIC *magʌ 'earth,' Proto-Indo-European *megĥ- 'earth,' Proto-Uralic *māγe 'earth,' Yukaghir mi-be 'underworld,' Korean ma 'earth,' Ainu ma 'peninsula, island,' Gilyak mi-f 'earth' = AMERIND *ʔamekʷa 'earth,' Proto-Salish *t-mixʷ 'earth,' Squamish t-mixʷ 'earth,' Thompson tə-mûxʷ 'earth,' Nootsack mixʷ 'earth,' Proto-Algonquian *-āmeHk(w)- 'earth, soil,' Fox -āmehk(w)- 'earth,' Menomini -āmɛhk(w)- 'earth,' Shawnee wāp-āmʔkwi 'white clay,' Arapaho mixta'amu 'earth,' Cheyenne -oma- 'ground,' Kutenai ammāk 'earth,' Santee maka 'earth,' Hidatsa ama 'earth,' Mandan ma'āk 'earth,' Biloxi amã 'earth,' Ofo amān 'earth,' Tutelo manáʔ ~ māʔ 'earth,' Nez Perce ʔáma 'island,' Yakima uma 'island,' Wappo ʔóma 'earth, world,' Chimariko ama 'earth,' Proto-Pomo *ʔa(h)mā 'earth,' Kashaya ʔamā 'earth, dirt,' Southern Pomo ʔaīna 'earth,' Northern Pomo mā 'earth,' Northeast Pomo ʔamã 'earth,' Southeast Pomo maṭ 'earth,' Proto-Yuman *ʔ-mat 'earth,' Cochimi emat 'earth,' Cocopa maṭ 'earth,' Maricopa amat 'earth,' Yuma ʔamaṭ 'earth,' Mohave amat 'earth,' Diegueño ʔemat 'earth,' Quinigua ama 'earth,' Jicaque ma 'earth,' Tarascan omequa 'island,' Yahgan mik'in 'earth,'

Mocochi mikuč 'earth,' Callahuaya makke ~ yamakan 'earth,' ?Tora timak 'earth,' Chapacura čimak 'earth,' Urupa manaka 'earth,' Wañam namakwam 'earth,' Yagua makane 'earth,' Aparai amato 'island,' Ouayana ahmonta 'island,' Sapiboca meči 'earth,' Cavineña meči 'earth,' Panobo maxpo 'earth,' Cashinawa mapo ~ mai 'earth,' Caripuna māi 'earth,' Otuke moktuhu 'earth,' Camacan hamiko 'earth,' Botocudo am 'island,' Patasho aham 'earth,' Macuni ām 'earth.' [IS 342; E EARTH₁; A 96]

26. EURASIATIC *man 'hand,' Proto-Indo-European *man-/mə-r- 'hand,' Yurak mana 'finger,' Tungus mana 'paw,' Korean manei 'touch,' Ainu amojn 'hand,' imeka 'gift,' Gilyak imγ- 'give,' man- 'measure by handspans,' tuń-miń 'finger,' Aliutor mənγ- 'hand,' Kerek mənəqal 'hand,' Itelmen man Ze 'palm' = AMERIND *man-/mak- 'hand, give,' Proto-Central Algonquian *mī 'hand,' Kwakiutl maχwa 'give potlatch,' Chinook m- 'hand (v.),' Maidu ma 'hand,' Central Sierra Miwok ammə 'give,' Choctaw ima 'give,' Mixe ma 'give,' Totonac makan 'hand,' Akwa'ala man 'arm,' East Pomo ma 'hold,' Salinan maa 'hand,' Tequistlatec mane 'hand, arm,' mage 'five,' Proto-Uto-Aztecan *ma 'hand,' *maka 'give,' Proto-Chinantec *man 'hand,' Kiowa mã 'hand,' mẽga 'give,' Proto-Tanóan *ma-n 'hand,' Colorado manta 'hand,' Ayoman man 'hand,' Mayna mani 'arm,' Quechua maki 'hand,' Ona mar 'arm, hand,' Ticuna mi 'hand,' Proto-Tupi *meʔeŋ 'hand,' Caranga maka 'receive,' Pilaga imak 'left hand,' Lengua amik 'hand,' Proto-Panoan *mɨkɨnɨ 'hand,' Kamakan mane 'give,' Bororo mako 'give,' Kaingan ma 'bring.' [E HAND₁; A 137]

27. NOSTRATIC *mene 'walk, step,' Proto-Indo-European *men- 'trample, step on,' Proto-Uralic *mene 'go, travel,' Yukaghir män- 'jump,' Old Turkish man- 'a step,' Tartar maŋda 'run,' Kamchadal emeneŋ 'a step' = AMERIND *mina 'go,' Santa Ana īma 'go!,' Chitimacha ʔami 'go, go away,' Kalapuya maʔa 'come,' Wappo mi 'go,' Taos mẽ 'go,' Proto-Uto-Aztecan *mi 'go,' Bribri mina 'go,' Rama mang 'go!,' Matanawi amī 'go!,' Colorado mai 'go,' Araucanian -me- 'go to . . . ,' Pehuenche amu 'walk,' Auake ma 'walk,' Yuracare ama 'come!,' Moseten mii 'go, walk,' Chulupi ma 'go,' Umotina a-menu 'go,' Proto-Ge *mõ(r) 'go, walk,' Dalbergia mũ 'go,' Kamakan emang 'go.' [IS 350, N 295; E WALK; A 126]

28. NOSTRATIC *mä 'we inc.,' Proto-Afro-Asiatic *m(n) 'we inc.,' Proto-Kartvelian *m- 'we inc.,' Proto-Indo-European *me-s 'we,' Proto-Uralic *mä-/me- 'we,' Yukaghir met 'I,' mit 'we,' Proto-Dravidian *mǎ 'we,' Proto-Altaic *bä- 'we ex.' (oblique mä-n), Gilyak me-ĝi 'we-2,' me-r 'we,' Chukchi muri 'we,' Chukchi -m 'let us,' Aleut -man/s 'we' = AMERIND *ma 'we inc., we,' Tsimshian -m 'we,' Takelma -am 'us,' Yokuts ma-k' 'we 2 inc.,' ma-i 'we inc.,' Rumsien ma-k 'we,' Mutsun mak-se 'we,' Coast Miwok mā 'we,' Yuki mī 'we inc.,' Santa Cruz Chumash miči 'we,' Yavapai magi 'we,' Maratino miŋ 'us,' Cuitlatec moguelo 'we,' Chimu mæ-ič 'we,' Cahuapana moki 'we,' Sabela

-mõni 'we,' Amaguaje may 'we,' Siona may 'we,' Yupua -mai- 'we,' Cubeo mahe 'we,' Särä mani 'we,' Desana mari 'we,' Tucano mani 'we,' Barasano màní 'we inc.,' Muinane -mo 'our,' Macuni mamai-aičohm 'we,' Came em 'we.' [N I:6; E G1; A G3]

29. NOSTRATIC *mo ~ *mu 'this, he, other,' Proto-Afro-Asiatic *m(w) 'they, this, he,' Proto-Kartvelian *m(a)- 'this, he,' Proto-Indo-European *mo- 'he, this,' Proto-Uralic *mū-/mō- 'other,' Proto-Altaic *bū/bō 'this' (oblique mu-n) = AMERIND *mo 'that, he, the,' Maidu mi 'he,' mō 'that one,' mɨ 'this, that,' Atakapa ma 'that,' Proto-Algic *m- (impersonal possessor), Proto-Uto-Aztecan *mo- 'himself,' Taos mo- 'himself,' Guarani amo 'that,' Arara mo 'he,' Barama mo(-ko) 'he, she,' mo(-ro) 'it,' Waiwai moro 'that one,' Moseten mo 'that, he,' Chama ma- 'that,' Northern Cayapo amu 'he,' Guato ma- (stage III article). [N 303; A G14]

30. EURASIATIC *mu(s) 'fly, gnat,' Afro-Asiatic: Musgu ammumi 'bee,' Gidder amama 'bee, honey,' Chibak məmɛ 'honey,' Iznacen (θ)ammem(θ) 'honey,' Proto-Indo-European *mū(s)- 'fly, gnat,' Ainu mose/moš 'fly, nettle,' Japanese musi 'insect, bug, worm' = AMERIND *mumu/mumi 'bee, fly,' Chemakum muumuuma 'bee,' Proto-Central Algonquian *amoa 'bee,' Bella Coola mamis 'fly,' Molala mumu-s 'fly,' Santa Cruz mumuru 'flies,' Natchez mom 'bee,' Huave muam 'bee,' Esselen mumirux 'flies,' Salinan le-me'm 'bee, wasp,' Proto-Uto-Aztecan *mumu/meme 'bee,' *mu 'fly,' Tucano mumi 'bee, honey,' Maku mime 'bee,' Bororo muiawo 'bee,' Northern Cayapo amiu 'wasp.' [E GNAT₁; A 27, AK 79, MG 117]

• The Afro-Asiatic forms are taken from Greenberg (1963: 52).

31. NOSTRATIC *na (locative), Proto-Afro-Asiatic *-n (locative), Proto-Kartvelian *-n (locative), Proto-Indo-European *en/n̥ (locative), Proto-Dravidian *-n(ʌ) (locative), Proto-Uralic *-na/-nä (locative), Yukaghir pure-n 'above,' ho-n (< *ko-n) 'where,' Proto-Altaic *-na (locative), Korean anh 'inside' (n.), Japanese asa-na 'in the morning,' Ryukyuan -ni 'in,' Ainu na-k-an 'whither,' rik-un 'above,' Gilyak –n (locative), Aleut -an (locative) = AMERIND *na ~ *ni (locative); examples of this affix are seen in the Amerind citations in etymologies 10 and 17 in Chapter 14, in conjunction with the k- and m-interrogatives, with the resultant meaning of 'where' or 'when.' [N I:11; E G30; A G47]

32. NOSTRATIC *NA 'this, that, he,' Proto-Afro-Asiatic *n(j) 'this,' Proto-Kartvelian *-n 'he,' Proto-Indo-European *ne-/no- 'this,' Proto-Uralic *nʌ- 'this,' Proto-Dravidian *nǎ 'this' = AMERIND *na ~ *ni 'this, that, he, here,' Paez ana 'this,' Colorado ne 'he,' Choco nan 'that,' Yahgan -n 'his,' Quechua -n 'his,' Kahuapana nana 'he,' Amuesha ña 'he,' Yuracare na 'that, he,' Suya ni 'this,' Arazaire nina 'here,' Galibi ini 'this,' Wayana ine 'he.' [N 332; A G15 & G23]

33. NOSTRATIC *-NA (plural of animate nouns), Proto-Afro-Asiatic *-ān (plural of animate nouns), Proto-Kartvelian *-en/-n (plural of animate nouns), Proto-Uralic *-Nʌ (plural), Proto-Altaic *-na/-nä (plural of animate nouns) = AMERIND *na (plural, especially of pronouns and nouns referring to humans), Kagaba nas-an 'we' (cf. nas 'I'), Lenca ana-nan 'they' (cf. ina 'he'), Zaparo ka-na 'we' (cf. ka 'I'), Jebero -nøn-na 'their' (cf. -nøn 'his'), Yamana sa-n 'you' (cf. sa 'thou'), Aguaruna -na (plural subj. of a verb), Tiquie nā 'they, their,' na- (plural of demonstratives and human nouns), Canichana -na (plural of human nouns). [N 333; A G30]

34. NOSTRATIC *ńangʌ 'tongue,' Proto-Kartvelian *nina/ena 'tongue,' Proto-Indo-European *dn̂ĝhū/jn̂ĝhū 'tongue,' Proto-Dravidian *nanc- 'lick,' Proto-Uralic *ńaŋkćʌ 'tongue,' = AMERIND *ñene 'tongue,' Maidu ʔèní 'tongue,' Proto-Uto-Aztecan *neni 'tongue,' Allentiac nanak 'tongue,' Millcayac nanat 'tongue,' Tschaawi nenera 'tongue,' Jebero ninra 'tongue,' Cahuapana ninegla 'tongue,' Tucano nene 'lick,' Saliba nene 'tongue,' Machiguenga -nene 'tongue,' Guarani ñẽʔẽ 'tongue,' Bare nu-nene 'tongue,' Ipurina ne-nene 'tongue,' Campa anene 'tongue,' Wapishana ninuk 'tongue,' Kariri nunu 'tongue,' Dzubucua ñunu 'tongue,' Kamaru nunuh 'tongue,' Wayoro o-nyon 'tongue,' Shuara inẽ 'tongue,' Taparita yonan 'tongue,' Tacana yana 'tongue,' Cavineña yana 'tongue,' Conibo ana 'tongue,' Chacobo hana 'tongue,' Proto-Ge *ñõ-tɔ 'tongue,' Apinage ño-to 'tongue,' Chavante da-non-to 'tongue,' Cayapo ño-to 'tongue,' Came none 'tongue,' Apucarana ñoñe 'tongue,' Arikapu i-nontä 'tongue,' Camacan nãnčo-nenkix 'tongue.' [N I:18; A 256, A 258]

35. NOSTRATIC *ñiKʼa 'neck vertebra, neck,' Proto-Uralic *ñika 'vertebra, neck,' Selkup nukka 'nape of the neck,' Proto-Altaic *ñika- 'neck vertebra, neck,' Khalkha nugas(-an) 'spinal cord' = AMERIND *nuqʼ 'neck, throat, swallow,' Kwakwala nəqwa 'swallow,' Nootka n'oʕaq- 'swallow,' Tutelo -nūksāʔ 'nape' (= 'neck-back'), Oneida -nuhs- 'shoulder,' North Sahaptin nuqʼ-waš 'neck,' Klamath n'awqs 'throat,' Proto-Muskogean *nukkʷi 'neck,' Creek nokwv 'neck,' Hitchiti nōkbebe 'neck,' Natchez naxts 'throat,' Alabama nokbi 'throat,' Huave onik 'neck,' Chorti nuk' 'neck,' Huastec nūk' 'neck,' Tzotzil nuk 'neck,' nuk'ulal 'throat,' Kekchi nuk' 'swallow,' Tequistlatec nuk' 'swallow,' Salinan (p-)ēnik'a 'throat,' Boncota anokua 'nape,' Tegria anukua 'nape,' Desano wɨ-nɨgɨ 'neck,' Tucano vee-nexko 'neck,' Siona naxe-seamu 'nape' (= 'neck-back'), Pioje naxe-mu 'neck,' Coto njaxe-teka 'nape, throat,' Curiari nõhũi 'neck,' Proto-Arawakan *nuki 'neck,' Piro noxi 'neck,' Waraquena nokane 'nape,' Carutana nouxe 'nape,' Waimare nukuluaka 'throat,' Tacana enaha 'neck,' Andoke ka-ñekkhə(ii)hih 'neck.' [N 330; A 255]

• In the Nostratic languages cited by Illich-Svitych (1976: 92), the first vowel is i in some forms, u in others. In his reconstruction of the Proto-Nostratic form, Illich-Svitych chose i. The Amerind family—an outgroup to Nostratic—indicates that the original vowel was *u*, and typological considerations would also favor deriving *i* from *u*, rather than vice versa.

36. NOSTRATIC *$nʌ$ 'we ex.,' Proto-Afro-Asiatic *$naḥnu$ 'we ex.,' Proto-Kartvelian *naj 'we ex.,' Proto-Indo-European *ne-/$nō$ 'we,' Proto-Dravidian *$nām$ 'we inc.,' Korean *na* 'I,' Ainu *en* 'me,' Gilyak *ńi* 'I,' *ni-te* 'we-2,' *ni-kta* 'we' = AMERIND *na 'we ex., we, I,' Nootka *newa* 'we,' Santa Ana Keres *hinu* 'I, we,' Proto-Algonquian *ne- 'I,' Tsimshian *n*- 'I,' Nez Perce *na* 'we,' Siuslaw *na* 'I,' Yokuts *naʔ* 'I,' Huave *-na-* 'I,' Karok *na* 'I,' Comecrudo *na* 'I,' Cotoname *na* 'I, we,' Proto-Aztec-Tanoan *$neʔ$ 'I,' Kiowa *nã* 'I, we,' Mixtec *n*- 'I, we ex.,' Popoloca *n*- 'I, we ex.,' Chinantec *n*- 'I, we,' Cuna *an* 'I,' Move *nu* 'we,' Rama *na* 'I,' Xinca *ni* 'I,' Kagaba *naui* 'our,' Guamaca *nabi* 'we,' Norteño *nu* 'we,' Bintucua *nan* 'I,' Timucua *ni-* 'I,' Guambiana *na* 'I,' Jaqaru *na-* 'I,' Yehubde *en* 'we,' Papury *yn* 'we,' Taulipang *ina* 'we,' Cariniaco *naana* 'we,' Galibi *ana* 'we,' Macusi *ana* 'we,' Proto-Panoan *no 'we,' Mataco *no-* 'my,' *na-* 'our ex.,' Vejoz *no* 'our ex.,' Pilaga *ien* 'we,' Guenoa *an-* 'our,' Vilela *nati* 'we.' [N I:7; E G3; A G1]

37. NOSTRATIC *$ońe$ 'hand,' Proto-Uralic *$ońe$ 'hand, handmade,' Proto-Altaic *$uńa$ 'obedient' = AMERIND *$ʔoni$ 'hand,' Nootka *hinī* 'give,' Kutenai *(ahq-)ʔān* 'handle,' Proto-Central Algonquian *$-en$ 'by hand,' Potowotami *-in* 'by hand,' Ojibwa *-in* 'by hand,' Blackfoot *-in-* 'hand,' Wiyot *an-* 'by hand,' Tuscarora *-ʔehn-* 'hand,' Onondaga *hônia* 'finger,' Mohawk *-aʔnye-* 'hand,' Seneca *ʔnya* 'hand, finger,' Tsimshian *an'ôn* 'hand,' Chinook *āyana* 'hand,' Takelma *oyon* 'give,' North Sahaptin *-ni-* 'give,' Nez Perce *-ni-* 'give,' Modoc *ney* 'give,' Lake Miwok *hiina* 'give,' Seri *ʔanol* 'hand, finger,' Proto-Central Otomi *$ʔuni$ 'give,' Timucua *huena* 'hand,' Mariusa *uhnä* 'hand,' Mura *haneai* 'hand,' Quechua *ayni* 'lend,' Yuri *-enoo* ~ *-unoo* 'hand,' Masaca *inæ* 'finger,' Ubde-Nehern *nooï* 'give,' Marahan *nonooi* 'give,' Amaguaje *hente* 'hand,' Siona *ente* 'hand,' Ticuna *hêntẽ* 'hand,' Proto-Nambikwara *$ō$ 'give,' Sabane *ʔō* 'give,' Uru *ona* 'give,' Kariri *una* 'share,' Callahuaya *jiana* 'give,' Taparita *yonga* 'hand,' Ocaina *onu* ~ *honōho* 'hand,' Kaliana *ay-eña-li* 'finger,' Jaricuna *uiena* 'hand, finger,' Macushi *uy-enθa* 'hand, finger,' Opone *ñeñe-taratara* 'finger,' Umaua *yēnyale* 'hand,' *yenya-gamulu* 'finger,' Galibi *yenarari* 'hand,' Acawai *y-enna-ru* 'hand,' Carare *ñiñae* 'hand,' Proto-Panoan *$ʔinã$ 'give,' Panobo *inai* 'give,' Shipibo *hinahue* 'give me,' Amahuaca *inanki* 'give,' Toba *ane* 'give,' Mocovi *yanni* 'give,' Chulupi *anhyut* 'give,' Lule *ni* 'give,' Kaskiha *nēēn-gi-ma* 'give,' Moseten *uñ* 'hand,' Proto-Ge *$ñĩ-kra$ 'hand,' Suya *$ñi(-ko)$ 'hand,' Came *ningue* 'hand, finger,' Palmas *niŋge* 'hand,' Catarina *ñonem* 'give,' Botocudo *en-ti* 'give,' Otuke *i-yuna* 'finger,' Opaie *e-ĩnye* 'hand,' Mashubi *ni(-ka)* 'hand.' [IS 362; A 138]

38. NOSTRATIC *$p'äkʌ$ 'hot, roast,' Proto-Indo-European *$pekʷ$- 'roast, boil, cook,' Proto-Uralic *$päkkʌ$ 'hot,' Yukaghir *pugolet* 'warm' (v.), Proto-Altaic

*päkü 'hot,' Nanai peku 'hot,' Korean pokk- 'roast,' Japanese wak- (< bak) 'boil,' Koryak pəɣpəɣ 'boil,' Kamchadal p'axp'aŋ 'boiled jukola,' Kuskokwim puqtla 'heat' = AMERIND *pek'u 'burn, hot,' Proto-North Wakashan *px- 'warm (v.), hot,' Kwakwala pəx 'heat' (v.), Squamish p'ač' 'hot,' ?Chippewa čibákwe 'cook,' ?Ojibwa tˢīpākkwe 'cook,' Modoc puk 'cook,' Takelma bok'o- bax 'boil,' Lake Miwok bok- 'boil,' Chitimacha pāči 'roast, fry,' Atakapa wak 'roast,' Tzotzil bak'ubel 'roast,' vok- 'boil,' Achomawi poxpoxʔus 'boil,' East Pomo pʰa- 'cook,' North Pomo pʰā 'cook,' Kashaya hpʰa 'bake,' Walapai pak 'boil,' Comecrudo pakiap 'boil, cook,' Tlappanec bahi 'boil,' Yurumangui baka-isa 'heat' (v.), Tewa p'ahāŋ 'be burnt,' Tübatulabal wā? 'broil,' Cayapa būke 'boil,' bextsu 'toasted,' Itonama ba?ɨ 'bake,' Catio bakoi 'roast,' Eten pokeiñ 'hot,' Atacameño bočon 'heat,' Guambiana pačig- 'hot,' Bribri patˢe 'kindle,' Paya pas 'kindle,' Sumu buswi 'burn,' Yahgan pūkū 'burn, cook,' Yamana amux-puka 'cook,' Barasano péka 'fire,' Capishana peikärä 'roast,' Siona poho 'roast,' Ubde-Nehern puhuitums 'boil,' ?Marahan woχyoi 'boil,' Waiana pexkume 'burn,' Puinave abag 'roast,' Tuyoneri epak 'burn,' Cayuvava boko 'hot,' Yuracare bože 'burn,' Kulina puku 'hot,' Karif abuga-dina 'roast,' Callahuaya -ppoke-na 'roast,' Wayoro pukwa 'burn,' Guayaki ᵐbaku 'cook, heat,' ?Witoto peiche 'roast,' Vejoz pokue 'roasted,' Pilaga apakata 'hot,' Amahuaca hobake 'cook,' Cavineña baho 'roast,' Botocudo pek 'burn,' apok 'roast,' Karaho puk 'burn,' Erikbatsa okpog(-maha) 'burn,' Caraho hepuk 'burn.' [IS 337; E HOT₁ & ROAST₁; CP 105 & 109, MG 18]

39. NOSTRATIC *p'alʌ 'burn,' Proto-Indo-European *pelH-/pleH- 'burn,' Proto-Uralic *pal'a- 'burn,' Yurak parada 'burn up,' Yukaghir par 'cook,' Proto-Dravidian *palʌ- 'sparkle,' Korean pul 'fire,' Ainu parase 'burn,' Gilyak paru 'catch fire' = AMERIND *pale 'burn, fire,' Nootka patˡ 'flaming, lit up,' .Nez Perce ipalataksa 'roast,' Patwin wala 'burn' (intr.), Chol pulem 'burn,' San Miguel Salinan (p)ōɬ 'toast,' Yuma ?apilʲ 'burn' (intr.), Diegueño upiɬ 'burn' (intr.), Akwa'ala ipil 'burn,' Isleta pʰaɬ 'burn,' Tarascan apare 'burn,' Kagaba pula 'burn, roast,' Ulua balpatˢi 'burn,' Guatuso cue-pala 'fire,' Paya piri-ha 'toast,' Itonama u-bari 'fire,' Catio pureai 'burn,' Cayapa biriju 'roast,' Yamana apurū 'roast,' Quechua wala 'burn,' Aymara pari 'hot,' Qawashqar obillia 'burn,' Yupua piɫo 'fire,' Tsöla hẹobale 'roast,' Chirango tsoebali 'roast,' Waiana paale 'roast,' Yuracare pele 'burn,' Arikem pureo- ipapa 'cook,' Chayma ipura 'roast,' Jaricuna ipuruda 'roast,' Surinam pūru 'roast,' Guarapuava poro 'burn,' Puri mbori 'burn.' [IS 337; E BURN₁; A 115]

40. NOSTRATIC *p'atʌ 'foot, footstep,' Proto-Afro-Asiatic *pt- 'go, leave,' Proto-Indo-European *pĕd/pŏd 'foot, footsteps,' Proto-Dravidian *paṭʌ 'foot- steps, palm,' Uralic: Ziryan pod 'foot, sole,' Ostyak petta 'sole,' Proto-Altaic *p'ad-ak 'foot, footsteps,' Korean padak 'bottom, sole,' Koryak apt- 'kick' = AMERIND *pati 'foot,' Zuni pačči 'sole,' Klamath peč 'foot,' Lutuami patˢ

'foot,' Maidu *paji* 'foot,' Santa Clara *(či-)pai* 'foot,' Quinigua *boi* 'deer's foot,' Tewa *po* 'leg,' Maku *(tˢe-)peči* 'shin,' Puinave *(a-)ped* 'shin,' Ticuna *para* 'tibia,' Kariri *bui* 'foot,' Baure *poj* 'foot,' Andoke *pa* 'leg,' Yabarana *petti* 'thigh,' Vilela *ape* 'foot,' Chiquito *piri* 'leg,' Proto-Ge **par* 'foot,' Opaie *(či-)para* 'foot,' Arikapu *(ši-)pra* 'foot,' Botocudo *po* 'foot, hand.' [N I:20; E FOOT₂; A 120, MC 66]

41. NOSTRATIC **p'at'ʌ* 'wide,' Proto-Afro-Asiatic **pt'-/pt-* 'wide, to open,' Proto-Indo-European **pet(H)-* 'wide, to spread,' Proto-Dravidian **pāt(t)ʌ* 'plot of land,' Proto-Altaic **pata-* 'field,' Ainu *para* 'broad, flat,' *pira* 'open, spread out,' Korean *pʌl-* 'become broad,' Old Japanese *pïrö-i* 'broad,' Gilyak *p'al-* 'floor,' Kamchadal *p'(ă)l-xaŋ* 'cheek' = AMERIND **patˡ'a* 'broad, flat,' Haisla *patˡ'à* 'flat,' Bella Bella *bātˡa* 'fathom, span,' Proto-Salish **pʌtˡ* 'broad,' Nisqualli *as-pel* 'broad,' Shuswap *c-pet* 'spread out,' Yurok *pel* 'broad,' Wiyot *bel* 'flat, wide,' Proto-Siouan **p-ra* 'flat, broad,' Biloxi *palači* 'broad,' Chiwere *blaθge* 'flat,' Tsimshian *baɬ* 'broad,' Nass *baɬ* 'spread out' (v.), Wishram *opēdˡ* 'stretch out,' Gashowu *phal* 'spread out,' Yawelmani *palin* 'flat,' Maidu *bat-batpe* 'flat, planar,' Southern Sierra Miwok *ṭappāle* 'broad,' Lake Miwok *pat'-* 'flat,' Koasati *patha* 'broad,' Alabama *patʰa* 'broad,' Natchez *patha* 'broad,' Tunica *pāl* 'flat,' Yana *-dʔpal-* 'flat,' North Pomo *bado* 'flat,' San Antonio Salinan *(p)elet'o* 'open,' Kiliwa *pataj* 'broad,' ?Cocopa *ʔaɬ* 'broad,' Comecrudo *papol* 'flat,' Quinigua *patama* 'broad,' Tequistlatec *ešpatˢ'gi* 'broad,' Mono *papa-haanoh* 'broad,' Ulua *pap-* 'opened on,' Timucua *pal-no* 'open,' Quechua *palta* 'broad,' Yamana *patux* 'flat country,' Yahgan *patuk* 'flat,' Otomi *pap-par* 'broad,' Guahibo *patajuobi* 'open,' Uru *pʰala* 'broad,' Callahuaya *ppejra* 'broad,' Wapishana *ibar* 'flat,' Muinane *aparide* 'open,' Ocaina *tʲa-pïïra* 'you open it,' Toba Guazu *pateta* 'flat,' Tacana *pai* 'flat,' Capasho *pato* 'broad,' Ramkokamekran *ipoti* 'broad.' [IS 372; E BROAD; A 52]

42. NOSTRATIC **pitʌ* 'hold,' Proto-Indo-European **pĕd/pŏd-* 'seize, hold,' Proto-Uralic **pitä* 'hold,' Proto-Dravidian **piṭʌ-* 'hold, seize,' Korean *pat* 'receive,' Japanese *wata-s-* 'receive,' Chukchi *pir-i-* 'carry,' Aleut *hid-u-sa-* 'carry away' = AMERIND **pitu* 'hand, hold,' Abenaki *u-pedi-n* 'his arm,' Pawnee *pīd/pīru* 'arm,' Chinook *pote* 'arm,' Yokuts *pʰutʰɔng* 'hand, arm,' Proto-Muskogean **put* 'touch,' Choctaw *potoli* 'handle, feel, touch,' Kalapuya *putukwi* 'arm,' Wappo *pito* 'touch,' Alabama *pota* 'take.' [IS 339; E SEIZE₁; AK 203, P 99, 243 & 260]

43. NOSTRATIC **p'ojʌ* 'child, baby,' Proto-Uralic **pojka* 'son,' Proto-Altaic **pö-/pi-* 'child, baby' = AMERIND **p'oj* '(younger) brother,' **p'ojp'oj* 'older brother,' Yurok *-pā* 'brother,' Lillooet *äpa* 'older brother,' ?Santa Ana *-w'ɪ* 'child,' Proto-California Penutian **bē* 'older brother,' Foothill North Yokuts *p'aj* 'baby,' *p'ajeeʔi* 'child,' Maidu *p'ü* 'boy,' *p'übe* 'son,' Wappo *ʔepa* 'older brother,' Zuni *papa* 'older brother,' Achomawi *apo* 'brother,' Atsugewi

pupa 'brother,' ?Yana p'au?ni 'son,' Shasta ?apu 'older brother,' Konomihu epput- 'brother,' Washo -peyu 'younger brother,' San Miguel Salinan apēu 'brother,' Salinan pepe? 'brother,' Taos p'ay-na 'younger brother,' popo-na 'older brother,' Tewa bibi 'brother,' Kiowa pabi 'brother,' San Ildefonso ep'i 'infant,' Proto-Uto-Aztecan *pa 'brother,' Mono papi 'older brother,' Kuwai-isu pabi-ne 'older brother,' Proto-Oto-Manguean *po 'younger brother,' *papi 'older brother,' Cacaopera pai-ka 'older brother,' Shiriana aba 'older brother,' Chumulu pava 'brother,' Sabanero pabaligu 'brother,' Cuaiquer paijpa 'son,' Nonama hamupui 'brother,' Matanawi upi ∼ opi 'brother,' Atacameño aba ∼ bija 'son,' Tehuelche abbo 'boy, child,' Kolan pua- 'brother,' Tuwituwey bibi 'younger brother,' Yahgan pepe 'child,' Cahuapana babi 'child,' Papury pui 'younger brother,' Waikina baĩ(-ga) 'brother,' Muniche ye-baę 'younger brother,' Ticuna bu?ɨ 'child,' Tucano po 'child,' Yuracare pe 'younger brother,' pi 'older brother,' Kariri popo 'older brother,' Dzubucua popo 'older brother,' Kamaru popo 'older brother,' Chamacoco pab 'child,' Turaha pab 'child,' Ebidoso pab 'son,' Paumari ibaii 'son,' Emerillon paa 'older brother,' pii 'child,' Arikem opoira 'son,' Hishcariana pepe 'older brother,' Yagua poen 'son,' rai-puipuin 'brother,' Peba pwɨɨ 'brother,' Taulipang pipi 'brother,' Pavishana upi 'brother,' Accawai poïto 'boy,' Proto-Panoan *poi 'sibling of opposite sex,' Shipibo pui 'brother,' Caripuna pui 'brother,' Pacawara eppa 'brother,' Proto-Tacanan *bui 'son, daughter,' Moseten voji 'sister,' voji-t 'brother,' Mascoy poije 'my son,' Botocudo po 'brother,' Guato be 'son,' Kaingan ve 'sibling,' Umotina abu 'older brother.' [IS 360; E CHILD2; A 53]

• Amerind shows the semantic innovation CHILD > BROTHER, with subsequent development of a contrast between plain and reduplicated roots, *p'oj 'younger brother' vs. *p'ojp'oj 'older brother,' as seen most clearly in the Taos examples above.

44. EURASIATIC *pol 'dark,' Proto-Indo-European *pel-/pol- 'pale, gray,' Proto-Uralic *pil'mʌ 'dark,' Old Turkish boz 'gray,' Mongolian bora 'gray,' Buriat balay 'dark,' Manchu balu 'blind,' Gilyak polm 'make blind,' Chukchi pylm 'dark,' pylmatyk 'become dark' = AMERIND *pol 'black,' Seri ko-opoɬ 'black,' Yana pal 'black,' Karankawa pal 'black,' Cuna polea 'be dark,' Tarascan vera- 'dark,' Cuitlatec puluši-li/puruši 'black,' Ulua bara 'black,' Itonama bola 'shadow,' Tehuelche epoln 'black,' Patagon apula 'night,' Qawasqar pal 'black,' Capixana vorone 'black.' [E DARK1; A 37, CP 18]

45. NOSTRATIC *p'učʌ 'body hair, down, feathers,' Proto-Kartvelian *pačw- 'body hair, feather,' Proto-Indo-European *pous- 'down, body hair,' Proto-Uralic *pučʌ 'down' = AMERIND p'ut'i 'hair, feather, bird down,' Bella Bella pātʰa 'feather,' Kwakwala p'aɬəm 'wool,' ?Nootka p'ayaɬ 'hair,' Lower Fraser stˡ'p'ɛl'qən 'feather,' Lummi stˡ'p'ɛl'qən 'feather,' Coeur D'Alene s-puɬt 'feather,' Quileute būɬku 'hair,' Wiyot bāɬ 'hair,' Caddo bāt 'hair,' Tsimshian

p'əlk'wa 'bird down,' Coos *watˡ* 'feather,' Alsea *pəlupəlu* 'feather,' Yaudanchi *paada* 'feather,' Wintu *p'it* 'feather,' Nomlaki *pute* 'feather,' Maidu *butú* 'hair,' Nisenan *butuj* 'feather,' Bodega Miwok *pútta* 'feather,' Plains Miwok *pútte* 'feather,' Lake Miwok *pottol* 'fur,' Clear Lake Yuki *p'oti* 'feather,' Wappo *pučiš* 'hair,' Atakapa *-puli* 'feathers,' Tunica *-puli* 'hair,' San Buenaventura Chumash *pakwan* 'hair,' Jicaque *pusus* 'feather,' Taos *p'o-na* 'hair,' Tewa *p'o* 'hair,' San Ildefonso Tewa *pʰō* 'hair,' Kiowa *phɔ-* 'hair, fur,' Proto-Uto-Aztecan **po* 'body hair,' Southern Paiute *pyhȳ* 'fur,' Ulua *butuka* 'body hair,' Sumu *butuni* 'pubic hair,' Nonama *paday* 'feather,' Choco *puda* 'hair,' Citara *puda* 'hair,' Saija *puda* 'hair of head,' Tucura *puda* 'hair,' Chami *buda* 'hair,' Catio *buda* 'hair,' Waunana *pura* 'hair,' Eten *purr* 'feather,' Guambiana *pušug* 'hair,' Moguex *puču-guizik* 'hair,' Colorado *apiču* 'hair,' Quechua *pʰuru* 'feather,' Aymara *phuyu* 'feather,' Cahuapana *ambolu* 'feather,' Tschaahui *amporo* 'feather,' Ubde-Nehern *pat* 'hair,' Dou *bata* 'head hair,' Papury *pad* 'hair,' Marahan *pat* 'hair,' Cubeo *pola* 'feather,' Palänoa *poali* ~ *poari* 'feather,' Waikina *poali* 'feather, hair,' Wanana *poali* 'feather,' Tucano *poali* ~ *poari* 'feather, hair,' Yupua *poa* 'feather,' Tuyuka *poa* 'feather,' Dyurumawa *poδa* 'hair,' Cayuvava *pote* 'feather,' Campa *ibiti* 'feather, hair,' Ipurina *piti* 'feather,' Machiguenga *ibiti* 'feather,' Quitemo *ipati-ko* 'feather,' Saliba *pule* 'hair,' Kandoshi *poro* 'hair, feather,' Chamacoco *ilepori* ~ *lapole* 'feather,' Yaruro *puru* 'feather,' Otomi *päro* 'head hair,' Arawak *bala* ~ *bara* 'hair, feather,' Wayana *ipot* 'feather,' Jaricuna *ipo* 'feather,' Roucouyenne *ïpotï* 'hair,' Cumanagote *ipotú* 'hair,' Aparai *ipoté* 'hair,' Waiwai *ke-poče* 'hair,' Chayma *ipot* ~ *ibot* 'hair,' Tamanaco *čipoti* 'hair,' Yabarana *čipotti* 'hair,' Apiaca *ire-put* 'hair,' Umana *putuhali* 'hair,' Urukuena *potuba* 'hair,' Witoto *ifote-say* 'hair,' Nonuya *ofotar(a)* 'hair,' Orejones *hupodiki* 'hair,' Galibi *apollire* 'feather,' Pavishana *ampulu* 'feather,' Pimenteira *uiu parü* 'feather,' *baburi* 'hair,' Ocaina *tyafóóro* 'feather,' Surinam *pērï* 'hair,' Lule *pyly* 'feather,' Moseten *beire* 'dance feather,' Cashibo *puiči* 'feather,' Chacobo *pɨʔi* 'feather,' Shipibo *puei* 'feather,' Caripuna *poe* 'feather,' Panobo *bu* 'hair,' Mayoruna *pu* 'hair,' Conibo *bu* 'hair,' Cashinawa *bô* 'hair,' Pacawara *vo* 'hair,' Pitacho *epatoy* 'hair,' *potoitan* 'feather,' Macuni *potegneinang* 'feather,' Umotina *ibotoka* 'feather,' Krenye *ipry* 'feather,' Apinage *-niabru* 'arrow feather,' Guarapuava *preia* 'feather,' Bororo *parikko* 'feather,' *bu* 'hair,' Malali *pöe* 'feather,' Came *fere* 'feather,' Tibagi *fēre* 'feather.' [N I:20; A 24, A 108, CA 45, EQ 42]

46. NOSTRATIC **p'ušʌ* 'blow,' Proto-Indo-European **peus-* 'blow,' Proto-Uralic **pušʌ-* 'blow,' Proto-Altaic **pusʌ-* 'blow' = AMERIND **putˢi* 'blow,' Oowekyala *piʔs-ḷa* 'whistle,' Santa Ana Keres *pūtˢa* 'blow,' Biloxi *pûsuh* 'blow,' Coos *pəš* 'blow,' Central Sierra Miwok *puṣēl* 'mouth,' Northern Sierra Miwok *pūče* 'mouth,' Chukchansi *pʰōsoʔ* 'blow,' Yahi *pus-* 'blow,' East Pomo

pušul 'blow,' Cocopa *p*s*ux* 'blow,' Tipai *psul* 'blow,' Kiliwa *pisil* 'blow,' Tequistlatec *fušk-* 'blow,' Comecrudo *pasekiau* 'blow,' Taos *pʰut*s*i* 'blow,' Proto-Uto-Aztecan **put*s 'blow,' Pipil *pitsa* 'blow,' Huichol *ipisiya* 'blow,' Itonama *i-pus-ne* 'blow,' Quechua *put*s*u* 'blow,' Aymara *pʰusa* 'blow,' Tehuelche *xapš* 'blow,' Cholon a-*xeposan* 'blow on the fire,' Tambe *pezu* 'blow,' Tupy o-*pežu* 'blow,' Cumanagote *y-pizma-ze* 'blow,' Yagua *pɔsató* 'blow,' Moseten *pisna* 'blow,' Amahuaca *pit*s*i* 'blow.' [IS 339; A 42, AK 26, H 17]

47. NOSTRATIC **qot'i* 'fire, set on fire,' Proto-Afro-Asiatic **ḫt'-/ḫt-* 'set on fire, catch fire,' Proto-Indo-European **Hĕt-* 'fire, hearth,' Proto-Dravidian **otʌ-* 'kindle,' Proto-Altaic **ōti* 'spark, fire,' Korean *tha* 'burn,' Gilyak *t'a* 'burn,' Proto-Eskimo **uutï-* 'burn, boil, roast,' Kuskokwim *ûtâ-* 'burn,' Aleut *ata* 'burn' = AMERIND **(ʔ)oti* 'fire; to burn,' Proto-Keresan **ʔiɾi* 'be hot,' Acoma *idi* 'fire,' Seneca *aʔta* 'fire,' Blackfoot *ototo* 'to burn' (tr.), Wiyot *ad* 'fire,' *dōw* 'burn,' Proto-California Penutian **ʔitV* 'roast,' Proto-Uto-Aztecan **ta(h)i* 'fire, to burn,' Proto-Oto-Manguean **ntah* 'warm, fever,' Paez *ot*s 'burn,' Tarascan *ete* 'burn,' Moseten *t*s*i* 'fire,' Proto-Tacanan **ti* 'fire,' Proto-Panoan **čiʔi* 'fire,' Fulnio *to* 'burn,' Caraja *hæote* ~ *eoti* 'fire.' [N 343; E BURN4; A 112, P 192]

• Illich-Svitych (1967: 352) gave the reconstruction **Hot'ʌ*.

48. NOSTRATIC **t'ä* 'this, that,' Proto-Afro-Asiatic **tʌ-* 'this' (fem.), Proto-Kartvelian **te-/ti-* 'this, that,' Proto-Indo-European **to-/te-* 'this, that,' Proto-Uralic **tä-* 'this,' Yukaghir *tiŋ* 'this,' *taŋ* 'that,' Proto-Dravidian **tā-* 'this,' Proto-Altaic **t'ä-* 'that,' Ainu *ta-p* 'this,' Kamchadal *tiʔ-n* 'this,' Chukchi *ət-lon* 'he,' *ʌt-ri* 'they,' Siberian Yupik *ta-na* 'this' = AMERIND **ta* ~ **ti* 'this, that, he[5], Stage III article,' Chumash *t-* (Stage III article), Proto-Algonquian **-t-* (fossilized article linking personal pronouns and vowel stems), Subtiaba *d-* (Stage III article), Proto-Mayan **t-* 'he,' Yupua *ti* 'this,' Tucano *toho* 'that,' Ona *ta* 'he, they,' Lule *tita* 'he,' *te* 'this,' Mataco *ta* 'that,' Cherente *ta* 'he,' Caraja *ti* 'he.' [N I:7; E G11; A G13]

49. NOSTRATIC **talHʌ* 'shoulder,' Proto-Dravidian **tōḷ* 'shoulder, upper part of the arm,' Proto-Altaic **tālu* 'shoulder, shoulder blade' = AMERIND **ta(ʔ)la* 'shoulder,' Nisqualli *talak*w 'shoulder,' Songish *t'ɛlaw* 'wing,' Musqueam *t*s*'ɛlɛʔ* 'breast,' Quileute *taɬ* 'heart,' Shawnee *telja* 'shoulder,' Achomawi *tala* 'shoulder blade,' Salinan *itaʔl* 'shoulder,' North Yana *dul* 'neck,' Xinca *taɬi* 'neck,' Ulua *salaχ* 'shoulder,' Lenca *thala* 'neck,' Tarascan *teru(-nhe-kua)* 'chest,' Chimu *altærr* 'neck,' Catio *osorro* 'throat,' Proto-Carib **mootali* 'shoulder,' Uitoto *emodo* 'back,' Yagua *namatɔ* 'shoulder.' [IS 355; A 228, AK 32, H 77, CP 30 & 131, MC 59]

---

[5] As used here, 'he' represents a third-person singular pronoun, without regard to gender.

• In the Macro-Carib forms *mo- appears to be the demonstrative discussed in No. 29 above.

50. NOSTRATIC *t'anʌ 'chop off,' Proto-Indo-European *ten- 'chop off,' Proto-Altaic *t'anu 'chop off' = AMERIND t'an 'cut,' Blackfoot no-toan 'knife,' Squamish tlač-tən 'knife,' Seshault łɛč'-tən 'knife,' Nootsack łač'-tn 'knife,' Tillamook huq-tən 'knife,' Lillooet xʷəēk-tən 'knife,' Sierra Popoluca tʌŋ 'cut down,' Jicaque t'ï 'chop,' Kiowa t'ã 'cut,' Isleta t'ē 'cut,' Towa tˢ'aʔ 'cut,' Proto-Oto-Manguean *Htaʔn 'break, cut, knife,' Viceyta tionko 'cut,' Tucano tune 'break,' Movima tan-na 'cut,' Munduruku t'ut'u 'cut,' Nomachiguenga tontimaroʔ 'cut,' Botocudo tan 'break,' Coroado tina(n) 'knife.' [IS 352; CA 23]

51. NOSTRATIC *t'ogʌ 'burn,' Proto-Afro-Asiatic *t'kʷ 'flame,' Proto-Indo-European *dhegʷh- 'burn,' Proto-Uralic *täγʌ(t) 'fire,' Proto-Altaic *t'oga 'fire,' Japanese tuk 'ignite, catch fire, burn,' tak- 'burn' (tr.), Gilyak t'uʁř 'fire' = AMERIND *t'ek'a/t'ok'a 'burn,' Shuswap t'ik 'fire,' Bella Bella t'iʔk'il 'burn,' Kwakiutl tˢexʲa 'kindle,' Lkungen čukku 'burn,' Kutenai tˢukʷ 'start a fire,' Proto-Siouan *atʰex 'burn,' Mohawk -atek- 'burn,' Huastec tek' 'cook,' Tzotzil tok'on 'cooked,' Havasupai tuka 'burn,' Coahuilteco tīxam(kō) 'burn,' Warrau doki-a 'burn,' Timucua toka 'fire,' Colorado tehe 'firewood,' Natu tika 'burn,' Shukuru itoka 'burn,' Amarakaeri taʔak 'fire.' [IS 337; E BURN3; A 54 & 251, AK 108]

52. NOSTRATIC *t'Ompʌ 'protuberant, bulging, to swell,' Proto-Uralic *tumpa 'protuberant, hill,' Cheremiss tema 'become full,' Hungarian töm/tem 'cram,' Yukaghir čumu 'all,' čemei 'finish,' Proto-Altaic *t'omp(ʌ) 'protuberant, to swell,' Old Turkish tüm- 'completely,' Manchu tome 'all,' Ainu tumak 'be humpbacked,' Korean tam (< Middle Korean tɔm-) 'all,' Japanese tom 'be rich in,' tumu 'heap,' Gilyak tam 'many,' Proto-Eskimo *tama 'all,' Aleut tamā 'all' = AMERIND *tumpa 'fill up, be full,' Cuitlatec tɨmpa 'all,' Xinca tumu 'finish,' tumuki 'all,' Warrau tobo 'full,' Allentiac topata 'be full,' Cayapa tuwa 'full,' Move debe 'enough,' Motilon tow 'all,' Tucano tubia 'stop up,' Choroti tipoi 'be full,' Tacana tupu 'it reaches,' Lule tump-s 'finish,' Cavineña tupu 'enough.' [IS 335; E ALL1; A 74, CP 83, MP 30]

53. NOSTRATIC *t'umʌ 'dark,' Proto-Afro-Asiatic *t'(w)m 'dark,' Proto-Indo-European *tem(H)- 'dark,' Proto-Uralic *tumʌ/tümʌ 'opaque, dark,' Proto-Altaic *t'umʌ- 'darkness, haze,' Korean ətu(u)m 'dark' = AMERIND *t'umak 'dark, black, night,' Nootka tum 'black, dark,' Kutenai tamoxu-intˢ 'be dark,' Yurok tˢmey 'be evening,' Keres tˢ'amištʲ 'dark,' North Sahaptin č(ə)muk 'black,' Nez Perce tsimux- 'black,' Klamath č'mog 'dark,' Yokuts čīmʔēk 'get dark,' Yaudanchi čümgutan 'black,' Wappo sumūaʔ 'evening,' Huchnom sūm 'night,' Coast Yuki sem 'night,' Chitimacha tˢ'ima 'night,'

Atakapa *tem* 'night,' Koasati *tamōxga* 'night,' Mixe *tˢoʔm* 'night,' Zoque *tsuʔ*
'night,' Sayula *tsuʔxit* 'evening,' Huastec *tˢamul* 'night,' Chimariko *himok*
'evening,' Salinan *smak'ai* 'night,' Esselen *tumas* 'dark,' Seri *iʔamok* 'night,'
Coahuilteco *čum* 'night, evening,' Jicaque *pox-tumo* 'dark,' Mono *tummuʔani-
ki* 'black,' Cora *šumoa* 'black,' Mixtec *tűű* 'black,' Amuzgo *matuma* 'evening,'
Xinca *tˢuma* 'black,' *čijmak* 'night,' Chiquimulilla *suʔmax* 'black,' Yupultepec
ts'yøma 'night,' Chibcha *suameca* 'evening,' Miskito *timia* 'night,' Ayoman
tem 'black,' Nonama *teamasi* 'black, night,' Catio *teamasi* 'night,' Araucanian
dumi 'dark,' Jaqaru *č'ama* 'nightfall,' Papury *tyum* 'night, evening,' Hubde
čomai 'dark,' Ubde-Nehern *čëmmai* 'night,' Curiariai *čęm* 'night,' Itene *tomi*
'black,' Caranga *sumči* 'dark,' Chipaya *somči* 'dark,' Callahuaya *thami* 'dark,
night,' Kulina *dzome* 'night,' Urupa *etim* 'night,' Bakairi *tamaɣeneŋ* 'black,'
Moseten *tomage* 'dark' (n.), *tomo* 'night,' Malali *aptom* 'night,' Chavante
tomanmara 'night,' Chiquito *timimi-s* 'evening.' [N I:36; E DARK3; A 76]

54. NOSTRATIC **t'upa* 'spit,' Proto-Afro-Asiatic **t(w)p* 'spit,' Proto-Kartvelian **t'ʌb-* 'spit,' Proto-Indo-European **pt(j)eu* (< **tp(j)eu-*) 'spit,' Proto-
Dravidian **tupp-* 'spit,' Proto-Altaic **t'upy-* 'spit,' Japanese *tuba(ki)* 'spittle,'
Ainu *tupe/topse* 'spit' = AMERIND **tupa* 'saliva,' Tutelo *čəpã* 'saliva,' Keres
šupɨ 'I spit,' Acoma *šúpə* 'saliva,' Laguna *šup'šup* 'spit,' Patwin *tuba* 'spit'
(v.), Choctaw *tufa* 'saliva,' Creek *tufkita* 'spit' (v.),' Koasati *tufka* 'spit' (v.),
Yucatec *tub* 'saliva,' Mam *tsup* 'saliva,' Tzotzil *tubal* 'saliva,' Quiché *č'ubinik*
'saliva,' Tewa *sóp'oh* 'saliva,' Nonama *ičituba* 'spit' (v.), Pehuenche *tufcun*
'spit' (v.), Saliba *čuva* 'saliva,' Wapishana *supit* 'spit' (v.), Urupa *çupe* 'saliva,'
Culino *nasopʰe* 'his saliva,' Witoto *tuva* 'spit' (v.), Moseten *čep* 'saliva.' [IS
354; E SPIT; AK 160]

55. NOSTRATIC **-t'ʌ* (causative), Proto-Afro-Asiatic **tʌ-/-t-* (reflexive),
Proto-Dravidian **-tt-* (causative), Proto-Uralic **-tt-/-t-* (causative, reflexive),
Yukaghir *-te-* (denominative), Proto-Altaic **-t-* (causative), Korean
-tʰi (causative), Japanese *-t* (causative), Ainu *-te* (causative), Gilyak *-d* (denominative), Chukchi *-et* (denominative), Kamchadal *t-* (causative), Eskimo
-ta/-ti (causative), Aleut *-ti* (causative) = AMERIND *t(')u* (causative), Seneca
-ʔt- (causative), Keres *-tʋ* (makes actions out of statives), Wiyot *-at* (transitivizer), Salish *-t* (transitivizer), Kutenai *-n't* (action by hand), Kwakwala *-d*
(transitivizer). [N I:13; E G49; A G92]

56. NOSTRATIC **t'ʌbʌ* 'suitable, appropriate,' Proto-Afro-Asiatic **t'jb/t'wb*
'good, fragrant,' Proto-Indo-European **dhabh-* (< **tabh-*) 'suitable, appropriate' = AMERIND **tˢ'upa* 'good,' ?Nisqualli *tlob* 'good,' San Juan Bautista
tappan 'good,' Yana *tˢ'up'* 'be good,' Salinan *tˢ'ep* 'good,' Coahuilteco *sap'ān*
'good,' Eten *tˢup* 'good,' Guambiana *tabig* 'good,' Nadobo *čabe* 'good,' Coche
čaba 'good,' Trumai *tˢipom* 'good,' Manao *sabi* 'good.' [IS 355; A 131]

57. NOSTRATIC *ʔejʌ 'come, go,' Proto-Afro-Asiatic *'j 'come,' Proto-Indo-European *ĥei- 'go,' Proto-Ugric *je(γ)- 'come,' Proto-Dravidian *ej- 'arrive, approach,' Proto-Altaic *ī- 'arrive, enter' = AMERIND *jaʔ 'go, come,' Proto-Central Algonquian *jā 'go,' Upper Chehalis ja 'road,' Catawba jã 'road,' Wishram ja 'go,' Choctaw ia 'go,' Alsea jax 'go,' Tsimshian jē 'go,' Wappo -ja- 'go,' Karankawa je 'go,' Tonkawa jaʔa 'several move,' Washo ijeʔ 'he goes,' Yana aja 'go,' Proto-Aztec-Tanoan *ja 'to go, carry,' Proto-Oto-Manguean *(n)ja(n) 'road,' Motilon ja 'walk,' Timucua eje 'road,' Chibcha ie 'road.' [N 130; E GO; A 128]

• In Illich-Svitych (1967: 357) the reconstruction was given as *je(Hʌ).

58. NOSTRATIC *ʔi/ʔe 'this, he,' Proto-Afro-Asiatic *j 'this, he,' Proto-Kartvelian *(h)i/(h)e 'that,' Proto-Indo-European *ĥei-/ĥe- 'this, he,' Proto-Uralic *i-/e- 'this,' Proto-Dravidian *ī/ē 'this,' Proto-Altaic *i-/e- 'this, he,' Korean i 'this,' Japanese i-ma 'now,' Ainu i- 'his, him,' Gilyak i/e- 'his, him' = AMERIND *(ʔ)i 'he, this, the,' Chinantec ʔi 'he,' Tewa ʔiʔ 'he,' Mono ʔi-hi 'this,' Borunca i ~ iæ 'he,' j- 'his,' Lenca i(-na) 'he,' i- (indef. obj.), Cuna i- (indef. obj.), Bribri i- (indef. obj.), Chiquito i- 'his,' Kraho iʔ- 'his,' Guarani i- 'he, his.' [N I:8; E G8; A G12]

REFERENCES

Barbujani, Guido, and Robert R. Sokal. 1990. "Zones of Sharp Genetic Change in Europe Are Also Linguistic Boundaries," *Proceedings of the National Academy of Sciences* 87: 1816–19.

Bengtson, John D. 1991a. "Notes on Sino-Caucasian," in Shevoroshkin, ed., 1991: 67–129.

——. 1991b. "Some Macro-Caucasian Etymologies," in Shevoroshkin, ed., 1991: 130–41.

Bengtson, John D., and Merritt Ruhlen. 1992. "Global Etymologies," Chapter 14 of this volume.

Bomhard, Allan. 1984. *Toward Proto-Nostratic.* Amsterdam.

——. 1991. "Lexical Parallels Between Proto-Indo-European and Other Languages," in L. Isebaert, ed., *Studia Etymologica Indoeuropaea.* Leuven, Belgium, 47–106.

Bouda, Karl. 1960–64. "Tungusisch und Ketschua," *Zeitschrift der Deutschen Morgenländischen Gesellschaft,* in two parts, 110: 99–113, 113: 602–23.

Bright, William. 1974. "North American Indian Languages," *Encyclopaedia Britannica,* 15th ed., Vol. 13: 208–13.

Bynon, Theodora. 1977. *Historical Linguistics.* Cambridge, Eng.

Campbell, Lyle. 1986. "Comment," *Current Anthropology* 27: 488.

——. 1988. Review of *Language in the Americas,* by Joseph H. Greenberg, *Language* 64: 591–615.

Campbell, Lyle, and Marianne Mithun, eds. 1979. *The Languages of Native America: Historical and Comparative Assessment.* Austin, Tex.

Cavalli-Sforza, L. L., Alberto Piazza, and Paolo Menozzi. 1994. *History and Geography of Human Genes.* Princeton, N.J.

Cavalli-Sforza, L. L., Alberto Piazza, Paolo Menozzi, and Joanna Mountain. 1988. "Reconstruction of Human Evolution: Bringing Together Genetic, Archeological and Linguistic Data," *Proceedings of the National Academy of Sciences* 85: 6002–6.

Diamond, Jared. 1992. *The Third Chimpanzee.* New York.

Dolgopolsky, Aron B. 1964. "Gipoteza drevnejšego rodstva jazykovyx semei severnoj Eurasii s verojatnostnoj točki zrenija," *Voprosy Jazykoznanija* 2: 53–63. [English translation in Vitalij V. Shevoroshkin and T. L. Markey, eds., *Typology, Relationship and Time,* 1986. Ann Arbor, Mich., 27–50.]

———. 1969. "Nostratičeskie osnovy s sočetaniem šumnyx soglasnyx," *Etimologija 1967* (Moscow), 296–313.

———. 1971. "Nostratičeskie etimologii i proisxoždenie glagol'nyx formantov," *Etimologija 1968* (Moscow), 237–42.

———. 1972. "Nostratičeskie korni s sočetaniem lateral'nogo i zvonkogo laringala," *Etimologija 1970* (Moscow), 356–69.

———. 1974. "O nostratičeskoj sisteme affrikat i sibiljantov: korni s fonemoj *ȝ,*" *Etimologija 1972* (Moscow), 163–75.

———. 1984. "On Personal Pronouns in the Nostratic Languages," in Otto Gschwantler, Károly Rédei, and Hermann Reichert, eds., *Linguistica et Philologica.* Vienna, 65–112.

Excoffier, Laurent, Béatrice Pellegrini, Alicia Sanchez-Mazas, Christian Simon, and André Langaney. 1987. "Genetics and History of Sub-Saharan Africa," *Yearbook of Physical Anthropology* 30: 151–94.

Golla, Victor, ed. 1984. *The Sapir-Kroeber Correspondence.* Berkeley, Calif.

Gould, Stephen Jay. 1989. "Grimm's Greatest Tale," *Natural History* 2: 20–25.

Greenberg, Joseph H. 1963. *The Languages of Africa.* Bloomington, Ind.

———. 1981. "Comparative Amerindian Notebooks," 23 vols. Mss. on file, Green Library, Stanford University, Stanford, Calif.

———. 1987. *Language in the Americas.* Stanford, Calif.

———. 1989. "Classification of American Indian Languages: A Reply to Campbell," *Language* 65: 107–14.

———. To appear. *Indo-European and Its Closest Relatives: The Eurasiatic Language Family.* Stanford, Calif.

Greenberg, Joseph H., Christy G. Turner II, and Stephen L. Zegura. 1986. "The Settlement of the Americas: A Comparison of Linguistic, Dental, and Genetic Evidence," *Current Anthropology* 27: 477–97.

Illich-Svitych, Vladislav M. 1967. "Materialy k sravnitel'nomu slovarju nostratičeskix jazykov," *Etimologija 1965* (Moscow), 321–96.

———. 1971–84. *Opyt sravnenija nostratičeskix jazykov,* 3 vols. Moscow.

Jefferson, Thomas. 1904. *The Writings of Thomas Jefferson,* Vol. 7. Washington, D.C.

Nikolaev, Sergei. 1991. "Sino-Caucasian Languages in America," in Shevoroshkin, ed., 1991: 42–66.

Ruhlen, Merritt. 1987. *A Guide to the World's Languages,* Vol. 1: Classification. Stanford, Calif.

———. 1989. "Nostratic-Amerind Cognates," in Vitaly Shevoroshkin, ed., *Reconstructing Languages and Cultures.* Bochum, Germany, 75–83.

———. 1990. "Phylogenetic Relations of Native American Languages," in *Prehistoric Mongoloid Dispersals* (Tokyo) 7: 75–96.

Shevoroshkin, Vitaly, ed. 1991. *Dene-Sino-Caucasian Languages.* Bochum, Germany.

Starostin, Sergei A. 1984. "Gipoteza o genetičeskix svjazjax sinotibetskix jazykov s enisejskimi i severnokavkazskimi jazykami," *Lingvističeskaja rekonstruktsija i drevnejšaja istorija vostoka* (Moscow) 4: 19–38.

———. 1989. "Nostratic and Sino-Caucasian," in Vitaly Shevoroshkin, ed., *Explorations in Language Macrofamilies.* Bochum, Germany, 42–66.

Swadesh, Morris. 1960. "On Interhemisphere Linguistic Connections," in Stanley Diamond, ed., *Culture and History: Essays in Honor of Paul Radin.* New York, 894–924.

Sweet, Henry. 1901. *The History of Language.* London.

Thomason, Sarah G. To appear. "Hypothesis Generation vs. Hypothesis Testing: A Comparison Between Greenberg's Classifications in Africa and in the Americas," in Allan R. Taylor, ed., *Language and Prehistory in the Americas.* Stanford, Calif.

Trombetti, Alfredo. 1905. *L'unità d'origine del linguaggio.* Bologna.

11

Amerind MALIQ'A 'Swallow, Throat' and Its Origin in the Old World

For Joseph H. Greenberg,
on the occasion
of his 75th birthday,
May 28, 1990

Probably the central myth of twentieth-century historical linguistics has been the belief that the comparative method is limited to a relatively short time depth—usually put at 5,000–10,000 years—beyond which all trace of genetic affinity has been erased by unrelenting waves of semantic and phonological change.* According to R. M. W. Dixon (1980: 237), "Generally, languages change at such a rate that after more than about three or four thousand years of separation genetic links are no longer recognizable." James Matisoff puts the boundary at 6,000 years (Matisoff 1990: 108), Hans Hock (1986: 566) opts for 7,000 years, and Terrence Kaufman (1990: 23) would extend the limits to around 8,000 years: "A temporal ceiling of 7,000 to 8,000 years is inherent in the methods of comparative linguistic reconstruction. We can recover genetic relationships that are that old, but probably no earlier than that." Finally, according to Sarah Thomason (to appear), "10,000 years is the standard guess about the outer limits of the applicability of the Comparative Method." Although one can only admire the precision these scholars have brought to determining the limits of comparative linguistics, one may legitimately ask what is the basis for this dating, whichever figure one chooses. Though I be-

---

* I would like to thank Lionel Bender, John Bengtson, Allan Bomhard, Dell Hymes, Joseph Greenberg, Vitaly Shevoroshkin, and William S.-Y. Wang for comments on an earlier version of this chapter.

lieve Thomason is correct—the figures are all just guesses—what exactly are these guesses based on? And why do such "guesses" range from 3,000–10,000 years, and not, say 40,000–50,000 years?

The main reason, I believe, is the *presumed* age of the Indo-European family itself, which has traditionally been put very close to these stated limits of the validity of comparative linguistics. Thus the fact that Indo-European cannot be shown to be related to any other family—yet another cherished myth—both establishes, and is "explained" by, the known limits of the comparative method in linguistics. This same (transparently circular) reasoning has been used by Americanists to argue that Joseph Greenberg's proposal of an Amerind family cannot be valid, because archaeologists agree that the Americas have been inhabited for more than 10,000 years, and the comparative method is valid only up to about 10,000 years, or, as Kaufman (1990: 26) puts it, "the proof of a common origin for the indigenous languages of this hemisphere is not accessible to the comparative method as we know it." All of these arguments, it must be stressed, are based on appeals to *archaeology*; no *linguistic* evidence points to *any* particular limits on the comparative method.

There is yet another "archaeological" argument for the limits of comparative linguistics, namely, the fact that there are no perceived connections between Old World languages and New World languages. Since the Americas are known through archaeological evidence to have been initially inhabited at least 12,000 years ago—and some anthropologists today would say 18,000 years or more—clearly no similarities between Old World languages and New World languages *could* survive after all this time, given what is "known" of the limits of the comparative method. In sum, the postulated "limits" of the comparative method have been determined by the "special status" of Indo-European, a family supposedly with no known relatives, and by the "archaeological evidence" showing that the peopling of the Americas occurred at too early a date for comparative linguistics to be of any value.

Such a tight fit between the archaeological evidence and the linguistic evidence could hardly have been anticipated. But *is* it really a tight fit, or just a gentleman's agreement? With regard to the age of Indo-European, the archaeologist Colin Renfrew (1987: 166) has recently written that "the dispersal [of Indo-European-speaking people] is thus set around 2500 B.C. This date is not based on any clear linguistic argument; it is not really a linguistic argument at all. It is a conclusion based upon consensus. Yet it is taken by archaeologists as linguistic evidence, and is used by them to support that very consensus. There is therefore a complete circularity. And in this case it would appear that the consensus may be in error." But if the age of Indo-European is in error, then the perceived limitations of the comparative method may also be in error.

In fact, the idea that Indo-European is unrelated to any other family has been demonstrated to be false by the Russian Nostraticists (Illich-Svitych 1971–84, Dolgopolsky 1984), by Greenberg (to appear), and by numerous precursors, and such an extreme position has in recent years been declining in acceptance. Of course the finding that Indo-European is related to other families is scarcely a new discovery. At the beginning of this century Henry Sweet (quoted at length in Chapter 6 herein) ridiculed the narrow-mindedness of Indo-Europeanists in doubting these relationships, in terms that, regrettably, are as apt today as they were then.

And around that same time Alfredo Trombetti (1905: 44) criticized the methodological inconsistency of the Indo-Europeanists in equally stark terms: "It is clear that in and of itself the comparison of Finno-Ugric *me* 'I,' *te* 'you' with Indo-European *me-* and *te-* [with the same meaning] is worth just as much as any comparison one might make between the corresponding pronominal forms in the Indo-European languages. The only difference is that the common origin of the Indo-European languages is accepted, while the connection between Indo-European and Finno-Ugric is denied."

In what follows I will argue that all of these notions—that Indo-European is not known to be related to any other language family, that Amerind languages cannot be shown to derive from a common source, and that there are no recognizable genetic connections between language families of the Old and New Worlds—are false. By examining a single etymology in some detail I will attempt to show that it is indeed possible to trace the evolution of a single root from North Africa, through Europe and Asia, and across the Americas. Let us begin by considering the following Amerind etymology for the root *MALIQ'A 'swallow, throat':

AN AMERIND ETYMOLOGY

ALMOSAN: Salish: Proto-Salish *məq' 'eat one's fill,' Chehalis *mq'ʷ* 'swallow,' Lower Fraser *məlqʷ* 'throat,' Pentlach *məkwəm* 'swallow,' Nisqualli *omikalekw* 'swallow,' Columbian *məlq ~ enmellik* 'tongue'; Wakashan: Nootka *m̉ukʷ* 'swallow,' Kwakwala *m̉lχʷ-ʔid* 'chew food for the baby,' *m̉lqʷa* 'moisten the fingers with the tongue,' Heiltsuk *m̉elqva* 'chew food for baby,' *m̉elχv-baút* 'lick the end of something,'; Algic: Yurok *mik'olum* 'swallow'; Kutenai *uʔmqoł* 'swallow.'

PENUTIAN: Chinook: Chinook *-mṓkuī-* 'throat,' *mlqʷ-tan* 'cheek,' Wishram *ō-mēqλ* 'lick'; Oregon: Takelma *mülk'* 'swallow,' Proto-Kalapuya *mílk* 'swallow' (v.), Tualatin *mílk ~ mílq* 'swallow,' *mílk'-wan* 'swallow,' Santiam *mílk* 'swallow,' Yonkala *k'andít-mílik* 'I swallowed it'; Plateau: North Sahaptin *malqmat* 'lick,' Molala *mil* 'throat'; California: Yokuts *mōk'i* 'swallow,' *mik'-is* 'throat,' Yaudanchi *mök* 'swallow,' *müküs* 'throat'; Gulf: Proto-Muskogean **mil* 'swallow,' Tunica *milu* 'choke,' *miru* 'swallow,' Atakapa *mol* 'gargle,' Wappo *malék'eʔ* 'swallow it,' Coast Yuki *mekup* 'throat,' Huchnom *meka* 'drink,' Yuki *mi* 'drink'; Mexican: Mixe *amuʔul* 'suck,' Zoque *muʔk* 'suck.'

HOKAN: Chumash: Santa Ynez *aqmil* 'drink' (? = *aq-mil* 'water-swallow'), Santa Cruz *akmil* 'drink'; Yuman: Yuma *malʲaqé* 'neck,' Walapai *malqi'* 'throat, neck,' Havasupai *milqé* 'throat,' Yavapai *melqí* 'neck,' Mohave *malʲaqé* 'throat,' Akwa'ala *milqí* 'neck,' Paipai *milqí* 'neck' (cf. also the obviously related Yuman forms where the initial nasal has assimilated the palatal nature of the following lateral: Yuma *anʲīlʲq* 'swallow,' Walapai *mi-nʲalq* 'swallow,' Diegueño *we-nʲaɬq* 'swallow,' Havasupai *kʷe-nʲálqika* 'swallow,' Akwa'ala *nʲelq* 'swallow,' etc.); ?Tlappanec *māga'ŋqɔ'* 'swallow.'

CHIBCHAN: Cuitlatec *eʔmeli* 'eat,' Cuna *murki-makka* 'swallow,' *murgi murgi sae* 'swallow food.'

ANDEAN: Quechuan: Cochabamba *malq'a* 'throat,' Huaraz *mallaqa* 'be hungry'; Aymara *maλq'a* 'swallow, throat' (probably a borrowing from Quechua); ? Cholon *amok* 'eat.'

MACRO-TUCANOAN: Curetu *mouku* 'drink,' Ticuna *mi* 'drink,' Iranshe *mokeʔi* 'neck.'

EQUATORIAL: Guamo *mirko* 'drink,' Arawak *amüküddun* 'swallow,' Callahuaya *maλk'a* 'throat' (almost certainly a loan from Quechua or Aymara).

MACRO-CARIB: Surinam *eʔmökï* 'swallow,' Faai *mekeli* 'nape of the neck,' Kaliana *imukulali* 'throat.'

One of the Penutian etymologies proposed by Greenberg (1987: 159) connected the Oregon and Gulf (excluding Yuki-Wappo) forms listed above in an etymology glossed 'swallow.' If the triconsonantal root of the Northwest Coast Penutian languages is archaic, then the original form might be reconstructed as **M-L-K'* (or **M-L-Q'*, if the uvular consonant is original). Furthermore, one of the Amerind etymologies proposed by Greenberg (No. 252), also glossed 'swallow,' connected some of the Almosan forms shown above (Pentlach, Nisquali, Yurok, and Kutenai) with certain Penutian forms (Chinook, Yokuts, Coast Yuki, Huchnom). Some of the Almosan forms (Kutenai, Yurok, Nisqualli) also suggest a triconsonantal root that might be reconstructed as **M-K'-L* or **M-Q'-L*, while the Wakashan forms retain the original order of the consonants, also preserved in Penutian. Given the virtual semantic identity of all these forms—and the fact that they appear to be based on a triconsonantal root that has metathesized the final two consonants in some Amerind subgroups—it seems more than likely that all these forms are historically related and should be joined in a single etymology.

Additional material taken from Greenberg's unpublished Amerindian note-books (Greenberg 1981) provides further support for the Amerind nature of the root in question. Of prime importance is the existence of the root in the Yuman branch of Hokan (Arizona) and the Quechuan (and perhaps Aymara[1]) branch of Andean (Peru, Ecuador, Bolivia). In Yuman the root is *M-L-K or *M-L-Q, whereas in Quechuan it is *M-L-Q' or *M-L-Q. Moreover, Cuna (a Chibchan language spoken in Panama) and Guamo (an Equatorial language of Venezuela) both exhibit the form *M-R-K. In the broader Amerind context we can see clearly that metathesis has occurred sporadically in Almosan and Macro-Carib, but the original order, *M-L-K', is too widely attested within Amerind to be doubted.

THE ORIGIN OF THE AMERIND ROOT

There are, moreover, indications that this particular root is not restricted to the Americas, but exists in Eurasia and perhaps North Africa as well. Illich-Svitych (1976: 57) reconstructed Proto-Nostratic *mälgi 'chest, udder' on the basis of Afro-Asiatic, Indo-European, and Uralic evidence. For Afro-Asiatic he posited *mlg 'breast, udder, suck' to account for Arabic mlğ 'to suck the breast' and Old Egyptian mnḏ (< *mlg) 'woman's breast, udder.' Illich-Svitych compared these forms with Proto-Indo-European *melĝ- 'to milk' and Proto-Uralic *mälɣe 'breast, thorax.' Rédei (1986: 267) suggests a slightly dif-ferent reconstruction, Proto-Finno-Ugric *mälke 'breast,' representing forms like Saami mielgâ 'breast, chest,' Mordvin mälhkä 'breast,' Vogul mägl 'breast' (with metathesis), and Hungarian mell 'breast.' Collinder (1977: 14) and Rédei (1986: 267) consider all these (and other) forms to be related. Further-more, both Collinder and Rédei suggest that Yukaghir melu(t) 'chest' may be related to the Uralic forms.

The Indo-European root is particularly interesting, for it illustrates how the failure of Indo-Europeanists to consider the extra-Indo-European context has led them to erroneous conclusions concerning both the semantic develop-ment and the phonological structure of Indo-European itself. The traditional reconstruction by Pokorny (1959: 722), *melĝ- 'to milk, milk' reflects forms such as Greek ἀμέλγω 'to milk,' Latin mulg-ēre 'to milk,' Irish bligim 'to milk,' mlicht 'milk,' Gothic miluks 'milk,' Old Norse mjolka 'to milk,' En-glish 'to milk, milk,' Lithuanian milžti 'to milk,' Old Church Slavic mlěsti 'to milk,' mlěko 'milk,' Albanian mjellë 'to milk,' Tocharian A mālk-lune 'milk-ing,' malke 'milk,' and Tocharian B malk-wer 'milk,' as well as Sanskrit mṛj-'wipe, stroke,' and Avestan marəz- 'touch.'

---

[1] The difficulties of distinguishing loanwords from common inheritance (or determining even the direction of loans) with regard to Quechua and Aymara are notorious.

The traditional explanation for the semantic development of this root has been that the Indo-Iranian meaning—'to wipe, stroke, rub'—was the original one, and that the development of RUB > MILK was an innovation characterizing European languages (Walde and Pokorny 1930, 2: 298). The extra-Indo-European context shows quite clearly that this semantic development—if it took place at all—worked in the opposite direction, since it is now clear that the Indo-European notion of 'milking' derives from the general Eurasiatic/Nostratic word for nursing, suckling, and the female breast. Any connection with rubbing and wiping must be thoroughly secondary. In fact, I am inclined to doubt, as did Illich-Svitych (1976: 58) and Gamkrelidze and Ivanov (1984: 569), that the Indo-Iranian root *marź- 'to rub, wipe' has anything at all to do with Proto-Indo-European *melĝ- 'to milk.'

In his discussion of this etymology Illich-Svitych (1976) notes that "Proto-Indo-European ĝ in place of the expected ĝh is unclear" (p. 58). The reason ĝh is expected, rather than ĝ, is that, according to Nostratic sound correspondences, Proto-Indo-European ĝ derives from Proto-Nostratic k, not from Proto-Nostratic g, which Illich-Svitych reconstructs for this root. It has long been known that the traditional reconstruction of the Proto-Indo-European stop system—with the three series k, g, and gh—is typologically implausible; such systems are not found in any existing languages. In order to remedy this (and other) problems with the traditional reconstruction, Thomas Gamkrelidze and Vyacheslav Ivanov (1972) and Paul Hopper (1973) independently arrived at the same solution to these problems. They proposed that the three series of Proto-Indo-European stops be reinterpreted as k, k', and g. Recently Allan Bomhard (1984, 1991) has begun investigating Nostratic using the glottalic interpretation of the Proto-Indo-European consonantism. According to the glottalic theory the Proto-Indo-European root under discussion should be reconstructed as *melk̂'- (Gamkrelidze and Ivanov 1984: 569), whose velar ejective perfectly matches that of the Amerind forms enumerated above. When considered in the wider context—and in the light of the glottalic theory of Proto-Indo-European consonantism—the "unexpected" ĝ of *melĝ- becomes the expected k̂' of melk̂'-.

There is additional evidence in Dravidian for the root in question. Burrow and Emeneau (1984: 459) group all of the following forms under etymology No. 5077: Tamil melku 'to chew, masticate,' Malayalam melluka 'to chew, champ,' Toda melk 'mouthful,' Kannada mellu 'to chew, masticate, eat with a muttering sound,' melaku 'bringing up again for rumination,' Telugu mekku 'to eat, gobble,' Gadba mekkap- 'to eat like a glutton.' The original meaning of 'nurse, suckle' appears lurking just below the surface in all these forms. Conspicuously absent from this etymology are any reflexes in the Kurux-Malto subgroup, generally regarded as the most divergent branch of Dravidian after the Brahui language of Pakistan. Yet there is another etymology in Burrow and Emeneau's dictionary, No. 5080, that I believe should be combined with the forms cited above: Kurux *melkhā* 'throat, neck' and Malto *melqe* 'throat.' It would appear that the Kurux-Malto branch has undergone a semantic shift typologically parallel to that which took place in Amerind.

There are also reflexes of this root in the Eskimo-Aleut family, which some Nostraticists include in Nostratic (Dolgopolsky 1984) and which Greenberg includes in his similar, but not identical, Eurasiatic family.[2] For example, in the Kuskokwim dialect of Central Yupik we find forms such as *milugâ* 'sucks it out,' *milûgarâ* 'licks (or sucks) it; kisses it (a child),' and *mulik* 'nipple'; similar forms may be found in the various Inupiaq dialects scattered from northern Alaska to Greenland. Aleut *umlix* 'chest, groin' probably also belongs with the Eskimo forms given above. As with the Dravidian forms, the notion of nursing a child is but a step away from the common Eskimo meanings.

On the other side of Bering Strait the Chukchi-Kamchatkan family has a root that might belong with the etymology under discussion in Proto-Chukchi-Kamchatkan *pilxə-* 'throat, food' (Mudrak 1989: 104), though the change $m > p$ is for the moment unexplained.

Finally, we should note that in their reconstruction of Proto-Caucasian, Nikolaev and Starostin (1992: 142) posit a root *$m\underline{V}q'\underline{V}lV$ 'throat, larynx' to account for forms such as Tindi *maq̄'ala* 'throat' and Bezhta *ris-muq* 'throat.' Since Caucasian is a family renowned for metathesis, it seems likely that the Proto-Caucasian form represents a metathesized form of the root discussed here.

CONCLUSIONS

The foregoing has traced the evolution of a single verbal root through a large number of supposedly "unrelated" families. We might reconstruct the original form and meaning of this root as *M-L-K* 'nurse, suckle, female breast.' Phonologically, the triconsonantal nature of the root is preserved in Afro-Asiatic, Caucasian, Indo-European, Uralic, Dravidian, Eskimo-Aleut, and Amerind. Afro-Asiatic preserves the original meaning, which has taken on slightly different connotations elsewhere. In Indo-European the meaning shifted from 'nursing' to 'milking' and, finally, in only a few branches, the product itself, 'milk.' In Uralic the meaning of 'breast' persists, but the verbal notion of 'nursing' has been lost. Both Dravidian and Eskimo-Aleut present

---

[2] For the differences between Nostratic and Eurasiatic—and the origin of these differences—see Chapter 1 and Chapter 10. Greenberg (to appear) posits a root under BREAST that encompasses the Indo-European, Uralic, and Eskimo-Aleut forms discussed here.

meanings only a shade different from nursing. In Dravidian the meaning is basically 'chew, eat (like a baby),' while in Eskimo-Aleut it is 'suck, lick, kiss, nipple.' A semantic innovation in Amerind characterizes the entire family, and at the same time distinguishes it from Eurasiatic/Nostratic: in Amerind the root lost all connotation of nursing (except in Wakashan?), becoming instead the general Amerind word for 'swallow' and 'throat.' A typologically similar development also occurred in Caucasian, if the root discussed above is truly cognate with the other forms.

As is well known, similarities in sound and meaning may have one of four explanations: onomatopoeia, chance, borrowing, or common origin (Greenberg 1957). I am aware of no suggestions in the linguistic literature that there is any intrinsic connection between the sounds and meanings discussed here. Furthermore, the fact that the root is found only in Amerind and Eurasiatic/Nostratic (and perhaps Caucasian) argues against an onomatopoeic explanation, as does the fact that the meaning varies slightly from family to family in semantically natural ways.

The role that chance resemblance plays in causing such similarities has been much bandied about by Greenberg's critics, who greatly exaggerate the frequency of this phenomenon. Many have offered their favorite chance resemblance, but all are invariably *binary* comparisons of *biconsonantal* roots. I have chosen to investigate a triconsonantal root that is found in no less than six "unrelated" families from Africa to the Americas for the simple reason that an explanation of chance is virtually ruled out from the start. (For more on the notion of chance resemblance, see Chapter 14 herein.)

As early as 1957 Greenberg emphasized that "while in particular and infrequent instances the question of borrowing may be doubtful, it is always possible to tell whether a mass of resemblances between two languages is the result of borrowing" (Greenberg 1957: 39), the two most important factors being outgroup comparison and the semantic nature of the borrowed items. In the present case the vast distribution of the root—which is also a part of the fundamental vocabulary, not a culture item easily borrowed—precludes any serious consideration of borrowing.

With all other possible explanations eliminated, we may conclude that we are here dealing with a case of common origin. There is no other sensible explanation for the facts outlined. Nor should one imagine that the lexical item discussed above is an isolated example. Recent work has shown, contrary to the cherished myths of many twentieth-century linguists, that there are *numerous* genetic connections between supposedly unrelated language families, if one is willing to take off the blinders (a summary of this work is given in Chapter 1). In particular, the resemblances between Amerind and Eurasiatic/Nostratic, above and beyond the etymology discussed in this paper, are abundant (see Chapters 10 and 14), and the linguistic family thus defined corresponds very closely to the vast North African–North Eurasian–Amerind population defined by Cavalli-Sforza et al. (1988) on the basis of the distribution of human genes.

REFERENCES

Bomhard, Allan. 1984. *Toward Proto-Nostratic.* Amsterdam.

——. 1991. "Lexical Parallels Between Proto-Indo-European and Other Languages," in L. Isebaert, ed., *Studia Etymologica Indoeuropaea.* Leuven, Belgium, 47–106.

Burrow, Thomas, and Murray B. Emeneau. 1984. *A Dravidian Etymological Dictionary.* Oxford, Eng.

Cavalli-Sforza, L. L., Alberto Piazza, Paolo Menozzi, and Joanna Mountain. 1988. "Reconstruction of Human Evolution: Bringing Together Genetic, Archeological and Linguistic Data," *Proceedings of the National Academy of Sciences* 85: 6002–6.

Collinder, Björn. 1977. *Fenno-Ugric Vocabulary.* Hamburg.

Dixon, R. M. W. 1980. *The Languages of Australia.* Cambridge, Eng.

Dolgopolsky, Aron. 1984. "On Personal Pronouns in the Nostratic Languages," in Otto Gschwantler, Károly Rédei, and Hermann Reichert, eds., *Linguistica et Philologica.* Vienna, 65–112.

Gamkrelidze, Thomas V., and Vyacheslav V. Ivanov. 1972. "Lingvisticheskaja tipologija i rekonstruktsija sistemy indoevropejskix smychnyx," *Konferentsija po sravnitel'no-istoricheskoj grammatike indoevropejskix jazykov,* Moscow, 15–8.

——. 1984. *Indoevropejskij jazyk i indoevropejtsy,* 2 vols. Tbilisi, Georgia.

Greenberg, Joseph H. 1957. "Genetic Relationship among Languages," in Joseph H. Greenberg, *Essays in Linguistics.* Chicago, 35–45.

——. 1981. "Comparative Amerindian Notebooks," 23 vols. Mss. on file, Green Library, Stanford University, Stanford, Calif.

——. 1987. *Language in the Americas.* Stanford, Calif.

——. To appear. *Indo-European and Its Closest Relatives: The Eurasiatic Family.* Stanford, Calif.

Hock, Hans Henrich. 1986. *Principles of Historical Linguistics.* Berlin.

Hopper, Paul. 1973. "Glottalized and Murmured Occlusives in Indo-European," *Glotta* 7: 141–66.

Illich-Svitych, Vladislav M. 1971–84. *Opyt sravnenija nostraticheskix jazykov,* 3 vols. Moscow.

Kaufman, Terrence. 1990. "Language History in South America: What We Know and How to Know More," in Doris L. Payne, ed., *Amazonian Linguistics*. Austin, Tex., 13–73.

Matisoff, James A. 1990. "On Megalocomparison," *Language* 66: 106–20.

Mudrak, Oleg. 1989. "Kamchukchee Roots," in Vitaly Shevoroshkin, ed., *Explorations in Language Macrofamilies*. Bochum, Germany, 90–110.

Nikolaev, Sergei L., and Sergei A. Starostin. 1992. "A Caucasian Etymological Dictionary," ms.

Pokorny, Julius. 1959. *Indogermanisches etymologisches Wörterbuch*. Bern.

Rédei, Károly, ed. 1986– . *Uralisches etymologisches Wörterbuch*. Budapest.

Renfrew, Colin. 1987. *Archaeology and Language: The Puzzle of Indo-European Origins*. Cambridge, Eng.

Ruhlen, Merritt. 1992a. "An Overview of Genetic Classification," in John A. Hawkins and Murray Gell-Mann, eds., *The Evolution of Human Languages*. Redwood City, Calif., 159–89. [A revised version appears as Chapter 1 of this volume.]

——. 1992b. "Linguistic Origins of Native Americans," Chapter 10 of this volume.

——. 1992c. "The Origin of Language: Retrospective and Prospective," Chapter 13 of this volume.

Sweet, Henry. 1901. *The History of Language*. London.

Thomason, Sarah Grey. To appear. "Hypothesis Generation vs. Hypothesis Testing: A Comparison Between Greenberg's Classifications in Africa and in the Americas," in Allan R. Taylor, ed., *Language and Prehistory in the Americas*. Stanford, Calif.

Trombetti, Alfredo. 1905. *L'unità d'origine del linguaggio*. Bologna.

Walde, Alois, and Julius Pokorny. 1930. *Vergleichendes Wörterbuch der indogermanischen Sprachen*. Berlin.

12

First- and Second-Person Pronouns in the World's Languages

It has long been known that first- and second-person singular pronouns are among the most stable meanings in language. Of the two, Aron Dolgopolsky (1986: 34) found that the first-person pronoun is the most stable meaning, and the second-person pronoun the third most stable. An immediate consequence of this stability has been the recognition by some linguists that pronouns are often indicative of deeper genetic connections. As we have seen elsewhere in this volume, both Henry Sweet and Alfredo Trombetti objected that the M/T 'I/you (sg.)' pronominal pattern, which is considered characteristic of Indo-European by all Indo-Europeanists, also occurs in neighboring families such as Uralic, Mongolian, Tungus, Gilyak, Chukchi-Kamchatkan, and Eskimo-Aleut. One (but not both) of these pronouns also occurs in Kartvelian, Turkic, Korean, and (Old) Japanese. This larger grouping, embracing all these groups and others, is defined essentially by the M/T pronominal pattern (though there is abundant additional evidence—grammatical and lexical—to confirm this initial conclusion), and it is the family called Eurasiatic by Joseph Greenberg and Nostratic by Russian scholars (and their non-Russian disciples). Pronouns have thus played a crucial role in debunking the myth of Indo-European's splendid isolation.

At the same time, pronouns have also been a central focus in the recent debate between Greenberg and his critics over the validity of Amerind (see Chapter 1). Greenberg (1987) claimed that the N/M 'I/you (sg.)' pronominal pattern—which had been previously noted by Trombetti, Edward Sapir, Morris Swadesh, and others—characterizes the Amerind family, and he presented evidence for this pattern from all eleven Amerind subgroups. In fact, a genetic explanation of this pattern was advocated as early as 1905, by Trombetti: "As can be seen, from the most northern regions of the Americas the pronouns NI 'I' and M 'thou' reach all the way to the southern tip of the New World, to Tierra del Fuego. Although this sketch is far from complete, due to the insufficient materials at our disposal, it is certainly sufficient to give an idea of the broad distribution of these most ancient and essential elements" (p. 208). A decade later Sapir too (1918; quoted in Darnell and Sherzer 1971: 27) was startled to find these two pronouns throughout the Americas, remarking, "Getting down to brass tacks, how in the Hell are you going to explain general American *n-* 'I' except genetically? It's disturbing, I know, but (more) non-committal conservatism is only dodging, after all, isn't it? Great simplifications are in store for us."

A genetic explanation of the N/M pronominal pattern was anathema to Sapir's mentor, Franz Boas, who favored diffusion of linguistic elements over common origin (see Chapter 6). The pronouns were, however, troublesome, since such grammatical elements are not known to diffuse, and Boas could do no better than to attribute them to "obscure psychological causes" (quoted in Haas 1966: 102). In the recent attack on *Language in the Americas* Greenberg's critics have offered even more fanciful explanations for the American pattern, attributing the N and M pronouns to the sucking reflex of nursing babies, or to an archaic residue of sounds that will quite naturally appear after long periods of time. Both putative "explanations" fail to come to grips with the fact that this particular pattern is characteristic of the Americas and rare or nonexistent elsewhere around the world. One can only wonder why the infant sucking sounds of African and Australian children have not produced the same pronouns found in the Americas.

What follows attempts to survey the first- and second-person pronouns in the world's languages. For each family I have consulted the basic sources in order to determine what pronouns have been posited for that family by specialists. Reconstructed pronouns are preceded by an asterisk; in families where reconstruction has not yet been carried out, pronouns that are widespread are cited without an asterisk. Roots presumed to be distinct are separated by ||, and alternate forms of the same root are separated by ~. First-person inclusive pronouns are indicated by [i]; exclusive pronouns, by [e]; and dual pronouns, by [d]. Lack of information following a language family indicates either that no such pronoun has been reconstructed for that family, or that no widespread pronoun has been identified for that family, or, in the case of extinct languages, that no such pronoun is attested.

THE PRONOUN "I"

KHOISAN: *tii* ‖ ŋ ~ na ~ ni ‖ *mi ~ *ma
NILO-SAHARAN: *akʷai
KORDOFANIAN: *ŋi
NIGER-CONGO: i ~ (m)i ~ (n)i ‖ a ~ (n)a
AUSTRALIAN: *ŋay
INDO-PACIFIC: na ‖ ta ‖ ka ‖ ya ‖ bo ~ mo ‖ u ~ -w
MIAO-YAO: *ku(ŋ) ‖ *weŋ ‖ *ia
AUSTROASIATIC: *ǰoo ‖ *eŋ ‖ *i
DAIC: *ku ‖ *ʔi ~ *ya ~ *i
AUSTRONESIAN *aku ‖ *'a(ŋ)kən
    FORMOSAN: *aku
    MALAYO-POLYNESIAN: *aku ‖ *'a(ŋ)kən
BASQUE: ni ~ neu
CAUCASIAN: *ðɔ̄ ‖ *nɤ̌
    WEST: *se ~ *sa
    EAST: *swo ~ *zu(n) ‖ *di(n) ~ *du ~ *tu
†HURRIAN: se- ~ es- ‖ -iww
†URARTIAN: ješə ~ šo ‖ -u
†HATTI: se- ~ es-
BURUSHASKI: ǰɛ ~ ǰa ‖ mi ~ mo ‖ aiya
NAHALI: ǰuo ‖ eŋge
SINO-TIBETAN: *ŋa ‖ *-ka
    CHINESE: *ŋo
    KAREN: ja (< *ŋa)
    TIBETO-BURMAN: *ŋa ~ *ŋay ~ aŋ ~ aŋ-ka ~ ka-ŋa ‖ *-ka
YENISEIAN: *ʔaǰ
NA-DENE: *šwí
    HAIDA: tˡa ‖ tea ~ dia
    TLINGIT: khut ~ hutt
    EYAK: chuu ‖ hŭtak
    ATHABASKAN: *šwí
AFRO-ASIATIC: *an ~ *anāku ‖ ʔ ~ a ‖ u ‖ i
†ETRUSCAN: mi ~ mi-ni
†SUMERIAN: ma
KARTVELIAN: *me(n) ‖ *xw-
DRAVIDIAN: yan ‖ i ~ y- ‖ ka ~ kan ‖ ut
ELAMITE: u ~ un ~ u- ‖ -kə
INDO-EUROPEAN: *me ‖ *eg ‖ *k

URALIC-YUKAGHIR: *me ‖ *k
ALTAIC: *mi ~ *bi
KOREAN-JAPANESE-AINU: mi ‖ na
GILYAK ñi ~ ñ-
CHUKCHI-KAMCHATKAN: -m ‖ -ka
ESKIMO-ALEUT: -ma ‖ -ka
AMERIND: na(ʔ) ‖ ʔi
  ALMOSAN: *ne-
  KERESIOUAN: hinʋ ‖ iʔi
  PENUTIAN: nV ‖ ʔi ~ hi
  HOKAN: na
  CENTRAL AMERIND: nV
  CHIBCHAN: na ‖ hi ~ i
  PAEZAN: na ‖ i
  ANDEAN: na ‖ hi ~ i
  MACRO-TUCANOAN: hi ~ yi
  EQUATORIAL: nV ‖ hi ~ he ~ yi ~ e
  MACRO-CARIB: awe ~ owi
  MACRO-PANOAN: nV ‖ i ~ e ~ ye
  MACRO-GE: nV ‖ he ~ i

THE PRONOUN "WE"

KHOISAN: *ʔi ~ *ʔe [i] ‖ *si(i) [e] ‖ *m- [i]
NILO-SAHARAN:
KORDOFANIAN:
NIGER-CONGO:
AUSTRALIAN: *ña [d] ~ *ñi-rrə [e] ‖ *ŋa-rrə [i] ~ *ŋali [d] ~ *ŋana
INDO-PACIFIC: ni ~ na ‖ pi ~ me [i] ‖ ki ‖ ti
MIAO-YAO: pe ~ (m)pua
AUSTROASIATIC: *ai [d] ‖ *he(i) [i] ‖ *bɨ(n) [i] ‖ *ye(h) [e] ‖ *le ~ *ne [e]
DAIC: raw [i] ~ ra [d] ~ ta [e] ~ tau [i] ~ daw ‖ tu [e]
AUSTRONESIAN (k)ita [di] ~ ita [i] ~ -nta [i] ‖ (k)ami [e] ~ ami [e] ~ -mai [e]
  FORMOSAN:
  MALAYO-POLYNESIAN:
BASQUE: gu ~ geu
CAUCASIAN: *ɮü [i] ‖ *ži [e]
  WEST: ħa ‖ š'ə ‖ te ~ de
  EAST: čun ~ uču ~ žu ~ tχuo [e] ‖ niž ~ nen ~ nuša ‖ ja ~ jin ~ jan [i]
  ‖ išši [e] ‖ waj [i] ‖ itˡi ~ iɬɬi ~ ile ~ tˡ'in [i]

†HURRIAN:

†URARTIAN:

†HATTI:

BURUSHASKI: *mi* ~ *mīmo* ~ *mī/ mēltʌlik* [d]

NAHALI: *māney* ‖ *tyē-ko* [d]

SINO-TIBETAN:

  CHINESE:

  KAREN:

  TIBETO-BURMAN:

YENISEIAN:

NA-DENE:

  HAIDA: *ítˡʼ* ~ *itˡa* ‖ *t'alaŋ*

  TLINGIT: *iann* ~ *ohann*

  EYAK: *kajuk* ‖ *khuinkhan*

  ATHABASKAN: *nakweni* ~ *xweni* ~ *naxeni* ~ *nàhí* ~ *náání*

AFRO-ASIATIC: **m(n)* [i] ‖ **nahnu* ~ *n-* [e]

†ETRUSCAN:

†SUMERIAN:

KARTVELIAN: **čwen* ‖ *m-* [i] ‖ *naj* ~ *n-* [e]

DRAVIDIAN: **ma* ~ *ām* [e] ~ *em* ‖ **nām* ~ *nam* [i] ‖ *-tat*

ELAMITE: *nikə* ‖ *-un(kə)*

INDO-EUROPEAN: **me-s-* ‖ **nō*

URALIC-YUKAGHIR: **mɛ-* ~ **me*

ALTAIC: **bɛ-* ~ **mɛ-n-* [e]‖ **(a)yɨn* [i] ‖ *mu-se* [i]

KOREAN-JAPANESE-AINU:

GILYAK *me-gi* [d] ~ *me-r* ‖ *nɨ* ~ *ńi* ~ *ńəŋ* [e]

CHUKCHI-KAMCHATKAN: **mu-r* ~ *mu-rx-*

ESKIMO-ALEUT:

AMERIND: *ma-k* [di] ‖ *ki* [di] ‖ *na* [e]

  ALMOSAN:

  KERESIOUAN:

  PENUTIAN: **mak*

  HOKAN: *magi* ‖ *ki* [d] ‖ *na*

  CENTRAL AMERIND: *nV*

  CHIBCHAN: *na*

  PAEZAN: *kV*

  ANDEAN: *moki* ~ *moni*

  MACRO-TUCANOAN: *maha* ~ *mani* ‖ *Vn*

  EQUATORIAL: *ki* ~ *ku* [i]

  MACRO-CARIB: *kV* [d,i] ‖ *ana* [e]

  MACRO-PANOAN: *nV*

  MACRO-GE: *na*

THE PRONOUN "THOU"

KHOISAN: *saa- ‖ *ʔa
NILO-SAHARAN: *ini ‖ u
KORDOFANIAN: *ŋa ~ ŋɔ ~ ŋo
NIGER-CONGO: u ~ o
AUSTRALIAN: *ŋiñ ~ *ŋin
INDO-PACIFIC: ka ‖ te ‖ ma ‖ na ~ ni ~ ŋi
MIAO-YAO: kɔn ‖ mwei
AUSTROASIATIC: *me ~ mo ~ mu ~ ma ~ nee ‖ *hai
DAIC: mai ~ miŋ ~ ma ~ mɨ ~ mu ~ mi ‖ su ‖ lu
AUSTRONESIAN *kaw ‖ *-mu
    FORMOSAN: isu ~ su ~ kasu
    MALAYO-POLYNESIAN: kaw ‖ imu ~ -mu
BASQUE: hi- ~ heu- ‖ zu ~ zeu
CAUCASIAN: *ɢu ‖ *wɔ̃
    WEST: wa ~ we
    EAST: ħuo ~ ħu ~ wun ~ vu ‖ mi(n) ~ me(n)
†HURRIAN: we- ~ -w ~ -û ~ -ô
†URARTIAN: -w ~ -aw
†HATTI: we-
BURUSHASKI: ūŋ ~ um ‖ go- ~ gu- ‖ -ko- ~ -ku-
NAHALI: nē- (Dravidian borrowing?)
SINO-TIBETAN: *naŋ ~ na ~ njo ~ nia
    CHINESE: njo ~ nja ‖ *kwə(j)
    KAREN: na
    TIBETO-BURMAN: *naŋ ~ na
YENISEIAN: *ʔu ~ *ʔəw ‖ *kə ~ ʔək-
NA-DENE: *wī
    HAIDA: tunga ~ dunga
    TLINGIT: weh
    EYAK: i ~ y
    ATHABASKAN: nani ~ nine ~ niŋ ~ nì
AFRO-ASIATIC: *'an-tə ~ *t- ‖ -ka ~ -ku
†ETRUSCAN:
†SUMERIAN:
KARTVELIAN: *sen- ~ *šwen ‖ *x-
DRAVIDIAN: nī(n̠) ~ nin̠ ~ ñ- ‖ -ti
ELAMITE: *ni ~ nin ~ -ni ‖ -ti
INDO-EUROPEAN: *tu ~ *te ‖ *-is ~ *-si

URALIC-YUKAGHIR: *ti ~ tet
ALTAIC: *ti- ‖ *si ~ *sen
KOREAN-JAPANESE-AINU: na ~ nə ‖ si
GILYAK či
CHUKCHI-KAMCHATKAN: (i-)ɣə-t ‖ *xəš- ~ *xən-
ESKIMO-ALEUT: -t
AMERIND: ma ~ mi
  ALMOSAN: *ke-
  KERESIOUAN: ʔīs ~ hísu
  PENUTIAN: ma ~ mi ‖ wiʔš
  HOKAN: ma ~ mi ‖ ika ~ hik ‖ p-
  CENTRAL AMERIND: ma ~ mu
  CHIBCHAN: ma ~ mo ‖ pe ~ pa ~ bo
  PAEZAN: paje ~ bü
  ANDEAN: ma ~ mi ‖ p- ~ bi
  MACRO-TUCANOAN: ma ~ mi
  EQUATORIAL: ma ~ mi ‖ pi ~ pa
  MACRO-CARIB: ama ~ amoro
  MACRO-PANOAN: mi ~ am
  MACRO-GE: ma ~ ama ‖ *ka ~ qa ~ aki

THE PRONOUN "YOU"

KHOISAN: *ʔi- ‖ *ʔu
NILO-SAHARAN:
KORDOFANIAN:
NIGER-CONGO:
AUSTRALIAN: *nu-rrə ~ *ñurra ~ *ñumpalə [d] ‖ *ku-rrə
INDO-PACIFIC: ki ‖ te ‖ mi ~ pi ‖ nik
MIAO-YAO: ʔmne ‖ ńew
AUSTROASIATIC: *be(n) [d] ‖ *pe ~ pa ‖ *yi ‖ *inaa
DAIC: su ~ sɨ ~ si ~ sau ‖ mo ~ mu ~ maɨ
AUSTRONESIAN
  FORMOSAN: kamu ~ amu ~ imu
  MALAYO-POLYNESIAN: kamu ~ -miw
BASQUE: zuek ~ zeuek
CAUCASIAN:
  WEST: š'ʷa ~ s'ʷe ~ fe
  EAST: šu ~ zu(r) ‖ biti ~ bišti ~ bissi ‖ meži ~ miže ‖ kün
†HURRIAN:
†URARTIAN:

†HATTI:
BURUSHASKI: *ma ~ maii ~ maimo*
NAHALI: *lā ~ lāla* ‖ *nēko ~ nāko* [d]
SINO-TIBETAN:
   CHINESE:
   KAREN:
   TIBETO-BURMAN:
YENISEIAN:
NA-DENE:
   HAIDA: *daleñ ~ dalunga*
   TLINGIT: *gigwann ~ yehwenn*
   EYAK: *liahshū* ‖ *kajuku*
   ATHABASKAN: *łan*
AFRO-ASIATIC: *t(ə)* ‖ *-kum ~ -kun ~ -kin*
†ETRUSCAN:
†SUMERIAN: *za*
KARTVELIAN: *(s₁)tkwen-*
DRAVIDIAN: **nīm ~ nim ~ num* ‖ *-tir*
ELAMITE:
INDO-EUROPEAN: *-te*
URALIC-YUKAGHIR: *tɛ ~ tit*
ALTAIC: *ta*
KOREAN-JAPANESE-AINU: *-s-i*
GILYAK
CHUKCHI-KAMCHATKAN: **tur ~ turx- ~ -tə-k*
ESKIMO-ALEUT: *-s-i* ‖ *-ti-k* [d] *~ -ti-t*
AMERIND: *mak ~ mik*
   ALMOSAN:
   KERESIOUAN:
   PENUTIAN: *makam*
   HOKAN: *mākaʔ ~ mal*
   CENTRAL AMERIND: *ʔima ~ yim*
   CHIBCHAN: *mi ~ mu*
   PAEZAN:
   ANDEAN: *mi ~ mai*
   MACRO-TUCANOAN: *mue ~ musa ~ mixsa*
   EQUATORIAL: *amos ~ mungui*
   MACRO-CARIB: *moki ~ amo*
   MACRO-PANOAN: *ami ~ mikuan ~ mil*
   MACRO-GE: *ma ~ makaija*

REFERENCES

Darnell, Regna, and Joel Sherzer. 1971. "Areal Linguistic Studies in North America: A Historical Perspective," *International Journal of American Linguistics* 37: 20–28.

Dolgopolsky, Aron. 1986. "A Probabilistic Hypothesis Concerning the Oldest Relationships among the Language Families of Northern Eurasia," in Vitalij V. Shevoroshkin and Thomas L. Markey, eds., *Typology, Relationship and Time.* Ann Arbor, Mich., 27–50.

Greenberg, Joseph H. 1981. "Comparative Amerindian Notebooks," 23 vols. Mss. on file, Green Library, Stanford University, Stanford, Calif.

——. 1987. *Language in the Americas.* Stanford, Calif.

Haas, Mary. 1966. "Wiyot-Yurok-Algonkian and Problems of Comparative Algonkian," *International Journal of American Linguistics* 32: 101–7.

Trombetti, Alfredo. 1905. *L'unità d'origine del linguaggio.* Bologna.

13

The Origin of Language:
Retrospective and Prospective

> *Il linguaggio . . . è l'archivo più copioso e più sicuro dell'umanità.*
>
> —Alfredo Trombetti (1905)

The question of the origin of language—all discussion of which was banned by the Société de Linguistique de Paris in 1866—has always been one of the few linguistic problems of interest to the general public.* Perhaps because of this widespread but uncritical attention, coupled with much amateurish work of no scientific value and the general reluctance of scholars to deal with such matters, the question has remained in a muddled state, its various components often not even clearly distinguished. I will explore here but a single aspect of the question, namely, whether or not all of the world's presently extant languages share a common origin. I will be seeking neither the *locus* of that origin nor its *antiquity*.

THE PROBLEM

The striking parallels between biology and linguistics, particularly in their evolutionary aspect, have been generally recognized since at least the mid-nineteenth century. In one of his few references to language, Charles Darwin

---

* A preliminary version of this chapter was presented at an International Conference on Language Change and Biological Evolution, Torino, Italy, May 1988. A Russian translation was published in *Voprosy Jazykoznanija* 1 (1991): 5–19.

pointed out in 1871 that "the formation of different languages and of distinct species, and the proofs that both have been developed through a gradual process, are curiously parallel." Were it not for these "curious" similarities it is doubtful that biologists and taxonomic linguists would ever conceive of a joint conference; historians and mathematicians seldom confer. Yet my focus here is on an area where the biological and linguistic perspectives appear to clash rather than to complement one another. For biologists the monogenetic origin of *Homo sapiens sapiens* is now generally accepted (though supporters of "Multiregional Evolution" would dispute this point), and for them, the notion that the Indo-European peoples have no known biological relatives would be ludicrous. Yet for most linguists a common origin of all human languages is very much in doubt, and the belief that Indo-European has no known linguistic relatives is not only a safe position, but practically a merit badge for sober scholarship. In practice, if not in theory, the linguistic approach is pre-Darwinian, in the sense that dozens, or even hundreds, of linguistic taxa are treated *as if* they were historically independent developments. Linguists seldom go so far as to deny the possibility that all these taxa are ultimately related; what they deny is that there is any *linguistic evidence* for such a hypothesis.

To be sure, the monogenetic origin of *Homo sapiens sapiens* need not *necessarily* entail the monogenesis of human language; the two topics are, and should be kept, distinct, and when we find correlations between biology and linguistics, we insist that these correlations be arrived at independently. Yet there is something strange about the spectacle of hundreds of supposedly unrelated language families, when the biological differences among the people who speak the tongues of the various language families are often minuscule. Surely no one imagines that each of these hundreds of language families represents an independent creation of language. But if they are not independent developments is it plausible, or even possible, that they have all been separated from each other for so long that any trace of deeper relationships has vanished? Is it not also strange that the comparative method, which was discovered in its broad outlines over two centuries ago, largely in terms of the Indo-European family, has never been able to connect that family with any other—at least to the satisfaction of the linguistic community? This mystery is compounded by the fact that Indo-European is in no sense an archaic or poorly distinguished family.

I believe the general rejection of attempts to connect Indo-European with other families, encouraged in an earlier day by chauvinistic arrogance, has effectively blocked consideration of the question of monogenesis by acting as a dike against *all* long-range comparison. For if Indo-European—that most studied and best understood of all families—cannot be convincingly connected

with any other family, then what confidence can we have in connections proposed between even less well studied families, often with a postulated time
depth many times that of Indo-European? Thus if the splendid genetic isolation of Indo-European can be maintained, the question of monogenesis is
moot.

Although the Paris interdiction of the study of the origin of language expressed primarily the European disenchantment with work on this topic, at
a time when Europe dominated the world, culturally and otherwise, in the
United States the historical linguist William Dwight Whitney (1867: 383) was
no less pessimistic: "Linguistic science is not now, and cannot ever hope to be,
in condition to give an authoritative opinion respecting the unity or variety
of our species." Although this remains the conventional wisdom among most
linguists to the present day, I believe it is largely a myth that scholars have
passed on uncritically from generation to generation for over a century. Aside
from barely concealed racism, there are multiple academic and institutional
reasons why this myth has persisted so long, the two most responsible being
the predominantly synchronic slant of twentieth-century linguistics and the
ever-increasing grip of specialization on academia. Although historical linguistics has never altogether succumbed, and indeed has always been considered
an integral part of general linguistics, there can be no doubt that during most
of the present century it has taken a back seat to synchronic exploration.
Moreover, even *within* historical linguistics, the increasing pace of publication
and specialization has discouraged most scholars from seeking to keep abreast
of developments outside of their own family or language of interest. There
has been a tacit assumption that developments in, say, Bantu linguistics can
be safely ignored by Romance scholars.[1]

AN ALTERNATIVE VIEW

Despite this generally hostile intellectual climate, and the risk of provoking
one's colleagues to consternation or condemnation, there have always been
some scholars who rejected the Paris edict and Whitney's admonition and
sought to find evidence of more comprehensive classifications of the world's
languages. Six such scholars bear mention here. In several works published
during the first quarter of the twentieth century, the Italian linguist Alfredo
Trombetti sought to establish the monogenesis of human language by comparing lexical and grammatical roots from languages and language families
around the world. Though one can hardly deny that some of Trombetti's

---

[1] In Ruhlen (1979) I sought to challenge that notion. See also the remarks of Henry Sweet
(1901) quoted in Chapter 6 herein.

proposals were incorrect, many others were later adopted (or independently discovered) and elaborated by other scholars. As early as 1905 he presented a strong *prima facie* case for the monogenesis of human language.

In the New World, from roughly 1910 to 1930, the American linguist Edward Sapir made a number of sweeping proposals for the consolidation of numerous Native American language families that had been identified only decades before, during the nineteenth-century catalog stage of linguistic taxonomy. Sapir was also the first to propose genetic affinity between Na-Dene and Sino-Tibetan, a connection that has recently been revived and extended (see Chapters 1 and 4). For a full discussion of Sapir's many contributions to Amerindian classification, see Ruhlen (1987).

Morris Swadesh, a student of Sapir's, shared both his mentor's interest in Amerindian linguistics and Trombetti's passion for global exploration. Though his early work was much in the spirit of Sapir, giving etymologies for various proposed groups, in his later work he shifted to his own technique of lexicostatistics, with mixed results. During this later phase he became interested in establishing a worldwide network of linguistic relationships, and the problem of a hierarchical classification of the world's languages became less important to him. His premature death in 1967 meant that his life's work was never adequately realized or summarized.

During the early 1960's two Russian scholars, Vladislav Illich-Svitych and Aron Dolgopolsky, revived an earlier proposal of the Dane Holger Pedersen that grouped Indo-European with several other families of Eurasia and North Africa in a Nostratic phylum. Though they had at first been unaware of each other's work, their results coincided to such an extent that Nostratic theory became a single unified field, and since Illich-Svitych's tragic death in 1966 the work of the field has been carried on by Dolgopolsky and others. In classical Nostratic theory, Indo-European is one of six related subgroups, the others being Afro-Asiatic, Kartvelian, Uralic, Altaic, and Dravidian. Roughly 400 etymologies supporting the Nostratic grouping have so far been published. Recently Dolgopolsky (1984) has proposed the inclusion of Elamite, Gilyak, and Chukchi-Kamchatkan as well.

The American linguist Joseph Greenberg has probably made the greatest contributions of all to linguistic taxonomy. Beginning with his revolutionary classification of African languages in the 1950's, he undertook to investigate those regions of the world where linguistic classification was least advanced. By 1963 he had classified all African languages into four phyla (Khoisan, Niger-Kordofanian, Nilo-Saharan, and Afro-Asiatic), and it is this classification that forms the basis of all contemporary research in African linguistics. In 1971 Greenberg offered evidence for an Indo-Pacific phylum that includes the very diverse Papuan languages of New Guinea and surrounding islands, and in 1987 he presented substantial evidence for an Amerind phylum that would include all New World languages except those belonging to the Na-Dene and Eskimo-Aleut families. He is currently at work on a book on Eurasiatic, a vast grouping that differs from Nostratic by the exclusion of Afro-Asiatic, Kartvelian, and Dravidian, and by the inclusion of Japanese, Ainu, Gilyak, Chukchi-Kamchatkan, and Eskimo-Aleut.

A CLOSER LOOK AT THE PROBLEM

Despite the pathbreaking work of these scholars, the majority of the linguistic community still adheres to the belief that Indo-European has no known linguistic relatives, and none is likely ever to be demonstrated, because—so the argument goes—beyond the time depth of Indo-European all trace of genetic affiliation has been obliterated by ceaseless phonetic and semantic erosion. This belief is so strong that even linguists in possession of evidence to the contrary will often provide an ad hoc explanation of the contradictory evidence rather than challenge the reigning tenets of comparative-historical linguistics.

The Australian language phylum is instructive in this regard. Humans have occupied Australia continuously since at least 40,000 years BP (before present), and there is no reason to think that Proto-Australian does not date from about that time (though the fact that Australia was not permanently cut off from New Guinea until about 10,000 years ago must be borne in mind). At the very least, Proto-Australian must be twice as old as Indo-European, and more likely seven or eight times as old. At this time depth, evidence of a primitive unity can no longer exist, according to the standard view of linguistic evolution, and yet the Australian phylum is universally accepted as a valid taxon.

In order to reconcile this clear contradiction R. M. W. Dixon (1980) discarded the principle of linguistic uniformitarianism and proposed that, because of their isolation, Australian languages have changed much more slowly than have languages elsewhere in the world:

Proto-Australian was probably spoken a considerable time in the past, perhaps some tens of millennia ago. It is this which makes it unlikely that it will ever be possible to demonstrate a genetic connection between Australian and any other language family. Any sister language that Proto-Australian may have left behind in South-East Asia, say, is likely to have changed out of all recognition over the intervening period, so that there would be insufficient points of similarity remaining for any connection to be recognizable. (Or it could well be that relatives of Proto-Australian have NO living descendants.) Generally, languages change at such a rate that after more than about three or four thousand years of separation genetic links are no longer recognizable. Australian languages have been relatively isolated from contact with other languages and cultures, and may well have changed at a comparatively slow rate; but any relative that they left behind in regions that were more linguistically cosmopolitan would not have been sheltered in this way. (p. 237)

This romantic notion of Australia as a Land That Time Forgot is most certainly unsupportable, and one should not lose sight of the fact that it is based on expectations rather than evidence. In any event, Dixon is categorical in his belief that "there is absolutely no evidence for a genetic connection between Australian languages and anything outside the continent; there is not even any remote 'possibility' that scholars could argue about. It seems that the languages of Australia have been so long in their present location that any evidence of connection with other languages has been, through time, eroded away." (p. 238)

Though the number of roots that have been reconstructed for Proto-Australian is rather small, some of these would appear to be cognate with roots found in other families (see Chapter 14). Consider, for instance, Proto-Australian *bungu 'knee,' which in various modern languages has semantic extensions to things that bend (wave, bend in a river, hump in a snake's body). This form is very similar in sound and meaning to the Indo-Pacific etymology for 'knee,' which includes forms such as Tobelo buku, Koianu poku, and Teri Kawalsch bugu. Traces of this root are also found in Eurasia. Ainu (he-) poki(-ki) 'bow down' appears to belong here, as do Proto-Indo-European *bheug(h) 'to bend,' and Proto-Altaic *bük(ä) 'to bend' (including forms such as Uighur bük 'to kneel,' Yakut bük 'to bend,' Khalkha bóx(ón) 'hump of a camel,' and Evenki buku 'bent, crooked'). In Africa, Proto-Bantu *bóngó 'knee' is virtually identical with the Australian form in both sound and meaning, and in the West Atlantic branch of Niger-Congo we find forms such as Baga -buŋ 'knee.' One may anticipate that additional reflexes of this root will be found elsewhere in the Niger-Congo family, but the lack of any kind of Niger-Congo etymological dictionary makes this difficult to verify for the moment. Finally, this same root is well attested in the Amerind family, where we find North American forms like Chumash (si-)buk 'elbow' and Walapai (mi-)puk 'knee' and South American forms like Guamaca buka 'knee, elbow' and Iranshe poku 'bow' (n.).

This example is by no means the only genetic connection between the Australian phylum and the rest of the world's languages. Dixon reconstructs *bula '2' for Proto-Australian, and Blake (1988) shows how this number has been used to form dual pronouns in the Pama-Nyungan subgroup: *nyuN-palV 'you-2' and *pula 'they-2.' Two of the extinct Tasmanian languages (considered by Dixon unrelated to Australian languages) exhibit similar forms, Southeastern boula '2' and Southern pooalih '2.' In the context of his Austro-Tai hypothesis Paul Benedict (1975) pointed out the similarity of the number 2 in all of the major families of Southeast Asia. Benedict reconstructs *ʔ(m)bar

'2' for Proto-Austroasiatic (cf. Santali *bar*, Jeh *bal*, Khmu' *bār*, Old Mon *ʔbar*) and **(a)war* '2' for Proto-Miao-Yao. He also considers Daic forms like Mak *wa* 'twin' and Austronesian forms like Javanese *kĕmbar* 'twin' to be cognate with the preceding. In Africa one of the pieces of evidence that Edgar Gregersen (1972) offered in support of Congo-Saharan (his proposal for joining Niger-Kordofanian and Nilo-Saharan in a single family) was forms for the number 2 that hardly differ from those we have seen so far. In Niger-Congo we have Temne *(kə)bari* 'twin,' Nimbari *bala* '2,' Mano *pere* '2,' and Proto-Bantu **bàdí* '2'; Nilo-Saharan has forms such as Nubian *bar(-si)* 'twin,' Merarit *warē* '2,' and Kunama *barā* 'pair.' In Eurasia one of Illich-Svitych's Nostratic etymologies appears related to the forms discussed so far, but in these families the meaning has shifted from '2' to 'half,' 'side,' and 'part.' Specifically, Illich-Svitych (1967) connects Proto-Indo-European **pol* 'half, side' (cf. Sanskrit *(ka-)palam* 'half,' Albanian *palë* 'side, part, pair,' Russian *pol* 'half,') with Proto-Uralic **pälä/*pole* 'half' (cf. Yurak Samoyed *peele* 'half,' Hungarian *fele* 'half, one side of two,' Vogul *pääl* 'side, half,' Votyak *pal* 'side, half') and Proto-Dravidian **pāl* 'part, portion' (cf. Tamil *pāl* 'part, portion, share,' Telugu *pālu* 'share, portion,' Parji *pēla* 'portion'). Finally, cognate forms are found in Amerind languages of North and South America (cf. Wintun *palo(-l)* '2,' Wappo *p'ala* 'twins,' Huave *apool* 'snap in two,' Colorado *palu* '2,' Sabane *paʔlin* '2').

The final piece of evidence I would like to offer for the proposition that the Australian phylum is demonstrably related to the rest of the world's languages involves an interrogative whose most usual form is *mi(n)* or *ma(n)* and whose meaning is 'what?, who?,' or some other interrogative. This root has been discussed in the work of Trombetti, Illich-Svitych, and Greenberg and appears to be one of the most broadly distributed formatives in human language. For Proto-Australian Dixon reconstructs **miNHa*[2] 'what,' with modern reflexes such as Dyirbal *minya* 'what' and Pitta-Pitta *minha* 'what.' These forms are strikingly similar to those contained in one of Greenberg's Indo-Pacific etymologies that includes forms such as Matap *mina* 'what,' Arapesh *mane* 'what,' Nyaura *məndə* 'what, thing,' Kati *man* 'something,' Biada *min* 'thing,' and Laumbe *mina* 'thing.'

In Eurasia there are a variety of forms that are in all likelihood cognate with those just mentioned. In the Austroasiatic phylum one can point to Kurku *amae* 'who,' Mon *mu* 'what,' Central Sakai *mā/mō* 'what.' Two isolated languages of the Indian subcontinent, Burushaski and Nahali, show reflexes of the interrogative under discussion. Burushaski has *men* 'who' and

---

[2] *NH* represents a correspondence between lamino-interdental *nh* and lamino-palatal *ny* that is found in the modern Australian languages.

amin 'which'; Nahali, miŋgay 'where' and miyan 'how much.' In the Caucasus *ma has been reconstructed as an interrogative particle in Proto-(North) Caucasian, and some languages show pronominal use of the m interrogative as well, e.g. Chechen mila 'who' and Bats me 'who.' For Kartvelian, G. Klimov (1964) has reconstructed *ma 'what' and *mi-n 'who.' Across Northern Eurasia the m interrogative is widely attested, its numerous occurrences having been emphasized in both Illich-Svitych's Nostratic etymologies and Greenberg's Eurasiatic etymologies. Examples include Proto-Indo-European *mo-, a base of interrogative adverbs; Proto-Uralic *mi 'what' (cf. Vogul män 'which, what,' Tavgy ma 'what,' Hungarian mi 'what, which,' Finnish mi/mi(-kä) 'what, which'); Proto-Turkic *mi 'what' (cf. Chuvash měn 'what' and Turkish mi, a sentence enclitic); Mongolian -ū (< *mu), a sentence interrogative, and Monguor amu/ama 'what'; Tungus -ma, an indefinitizer; Korean muŏt 'what' and Old Korean mai 'why'; Ryukyuan (the language most closely related to Japanese) mī 'what'; Ainu mak/makanak 'what,' makan 'what kind'; Chukchi mikin 'who,' Kamchadal min 'which, what sort.'

In the New World the m interrogative is not found, to the best of my knowledge, in either Eskimo-Aleut or Na-Dene, but it is widespread in Amerind. North American examples include North Sahaptin mēn/mna 'where,' Central Sierra Miwok minni 'who,' San Jose mani 'where,' Choctaw mana 'when,' and Chickasaw mano 'where.' In South America we have Kagaba mai 'who,' mani 'where,' Paez maneh 'when,' Allentiac men 'who,' Catio mai 'where,' Guajajara mon 'who,' Maripu manub 'in which direction,' Cofan mañi 'where,' Krenje menõ 'who,' and Botocudo mina 'who.'

In Africa the m interrogative is widely attested in Afro-Asiatic and is perhaps found in Khoisan as well. The Khoisan examples are relatively few (cf. Kxoe mấ 'who,' mấ 'which,' Naron kama 'if, when,' Nama maba 'where'), but in Afro-Asiatic it is attested in every branch of the family. Examples include Akkadian mīn 'what,' mann 'who,' Amharic mɨn 'what,' Arabic man/min 'who,' Tuareg ma 'what,' mi 'who,' Saho mā 'what,' mi 'who,' Somali máḥấ 'what,' Oromo mấni 'what,' Kaffa amone 'what,' Hausa mè/mì 'what,' Bata mən 'what,' and Logone mini 'who.'

In all of the above forms I would maintain that the initial m- portion of the root is cognate. The final -n portion, however, has multiple sources, one of which is locative. A k interrogative, which can be seen in some of the forms above, is the chief rival of the m interrogative in the world's languages, sometimes joining with it, sometimes supplanting it, and sometimes being replaced by it. The complex interplay of these two interrogatives (as well as a third, j) has been discussed by Trombetti, Illich-Svitych, and Greenberg, all of whom have called attention to the generally personal character of the k interrogative (who?), which contrasts with the generally nonpersonal character of the m interrogative (what?). Finally, it may be significant that despite the enormous geographic distribution of this root—from Africa to the Americas—it appears not to occur in Niger-Kordofanian or Nilo-Saharan, a point to which I will return.

Notwithstanding the very widespread distribution of these roots, many of which have been known from at least the time of Trombetti, they have had little impact on comparative-historical linguistics, which, from a theoretical perspective, has remained devoutly Eurocentric. Indo-European, as an examination of any of the introductory textbooks will reveal, is still almost universally regarded as unrelated to any other family. The Americas have actually seen retrogression in linguistic taxonomy during this century, the number of supposedly independent families growing to over 200 by the time that Greenberg (1987) offered compelling evidence that there are in fact just three (see Chapter 6). In Asia many Altaicists have come to reject any connection among the three Altaic branches, and even the Uralic affinity of Yukaghir is sometimes denied or questioned. The reasons for the rejection of more comprehensive classifications are multiple and have been amply discussed in Greenberg (1987) and Ruhlen (1987). Rather than cover that ground once again I will merely cite a few particular criticisms that exemplify the flavor of the opposition to long-range comparison.

Traditionally, the most common criticism of long-range comparison has been that the proposed cognates were semantically and/or phonologically too disparate to be historically related. This is hardly the case with the etymologies discussed above, which are in fact criticized as being *too similar* in sound and meaning to be related at the time depths proposed. The putative cognates cited in these etymologies are sufficiently extensive and sufficiently similar in sound and meaning that their genetic affinity would not be controversial if they represented merely some group of South American Indian languages, but because they represent instead supposedly unrelated language families from every corner of the earth the actual substance of the etymologies is given less weight than are the expectations of scholars about what genetic connections are possible. What would be considered an obvious etymology at a low level of classification becomes "random noise" at higher levels—with no change in content at all. Trombetti (1905: 44) criticized this inconsistency as follows: "It is clear that in and of itself the comparison of Finno-Ugric *me* 'I,' *te* 'you' with Indo-European *me-* and *te-* [with the same meaning] is worth just as much as any comparison one might make between the corresponding pronominal forms in the Indo-European languages. The only difference is that the common origin of the Indo-European languages is accepted, while the connection between Indo-European and Finno-Ugric is denied."

No one would deny that the member languages of low-level groups like Romance often display cognates that are very similar or even identical. What is in dispute is (1) whether supposedly independent, higher-level groupings (e.g. Indo-European, Australian, and Amerind) can share cognates that are similar in form and meaning and (2) whether a reconstructed proto-language (e.g. Proto-Indo-European, Proto-Nostratic, or Proto-Australian) can show reflexes in its extant daughter languages that are similar or identical to the reconstructed form. The answers to both of these questions depend on the rate and nature of linguistic change. As Dixon's comments indicate, many linguists believe that the rate of linguistic change is such that all trace of genetic affiliation is effaced after only several thousand years, so for him the answer to both questions is no. But if all of the supposedly independent linguistic families do derive from a common origin, then the fact that the earliest reconstructable items in the various families look alike should hardly be surprising. *Greater convergence with greater depth is what one would expect.*

As regards the second question I would point out only that, in every etymological dictionary I have examined, some of the reconstructed forms for the proto-language are similar or identical to some of the reflexes in its extant daughter languages. Pokorny (1959) reconstructs Proto-Indo-European **nepōt* 'nephew, grandson,' a form that must have existed at least 5,000 years ago. Yet this same form, with the same meaning, is preserved to this day intact in Rumanian *nepot* 'nephew, grandson.' At least in this instance Dixon's inexorable erosion seems not to have taken place. And even phyla that are much older than Indo-European show the same phenomenon. In the first etymology above, for example, Proto-Australian **bungu* 'knee' shows the reflex *bungu* 'knee' in many modern languages (e.g. Guugu Yimidhir, Yidiny, Dyirbal). Now if Proto-Australian, which in all likelihood dates from 40,000 BP or more, can be accorded reflexes in contemporary languages that are identical to the reconstructed form, on what grounds can one object to a similar phenomenon between Proto-Sapiens and modern languages, given that Proto-Sapiens could be only 20,000–30,000 years older than Proto-Australian?

Furthermore, the assumption that linguistic change has been constant and continuous since the emergence of *Homo sapiens sapiens* may be incorrect. It is well known among anthropologists, archaeologists, and even historians that cultural evolution in general appears to have developed at an ever accelerating pace as one approaches the present, and the same may well be true for linguistic evolution. Biological evolution, too, is no longer necessarily conceived of as a very long, slow process of gradual and constant change; scholars like Niles Eldredge and Stephen Jay Gould have argued instead for a more episodic character to evolution, in which little change may occur over very long periods of time (see Eldredge 1985), and recent research on catastrophes and mass extinctions tends to support that mode. Given that we do not *know* what linguistic evolution was like during the past 100,000 years, it would seem premature to rule out any of the possibilities on a priori grounds.

Some linguists, of course, are simply unaware that other language families often have roots similar to those in the family they are interested in, and I suspect that this is the case with Dixon. Other linguists, however, are aware of such roots but choose to ignore them. One of the most cogent pieces of evidence that Greenberg (1987) offered in support of the Amerind phylum was the presence of first-person *n* and second-person *m* in all eleven branches. As noted in Chapter 12, the first- and second-person pronouns are known to be among the most stable meanings over time. Dolgopolsky (1964) found that the first-person pronoun is the most stable item, and the second-person pronoun ranked third in stability (following the number 2). It is also well known that initial nasal consonants are among the most stable sounds, and the conjunction of stable sounds with stable meanings has meant that even after 12,000 years these pronouns have been preserved in every branch of the Amerind phylum. Greenberg did not claim to be the first to notice the broad distribution of these two pronouns in North and South America. Swadesh (1954) had underscored their distribution in an article containing additional evidence for Amerind (not yet so named), and a year later Greenberg, unaware of Swadesh's article, discovered the same distribution. Greenberg observes, "That two scholars should independently make the same basic observation is an interesting sidelight in the argument for the Amerind grouping as I have defined it" (1987: 54).

Lyle Campbell, an Amerindian scholar and one of Greenberg's chief critics, sees things differently: "The widespread first-person *n* and less widespread second-person *m* markers . . . have been recognized from the beginning without significant impact on classification" (Campbell 1986: 488). Lamentably, Campbell is correct, but that such crucial evidence has been overlooked—or, worse, scorned—is not something to take pride in. Were a biologist to remark smugly, "That group of animals you keep mentioning, the ones with a backbone, has been recognized for a long time and I am not impressed," his colleagues would chuckle and move on to other business. Here we see perhaps one measure of the difference between biology and linguistics, especially as they present themselves today. Greenberg (1987) summarizes the fundamental and obvious importance of the two Amerind pronouns as follows:

It is the business of science to note non-random phenomena and to explain them. Were we to plot the occurrence of specific first- and second-person markers on a world map, we would not fail to notice a clustering of first-person *m* and second-person *t* (along with *s*) in Europe, northern Asia, and the northern part of North America as far as Greenland, with a second clustering of first-person *n* and second-person *m* covering the rest of the Americas, outside of the Eskimo-Aleut and Na-Dene areas.

In my opinion, this observation alone would suffice to lead any historically minded anthropologist to the view that there must be at least one very large stock to account for the first set and another to account for the second set. (p. 55)

AN END TO MYTHOLOGY

I have suggested here that the currently widespread beliefs, first, that Indo-European has no known relatives, and, second, that the monogenesis of language cannot be demonstrated on the basis of linguistic evidence, are both incorrect. Belief in these erroneous assertions is based largely on extra-linguistic criteria and a priori assumptions, rather than on a serious survey of the world's linguistic literature. A growing, though still small, number of linguists are coming to realize that all the world's languages do share a common origin, and they are beginning to work on that basis. In the remainder of this chapter I shall discuss several implications of monogenesis for linguistic taxonomy.

First, the search for linguistic "relationships" is now over (or should be), since it no longer makes sense to ask if two languages (or two language families) are related. *Everything* is related, and the question to be investigated within or among different families is the *degree* of their relationship, not the fact of it. All taxonomic questions dissolve into one: discovering the hierarchical subgrouping of the human family on the basis of linguistic traits. Such traits may be either lexical (i.e. roots, affixes) or typological (e.g. nasal vowels, the SOV word order, an inclusive/exclusive distinction for 'we'). The use of lexical evidence to support a particular subgrouping needs no justification, since it has long been an essential technique of the comparative method. It is the *total distribution* of a root that reveals its taxonomic significance, not its mere presence in this or that family. Within that total distribution, particular developments within particular subgroups, such as Grimm's Law within Indo-European, may provide additional evidence for subgrouping.

The use of typological traits in genetic classification is more controversial, the generally accepted view being that such traits are in fact not indicative of genetic relationships. As is well known, the use of typological traits in some of the earlier work on African linguistics led to classifications that were definitely not phylogenetic, but the error of those early taxonomists lay more in their reliance on too few traits (sometimes just one) than in the traits themselves. Thus from a strictly historical perspective the use of sex gender, nasal vowels, or word order alone to classify languages would lead to absurd results. Still, such features, no less than grammar or the lexicon, are genetically transmitted as a part of language, and thus have some, if not absolute, evidentiary value. It can hardly be an accident of nature that the 700 or so Papuan languages are uniformly SOV in basic word order (with a few notable exceptions under Austronesian influence). The fact that the Indo-European sex-gender system is not cognate with gender systems in other families does not imply that gender has not been a genetically transmitted trait during the history of Indo-European (and of course in other families where it has developed independently). In a preliminary taxonomic analysis of the world's linguistic phyla (Darlu, Ruhlen, and Cavalli-Sforza 1988), we found, using typological traits such as consonants (presence or absence of *p, m, s*, etc.), vowels (presence or absence of *i, e, a*, etc.), pronouns (presence or absence of a first-person dual inclusive pronoun), and word order (presence or absence of SOV word order in the basic declarative sentence), that often those phyla that linguists had previously connected on the basis of cognates also were immediately affiliated with each other on the basis of typological traits (e.g. Uralic and Altaic, Chukchi-Kamchatkan and Eskimo-Aleut, Na-Dene and Caucasian, Niger-Kordofanian and Nilo-Saharan, Indo-European and Afro-Asiatic). These preliminary data indicate that there is a greater genetic component in typology than has previously been assumed.

A second consequence of monogenesis is that it becomes possible, at least theoretically, to compare a phylogenetic tree of the human family based on linguistic traits with one based on biological traits. Many linguists still believe that there is little correlation between linguistic and biological traits. According to Campbell (1986: 488), "repetition of the obvious seems required: there is no deterministic connection between language and gene pools or culture." However, recent work by L. L. Cavalli-Sforza et al. (1988) shows that the correlations between biological and linguistic classifications are of a most intimate nature: "Linguistic families correspond to groups of populations with very few, easily understood overlaps, and their origin can be given a time frame. Linguistic superfamilies show remarkable correspondence . . . , indicating considerable parallelism between genetic and linguistic development."

As we saw in Chapter 1, many linguistic taxa correspond almost exactly to biological taxa, not only in the lower levels of classification (e.g. Eastern Austronesian, Altaic), but in the higher levels as well (e.g. Congo-Saharan, Austric, Nostratic/Eurasiatic, Amerind). This being the case, one is left to wonder whether the basic biological dichotomy between Sub-Saharan Africa and the rest of the world will be matched by a basic linguistic dichotomy between Congo-Saharan (for which Gregersen 1972 offered lexical and grammatical evidence) and non-Congo-Saharan. As will be shown in Chapter 14, some of the roots posited by Gregersen for Congo-Saharan are in fact even more widespread, occuring elsewhere in the world, and hence cannot be innovations within Congo-Saharan. Gregersen's etymologies thus involve a mixture of those restricted to Congo-Saharan and those shared by Congo-Saharan and other families. The interrogative etymology *min* 'what' discussed above is interesting in this regard, for it seems to be found everywhere *but* in Congo-Saharan, and thus could be an innovation of the non-Congo-Saharan grouping, if this turns out to be a valid linguistic taxon.

A final consequence of monogenesis, should it be accepted, is that it will necessarily lead to a reappraisal of a good many family-internal explanations of various phenomena. One such example is Dixon's (1980) explanation of the origin of the Australian interrogative *miNHa* 'what':

Languages in North Queensland which do not have *miNHa* as an indefinite-interrogative form generally have a lexical item *miNHa* 'meat, (edible) animal.' It is likely that there has been semantic shift, with the generic noun *miNHa* 'animal' shifting to become an indefinite term 'something'; like other indefinites in most Australian languages this also had an interrogative sense 'what.' *miNHa* is now found with indefinite-interrogative sense over a large region centered in New South Wales (and in a few scattered languages outside this area), suggesting a pattern of areal diffusion." (p. 376)

Thus Dixon derives the interrogative *miNHa* 'what' from a phonologically identical root meaning 'meat' via an intermediate stage meaning 'something.' Even if there were not abundant evidence that the Australian interrogative *miNHa* is cognate with similar forms in many other phyla, as we saw above, I believe Dixon's family-internal explanation would still have to be rejected. The semantic shift MEAT > SOMETHING is unusual, to say the least, and quite probably unattested in the world's languages. Furthermore, the normal semantic evolution is from INTERROGATIVE to INDEFINITE, not vice versa. All in all, Dixon's family-internal explanation is most improbable, whereas the family-external explanation is simple and straightforward. Greenberg (1990, 1991) illustrates the value of a broad perspective for understanding certain phenomena within Indo-European, a theme that has been one of the major contributions of Nostratic research as well. Biological taxonomists have long understood the crucial importance of the broad perspective, and one may hope that linguistic taxonomists will soon gain a similar appreciation.

We are only beginning to understand the structure of the human population as it is reflected in biological and linguistic traits. For the highest levels of human classification, biological taxonomy seems to be in a more advanced state for the moment, but clearly both biology and linguistics have their own separate and important roles to play in unraveling the phylogeny of our species. Perhaps when both biological and linguistic taxonomy have been elaborated more confidently and in greater detail, the many parallels and similarities between the two fields will come to be viewed not as "curious" but as natural.

REFERENCES

Benedict, Paul K. 1975. *Austro-Thai: Language and Culture.* New Haven, Conn.

Bengtson, John D., and Merritt Ruhlen. 1992. "Global Etymologies," Chapter 14 of this volume.

Blake, Barry J. 1988. "Redefining Pama-Nyungan: Towards the Prehistory of Australian Languages," *Yearbook of Australian Linguistics* 1.

Campbell, Lyle. 1986. "Comment," on an article by Joseph H. Greenberg, Christy G. Turner, and Stephen L. Zegura, *Current Anthropology* 27: 488.

Cavalli-Sforza, L. L., Alberto Piazza, Paolo Menozzi, and Joanna Mountain. 1988. "Reconstruction of Human Evolution: Bringing Together Genetic, Archeological and Linguistic Data," *Proceedings of the National Academy of Sciences* 85: 6002–6.

Darlu, Pierre, Merritt Ruhlen, and L. L. Cavalli-Sforza. 1988. "A Taxonomic Analysis of Linguistic Families," ms.

Darwin, Charles. 1871. *The Descent of Man.* London.

Dixon, R. M. W. 1980. *The Languages of Australia.* Cambridge, Eng.

Dolgopolsky, Aron B. 1964. "Gipoteza drevnejšego rodstva jazykovyx semei severnoj Eurasii s verojatnostnoj točki zrenija," *Voprosy Jazykoznanija* 2: 53–63. [English translation in Vitalij V. Shevoroshkin and Thomas L. Markey, eds., *Typology, Relationship and Time,* 1986. Ann Arbor, Mich., 27–50.]

———. 1984. "On Personal Pronouns in the Nostratic Languages," in Otto Gschwantler, Károly Rédei, and Hermann Reichert, eds., *Linguistica et Philologica.* Vienna, 65–112.

Eldredge, Niles. 1985. *Time Frames.* New York.

Greenberg, Joseph H. 1963. *The Languages of Africa.* Bloomington, Ind.

———. 1971. "The Indo-Pacific Hypothesis," in Thomas A. Sebeok, ed., *Current Trends in Linguistics,* Vol. 8. The Hague, 807–71.

———. 1987. *Language in the Americas.* Stanford, Calif.

———. 1990. "The Prehistory of the Indo-European Vowel System in Comparative and Typological Perspective," in Vitaly Shevoroshkin, ed., *Proto-Languages and Proto-Cultures.* Bochum, Germany, 77–136. [Russian translation in *Voprosy Jazykoznanija* (1989), No. 4: 5–31.]

———. 1991. "Some Problems of Indo-European in Historical Perspective," in Sydney M. Lamb and E. Douglas Mitchell, eds., *Sprung from Some Common Source: Investigations into the Prehistory of Languages.* Stanford, Calif., 125–40.

————. To appear. *The Eurasiatic Language Family: Indo-European and Its Closest Relatives*. Stanford, Calif.

Gregersen, Edgar A. 1972. "Kongo-Saharan," *Journal of African Languages* 11: 69–89.

Illich-Svitych, Vladislav. 1967. "Materily k sravnitel'nomu slovarju nostratičeskix jazykov," *Etimologija 1965* (Moscow), 321–73. [English translation in Vitaly Shevoroshkin, ed., *Reconstructing Languages and Cultures*. Bochum, Germany, 125–76.]

————. 1971–84. *Opyt sravnenija nostratičeskix jazykov*, 3 vols. Moscow.

Klimov, G. A. 1964. *Etimologičeskij slovar' kartvel'skix jazykov*. Moscow.

Pokorny, Julius. 1959. *Indogermanisches Etymologisches Wörterbuch*. Bern.

Ruhlen, Merritt. 1979. "On the Origin and Evolution of French Nasal Vowels," *Romance Philology* 32: 321–35.

————. 1987. *A Guide to the World's Languages*, Vol. 1: Classification. Stanford, Calif.

————. 1991. "Proisxoždenije jazyka: retrospektiva i perspektiva," *Voprosy Jazykoznanija* 1: 5–19. [Russian translation of this chapter.]

Swadesh, Morris. 1954. "Perspectives and Problems of Amerindian Comparative Linguistics," *Word* 10: 306–32.

Sweet, Henry. 1901. *The History of Language*. London.

Trombetti, Alfredo. 1905. *L'unità d'origine del linguaggio*. Bologna.

Whitney, William Dwight. 1867. *Language and the Study of Language*. New York.

14

Global Etymologies

John D. Bengtson and Merritt Ruhlen

> *If the strength of Indo-European studies*
> *is largely based on the existence,*
> *in a few instances at least,*
> *of very old sources, the strength*
> *of Amerindian studies is simply*
> *the vast number of languages.*
> *Thus synchronic breadth becomes*
> *the source of diachronic depth.*
>
> —Joseph H. Greenberg (1987)

How does one know that two languages are related? Or that two language families are related? Every linguist purports to know the answers to these questions, but the answers vary surprisingly from one linguist to another. And the divergence of views concerning what *is* actually known is even greater than that exhibited on the question of how one *arrives at* this body of information. This is not a particularly satisfactory state of affairs. In what follows we will explore these questions in a global context. We conclude that, despite the generally antipathetic or agnostic stance of most linguists, the case for monogenesis of extant (and attested extinct) languages is quite strong. We will present evidence that we feel can only be explained genetically (i.e. as the result of common origin), but we will also attempt to answer some of the criticism that has been leveled at work such as ours for over a century.

THE BASIS OF LINGUISTIC TAXONOMY

That ordinary words form the basis of linguistic taxonomy is a direct consequence of the fundamental property of human language, the *arbitrary* relationship between sound and meaning. Since all sequences of sounds are equally well suited to represent any meaning, there is no tendency or predisposition for certain sounds or sound sequences to be associated with certain meanings (leaving aside onomatopoeia, which in any event is irrelevant for classification). In classifying languages genetically we seek, among the available lexical and grammatical formatives, similarities that involve *both* sound and meaning. Typological similarities, involving sound alone or meaning alone, do not yield reliable results.

The fundamental principles of taxonomy are not specific to linguistics, but are, rather, as applicable in fields as disparate as molecular biology, botany, ethnology, and astronomy. When one identifies similarities among molecular structures, plants, human societies, or stars, the origin of such similarities can be explained only by one of three mechanisms: (1) common origin, (2) borrowing, or (3) convergence. To demonstrate that two languages (or language families) are related, it is thus sufficient to show that their shared similarities are not the result of either borrowing or convergence. As regards convergence— the manifestation of motivated or accidental resemblances—linguists are in a more favorable situation than are biologists. In biology, convergence may be accidental, but is more often motivated by the environment; it is not by accident that bats resemble birds, or that dolphins resemble fish. In linguistics, by contrast, where the sound/meaning association is arbitrary, convergence is *always* accidental.

It is seldom emphasized that similarities between language *families* are themselves susceptible to the same three explanations. That we so seldom see mention of this corollary principle is largely because twentieth-century historical linguistics has been laboring under the delusion that language families like Indo-European share *no* cognates with other families, thus offering nothing to compare. At this level, it is alleged, similarities simply do not exist.

What is striking is that this position—for which considerable evidence to the contrary existed already at the start of this century (Trombetti 1905) and which on a priori grounds seems most unlikely (Ruhlen 1988a)—came to be almost universally accepted by linguists, most of whom have never investigated the question themselves. Those few scholars who have actually investigated the question, such as Trombetti (1905), Swadesh (1960), and Greenberg

(1987), have tended to favor monogenesis of extant languages. Even Edward Sapir, often considered an exemplar of linguistic sobriety (despite his alleged excesses in the Americas), looked favorably upon the work of Trombetti, as seen in a letter to Kroeber in 1924: "There is much excellent material and good sense in Trombetti in spite of his being a frenzied monogenist. I am not so sure that his standpoint is less sound than the usual 'conservative' one" (quoted in Golla 1984: 420). We maintain that a comparison of the world's language families *without preconception* reveals numerous widespread elements that can only be reasonably explained as the result of common origin.

BORROWING

Linguists employ a number of well-known techniques to distinguish borrowed words from inherited items. Most important, clearly, is the fact that basic vocabulary, as defined by Dolgopolsky (1964) and others, is highly resistant to borrowing. Though it is no doubt true that *any* word may on occasion be borrowed by one language from another, it is equally true that such basic items as pronouns and body parts are rarely borrowed. Furthermore, borrowing takes place between two languages, at a particular time and place, not between language families, across broad expanses of time and place. Thus to attribute the global similarities we document here to borrowing would be ludicrous. And as regards the alleged cases of *mass* borrowing in the Americas (the so-called "Pan-Americanisms"), Greenberg (1990: 11) quite rightly protests "that basic words and pronouns could be borrowed from Tierra del Fuego to British Columbia . . . is so utterly improbable that it hardly needs discussion." It seems to us even less likely that basic vocabulary—the grist for most of the etymologies we offer herein—could have been borrowed from one language to another all the way from Africa across Eurasia to South America.

CONVERGENCE

A common criticism of work like ours is that, with around 5,000 languages to choose from, it cannot be too hard to find a word in some African language that is semantically and phonologically similar to, or even identical with, some word in an American Indian language.[1] There are so many possibilities, runs this argument, that one can hardly fail to find accidental "look-alikes" everywhere (Goddard 1979, Campbell 1988). But this sort of mindless search is exactly the reverse of how the comparative method proceeds. The units we are comparing are *language families*, not individual languages (a language isolate like Basque has traditionally been considered, taxonomically,

---

[1] For a more fundamental discussion of convergence, see Chapter 2.

a family consisting of a single language). Specifically, we will be comparing items in the following 32 taxa, each of which we believe is a genetically valid group at some level of the classification: Khoisan, Niger-Congo, Kordofanian, Nilo-Saharan, Afro-Asiatic, Kartvelian, Indo-European, Uralic, Dravidian, Turkic, Mongolian, Tungus, Korean, Japanese-Ryukyuan, Ainu, Gilyak, Chukchi-Kamchatkan, Eskimo-Aleut, Caucasian, Basque, Burushaski, Yeniseian, Sino-Tibetan, Na-Dene, Indo-Pacific, Australian, Nahali, Austroasiatic, Miao-Yao, Daic (= Kadai), Austronesian, and Amerind.

One may legitimately wonder why, for the most part, we are comparing relatively low-level families like Indo-European and Sino-Tibetan rather than higher-level taxa like Eurasiatic/Nostratic and Dene-Caucasian, especially since both of us support the validity of these higher-level families (Bengtson 1991a,b, Ruhlen 1990a). We do this to emphasize that higher-level groupings do not require the prior working out of all the intermediate nodes, contrary to the opinion of most Amerindian specialists (the field is all but bereft of generalists!). As is well known, both Indo-European and Austronesian were recognized as families from the early years of their investigation, long before specialists had reconstructed all their intermediate levels (a task that is, of course, still incomplete). In taxonomy it is a commonplace that higher-level groupings are often more obvious—and easier to demonstrate—than are lower-level nodes. We maintain that this is particularly so when one considers the entire world. Current contrary opinion notwithstanding, it is really fairly simple to show that all the world's language families are related, as we shall see in the etymologies that follow. Discovering the correct intermediate groupings of the tree—the subgrouping of the entire human family—is a much more difficult task, and one that has only begun. Exactly the same is true of Amerind, which itself is a well-defined taxon (Greenberg 1987, Ruhlen 1991a); the subgrouping *within* Amerind involves far more difficult analyses and taxonomic decisions (Ruhlen 1991c).

Each of our 32 genetic groups is defined by a set of etymologies that connects grammatical and lexical items presumed to be cognate within that group; the postulated membership and putative subgrouping within each of these groups is given in Ruhlen (1987a). The precise number of etymologies defining each of the 32 groups ranges from several thousand (for close-knit and/or well-documented groups like Dravidian or Indo-European) to several dozen (for ancient and/or poorly studied groups like Indo-Pacific or Australian). For the most part the many etymologies defining each group have been discovered independently, by different scholars. (In this regard Greenberg's work—in Africa, New Guinea, and the Americas—represents an exception to the rule.) So instead of drawing our etymologies from thousands of *languages,* each containing thousands of words, we are, rather, limited to less than three-dozen *families,* some of which have no more than a few hundred identifiable cognates. The pool of possibilities is thus greatly reduced, and accidental look-alikes will be few.

We believe that the failure of our critics to appreciate the truly minuscule probability of accidental similarities is the chief impediment to their understanding why all the world's languages must derive from a common origin. Accordingly, let us consider this question in some detail. Each of the etymologies we cite involves at least a half-dozen of the 32 supposedly independent families, precisely because the probability of finding the same accidental resemblance in six different families is close to zero. The multiplication of the (im)probabilities of accidental resemblance, as more and more families are considered, quickly assures the attentive taxonomist that similarities shared by numerous families, often separated by vast distances, cannot be due to chance. This crucial point has been emphasized by Collinder (1949), Greenberg (1957, 1963, 1987), and Dolgopolsky (1964), among others, but even Trombetti (1905) was well aware of the statistical importance of attestation in multiple families, rather than in just two. The biologist Richard Dawkins (1987: 274) makes the same point: "Convergent evolution is really a special kind of coincidence. The thing about coincidences is that, even if they happen once, they are far less likely to happen twice. And even less likely to happen three times. By taking more and more separate protein molecules, we can all but eliminate coincidence."

To see just how unlikely accidental look-alikes really are, let us consider two languages that each have just seven consonants and three vowels:

p	t	k		i	u
	s				a
m	n				
	l				

With a few notable exceptions the vast majority of the world's languages show at least these phonological distinctions. Yet even this minimal inventory is capable of producing 147 CVC roots, as shown in Table 5. The probability of accidental phonological *identity* is only 1/147, though the probability of accidental phonological *resemblance* might be 2/147, 3/147, etc., depending on how many other phonological shapes in Table 5 are deemed sufficiently similar. A perusal of Table 5 suggests, however, that most of these putative roots are quite distinct phonologically and are not readily connected by common phonological processes.

TABLE 5 Possible CVC Roots for a Language with Seven Consonants and Three Vowels

KAK	LAK	MAK	NAK	PAK	SAK	TAK
KAL	LAL	MAL	NAL	PAL	SAL	TAL
KAM	LAM	MAM	NAM	PAM	SAM	TAM
KAN	LAN	MAN	NAN	PAN	SAN	TAN
KAP	LAP	MAP	NAP	PAP	SAP	TAP
KAS	LAS	MAS	NAS	PAS	SAS	TAS
KAT	LAT	MAT	NAT	PAT	SAT	TAT
KIK	LIK	MIK	NIK	PIK	SIK	TIK
KIL	LIL	MIL	NIL	PIL	SIL	TIL
KIM	LIM	MIM	NIM	PIM	SIM	TIM
KIN	LIN	MIN	NIN	PIN	SIN	TIN
KIP	LIP	MIP	NIP	PIP	SIP	TIP
KIS	LIS	MIS	NIS	PIS	SIS	TIS
KIT	LIT	MIT	NIT	PIT	SIT	TIT
KUK	LUK	MUK	NUK	PUK	SUK	TUK
KUL	LUL	MUL	NUL	PUL	SUL	TUL
KUM	LUM	MUM	NUM	PUM	SUM	TUM
KUN	LUN	MUN	NUN	PUN	SUN	TUN
KUP	LUP	MUP	NUP	PUP	SUP	TUP
KUS	LUS	MUS	NUS	PUS	SUS	TUS
KUT	LUT	MUT	NUT	PUT	SUT	TUT

Now were we to compare two languages with a more typical phonemic inventory, say, fourteen consonants and five vowels,

p	t	k		j	w		i	u
b	d	g					e	o
	č							
	s						a	
m	n							
	l							
	r							

we would find that the number of possible CVC roots in each language jumps to 980. Again, of course, the probability of chance resemblance will depend on certain phonological assumptions, but precious few accidental identities *or* resemblances, vis-à-vis the stock of some other language or group of languages, could be expected.

One may appreciate just how unlikely an explanation of chance resemblance —independent development in each family—really is by considering the probability that the resemblances noted in etymology 21 (below) arose by convergence. We have chosen this etymology for our argument because the meaning involved is rarely borrowed and has no onomatopoeic connections. It thus offers a clear case, where the similarities must be due either to common origin or to accidental convergence. Let us try to calculate the probability that these similarities arose independently. To do this we must make certain assumptions, and at each such stage we shall adopt a minimalist approach that in fact underestimates the true probability. Let us assume, as we did above, that each language family uses only seven consonants and three vowels, yielding the 147 syllable types shown in Table 5. What, then, is the probability that two languages will accidentally match for a particular semantic/phonological domain, in the present case 'female genitalia'? Clearly it is 1/147 or .007. Whatever the form that appears in the first language family, the second family has only one chance in 147 of matching it. And the probability that a third family will offer a match will be $(1/147)^2$ or .000049; that of a fourth family, $(1/147)^3$ or .0000003; and so forth. In the etymology we give, 14 of the 32 taxa show apparent cognates, though the evidence is for the moment slim in Australian and the vowel in Austronesian (and many Amerind forms) is *e* rather than the expected *u*. But if we ignore these details, then the probability that the particular sound/meaning correlation "PUT/female genitals" arose independently *fourteen times* will be $(1/147)^{13}$, or about one chance in ten octillion, by our rough calculations. We feel that this qualifies as a long shot; certainly descent from a common source is the more likely explanation.

The foregoing constitutes what we consider to be the basis of genetic classification in linguistics. The application of these basic principles to the world's language families leads inevitably, in our opinion, to the conclusion that they all derive from a single source, as suggested by the 27 etymologies presented below. We have not yet dealt, however, with a number of other topics that in the minds of many linguists are inextricably tied up with taxonomy, questions like reconstruction, sound correspondences, and the like. We believe that these topics are not in fact of crucial importance in linguistic taxonomy, and that mixing the basic taxonomic principles with these other factors has led to much of the current confusion that we see concerning the classification of the world's languages. So that these ancilary topics not be invoked yet again, by those opposed to global comparisons, we will take them up one by one and explain why they are not relevant to our enterprise. Let us begin with a topic that is at the heart of many current disputes, the alleged incompatibility between Greenberg's method of multilateral comparison and the traditional methods of comparative linguistics.

MULTILATERAL COMPARISON VS. THE TRADITIONAL METHOD

Many linguists feel that Greenberg's use of what he calls multilateral comparison to classify languages in various parts of the world is incompatible with—or even antagonistic to—the methods of traditional historical linguistics, which emphasize reconstruction and sound correspondences (about which, see below). Thus, Bynon (1977: 271) claims that "the use of basic vocabulary comparison not simply as a *preliminary* to reconstruction but as a *substitute* for it is more controversial. . . . Traditional historical linguists . . . have not been slow in pointing out the inaccuracies which are bound to result from a reliance on mere similarity of form assessed intuitively and unsubstantiated by reconstruction." In a similar vein, Anna Morpurgo Davies (1989: 167) objects that "we do not yet know whether superfamilies outlined in this way have the same properties as families established with the standard comparative method. If they do not, there is a serious risk that the whole concept of superfamily is vacuous." And Derbyshire and Pullum (1991: 13) find Greenberg's Amerind hypothesis "startling, to say the least, when judged in terms of the standard methodology . . . ."

The confusion displayed in the previous three quotes (and one could give many others) results from a failure to realize that the comparative method consists essentially of two stages. The first stage is *classification,* which is really no different from what Greenberg calls multilateral comparison. The second stage, which might be called *historical linguistics,* involves family-internal questions such as sound correspondences and reconstruction. In practice, there is no name for this second stage simply because the two stages are seldom distinguished in the basic handbooks on historical linguistics, in which, almost without exception, the initial stage, classification, is overlooked (Bynon 1977, Hock 1986, Anttila 1989). Also overlooked in these basic texts are language families other than Indo-European. The origin of this anomaly—which knows no parallel in the biological world—is a consequence of the primogeniture of Indo-European in the pantheon of identified families, and the subsequent elaboration of the family by Europeans in the nineteenth century.

That the initial stage of comparative linguistics, classification, is so systematically overlooked today lies in the origin of the Indo-European concept itself. When Sir William Jones announced in 1786 that Sanskrit, Greek, and Latin—and probably Gothic and Celtic as well—had all "sprung from some common source," he essentially resolved the first stage of comparative linguistics at the outset: he identified five branches of Indo-European and hypothesized that all five were altered later forms of a single language that no longer existed. What was left unstated in Jones's historic formulation was the fact that languages such as Arabic, Hebrew, and Turkish—languages that Jones knew well—were excluded from his Indo-European family.[2] For Indo-European, and for the Indo-Europeanists who came to dominate historical linguistics, the problem of classification was essentially resolved by Jones, and the later additions of a few more obvious branches, such as Tocharian and Anatolian, did not alter this state of affairs.

The problems that Greenberg confronted, however, when he set out to classify the languages of Africa, were quite different from those facing a historical linguist investigating an already-defined family. Greenberg was confronted by over 1,000 languages, only some of which fit into well-defined families (e.g. Semitic, Bantu), and among which there was little understanding of the relationships. Under these circumstances, where does one start? Obviously the only way to begin is by the comparison of basic lexical items and grammatical formatives in *all* the languages, which inevitably leads to a classification of the languages into a certain number of groups defined by recurring similarities. This is exactly what Jones had done when he identified Indo-European, stressing, as he did, "a stronger affinity, both in the roots of verbs and in the forms of grammar, than could possibly have been produced by accident." He said nothing of sound correspondences or reconstruction, for in fact these concepts came to prominence (despite the earlier work of Rask, Grimm, and Bopp) only in the second half of the nineteenth century.

We believe, in short, that there is really no conflict between Greenberg's method of classifying languages and what is often referred to rather inexplicitly as "the standard methodology." The standard methodology is used to investigate family-internal problems; it does not—at least as it is explained in the basic textbooks referred to above—tell one how to identify language families. Accordingly, it does not tell one how to classify the world's languages. This, rather, is what Greenberg's work does, and it is, furthermore, how Greenberg views what he does. It has recently been alleged that he himself subscribes to the view that his methods differ from the standard methodology: "Greenberg (1987) makes clear that he believes such groupings [as Altaic, Hokan, and Amerind] cannot be reached by the standard comparative method; a wholly different method, MASS COMPARISON, is required" (Nichols 1990: 477). That this is, in fact, exactly the opposite of Greenberg's views is shown in the following:

Statements from certain American Indianists that I have rejected comparative linguistics and have invented a new unorthodox method called mass or multilateral comparison are repeated again and again in the press. However, as I clearly stated in Greenberg (1987: 3), once we have a well-established stock I go about comparing and reconstructing just like anyone else, as can be seen in my various contributions to historical linguistics. However, as I pointed out long ago in regard to my generally accepted African classification, the first step has to be to look very broadly,

---

[2] The term Indo-European was not introduced until the nineteenth century.

on at least a continent-wide scale, to see what the obvious groupings are. How can one start to apply the comparative method until one knows what to compare? (Greenberg 1990: 8)

RECONSTRUCTION

It is remarkable how frequently reconstruction is confounded with taxonomy. For a moment's reflection should make it clear that one can only begin reconstructing a proto-language *after* one has decided which languages belong to the putative family. Until one has delineated a set of seemingly related languages, collectively distinct from all others, by the methods outlined at the outset of this chapter, there is simply nothing to reconstruct. (After the fact, of course, reconstruction and (re)classification may enjoy a fruitful feedback.) And as for the supposed validating effect of reconstruction, would anybody claim that a bad reconstruction invalidates a well-defined family such as Indo-European? Or that a brilliant reconstruction could show that Slavic, Ob-Ugric, and Basque form a valid family? As a process, reconstruction is entirely different from taxonomy, and the two should not be confused. It is for this reason that Bynon's claim that Greenberg uses multilateral comparison as a "substitute" for reconstruction really makes no sense, and it is certainly not anything that Greenberg has ever written or said or even suggested.

SOUND CORRESPONDENCES

Perhaps the greatest source of confusion in recent taxonomic debates has been the role that sound correspondences, for example Grimm's Law, play in classification. It is clear that many historical linguists see regular sound correspondences as playing some crucial role in identifying valid linguistic taxa. In reality, sound correspondences are discovered only *after* a linguistic family has been identified, for the simple reason that sound correspondences are properties of particular linguistic families. They are not—and could not be—a technique for discovering families. When the Indo-European sound correspondences were worked out in the nineteenth century, not for a minute did any of the Indo-Europeanists imagine that they were "proving" Indo-European, the validity of which had not been in doubt for decades.

There are several reasons why sound correspondences have become enmeshed with taxonomic questions. First, it is sometimes alleged that it is only by means of regular sound correspondences that borrowings can be discriminated from true cognates. It has long been recognized, however, that loanwords often obey regular sound correspondences as strictly as do true cognates, a point emphasized on several occasions by Greenberg (1957, 1987). Campbell (1986: 224) makes the same point: "It ought to be noted that such agreements among sounds frequently recur in a number of borrowed forms, mimicking recurrent sound correspondences of true cognates."

Another alleged use of sound correspondences is to discriminate superficial look-alikes from true cognates (see the quote by Bynon above), and cognates, it is claimed, do not look alike and can only be recognized by means of sound correspondences. Thus, the commonly accepted Indo-European sound correspondences show that Armenian *erku* '2' and Latin *duo* '2' are cognate, despite their different form, whereas English bad and Farsi *bad* are not cognate, despite their identity of form. Campbell has aptly criticized such views:

Identical or very similar sound matchings do not necessarily imply loans or weak evidence of genetic connection. . . . With a time depth approaching that of the Indo-European languages of Europe, the Mayan correspondences are on the whole identical or are the result of single natural and recurrent changes. Proto-Mayan *p, *m, *n, and *y are reflected unchanged, with identical correspondences, in all of the over thirty Mayan languages. All other correspondences are very similar. Even English, after its many changes, reflects Proto-Indo-European *r, *l, *m, *n, *s, *w, and *y unchanged, on the whole.

A quick survey of once-disputed but now established remote genetic relationships reveals that identical (or very similar) sound correspondences are not that unusual . . . .

Therefore, identical correspondences should not be shunned nor too speedily attributed to borrowing. While longer separation may provide greater opportunity for unusual and exotic correspondences to develop in cases of distant genetic relationship, it is in no way necessary for such developments to have taken place nor for correspondences to be non-identical" (1986: 221–23).

Indeed, when one looks at the reconstructions that have been proposed for almost any family, one is able to find modern languages that preserve the proposed ancestral forms virtually unchanged. To cite just a few examples, Proto-Indo-European *nēpot- 'nephew, son-in-law' is strikingly similar to modern Rumanian *nepot*, and Proto-Indo-European *mūs 'mouse' was preserved without change in Latin, Old English, and Sanskrit. Proto-Austronesian *sepat '2' is almost identical with Rukai *sepate*, and Proto-Autronesian *matˢa 'eye' is identical with Rukai *matˢa*. Proto-Uralic *tule 'fire' is preserved in Finnish *tule-*, and Proto-Uralic *mośka 'to wash' differs little from Estonian *mõske-*. At an even greater time depth, we find that Proto-Nostratic *nato 'female relation by marriage' has survived, in Uralic, as Finnish *nato 'husband's or wife's sister' and, in Dravidian, as Malayalam *nāttūn 'husband's sister, brother's wife,' while Proto-Nostratic *pʰalV 'tooth' survives in Dravidian as Telugu *palu* and in Altaic as Ulch *palu*. At a time depth perhaps even greater than that of Nostratic, we find Proto-Australian *buŋku 'knee' preserved in Dyirbal *buŋku*.

In the etymologies we present below, connecting all of the world's language families, the situation is not all that different from that within the families just discussed. There are, in fact, many examples of sound correspondences of the transparent variety discussed by Campbell. This initial stage of the analysis is necessarily characterized by the identification of easily recognizable similarities, just as was the discovery of Indo-European or any other family. The refinement represented by exotic sound correspondences of the *erku–duo* variety inevitably awaits a later stage in the analysis—the second stage, which we have called "historical linguistics." And it is important to recognize that the work of this stage leads almost invariably to a refinement of the *etymologies,* rather than a refinement of the *classification.*

Among the world's language families, there are no doubt exotic sound correspondences as well that we have not detected. It should be noted, nevertheless, that as early as 1986 one of us (Bengtson) proposed some global sound correspondences, and the Russian scholar Sergei Starostin (1991) has recently published the most explicit statement of interphyletic sound correspondences to date. His brief table of Nostratic–Dene-Caucasian correspondences, though not quite global in scope, accounts for a vast expanse of the linguistic world. Nostratic, for Starostin, includes ten of our 32 taxa (Kartvelian, Indo-European, Uralic, Dravidian, Turkic, Mongolian, Tungus, Korean, Japanese-Ryukyuan, and Eskimo-Aleut), and Dene-Caucasian, for Starostin, includes Caucasian, Sino-Tibetan, Yeniseian, and Na-Dene—to which one may confidently add both Basque and Burushaski (Bengtson 1991a,b). Thus, Starostin's equations account for roughly half of our 32 taxa, as well as the vast majority of the Eurasian land mass. We find nothing in Starostin's correspondences that is inconsistent with the etymologies proposed below.

ON THE LIMITS OF THE COMPARATIVE METHOD

It has recently been widely asserted that the comparative method in linguistics produces reliable results only for the past 5,000–10,000 years. According to Kaufman (1990: 23), "A temporal ceiling of 7,000 to 8,000 years is inherent in the methods of comparative linguistic reconstruction. We can recover genetic relationships that are that old, but probably no earlier than that. The methods possibly will be expanded, but for the moment we have to operate within that limit in drawing inferences." Similar statements from a host of other scholars are given in Chapter 11, where such beliefs are identified as the central myth of historical linguistics (Chapter 13 further analyzes such myths). The origin of this myth, we believe, is an attempt by Indo-Europeanists to "explain" why Indo-European has no known genetic connections—in our view yet another myth. The fact that Indo-European is intimately connected with numerous other families has been demonstrated beyond a reasonable doubt by the Russian Nostraticists (Illich-Svitych 1971–84), a demonstration that is complemented and extended by Greenberg (to appear).

We have shown that in numerous cases sounds (particularly stable ones like nasal consonants and liquids)—and even entire words—have persisted over time spans greater than 8,000 years virtually unchanged. This raises the question why these evidently quite stable sounds must suddenly change beyond recognition, or disappear entirely, beyond the supposedly insuperable threshold of 10,000 years. If we can use modern languages to reconstruct proto-languages that existed at least 6,000–8,000 years ago (e.g. Proto-Indo-European, Proto-Uralic, Proto-Dravidian, Proto-Austronesian), why cannot such earlier languages themselves be compared (as in fact we will do) in order to discern still earlier groupings? Would it not be one of the more remarkable coincidences in the history of science if Indo-European, the family in terms of which comparative linguistics was discovered, turned out to define the temporal limit of comparative linguistics as well? That there is no such coincidence is amply demonstrated in the etymologies we give below. We feel it is time for linguists to stop selling the comparative method short and to apply it consistently to the world's linguistic taxa, *without preconception*. The present chapter represents a step in this direction, an initial step that shows that all of the world's populations are linguistically connected. The culmination of these efforts will be a comprehensive subgrouping of this single linguistic family.

BAD SEMANTICS

Another criticism of global etymologies in particular, and of long-range comparison in general, is that such liberties are taken with semantic change that literally anything can be connected with anything else, and it is certainly true that many global etymologies proposed over the years have been semantically unconvincing. But for just that reason we have constrained the semantic variation of each etymology very tightly, and few of the semantic connections we propose would raise an eyebrow if encountered in any of the standard etymological dictionaries. They are in fact semantically more conservative than many proposed connections in Pokorny (1959), the standard Indo-European etymological dictionary. Whatever damage this often alleged defect may have done to earlier programs of long-range comparison, we believe that it does not affect the etymologies presented below.

ERRORS IN THE DATA

Another often-cited criticism of long-range comparison is the presence of errors in the data, errors that invalidate the overall hypothesis. This is a specious argument, for it ignores both common sense and the standard measures of statistical significance. Genetic classification is not analogous to a mathematical proof, wherein one false step undermines the complete demonstration. Rather, the cumulative weight of all the evidence completely swamps the effects of whatever random errors may be scattered through the work. As Greenberg has often stressed—and has in fact shown in his work—multilateral comparison yields valid genetic classifications even from decidedly degenerate data. An example was Greenberg's classification of Australian languages in 1953, using little more than the vocabularies published by E. M. Curr in 1886–87. The notion that data must be pristine and copious flies in the face of commonly accepted historical method. It is all well and good for Kaufman (1990: 18) to demand at least 500 items of basic vocabulary and 100 points of grammar before "serious comparative work" can be carried out, but the fact remains that Indo-Europeanists have classified Lydian as Indo-European, without dissent, on the basis of a handful of words, as noted by Greenberg (1990: 10). Similarly, David Payne (1991: 362) reports that "all that remains of the [Shebayo] language is a vocabulary list of fifteen words collected at the end of the 17th century. . . . Despite the paucity of data from this language, it is quite clear that it is Arawakan." Historians and historical linguists—not to mention paleontologists working from handfuls of bashed fossils—use whatever material is available; they do not demand that the evidence be complete or immaculate.

DISTRIBUTIONAL DIFFERENCES

It is often alleged that one can find anything in linguistic data if one looks for it hard enough. Thus the global etymologies we present below are a tribute more to our industry and enterprise than to real genetic connections. Such a view is widespread among linguists who have never actually compared large numbers of languages (or language families), but those of us who *have* done this kind of work know the reverse to be true. "Wanting" to find something is of very little help if it is not there. Greenberg (1987) points out that the Amerind family has two general words for females, TUNA 'girl' and KUNA 'woman.' Both roots are abundantly attested throughout North and South America, and both are found in all eleven branches of the Amerind family. What is interesting about their distribution, however, is that whereas KUNA is widely attested in the Old World, as we show in etymology 11 below, we have found no trace of TUNA in the Old World. If it were really so easy to find anything one looks for, why did we fail to find TUNA in the roughly 4,500 Old World languages, when it is so readily observed in the approximately 500 New World languages? The evolutionary analysis provides a simple and natural explanation: when the Amerind forebears first entered the New World they brought with them the word KUNA 'woman,' and only later did they invent the word TUNA 'girl.' That there is no trace of TUNA 'girl' in the Old World is because it never existed there.

GLOBAL ETYMOLOGIES

For each etymology, in what follows, we present a phonetic and semantic gloss,[3] followed by examples from different language families. Though we have not attempted to present a unified phonetic transcription for all sources, we *have* adjusted certain transcriptions from time to time to avoid potential ambiguity. In the first etymology (but not elsewhere) yod has been normalized to *j* in all citations. Ejectives have been normalized to *p'*, *t'*, *k'*, etc.; V represents a vowel of indeterminate timbre; ĭ is used for the Old Church Slavic soft sign and ŭ for the hard sign; and ~ separates alternative forms. In the two interrogative etymologies (10, 17), interrogative and relative uses are not distinguished ('who?' as in "Who is that man?" vs. 'who' in "The man who came to dinner."). The intimate connection between the two is well known and uncontroversial. Most of the cited forms are, however, true interrogatives.

The source of the information for each family represented in a given entry is indicated by an abbreviation in brackets at the end of the entry. The number following the abbreviation is either the etymology number in the original source (if there is one) or the page number there. Since the existence of these roots as characteristic features of the language families cited has already been established by other scholars, and is not for the most part in question, we do not give the complete documentation for each family, limiting ourselves in most instances to an indication of the range of semantic and phonological variation within the family. The reader who wishes to see every relevant form for a given family should consult the sources cited. For Amerind, however, we give extensive citations, in order to counterbalance the fallacious criticism that has been directed at Greenberg's work. Parts of etymologies that are problematic, by dint of either phonetic or semantic divergence, or by restricted distribution, are preceded by a question mark. The lack of a semantic gloss following a form means that that form has the same meaning as the preceding form.

We make no claim to being the first to discover any of the etymologies listed below. The pioneering work of Trombetti, Swadesh, Greenberg, Illich-Svitych, Dolgopolsky, and Starostin has identified numerous widespread roots. What we *have* tried to do is to make each etymology more complete and more soundly documented in this incarnation than it may have been in previous ones. With this goal in mind we have weeded out certain families from pre-

---

[3] We do not deal here with reconstruction, and these glosses are intended merely to characterize the most general meaning and phonological shape of each root. Future work on reconstruction will no doubt discover cases where the most widespread meaning or shape was not original.

vious proposals, where the root was phonologically or semantically too divergent, or too weakly attested, to be convincing. But we believe we have also uncovered some additional etymological connections that had previously gone unnoticed. To a very great extent the recognition of these similarities has been made possible by the lower-level classificatory work of Greenberg in Africa, the New Guinea area, and the Americas, and by that of Russian scholars on Kartvelian, Caucasian, and other families of the former Soviet Union. Before all this work appeared, in recent decades, it was difficult, if not impossible, for a taxonomist to be sure that a root was truly diagnostic of some family, simply because there was no understanding of what the valid genetic families were, much less what cognates defined them. Trombetti, for example, dealt in terms of languages only where he was forced to by a lack of any general overall classification. Wherever possible, he worked with established language families (e.g. Indo-European, Uralic, Bantu), since he was well aware of the unavoidable methodological quandary presented by poorly documented families.

We harbor no illusions, of course, that every etymological connection we propose will be found, ultimately, to be correct, but we do believe that the removal of such errors as may exist in these etymologies will not seriously affect the basic hypothesis, which does not depend on any specific link for its validity. Furthermore, the number of widespread etymologies can be vastly increased over the fragment we present here. In the long run we expect the evidence for monogenesis of extant languages to become so compelling that the question will be not whether all the world's languages are related, but why it took the linguistic community so long to recognize this obvious fact.

1 AJA 'mother, older female relative'

KHOISAN: ≠Au.//eî *ai* 'female, mother,' !Kung *ʔai* 'mother'; Naron *ai*, Hadza *aija* ~ *aijako* 'mother, grandmother, aunt'; /'Auni *aija* 'mother.' [BD 6]

NIGER-CONGO: Temne *-ja* 'mother,' Bulom *ja*, Yoruba *ija*; Bantu: Proto-Bantu *jíjà* ~ *jíjò*. [BA IV: 190]

NILO-SAHARAN: Saharan: Daza *aja* 'mother,' Kanembu *jia* ~ *ja*, Kanuri *ja*; Fur *ija*; Maban: Runga *ja*; Koman: Gumuz *ijo*; Central Sudanic: Mangbetu *aja*, Madi *ia*, Lombi *jaija*; East Sudanic: Gulfan *aja*, Midob *ija*, Suk *iju*, Nyangiya *joijao* 'thy mother.' [NS 95, CN 67, ES 77, NSD 43]

AFRO-ASIATIC: Omotic: Wolamo *ajē* 'mother'; Cushitic: Oromo *ajo*, Somali *hoojo*; Chadic: Kotoko *īja* ~ *ija* ~ *ja*, Mubi *íjà*. [WM 64]

DRAVIDIAN: Tamil *āj* ~ *ãji* ~ *jaj* 'mother,' *ājāḷ* 'mother, grandmother,' Kannada *āji* 'mother,' Kolami *aj*, Parji *ajal* 'woman, wife,' *ija* 'mother,' Gadba *aja* 'mother,' *ajal* 'woman, wife,' Gondi *ajal* 'mother,' Konda *aja*, Pengo

aja ~ ija, Manda aja, Kui aia ~ aja ~ ija, Kuwi īja 'mother,' aja 'woman,'
Kurux ajaŋg ~ ajo 'mother,' Malto ajā 'my mother.' [D 364, NSD 43]
BURUSHASKI -ʌi 'daughter, girl.' [B 455]
?INDO-PACIFIC: Isabi aijo 'mother,' Korafe aja. [FS 99]
NAHALI aji 'husband's younger sister.' [NA 59]
AUSTROASIATIC: Munda: Sora ajaŋ-tsɔr 'bitch' (= female-dog, cf. kin-tsɔr
'male dog'); Mon-Khmer: Proto-Mon-Khmer *jaʔ 'grandmother.' [PB 482,
SB 34]
MIAO-YAO: Proto-Yao *ja 'father's sister.' [PB 339]
DAIC: Tai: Proto-Tai *ja 'father's mother'; Sek ja; Kam-Sui: Proto-Kam-
Sui *ja 'grandmother,' Sui ja 'grandmother, old woman'; Li: Proto-Li *ja
'mother, grandmother,' Small Cloth Loi ja 'mother'; Lakkia jə 'grand-
mother.' [PB 339]
AUSTRONESIAN: Proto-Austronesian *'ajah 'father,' Atayal jajaʔ 'mother,'
Pazeh jah 'older sister,' Malay 'ajah 'father,' Javanese (j)ajah 'father.'
[AN 13, WW 74, PB 339]
AMERIND: Penutian: North Sahaptin ájaD 'woman,' Nez Perce ʔajat, Tzotzil
jaja 'grandmother'; Hokan: Washo -ja 'paternal aunt,' Quinigua ʔjaak,
Tonkawa ʔejan 'woman's sister'; Central Amerind: Tewa jia 'mother,'
Proto-Oto-Manguean *ja 'female,' Proto-Uto-Aztecan *je 'mother,' Tara-
humara ije, Yaqui ʔaije, Nahua -jeʔ; Chibchan-Paezan: Xinca aja 'woman,'
Matagalpa joaja, Cuna jaa-kwa 'young woman,' Colorado aja 'mother';
Andean: Ona joj 'grandmother,' Auca -jǽjǽ; Macro-Tucanoan: Amaguaje
ajo 'old woman,' Masaka jaja 'older sister,' Ticuna jake 'old woman';
Equatorial: Mapidiana aja 'aunt,' Tora ije 'paternal grandmother,' Arikem
haja 'aunt'; Macro-Panoan: Mayoruna jaja, Shipibo jaja 'paternal aunt,'
Moseten eje 'grandmother,' jaja 'mother-in-law'; Macro-Carib: Accawai
aja 'mother'; Macro-Ge: Coropo ajan, Coroado ajan, Palmas jã. [CA 55,
AMN]

2 BU(N)KA 'knee, to bend'

NIGER-CONGO: Baga -buŋ 'knee,' Pajade -paŋ, ?Lefana -ŋko; Bantu: Proto-
Bantu *bóŋgó, Swahili bong'oa 'to stoop, bend down.' [BA III: 57]
KORDOFANIAN: Tegele mbo 'knee' (pl. aboan ~ abuaŋ). [VB]
AFRO-ASIATIC: Omotic: Dime boq 'knee,' Bako boɣa, Basketo buka, Oyde
bunke; Chadic: Fyer fuŋ 'knee,' Bura bunji 'knee.' [VB]
INDO-EUROPEAN: Proto-Indo-European *bheug(h) 'to bend'; Indic: Sanskrit
bhugná 'bent'; Germanic: Gothic biugan 'to bend,' Old Icelandic bogenn
'bent,' English bow, elbow; Celtic: Proto-Celtic *buggo 'flexible, mal-
leable,' Irish bog 'soft'; Albanian butë (< bhug(h)-to) 'soft'; Baltic: Latvian baũgurs 'hill, rising ground.' [IE 152, N 25]

TURKIC: Proto-Turkic *bük(ä) ~ *bök(ä) 'to bend,' Chuvash pĕk ~ pŏk 'to
bend,' Yakut bük, Khakas bükri 'bent,' Old Uighur bük ~ bök 'to twist,'
Uighur bük ~ bök 'to kneel.' [N 25]

MONGOLIAN: Proto-Mongolian *böke 'to bend,' Written Mongolian bökeji ~
bököji 'to cave in, sag' böken 'hump of a camel,' bökötür 'bent,' Khalkha
bóx(ón) 'hump of a camel,' Kalmyk bökṇ 'hump, humped.' [N 25]

TUNGUS: Proto-Tungus *bök(ä) 'to bend,' Manchu buk(-da), Nanai bukun
'hump,' Evenki bukä 'to bow,' buku 'bent, crooked,' bäkä 'hump.' [N 25]

AINU he-poki-ki 'bow down,' he-poki-poki 'to nod the head.'

INDO-PACIFIC: Halmahera: Tobelo buku 'knee,' Modole bubuqu, Loda wuwu-
ku; Bougainville: Koianu poku; South New Guinea: Teri Kawalsch bugu;
Northeast New Guinea: Saker bakbakan. [IP 43]

AUSTRALIAN: Proto-Australian *puŋku 'knee,' Tyeraity böŋgöl, Maranunggu
biŋgar, Guugu Yimidhir buŋgu, Kok-Nar poŋk ~ púŋkuwál, Gugu-Badh-
un buŋguyal, Kukatj poŋkɨpal, Dyirbal buŋgu 'knee, bend in the river,
wave,' Yidiny buŋgu 'knee, hump in a snake's body.' [NP 232, RD 110, 123,
223]

AMERIND: Proto-Algonquian: *wāk- 'bend,' Blackfoot woxos 'shin' (from an
earlier meaning of 'knee,' as seen in Maidu pok'ósi), Bella Bella wak-
'bent,' Crow išbaxe 'elbow,' Hidatsa išpahi 'elbow,' Caddo buko 'knee';
Penutian: Tfalatik pɔsq 'bow' (with metathesis, from earlier *pɔqVs),
Kalapuya oposqu 'bow' (with metathesis), Maidu pok'ósi 'knee,' Nisenan
p'əkkasi 'elbow,' Zuni poʔku 'to fold,' Texistepec boka 'elbow,' Pokonchi
bak 'crooked,' Sierra Popoluca pikši 'bow,' Mixe kupokš 'elbow'; Hokan:
Shasta ʔičipka 'knee,' Achomawi lupuʔisi 'bow,' Chumash sibuk ~ šipuk
'elbow,' Walapai mipuk 'knee,' phúʔ 'bow'; Central Amerind: Varohia
čopokori 'knee'; Chibchan-Paezan: Guamaca buka 'knee, elbow,' Rama
buk 'twist,' Atanque buküh-köna 'knee,' Warrao oboka 'elbow,' Colorado
te-bunga 'elbow,' Cayapa ne-bumbuka 'knee,' Chimu č'epuk; Andean:
Jebero pöktenja 'bow,' Ona epekten 'elbow,' Alakaluf kolpakar 'knee';
Macro-Tucanoan: Iranshe poku 'bow (n.),' Proto-Nambikwara *pako
'crooked,' *pok 'bow (n.)'; Equatorial: Paumari amabokoi 'elbow,' Guara-
ñoca pokà 'bow,' Cuiva tabóko 'knee,' Palicur ubowɣi, Karif bugunuge
'elbow'; Macro-Carib: Miranha thüboqua 'bow,' Apiaca topkat; Macro-
Panoan: Mayoruna mupukušau 'elbow,' Panobo waʔpuško 'elbow' (with
metathesis), Sapiboca embako 'elbow,' Tiatinagua waku; Macro-Ge:
Mohačobm pokai 'bow,' Umotina boika, Bororo boiga, Opaie či-p̃ege-ri
'elbow.' [AM 157, MT 16, AMN]

3 BUR 'ashes, dust'

NILO-SAHARAN: Songhai: Gao *bonni* 'ashes,' Djerma *boron*; Berta *bub(u)ʔda*; Central Sudanic: Bongo *buru-ku*, Keliko *ɔfɔrago*; East Sudanic: Kenzi, Birgid *u-burti*, Murle *būr*, Mursi *burr*, Balé *bur*, Shilluk, Bor *bur*, Lango *buru*, Alur *burru*. [NS 9, CN 7, ES 5, NSD 6, NSB]

AFRO-ASIATIC: Proto-Afro-Asiatic **b(w)rH* 'loose soil, sand, dust'; Semitic: Proto-Semitic **br* 'dust,' Arabic *baraj* 'dust, soil,' Mehri *berōr* 'sandy seashore,' Classical Hebrew *bar* 'field, open space,' Proto-Semitic **bwr* '(fallow) ground,' Arabic *bawr* 'fallow ground,' Syriac *būrō*, Akkadian *bāru* 'open space'; ?Berber: Shilha *tamurt* 'soil'; Cushitic: Beja *būr* 'soil,' Bilin *birā* 'soil,' Saho *baro*, Afar *baḷō*, Somali *bɛrri*; Chadic: Proto-Chadic **'bwr* 'sand,' Angas *'bur* 'sand, dust,' Logone *búrá*, Gider *burduku* 'soil.' [CS 398, N 22]

KARTVELIAN: Svan *burɣw* 'to raise dust,' *birɣw* (< **burɣw-i*) 'dust, ashes,' ?Middle Georgian *bre*. [N 22]

URALIC: Proto-Uralic (Illich-Svitych) **porV* 'dust, sand, dirt'; Samoyed: Kamassian *püre* 'sand'; Ugric: Ostyak *per* 'ashes'; Finnic: Finnish *poro* 'hot ashes, course dust,' Estonian *pori* 'mud,' Mansi *pors* 'sweepings.' [U 68, N 22]

DRAVIDIAN: Proto-Dravidian **pūṛV* ~ **poṛV* 'loose soil, sand, dust,' Malto *porsi* 'sweepings,' Naikri *burdi* 'ash,' Telugu *būḍida* 'ashes,' Tulu *poyyè* 'sand,' Malayalam *puruti* 'dust, earth,' *pūyi* 'sand,' Tamil *puṛuti* 'dust, dry earth,' *pūṛi* 'powder, dust.' [D 4316, N 22, NSD 6]

TURKIC: Proto-Turkic **bōr*, Chuvash *pur(ă)* 'chalk,' Tuva *por* 'clay,' Jakut *buor* 'soil, clay, dust,' Altai *pur* 'ashes,' Uighur *bor*, Kazakh *bor* 'chalk.' [N 22]

MONGOLIAN: Khalkha *bur* 'dirty, muddy, dark,' Buriat *bur* 'silt, swamp, clay.' [N 22]

TUNGUS: Manchu *buraki* 'dust, sand,' Nanai *buräxin* 'dust,' Oroch *buräxi*. [N 22]

?ESKIMO-ALEUT: Proto-Eskimo-Aleut **pujV* ~ **apju* 'dust, mud, soot.' [EA]

BURUSHASKI *bur-di* 'the ground.'

?INDO-PACIFIC: Tasmanian *būrana* 'smoke.'

AUSTRALIAN: Proto-Australian **burin* ~ **burinj* 'smoke.' [AC 75]

AMERIND: Chibchan-Paezan: Cuna *piru* 'ashes,' Uncasica *bura*, Manare *oka-bora*, Move *ñio-bru*, Guatuso *purun*, Catio *pora* 'dust'; Andean: Lupaca *purka* 'ashes'; Equatorial: Shuara *pupuur* 'dust,' Bare *baridi* 'ashes,' Wapishana *parati*, Goajiro *purpura* 'dust'; Macro-Panoan: Taruma *gula-paru* 'powder'; Macro-Carib: Yagua *pupāndru* 'ashes'; Macro-Ge: Proto-Ge **prə* 'ashes,' Krenje *pro*, Cayapo *pra* 'embers,' Guato *(ma-)fora(-ta)* 'ashes,' Caraja *brībi*. [AM 11, AMN]

4 ČUN(G)A 'nose; to smell'

KHOISAN: ≠Au.//eî *č'ū* 'nose,' !Kung *tˢ'ū* ~ *sū̃*, !O-!Kung *tˢn* ~ *čn*; G//abake
čui, Naron *sō̃* 'to snuff,' Nama *suni* 'sniff, smell from'; /Xam *sū* 'snore,'
//Ng-!'e *sū?wa* 'blow the nose,' Kakia /nuha *čuni* 'nostrils.' [K 89, SAK
488, 489, HF 1:10]

NILO-SAHARAN: Saharan: Zagawa *sina* 'nose,' Berti *sano*; East Sudanic: Mei-
dob *i-siŋi* 'nose,' Ongamo *(a-ta-)sɪŋa* 'to sneeze,' Ik *sik'wa* 'to sneeze';
Central Sudanic: Shabo *čona* ~ *šona* 'nose.' [NSB, KER, HF 12]

AFRO-ASIATIC: Proto-Afro-Asiatic **t̠(w)n* ~ **t̠(j)n* 'smell; Ancient Egyptian
śn 'to smell,' *śnśn* 'to breathe'; Omotic: Proto-Omotic **sin-t* 'nose,' Basketo *sinča*, Chara *sindā*, Gimira *sint*, Mao *šinto*; Cushitic: Burgi *suna*,
Konso *sona*, Tambaro *sana*, Somali *san*, Kaffa *činno* 'odor,' Saho *sīn* 'to
smell'; Chadic: Hausa *súnsùnā* ~ *sánsànā* 'to smell,' Bachama *šine*, Bata
činne, Klesem *siŋ*, Bana *činan*, Dari *šin*. [AA 54, N 51, HF 1:10]

KARTVELIAN: Georgian *sun* 'odor, to smell.' [N 51]

INDO-EUROPEAN: Proto-Indo-European **snā* 'to flow, dampness, nose'; Germanic: Proto-Germanic **snu* 'to smell, nose,' Swedish *snus* 'snuff,' *snuva*
'runny nose,' German *snau* 'snout, beak,' Old Icelandic *snoppe* 'to snuff,'
Norwegian *snūt* 'nose,' English 'snout, sniff'; Baltic: Lithuanian *snukkis*
'snout.' [IE 971]

URALIC: Proto-Uralic (Illich-Svitych) **čüŋV* 'to smell, odor, smoke,' (Rédei)
*śaŋkɜ 'smell, taste'; Samoyed: Nenets *t'üńē* ~ *tińē* 'to smell'; Ugric:
Vogul *seeŋkw* 'mist, vapor'; Finnic: Votyak *čyŋ* ~ *šyŋ* 'smoke,' Zyrian
čyn 'smoke,' ?Finnish *henki* 'breath, spirit.' [U 97, N 51, KR 462]

DRAVIDIAN: Tamil *cuṇṭu* 'bill, beak,' Malayalam *cuṇṭu* 'beak, lips, snout,'
Kannada *cuṇḍu* 'a bird's beak,' Parji *coṇḍ* 'mouth, beak,' Pengo *coṇḍi*
'beak of a bird,' Kui *suḍa* 'mouth, beak,' Kuwi *hoṇḍi* 'mouth.' [D 2664]

CAUCASIAN: Proto-Caucasian **sHwiḻnt'* 'to smell, snot,' Proto-Avar-Andi
*s̄ʷint'V 'to smell, snuff,' Avar *s̄unt'* 'snuff,' *sunt'(-ize)* 'to smell,' Dargi
sunt' 'scent, odor,' Lak *s̄unt'* 'snuff,' Proto-Lezghian **s̄ʷiḻnt'* 'snot,' Tsaxur
suḻnt' 'snot,' ?Hurrian *sunA* 'breath, soul.' [HF 1:10, C 190]

BASQUE *su-dur* 'nose,' *sun-da* 'smell.'

BURUSHASKI *šūŋ* (εtʌs) ~ *s̄ū* (εtʌs) 'to smell.' [B 335]

SINO-TIBETAN: Karen *suŋ* 'odor'; Tibeto-Burman: Proto-Tibeto-Burman
*sVna 'nose,' **suŋ* 'smell,' Tibetan *sna*, *bsuŋ* 'smell (sweet),' Nung *sƏna*,
Janggali *sina*, Digaro *hƏna(-gam)*, Burmese *hna*, *sàŋ* 'emit a pleasant
odor.' [ST 101, 405, HF 1:10]

NA-DENE: Haida *sánjuu* 'smell,' *sīnaŋ* 'sniffling'; Tlingit *čan* 'stench'; Eyak
čãh ~ *čã?* 'stink'; Athabaskan: Proto-Athabaskan **-čin-ɬ* 'nose,' Galice
šan ~ *šãã* 'smell,' Kato *čƏn* 'smell.' [ND]

INDO-PACIFIC: Baruya *sinna* 'nose,' Musak *sinami-* 'to smell.' [FS 105]

NAHALI *čōn* 'nose.' [NA]

MIAO-YAO: Miao *tsinyu* 'nose,' Yao *(pu-)tsoN*. [HF 1:10]

DAIC: Ong Be *zoŋ* 'nose,' *suŋ (mu)* 'to blow the nose' (= to-blow [nose-mucus]). [PB 345]

AUSTRONESIAN: Proto-Austronesian **iğuŋ* ~ **uğuŋ* 'nose,' Kuvalan *uğuŋ*, Proto-Philippine **suŋaD*, Proto-Oceanic **isu(ŋ)* ~ **untsu(ŋ)*, Fijian *utsu*, Proto-Polynesian **isu*; Proto-Austronesian **t'uŋaḷ* ~ **suNar* 'to sneer, turn up the nose.' [AN 67, 158; WW 139, 227; PB 345]

AMERIND: Almosan-Keresiouan: Seneca *ʔosēnōʔ* 'smell,' Chiwere *sīŋe*, Tutelo *sūw* 'stink'; Penutian: Wintu *sono* 'nose,' Chukchansi *sinik'*, Gashowu *sīn-wiyi* 'to blow the nose,' Yokuts *s̩ēniṭ'* 'smell,' Yaudanchi *senk'a* 'smell,' Huave *šink* 'nose,' Santa Cruz *suunta* 'snot,' Lake Miwok *s̩in-* 'blow the nose,' Central Sierra Miwok *sēŋ-aH* 'smelly thing'; Central Amerind: Tewa *sū* 'smell,' Kiowa *sē*, Proto-Central Otomi **šiñū* 'nose,' South Pame *šinyû*; Chibchan-Paezan: Atanque *sun-köna* 'beak,' Binticua *misun-a* 'nose,' Move *inson*, Colorado *sin*, Timicua *čini*; Andean: Sek *čuna*, Leco *(bi-)činua*, Proto-Quechuan **sinqa*; Macro-Tucanoan: Ubde-Nehern *činuehei* 'smell,' Yuri *čunama*; Equatorial: Campa *asanki-ro*, Callahuaya *čini* 'nose,' Caranga *čonanğa* 'stink.' [AK 175, CP 133, A 79, 106, AMN]

5 KAMA 'hold (in the hand)'

KHOISAN: Zhu *xóm(-xéi)* 'rub back and forth'; Kxoe *xôm* 'crush with the hands.' [SAK 852]

NIGER-CONGO: Dagomba *kam* 'squeeze,' Nupe *kã*, Proto-Bantu **kama*, Swahili *kama* 'to squeeze, to milk,' *kama-ta* 'to take hold, seize, grasp.' [KS 59, BA III: 263]

?NILO-SAHARAN: Songhai *kaŋkam* 'squeeze' (< **kamkam* ?). [KS 59]

AFRO-ASIATIC: Proto-Afro-Asiatic **km* 'seize, take, squeeze'; Semitic: Akkadian *kamū* 'to capture,' Arabic *kamaša* 'seize, grasp'; Cushitic: Dahalo *kam* 'to hold,' Kwadza *komos* 'to grip,' Iraqw *kom* 'to have'; Berber: Tuareg *ekmem* 'squeeze'; Chadic: Hausa *kāma* 'to catch,' Musgu *kaw* 'seize,' Gidar *gəma* 'to take,' Masa *čum*. [AA 63, N 157, AB 160]

INDO-EUROPEAN: Proto-Indo-European **gem* ~ **gemō* 'to grasp with both hands, seize'; Armenian *čmlem* 'I squeeze'; Greek *geuto* 'he took' (< **gem-to*); Celtic: Old Irish *gemel* 'fetters'; Germanic: Old Swedish *kumla* 'to crumple'; Baltic: Latvian *gùmstu* 'to seize, grasp'; Slavic: Old Church Slavic *žĭmǫ* 'I press, squeeze.' [IE 368, N 157, AB 171]

URALIC: Proto-Uralic (Illich-Svitych) **kama-lV* ~ **koma-rV* 'handful,' (Rédei) **komɜ(rɜ)* 'palm of the hand,' (Rédei) **käme(-ne)*; Samoyed: Yenisei Samoyed *hammara* 'hand'; Finnic: Finnish *kamahlo* ~ *kahmalo* 'double handful,' Estonian *kamal* 'handful,' Mordvin *komoro*, Saami *goab-mer* 'double handful.' [U 42, N 157, KR 137, 175]

DRAVIDIAN: Proto-Dravidian **kamV* 'to seize, take, hold,' Koraga *kamḍi* 'to steal,' Telugu *kamucu* 'to hold, seize,' Malto *kam* 'to gather (by oneself).' [D 1326, N 157]

TURKIC: Proto-Turkic **kam-a* ~ **qam-a* 'to take, seize,' Old Uighur *qama* 'to take prisoner, surround,' Kirghiz *kama* 'to surround, arrest,' Tatar *kama* 'to herd cattle into a pen,' Nogai *kam-ty* 'to seize.' [N 157]

MONGOLIAN: Written Mongolian *qamu* 'to gather, pick up,' Khalkha *xamă* 'to gather, pick up.' [N 157]

TUNGUS: Proto-Tungus **kama* ~ **kamu* 'to press, oppress, forbid,' Nanai *kama-le* 'to press, clasp,' Olcha *kama-lu* 'to forbid,' *kama-lğu* 'to press,' Orok *kamu-i* 'to take in one's arms, seize,' Evenki *kama* 'deny assistance to, oppress.' [N 157]

CAUCASIAN: Proto-Caucasian **k'ēmV* 'armful, handful,' Proto-Lak **k'ama* 'handful,' Proto-Lezghian **k'em(a)* 'armful.' [C 124]

?INDO-PACIFIC: North New Guinea: Arapesh *kum* 'to steal,' Bosngun *kamba* 'to steal,' Siaute *kupi* 'to take.' [NNG 45]

MIAO-YAO: Proto-Miao-Yao **ŋgam* 'to crush, squeeze' (< **kamgam*), Hai-ninh Yao *gam* 'to crush or squeeze with the hand.' [PB 315]

DAIC: Tai: Proto-Tai **hŋam* 'to lay hold of, grasp' (< **kamgam*), **kum* 'hold with the hand'; Kam-Sui: Sui *ʔñam* 'to hold,' Mak *ñam* 'to clench the fist, take hold of' (< **ʔŋam* < **kamgam*); Li: Proto-Li **kəm* 'to press with the hand, squeeze,' Southern Li *kom (luoi)* 'to squeeze' (= press [down]); Ong-Be *kom* 'to press down.' [PB 315]

AUSTRONESIAN: Proto-Austronesian **kem* 'enclose, cover, grasp,' **gemgem* 'hold, grasp in the fist, make a fist,' Rukai *(wa-)gəmgəm* 'to squeeze in the hand.' [AN 54, 74, 78; WW 103; PB 315-16]

6 KANO 'arm'

KHOISAN: /Xam //kũ 'arm,' /Nu-//en //kan 'branch'; Naron //k'õã 'arm,' Nama //õa(-b); !Kung //kãũ 'branch,' ?≠hã ~ ≠hã 'arm.' [SAK 130, 186]

NIGER-CONGO: Yingulum *kəní* 'arm,' Fali *kʌn*; Bantu: Proto-Bantu **kónò* '(fore)arm,' Nyali *(i-)kón(-do)* 'hand,' Swahili *(m-)kono* 'arm, forearm, hand, front paw.' [BA 297, AT 11]

NILO-SAHARAN: Kunama *kò'nà* 'hand,' *u-kun-kula* 'armpit, elbow' (= arm-hole), Ilit *kon* 'hand,' Berta *k'oŋ-k'oloŋ* ~ *kʷɔn-kʷɔlɔŋ* 'elbow,' Teso *(á-)kànì* 'hand,' Masai *(eŋ-)káíná* 'hand.' [CN 5, AT 79, NSB]

?AFRO-ASIATIC: Chadic: Proto-West Chadic **ḥA-ganA* 'arm, shoulder,' An-gas *gwon* 'shoulder,' Bokkos *kôŋ* 'arm,' Sha *g̃aan*; Cushitic: Iraqw *kun(-day)* 'foot.' [AT 86, OS 683]

?INDO-EUROPEAN: Proto-Indo-European *kon-t-* ~ *kn-t-* '10,' Germanic: Proto-Germanic *handu(-z)* 'hand,' English hand.

URALIC: Proto-Uralic (Rédei) *konɜ* ~ *konɜ-ala* 'armpit'; Yukaghir *kun(-el)* '10,' *xanba* 'hand'; Ugric: Hungarian *hón* ~ *hón(-alj)* 'armpit' (-alj 'that which is beneath'), Vogul *kan(-l)* 'armpit'; Finnic: Finnish *kain (-alo)*, Votyak *kun(-ul)*, Zyrian *kon(-uvt)*, (-uvt 'that which is beneath'). [U 101, KR 178]

DRAVIDIAN: Tulu *kaŋkuḷa* 'armpit' (= arm-hole), Kannada *kaŋkuṟ* ~ *gaŋkəlu* 'armpit,' Kota *ganjguly*. [D 1234, N 220]

CAUCASIAN: Proto-Caucasian *ᴳHwi̯nĀ* 'arm, shoulder,' Proto-Lezghian *q̄ün* 'shoulder,' Krytz *qunä*, Archi *qIun*. [C 156]

YENISEIAN: Proto-Yeniseian *ken* 'shoulder.' [Y 28]

SINO-TIBETAN: Ancient Chinese *kēn* 'shoulder'; Proto-Tibeto-Burman *kan* 'arm.' [Y 28, TB 438]

NA-DENE: Proto-Eyak-Athabaskan *gàn* 'arm,' Tanana *gan*, Tlatskanai *okane*, Ingalik *gàn*, Galice *gaane?* 'arm, branch,' Navajo *gaan* 'arm.' [SN, ND]

INDO-PACIFIC: Tasmanian: Southeastern *gouna* ~ *guna* ~ *gouana* ~ *wana* 'arm, hand,' Parawen *konɛnɛ* 'arm,' Jilim *kanan* 'left (arm),' Dumpu *kiñɛn* 'shoulder,' Gapun *akan* 'arm.' [T 83, FS 107, IP 820]

?NAHALI *khanḍa* 'shoulder,' *akhanḍi* 'finger.' [NA 59, 85; Kuiper believes *khanḍa* is probably a borrowing from Kurku.]

?AUSTROASIATIC: Vietnamese *cánh* ~ *cành* 'arm, branch, wing.'

DAIC: Tai: Proto-Tai *xeen* 'arm,' Dioi *kien* 'arm, sleeve,' Sek *keen*; Kam-Sui: Sui *ćhin*, Then *khyin* 'sleeve'; Ong-Be *kan (mo)* 'forearm,' *gen (mo)* 'upper arm.' [PB 379]

AMERIND: Almosan-Keresiouan: Blackfoot *kin(-ists)* 'hand,' Kutenai *kin*, Kalispel *axən* 'arm,' Okanagan *-aqan*, Kwakwala *-xaina* 'shoulder'; Penutian: Tunica *hkeni* 'hand,' Chitimacha *ʔokun* 'shoulder,' Sayula *konik* 'carry on the shoulder'; Central Amerind: Chichimec *kan'a* 'hand,' Otomi *xĩʼnyí* 'shoulder'; Chibchan-Paezan: Murire *kana* 'arm,' Bintucua *guna* 'arm, hand,' Guamaca *guna* 'arm,' Atanque *guna* 'hand,' Chimu *aken* 'arm'; Andean: Ona *haken* 'arm,' Tehuelche *aken* 'shoulder blade,' Simacu *kanúxua* 'shoulder,' Selknam *k'ojjn*; Macro-Tucanoan: Särä *axkono* 'shoulder,' Uaiana *akono* 'shoulder, armpit,' Omoa *naxkono* 'shoulder'; Equatorial: Piro *kano* 'arm,' Parecis *-kano-*, Canamari *kano* 'shoulder,' Timote *-kiñem* 'hand,' Mocochi *kiñien*, Tinigua *kwana*, Trumai *kanap*; Macro-Carib: Miranya *gano-aga* 'hand,' *gano-múhtee* 'armpit,' Coeruna *kunia* 'hand'; Macro-Panoan: Proto-Panoan *mï-kïnï* 'hand,' Lengua *kanyama* 'armpit'; Macro-Ge: Bororo *kana* 'upper arm,' Camican *guangäni* 'arm,' Botocudo *kinaon* 'shoulder,' Opaie *(či-)kã* 'shoulder.' [AK 6, CP 4, AM 16, AMN]

7 KATI 'bone'

?KHOISAN: /Xam /kuttən 'bone behind the ear,' //Ng-!'e ketn 'bone.' [BD 87, 326]

NILO-SAHARAN: ?Berta k'ara 'bone,' East Sudanic: Nera kətii(n), Kenuzi kīd, Kundugr koidu, Turkana ako-, Lotuko -γōtyu, Bari kuyu, Debri kwedu, Proto-Southeast Surmic *gigec. [ES 21, NSB, SES]

AFRO-ASIATIC: Proto-Afro-Asiatic *qš 'bone'; Ancient Egyptian qś 'bone'; Semitic: Arabic qaṣṣ ~ gaṣṣ 'sternum'; Cushitic: Proto-Cushitic *(m-)qS 'bone,' Kambata miqqa-ta (qq < *qS); Omotic: Jeba ʔúús-u (< *k'us), Badditu miqi-tē, Wolamo maqa-tta; Berber: Proto-Berber *ġs(j) 'bone,' Shilha ixs, Kabyle iġes, Tuareg eġēs; Chadic: Proto-Chadic k'ṣ(j) 'bone,' Proto-West Chadic *ḥa-k'asi, Hausa k'āśi, Musgu keṣ'ke, Gerka γas, Somrai guseŋ, Karbo kāso ~ kāsi. [CS 225, AA 11, N 219, OS 620, HF 12]

INDO-EUROPEAN: Proto-Indo-European *kos-t 'bone'; Italic: Latin costa 'rib'; Slavic: Old Church Slavic kostĭ 'rib,' Serbo-Croatian kôst, Russian kostʲ. [IE 616, N 219]

?URALIC: Samoyed: Kamassian kot 'rib'; Finnic: Mordvin kaskǎ ~ kaske 'sacrum.' [N 219, SUL 492]

DRAVIDIAN: Kurux xōc(-ol) 'bone,' Malto qoc(-lu). [D 1288]

CHUKCHI-KAMCHATKAN: Proto-Chukchi-Kamchatkan *(χ)ətʌ-χəmV 'bone.' [CK 1]

?ESKIMO-ALEUT: Proto-Eskimo-Aleut *qat'ɨ 'breast, ribs.' [EA]

CAUCASIAN: Proto-Caucasian *kŏtˢ'a 'kind of bone,' Proto-Dido *k'otˢ'u 'back of head,' Proto-Lezghian *k'atˢ'a 'vertebra, shin,' Proto-Xinalug *kɨz 'thigh, hip.' [C 116]

BASQUE gar-khotx(e) 'nape' (gara = 'skull').

?BURUSHASKI kʌnǰa 'back of neck, neck joint.'

SINO-TIBETAN: Proto-Sino-Tibetan *kut 'bone,' Old Chinese *kwət. [SC 57]

NA-DENE: Haida (s)kuts ~ (s)kuǧi 'bone,' Eyak q'ahš. [ND]

INDO-PACIFIC: South New Guinea: Dabu kut 'bone,' Dibolug kute, Ngamai kuta, Kawam kutra, Parb kwod, Tunjuamu guat, Tokwasa kuart, Bangu kuar, Keladdar kadrowa. [SNG 9]

AMERIND: Almosan-Keresiouan: Bella Bella k'ōdᶻo 'bone, rib' (borrowing from Chinook?), Pawnee kīsu 'bone,' Wichita kīsʔa, Acoma ya-gətsʲ-əni 'rib'; Penutian: Chinook qotˢo 'bone,' Northern Sierra Miwok kyččyč, Plains Miwok kəčəč, Yuki k'iʔt, Wappo kúțe 'rib,' Chitimacha katˢi 'bone,' Uspantec k'alk'aš 'rib'; Chibchan-Paezan: Binticua katia ~ kiasi 'rib,' Matanawi kisi, Atacameño kada 'bone,' Itonama čɨdɨki, Chimu čotti, Colorado čide; Andean: Selknam q'ejt' 'breastbone,' Mapudungu kadi 'rib,' Genneken uguets 'bone,' Alakaluf akšiase 'rib'; Macro-Tucanoan:

Kapishana *nya-kotsī*; Equatorial: Caranga *kaiču* 'bone'; Macro-Panoan: Cavineña *(epere-)'katse* 'rib,' Komlek *kadekotti* 'bone,' Caduveo *koda-uek'o* 'rib.' [AM 141, P 102, CP 23, AIW, AMN]

8 K'OLO 'hole'

KHOISAN: ≠Au.//eî *!kuru* 'quiver' (n.), !Kung *!kɔro* 'hole,' *!kuru* 'quiver' (n.), *!koro* 'hole, grave,' !O-!Kung *kɔlɔ* 'hollow'; G//abake *koro* 'hole in tree,' *(čui) kxolo* 'nostrils' (= nose hole); /Xam *!kɔrro* 'to be hollow,' /*huru* 'hole,' /*ūru* 'anus,' /'Auni *!kuru* 'quiver' (n.). [SAK 371]

NILO-SAHARAN: Songhai *nkoro* 'buttocks'; Saharan: Kanuri *kuli* 'anus,' Teda *kulo*; Berta *k'oŋ-k'oloŋ* ~ *kʷɔn-kʷɔlɔŋ* 'elbow' (= arm-hole, cf. the Kunama form below); Koman: Buldiit *kul(ma)* 'buttocks'; Kunama *kura* 'anus,' *ukunkula* 'armpit, elbow' (< **kan-kul* 'arm-hole'); East Sudanic: Temein *kukuruk(it)* 'buttocks,' Nandi *kulkul* 'armpit,' So *ukɔlkɔl* 'armpit,' Gaam *kura-n* 'hollow (in ground).' [NS 4, CN 2, 5, ES 3, NSD 3, KER 432]

INDO-EUROPEAN: Proto-Indo-European **(s)kūlo* 'hiding place, back part'; Indic: Sanskrit *kūlam* 'rear of army'; Italic: Latin *cūlus* 'buttocks, anus,' *clūnis* 'buttock, hip'; Celtic: Old Irish *cūl* 'back, rear,' Welsh *cil* 'back,' *clùn* 'buttock'; Germanic: Proto-Germanic **hulo* 'hole,' Gothic *hulundi* 'cave,' English hole, Swedish *näs-håla* 'nostril.' [IE 951]

URALIC: Proto-Finno-Ugric **köl* 'hole'; Ugric: Vogul *kal* ~ *hal* 'crack,' Ostyak *kŏl* ~ *hul*, Hungarian *halok* 'incision'; Finnic: Finnish *kolo* 'hole, crack,' Saami *golo* 'fissure,' Zyrian *kolas* 'crack,' Cheremis *kongəla* 'armpit,' Southern Estonian *kaŋgel* 'shoulder.' [U 101, 106, N 220, EU]

KOREAN *kul* 'cave.' [EU]

JAPANESE-RYUKYUAN: Japanese *kur* 'hollow, scoop out.' [EU]

DRAVIDIAN: Tulu *kulligè* 'buttocks,' *kaŋkuḷa* 'armpit' (= arm-hole), Kolami *kūla* 'buttock,' *ganjgūly* 'armpit,' Gondi *kula* 'buttock,' *kākri* 'armpit,' Kannada *kaŋkur* ~ *gaŋkəlu* 'armpit,' Telugu *kauŋgili* 'breast,' *tsaŋkili* ~ *tsakkili* 'armpit' (= arm-hole), Malayalam *akkuḷam* 'armpit, tickling,' Tamil *akkuḷ* 'armpit,' *akkuḷu* 'to tickle.' [D 1234, 2274, Supplement 30; N 220, NSD 3]

CAUCASIAN: Proto-Caucasian **kHwɔrV* 'hole, pit, ravine,' Proto-Nax **kōr* 'window,' Proto-Dido **kurV* 'ravine,' Proto-Lak **kuIru* 'nest,' Proto-Dargi **kur* 'pit,' Proto-Lezghian **kur* 'pit, river,' Lezgi *k'ul-ux* 'backwards,' *k'ul-ux-k'il* 'hip, posterior, buttocks,' Kurin *qula* 'loins, buttocks.' [C 113, JR 58]

SINO-TIBETAN: Tibeto-Burman: Proto-Tibeto-Burman **kor* ~ **kwar* 'hole,' **kali* 'armpit, tickle,' Tibetan (West) *kor* 'hollow in the ground, pit,' Lushei *khuar* ~ *khur* 'hole,' *kor* 'ravine,' Dimasa *ha-khor* 'cave' (= earth-hole), *sisi-khor* 'armpit' (= tickle-hole), Bodo *ha-khor* 'hole, valley,' Bur-

mese *kălí* 'tickle,' *tshak-kăli* ∼ *lak-kăli* 'armpit' (= arm-hole, cf. the Telugu form above), Lakher *kili* 'tickle,' *ba-kəli* 'armpit.' [ST 265, 349, 350]
NA-DENE: Haida *kunts-qul* ∼ *kwun-zool* 'nostril' (= nose-hole). [ND]
DAIC: Khamti *kăle* 'tickle,' *kap kăle* 'armpit' *tsuŋ kări* 'tickle,' Shan *sop kălit*
'armpit'; Tai: Proto-Tai **xru* ∼ **ru* 'hole,' **xru ʔdaŋ* 'nostril'
(= hole nose). [PB 316, 410]
AUSTRONESIAN: Proto-Austronesian **kili* 'shoulder,' **kilikili* 'armpit,' Taga-
log *kili(ti)* 'tickling,' *kilikili* 'armpit,' Cham *kəlĕk* 'tickle,' Fijian *kili* ∼
kiri 'armpit,' Nggela *kilikili* 'tickle a tired pig to make it go.' [AN 80, 121,
WW 187, PB 230, 410]

9 KUAN 'dog'

KHOISAN: /Xam *!gwãĩ* 'hyena,' //Ng-!'e /*xãĩ*, /'Auni /*kãĩn*, Kakia /*xãĩ*, /Nu-
//en /*ūn*, !Kung /*gwí*, !O-!Kung /*gwĩ*. [SAK 380, DB 48]
AFRO-ASIATIC: Proto-Afro-Asiatic **k(j)n* 'dog, wolf'; Omotic: Haruro *kānō*,
Basketo *kanā*, Kullo *kana*, Gimira *kjan*, Kaffa *kunānō*, Mao *kano*; Chadic:
Gamergu *kenē*, Jegu *káń*. [CS 189, N 238, UOL 175]
INDO-EUROPEAN: Proto-Indo-European **kwon* ∼ **kun* 'dog'; Phrygian *kan*;
Greek *kuōn*; Italic: Latin *can(-is)*; Armenian *šun* ∼ *šan*; Indic: Sanskrit
çvan; Iranian: Avestan *span*; Tocharian *ku* ∼ *kon*; Germanic: Old English
hund, English hound. [IE 632, UOL 175, N 238, EU]
URALIC: Proto-Uralic (Illich-Svitych) **küjnä* 'wolf'; Finno-Ugric: Northern
Saami *gâidne* 'wolf,' Udmurt *kẙjon* 'wolf,' Komi *kȯin* 'wolf'; Samoyed:
Ostyak Samoyed *kana(-k)* 'dog' (probably a borrowing) [N 238, UOL 175,
EU]
TURKIC: Old Turkish *qančiq* 'bitch.' [EU]
MONGOLIAN: Mongol *qani* 'a wild masterless dog.' [EU]
TUNGUS: Proto-Tungus **xina* 'dog,' Manchu *(inda-)xun*, Udej *in'ai*, Oroch
inaxki, Evenki *ina, inakin*, Lamut *ŋen*, Orok *ŋinda*. [N 238, EU]
KOREAN: *ka* 'dog' (< *kani*). [N 238, EU]
GILYAK: *qan* ∼ *kan* 'dog.' [EU]
ESKIMO-ALEUT: Sirenik *qanaɣa* 'wolf.' [EU]
CAUCASIAN: Proto-Caucasian **χHwĕje* 'dog,' Proto-Avar-Andi **χʷoʔi* 'dog,'
Proto-Lezghian **χ̄ʷäja* 'dog.' [C 212]
BASQUE: *haz-koin* 'badger' (lit. 'bear-dog').
YENISEIAN: Proto-Yeniseian **kūń* ∼ **gūń* 'wolverine.' [Y]
SINO-TIBETAN: Proto-Sino-Tibetan **qhʷĩj* 'dog,' Archaic Chinese **kʰiwən*
'dog'; Tibeto-Burman: Proto-Tibeto-Burman **kwiy*, Tibetan *khyi*, Kana-
uri *kui*, Thebor *khui*, Vaya *uri*, Chepang *kwi*, Karen *gwi*. [ST 159, UOL
175]
?INDO-PACIFIC: Pila *kawun* 'dog,' Saki *kawuŋ*, Wodani *kawino*. [FS 14]

?AUSTRONESIAN: Proto-Oceanic *nkaun* 'dog.' [WW 60]

AMERIND: Hokan: Achomawi *kuān* 'silver fox,' Tonkawa *ʔekuan* 'dog,' North Yana *kuwan-na* 'lynx,' Yurimangui *kwan* 'dog'; Central Amerind: Jemez *kiano*, Isleta *kuyanide*, Taos *kwiane-*, Tewa *tuxʷana* 'fox, coyote,' Zacapoaxtla *itˢkwiin-ti* 'dog,' Chatina *čuni*, Popoloca *kuniya*, Ixcatec *ʔuniña*, Chocho *ʔuña*; Chibchan-Paezan: Guamaca *kensi*; Equatorial: Esmeralda *kine*; Macro-Ge: Came *okong*, Serra do Chagu *hong-kon*. [A 86, CAN, UOL 176, AMN]

10 KU(N) 'who?'

KHOISAN: ≠Au.//eî *kama* 'when, if,' *xa* (interrogative particle), !Kung *ka* 'when,' !*kũ(-de)* 'who'; G//abake /*kam* 'when,' Naron *kama* 'when, if,' Nama *hamo* 'when,'; /Xam !*ku(dɛxa)* 'who,' *xa* (interrogative particle). [SAK 384, 388, 757, 764, UOL 70]

NIGER-CONGO: Pam *kɔ̄gé* 'which,' Dama *káʔī* 'which,' Jukun *áké* 'what,' Proto-Bantu *kí∼ ká* 'which,' Swahili *ga-ni* 'what, why, what kind.' [BA]

NILO-SAHARAN: Fur *kii* 'who,' *ka* 'what,' Daza *ka* 'which,' Masai *ka* 'which,' Didinga *ŋani* 'who' (< *kani* ?), Liguri *keneen* 'who,' Nyala *k-rem* 'how many,' Shatt *k-reñ* 'how many,' Shabo *kukne* 'who.' [NS 149, CN 126, HF 12]

AFRO-ASIATIC: Proto-Afro-Asiatic *k(w)* ∼ *q(w)* 'who'; Semitic: Proto-Semitic *kV* 'how,' Arabic *ka*, Geez *kama*, Aramaic *kə*, Akkadian *kima* ∼ *ki* 'how,' South Arabian *ko* 'how, why,' Mehri *ūkō* 'why'; ?Berber: Tuareg *akken* 'how,' Gdames (*mə-*)*k*; Cushitic: Proto-Cushitic *kw* 'who,' Somali *kú-ma* 'who (masc.),' Oromo *ka-mi* 'who,' *aka* 'how'; Omotic: Kaffa *kō-nē* 'who,' Mao *konne*, Kullo *hone*, Wolamo *ōne*, Beja *kāk(u)* 'how'; Chadic: Proto-Chadic *k'(w)* 'who,' Hausa *k'à*, Bura *ga* 'what,' Logone *ɣwani*, Somrai *kāna* 'who,' Mubi *gin*. [N 232, UOL 70]

INDO-EUROPEAN: Proto-Indo-European *kʷo* ∼ *kʷi* 'who,' *-kʷe* (coordinating conjunction); Indic: Sanskrit *kas* 'who'; Iranian: Avestan *kō*; Armenian *o* (< *kʷo*); Anatolian: Hittite *kuiš* 'who,' *kuit* 'what,' Luwian *kui* 'who,' Lydian *qis* 'who,' *qid* 'what'; Albanian *kë* 'whose'; Italic: Latin *quis* 'who,' *quis-que* 'whoever,' *quod* 'what,' *quam* 'how, as,' *quom* 'when,' (*arma virum*)-*que* '(arms) and (the man)'; Celtic: Old Irish *cia* 'who,' *cid* 'what'; Germanic: Gothic *hwas* 'who,' English *who, what, when, where, why, how*; Baltic: Old Prussian *kas* 'who,' *ka* 'what'; Slavic: Old Church Slavic *kъto* 'who'; Tocharian: Tocharian A *kus* 'who, what.' [IE 644, N 232, EU, UOL 70]

URALIC: Proto-Uralic (Rédei) *ke* ∼ *ki* 'who,' (Rédei) *ku* ∼ *ko* 'who, which, ?what'; Yukaghir *kin* 'who,' *hon* 'where,' *hadi* 'which,' *hodier* 'why'; Proto-Uralic (Illich-Svitych) *ke* ∼ *ko* ∼ *ku* 'who'; Samoyed:

Yurak *hu* 'who,' *huna* 'where,' Tavgy *kua* 'which,' *kuninu* 'where,' *kune* 'when,' Selkup *kutte* 'who,' *kun* 'where,' Kamassian *kaamõn* 'when'; Ugric: Vogul *kon* 'who,' *qun* 'when,' Ostyak *hŏjə* 'who,' *hŏtə* 'what,' *hun* 'when,' Hungarian *ki* 'who'; Finnic: Finnish *ken* ~ *kene* ~ *ke* ~ *ku* ~ *kuka* 'who,' *kussa* 'where,' *koska* 'when,' Saami *gi* ~ *gæ* ~ *gutti* 'who,' *goktĕ* 'how,' Mordvin *ki* 'who,' Cheremis *ke* ~ *kö* ~ *kü* ~ *kudõ*, Votyak *kin* 'who,' *kin-ke* 'someone,' *ku* 'when,' Zyrian *kin* 'who,' *kod* 'which,' *ko* 'when.' [U 44, 46, N 223, 232, EU, KR 140, 191]

TURKIC: Proto-Turkic **k'Em* 'who,' **ka* ~ **qa* (interrogative base), Chuvash *kam* 'who,' Old Turkish *käm* 'who,' *qa-ñu* 'which,' *qa-na* 'where,' Old Uighur *kim* 'who,' *qaju* 'which,' *qajda* 'where,' Tatar *kem* 'who,' Karagas *kum* ~ *kym*, Jakut *kim*, Old Oguz *qanda* 'where.' [N 223, 232, EU, UOL 70]

MONGOLIAN: Proto-Mongolian **kè-n* 'who,' **ka* 'where, whither,' Written Mongolian *ken* 'who,' *qa-mi-ga* 'where,' Khalkha *xeŋ* 'who,' *xāna* (< **ka-ga-na*) 'where,' Kalmyk *ken* 'who,' *xā* (< **ka-ga*) 'where, whither,' Moghol *ken* 'who.' [N 223, 232, EU]

TUNGUS: Proto-Tungus **xa* 'what, how, how much,' Nanai *xaj* 'what,' *xadu* 'how much,' *xoni* 'how,' Manchu *aj* 'what,' *udu* 'how much,' Udihe *ī* 'what,' *adi* 'how much,' *ono* 'how,' Even *ī-räk* 'how,' *adi* 'how much,' *ōn(i)* 'how.' [N 232, EU]

KOREAN *ka* (interrogative particle). [N 232, EU]

JAPANESE-RYUKYUAN: Japanese *ka* (interrogative particle, indefinitizer), *ka* . . . *ka* (alternating conjunction), Ryukyuan *ča* 'what.' [EU]

AINU *ka* (interrogative particle, indefinitizer), *ka* . . . *ka* (coordinating conjunction). [EU]

GILYAK *ka* (interrogative particle), *ko* . . . *ko* (coordinating conjunction). [EU]

CHUKCHI-KAMCHATKAN: Kamchadal *k'e* 'who' (genitive *k'en*), Chukchi *mik* ~ *mek* 'who,' *req* ~ *raq* 'what,' Koryak *qej* . . . *qej* 'either . . . or,' *kur* 'to be who?, to be what?,' Kerek *jaq* 'who, what.' [EU]

ESKIMO-ALEUT: Proto-Eskimo-Aleut **ken* 'who,' **qa-* (interrogative pronoun), Aleut *ki-n* 'who,' *qata* 'where, whither, what,' *qanangun* 'where,' *qanayam* 'when,' *qanagan* 'whence,' Eskimo *ki-na* 'who,' Greenlandic *qaŋga* 'when,' *qanuq* 'how,' Siberian Yuit *qafsina* 'how many,' Alaskan Yuit *-ka* (question particle). [EU, EA 118, 121]

CAUCASIAN: Proto-Caucasian **kʷi* 'who, which,' Kurin *ku-* 'what,' Archi *kʷi-* 'who,' Avar *kʰi-n* 'how.' [UOL 70, SC 149]

BURUSHASKI *kɛ* 'if, when,' *kɛ* 'and,' *kɛ* . . . *kɛ* 'both . . . and,' *(men . . .)* *kɛ* '(who)ever.' [B 231, 265]

SINO-TIBETAN: Old Chinese **kjei* 'how much,' Hruso *kʰi-nia* 'how many,' *kʰi-mia* 'how far.' [SC 149]

NA-DENE: Haida *gyis-to* ~ *kiš-to* 'who,' *gōsu* ~ *guu(s)* 'what,' *gyinu* 'where,' *giisant* 'when'; Tlingit *kusu* ~ *gùsú* ~ *gū* 'where,' *kūnsa* 'how much.' [ND]

?AUSTRALIAN: Maung *gunuga* ~ *gigi* 'what,' Tiwi *kuwa* 'who,' *kamu* 'what.' [RD 373, 376]

NAHALI *(nani) ka* 'anyone' *(nani* 'who'), *(nan) ka* 'anything' *(nan* 'what'). [NA 92]

AUSTROASIATIC: Munda *o-ko-e* 'who,' *o-ka* 'what,' *če-le* 'which'; Mon-Khmer: Vietnamese *gi* 'what,' Nicobarese *či* 'who,' *či-n* 'who, what,' *kahä* 'what,' *čan* ~ *ču* 'where.' [UOL 70]

AUSTRONESIAN: Proto-Austronesian **ku'a[']* 'how.' [AN]

AMERIND: Almosan-Keresiouan: Kutenai *ka* 'where,' Wiyot *gu-* 'when, where,' Yurok *kus* 'when, where,' Passamaquoddy *kekʷ* 'what,' Chemakum *āč'is* 'what,' Quileute *ak'is* 'what,' *qo-* 'where,' Nootka *ʔaqi-* 'what,' Bella Bella *akoiqkan* 'who,' Pentlatch *kwǝnča* 'where,' *kwǝs* 'when,' Upper Chehalis *ka-n* 'do what?,' Keres *hēko* 'whither,' Quapaw *ka* 'what,' Ofo *kaka* 'what,' Wichita *ʔēkiyaʔ* 'who,' Caddo *kwit* 'where,' Cherokee *gago* 'who,' Onondaga *kanin* 'where,' Seneca *kwanu* 'who,' Mohawk *ka* 'where'; Penutian: Tsimshian *gu* 'who,' Alsea *qau*, Kalapuya *ūk*, Coos *qanč* 'where,' Siuslaw *qani*, Klamath *kani* 'who,' *ka* 'which,' Bodega Miwok *ʔeke* 'what,' *ʔeketto* 'where,' Zuni *kāk'i-pi* 'when,' Tunica *kaku* 'who,' *kanahku* 'what,' *kaʔaš* 'when,' Natchez *kanne* 'someone,' *gōš* 'what,' Huave *xaŋ* 'who,' *key* 'what,' Quiche *xan* 'when'; Hokan: Achomawi *kī* 'who,' Washo *kudiŋa* 'who,' *kuŋate* 'what,' *kuŋa* 'where,' East Pomo *kia* 'who,' *k'owa* 'what,' Chumash *kune* 'who,' *kenu* 'why,' Esselen *kini* 'who,' *ke* 'where,' Walapai *ka* 'who,' Seri *kiʔ*, Coahuilteco *ka* 'what,' Chontal *kanaʔ* 'when,' Tlappanec *gwana*, Jicaque *kat* 'where,' Yurimangui *kana* 'what,' *kuna* 'where'; Central Amerind: Proto-Aztecan **kaan* 'where,' **keem* 'how,' **kee-ski* 'how much, how many,' Nahua *aʔkon* 'who,' Zacapoaxtla *akoni*, Yaqui *hakuni* 'where,' Isthmus Zapotec *gunaʔ*, Mazatec *kʔia* 'when'; Chibchan-Paezan: Cuna *kana* 'when,' Miskito *ajkia*, Paya *agini*, Terraba *kene* 'where,' Tirub *koñe*, Totoro *kin* 'who,' Paez *kim* 'who,' *kīh* 'what,' Catio *kai* 'who,' Moguex *kina* 'who, what,' Tucura *karea* 'why'; Andean: Yahgan *kunna* 'who,' *kanin(a)* 'to whom,' *kana* 'where,' Tehuelche *keme* 'who,' *ken* 'which,' *kenaš* 'when,' *kienai* 'where,' Araucanian *kam* 'how,' Aymara *kuna* 'what,' *kamisa* 'how,' Iquito *kanʌʌka* 'who,' Aymara *kuna* 'what,' *kauki* 'where'; Macro-Tucanoan: Ticuna *karo* 'where,' *kejaito* 'when'; Equatorial: Ayore *gōsi* 'who,' Tuyoneri *kate* 'what,' Yaruro *kanemo* 'when,' Uru *kanč014*, Wapishana *kanum* 'what,' Puquina *kin*; Macro-Carib: Yabarana *ekkwarijawa* 'when,' *akǝtto* 'where,' Witoto *akö* 'what,' Miranya *kia* 'where,' Faai *kiati*, Andoke *koide* 'who'; Macro-Panoan: Lule *kine-kinema*, Macca *katˢik* 'who,' *kona* 'when' (rel.), Taruma *gaga* 'what,' Tacana *ketsunu* 'when,' *kepia* 'where.' [AM: G102; UOL 70, AMN]

11 KUNA 'woman'

AFRO-ASIATIC: Proto-Afro-Asiatic *k(w)n ~ *knw 'wife, woman'; Omotic: Chara gänēts 'woman,' Kaffa geñe 'lady,' Mocha gäñe 'lady, woman,' Shinasha geña 'lady'; Cushitic: Proto-Cushitic *H-kwn 'wife,' Bilin ' 'əxʷina (pl. 'əkʷin) 'wife,' Xamta eqʷen 'wife,' Dembia kiūnā 'wife,' Avija xuonā 'wife,' Oromo qena 'lady'; Semitic: Akkadian kinītu ~ qinītu 'one of the wives in a harem'; Berber: Proto-Berber *t-knw 'wife,' Tuareg tēkne 'wife,' Kabyle ṭakna 'one of the wives in polygamy'; Chadic: Margi ŋkwà 'girl' (< *m-kwà), Igala ginum 'woman,' Makari gerim 'woman,' Logone gənəm 'woman.' [N 178, UOL 179]

INDO-EUROPEAN: Proto-Indo-European *gʷen ~ *gʷenā 'wife, woman'; Anatolian: Lydian kâna 'woman, wife,' Luwian wanā; Indic: Sanskrit gnā 'goddess'; Iranian: Avestan gənā 'wife'; Armenian kin (pl. kanai-kʻ); Greek: Mycenaean ku-na-ja; Albanian grue ~ grua; Celtic: Old Irish ben; Germanic: Gothic qino, Old High German quena, English queen; Baltic: Old Prussian genno 'wife'; Slavic: Old Church Slavic žena; Tocharian: Tocharian B śana. [IE 473, N 178, EU, LC 922, UOL 179]

TURKIC: Proto-Turkic *küni 'one of the wives in polygamy,' Old Turkic küni 'wife,' Kirghiz künü, Azerbaijani günü. [N 178]

ESKIMO-ALEUT: Proto-Eskimo-Aleut *ʔaʁ(i)na- 'woman,' Eskimo: Alaskan aganak, Greenlandic arnaq, Yuit arnaq 'female person, woman.' [EU]

CAUCASIAN: Proto-Caucasian *q(w)änV 'woman,'   Proto-Dagestan *qonV(p̄V). [EC, NSC 59]

?INDO-PACIFIC: Andaman Islands: Bea chána 'woman,' chana-da 'mother'; Tasmanian: Southeast quani 'wife, woman'; Mugil kanen 'mother.' [T 471, UOL 180]

AUSTRALIAN: Warrgamay gajin 'female of human or animal species,' Gamilaraay gunijarr 'mother,' Ngaanyatjara ngunytju, Jalnguy guyŋgun 'spirit of a dead woman.' [RD 119, UOL 180]

?AUSTROASIATIC: Mon-Khmer: Nancowry kān ~ kāne 'woman.' [UOL 179]

AMERIND: Almosan-Keresiouan: Shawnee kwan-iswa 'girl,' Nootka ganəmo, Bella Bella ganəm 'woman, wife,' Lkungen kaŋi 'girl,' Spokane en-okhono 'wife,' Siletz qenaʔs 'grandmother,' Santa Ana k'uwi 'woman, wife,' Dakota hun 'mother,' Yuchi wa-hane 'old woman'; Penutian: Tsimshian hanāɢ 'woman,' Cayuse kwun-asa 'girl,' Yawelmani gaīna 'woman,' Konkow kónoj 'woman, wife,' Nisenan kono 'girl,' San Juan Bautista atsia-xnis, Lake Miwok ʔunu 'mother,' Zuni k'anakʷayina 'woman,' Yuki aŋ-k'an 'mother'; Hokan: Chumash kunup 'girl,' Diegueño kux-kʷanʲ 'mother,' xe-kʷanʲ 'daughter,' Seri kuãam 'female,' koŋkáii 'wife,' Tonkawa kʷān 'woman,' Karankawa kanin 'mother,' Tequistlatec (ɬ-)agaʔno 'woman, female'; Central Amerind: Proto-Tiwa *k*ʷ*iem* 'maiden,' Papago *hóoñigï* 'wife,' Isthmus Zapotec *gunáa* 'woman'; Chibchan-Paezan: Boncota *güina* 'female,' Ulua *guana*, Pedraza *konui-xa* 'daughter,' Choco *huena* 'woman,' Paez *kuenas* 'young woman'; Andean: Simacu *kaxkanu* 'daughter-in-law,' Yahgan *čou-kani-kipa* 'young woman,' Kulli *kañi* 'sister,' Cholon *akiñiu*, Alakaluf *ekin-eč* 'woman,' Tsoneka *na-kuna*; Macro-Tucanoan: Nadobo *kuñan*, Särä *kana* 'mother'; Equatorial: Yurucare *igūn* 'girl,' *ti-gūn* 'daughter,' Cuica *kuneu-ksoy* 'girl,' *kunakunam* 'woman,' Proto-Tupi *kuyã*, Guarani *kuña* 'female,' *kuña-taī* 'girl,' Guarayo *ekuna* 'woman,' Canoeiro *kuña-tain* 'small girl,' Kamayura *kunja* 'woman,' Guahibo *kvantua* 'first wife,' Amuesha *kuyan-iša* 'woman'; Macro-Carib: Palmella *ena-kone* 'mother,' Accawai *kana-muna* 'girl,' Muinane *kini-ño*, Miranya *guaniu* 'mother'; Macro-Panoan: Chama *egʷan-asi* 'woman,' Lengua *iŋ-kyin* 'mother,' Sanapana *küli-guana-man* 'old woman,' ?Chacobo *huini* 'female,' ?Cavineña *ekwaʔa* 'mother'; Macro-Ge: Suya *kuña* 'woman,' Cherente *pi-kon*, Capaxo *konjan*, Caraja *hanökö*. [AM 272, P 283, H 164, LC 922, AMN]

12 MAKO 'child'

?NIGER-CONGO: Bantu: Ngoala *maŋku* 'child,' Yaunde *moŋgo*, Pande *maŋga*, Mbudikum-Bamum *muŋke*. [HJ II: 271]

INDO-EUROPEAN: Proto-Indo-European *maghos* 'young,' *maghu* 'child, boy'; Iranian: Avestan *maγava* 'unmarried'; Celtic: Old Irish *macc* 'son'; Germanic: Gothic *magus* 'boy,' Old English *magu* 'child, son, man,' Swedish *måg* 'son-in-law'; Baltic: Latvian *mač* (gen. *maǵa*) 'small.' [IE 696, AB 371]

DRAVIDIAN: Tamil *maka* 'child, young of an animal, son or daughter,' Malayalam *makan* 'son,' *makkaḷ* 'children (esp. sons),' Kota *mog* 'child,' Toda *mox* 'child, son, male, daughter,' Kannada *maga* 'son, male person,' *makan* 'son,' *magu* 'infant, child of either sex,' Kodagu *makka* 'children,' Tulu *mage* 'son,' *magaḷu* 'daughter,' Telugu *maga* 'male,' Konda *moga koṛo* 'boy child,' *gālu* 'daughter' (< *mgālu*), Pengo *gāṛ* 'daughter,' Kuwi *maka* (vocative used to daughters and sisters in affection), Malto *maqe* 'boy,' *maqi* 'girl,' *maqo* 'small, little, young,' *maqu* 'young of an animal.' [D 4616, AB 371]

CAUCASIAN: Proto-Caucasian *mik'wV* 'small, young one,' Proto-Avar-Andi *mok'i* ~ *mik'i* 'small, child,' Proto-Dido *mik'V* 'small, little,' Proto-Lezghian *mik'ʷV* 'young.' [C 151]

SINO-TIBETAN: Tibeto-Burman: Proto-Tibeto-Burman *māk* 'son-in-law,' Miri *mak(-bo)*,' Burmese *(sa-)mak*, Lushei *māk(-pa)*. [ST 324]

INDO-PACIFIC: Southwest New Guinea: Jaqai *mak* 'child,' Aghu *amoko*, Madinava *imega(-kaivagu)*. [SWNG 12]

AMERIND: Almosan-Keresiouan: Natick *mukketchouks* 'boy,' Beothuk *maga-raguis* 'son,' Santa Ana -*ma'kə* 'my daughter,' Acoma *magə* 'girl,' Hidatsa *makadištamia*; Penutian: Cayuse *m'oks* 'baby,' Modoc *mukak*, Gashowu *mokheta* 'girl,' Santa Cruz *mux-aš*, Zuni *maki* 'young woman,' Yuki *muh* 'young,' Mixe *mahntk* 'son,' ?*miš* 'girl, boy'; Hokan: Achomawi *mik-tsan* 'child' (-*tsan* = dim.), Yana *ʔimx* 'young,' Washo *mèhu* 'boy,' Chumash (Santa Barbara) *mičamo* 'boy,' *amičanek* 'girl,' Chumash (Santa Ynez) *makčai* 'daughter,' *mak-isi-huanok* 'girl,' Cocopa *xmik* 'boy,' Walapai *mik*, Maricopa *maxay*, Yuman *maša-xay* 'girl,' Tequistlatec *(ɬa-)mihkano* 'boy'; Central Amerind: Tewa *mogè* 'young,' ?Otomi *metsi* 'boy'; Chibchan-Paezan: Cuna *mači(-gua)*, Ulua *muix-bine* 'child,' Chimila *muka* 'son-in-law,' *muka-yunkvir* 'daughter,' Shiriana *moko* 'girl,' Nonama *mukua* 'daughter,' *mučaira* 'son'; Andean: Yahgan *maku* 'son,' *makou-esa* 'daughter-in-law,' Yamana *māku-n* 'son'; Macro-Tucanoan: Yeba *mākēē* 'child,' *yimaki* 'son,' Waikina *maxkē* 'child,' *mehino* 'boy,' Dyurumawa *(ma-)maki* '(small) child,' Coto *ma-make* 'boy,' Tucano *muktuia* 'boy, girl,' *vimago* 'girl,' *dyemaxkī* 'child,' Curetu *si-magö* 'daughter,' *si-mugi* 'son,' Waiana *yemakə* 'daughter,' Ömöa *yemaxke* 'son,' Ticuna *mākan* 'child,' Desana *mague* 'son,' Auake *makuamē*, Waikina *make*; Equatorial: Mehinacu *yamakui* 'boy,' Paumari *makinaua* 'boy, young,' -*makhini* 'grandson,' Marawan *makibmani* 'boy,' Uru *mači* 'daughter,' Caranga *mač* 'son,' Oyampi *kunyā-muku-* 'girl,' Maue *makubdia*, Tambe *kusa-muku* 'young woman'; Macro-Carib: Yabarana *mūku* 'boy,' Galibi *magon* 'young of animals,' Cumanagote *miku* 'child,' Pavishana *mu'gi* 'daughter,' Taulipang *muku* 'son,' Accawai *mogo*; Macro-Panoan: Tiatinagua *mahi*; Macro-Ge: Apinage *mäaukride* 'girl,' Ramkokamekran *mäggepru*, Coroado *meke-šambe* 'son.' [AM 62, AMN]

13 MALIQ'A 'to suck(le), nurse; breast'

AFRO-ASIATIC: Proto-Afro-Asiatic: **mlg* 'breast, udder, suck,' Arabic *mlğ* 'to suck the breast,' Old Egyptian *mnḏ* (< **mlg*) 'woman's breast, udder'; Cushitic: Somali *maal-* 'to milk,' Rendille *ṃaal-*. [N 291, LN 291]

INDO-EUROPEAN: Proto-Indo-European **melĝ-* 'to milk'; Greek ἀμέλγω; Italic: Latin *mulg-ēre*; Celtic: Irish *bligim* 'to milk,' *mlicht* 'milk'; Germanic: Gothic *miluks* 'milk,' Old Norse *mjolka* 'to milk,' English 'to milk, milk'; Baltic: Lithuanian *milžti* 'to milk'; Slavic: Old Church Slavic *mlěsti*; Albanian *mjellë*; Tocharian: Tocharian A *mālk-lune* 'milking,' *malke* 'milk,' Tocharian B *malk-wer* 'milk.' [IE 722]

URALIC: Proto-Uralic (Illich-Svitych) **mälγe* 'breast,' Proto-Finno-Ugric (Rédei) **mälke*; Saami *mielgâ* 'breast, chest,' Mordvin *mälhkä* 'breast,' Vogul *mägl* (with metathesis), Hungarian *mell*, Yukaghir *meɫu-t*. [N 291, R 267]

DRAVIDIAN: Kurux *melkhā* 'throat, neck' and Malto *melqe* 'throat,' Tamil *melku* 'to chew, masticate,' Malayalam *melluka* 'to chew, champ,' Toda *meḻk* 'mouthful,' Kannada *mellu* 'to chew, masticate, eat with a muttering sound,' *melaku* 'bringing up again for rumination,' Telugu *mekku* 'to eat, gobble,' Gadba *mekkap-* 'to eat like a glutton.' [D 5077, 5080]

ESKIMO-ALEUT: Aleut *umlix* 'chest,' Kuskokwim *milugâ* 'sucks it out,' *mulik* 'nipple,' *milûgarâ* 'licks (or sucks) it; kisses it (a child).' [EU]

CAUCASIAN: Proto-Caucasian **mVq'VlV* 'throat, larynx,' Proto-Avar-Andi **maq̄'ala* 'throat,' Proto-Dido **muq'*, Proto-Dargi **muq'luq'* 'chute, gutter.' [C 142]

AMERIND: Almosan: Lower Fraser *məlqᵂ* 'throat,' Nootka *m̓ukᵂ* 'swallow,' Kwakwala *m̓lχᵂ-ʔid* 'chew food for the baby,' *m̓lqᵂa* 'moisten the fingers with the tongue,' Heiltsuk *m̓elqva* 'chew food for baby,' *m̓elχv-baút* 'lick the end of something,' Yurok *mik'olum* 'swallow,' Kutenai *uʔmqoł*; Penutian: Chinook *-mókuī-* 'throat,' *mlqᵂ-tan* 'cheek,' Wishram *ō-mēqλ* 'lick'; Oregon: Takelma *mülk'* 'swallow,' Tfalatik *milq*, Kalapuya *malq-mat* 'lick'; Yokuts *mōk'i* 'swallow,' *mik'-is* 'throat,' Mixe *amuʔul* 'suck,' Zoque *muʔk*; Hokan: Yuma *malʲaqé* 'neck,' Walapai *malqi'* 'throat, neck' Havasupai *milqé* 'throat,' Yavapai *melqí* 'neck,' Mohave *malʲaqé* 'throat,' Akwa'ala *milqí* 'neck,' Paipai *milqí*; Chibchan: Cuna *murki-makka* 'swallow,' *murgi murgi sae* 'swallow food'; Andean: Quechua (Cochabamba) *malq'a* 'throat,' Quechua (Huaraz) *mallaqa* 'be hungry'; Aymara *maλq'a* 'swallow, throat' (a borrowing from Quechua?) Equatorial: Guamo *mirko* 'drink.' [P 239, AMN; this etymology is explored in greater detail in Chapter 11.]

14 MANA 'to stay (in a place)'

?NILO-SAHARAN: Tatoga *miṅ* 'to stand,' Shabo *maŋ-ka* 'to sit.' [NSB, HF 12]

AFRO-ASIATIC: Proto-Afro-Asiatic **mn* 'to remain, be firm'; Ancient Egyptian *mn* 'to remain,' Coptic *mun*; Semitic: Proto-Semitic **'mn* 'to be firm, safe,' Arabic *'munu* 'to be loyal to someone,' *'manu* 'to be safe,' Geez *'mn* 'to be faithful,' Syriac *'amīn* 'firm,' Classical Hebrew *(n-)'mn* 'to be permanent, safe'; Omotic: Gofa *min* 'to be firm, strong'; Cushitic: Oromo *manā* 'house, home,' Somali *mīn*; Chadic: Musgu *mine* 'to be.' [CS 38, N 287, UOL 192]

?KARTVELIAN: Georgian *mena* 'dwelling' (possibly a borrowing from Iranian languages). [N 287]

INDO-EUROPEAN: Proto-Indo-European **men* 'to remain'; Indic: Sanskrit *man* 'to linger, not budge from a place'; Iranian: Old Persian *man* 'to remain, wait for'; Armenian *mnam* 'I remain, wait for'; Italic: Latin *man(-ere)* 'to remain'; Tocharian: Tocharian A *mñe* 'waiting,' *mäsk* (< **men-sk*) 'to be.' [IE 729, N 287, UOL 192]

DRAVIDIAN: Proto-Dravidian *man 'to remain in a place,' Brahui *manning* 'to become, be,' Malto *mene*, Kurux *mannā*, Kuwi *man* 'to be, remain, stay,' Konda *man* 'to be, stay, dwell,' Parji *men* 'to be, stay,' Telugu *manu* 'to live, exist,' *mannu* 'to last, be durable,' Malayalam *mannuka* 'to stand fast,' Tamil *maṉṉu* 'to be permanent, remain long, stay.' [D 4778, N 287]

TUNGUS: Evenki *mānā* 'to live settled, stay in camp for a long time in one place,' Negidal *mänägä* 'to remain.' [N 287]

CAUCASIAN: Proto-Caucasian *ʔi-ma(n)- 'to stay, be,' Hurrian *mann-* 'to be.' [NSC 111]

BASQUE *min* 'to place, set up, settle.'

BURUSHASKI *mʌn(-ʌs)* 'to be, become.' [B 257]

INDO-PACIFIC: South New Guinea: Makleu *man* 'to sit,' Jab *mön*; Central New Guinea: Siane *min* 'to stay, sit,' Gende *mina* 'stay,' Mogei *mana(-munt)* 'to sit,' Kuno *amen(-nyint)*; Northeast New Guinea: Langtub *min* 'to stay'; Unclassified New Guinea: Waruna *mana* 'to dwell,' Gogodala *mana* 'to sit, stay.' [IP 65]

AMERIND: Almosan-Keresiouan: Nootka *ma-* 'dwell'; Penutian: Tsimshian *mān* 'remain,' Kalapuya *mānɨ-* 'wait,' Maidu *ma* 'be,' Zuni *ʔīma* 'sit'; Hokan: Subtiaba *-ama*; Chibchan-Paezan: Cacaopera *ima* 'wait,' Puruha *ma* 'be,' Timicua *-ma* 'inside'; Andean: Cholona *-man* 'in,' Aymara *mankxa* 'inside,' Araucanian *minu*, Quechua *ma-* 'be,' Yahgan *mani* 'be,' *jumanana* 'live,' *möni* 'remain,' *kamani* 'stand'; Equatorial: Dzubucua *mañe* 'remain,' Otomi *yamania* 'live,' Paumari *gamanani* 'stand,' Coche *xamnan* 'be'; Macro-Carib: Yameo *mune* 'sit down,' Ocaina *mūnʔxo* 'remain,' Apiaca *umano* 'wait'; Macro-Panoan: Cashinawa *mana*, Shipibo *manei* 'remain,' Chacobo *man-* 'wait,' Panobo *manai*, Lule *-ma* 'in'; Macro-Ge: Botocudo *mēn* 'remain,' Crengez *moinj* 'to sit,' Capoxo *moinjam*, Bororo *amu* ~ *ami* 'to rest,' Cayapo *kaimaniun* 'stand,' *kaman* 'inside,' Tibagi *ema* 'dwell,' [AM: G46, A 59, MG 99, AMN]

15 MANO 'man'

?NIGER-CONGO: Bantu: Mbudikum-Bamum *-mani* 'man,' Rwanda *mana*, Nyanja *-muna*, Ci-ambo *-mna*.

NILO-SAHARAN: East Sudanic: Me'en *mɛʔɛn-* 'person,' Maban *mɛṉṉu*, Tama *ma*, Ik *am*, Didinga *matˢ* 'male,' Merarit *mo*, Dinka *motˢ*, Maban: Mabang *ma-šu* 'person.' [ES70, NSB]

AFRO-ASIATIC: Proto-Afro-Asiatic *mn 'male, man, person'; Ancient Egyptian *mnw* 'Min, a phallic deity,' Old Egyptian *mnyw* 'herdsman'; Omotic: Wolamo *minō* 'warrior,' Janjero *monō* 'people'; Cushitic: Proto-Cushitic *mn 'man,' Burji *méen-a* 'people,' Somali *mun* 'male,' Hadiyya *manna* 'people,' *man-čo* 'person,' Tembaro *mana*, Iraqw *ameni* 'woman'; Berber:

Zenaga *uman* 'kin,' Ghadames *iman* 'person,' Zwawa *iman*, Qabyle *iman*;
Chadic: Proto-Chadic **mn(j)* 'man,' Proto-West Chadic **mani* 'man, husband,' Karekare *men* 'people,' Kanakuru *minja*, Bata *māno* 'man,' Musgu
muni 'woman,' Logone *mēni* 'man, person,' Dari *mānji* 'person.' [AA 78,
N 292, OS 801, LN 292]

INDO-EUROPEAN: Proto-Indo-European **manu(-s)* ~ **monu(-s)* 'man'; Indic:
Sanskrit *mánu* ~ *mánus* 'man, person'; Iranian: Avestan **manus* 'man';
Germanic: Gothic *manna*, Old High German *man*, English *man* (pl. *men*),
woman (< wife + man); Slavic: Old Church Slavic *mǫžĭ* (< **mon-g-jo-*),
Russian *muž* 'husband.' [IE 700, N 292]

URALIC: Proto-Uralic (Illich-Svitych) **mäńće* 'man, person'; Ugric: Vogul
mɛńći ~ *mańśi* (self-name), Ostyak *mańt'* ~ *mońt'* ~ *məś* ~ *maś* (self-
name of one Ostyak clan), Hungarian *magyar* (self-name); Finnic: Finnish
mies, Estonian *mees*. [U 114, N 292]

DRAVIDIAN: Kolami *mās* 'man,' *māc* 'husband,' *māca* 'wife,' Naikri *mās*
'man,' *māsal* 'woman,' Naiki *mās* 'husband,' *māsa* 'wife,' Parji *mañja* ~
mañña 'man,' Gondi *manja* 'man, person,' Konda *māsi* 'husband,' Kurux
mēt ~ *mēt* 'adult man, husband,' Tamil *māntar* 'people, men.' [D 4791;
Illich-Svitych's comparison (N 292) is with D 4774: Tamil *maṉ* 'king, chief, husband,'
etc. The two are probably related.]

JAPANESE-RYUKYUAN: Old Japanese *(wo-)mina* 'woman' (mod. *onna*). [SY]

AINU *meno(-ko)* ~ *mene(-ko)* 'woman.'

CAUCASIAN: Proto-Caucasian **mVnxV* 'man, male.' [NSC 116]

YENISEIAN: Proto-Yeniseian **pix-* 'man.' [NSC 116]

INDO-PACIFIC: Bilakura *munan* 'man,' Warembori *mando*, Osum *aminika*
'woman,' Ikundun *mundu* 'man.' [FS 92, 93, 106]

NAHALI *mancho* ~ *manco* 'man,' *man-ṭa* 'men.' [NA 89]

MIAO-YAO: Proto-Miao-Yao **hmən* 'person,' Miao *hmoŋ* ~ *hmuŋ* (self-name
of the Miao), Yao *man* ~ *myen* ~ *mun* (self-name of the Yao). [PB 336]

AMERIND: Almosan-Keresiouan: Bella Coola *man* 'father,' Pentlatch *mān*,
Squamish *man*, Blackfoot *no-ma* 'husband'; Penutian: Coos *ma* 'person,' Kalapuya *menami*, Nisenan *manai* 'boy,' Rumsien *ama* 'person,'
Hokan: Chumash *s-mano* ~ *ɬ-mano* 'man'; Chibchan-Paezan: Ayoman
ayoman 'husband,' Warrau *moana* 'people'; Andean: Iquito *komano* 'father,' Yahgan *imun-* 'father,' *yamana* 'person'; Macro-Tucanoan: Yahuna
meni 'boy,' *manehẽ* 'husband,' Yupua *manape̥*, Yuyuka *yemane*, Coto
ömuna 'man,' Proto-Nambikwara **mĩn* 'father,' Kaliana *mĩnõ* 'man, person,' *imone* 'father-in-law,' Wanana *meno* 'man,' *manino* 'her husband,'
Waikina *emeno* 'man'; Equatorial: Guahibo *amona* 'husband,' *itsa-mone*
'person,' Callahuaya *mana*, Achual *aišman* 'man,' Marawan *maki-b-mani*
'boy,' Chamicuro *θamoni* 'my father,' Manao *re-manao* 'person,' Proto-

Tupi *men 'husband,' Guarani mena, Guajajara man; Macro-Carib: Apiaca moni 'boy,' Ocaina moon 'father,' Paravithana mei-moen 'son,' Miranya itse-meni; Macro-Panoan: Moseten moinči 'person,' Charrua itojman 'boy,' Guana emmanabie 'man'; Macro-Ge: Cayapo män 'person,' miän 'husband,' Chicriaba aimaman 'boy,' mamaŋ 'father,' Coroado kuoyman 'man.' [AM 154, AMN]

16 MENA 'to think (about)'

?KHOISAN: Sandawe mĕ:na 'to like.'

NIGER-CONGO: Fulup -maman 'know,' Mambila mini 'think,' Malinke mɛn 'understand,' Bambara mɛ, Proto-Bantu *màni ~ *mèni ~ *mèny ~ *màn 'know,' Namshi meĭ, Ibo ma, Mandyak me. [NC 28, KS 45, BA IV: 8, 12]

KORDOFANIAN: Tumale aiman 'think.' [NK 41]

NILO-SAHARAN: Songhai ma 'understand,' Daza monər 'know,' Dinik máì, Lotuko mij, Proto-Daju *minaŋe 'to dream,' Shatt miniŋ, Ik miin-es 'to love,' Teso a-min. [KS 45, NSB, KER]

AFRO-ASIATIC: Proto-Afro-Asiatic *man 'think, understand, wish, desire, count'; Semitic: Sokotri mnj 'wish,' Tigrinya tämännäjä, Arabic mnw 'understand,' Hebrew mānāh 'count,' Akkadian manū, Aramaic mənā; Cushitic: Somali mān 'mind'; Chadic: Angas man 'know,' Boleva mon, Masa min 'wish.' [N 281, AB 348]

INDO-EUROPEAN: Proto-Indo-European *men 'to think'; Anatolian: Hittite me-ma-a-i (< *me-mn-eA-) 'to say'; Italic: Latin men(s) 'mind,' meminī 'to remember,' mon(-ēre) 'to remind, warn'; Indic: Sanskrit mányatē 'to think,' mánas 'mind'; Greek mimnēskein 'to remember'; Germanic: Gothic munan 'to think,' muns 'thought'; Baltic: Lithuanian menù, miñti 'to remember'; Slavic: Old Church Slavic mǐněti 'to count,' pa-mę tǐ 'mind, memory'; Albanian mund 'I can'; Armenian i-manam 'I understand'; Tocharian: Tocharian A mnu 'thought,' Tocharian B mañu 'wish (n.), desire (n.).' [IE 726, N 281, AB 348]

URALIC: Proto-Uralic (Illich-Svitych) *manV ~ *monV 'guess, speak, conjure,' (Rédei) *monꟍ- 'say'; Yukaghir mon; Samoyed: Yurak maan, Tavgy muno 'say, command'; Ugric: Hungarian mon(-d) 'say'; Finnic: Finnish manaa 'to warn, admonish, curse, bewitch,' Estonian mana 'abuse, curse,' Saami moanâ 'to conjecture,' Mordvin muńa 'bewitch,' Cheremis mana 'speak, order.' [U 53, N 281, AB 348, KR 290]

DRAVIDIAN: Tamil maṇu 'prayer, request, word,' Kannada manuve 'request,' Telugu manavi 'prayer, humble request,' Irula maṇi 'talk, speak,' Kota mayṇ- 'talk, scold, abuse.' [D 4671, 4775, N 281]

?TURKIC: Turkish mani 'folk song,' Crimean Turkish manä 'folk song, melody.' [LN 281]

BASQUE *mun* 'medulla,' *munak* (pl.) 'brains.' [LC 916]

?BURUSHASKI *minʌs* 'story, tale.' [B 506]

?SINO-TIBETAN: Tibeto-Burman: Proto-Tibeto-Burman **r-miŋ* 'name,' Tibetan *miŋ,*' Magari *armin*, Limbu *miŋ*, Garo *miŋ* 'to name,' Burmese *mań* 'to be named,' Mikir *mon* 'mind,' *mun-t'i* 'to think, understand, guess, assume, appreciate,' Midźu *moŋ* 'to summon.' [ST 83] Cf. also Proto-Tibeto-Burman **maŋ* 'dream,' often in composition with Proto-Tibeto-Burman **ip* 'sleep,' as in Nung *ip-maŋ* 'to dream,' Burmese *ip-mak* 'dream,' *hmaŋ(-tak-mi)* 'to be possessed (applied to somnambulism).' [ST 82]

AMERIND: Almosan-Keresiouan: Shawnee *menw* 'prefer, like,' Laguna *amū* 'love,' Catawba *mu?e* 'wish,' Thompson *iomin-* 'have friendly feelings,' Okanagan *iqamēn* 'love,' Kalispel *x̄amenč*, Spokane *-manən* 'wish,' Nootka *māna* 'try, test'; Penutian: Lake Miwok *mēna* 'think,' *menaw* 'try,' Bodega Miwok *munu* 'be hungry,' Patwin *meina* 'try'; Hokan: Chimariko *mi?inan* 'like,' Karok *?īmnih* 'love'; Central Amerind: Chichimec *men*, Mixtec *manī*; Chibchan-Paezan: Chimila *mojnaya* 'wish,' Binticua *meyuno* 'seek,' Timucua *mani* 'wish,' Andaqui *miña-za* 'I sought,' Colorado *munai* 'love,' *muna-ha* 'wish'; Andean: Araucanian *mañumn* 'love,' Aymara *muna*, Sabella *mẽ-* 'seek,' Cholona *men* 'wish,' Quechua *muna*; Equatorial: Otomi *manenianda* 'love,' *momene* 'think,' Baure *emeniko* 'love,' Kamayura *emanhau*; Macro-Panoan: Lengua *min-* 'wish,' Mataco *hemen* 'love,' Vejoz *humin*, Mascoy *emeni*, Caduveo *addemane* 'do you love me?'; Macro-Ge: Kamakan *mã* 'seek,' Krêye *mã-* 'wish, love,' Apinage *amnõnmõn* 'think.' [AM 270, AMN]

17 MI(N) 'what?'

KHOISAN: ≠Au.//eî *kama* 'if, when,' G//abake /*kam* 'when,' Naron *kama* 'if, when,' Nama *hamo* 'when,' *maba* 'where,' Kxoe *ma* 'who, which,' /Nu-//en *maba* 'where.' [SAK 384, 757, 758, UOL 71]

AFRO-ASIATIC: Proto-Afro-Asiatic **m(j)* 'what, who'; Semitic: Akkadian *mīn* 'what,' *mann* 'who,' *man-ma* 'whoever,' Geez *mi* 'what,' Amharic *mɨn* 'what,' Arabic *man* ∼ *min* 'who,' *mah-mā* 'whatever,' Aramaic *man* 'who,' Classical Hebrew *mī̆*; Ancient Egyptian *m(j)* 'who,' *m* 'what'; Berber: Tuareg *ma* 'what,' *mi* 'who,' Shilha *ma(t)* 'who, what,' *mīt* 'who'; Cushitic: Proto-East Cushitic **ma?* 'what,' Saho *mi* 'who,' *mā* 'what,' Somali *máh̬â* 'what,' Oromo *máni* 'what,' *-mi* (interrogative particle), Sidamo *ma* 'what,' Darasa *ma* 'what,' *māta* 'who'; Omotic: Kaffa *amone* 'what,' Mocha *ámo*, Alagwa *mi* 'what,' *miya* 'who'; Chadic: Hausa *mḕ* ∼ *mì* 'what,' Karekare *mija*, Margi *mì*, Bata *mən*, Ngala *mena*, Logone *mini* 'who,' Sokoro *-ma* (interrogative particle). [AA 77, N 300, UOL 71, LN 300]

KARTVELIAN: Proto-Kartvelian *ma ~ *maj 'what,' *mi-n 'who,' Georgian ma 'what,' win 'who,' win-me 'whoever,' Chan mu 'what,' min 'who,' Svan maj 'what.' [KA 124, 135, N 300, UOL 71]

INDO-EUROPEAN: Proto-Indo-European *mo- (base of interrogative adverbs); Anatolian: Hittite ma-ši-š 'how much,' maḫḫan 'when,' Luwian mān, Hieroglyphic Hittite mana 'if, when'; Celtic: Old Irish má 'if,' Middle Breton ma 'what'; Tocharian: Tocharian A mänt 'how.' [N 300, EU]

URALIC: Proto-Uralic (Illich-Svitych) *mi 'what,' (Rédei) *mɜ; Yukaghir me-neme 'something'; Samoyed: Tavgy ma 'what,' Yenisei Samoyed mii', Kamassian mo 'why'; Ugric: Vogul män 'which, what,' Hungarian mi 'what, which'; Finnic: Finnish mi ~ mi-kä, Saami mi ~ mâ, Cheremis ma ~ mo, Votyak ma 'what.' [U 54, N 300, EU, R 296]

?DRAVIDIAN: Kajkadi midā 'what,' Burgendi mī, Tamil (even-)um '(who)ever.' [N 300, UOL 71]

TURKIC: Proto-Turkic *mi 'what,' Chuvash měn 'what,' miśe 'how much,' měnle 'what kind of,' Old Uighur mu ~ mü (sentence question enclitic), Turkish mi (sentence question enclitic). [N 300, EU]

MONGOLIAN: Mongolian -ū (< *wu < *mu) (sentence interrogative), Monguor amu ~ ama 'what.' [EU]

TUNGUS: Tungus -ma (indefinitizer), (ēku-)ma '(what)ever.' [EU]

KOREAN muõt 'what,' mjet 'how much,' Old Korean mai 'why.' [EU]

JAPANESE-RYUKYUAN: Ryukyuan mī 'what,' -mi (sentence interrogative enclitic). [EU]

AINU mak ~ makanak 'what,' makan 'what kind.' [EU]

CHUKCHI-KAMCHATKAN: Proto-Chukchi-Kamchatkan *m-ənqV 'what,' *m-ke 'who,' *maʔ 'when,' *miŋ 'which,' Chukchi mikin 'who', mi-k 'where,' Kamchadal min 'which, what sort.' [EU, CK]

CAUCASIAN: Proto-Caucasian *ma (interrogative particle), Chechen mila 'who,' Bats me. [KA 135]

BURUSHASKI mɛn 'who,' amin 'which,' mɛn (. . . kɛ) 'who(ever).' [L 265]

YENISEIAN: Proto-Yeniseian *wi- ~ *we- 'what.' [Y]

INDO-PACIFIC: Andaman Islands: Biada min 'thing,' Bale ming; Central Melanesian: Laumbe mina, Reef (kele)mengge 'this (thing)'; North New Guinea: Nyaura məndə 'thing, what,' Arapesh mane 'what'; Southwest New Guinea: Kati man 'something'; Central New Guinea: Matap mina 'what.' [IP 75]

AUSTRALIAN: Proto-Australian *minha ~ *minya 'what,' Dyirbal minya, Pitta-Pitta minha, Gumbaynggir minya, Malyangapa minhaga, Yota-Yota minhe, Diyari minha. [RD 373, 376]

NAHALI miŋgay 'where,' miyan 'how much.' [NA 91]

AUSTROASIATIC: Munda: Kurku *amae* 'who,' Mundari *ci-mae* 'why'; Mon-Khmer: Mon *mu* 'what,' Sakai *ma'*, *āmai* 'who,' Central Sakai *mō*, *mā* 'what.' [NA 91, UOL 71]

AMERIND: Almosan-Keresiouan: Kwakwala *m'as* 'what,' Mandan *mana* 'who,' *matswɛ* 'what,' Tutelo *māʔtu* 'when'; Penutian: Siuslaw *mînč*, North Sahaptin *mēn* 'where,' *mūn* 'when' *miš* 'how, why,' Nez Perce *mana* 'what,' *mine* 'where,' *maua* 'when,' Patwin *mena* 'where,' Central Sierra Miwok *manaχ-* 'who,' *mičy* 'do what,' Northern Sierra Miwok *mini* 'where,' *mi-tan* 'when,' Bodega Miwok *manti* 'who,' San Jose Costanoan *mani* 'where,' San Francisco Costanoan *mato* 'who,' Chitimacha *ʔam* 'what,' Atakapa *ma* 'where,' Choctaw *mano* 'when,' *imato* 'where,' Yuki *im* 'who,' Coast Yuki *im* 'where,' Wappo *may* 'who,' Chontal *max*, Yucatec *ma-š*, Tzeltal *mač'a*, Jacaltec *mat^s(a)*; Hokan: Yana *ʔambi*, East Pomo *am*, Chumash *muski*, Cocopa *makaya* 'where,' Diegueño *maap* 'who,' *maʔyum* 'when,' *maay* 'where,' Mohave *makač* 'who,' *maki* 'where,' Yuma *meki*, Maricopa *mekyenye* 'who,' *miki* 'where,' Akwa'ala *mukat* 'who,' Karankawa *muda* 'where'; Central Amerind: Mazatec *hme* 'what'; Chibchan-Paezan: Tarascan *ambe*, Guamaca *mai* 'who, how,' Kagaba *mai* 'who,' *mani* 'where,' *mitsa* 'when,' *mili* 'which,' Cacaopera *ma(-ram)* 'where,' Matagalpa *man*, Bribri *mîk* 'when,' Sumu *manpat*, Cabecar *mānē* 'which,' Move *ama* 'where,' Chimila *miki* 'who,' *muru* 'when,' *me-ma* 'to where,' *me-k* 'from where,' Guambiana *mu* 'who,' Totoro *man* 'how many,' Paez *manč* 'when,' *manka* 'where,' *manzos* 'how often,' *mants* 'how many,' *mau* 'how,' Cayapa *muŋ* ~ *maa* 'who,' Allentiac *men*, Catio *mai* 'where,' Colorado *moa* 'who,' *matuši* 'when'; Andean: Sek *xam-anmi* 'where,' Jebero *maʔ* 'what,' Cahuapana *ma-e* 'what,' *impi* 'when,' Quechua *ima* 'what,' *may* 'where'; Equatorial: Guamo *miku* 'what,' Yurucare *ama* 'who, which,' Tinigua *mné'á* 'who,' Yuruna *mane*, Paumari *-mani-* (interrogative), Candoshi *maya* 'what,' Esmeralda *muka*, Timote *mape* 'when,' Turiwara *maape* 'when, where,' Saliba *imakena* 'when,' Tuyoneri *menoka* 'when,' *me-yo* 'where,' Guajajara *mɔn* 'who,' Guayaki *ma* 'what, how,' Guarani *mba'e* 'what,' *mamo* 'where,' Cofan *mã-ni*, Maripu *manu(b)* 'in which direction,' Kandoshi *maja* 'what'; Macro-Carib: Witoto *mika*, Miranya *mukoka* 'when,' *mu* 'whose,' Witoto-Kaimö *muka* which'; Macro-Panoan: Nocten *emetta* 'what,' *mequie* 'when,' Toba-Guazu *mi* 'who'; Macro-Ge: Caraho *ampo* 'what,' *manēno* 'when,' *ampô-mē* 'which,' Puri *ya-moeni* 'when,' Aponegicran *muena* 'what,' Cayapo *mã* 'where,' Umutina *mašika* 'where,' *matuni* 'why,' Krẽye *menõ* 'who,' *ampô-ny* 'why,' Botocudo *mina* 'who.' [AM: G103, AMN]

18 PAL '2'

NIGER-CONGO: Temne *(kə)bari* 'twin,' Mano *pere* '2,' Nimbari *bala*, Daka *bara*, Proto-Bantu **bàdí* ~ **bìdí* '2,' **bádì* 'side.' [NC 48, KS 76, UOL 92, BA III: 21, 22, 43]

NILO-SAHARAN: Nubian *bar(-si)* 'twin,' Merarit *wírre* '2,' Kunama *báarè* '2,' *ibā* 'twin,' Maba *mbar* '2,' Mesalit *mbarrá*, Tama *warri*, Baka *brūe*, Ilit *ball-ame*. [ES 119, KS 76, UOL 92, NSB]

AFRO-ASIATIC: Omotic: Kafa *bara* 'other,' Mocha *baro*, Dime *bal*; Cushitic: Saho *baray* '2nd,' Oromo *bíra*; Chadic: Proto-Central Chadic **(kV-)bwVr* '2.' [VB]

INDO-EUROPEAN: Proto-Indo-European **pol* 'half, side'; Indic: Sanskrit *(ka-)palam* 'half'; Albanian *palë* 'side, part, pair'; Slavic: Old Church Slavic *polŭ* 'side, half,' Russian *pol* 'half.' [IE 802, 986, IS 356]

URALIC: Proto-Uralic (Illich-Svitych) **pälä* ~ *pole* 'half,' (Rédei) **pälä* 'half, side'; Samoyed: Yurak Samoyed *peele* 'half,' Selkup *pɛle*, Kamassian *pjeel* 'half, side'; Ugric: Hungarian *fél* ~ *fele* 'half, (one) side (of two),' Vogul *pääl* 'side, half'; Finnic: Saami *bælle* ~ *bæle* 'side, half, one of a pair,' Mordvin *pel'* 'side,' *pele* 'half,' Votyak *pal* 'side, half.' [U 67, IS 356, R 362]

DRAVIDIAN: Proto-Dravidian **pāl* 'part, portion,' Tamil *pāl* 'part, portion, share,' Malayalam *pāl* 'part,' Kannada *pāl* 'division, part,' Tulu *pālụ* 'share, portion, part,' Telugu *pālu* 'share, portion,' Parji *pēla* 'portion.' [D 4097, IS 356]

INDO-PACIFIC: Andaman Islands: Biada *(ik-)pāūr(-da)* '2,' Kede *(ír-)pōl*, Chariar *(nér-)pól*, Juwoi *(ró-)pāūr*; New Guinea: Ndani *bere*, Sauweri *pere*; Tasmanian: Southeastern *boula* ~ *bura*, Southern *pooalih*. [T 331, VB]

AUSTRALIAN: Proto-Australian **bula* '2,' Proto-Pama-Nyungan **(nyuN)palV* '(you) two,' **pula* 'they two,' Ngiyambaa *bulā* 'one of a pair.' [RD 356, BB 7, 31]

AUSTROASIATIC: Proto-Austroasiatic **ʔ(m)bar* '2'; Munda: Santali *bar*, Kharia *(u-)bar*, *(am-)bar* 'you two,' Juang *ambar*, Remo *ʔmbār* '2'; Mon-Khmer: Khmu' *bār*, Bahnar *ʔbar*, Jeh *bal*, Old Mon *ʔbar*, Old Khmer *ber*, Sakai *hmbar*, Khasi *ār*, Riang *(k-)ār*, Palaung *ār* ~ *a*, *par* 'you two,' Temiar *bər(-nar)* '2,' Central Nicobarese *ã*. [PB 135, UOL 94]

MIAO-YAO: Proto-Miao-Yao **(a)war* ~ **(ə)wər* '2,' Proto-Miao **way* (< **war*), Proto-Yao **(w)i*. [PB 415]

DAIC: Mak *wa* 'twin,' Ong Be *von* '2.' [PB 415]

AUSTRONESIAN: Proto-Austronesian **kə(m)bal* ~ **(ŋ)kə(m)bar* 'twin,' Javanese *kĕbar* 'doubled,' *kĕmbar* 'twin,' Motu *hɛ-kapa* 'twins,' Roro *aka-bani* '8' (= 4-pair). [AN 76, WW 227, PB 415]

AMERIND: Penutian: Wintun *palo(-l)* '2,' Wappo *p'ala* 'twins,' Atakapa *happalst* '2,' Huave *apool* 'snap in two'; Chibchan-Paezan: Chiripo *bor* '2,' Xinca *bial* ~ *piar*, Bribri *bul* ~ *bur*, Cacaopera *burru*, Sanuma *-palo* (repetitive), *polakapi* '2,' Cayapo *palʲu*, Colorado *palu*, Atacameño *poya*; Andean: Quechua *pula* 'both,' Aymara *paja* '2,' Yamana *sa-pai* 'we-2' (*sa-* = 'thou'), Yahgan *(i-)pai* '(we) two'; Macro-Tucanoan: Tuyuka *pealo* '2,' Wanana *pilia*, Desana *peru*, Yupua *apara*, Proto-Nambikwara **p'āl(-in)*, Catuquina *upaua*, Hubde *mbeere*, Ticuna *peia*; Macro-Ge: Caraho *pa-* 'we-2-inc.' [AM 262, AMN]

19 PAR 'to fly'

NIGER-CONGO: Proto-West Sudanic **pil* 'to fly,' Serer *fol*, Same *pere*, Ewe *flò* 'to jump,' Yoruba *fò* 'fly,' Grebo *fri*, Igbo *fé*, Ijo *fin*. [KS 32]

NILO-SAHARAN: Dinka *par* 'to fly,' Nubian *fire* 'to flutter,' Teso *a-poror* 'to fly,' Teda *bur-ci* 'to jump,' Songhai *firi* 'to fly,' Ik *por-ɔn*, Maasai *-biri*, Majang *pir*. [KS 32, NSD 27, UOL 193, KER, HF 12]

AFRO-ASIATIC: Omotic: Proto-Omotic **pyaRR* 'to fly'; Ancient Egyptian *pꜣ* 'to fly, flee'; Semitic: Aramaic *parr* 'flee,' Arabic *farra*, South Arabian *ferfir* 'wing,' Amharic *barrara* 'fly away, flee'; Cushitic: Beja *fār* 'jump, hop,' Boyo *firy* 'flee'; Berber: Shilha *firri* to fly,' Ait Izdeg *afru*; Chadic: Ankwa *p'ār* 'jump,' Angas *piar* 'jump, leap,' Buduma *fər* 'fly, jump.' [CS 366, AA 32, IS 346]

KARTVELIAN: Proto-Kartvelian **p'er* 'to fly,' Georgian *p'er*, Svan *p'er*; Proto-Kartvelian **prin* 'to fly,' Georgian *prin* ~ *pren*, Mingrelian *purin*, Chan *purtin*. [KA 152, 190, IS 346]

INDO-EUROPEAN: Proto-Indo-European **(s)per* 'to fly'; Indic: Sanskrit *parṇá* 'feather'; Iranian: Avestan *parəna* 'feather, wing'; Slavic: Old Church Slavic *perǫ* 'to fly,' *pero* 'feather.' [WP II: 21, IE 850, IS 346, EU]

URALIC: Yukaghir *perie* 'feathers,' *perienze* 'feathered,' *perień* 'have wings'; Proto-Uralic **parV* 'to fly'; Ugric: Ostyak *pɔr* ~ *pur* 'to fly.' [IS 346]

DRAVIDIAN: Proto-Dravidian **parV* ~ **par̲V* 'to fly, run, jump,' Tamil *para* 'to fly, hover, flutter, move with celerity,' Malayalam *parakka* 'to fly, flee,' *para* 'bird,' *paru* 'flight,' Kota *parn-* 'to fly,' Toda *pōr̲*, Kannada *pār̲* 'to leap up, run, jump, fly,' Kodagu *pār* 'to fly, leap,' Telugu *paracu* 'to run away, flee,' *parika* 'a kind of bird,' Kui *pāsk* 'to fly,' Kuwi *prāḍ* 'to run away.' [D 4020, NSD 27, IS 346]

?TUNGUS: Evenki *hār* 'to soar.' [IS 346]

GILYAK *parpar* 'to hover, fly about.' [EU]

CAUCASIAN: Proto-Caucasian **pirV* 'to fly,' Proto-West Caucasian **pərə*, Ubyx *pərə*, Abkhaz *pir*; Proto-Lezghian **pVr-*, Udi *pur*, Archi *parx*, Proto-Avar-Andi **par-pV-*; Proto-Caucasian **părVpălV* 'butterfly, moth,'

Proto-West Caucasian *parəpalə 'moth,' Proto-Lezghian *pa(r)pal- 'butterfly.' [C 162, 167; KA 152, 190]

BASQUE pimpirina 'butterfly' (< *pir-pir-).

SINO-TIBETAN: Proto-Sino-Tibetan *phur ~ *bhur 'to fly'; Archaic Chinese *pjwər 'to fly'; Tibeto-Burman: Proto-Tibeto-Burman *pur ~ *pir 'to fly,' Tibetan 'phur-ba, Central Tibetan 'phir-ba, Nung əphr 'to shake,' khoŋ-phr 'moth,' Garo bil 'to fly,' Dimasa bir, ?Bahing byer, ?Abor-Miri ber. [ST 181, 398, NSC 152]

?INDO-PACIFIC: Baham paru-baru 'bird,' Kondo boro, Kare purupuru, Bunabun piropir 'butterfly.' [FS 8, 135]

NAHALI aphir 'to fly.' [NA 59; according to Kuiper this is a borrowing from Kurku]

AUSTROASIATIC: Munda: Proto-Munda *apir 'to fly'; Mon-Khmer: Mon pau, Khmer par, Bahnar par, Jeh pal, Vietnamese bay. [PB 482]

DAIC: Tai: Proto-Tai *?bin 'to fly,' Dioi bin; Sek bil ~ ?bil; Kam-Sui: Proto-Kam-Sui *pwen ~ *bwen, Kam pen, Sui win ~ vyen, Mak vin; Lakkia pon; Ong-Be vin. [PB 394]

AUSTRONESIAN: Proto-Formosan *(maq)baR 'to fly,' *(mi-)pəRpəR. [PB 394]

20 POKO 'arm'

?KHOISAN: Hadza upukwa 'leg, hind leg, foot,' ufukwani 'thigh.' [BD 247, 249]

NIGER-CONGO: Dagomba boɣo 'arm,' Gbaya baxa, Ewe abo, Zande bo, Proto-Bantu *bókò, Sotho le-boko 'arm,' ?Wolof, Gbaya buko '10,' ?Mossi piga, ?Tiv puwə, ?Grebo pu, ?Vere bo. [KS 4, NC 44, UOL 194]

NILO-SAHARAN: Bagirmi boko 'arm,' Baka baka, Berta buá, Didinga iba. [KS 4, CN 3, UOL 194]

INDO-EUROPEAN: Proto-Indo-European *bhāghu(s) 'arm, forearm, elbow'; Indic: Sanskrit bāhúḥ 'arm'; Iranian: Avestan bāzus; Armenian bazuk 'forearm' (a loan from Iranian languages, according to Pokorny); Tocharian: Tocharian A poke 'arm,' Tocharian B pauke; Greek pakhus 'elbow, forearm'; Germanic: Old English bōg 'arm, shoulder, bough,' English bough. [IE 108, UOL 194]

DRAVIDIAN: Kurux pāknā 'to take up into one's arms,' Malto páke 'to take in the lap.' [D 4050]

MONGOLIAN: Proto-Mongolian *baɣu- 'upper arm.' [AD 20]

BURUSHASKI: Hunza bʌɣu 'double armful,' Werchikwar bʌɣ'o 'taking or embracing in two arms.' [B 65, W 38]

YENISEIAN: Proto-Yeniseian *boq 'hand, palm.' [Y 28]

SINO-TIBETAN: Tibeto-Burman: Proto-Tibeto-Burman *pow ~ *bow 'arm' (cf. English bough for a similar phonetic development). [TB 442]

?INDO-PACIFIC: Andaman Islands: Bea pag 'claw,' Bale poag; Tasmanian *pögaréna* 'shoulder'; New Britain: Sulka *paaga* 'fingernail'; West New Guinea: Baham *pag*; North New Guinea: Nafri *faxa*; East New Guinea: Amara *foka*; Unclassified New Guinea: Tate *faha* 'claw.' [IP 858]

NAHALI *boko* ~ *bokko* 'hand.' [NA 74]

?AUSTROASIATIC: Semang *pāk* 'hand,' *ta-pak* 'to slap.' [NA 63]

DAIC: Tai: Proto-Tai *ʔba* 'shoulder'; Sek *va*; Kam-Sui: Mak *ha*; Ong-Be *bea*; Li: Proto-Li *va*; Laqua *muə* 'shoulder' (< *mb(γ)a). [PB 378]

AUSTRONESIAN: Proto-Austronesian *(ʔa)-baγa* 'shoulder,' Proto-Formosan *qa-baγa-(a)n*, Proto-Oceanic *(qa-)paγa*, Mukawa *kabara*, Paiwa *kavara*. [AN 19, WW 187, PB 378]

AMERIND: Almosan-Keresiouan: Mandan *sūpaxe* 'arm,' Dakota *xupahu*, Biloxi *sōpka* 'fin'; Penutian: Natchez *ilbak* 'hand,' Choctaw *ibbok* 'hand, arm,' Chitimacha *pākta* 'armpit,' Totonac *paqniʔ* 'arm,' Huastec *pahāb* 'hand,' Quiche *sipax* 'give'; Hokan: Yana *dac-buku* 'arm,' Salinan *puku*, Chumash *pu*, Cochimi *ginyakpak*, Mohave *hivipuk*, Havasupai *vuy-eboka*, Subtiaba *paxpu*; Chibchan-Paezan: Shiriana *poko* ~ *boko*, Cuitlatec *poxja*, Jutiapa *paxa*, Chiquimulilla *pux* 'hand,' Xinca *pahal* 'arm,' Paya *bakapu* 'give,' Cayapa *pexpex* 'arm,' Colorado *pexpe*, Mura *apixi*, Chimu *pīk* 'give,' Puruha *pux*; Andean: Culli *pui* 'hand,' Simacu *bixi*, Allentiac *pux* 'give,' Auca *po* 'hand,'; Macro-Tucanoan: Canamari *pöghy* 'hand,' Papury *mbake*, Tiquie *(m)bake* 'arm,' Kaliana *kijapakuba*, Catauxim *ču-bakō* 'hand,' Proto-Nambikwara *pik*'; Equatorial: Chamacoco *pukē* 'arm,' Turaha *pogo*, Camsa *buakua-ha*, Coche *buakwače* 'hand, forearm,' Ramarama *i-pāŋua* 'arm,' Karif *bugalaga* 'armpit,' Omagua *poa* 'hand,' Proto-Tupi *po*, Yuracare *popo*, Kamaru *bo* 'arm,' Aruashi *bu* 'hand'; Macro-Carib: Muinane *ɔnɔ-bwɨkɨ* 'arm,' Mocoa *apo*, Ocaina *ooʔpo* 'hand,' Tamanaco *(j-)apa(-ri)* 'arm,' Coeruna *(ko-)ipai*; Macro-Panoan: Chulupi *pakat* 'hand,' Suhin *pakat-ai*, Sanapana *in-apheik*, Charrua *(is-)bax* 'arm,' Toba *apige*, Chacobo *baš* 'elbow, forearm,' Proto-Tacanan *bai* 'arm'; Macro-Ge: Botocudo *po* 'hand,' Proto-Ge *pa* 'arm,' Kaingan *pe*, Chiquito *(i-)pa*, Guato *(ma-)po*. [AM 7, MT 46, AMN]

21 PUTI 'vulva'

NIGER-CONGO: Mande: Malinke *butu* 'vulva,' Guro *buri*, Bobo-Fing *bido*, Bisa *bid*; Bantu: Luganda *-butɔ* 'womb,' Kunda *-budu*, Swazi *-ŋgo-bɔti*, Ki-sikongo *-buti*. [HJ, M]

NILO-SAHARAN: Songhai: Gao *buti* 'vulva,' Djerma *bute*; Koman: Ganza *pit*, Koma *bitt*. [NS 145, NSD 59]

AFRO-ASIATIC: Proto-Afro-Asiatic *pwt* 'hole, anus, vulva'; Omotic: Ganjule *pote* 'vagina'; Semitic: Hebrew *pot* 'vulva' ("secret parts" in the King James Version, Isaiah 3:17); Cushitic: Somali *fúto* 'anus,' Darasa *fīdo* 'genitals,' Oromo *fuǧi* 'vulva'; Chadic: Jegu *paate*, 'vulva,' *paato* 'penis,' Angas *fut* 'hole.' [CS 381, IS 340, WM 64]

KARTVELIAN: Proto-Kartvelian **put'* 'hole,' Svan *put'u*. [IS 340]

INDO-EUROPEAN: Proto-Indo-European **puto* 'cunnus'; Indic: Sanskrit *pŭtau* 'buttocks'; Italic: Vulgar Latin **putta* 'girl,' Old French *pute* (mod. *putain*) 'whore,' Provençal *puta(-na)*, Spanish *puta*; Germanic: Old Icelandic *fuð* 'cunnus,' Middle High German *vut* 'vulva,' Swiss German *fotz* ~ *fotza*, Swedish *fitta*, *fod* 'rear end' (dialectal). [WP II: 21, IE 848, SM 1013]

URALIC: Proto-Uralic (Illich-Svitych) **putV* 'rectum,' (Rédei) **putɜ* 'rectum, colon'; Ugric: Ostyak *pŭti* 'rectum'; Finnic: Saami *buttĕgĕ*. [U 91, IS 340, R 410]

DRAVIDIAN: Brahui *puṇḍū* 'anus, buttocks,' *pōs* 'vulva,' Tamil *puṇṭai* 'vulva,' *pūṟu* ~ *pīṟu* 'anus,' *poccu* 'vulva, anus,' Malayalam *pūṟu* 'buttocks, vulva,' Kannada *pucci* 'vulva,' Telugu *pūḍa* 'anus,' Tulu *pūṭi* 'vulva,' Kodagu *purï*, Kota *piḍ*, Toda *pïḍy* 'penis,' Kuwi *putki*. [D 4273, 4379, 4476, NSD 59]

MONGOLIAN: Middle Mongolian *hütü-gün* 'vulva.'

JAPANESE-RYUKYUAN: Old Japanese *pʰɔto* 'vulva' (mod. *hoto*). [SY]

ESKIMO-ALEUT: Proto-Eskimo-Aleut **putu* 'hole.' [EA]

CAUCASIAN: Proto-Caucasian **pŭt'i* 'genitals (mostly female),' Proto-Nax **but'* 'vulva,' Proto-Avar-Andi **but'a*, Proto-Lak **put'i* 'tube,' Proto-Dargi **put'i* 'anus,' Proto-Lezghian **p̄ot'* 'penis.' [C 168]

BASQUE *poto-rro* 'pubis, vulva.'

?AUSTRALIAN: Luridya *pudă* 'vulva.' [VB]

?AUSTRONESIAN: Proto-Austronesian **betik* 'vagina,' **puki* 'vulva' (< **puti* ?; cf. East Rukai *pati* 'vulva'), Ami *puki*, Tsou *buki* 'penis.' [AN 121, WW 231, 233, PB 417]

AMERIND: Almosan-Keresiouan: Delaware *saputti* 'anus,' Mohegan *sebud*, Wiyot *beš* 'vagina,' Upper Chehalis *-pš* 'anus'; Penutian: Chinook *puč*, Yaudanchi *poto* 'penis,' San Juan Bautista *lapus* 'anus,' Southern Sierra Miwok *pōtol*; Hokan: Washo *(d-)ībis* 'vagina,' Karok *vīθ*, Diegueño *hapïcatt*, Tequistlatec *(la-)bešuʔ*; Chibchan-Paezan: Move *butie*, Paya *pɛta-is-tapcca* 'anus,' Chimu *pot*, Ayoman *busi* 'vagina,' Allentiac *poru*; Andean: Quechua *upiti* 'anus,' Yamana *pūta* 'hole,' Aymara *pʰutʰu*; Macro-Tucanoan: Gamella *sebu* 'vulva,' Uaiana *mbitikope* 'anus,' Uasöna *hibitikope*; Equatorial: Guahibo *petu* 'vagina,' Guayabero *sil-fʰuta* 'vulva,' Kandoshi *apčir(-ič)*, Toyeri *apuit* 'vagina,' Wachipairi *ped*, Piapoko *afʰutani* 'buttocks,' Tariana *pāti-niawa* 'vagina,' Warakena *pēde* 'clitoris,' Caranga *pïče* 'vulva,' Uro *piši*, (cf. also such Equatorial forms as Siusi *tˢu-pote* 'vagina,' Campa *sibiči* 'vulva,' *šibiči* 'penis,' Uro *šapsi* 'genital organ'); Macro-Carib: Jaricuna *poita* 'vagina,' Pimenteira *pütze-maung*, Waiwai *boči* 'pubic hair,' Motilon *pirri* 'penis'; Macro-Panoan: Cavineña

busu-kani 'anus,' Tagnani *opet*, Tiatinagua *besi* 'penis,' Panobo *buši*,'
Lule *pesu*; Macro-Ge: Mekran *putote*. [AM 263, EQ 121, AMN]

22 TEKU 'leg, foot'

NIGER-CONGO: Konyagi *-tak* 'heel,' Gurmana *-duge*, Jarawa *-dudug-ul*, Ki-
kuyu *-togigo*. [HJ II]

NILO-SAHARAN: Proto-Kuliak **tak'a* 'foot, shoe,' *takw* 'step on, tread on,'
So *tɛg* 'foot'; Saharan: Daza *dige* 'leg,' Kanuri *dəŋgʌl* 'wade,' Kanembu
dõ ~ *duu* 'leg,' Berti *taki* 'thigh,' Karda *dìgì* 'foot.' [VB, NSB]

AFRO-ASIATIC: Omotic: Male *toki* 'leg,' Koyra *toke*, Kachama *tuke*, Bambeshi
tugɛ 'foot,' Nao *tego* 'to go,' Dime *tiŋgo*; Cushitic: Proto-East Cushitic
*tāk-, Somali *tag-* 'to go,' Dahalo *ḍaka'a* 'foot'; Chadic: Proto-West Chadic
*tak- 'to walk with somebody, accompany,' Muzgum *túgu* 'foot,' Gollango
tah 'to go.' [VB, LN 255, OS 166]

DRAVIDIAN: Proto-Central Dravidian **tāk* 'to walk,' Parji *tāk*, Pengo *tāŋ(g)*,
Kui *tāka*. [D 3151, LN 255] Cf. also Telugu *ḍekka* 'hoof,' Naikri *ḍekka*,
Konda *ḍeka*, Kuwi *dekka*. [D 2970]

CAUCASIAN: Proto-Caucasian **t'H̥ǎlq'ʷV* 'part of the leg,' Proto-East Caucasian **t'ʷehʷV* 'foot,' Proto-Dido **t'iq'ʷV* 'sole of the foot,' Proto-
Lezghian **t'elq'ʷI* 'shin, ankle.' [C 196]

NA-DENE: Proto-Eyak-Athabaskan **t'ằx* ~ **t'ằh* 'foot.' [DC]

INDO-PACIFIC: Tasmanian *tokăna* 'foot'; Timor-Alor: Abui *tuku* 'leg, foot';
Halmahera: Ternate *tagi* 'to walk'; Central Melanesian: Savo *tetegha* 'foot,
lower leg'; Tasmanian: Northeast *tage(-na)* 'to walk,' North *taka(-ri)*,
Southeast *taga(-ra)*; North New Guinea: Arso *taka* 'foot'; Southwest New
Guinea: Marind *tagu* 'to walk,' Telefol *tek* 'to go'; South New Guinea:
Mombum *itögh* 'foot,' Bara *togoi* 'leg'; Central New Guinea: Ekari *togo*
'to walk,' Matap *tag* 'hip'; East New Guinea: Jegasa Sarau *tegi* 'foot.' [IP
80, T 458]

AMERIND: Almosan-Keresiouan: Mandan *dok'a* 'leg,' Hidatsa *idiki*; Penutian: Siuslaw *tsīkʷ* 'foot,' North Sahaptin *təχp* 'with the foot,' Nez Perce
teχé?p 'foot,' Wintu *t'ek-* 'move,' Mixe *tek* 'foot,' Huastec *tˢ'ehet* 'upper leg'; Hokan: Jicaque *tek* 'leg'; Chibchan-Paezan: Borunca *tek* ~ *dek*
'walk,' Move *dikeko*, Atanque *dukakana* 'leg,' Baudo *tači-kini* 'foot'; Andean: Simacu *tixea* 'foot,' Yahgan *kadek* 'walk'; Macro-Tucanoan: Tiquie
do(γ) 'leg,' Wanana *dexso* 'thigh'; Equatorial: Tinigua *diki* 'foot,' Piaroa *tsihẽpẽ*, Wapishana *čikep* 'walk,' Arawak *adikki-hi* 'footprint,' Miguri
guateke 'walk,' Guayabero *tuk* 'foot,' Yurucare *tekte* 'leg,' Guahibo *taxu*
'foot'; Macro-Carib: Bora *take* 'leg,' Andoke *(ka-)dekkhe* 'foot'; Macro-
Panoan: Cavineña *edači*, Panobo *taeg*, Mayoruna *taku*, Amahuaca *taku*;
Macro-Ge: Oti *etage* 'leg,' Cotoxo *täxkatse*, Camican *tako-emaŋ* 'walk,'
Proto-Ge **tɛ* 'leg.' [AM 165, AMN]

23 TIK 'finger; one'

NIGER-CONGO: West Atlantic: Fulup *sik ~ sex* 'finger,' Nalu *te*; North-Central Niger-Congo: Gur *dike* '1'; South-Central Niger-Congo: Gwa *dogbo*, Fon *dòkpá* Ewe *dèká*; Bantu: Tonga *tiho* 'finger,' Chopi *tˢiho*, Ki-Bira *zika*, Ba-Kiokwa *zigu*. [KS 55, UOL 91, HJ II: 295]

NILO-SAHARAN: Fur *tɔk* '1,' Maba *tək*, Dendje *doko* 'ten,' Nera *dɔkk-u* '1,' Merarit *tok* 'ten,' Dinka *tok* '1,' Berta *dúkóni*, ?Mangbetu *t'ɛ*, Kwama *seek-o*, Bari *to*, Jur *tok*, Twampa *dèʔ*, Komo *dé*. [NS 103, CN 72, ES 83, KS 55, UOL 91, NSB]

AFRO-ASIATIC: Proto-Afro-Asiatic **tak* '1'; Semitic: Peripheral West Gurage *təgu (əmmat)* 'only 1'; Cushitic: Oromo *toko* '1,' *takku* 'palm (of hand),' Yaaku *tegei* 'hand,' Saho *ti* '1,' Bilin *tu*, Tsamai *dōkko*; Berber: Nefusa *tukoḍ* 'finger'; Chadic: Hausa *(ḍaya) tak* 'only 1,' Gisiga *tēkoy* '1,' Gidder *te-teka*, Logone *tku* 'first.' [AAD 3: 10]

INDO-EUROPEAN: Proto-Indo-European **deik* 'to show, point,' **dekm̥* '10'; Italic: Latin *dig(-itus)* 'finger,' *dic(-āre)* 'to say,' *decem* '10'; Germanic: Proto-Germanic **taihwō* 'toe,' Old English *tahe* 'toe,' English toe, Old High German *zêha* 'toe, finger.' [IE 188, 191, EU]

URALIC: Votyak *odik* '1,' Zyrian *õtik*. [U 138, EU]

TURKIC: Chuvash *tek* 'only, just,' Uighur *tek* 'only, merely,' Chagatai *tek* 'only, single,' Turkish *tek* 'only,' *teken* 'one by one.' [EU]

KOREAN *(t)tayki* '1, thing,' *teki* '1, guy, thing,' Old Korean *tēk* '10.' [EU]

JAPANESE-RYUKYUAN: Japanese *te* 'hand.' [UOL 195]

AINU *tek ~ teke* 'hand,' *atiki* 'five.' [UOL 195, EU]

GILYAK *řak* 'once.' [EU]

CHUKCHI-KAMCHATKAN: Kamchadal *itygin* 'foot, paw.' [EU]

ESKIMO-ALEUT: Proto-Eskimo-Aleut **q(i)tik* 'middle finger'; Eskimo: Kuskokwim *tik(-iq)* 'index finger,' Greenlandic *tik(-iq)* 'index finger,' *tikkuag-paa* 'he points to it'; Aleut: Attu *tik(-laq)* 'middle finger,' *atgu* 'finger,' *taγataq* '1,' Atka *atakan*. [EU, EA 121]

YENISEIAN: Proto-Yeniseian **tok* 'finger.' [VT]

SINO-TIBETAN: Archaic Chinese **t'iek* 'single, 1'; Tibeto-Burman: Proto-Tibeto-Burman **tyik* '1,' Rai *tik(-pu)*, Tibetan *(g-)tśig*. [ST 94]

NA-DENE: Haida *(s-)tˡa* 'with the fingers'; Tlingit *tˡeeq* 'finger,' *tˡek* '1'; Eyak *tikhi*; Athabaskan: Sarsi *tlik'-(aza)*, Kutchin *(ĩ-)łag*, Hupa *łaʔ*, Navajo *łàʔ*. [ND]

INDO-PACIFIC: Tasmanian: Southern *motook* 'forefinger,' Southeastern *togue* 'hand'; West New Guinea: Proto-Karonan **dik* '1'; Southwest New Guinea: Boven Mbian *tek* 'fingernail,' Digul *tuk*. [IP 37, SWNG 39, SNG 42, UOL 195]

AUSTROASIATIC: Proto-Austroasiatic *(k-)tig 'arm, hand'; Munda: Kharia
tiʔ; Mon-Khmer: Riang tiʔ, Wa taiʔ, Khmer ṭai, Vietnamese tay, Proto-
Aslian *tik ~ *tiŋ. [PB 467, UOL 195]
MIAO-YAO: Proto-Miao-Yao *ntoʔ 'finger'; Proto-Yao *doʔ; Proto-Miao *ntai
'point with the finger.' [PB 356]
DAIC: Proto-Li *dliaŋ 'finger,' Northern Li tleaŋ ~ theŋ, Loi thɛŋ ~ ćiaŋ.
[PB 356]
?AUSTRONESIAN: Proto-Austronesian *(tu-)diŋ 'point with the finger.' [AN
140, WW 156, PB 356, UOL 195]
AMERIND: Almosan-Keresiouan: Nootka takʷa 'only,' Bella Coola tˢ'iʔxʷ
'five,' Kalispel tˢ'oqʷ 'point with the finger,' Kwakwala sokʷ 'five,' Nitinat
-tsoq- 'in hand,' Cherokee sakwe '1,' Acoma ʔiskaw, Pawnee uska, Mohawk tsiʔer 'finger,' Hidatsa šaki, Winnebago sāk, Quapaw čak, Biloxi
ičaki 'fingers,' Yuchi saki 'hand'; Penutian: Southern Sierra Miwok tˢik'aʔ
'index finger,' Wintun tiq-eles '10,' Nisenan tok- 'hand,' Mixe toʔk ~
tuk' '1,' Sayula tuʔk, Tzeltal tukal 'alone,' Quiche tik'ex 'carry in the
hand,' Hokan: Proto-Hokan *dɨk'i 'finger,' Karok tīk 'finger, hand,' Achu-
mawi (wa-)túči 'finger,' Washo tsek, Yana -tˢ'gi- 'alone,' East Pomo bī'ya-
tsūkai 'finger,' Arraarra teeh'k 'hand,' Pehtsik tiki-vash, Akwa'ala ašit-
dek '1'; Central Amerind: Nahua tˢïikiaʔa, Pima Bajo čīč, Tarahumara
sika 'hand,' Mazatec čikaʔã 'alone,' Mangue tike '1,' Cuicatec diči '10';
Chibchan-Paezan: Chibcha ytiquyn 'finger,' ačik 'by ones,' Borunca e'tsik
'1,' Guatuso dooki, Shiriana ĩthak 'hand,' Ulua tinka-mak 'finger,' Paez
tɛ ɛč '1,' Allentiac tukum '10,' Warrau hisaka 'finger, 1'; Andean: Cahuapana itekla 'finger, hand,' Jebero itökla, Alakaluf tākso '1,' Quechua sōk;
Macro-Tucanoan: Siona tekua, Siona teg-li '5,' Canichana eu-tixle 'finger,' Ticuna suku 'hand,' Yupua di(x)ka 'arm,' Uasöna dikaga; Equatorial: Upano tˢikitik '1,' Aguaruna tikij, Murato tˢiči 'hand,' Uru tˢī '1,'
Chipaya zek, Itene taka, Guamo dixi 'finger,' Katembri tika 'toe,' Yuracare teče 'thumb'; Macro-Carib: Kukura tikua 'finger,' Accawai tigina
'1,' Yagua teki; Imihita meux-tsekoa 'finger,' Trio tinki '1,' Ocaina dikabu
'arm'; Macro-Panoan: Mataco otejji '1,' Tagnani etegueno 'finger,' Sensi
(nawiš)-tikoe '1 (finger)' Cavineña eme-toko 'hand,' Moseten tak '10';
Macro-Ge: Botocudo (po-)čik '1 (finger),' ǧik 'alone,' Proto-Ge *(pɨ-)tˢi
'1 (finger).' [AM 110, MT 1, DL 56, AMN]

24 TIKA 'earth'

?NIGER-CONGO: Proto-Bantu *tàkà 'earth, mud, ground, soil,' Swahili taka
'dirt, refuse.' [BA IV: 87]
?NILO-SAHARAN: Berta adok'o(ŋ) ~ atok'o(ŋ) 'mud.' [Bender 1989]

KARTVELIAN: Proto-Kartvelian *tiqa ~ *diqa 'soil, clay,' Georgian tixa 'clay, dirt' (< Old Georgian tiqa), Mingrelian dixa ~ dexa 'soil, earth,' Chan (n)dixa 'soil.' [KA 94, N 69]

INDO-EUROPEAN: Proto-Indo-European *dhghem 'earth'; Anatolian: Hittite te-e-kan; Indic: Sanskrit kṣam; Iranian: Avestan zā̊; Albanian dhe; Italic: Latin humus; Celtic: Old Irish dū 'place'; Baltic: Latvian zeme 'earth'; Slavic: Old Church Slavic zemlja; Tocharian: Tocharian A tkaṃ. [IE 414, N 69]

DRAVIDIAN: Tamil tukaḷ 'dust,' Telugu dūgaṟa 'dust, dirt,' Kolami tūk 'dust, earth, clay,' Naikri tuk 'earth, clay,' Parji tūkud 'earth, clay, soil,' Gadba tūkuṟ 'earth, clay.' [D 3283]

JAPANESE-RYUKYUAN: Old Japanese tukï 'mud,' tuki 'land' (mod. tˢuki ~ tˢuči). [SY]

BURUSHASKI tīk ~ tik 'earth, ground.' [B 351]

YENISEIAN: Proto-Yeniseian *təq- 'clay, dirt,' Ket tag-ar 'clay,' Kot tʰag-ar 'dirt.' [SC 76]

SINO-TIBETAN: Lushei diak 'mud,' Sho dʰek ~ dek 'earth.' [IST 221]

NA-DENE: Haida tˡig ~ tˡga ~ klik 'earth, ground' (cf. TIK 'finger' above for a similar shift of t > tˡ before i); Tlingit (tˡit-)tik ~ tˡiak-ū ~ klatk 'earth'; Eyak (Yakutat) (tza)tˡkh 'earth.' [ND]

NAHALI tˢikal ~ sikal 'earth.' [NA 67; probably a borrowing of Kurku tˢikal 'mud,' according to Kuiper.]

AMERIND: Almosan-Keresiouan: Bella Bella təqʷum 'dirty,' Nootka tˢʼakʼumtˢ 'earth,' Kwakwala dzəqwa 'mud,' Squamish tíqʷ 'muddy,' Lower Fraser s-tʼiqəl, Seneca -tki- 'dirty,' Yuchi sʼakʼɔ 'mud,' Hidatsa iḥatsaki 'dirty,' Acoma háʔatˢʼi 'land'; Penutian: Tsimshian maʔtks 'dirty,' Pokonchi tˢikot, Mam čokš 'earth,' Mixe məʔəts 'mud,' Sayula moʔts, Ixil šokʼol, Quiche šoqʼox 'muddy'; Hokan: Shasta tˢʼik 'mud,' Achomawi teqade 'earth,' Diegueño taketak 'dirty'; Central Amerind: Cora tˢiʔitˢa, Hopi tïtˢkia 'earth,' Chatina tˢuuh 'dirty,' Proto-Central Otomi *tˢʼo, Chinantec suh 'dirt'; Chibchan-Paezan: Xinca tuxa 'mud,' Binticua tikan, Bribri ičuk 'earth,' Rama taki, Cabecar du-čeka 'mud,' Guambiana čig, Alllentiac toko, Cayapa tu 'earth'; Andean: Quechua čʼiči 'dirty,' Pehuelche atek 'earth,' Tehuelche takhs 'dirty'; Macro-Tucanoan: Papury tixsa, Yupua tīxta 'earth,' Tucano dixta, Särä sixta, Canichana ni-čixiči, Nadobo togn 'mud'; Equatorial: Tinigua tokwana 'earth,' Caranga tˢuxtˢi 'dirty,' Chamicuro tˢixta 'earth,' Cocoma tuguka; Macro-Carib: Yabarana ašikipe 'dirty,' Witoto sagope 'mud'; Macro-Panoan: Toba-Guazu toko 'dirty,' Lengua atits, Chulupi tīs 'wet ground,' Tacanaači 'dirty'; Macro-Ge: Chiquito tuki-s, Bororo txu, Chavante tika 'earth,' Apinage tugu 'dirty,' Cayapo tuk. [AMN]

25 TSAKU 'leg, foot'

?NIGER-CONGO: Bantu: Proto-Bantu *tᵃkù 'calf of the leg.' [BA 79]

NILO-SAHARAN: East Sudanic: Jur čok 'foot,' Zilmamu šowa 'foot,' Nera šokna 'foot, claw,' Proto-Dinka-Nuer *tˢok 'foot'; Gumuz: Proto-Gumuz *tˢogwa, Proto-Koman *šok, Komo šawkʰ, Twampa šòg, Kwama sɔŋk'. [VB, NSB]

AFRO-ASIATIC: Cushitic: Beja sikwina 'foot,' Quara sukanā; Semitic: Hebrew šoq 'leg,' Arabic sāq; Berber: Shilha (ta-)zux(-t) 'foot'; Chadic: Proto-West Chadic *sAkA 'leg,' Bolewa šeke 'foot,' Fali sika. [CS 265, AA 34, OS 292]

INDO-EUROPEAN: Indic: Sanskrit sak(-thi) 'thigh'; Iranian: Avestan hax(-ti); Celtic: Welsh heg(-ol) 'leg, shank.' [IE 930]

URALIC: Yukaghir tˢoγ(-ul) 'foot, leg'; Ugric: Ostyak săg(-ənt') ~ soh(-ət') ~ śog(-əś) 'back side of the leg from the heel to the bend of the knee (of a human being); back hoof (of a horse); Finnic: Saami čæwǧa ~ čæwǧe 'hock of reindeer or other quadruped.' [U 92]

CHUKCHI-KAMCHATKAN: Kamchadal tˢk(-ana) ~ tˢki 'foot, leg, paw.' [Swadesh 1962]

CAUCASIAN: Proto-Caucasian *č'V[l]k'ʷV 'foot, hoof,' Proto-Avar-Andi *c̄'ik'ʷa 'foot.' [C 75, DC]

BURUSHASKI: Hunza šʌk 'arm, forearm (of a human being); thigh, upper part of the leg (of an animal),' Werchikwar šʌk. [B 320, W 215]

?SINO-TIBETAN: Ancient Chinese *tsⁱwok 'foot,' Cantonese tsuk.

INDO-PACIFIC: Andaman Islands: Onge tˢige 'leg,' Biada tˢag, Puchikwar tˢok, Juwoi čok; Central New Guinea: Mikaru saga 'foot,' Grand Valley Dani (ne-)sok '(my) foot'; East New Guinea: Korona sogo 'foot,' Sikube suku, Mafulu soge, Kambisa suga. [IP 80, T 458]

AUSTROASIATIC: Munda: Kharia dᶻuŋ 'foot'; Mon-Khmer: Mon tˢöŋ 'foot, leg,' Khmer dᶻɤŋ 'leg, foot,' Temiar dᶻoŋ ~ dᶻukⁿ, Mah Meri dᶻogn, Shompen čuk 'foot.' [VB]

AMERIND: Almosan-Keresiouan: Proto-Algic *-sōʔk-ani ~ -šōʔk-ani 'hip,' Kutenai saq' 'leg,' Quileute t-tˢ'oqʷ 'foot,' Squamish -čq' 'hip, side,' Okanagan s-tˢ'ōqan 'leg,' Yuchi go-čuko 'thigh'; Penutian: Nass asāx 'foot,' Siuslaw tˢīkʷ, Klamath č'ōg 'leg,' bo-sak-l' 'thigh,' Lake Miwok čúki 'hip,' Wappo čoke 'hip bone,' Zuni sakʷi 'leg,' Atakapa ʔaška 'foot,' Huave tsāk 'leg,' Mam čog, Tzotzil čakil 'hip'; Hokan: Achomawi šakō 'leg,' Northern Pomo šaku, Eastern Pomo šāko, Kashaya šahku, Yana dᶻūk'uwalla 'hip,' Mohave tˢakas; Central Amerind: Mazatec n-tˢaku 'his foot,' Popoloca tˢāgu 'leg,' Mixtec tˢaha 'hip,' Ixcatec tˢaku 'leg,' Chocho tˢagua; Chibchan-Paezan: Tarascan tˢika-hta-kua 'thigh,' Murire sokua-

gete, Sabanero *suaguet* 'leg,' Binticua *júkue,* Andaqui *sogua-para* 'foot,'
Itonama *uj-sahua-no* 'leg,' Jirajira *a-sagan-ipipo,* Timucua *secah;* Andean: Proto-Quechuan **čaki* 'foot,' Yahgan *čikan* 'leg,' Alacaluf *čekur*
'foot'; Macro-Tucanoan: Särä *tsagalo* 'thigh,' Buhugana *sakalo,* Yuri
sokehry 'hip'; Equatorial: Campa *no-tsaki,* Piaroa *tsiha* 'thigh,' Mocochi
čuko 'leg,' Otomi *čučuga* 'thigh,' Chapacura *čiki-či* 'foot'; Macro-Carib:
Trio *sako* 'leg,' Mocoa *saku,* Ocaina *iʔžóóga* 'foot'; Macro-Panoan: Toba-
Guazu *čagañi* 'thigh,' Cavineña *etsaka* 'leg,' Sapiboca *ečuxu* 'thigh';
Macro-Ge: Botocudo *žäk-merum* 'tibia,' Masacara *šüöku* 'leg,' Kaingan
(in)-tˢo '(my) leg.' [AM 165, AK 113, CP 114, AIW, PP 133, AMN]

26 TSUMA 'hair'

KHOISAN: !Kung *čum* 'shell,' *š'um* 'skin,' Eastern ≠Hua *č'ū* ~ *tˢ'ū* ~ *dtˢ'ū*
'skin'; G//abake *čā* ~ *čo* 'skin'; /Xam *tū* 'shell.' [SAK 597, 807]

NILO-SAHARAN: Nyangiya *sim-at* 'hair,' Nandi *sum.* [KER 445]

AFRO-ASIATIC: Omotic: Proto-Omotic **somm-* 'pubic hair'; Cushitic: Sidamo
šomb-, Proto-Southern Cushitic **seʔem-* 'hair'; Old Egyptian *zmɜ;* Semitic: Proto-Semitic **šmġ* 'fine hair shed by a camel'; Chadic: Hausa
suma 'growth of hair.' [OL 47, CCE]

CAUCASIAN: Proto-Caucasian **tˢ'ñwĕme* 'eyebrow,' Proto-Lezghian **tˢʷem,*
Proto-Nax **tˢ'a-tˢ'ʔVm.* [C 70]

BASQUE *zam-ar(r)* 'lock of wool, shock of hair.' [SC 12]

YENISEIAN: Proto-Yeniseian **tˢəŋe* 'hair.' [SC 12]

SINO-TIBETAN: Proto-Sino-Tibetan **tˢʰām* 'hair'; Archaic Chinese **sam* ~
*ṣam 'hair, feather'; Tibeto-Burman: Proto-Tibeto-Burman **tsam* 'hair,'
Lepcha *ătsom,* Tibetan *(ʔag-)tshom* 'beard of the chin' (= [mouth]-hair),
Kanauri *tsam* 'wool, fleece,' *(mik-)tsam* 'eyebrow' (= [eye]-hair), Magari
tśham 'hair, wool,' Burmese *tsham,* Lushei *sam* 'hair (of the head),' Dhi-
mal *tśam* 'hide, bark,' Garo *mik sam* 'eyebrow,' Nung *əŋsam* 'hide.' [ST
73, 191, UOL 194, SS 23]

MIAO-YAO: Proto-Miao-Yao **śjām* ~ **sjām* 'beard, moustache.' [PB 307]

AMERIND: Almosan-Keresiouan: Pawnee *ošu* 'hair,' Dakota *šū* 'feather,' Woc-
con *summe* 'hair'; Penutian: North Sahaptin *šəmtai* 'pubic hair,' Nez
Perce *simtey,* Kekchi *tˢutˢum* 'feather,' *ismal* 'hair,' Mam *tsamal,* Quiche
isumal; Hokan: Proto-Hokan **čʰemi* 'fur,' North Pomo *tˢime* 'hair,' Kashaya *sime* 'body hair, fur,' Northeast Pomo *čʰeme* 'body hair,' Mohave
sama 'root,' Cocopa *išma* 'hair,' Tlappanec *tˢūŋ* 'hair, root'; Central
Amerind: Tubatulabal *tˢomol* 'hair, head'; Chibchan-Paezan: Matagalpa
susum 'beard,' Xinca *susi* 'beard'; Andean: Tsoneka *čomki* 'pubic hair,'
Quechua *sunk'a* 'beard'; Equatorial: Caranga *čuma* 'hair,' Quitemo *čumi-
či,* Aguaruna *susu* 'beard,' Candoshi *sosi.* [AM 136, EQ 54, UOL 194, DL 4,
AMN]

27 ʔAQ'WA 'water'

KHOISAN: Northern: !o !kung *kãũ* 'to rain,' !kung *k"ā* 'drink'; Central: Naron *k"ā* 'drink'; Southern: /kam-ka !ke *k"wã* ~ *k"wẽ* 'drink,' *kãũ* 'to rain,' //ng !ke *k"ã* ~ *k"ẽī* 'drink,' *kãũ* 'to rain,' Batwa *k"ã* ~ *k"ẽ* 'drink,' /auni *k"āa* 'drink,' Masarwa *k"ã* 'drink,' /nu //en *k"ã* 'drink.' [KE 261]

NILO-SAHARAN: Fur *kɔí* 'rain'; East Sudanic: Nyimang *kwe* 'water,' So *kwɛʔ*, Ik *čuɛ*; Central Sudanic: Mangbetu *éguo*; Berta *kɔ̀ì* 'rain, cloud'; Koman: Kwama *uuku* 'water,' Anej *agu-d* 'cloud.' [NSB, KER]

AFRO-ASIATIC: Proto-Afro-Asiatic (Illich-Svitych) *ʕq(w)* 'water,' (Ehret) *ak'ʷ-*; Omotic: Proto-North Omotic *ak'-*, She *k'ai* 'wet,' Janjero *ak(k)a* 'water,' Kaffa *ačō*, Mocha *āč'o*, Gofa *haččā*, Shinasha *ač'č'o*, Badditu *watˢ'ē*; Cushitic: Proto-Cushitic (Ehret) *-k'ʷ-* 'to be wet,' (Illich-Svitych) *ʕqw* 'water,' Agaw *aqʷ*, Bilin *ʕaqʷ*, Xamir *aqʷā* 'drops of water,' Damot *agʷo* 'water,' Proto-East Cushitic (Ehret) *k'oy-* 'wet,' Hadiyya *wo'o* 'water,' Tambaro *waha*, Sidamo *waho*, Iraqw *āha* 'drink.' [N 139, EU, AM 87, CE 348]

INDO-EUROPEAN: Proto-Indo-European (Pokorny) *akʷā-* 'water,' (Puhvel) *egʷ-*, (Bomhard) *ek'ʷ-*; Anatolian: Hittite *eku-*, Luwian *aku-*, Palaic *ahu-* 'drink'; Italic: Latin *aqua* 'water'; Germanic: Gothic *ahwa* 'river'; Tocharian: Tocharian A *yok-* 'drink.' [IE 23]

URALIC: Proto-Uralic (Rédei) *yoka* 'river.' [R 99–100]

JAPANESE *aka* 'bilge water.' [JP 100]

AINU *wakka* 'water,' *ku* 'drink.' [JP 100]

CAUCASIAN: Proto-Caucasian *-VqV* 'suck,' Proto-Lezghian *ʔoχʷa* 'drink,' Lezghian *χʷa-l*, Agul *uχas*, Proto-Lezghian *ʔoq̄ʷa-* 'rain,' Lezghian *q̄ʷa-z*, Rutul *huʁʷas*, Tsakhur *joʁʷi*; Proto-Nax *-aq-* 'suck(le),' Chechen *-aq-* 'suck'; Proto-Dargi *-uq-* 'suck(le).' [C 3, 16]

?BURUSHASKI *hʌγ-um* 'wet.'

SINO-TIBETAN: Proto-Sino-Tibetan *Ku* 'fluid, spill,' Newari *kʰwo* 'river,' Khaling *ku* 'water,' Kachin *kʰu*. [NSC 43]

INDO-PACIFIC: Awyu *okho* 'water, river,' Syiagha *okho* 'water,' Yareba *ogo*, Yonggom *oq*, Ninggirum *ok*. [FS 96, 134]

AUSTRALIAN: Proto-Australian *gugu* 'water.' [AC]

AMERIND: Almosan-Keresiouan: Proto-Central Algonquian *akwā* 'from water,' Kutenai *-qʷ* 'in water,' Quileute *kwāya'* 'water,' Snohomish *qʷa?*, Caddo *koko*; Penutian: Nass *akʲ-s*, Takelma *ugʷ* 'drink,' Wintun *wak'ai* 'creek,' Zuni *k'a* 'water,' Atakapa *ak*, Yuki *uk'*, Tetontepec *uu?k* 'drink,' Yucatec *uk'* 'be thirsty'; Hokan: Chimariko *aqa* 'water,' Kashaya *ʔahqha* 'water,' *q'o* 'drink,' Seri *ʔax* 'water,' Diegueno *ʔaxā*, Quinigua *kwa*, Tonkawa *ʔāx*, Tequistlatec *l-axaʔ*; Central Amerind: Proto-Chinantec *gʷa* 'stream, river'; Chibchan-Paezan: Shiriana *koa* 'drink,' Chimila *uk-*, Binticua *agu*, Allentiac *aka* 'water'; Andean: Iquito *aqua*, Quechua *yaku*, Yamana *aka* 'lake'; Macro-Tucanoan: Auake *okõa* 'water, river,' Cubeo *oko* 'water,' Tucano *axko*; Equatorial: Amniape *äkü*, Quitemo *ako*, Uaraicu *uaka* 'wash,' Terena *oko* 'rain,' Chipaya *ax^w* 'wash'; Macro-Carib: Yagua *xa* 'water,' Witoto *joko* 'wash,' Macushi *u-wuku* 'my drink,' Waiwai *woku* 'drink,' Taulipang *ai'ku* 'wet'; Macro-Panoan: Lule *uk* 'drink,' Mayoruna *uaka* 'water,' Culino *yaku* 'water,' *waka* 'river,' Huarayo *hakua* 'wash'; Macro-Ge: Koraveka *ako* 'drink,' Fulnio *waka* 'lake,' Kamakan *kwa* 'drink,' Chavante *kō* 'water,' Aponegicran *waiko* 'drink.' [AM 87, AMN]

ABBREVIATIONS

A	Andean, Greenberg 1987
AA	Afro-Asiatic, Greenberg 1963
AAD	Afro-Asiatic Dictionary, Diakonov 1981–
AB	Allan Bomhard, 1987
AC	A. Capell, 1956
AD	Anna Dybo, 1988
AIW	Mary Key, 1987
AK	Almosan-Keresiouan, Greenberg 1987
AM	Amerind, Greenberg 1987
AMN	Amerindian Notebooks, 23 vols., Greenberg 1981
AN	Austronesian, Dempwolff 1934–38
AT	A. N. Tucker and M. A. Bryan, 1957
B	Burushaski, Lorimer 1938
BA	Bantu, Guthrie 1967
BB	Barry Blake, 1988
BD	Bushman Dictionary, Bleek 1956
C	Caucasian, Nikolaev and Starostin 1992
CA	Central Amerind, Greenberg 1987
CAN	Central Amerind Notebook, Greenberg 1981
CCE	Vladimir Orel and Olga Stolbova, 1988
CE	Christopher Ehret, 1989
CK	Chukchi-Kamchatkan, Mudrak 1990
CN	Chari-Nile, Greenberg 1963
CP	Chibchan-Paezan, Greenberg 1987
CS	Marcel Cohen, 1947
D	Dravidian, Burrow and Emeneau 1984
DB	Dorothea Bleek, 1929
DC	Dene-Caucasian, Nikolaev 1991

DL	D. R. Leshchiner, 1989
EA	Eskimo-Aleut, Mudrak 1989
EC	East Caucasian, Starostin and Nikolaev 1975
EQ	Equatorial, Greenberg 1987
ES	East Sudanic, Greenberg 1963
EU	Eurasiatic, Greenberg to appear
FS	F. Seto, 1988
H	Hokan, Greenberg 1987
HF	Harold Fleming, ed., *Mother Tongue,* 1986–
HJ	Harry Johnston, 1922
IE	Indo-European, Pokorny 1959
IP	Indo-Pacific, Greenberg 1971
IS	V. M. Illich-Svitych, 1967
IST	Robert Shafer, 1974
JB	John Bengtson, 1986
JP	James Patrie, 1982
JR	Johannes Rahder, 1963
K	Khoisan, Greenberg 1963
KA	Kartvelian, Klimov 1964
KE	Khoisan Etymologies, Ruhlen 1987b
KER	Harold Fleming, 1983a
KS	Kongo-Saharan, Gregersen 1972
LC	Morris Swadesh, 1960
LN	Vaćlav Blažek, 1990
M	Mande, Mukarovsky 1966
MG	Macro-Ge, Greenberg 1987
MT	Macro-Tucanoan, Greenberg 1987
N	Nostratic, Illich-Svitych 1971–84
NA	Nahali, Kuiper 1962
NC	Niger-Congo, Greenberg 1963
ND	Na-Dene Notebook, Greenberg 1981
NK	Niger-Kordofanian, Greenberg 1963
NNG	North New Guinea, Greenberg 1971
NP	Norman-Paman, Black 1980
NS	Nilo-Saharan, Greenberg 1963
NSB	Nilo-Saharan, Bender 1980
NSC	Nostratic–Sino-Caucasian, Starostin 1991
NSD	Nilo-Saharan–Dravidian, Greenberg 1986
OL	Václav Blažek, 1989
OS	Olga V. Stolbova, 1987
P	Penutian, Greenberg 1987

PB   Paul Benedict, 1975
PP   Paul Proulx, 1984
R   Károly Rédei, 1986–88
RB   Robert Blust, 1980
RD   Robert Dixon, 1980
SAK   Southern African Khoisan, Ruhlen 1987b
SB   S. Bhattacharya, 1966
SC   Sino-Caucasian, Bengtson 1991a
SES   Southeast Surmic, Fleming 1983b
SM   Stuart Mann, 1984–88
SN   Sergei Nikolaev, 1991
SNG   South New Guinea, Greenberg 1971
SS   Sergei Starostin, 1984
ST   Sino-Tibetan, Benedict 1972
SUL   Björn Collinder, 1957
SWNG   Southwest New Guinea, Greenberg 1971
SY   S. Yoshitake, 1934
T   Tasmanian, Plomley 1976
TB   Tibeto-Burman, Matisoff 1985
U   Uralic, Collinder 1977
UOL   Alfredo Trombetti, 1905
VB   Václav Blažek, 1988
VT   V. N. Toporov, 1967
W   Werchikwar, Lorimer 1962
WM   Walter Müller, 1975
WP   Alois Walde and Julius Pokorny, 1930
WW   S. A. Wurm and B. Wilson, 1975
Y   Yeniseian, Starostin 1984

REFERENCES

Anttila, Raimo. 1989. *Historical and Comparative Linguistics.* Amsterdam.
Bender, M. Lionel. 1980. "Nilo-Saharan Comparative Wordlist," ms.
———. 1989. "Berta Lexicon," in M. Lionel Bender, ed., *Topics in Nilo-Saharan Linguistics.* Hamburg, 271–304.
Benedict, Paul K. 1972. *Sino-Tibetan: A Conspectus.* Cambridge, Eng.
———. 1975. *Austro-Thai: Language and Culture.* New Haven, Conn.
Bengtson, John D. 1986. "Toward Global Sound Correspondences," ms.
———. 1987. "Notes on Indo-European '10,' '100,' and '1,000,'" *Diachronica* 4: 257–62.

———. 1991a. "Notes on Sino-Caucasian," in Vitaly Shevoroshkin, ed., *Dene-Sino-Caucasian Languages.* Bochum, Germany, 67–129.

———. 1991b. "Some Macro-Caucasian Etymologies," in Vitaly Shevoroshkin, ed., *Dene-Sino-Caucasian Languages.* Bochum, Germany, 130–41.

Bhattacharya, S. 1966. "Some Munda Etymologies," in Norman H. Zide, ed., *Studies in Comparative Austroasiatic Linguistics,* The Hague, 28–40.

Black, Paul. 1980. "Norman Paman Historical Phonology," Bruce Rigsby and Peter Sutton, eds., *Papers in Australian Linguistics* 13, *Pacific Linguistics* A59. Canberra, 181–239.

Blake, Barry. 1988. "Redefining Pama-Nyungan: Towards the Prehistory of Australian Languages," *Yearbook of Australian Linguistics* 1.

Blažek, Václav. 1988. "Additions to the Global Etymological Dictionary of Ruhlen-Bengtson 1988, part 2," ms.

———. 1989. "Omotic Lexicon in Afroasiatic Perspective: Body Part Cognates," paper given at the Second International Symposium on Cushitic and Omotic.

———. 1990. "Lexica nostratica: Addenda et corrigenda II," *Archív orientální* 58: 205–18.

Bleek, Dorothea F. 1929. *Comparative Vocabularies of Bushman Languages.* Cambridge, Eng.

———. 1956. *A Bushman Dictionary.* New Haven, Conn.

Blust, Robert. 1980. "Austronesian Etymologies," *Oceanic Linguistics* 19: 1–189.

———. 1988. *Austronesian Root Theory.* Amsterdam.

Bomhard, Allan R. 1987. "A Sample of the Comparative Vocabulary of the Nostratic Languages," ms.

Boyd, Raymond. 1978. "A propos des ressemblances lexicales entre langues niger-congo et nilo-sahariennes," *Bulletin de SELAF (Paris)* 65: 43–94.

Burrow, Thomas, and Murray B. Emeneau. 1984. *A Dravidian Etymological Dictionary.* Oxford, Eng.

Bynon, Theodora. 1977. *Historical Linguistics.* Cambridge, Eng.

Campbell, Lyle. 1986. "Cautions about Loan Words and Sound Correspondences," in Dieter Kastovsky and Aleksander Szwedek, eds., *Linguistics across Historical and Geographical Boundaries.* Berlin, 221–24.

———. 1988. Review of *Language in the Americas,* by Joseph H. Greenberg, *Language* 64: 591–615.

Campbell, Lyle, and Ronald W. Langacker. 1978. "Proto-Aztecan Vowels: Part III," *International Journal of American Linguistics* 44: 262–79.

Capell, A. 1956. *A New Approach to Australian Linguistics.* Sydney.

Cohen, Marcel. 1947. *Essai comparatif sur le vocabulaire et la phonétique du chamito-sémitique.* Paris.

Collinder, Björn. 1949. "La parenté linguistique et le calcul des probabilités," *Uppsala universitets årsskrift* 13: 1–24.

———. 1957. *A Survey of the Uralic Languages.* Uppsala.

———. 1977. *Fenno-Ugric Vocabulary.* Hamburg.

Curr, E. M. 1886–87. *The Australian Race.* Melbourne.

Dawkins, Richard. 1987. *The Blind Watchmaker.* New York.

Dempwolff, Otto. 1934–38. *Vergleichende Lautlehre des austronesischen Wortschätzes,* 3 vols. Berlin.

Derbyshire, Desmond C., and Geoffrey K. Pullum, eds. 1991. *Handbook of Amazonian Languages,* Vol. 3. Berlin.

Diakonov, I. M., ed. 1981– . *Sravnitel'no-istoričeskij slovar' afrazijskix jazykov.* Moscow.

Dixon, R. M. W. 1980. *The Languages of Australia.* Cambridge, Eng.

Dolgopolsky, Aron. 1964. "Gipoteza drevnejšego rodstva jazykovyx semei severnoj Eurasii s verojatnostnoj točki zrenija," *Voprosy Jazykoznanija* 2: 53–63. [English translation in Vitalij V. Shevoroshkin and Thomas L. Markey, eds., *Typology, Relationship and Time,* 1986. Ann Arbor, Mich., 27–50.]

Dybo, Anna. 1988. "Methods in Systemic Reconstruction of Altaic and Nostratic Lexics," paper given at the International Conference on Language and Prehistory, University of Michigan.

Ehret, Christopher. 1989. "A Reconstruction of Proto-Afroasiatic," ms.

Fleming, Harold. 1983a. "Kuliak External Relations: Step One," in Rainer Vossen and Marianne Bechhaus-Gerst, eds., *Nilotic Studies.* Berlin, 375–421.

———. 1983b. "Surma Etymologies," in Rainer Vossen and Marianne Bechhaus-Gerst, eds., *Nilotic Studies.* Berlin, 525–55.

Fleming, Harold, ed. 1986– . *Mother Tongue.* Boston.

———. 1990. "Omotica, Afrasiana and More: Ethiopia as the Ever-Flowing Vase," *Mother Tongue* 12: 22–30.

Goddard, Ives. 1979. "The Languages of South Texas and the Lower Rio Grande," in Lyle Campbell and Marianne Mithun, eds., *The Languages of Native America: Historical and Comparative Assessment.* Austin, 355–89.

Golla, Victor, ed. 1984. *The Sapir-Kroeber Correspondence.* Berkeley, Calif.

Greenberg, Joseph H. 1953. "Historical Linguistics and Unwritten Languages," in A. L. Kroeber, ed., *Anthropology Today.* Chicago: 265–86.

———. 1957. "Genetic Relationship among Languages," in *Essays in Linguistics,* by Joseph H. Greenberg. Chicago, 35–45.

———. 1963. *The Languages of Africa.* Bloomington, Ind.

———. 1971. "The Indo-Pacific Hypothesis," in Thomas A. Sebeok, ed., *Current Trends in Linguistics,* Vol. 8. The Hague: 807–71.

―――. 1981. "Amerindian Comparative Notebooks," 23 vols., Mss. on file, Green Library, Stanford University, Stanford, Calif.

―――. 1986. "Nilo-Saharan–Dravidian Etymologies," ms.

―――. 1987. *Language in the Americas*. Stanford, Calif.

―――. 1990. "The American Indian Language Controversy," *Review of Archaeology* 11: 5–14.

―――. To appear. *Indo-European and Its Closest Relatives: The Eurasiatic Language Family*. Stanford, Calif.

Gregersen, Edgar A. 1972. "Kongo-Saharan," *Journal of African Languages* 11: 69–89.

Guthrie, Malcolm. 1967. *Comparative Bantu*, 4 vols. Farnborough, Eng.

Hock, Hans Henrich. 1986. *Principles of Historical Linguistics*. Berlin.

Illich-Svitych, V. M. 1967. "Materialy k sravnitel'nomu slovarju nostratičeskix jazykov," *Etimologija 1965* (Moscow): 321–96.

―――. 1971–84. *Opyt sravnenija nostratičeskix jazykov*, 3 vols. Moscow.

Johnston, Harry H. 1922. *A Comparative Study of the Bantu and Semi-Bantu Languages*, 2 vols. Oxford, Eng.

Kaufman, Terrence. 1990. "Language History in South America: What We Know and How to Know More," in Doris L. Payne, ed., *Amazonian Linguistics: Studies in Lowland South American Languages*. Austin, Tex., 13–73.

Key, Mary R. 1968. *Comparative Tacanan Phonology*. The Hague.

―――. 1987. "American Indian Wordlist," ms.

Klimov, G. A. 1964. *Etimologičeskij slovar' kartvel'skix jazykov*. Moscow.

Kuiper, F. B. J. 1962. *Nahali: A Comparative Study*. Amsterdam.

Leshchiner, D. R. 1989. "Rekonstruktsija nazvanij častej tela v jazykax sem'i xoka," *Lingvističeskaja rekonstruktsija i drevnejšaja istorija vostoka* (Moscow) 1: 159–66.

Lorimer, D. L. R. 1938. *The Burushaski Language*, vol. 3. Oslo.

―――. 1962. *Werchikwar English Vocabulary*. Oslo.

Mann, Stuart E. 1984–88. *An Indo-European Comparative Dictionary*. Hamburg.

Matisoff, James A. 1985. "Out on a Limb: Arm, Hand and Wing in Sino-Tibetan," in Graham Thurgood, James A. Matisoff, and David Bradley, eds., *Linguistics of the Sino-Tibetan Area: The State of the Art*. Canberra, 421–49.

Matteson, Esther, ed. 1972. *Comparative Studies in Amerindian Languages*. The Hague.

Morpurgo Davies, Anna. 1989. Comments on "Models of Change in Language and Archaeology," by Colin Renfrew, *Transactions of the Philological Society* 87(2): 156–71.

Mudrak, Oleg A. 1984. "K voprosu o vnešnix svjazjax eskimosskix jazykov," *Lingvističeskaja rekonstruktsija i drevnejšaja isorija vostoka* (Moscow) 1: 64–68.

———. 1989. "Eskaleutian Roots," in Vitaly Shevoroshkin, ed., *Reconstructing Languages and Cultures.* Bochum, Germany, 112–24.

———. 1990. "Kamchukchee Roots," in Vitaly Shevoroshkin, ed., *Explorations in Language Macrofamilies.* Bochum, Germany, 90–110.

Mukarovsky, Hans G. 1966. "Zur Stellung der Mandsprachen," *Anthropos* 61: 679–88.

Müller, Walter W. 1975. "Beiträge zur hamito-semitischen Wortvergleichung," in James Bynon and Theodora Bynon, eds., *Hamito-Semitica.* The Hague, 63–73.

Newman, Stanley. 1964. "Comparison of Zuni and California Penutian," *International Journal of American Linguistics* 30: 1–13.

Nichols, Johanna. 1990. "Linguistic Diversity and the First Settlement of the New World," *Language* 66: 475–521.

Nikolaev, Sergei. 1991. "Sino-Caucasian Languages in America," in Vitaly Shevoroshkin, ed., *Dene-Sino-Caucasian Languages.* Bochum, Germany, 42–66.

Nikolaev, Sergei, and Sergei Starostin. 1992. "A (North) Caucasian Etymological Dictionary," ms.

Orel, Vladimir E., and Olga V. Stolbova. 1988. "Cushitic, Chadic, and Egyptian: Lexical Relations," paper presented at the International Conference on Language and Prehistory, University of Michigan.

Patrie, James. 1982. *The Genetic Relationship of the Ainu Language.* Honolulu, Hawaii.

Payne, David L. 1991. "A Classification of Maipuran (Arawakan) Languages Based on Shared Lexical Retentions," in Desmond C. Derbyshire and Geoffrey K. Pullum, eds., *Handbook of Amazonian Languages,* Vol. 3. Berlin, 355–499.

Plomley, N. J. B. 1976. *A Word-List of the Tasmanian Aboriginal Languages.* Launceston, Australia.

Pokorny, Julius. 1959. *Indogermanisches Etymologisches Wörterbuch.* Bern.

Proulx, Paul. 1984. "Proto-Algic I: Phonological Sketch," *International Journal of American Linguistics* 50: 165–207.

Rahder, Johannes. 1963. "Etymological Vocabulary of Chinese, Japanese, Korean, and Ainu, Part 5," *Orbis* 12: 45–116.

Rédei, Károly, ed. 1986–88. *Uralisches Etymologisches Wörterbuch.* Budapest.

Ruhlen, Merritt. 1987a. *A Guide to the World's Languages,* Vol. 1: Classification. Stanford, Calif.

———. 1987b. "Khoisan Etymologies," Chapter 3 of this volume.

———. 1988a. "The Origin of Language: Retrospective and Prospective," Chapter 13 of this volume. [Russian version in *Voprosy Jazykoznanija* 1 (1991): 5–19.]

———. 1988b. "Na-Dene Etymologies," Chapter 5 of this volume.

———. 1991a. "Amerind T'ANA 'Child, Sibling,'" Chapter 9 of this volume.

———. 1991b. "The Emerging Synthesis: A View from Language," paper presented at the International Conference on Genetics, Linguistics, and Archaeology, Florence, Italy, May 1991.

———. 1991c. "The Amerind Phylum and the Prehistory of the New World," in Sydney M. Lamb and E. Douglas Mitchell, eds., *Sprung from Some Common Source: Investigations into the Prehistory of Languages.* Stanford, Calif., 328–50.

———. 1992. "An Overview of Genetic Classification," in John Hawkins and Murray Gell-Mann, eds., *The Evolution of Human Languages.* Redwood City, Calif. [Also Chapter 1 of this volume.]

Schmidt, Wilhelm. 1952. *Die Tasmanischen Sprachen.* Utrecht.

Seto, F. 1988. *Tropical Pacific Historical and Linguistic Selections,* vol. 5. Tokyo.

Shafer, Robert. 1965. "The Eurasial Linguistic Superfamily," *Anthropos* 60: 445–68.

———. 1974. *Introduction to Sino-Tibetan.* Wiesbaden, Germany.

Shevoroshkin, Vitaly, ed. 1991. *Dene-Sino-Caucasian Languages.* Bochum, Germany.

Starostin, Sergei A. 1982. "Prajenisejskaja rekonstruktsija i vneshnie svjazi enisejskix jazykov," *Ketskij sbornik.* Leningrad, 144–237.

———. 1984. "Gipoteza o genetičeskix svjazjax sinotibetskix jazykov s enisejskimi i severnokavkazskimi jazykami," *Lingvističeskaja rekonstruktsija i drevnejšaja istorija vostoka* (Moscow) 4: 19–38. [English translation in Vitaly Shevoroshkin, ed., *Dene-Sino-Caucasian Languages,* 1991. Bochum, Germany, 12–41.]

———. 1991. "Nostratic and Sino-Caucasian," in Vitaly Shevoroshkin, ed., *Explorations in Language Macrofamilies.* Bochum, Germany, 42–66.

Starostin, Sergei, and Sergei Nikolaev. 1975. "List of Proto-Daghestanian and Proto-Nakh-Daghestanian (ND) Nominal Roots (with Extra-Caucasian Comparisons by Aron Dolgopolsky)," ms.

Stolbova, Olga V. 1987. "Sravnitel'no-istoričeskaja fonetika i slovar' zapadno-čadskix jazykov," in V. J. Porxomovskij, ed., *Afrikanskoje istoričeskoje jazykoznanije.* Moscow, 30–268.

Swadesh, Morris. 1960. "On Interhemisphere Linguistic Connections," in Stanley Diamond, ed., *Culture in History.* New York, 894–924.

————. 1962. "Linguistic Relations across Bering Strait, *American Anthropologist* 64: 1262–91.

Thelwall, Robin. 1981. "Lexicostatistical Subgrouping and Lexical Reconstruction of the Daju Group," in T. C. Schadeberg and M. L. Bender, eds., *Nilo-Saharan*. Dordrecht, Netherlands, 167–84.

Toporov, V. N. 1967. "Iz etimologii enisejskix jazykov," *Etimologija 1965* (Moscow): 311–20.

Trombetti, Alfredo. 1905. *L'unità d'origine del linguaggio.* Bologna.

Tucker, A. N., and M. A. Bryan. 1957. *Linguistic Survey of the Northern Bantu Borderland,* vol. 4. London.

Walde, Alois, and Julius Pokorny. 1930. *Vergleichendes Wörterbuch der indogermanischen Sprachen.* Berlin.

Wurm, S. A., and B. Wilson. 1975. *English Finderlist of Reconstructions in Austronesian Languages.* Canberra.

Yoshitake, S. 1934. *The Phonetic System of Ancient Japanese.* London.

Index

No attempt has been made in the following index to list every language—or even every language family—mentioned in this book. Such an index would have been excessively long, cumbersome, and of very little use to most readers. In fact, since each chapter deals with a specific topic, even the table of contents provides a rough index to the book. The present index is for the most part limited to higher-level families that are traditionally considered to represent the limits of the comparative method in linguistics (e.g. Indo-European, Uralic, Austronesian), and to individual languages that are often considered "unrelated" to other languages or language families (e.g. Basque, Burushaski, Japanese). General topics and authors are also included.

In the index an "f" following a page number indicates a separate reference on the following page, and "ff" indicates a separate reference on the following two pages. An "n" indicates the reference is contained in a footnote. A continuous discussion over two or more pages is indicated by a span of page numbers, e.g., "115–22." *Passim* is used to indicate a cluster of references on close by not consecutive pages.

Library of Congress Cataloging-in-Publication Data

Ruhlen, Merritt, 1944–
    On the origin of languages : studies in linguistic taxonomy /
Merritt Ruhlen.
        p.   cm.
    Includes index.
    ISBN 0-8047-2321-4 (acid-free paper)
    1. Comparative linguistics.   2. Language and languages—
Classification.   3. Language and languages—Origin.   I. Title
P143.R84   1994
410—dc20
                                                    93– 39188
                                                        CIP

⊗ This book is printed on acid-free paper. It has been typeset by the
   author in T$_E$X.